This book is dedicated to my mother,
Themis, who managed to keep my soul
alive through years of defeat and despair;
to my brother, George, who believed in
beauty to the end; to all the little film
magazines that have kept the faith
despite inadequate financing.

Acknowledgements

I am deeply indebted to Robert M. Ockene for his editorial tenacity in this difficult enterprise. I am indebted also to Sharland Trotter, Beatrice Spencer, Wallis Ammerman, Joseph Weill, Ernest Callenbach, Ian Cameron, Jean-Louis Comolli, Edwin Fancher, Rudi Franchi, Gordon Hitchens, Penelope Houston, Marshall Lewis, Jonas Mekas, Gerald Pratley, James Stoller, Herman G. Weinberg, and Daniel Wolf.

For permission to reprint interviews with, and statements on and by, the directors mentioned, I am grateful to the following:

Cahiers du Cinema for Antonioni, Bergman, Dreyer, Eisenstein, Fellini, Ford, Godard, Hawks, Ophuls, Riefenstahl, and Welles. Copyright © 1955, 1956, 1958, 1963, 1965, 1966.

Cahiers du Cinema in English for translations of interviews with the above directors. Copyright © 1966, 1967.

Film Comment for Preminger. Copyright © 1965.

Film Culture for Bunuel, Cukor, Lubitsch, Pasolini, Rossellini, von Sternberg, von Stroheim, and Preston Sturges. Copyright © 1955, 1958, 1962, 1964.

Film Quarterly for Huston, Keaton, Peckinpah, Abraham Polonsky, and Satyajit Ray. Copyright © 1958, 1962, 1963, 1964, 1965.

Movie for Bresson, Bunuel, Chabrol, Donner, Hitchcock, Lang, and Preminger. Copyright © 1962, 1963, 1965, 1966.

Moviegoer for Ophuls. Copyright © 1966.

The Museum of Modern Art for Von Sternberg. Copyright © 1966.

New York Film Bulletin for Godard, Resnais, Truffaut. Copyright © 1962, 1963, 1964.

Gerald Pratley for Lean. Copyright © 1965.

Sight and Sound for Brook, Chaplin, Kurosawa, Losey, Nicholas Ray, and Renoir. Copyright © 1957, 1961, 1962, 1963, 1964.

Table of Contents

The Fall and Rise
of the Film Director

by Andrew Sarris

Greta Garbo's creakiest vehicle of the Thirties was an opus entitled *Susan Lenox—Her Fall and Rise*. Film historians and archivists have repeatedly restored the classical cadence of "Rise and Fall" to the title in defiance of the plot line and the aggressively American optimism it presents. Film directors are comparable to sudsy Susan Lenox in that their tarnished professional image has regained its gloss after a long period of neglect and downright disrepute. In fact, the renewed awareness of the film director as a conscious artist is one of the more interesting cultural phenomena of the past decade. This renewal can be described as a rise only in the most relative terms. The director has risen no more than the sun rises. As the latter is a figure of speech describing the diurnal rotation of the earth from the point of view of the fallible human eye, the pre-eminence of the director has been a matter of public and critical fancy.

Like the sun, the director has always been out there on the set, and his turn to be worshiped has come full circle from the earliest days of his solitary pre-eminence behind primitive tripod cameras pointed at a world still visually virginal. This intimation of lost innocence is invoked in Billy Wilder's *Sunset Boulevard* when Erich von Stroheim commands the newsreel cameras to turn on Gloria Swanson as she descends the staircase to utter madness. There is more than the numbing nostalgia for a burnt-out star in this sequence; there is also the evocation of an era when movie-making was more individual, less industrial. It is immaterial whether there ever was an era of directional enlightenment. Many film historians have testified to the

9

existence of a Golden Age in order to create a frame of reference. The gold may have turned to brass before 1925 or 1920 or 1915, but somewhere along the line, the legend persists, the film director lost all his freedom and integrity to some monstrous entity known as the motion picture industry—code name: Hollywood.

Confirmation of this legend of directorial decline and decadence has been provided by veteran Hollywood director George Stevens: "When the movie industry was young, the film-maker was its core and the man who handled the business details his partner . . . When [the director] finally looked around, he found his partner's name on the door. Thus the film-maker became the employee, and the man who had the time to attend to the business details became the head of the studio."

Studio head Samuel Goldwyn put the matter somewhat more brutally when a reporter had the temerity to begin a sentence with the statement: "When William Wyler made *Wuthering Heights* . . ." The reporter never passed beyond the premise. "*I* made *Wuthering Heights*," Goldwyn snapped. "Wyler only directed it."

"Only directed" is more precisely defined in the appendix of *The Film Till Now* by Paul Rotha and Richard Griffith: "Director—(a) In feature films the Director is usually the technician who directs the shooting of the film, that is, he tells the players what to do and the cameraman what to shoot, and usually supervises the editing. Most feature films are directed from scripts written by the script department or by an independent script-writer. The editing is carried out by a department under a supervising editor working in consultation with the director and producer. Sometimes a director will write his own shooting-script and do his own editing; thus the film will tend much more to carry his individual mark.

"(b) In documentary films the Director usually writes his own script after first-hand investigation of the subject, although sometimes he may employ a dialogue writer. He not only directs the action of the film, but controls it through all stages of editing, music, dubbing, etc. Wartime developments have tended to departmentalize documentary production as in story films."

The most interesting aspect of this duplex definition, devised during the Forties, is its ingrained bias in favor of the documentary director. Directors of "feature" or "story" films were presumably less artists than artisans not

10

only because they were more closely supervised, but also because "feature" films were considered more frivolous than documentary films. Thus, most movie directors were doubly denigrated in the scholarly texts of the period. On the one hand, most directors were charged with having too little control over their movies, and on the other, their movies were not considered worth doing in the first place.

Not that scholarly texts had any appreciable influence on the motion picture industry. Like so many other products of capitalism, movies were designed for immediate consumption and rapid expendability. Once a movie became "old," it was returned to the vaults, never to be shown publicly again. Thus, even if there had been any interest in directorial careers, the necessary research materials were not available. To make matters worse, film history was split in two by the advent of sound in the late Twenties.

People who grew up in the Thirties were completely unaware of the cinema of the Twenties except for infrequent custard pie two-reelers or an occasional revival of the foreign repertory—from *Caligari* to *Potemkin*. By about 1934, censorship had placed many movies of the early Thirties out of bounds, a condition that existed until the Forties and Fifties when television gold made it lucrative for studios to open their vaults. We are still a long way from the day when scholars can obtain the films they need from film libraries, but the proliferation of old films has had its effect on contemporary criticism. A greater awareness of the past, a sense of stylistic continuity in the works of individual directors, a cyclical pattern of period mannerisms—these are some of the dividends of the improved distribution of movies in the Sixties. The most hardheaded businessman in the movie industry must now be at least marginally concerned with the burgeoning scholarship in the medium. By the same token, the most serious-minded scholar cannot avoid taking movies more seriously than heretofore, particularly when it is now possible to trace links between the Marx Brothers and Ionesco, between Buster Keaton and Samuel Beckett.

Unfortunately, most scholarly works on the cinema are still written from a predominantly sociological viewpoint, and most directors are still subordinated to both the studio and the star system that allegedly enslave them. Indeed most directors have always been considered less as creators than as decorators of other people's scenarios. That most

11

directors do not write their own scripts is enough to discredit these directors in the eyes of the literary establishment. Such discredit is often unjustified even on literary grounds simply because many directors decline to take credit for collaboration on the writing of their films.

Furthermore, screenwriting involves more than mere dialogue and plot. The choice between a close-up and a long-shot, for example, may quite often transcend the plot. If the story of Little Red Riding Hood is told with the Wolf in close-up and Little Red Riding Hood in long-shot, the director is concerned primarily with the emotional problems of a wolf with a compulsion to eat little girls. If Little Red Riding Hood is in close-up and the Wolf in long-shot, the emphasis is shifted to the emotional problems of vestigial virginity in a wicked world. Thus, two different stories are being told with the same basic anecdotal material. What is at stake in the two versions of Little Red Riding Hood are two contrasting directorial attitudes toward life. One director identifies more with the Wolf—the male, the compulsive, the corrupted, even evil itself. The second director identifies with the little girl—the innocence, the illusion, the ideal and hope of the race. Needless to say, few critics bother to make any distinction, proving perhaps that direction as creation is still only dimly understood.

As a consequence, contemporary film criticism has tended to diverge into two conflicting camps, the poor film director caught in the middle. First and foremost, we have the literary establishment, which relegates visual style to subordinate paragraphs in reviews. Then we have the visualists, who disdain plots and dialogues as literary impurities. Since most directors worthy of note work in the impure realm of the dramatic sound film, it is difficult to isolate their personal contributions to the cinema. The literary critics prefer to synopsize the plot, discuss the theme, if any, evaluate the performances, comment on the photography, editing, etc., and credit the director only for "pacing," usually in the three speeds—fast, deliberate, and most often of all, too slow. Conversely, the visual critics concentrate on landscapes and abstractions as "pure" cinema, and castigate dramatic scenes as "talky," "stagey," "literary," etc. That is why the coming of sound was such a traumatic experience for serious film aestheticians of the late Twenties and early Thirties, and why much of what we call film history is actually the thinly disguised nostal-

12

gia of elderly film historians for the mute movies of their youth.

Through the haze of selective recollection, the silent film had apparently flown to an extraordinary elevation in the Twenties only to crash through the sound barrier with a screech and a squeak. It became fashionable to mourn the tragedy of talkies until well into the Forties, and after to talk about the cinema in terms of artistic decline until well into the Fifties.

The biographical pattern of almost every director went something like this: He started off very promisingly, but was soon corrupted by Hollywood (if he were foreign), or by big budgets (if he were American). His work became more and more "commercial," less and less "significant." Because distribution was so erratic, it was always reasonbly safe to say that yesterday's movies were superior to today's.

On the whole, however, directors were penalized more by critical indifference than by critical captiousness. Few people cared to read about directors; a volume of interviews of directors would have been inconceivable even as late as ten years ago. If the role of the director is now taken more seriously, it is because the cinema itself is taken more seriously. The director never really had any serious rival in the creative process. No one, least of all the serious scholar, was ever taken in by the pufferies of the producers. Selznick, Zanuck, Hughes, Goldwyn, and Thalberg did exercise great control over their productions, but few of their contributions were regarded as genuinely creative. Mostly, they maintained a certain level of technical quality in their productions, but production control without creative responsibility falls generally under the heading of interference.

The writer was even less serious a challenge to the director. Although the director was shackled to some extent by the studio system through the Thirties and Forties, the writer was virtually deprived of his identity. As far as studios were concerned, there was never a question of too many scribes spoiling the script. Quite to the contrary, most producers believed strongly in the safety of numbers, and the multiple writing credits on the screen made it difficult for screenwriters to be taken seriously as screen authors.

By contrast, directors almost invariably received sole credit for their efforts, however craven and controlled

13

these efforts may have been considered. In addition, the director's credit always appeared last on the screen—or almost always—one contractual exception being the aforementioned Samuel Goldwyn, a producer with a passion for having his name follow the director's. Nevertheless, the director's position, even in Hollywood, has always been strategically superior to the writer's. In the early Forties, the Screenwriter's Guild felt obliged to agitate for greater critical recognition, and the conflict became so exaggerated that, at one point, Stephen Longstreet attacked Vincente Minnelli for distracting audiences from dialogue with fancy camera angles in the 1945 Judy Garland-Robert Walker romance, *The Clock*. Needless to say, no screenwriter today would dare make a comparable objection.

Even today, however, the film director faces massive obstacles to critical recognition. Writers, actors, producers, and technicians challenge him at every turn. Also, the analogous and yet anomalous relationship with stage directors tends to confuse the issue. It is fashionable to say that the screen is a director's medium and the stage a writer's medium, but it is difficult to demonstrate that a Broadway-to-Hollywood-and-back director like Elia Kazan is any less in command in one medium than in another. To some extent, of course, the role of the director, stage or screen, depends on the person playing it. Many, if not most, film directors are little more than glorified stage managers charged with maintaining a schedule for the execution of the preordained plans of the studio, the stars, the producer, the writer or writers, the technicians, the distributors, and even the vulgar public. At his least or his worst, the director is reduced to the level of a technician without the technician's pride in his craft. Such directors are like absolute despots compelled to act as constitutional monarchs, but lacking the style to conceal or circumvent their subservience.

At the other extreme, we have a new breed of film-makers who do not even call themselves "directors." These are the so-called independents, the "poets," the perpetual avant-garde of the cinema. They scorn or pretend to scorn the elaborate technical and industrial processes of movie production for the sake of a more individualized creation. They are descended, if only atavistically, from the first film-makers, the curious cameramen who were playing with a new toy. Ironically, the avant-garde has generally

14

resisted the stylistic and technological innovations initiated by so-called commercial movie-makers. Sound, color, music, variable screens were all developed by the film industry while the avant-garde was publishing manifestoes against them. The avant-garde has thus led the way not in form, but in content—anarchic, subversive, sacrilegious, scatological, and pornographic.

Through the years and decades, however, avant-garde attitudes in America have relied on the foreign "art film" for intellectual authority. The Germans and the Russians were particularly fashionable in the Twenties, before Hitler and Stalin stultified experimentation. Movies like *The Last Laugh* and *Variety* dramatized the expressive potentialities of the moving camera along with downbeat subjects considered too grim for Hollywood, but it was Sergei Eisenstein's *Potemkin* that galvanized a whole generation of intellectuals and aesthetes into wild enthusiasm over the creative possibilities of montage, a term that reverberated through the Twenties and Thirties the way *mise en scène* has reverberated through the Fifties and Sixties. Normally, montage is merely a fancy word for editing or cutting, but Eisenstein gave montage a mystique by linking it to the philosophical processes of dialectical materialism. As Eisenstein conceived of film-making, images equaled ideas, and the collision of two dynamically opposed images created a new idea. Eisenstein's montage theory was ideal for describing the collisions of the Russian Revolution, but there did not seem to be many other plots for which incessant montage was appropriate. The great majority of movies developed a dramatic style of expression to enhance audience identification with star personalities. Since in the world cinema the mystique of montage was thereafter honored more in the breach than in the observance, film histories turned sour with acid critiques of alleged betrayals of the medium. As the gap widened between what was popular and what was intellectually fashionable, Eisensteinian aesthetics were supplemented by Marxist politics. Movies were not merely vulgar; they were instruments of capitalism in the never-ending class struggle. Film directors were thus presented with two choices: fight the establishment, or "sell out."

It remained for the illustrious French film critic André Bazin to eliminate much of the confusion arising from Eisenstein's half-digested montage theories. Bazin pinpointed psychological and physical situations in which montage

15

disrupted the unity of man with his environment. Indeed it was French criticism in the late Forties and early Fifties that introduced the mystique of *mise en scène* to counterbalance that of montage. The more extreme of Eisenstein disciples had reached a stage of absurdity in which what was actually on the screen was secondary to the "rhythm" of the film. The montage maniacs had thus enthroned punctuation at the expense of language. At times, it seemed that the camera was merely an excuse to get into the cutting room.

Ironically, the producers shared the highbrow enthusiasm over montage. "We'll save it in the cutting room" became one of the hackneyed slogans of bad producers. *Mise en scène,* with its connotation of design and decor, reintroduced pictorial values to a medium that had become obsessed with the musical rhythms of images flashing by to be slashed on the moviola.

Because French critics were less awed by montage, they tended to be more appreciative of Hollywood than their cultivated counterparts in America and England. Most Hollywood directors of the Thirties were disqualified from serious consideration because they did not supervise the final editing (montage) of their films, for editing was then considered, by the aestheticians, the supreme function of cinematic creation. With the collapse of the montage mystique, however, many directors of the Thirties have been rediscovered as undeniably personal artists. Not only do the best directors cut "in the mind" rather than in the cutting room, but montage is only one aspect of a directorial personality.

Nonetheless, the Hollywood director is still taken less seriously than his foreign counterpart, and, in interviews, he generally regards himself with the same lack of seriousness. Part of his problem is the Hollywood ethos of the "team"; part is the tendency of Hollywood movies to conceal the inner workings for the sake of popular illusionism. Audiences are not supposed to be conscious that a movie is directed; the movie just happens by some mysterious conjunction of the players with their plot. Quite often, Hollywood directors have labored in obscurity to evolve an extraordinary economy of expression that escapes so-called highbrow critics in search of the obvious stylistic flourish. Consequently, there has been a tendency to overrate the European directors because of their relative articulateness about their artistic *angst,* and now a reaction has set in against some of the disproportionate pomposity that has ensued. Some of the recent cults for Ingmar Bergman, Federico Fellini, and Michelangelo Antonioni create the impression that the cinema was born sometime between 1950 and 1960. Not that European directors are entirely to blame for occasionally appearing pretentious. They are merely playing the role that is expected of them, just as Hollywood directors are conditioned to pretend that they are all hardheaded businessmen. But here, too, the gap is narrowing as Hollywood directors venture to be more explicit about their artistic intentions and European directors dare to be more candid about commercial and professional problems.

As film scholarship becomes more sophisticated, the facile distinctions between so-called "art" films and so-called "commercial" films become less meaningful. Out of the sifting and winnowing emerges a new division of good "art" and "commercial" films on one side and bad "art" and "commercial" films on the other. Not only do art and commerce intersect; they are intertwined with the muddled processes of film-making. Even art films have to make money, and even commercial films have to make some statement. To put it another way, more and more critics are demanding that there should be more fun in art, and more art in fun. The post-Marxist pop and camp movements have perhaps overreacted to the socially conscious solemnity of the past, but the increasing skepticism about mere good intentions is a healthy sign of higher standards. Unfortunately, the pendulum has swung from the extreme of sobriety to the extreme of silliness. In the process, however, it has become possible to speak of Alfred Hitchcock and Michelangelo Antonioni in the same breath and with the same critical terminology. Amid the conflicting critical camps, both Rays, Nicholas and Satyajit, have gained a respectful hearing. Suddenly every director is . entitled to equal time on the international critical scene in which critics are compelled to abandon many of their cherished prejudices and snobberies. In a more open-minded atmosphere of critical recognition, it is only natural that film directors should abandon some of their defensive attitudes toward their roles. However, as instructive as the new frankness of film directors may be, interviews with directors cannot usurp the role of critical analysis.

André Bazin has summed up the situation admirably: "There are, occasionally, good directors, like René Cle-

17

ment or Lattuada, who profess a precise aesthetic consciousness and accept a discussion on this level, but most of their colleagues react to aesthetic analysis with an attitude ranging from astonishment to irritation. Moreover, the astonishment is perfectly sincere and comprehensible. As for the irritation, this often springs from an instinctive resistance to the dismantling of a mechanism whose purpose is to create an illusion, and only mediocrities gain, in effect, from malfunctioning mechanisms. The director's irritation springs also from his resentment at being placed in a position that is foreign to him. Thus, I have seen a director as intelligent (and conscious) as Jean Grémillon play the village idiot and sabotage our discussion of *Lumière d'été* evidently because he did not agree with me. And how can I say he is wrong? Is not this impasse reminiscent of Paul Valéry leaving the lecture hall where Gustave Cohen has presented his famous commentary on *Cimitière Marin* with a word of ironic admiration for the professor's imagination? Must we conclude therefore that Paul Valéry is only an intuitive artist betrayed by a pedant's textual analysis and that *Cimitière Marin* is merely automatic writing?

"As a matter of fact," Bazin declares, "this apparent contradiction between the critic and the author should not trouble us. It is in the natural order of things, both subjectively and objectively. Subjectively, because artistic creation—even with the most intellectual temperaments—is essentially intuitive and practical: it is a matter of effects to attain and materials to conquer. Objectively, because a work of art escapes its creator and bypasses his conscious intentions, in direct proportion to its quality. The foundation of this objectivity also resides in the psychology of the creation to the inappreciable extent to which the artist does not really create but sets himself to crystallize, to order the sociological forces and the technical conditions into which he is thrust. This is particularly true of the American cinema in which you often find quasi-anonymous successes whose merit reflects, not on the director, but on the production system. But an objective criticism, methodically ignoring "intentions," is as applicable to the most personal work imaginable, like a poem or a painting, for example.

"This does not mean that knowing authors (*auteurs*) personally, or what they say about themselves and their work, may not clarify the critic's conception, and this is proven by taped interviews we have published in *Cahiers du Cinema* through the Fifties. These confidences, on the contrary, are infinitely precious, but they are not on the same plane as the criticism I am discussing; or, if you will, they constitute a pre-critical, unrefined documentation, and the critic still retains the liberty of interpretation."

Bazin's actual acceptance of the director as author or *"auteur"* is typical of the French critical orientation toward the director as the sole creative artist of consequence in the cinema. Although the personal and poetic artistry of Ingmar Bergman and Federico Fellini in their films of the early Fifties helped encourage a resurgence of serious interest in the cinema, it was not until the *nouvelle vague* emerged that the role of the director became fully romanticized for young people around the world. Bergman and Fellini were, after all, mature artists and remote figures to most of their admirers. Truffaut and Godard were young men in their twenties without practical experience. They were critics and enthusiasts, and they obviously loved movies with none of the dead chill of professionals. They also admired many of their predecessors, artists as disparate as Jean Renoir and Alfred Hitchcock. Above all, they had resurrected many directors from the limbo of low regard and had popularized the *Politique des Auteurs,* a mystique for reviewing directorial careers rather than individual films.

Overnight the director was king. Truffaut expressed the lyricism of being a director simply by freezing Jeanne Moreau on the screen, thus immortalizing her in a medium where montage implies mortality. Rouben Mamoulian did almost the same thing with Garbo in *Queen Christina* in 1933, but he could never go the whole way to freeze her, not because he didn't know how, but because the world of the Thirties was not interested in how Mamoulian felt about Garbo. Mamoulian had been hired simply to present Garbo to her public. By contrast, Truffaut felt empowered to tell the whole world how he felt about Moreau. Jean-Luc Godard has been even more audacious in breaking every possible rule imposed upon a director by producers and aestheticians. If Godard has been abused for his impudence, Federico Fellini (*8½*), Richard Lester (*A Hard Day's Night*), and Tony Richardson (*Tom Jones)* have struck a post-*Breathless* bonanza by exploiting Godard's gimmicks to the hilt. The meaning of all the freezes, jump cuts, and zany camera speeds of the Sixties

19

is simply that directors have found the courage at long last to call attention to their techniques and personalities.

The interviews in this book do not in any sense constitute a definitive critical evaluation of the directors involved. The interviews are instead a kind of supplementation to the evidence on the screen. The film is still the thing, say what its director will, and it still takes more than giving a good interview to make a good film. The most articulate director in the world can also be the most inept film-maker, and, needless to say, the great master can be made to sound like a blithering idiot. In addition to the age-old barrier between the artist and the critic, there is the problem of a largely, though not entirely, visual art form being described in words, words, words. A somewhat frustrated film critic once observed that the only adequate critique of one film is another film. An extreme position, granted, but conversation under even the most ideal circumstances must remain secondary to creation. There will always be more (or less) on the screen than the most artful interview can express. More if the art is superior to its articulation, less if the articulation is revealed on the screen as mere rationalization. Perhaps Soren Kierkegaard anticipated the ultimate mystery of cinematic expression in *Either/Or:* "I call these sketches Shadowgraphs," he writes, "partly by the designation to remind you at once that they derive from the darker side of life, partly because like other shadowgraphs they are not directly visible. When I take a shadowgraph in my hand, it makes no impression on me, and gives me no clear conception of it. Only when I hold it up opposite the wall, and now look not directly at it, but at that which appears on the wall, am I able to see it. So also with the picture which I wish to show here, an inward picture which does not become perceptible until I see it through the external. This external is perhaps quite unobtrusive, but not until I look through it do I discover that inner picture which I desire to show you, an inner picture too delicately drawn to be outwardly visible, woven as it is of the tenderest moods of the soul."

Michelangelo Antonioni

Michelangelo Antonioni burst into prominence at the 1960 Cannes Film Festival where an audience of philistines booed and hissed L'Avventura *as though it were* Le Sacré du Printemps. *From that moment of martyrdom, Antonioni has risen steadily to become one of the mainstays of the modern cinema. In a more personal context, his films from* L'Avventura *to* The Red Desert *signalize his working relationship with Monica Vitti, his star and symbol of anxiety in a world whose technology has outdistanced its sentimental psychology.*

Next to Resnais, Antonioni is the most abstract film-maker in the world of commercial film-making. The director envisages the world as a chessboard on which the kings and queens, the knights and bishops of old have been replaced by pawns whose moves are hopelessly confused by the application of obsolete rules. His first film, Cronaca di un Amore, *focuses on two lovers who are parted by the accidental deaths of a friend and a husband, deaths willed but not executed by the couple. Ever since, Antonioni has been preoccupied with the shadow of guilt that hovers over human relationships before the police arrive. No director in history has been as fascinated by moral permutations of suicides and fatal accidents. Hitchcock and Bunuel have derived dark humor from this casuistic problem that apparently torments Antonioni.*

However, Antonioni's films before L'Avventura-Cronaca di un Amore, La Signora Senza Camelia, Le Amiche, I Vinti, Il Grido—*were concerned also with problems arising from class distinctions and economic calculations. The key to the director's treatment of the relationship between men and women is stated by a character in* Le Amiche:

"Every woman who lives with a man to whom she is superior is unhappy." L'Avventura *and* La Notte *derive their maddening rhythm from the idea that the duration of time drains away human emotions, and their distinctive visual shape from the suggestion that spatial forms create psychological barriers. The unique aesthetic developed by Antonioni has led him to abandon the lower and middle classes in which lives are constricted by necessity and to concentrate on the idle rich who have the time to torture each other.*

Antonioni's camera style represents an evolution of anti-Eisenstein esthetics in the European cinema. The director is noted for his two-shots within which his alienated characters never look at each other. His use of nature is not limited to background effects, but forms the very subject of his dramas. Sicilian landscapes and seascapes furnish the scenario as well as the scenery of L'Avventura, *and industrially ravaged Ravenna provides a similar motif in* The Red Desert.*—A.S.

GODARD—*Your three previous films,* L'Avventura, La Notte, L'Eclisse, *gave us the impression of being in a straight line, going ahead, searching; and now, you arrived in a new area, which is called, perhaps, the* Red Desert, *which is perhaps a desert for this woman but which, for you, is, on the contrary, a film about the entire world, and not only about some fuller and more complete world or other: it's a film about the entire world, and not only about today's world . . .*

ANTONIONI—It is very difficult for me to talk about this film now. It's too recent. I am still too tied up with the "intentions" that pushed me to make it; I have neither the lucidity nor the detachment necessary in order to be able to judge it. I believe I can say, however, that this time it's not a question of a film about sentiments. The results (whether they be good or bad, beautiful or ugly) obtained in my previous films are here out-dated, null and void. This is another matter altogether. Before, it was the relationship of one character to another that interested me.

* *Jean-Luc Godard's interview with Michelangelo Antonioni appeared originally in* Cahiers du Cinema, *No. 160, November 1964. Rose Kaplin's translation appeared in* Cahiers du Cinema *in England, No. 1, January 1966.*

Here, the central character is confronted with a social milieu as well, and this means I must treat my story in a completely different way. It simplifies things too much (as many have done) to say that I accuse this inhuman, industrialized world in which the individual is crushed and led to neurosis. My intention, on the contrary (moreover, we may know very well where we start but not at all where we'll end up), was to translate the beauty of this world, in which even the factories can be very beautiful. . . . The line, the curves of factories and their smoke-stacks, are perhaps more beautiful than a row of trees—which every eye has already seen to the point of monotony. It's a rich world—living, useful. As for me, I hold that the sort of neurosis seen in *Red Desert* is above all a question of adaptation. There are people who adapt themselves, and others who haven't yet done this, for they are too tied to structures, or life-rhythms, that are now out of date. This is the case with Giuliana. The violence of the variation, the wedge between her sensitivity, intelligence and psychology and the cadence that is imposed on her, provoke the character's breakdown. It is a breakdown concerning not only her epidermic contacts with the world, her perception of the noises, colors, cold personalities surrounding her, but also her system of value (education, morality, faith), which are no longer valuable and no longer sustain her. She finds herself, thus, in the position of needing to renew herself completely, as a woman. This is what the doctors advise and this is what she strives to do.

GODARD—*What is the explanation for the insert of the episode of the story she tells the little boy?*

ANTONIONI—There is a woman and a sick child. The mother must tell the child a story, but he has already heard all the ones she knows. She must therefore invent one. Giuliana's psychology being given, it seems natural to me that this story become, for her—unconsciously—an evasion of the reality surrounding her, towards a world where the colors belong to nature: the blue sea, the pink sand. The rocks themselves take on human form, embrace her and sing sweetly.

Do you remember the scene in the room, with Corrado? She says, leaning against the wall, "Do you know what I'd like? . . . Everyone who ever loved me . . . to have them here, around me, like a wall." She needs them, in fact, to help her live, because she is afraid she won't be able to arrive at it alone.

23

GODARD—*The modern world is therefore only the revealer of an older and more profound neurosis?*

ANTONIONI—The milieu in which Giuliana lives accelerates the personality's breakdown, but, naturally, the personality must carry within itself a favorable terrain for this breakdown. It isn't easy to determine the causes and origins of neurosis; it is manifested in such different forms, at times going as far as schizophrenia, whose symptoms often resemble neurotic symptoms. But it is by means of a like exasperation that one arrives at encompassing a situation. I have been reproached for having chosen a pathological case. But, if I had chosen a normally adapted woman, there would no longer be a drama; the drama concerns those who do not adapt.

GODARD—*Aren't there already traces of this character in the one in* L'Eclisse?

ANTONIONI—The character of Vittoria in *L'Eclisse* is the opposite of that of Giuliana. In *L'Eclisse,* Vittoria is a calm and well-balanced girl, who thinks about what she does. There isn't a single neurotic element in her. The crisis, in *L'Eclisse,* is a crisis of the sentiments. In *Red Desert,* the sentiments are a ready-made fact. Morever, the relationship between Giuliana and her husband is normal. If you were to ask her, "Do you love your husband?," she would answer yes. Until her attempt at suicide, the crisis is underground, it is not visible.

I want to underline the fact that it isn't the milieu that gives birth to the breakdown: it only makes it show. One may think that outside of this milieu, there is no breakdown. But that's not true. Our life, even if we don't take account of it, is dominated by "industry." And "industry" shouldn't be understood to mean factories only, but also and above all, products. These products are everywhere, they enter our homes, made of plastics and other materials unknown barely a few years ago; they overtake us wherever we may be. With the help of publicity, which considers our psychology and our subconscious more and more carefully, they obsess us. I can say this: by situating the story of *Red Desert* in the world of factories, I have gone back to the source of that sort of crisis which, like a torrential river, swelled a thousand tributaries, divides in a thousand arms in order, finally, to submerge everything and spread everywhere.

GODARD—*But isn't this beauty of the modern world also the resolution of the characters' psychological difficulties, doesn't it show vanity?*

ANTONIONI—One must not underestimate the drama of man thus conditioned. Without drama, there are perhaps no longer men. Furthermore, I do not believe that the beauty of the modern world in itself can resolve our dramas. I believe, on the contrary, that once adapted to new life-techniques we will perhaps find new solutions to our problems.

But why have me speak of these things? I am not a philosopher and all these observations have nothing to do with the "invention" of the film.

GODARD—*Was the presence of the robot in the little boy's room benevolent or malevolent?*

ANTONIONI—In my opinion, benevolent. Because the child, by playing with this genre of toy, will adapt very well to the life waiting for him. But here we come back to what we were just talking about. The toys are produced by industry, which in this way even influences the education of children.

I am still stupefied by a conversation I had with a cybernetics professor from the University of Milan, Silvio Ceccato, considered by the Americans to be another Einstein. A formidable type, who has invented a machine that looks and describes, a machine that can drive a car, make a report from an aesthetic point of view—or ethical or journalistic, etc. And it's not a matter of television: it's an electronic brain. This man, who, moreover, proved to be extraordinarily lucid, never spoke one technical word in the course of a conversation I didn't understand. Well, I went crazy. At the end of each minute, I no longer understood anything of what he had just said to me. He forced himself to use my language, but he was in another world. With him was a young girl, 24 or 25 years old, pretty, of *petit bourgeois* origin—his secretary. Now she understood it perfectly. In Italy, these are generally very young and very simple girls, who have only a modest diploma, who work at programming electronic brains: for them, it's very simple and very easy to program an electronic brain— while it isn't easy at all for me.

Another savant, Robert M. Stewart, came to see me, six months ago, in Rome. He had invented a chemical brain and presented himself at a cybernetics congress in Naples to give an account of his discovery, which is one of the most extraordinary discoveries in the world. It's a very small box, mounted on tubes: it's a matter of cells, into whose composition gold enters, mixed with other substances. The cells are alive in a liquid chemical and they live an autonomous life; they have reactions: if you come into the room, the cell takes on a certain form; and if I come in, it takes on another form, etc. In this little box there are only a few million cells, but starting from that, one can arrive at remaking the human brain. This savant feeds them, puts them to sleep . . . he talked to me about all that, which was very clear but so unbelievable that at a certain point I was no longer following him. By contrast, when he gets a little older, the little boy who plays with the robot from earliest childhood will understand very well; he will have no trouble at all in going, if he wants to, out to space in a rocket.

I look at all that with a great deal of envy, and would like to be already in this new world. Unfortunately, we aren't there yet; it's a drama that will last several generations—mine, yours, and the generation of those born right after WW II. I think that, in the years to come, there are going to be very violent transformations, both in the world and in the individual's interior. Today's crisis comes from this spiritual confusion, from this confusion of conscience, of faith and of politics; there are so many symptoms of the transformations to come. Then I said to myself, "What does one say, today, in the cinema?" And I wanted to tell a story based on these motivations I was talking about before.

GODARD—*However, the heroes of this film are integrated with this mentality, these are engineers, they're part of this world. . . .*

ANTONIONI—Not all of them. The character played by Richard Harris is almost a romantic, who thinks about fleeing to Patagonia and has no idea at all about what he must do. He is taking flight and believes he is resolving, in this way, the problems of his life. But this problem is inside, not outside, of him. All the more true that it is enough for him to meet a woman in order to provoke a crisis, and he no longer knows whether he will leave or not; the whole thing turns him around. I would like to point out a moment in the film which is an accusation of the old world: when, at the breaking point, this woman needs someone to help her, she finds a man who profits from her and from that crisis. She finds herself face-to-face with old things, and it is the old things that shake her and sweep her off her feet. If she had met someone like her husband, he would have acted differently; he would have, first of all, tried to take care of her, then, after that,

26

perhaps. . . . When there, it's her own world that betrays her.

GODARD—*At the end of the film is she going to become like her husband?*

ANTONIONI—I believe that, following the efforts she makes to find a link with reality, she ends by finding a compromise. Neurotics have crises, but also moments of lucidity which may last all their lives. Perhaps she finds a compromise, but the neurosis stays with her. I believe I have given the idea of this continuity of illness by means of the slightly soft image: she is in a static phase. What is she going to become? Another film would have to be made in order to know that.

GODARD—*Do you think that this new world's heightened consciousness may have repercussions on aesthetics, on the conception of the artist?*

ANTONIONI—Yes, I believe so. That changes the way of seeing, of thinking: everything changes. Pop Art demonstrated that something else is sought. One must not underestimate Pop Art. It is an "ironic" movement, and this conscious irony is very important. The Pop Art painters know very well that they are making things whose aesthetic value is not yet ripe—except for Rauschenberg, who is more of a painter than the others. . . . even though Oldenburg's "soft typewriter" is very fine. . . . I like it very much. It believes it is good that all that is coming out. That can only accelerate the transformation process in question.

GODARD—*But does the savant have the conscience we do? Does he reason as we do, in respect to the world?*

ANTONIONI—I asked that of Stewart, the inventor of the chemical brain. He answered that his very specialized work, without a doubt, had reverberations in his private life, even including his relationship with his family.

GODARD—*And must the sentiments be preserved?*

ANTONIONI—What a question! Do you think it is easy to answer that? All I can say about sentiments is that they must change. "Must" isn't what I mean to say. They are changing. They have already changed.

GODARD—*In the science-fiction novels, there are never artists, poets. . . .*

ANTONIONI—Yes, it's curious. Perhaps they think that one can do without art. Perhaps we are the last to produce things so apparently gratuitous as are works of art.

27

GODARD—*Does* Red Desert *also help you to settle personal problems?*

ANTONIONI—While making a film, we live, and nevertheless, we are always settling personal problems. Problems which concern our work, but also our private life. If the things we talk about are not those we were talking about right after the war, it is because the world around us has, in fact, changed and, also, we ourselves have changed. Our requirements have changed, our purposes, our themes.

Right after the war, there were numerous things to be said; it was interesting to show social reality, the social condition of the individual. Today, all that has already been seen and done. The new themes we can treat of today are those about which we were just speaking. I don't know yet how we can approach them, present them. I have tried to develop one of these themes in *Red Desert* and I don't think I exhausted it. It is only the beginning of a series of problems and aspects of our modern society and of the way of life that is ours. Moreover, you too, Godard, you make very modern films, your way of treating subjects reveals an intense need to break with the past.

GODARD—*When you begin or end certain sequences with quasi-abstract forms of objects or details, do you do it in a pictorial spirit?*

ANTONIONI—I feel the need to express reality in terms that are not completely realistic. The abstract white line that enters the picture at the beginning of the sequence of the little gray street interests me much more than the car that arrives: it's a way of approaching the character in terms of things rather than by means of her life. Her life, basically, interests me only relatively. It is a character that participates in the story as a function of her femininity; her feminine aspect and character are the essential things for me. It is exactly for that reason that I had this role played a bit statically.

GODARD—*Thus, there is also on this point a break with your previous films.*

ANTONIONI—Yes, it is a less realistic film, from a figurative point of view. That is to say, it is realistic in a different way. For example, I used the telescopic lens a great deal in order not to have deep-focus, which is for good reason an indispensable element of realism. What interests me now is to place the character in contact with things, for it is things, objects and materials that have weight

28

today. I do not consider *Red Desert* a result: it is a research. I want to tell different stories with different means. Everything that's been done, everything I've done until now no longer interests me, it bores me. Perhaps you, too, feel the same thing?

GODARD—*Was filming in color an important change?*

ANTONIONI—Very important. I had to change my technique because of it, but not only because of it. I already had a need to change my technique, for the reasons we've spoken about. My requirements were no longer the same. The fact of using color accelerated this change. With color, you don't use the same lenses. Also, I perceived that certain camera movements didn't always jell with it: a rapid panoramic sweep is efficacious on brilliant red, but it does nothing for a sour green, unless you're looking for a new contrast. I believe there is a relationship between camera movement and color. A single film is not sufficient for studying the problem in depth, but it's a problem that must be examined. I made, for this reason, some 16mm tests. They were very interesting, but I was unable to achieve, in the film itself, certain effects I had found by this means. Up to this point, I've been in too much of a corner.

You know that a psycho-physiology of color exists; studies, experiments have been done on this subject. The interior of the factory seen in the film was painted red; two weeks later the workers were fighting amongst one another. It was re-painted in pale green and everyone was peaceful. The workers' eyes must have a rest.

GODARD—*How did you choose the colors for the store?*

ANTONIONI—It was necessary to choose between warm colors and cool colors. Giuliana wants cool colors for her store. These are colors that are less discordant with the objects displayed. If you paint a wall orange, this color will kill any object nearby, while sky-blue or pale green will set the objects off without overwhelming them. I wanted this contrast between warm colors and cool colors: there is an orange, a yellow, a maroon ceiling, and my character discovers that, for her, they don't go well together.

GODARD—*The film's title was* Celeste E Verde (*Heavenly Blue And Green*).

ANTONIONI—I abandoned it, because it didn't seem to be a virile enough title; it was too directly linked to the color. Moreover, I had never thought about color in itself. The film was born in colors, but I always thought, first of all, of the thing to be said—this is natural—and thus aided the expression by means of the color. I never thought: I'm going to put a blue next to a maroon. I dyed the grass around the shed on the edge of the marsh in order to reinforce the sense of desolation, of death. The landscape had to be rendered truthfully: when trees are dead, they have that color.

GODARD—*The drama is thus no longer psychological, but plastic. . . .*

ANTONIONI—It's the same thing.

GODARD—*Thus, all those shots of objects during the conversation about Patagonia? . . .*

ANTONIONI—It's a sort of "distraction" on the character's part. He is tired of listening to all these conversations. He is thinking of Giuliana.

GODARD—*The dialogue is simpler, more functional than that of your previous films; isn't their traditional role of "commentary" taken by the color?*

ANTONIONI—Yes, I believe that is true. Let us say that, here, the dialogue is reduced to an indispensable minimum and that, in this sense, it is linked to the color. For example, I would never have done the scene in the shack where they talk about drugs, aphrodisiacs, without using red. I would never have done it in black and white. The red puts the spectator in a state of mind that permits him to accept this dialogue. The color is correct for the characters (who are justified by it) and also for the spectator.

GODARD—*Do you feel yourself to be closer to the researches of painters than to those of novelists?*

ANTONIONI—I don't feel too distant from the researches of the New Novel, but they help me less than the others: painting and scientific research interest me more. I don't believe they influence me directly. There is, in this film, no pictorial research at all; we are far from painting, it seems to me. And, naturally, the requirements of painting have nothing to do with narrative content, where one is found in the cinema: this is where the novel's researches join those of painting.

GODARD—*Did you re-work the color in the laboratory, as is permitted with Technicolor?*

ANTONIONI—I placed no confidence at all in the laboratory, during the shooting. That is to say, I tried, during the shooting, to put the colors I wanted on the things themselves, on the landscapes. I painted directly, instead of trafficking with color in the laboratory. After that, what I demanded from the laboratory was a faithful reproduction of the effects I had obtained. It wasn't easy, for Technicolor, as you know, requires numerous operations involving the master print: the job was very long and delicate.

GODARD—*You verified things during the shooting, as you went along. . . .*

ANTONIONI—Exactly. I believe one mustn't place too much trust in the work that can be done in the laboratory. It's not their fault. It's just that technically, color is still a long way behind.

GODARD—*In your opinion, does Giuliana see the color as you show it?*

ANTONIONI—You know, there are neurotics who see color differently. Doctors have done experiments on this subject, with mescaline for example, in order to try to know what they see. At a certain point, I had the intention of having some effects of this nature. But now there is no longer anything of this but one single moment, when you see stains on a wall. I also thought of modifying the color of certain objects, and then the fact of using all those "tricks" very quickly seemed to me to become artificial; it was an artificial way of saying things which could be said in a much more simple way. Well, I eliminated these effects. But we may think that she sees color differently.

It's amusing: at this moment, I am speaking with Godard, one of the most modern talented *cinéastes* of today, and just a little while ago, I lunched with René Clair, one of the greatest directors of the past: it wasn't at all the same genre of conversation . . . he is preoccupied with the future of the cinema. We, on the contrary (you agree, I believe), have confidence in the future of the cinema.

GODARD—*And what are you going to do now?*

ANTONIONI—I am going to do a sketch with Soraya. . . . This sketch interests me because I am going to pursue my researches with color, push ahead the experiments I did with *Red Desert*. After that, I'm going to make a film that interests me more. If I find a producer who will let me do it. . . .

Michelangelo Antonioni (1912–   ):
Filmography:
Documentaries: 1943–1947—Gente Del Po. 1948—N.U. 1948–1949—
L'Amorosa Menzogna, Superstizione. 1949—Sette Canne Un Vestito.
1950—La Funivia Del Faloria, La Villa Dei Mostri. 1955—Uomini in Piu.
Features: 1950—Cronaca Di Un Amore. 1952—I Vinti. 1952–1953—

Ingmar Bergman

Ingmar Bergman, perhaps more than any other director, has made the cinema fashionable for intellectuals and aesthetes normally hostile to movies as such. The allegorical awesomeness of The Seventh Seal *aroused American high-brows in the late Fifties much as the montage dialectics of* Potemkin *did a generation before. Bergman's tone was generally somber, his subjects the very gravest. Cults arose to hail him for his profoundity, and counter-cults assailed him for his ponderousness. Bergman himself used* The Devil's Eye (1960) *as a means to chide his more solemn critics with a spoof of the Don Juan legend as it affects the perverse Swedish temperament. Gunnar Bjornstrand steps in front of the screen, so to speak, to explain that the audience is not to take the proceedings too seriously, particularly the Hollywood hell with central heating that might have graced Ernst Lubitsch's* Heaven Can Wait. *However, when Bergman gets down to earth with a classical male and a modern female, he is curiously intense about the nature of love. As always, there are serious overtones to his lightest scenes and a suggestion of amusement at his gravest moments. It is this perpetual counterpoint that is part of the magic and mystery of Ingmar Bergman.*

Bergman's personality is stamped on his films from the beginning of his career. The wry wit and metaphysical morbidity are inimitable trademarks of a peculiarly incisive sensibility. In addition, films like Monika, The Naked Night, *and* The Silence *are among the most erotic works ever executed by a film director. Bergman's violence does in fact save his cinema from deadening gentility and re-*

finement. As Antonioni is sometimes criticized for the fallacy of expressive form, that is showing boredom boringly, Bergman is more often criticized for the fallacy of impressive content because of a tendency to overload dramatic psychology with gratuitous theology. Nonetheless Bergman has displayed an extraordinary range of themes and subjects, and he is incontestably one of the great directors of actors in the history of the cinema. Along with Ophuls, Mizoguchi, and Antonioni, Bergman is an eloquent pleader for women as the instruments of the life force. Ultimately, Bergman has ennobled the cinema by entrusting to it the gravest issues of Western Civilization and by staking his own personality on the outcome of his art. Above all, Bergman has managed not infrequently to be as entertaining as he is edifying.*—A.S.

"Making films" is for me a necessity of nature, a need comparable to hunger and thirst. Some achieve self-expression by writing books, climbing mountains, beating their children, or dancing the samba. I happen to express myself by making films.

In *The Blood of a Poet*, the great Cocteau shows us his alter ego staggering down a nightmarish hotel corridor and makes us peer behind every door at those hallucinatory self-projections which constitute his "I."

Without pretending today to equate my personality with Cocteau's, I have thought of conducting you on a tour of my interior studios, there where my films unfold invisibly. I fear this visit will disappoint you: The equipment is always scattered about because the proprietor is too taken up with business problems to find the time to arrange things in order. In addition, the light is rather bad in certain places, and some doors feature signs boldly lettered: "PRIVATE." Finally, the guide himself sometimes wonders what there is worth showing.

Be that as it may, we will push a few doors ajar. That is not to say that you will find exactly the answer to the questions you have put to yourself, but perhaps, despite all, you may be able to assemble some pieces of a complicated puzzle that represents the unfolding of a film.

* Ingmar Bergman's article "What Is Making Films" originally appeared in Cahiers du Cinema, No. 61, July 1956. Alice Turner provided the English translation.

If we consider the most fundamental element of cinematographic art, the perforated strip of film, we note that it is composed of small rectangular images—fifty-two to the meter—with each separated from its neighbors by a black band. Looking more closely, we discover that these tiny rectangles, which at first glance seem to contain the same details, differ one from the next only by an almost imperceptible modification of these details. And when the feeding mechanism of the projector presents these successive images on the screen in such a manner that we see each image for only one twenty-fourth of a second, we have the illusion of movement.

Between each of these little rectangles the aperture passes before the lens and plunges us into complete darkness before restoring us to full light with the following rectangle.

When I was ten years old and I operated my first magic lantern—with its chimney, its petrol lamp, and its constantly repeating films—I found the above phenomenon exciting and mysterious. Even today, I feel in myself the nervous excitement of childhood when I realize that I am actually an illusionist, since cinema exists only because of an imperfection in the human eye, its inability to perceive separately pictures that follow one another rapidly and are essentially similar.

I have calculated that if I see a film that lasts an hour, I am in fact plunged into absolute blackness for twenty minutes. In making a film, I am thus guilty of fraud; I make use of an apparatus built to take advantage of a human physical imperfection, of an apparatus thanks to which I carry my audience, as if on a pendulum, from one mood to another mood at the opposite extreme: I make it laugh, cry out with fright, smile, believe in legends, become indignant, take offense, become enthusiastic, become bawdy, or yawn with boredom. Thus, I am no better than a fraud, no better than—considering that the public is aware of the deceit—an illusionist. I mystify, and I have at my disposition the most precious and the most amazing magical apparatus that has ever been, in all the history of the world, in the hands of a mountebank.

There is here, or there ought to be here, for all those who make or sell films, the source of an insoluble moral conflict.

As for our commercial partners, this is not the moment to go into the mistakes that they have made from one year

35

to the next, but it would be worthwhile if a scientist would one day discover a system of weights or measures capable of computing the amount of natural gifts, of initiative, of talent and creative force which the film industry has mangled in its formidable machinery. Clearly, he who wishes to enter the race must accept the rules in advance, and there is no reason why work in the cinema should be more respected than work in any other field. The difference seems to be chiefly that, in our specialty, brutality manifests itself more openly, but in a way this is an advantage.

Loss of equilibrium has consequences more dire for the conscientious film-maker than for a tightrope walker or an acrobat who performs under the circus tent without a net. For the film-maker and the tightrope artist, the risk is of the same order: *Falling and killing oneself.* Doubtless you think this an exaggeration: making a film is not nearly so dangerous! Nevertheless I stick to my statement: The risk is equal. Even if, as I said, one is somewhat of a magician, one cannot deceive the producers, the bank directors, the theater owners, or the critics when the public will not go to see a film and pay out the money from which the producers, bank directors, theater owners, critics, and magicians must earn their livings.

I can cite you the example of a recent experience, the memory of which still makes me tremble and in which I nearly lost my own equilibrium. An unusually courageous producer invested money in one of my films that, after a year of intense activity, appeared under the title *The Naked Night (Gycklarnas afton)*. The critics were generally unfavorable, the public stayed away, the producer calculated his losses, and as for me, I had to wait several years before I could get another project.

If I make two or three more films that show a financial loss, the producers will conclude justifiably that it would be better to stake no more money on my talents.

Thus I would become immediately suspect, a loser, and I would be able to reflect at leisure how to use my so-called artistic gifts: the magician would be deprived of his apparatus.

When I was younger, I did not resent these uncertainties. The work was an exciting game for me, and whether the results were successful or unsuccessful, I rejoiced in my activities like a child with his castles of sand or clay. The performer danced on his rope, unconscious of and therefore careless of the abyss and the hard ground of the circus ring.

The game has changed into a bitter struggle. The walk along the tightrope is made now with full knowledge of danger, and the points to which the cord is attached are called fear and incertitude. Each work calls forth all my resources of energy. Creation has become, under the effect of causes not so much interior as exterior and economic, a demanding duty. Failure, criticism, public indifference today make more painful wounds. The wounds take time to heal, and the scars are deeper and last longer.

Before undertaking a project or after having started it, Jean Anouilh used to concentrate on a little game in order to exorcise fear. He said to himself: "My father is a tailor. He takes deep pleasure in what his hands have created, handsome trousers or an elegant coat. It is the pleasure and satisfaction of the artisan, the pride of a man who knows his trade."

I do this also. I recognize the game, I play it often and I succeed in fooling myself and others, even though this game is played only as an ineffective sedative: "My films are good work. I am dedicated, conscientious, extremely attentive to details. I work for my contemporaries and not for eternity; my pride is the pride of the artisan."

However, I know that, if I speak this way, it is in order to deceive myself, and an uncontrollable restlessness cries: "What have you made that can last? Is there in your films a single meter of film worth passing on to posterity, a single line, a single situation that is really and indisputably true?"

To this I must reply—perhaps still under the effect of an ineradicable disloyalty, but most sincerely: "I don't know, I hope so."

You must excuse my having described at such length and with so much commentary the dilemma which is imposed on the creators of films. I wanted to try to explain to you why so many of those who work in the cinema succumb to a temptation that is invisible and difficult to explain. Why we fear, why sometimes we lose heart in the work, why we become stupid and allow ourselves to be annihilated in tarnished and poisoned compromises.

I would like however to linger a little longer on one of the aspects of the problem, on the most important and the most difficult to grasp, the public. The creator of films deals with a medium of expression that interests not only

37

himself but also millions of other people, and most of the time he feels the same desire as other artists: "I want to succeed *today*. I want fame *now*. I want to please, to delight, to move *at once*."

Midway between this wish and its realization is the public—and they want only one thing from a film: "I've paid. I want to be diverted, caught up, involved. I want to forget my troubles, my surroundings, my work. I want to get away from myself. I am here, seated in the darkness, and like a woman about to give birth, I want to be *delivered*."

The film-maker who recognizes this need and who lives off the public's purse is placed in a difficult situation that imposes certain obligations. In making his film, he must always take into consideration the reaction of the public. For me personally, I continually ask myself the question: "Can I express myself more simply, more purely, more briefly? Will everyone be able to understand what I am saying now? Will the most simple soul be able to follow the line of action? And this, which is the most important: Up to what point have I the right to compromise, and where does my obligation to myself begin?"

All experimentation necessarily implies great risk, because it always alienates the public. But, the alienation of the public can lead to sterility, to isolation in an ivory tower.

It would be wonderful if producers as well as other directors of film techniques put laboratories at the disposition of the creators. But this is never the case in our day. Producers trust only engineers and imagine stupidly that the health of the film industry depends on invention and technical complications.

Nothing is easier than to frighten a spectator. He can be literally maddened, for most people have in some part of their being a fear always ready to come forth. It is much more difficult to make him laugh, to make him *really* laugh. It is easy to put a spectator into a state worse than the one he arrived in, it is difficult to put him into a better state; still it is this that he wants each time he goes into the darkness of the cinema. But how often and by what methods do we give him this satisfaction?

It is thus that I reason, at the same time knowing very well and with absolute evidence that this reasoning is dangerous, that it takes the risk of condemning all failure, of confounding idealism with pride, of considering as absolutes the frontiers that the public and the critics mark out for you even when you do not acknowledge them and they are not your own, since your personality is always in evolution. On the one hand, I am tempted to adopt myself, to make myself what the public wants me to be, but on the other hand, I sense that this would be the end of everything, this would suppose total indifference in me. Also I count myself happy not to have been born with exactly as much intelligence as feeling; it is nowhere written that a film-maker must be content, happy, or satisfied. Who has said that he must not make noise, break barriers, battle against windmills, send robots to the moon, have visions, play with dynamite, or tear pieces of flesh from himself or others? Why can't someone frighten film producers? It's their job to be frightened; they are paid for their stomach ulcers!

But "film-making" is not only running up against problems, dilemmas, economic cares, responsibilities, and fears. There are also games, dreams, secret memories. It often begins with a picture: a face suddenly and forcefully illuminated, a hand lifting, a moment at dawn with some old women seated on a bench, separated by a sack of apples. Or sometimes it is an exchange of words: two persons, suddenly, say something to each other in a completely personal tone of voice; perhaps their backs are turned, I cannot even see their faces and thus I am forced to listen, to wait until they speak again, till they repeat the same words, unimportant but charged with a secret tension, a tension of which I am not yet clearly conscious but which acts like a surreptitious filter. The illuminated face, the hand lifted as if for an incantation, the old women in the square, the banal words, all these images come to attach themselves to my line like brilliant fish, or more exactly, I myself am caught by a line the texture of which I happily ignore.

Soon enough, well before the theme is entirely drawn out in my mind, I submit the games of my imaginaton to the test of reality. I pose, as in a game, my sketch, still very fragile and incomplete, on an easel in order to judge it from the point of view of all the technical resources of the studios. This imaginary test of "viability" acts on the motif like a coating of rust. Does it hold up? Will the motif hold on to its worth when it is plunged into the daily and murderous routine of the studios, far from the shadowy bright dawns in the games of the imagination?

Some of my films come to fruition very quickly and are quickly finished. These are the films that come up to general expectation. The children are always undisciplined, but always healthy; one can at once predict that they will carry on the family line.

Then, there are the other films—those that come slowly, that take years, that refuse to let themselves be imprisoned by a technical or formal solution, that usually refuse any concrete solution. They stay in the shadow; if I want to find them again, I must follow them, find a context, persons, situations. Here, the faces turned away start to speak, the roads are strange, some few persons glance out through the casement window, an eye gleams in the twilight or changes itself into a carbuncle, then bursts with the sound of a shattering crystal. The square, on this autumn morning, is a sea, the old women have transformed themselves into ancient trees, and the apples are children who build cities of sand and stone near the spray of the waves. *VISUAL IMAGES WHICH TURN INTO FILM.*

What is it then to "shoot a film"? If I asked all of you this question, I would doubless get somewhat different replies, but you would agree perhaps on one point: To shoot a film is to do what is necessary to put the contents of the script on film. In this you would say much, and at the same time too little. For me, shooting a film represents days of inhumanly maddening work, backaches, eyes full of dust, smells of makeup, sweat and lights, a never-ending series of tensions and delays, an uninterrupted battle between will and duty, between vision and reality, conscience and laziness. I bear in mind the morning risings, the nights without sleep, of the most acute sentiment in life, a sort of fanaticism centered around the one work, by means of which I finally become an integral part of the film, an apparatus, ridiculously small, whose sole fault is to require food and drink.

It happens sometimes that in the middle of this excitement, when all the studios buzz with so much life and work that they seem ready to burst, I find the idea for my next film. You would be wrong, however, if you think that the activity of a film-maker takes on at this moment a sort of ecstatic vertigo, an uncontrollable excitation, and a dreadful disorganization. To shoot a film is to undertake to train a hard-to-handle horse for the grand prize; one must have a clear head, meticulousness, firm and exact calculations. Add to this an always even disposition and a patience that is not of this world.

To shoot a film is to organize an entire universe, but the chief elements are the industry, the money, the fabrication, the point of view, the development and the print, a schedule to follow, though it is rarely followed, a meticulous plan of action in which irrational factors make up the highest percentage. The sentry has on too much eye make-up—fifteen thousand dollars to begin the scene again. One day the water from the pipes has too much chlorine in it: the negatives are spoiled—begin again! Another day, death does you the bad turn of removing an actor—begin again with another—and there are millions of other pitfalls waiting for you. It thunders, the electric transformer has a breakdown, and we wait, all covered with makeup, in the pale daylight while the hours roll by and the money rolls by with them.

Idiotic examples, taken at random. But they are able to be idiotic because they touch on the great and sublime idiocy: that of transforming shadowy dreams, dividing a tragedy into five little pieces, playing with each one of them, then putting together all these pieces in such a way as to reconstitute a unity that will be once again a tragedy: that of fabricating a tape of 2,500 meters that conforms to the life and soul of actors, producers, and directors. To shoot a film is all that, but is still more, and it is still worse.

To make films is also to plunge again by its deepest roots down to the *world of childhood*. Let us descend, if you would like to, into the interior studio situated in the most intimate recess in the life of the director. We open for a moment the most secret of his rooms to see there a picture of Venice, an old window-blind, and the first magic-lantern apparatus.

At Upsala, my grandmother lived in a very old apartment. I slid along there under the dining room table, dressed in an apron with a pocket in front, and there I listened to the voice of the rays of sunlight that came in through the immensely high windows. The rays of sun moved continually, the bells of the cathedral resounded; the rays moved and their movement engendered something like a special sound. It was a day between winter and spring; I had had the measles, and I was five years old. In the next-door apartment someone was playing the piano —always waltzes—and on the wall hung a large picture

41

representing Venice. As the sun rays and the shadows passed in waves over the picture, the water in the canal began to flow, the pigeons to rise above the pavement of the square, the people to talk to each other noiselessly with gestures of their hands and heads. The sound of bells came not from the cathedral, but from the picture, the same with the piano tunes. This picture of Venice had something altogether strange about it. Almost as strange as the fact that the rays of sunlight in my grandmother's salon were not silent, but had a sound. It was perhaps all those bells . . . or maybe the big pieces of furniture that talked with each other in a continual murmur.

I think I can remember, however, an experience even older than that of the measles year, the perception—impossible to date—of the movement of a window-blind. It was a black window-blind of the most popular type that I saw in my child's room, at dawn or in the evening, when everything becomes alive and a little frightening, when even the playthings turn into hostile things, or simply strange and indifferent things. So the world was no longer the everyday world with my mother's presence, but a silent and dizzying solitude. It was not that the window-blind moved; no shadow appeared there. It was on the surface itself that the shapes were found: not men, not animals, not heads, nor faces, but things for which there is no name! In the dimness crossed with bars of light, these shapes detached themselves from the blind and advanced toward the green screen or toward the desk with its carafe of water. They were unpitying, impassive, and frightening: they disappeared only when it became really dark or really light or when sleep overtook me.

He who, like myself, is born into a minister's family learns very early to look behind the scenes at life and at death. Father has a burial, a marriage, a baptism, a retreat, he writes a sermon. One makes a very early acquaintance with the devil; one needs to give him a concrete form. But it is here that the game of the magic lantern comes in, the little iron box with the gas lamp (I can still smell the odor of the heated iron) and the color projections. There was, among others, Little Red Riding Hood and the Wolf. The Wolf was the devil, a devil without horns, but with a tail and bright red jowls, a devil curiously palpable and at the same time ungraspable, the representative of evil and persecution on the flowered paper of a child's room.

42

The first film that I had in my possession was three meters long and was brown. It represented a young girl asleep in a field; she awoke, stretched, got up, and, arms outstretched, disappeared on the right side of the picture. That was it. On the box in which the film was put again was drawn a blushing picture with the words "Frau Holle." No one in my circle knew who Frau Holle was, but it hardly mattered; the film was a great success and was played every evening until it disintegrated to the point where it could no longer be repaired.

This shaky little cinema was my first magician's box. In fact, strangely enough, the toy was mechanical, the people and things never changed. I often ask myself how it was able to fascinate me so much, that which, still today, fascinates me in exactly the same way. This thought comes to me sometimes in the studio or in the darkness of the editing room, where I have in front of me the little picture and the film passes between my fingers, or again during the fantastic childbirth that represents the recomposition when the finished film slowly unveils itself. I cannot stop myself from thinking that I handle an instrument so refined that it is possible for us to illuminate with it the human soul with a light infinitely *more* vivid, to unveil it still more brutally, and to add to our knowledge new domains of reality. Perhaps we will even discover a crack that will let us penetrate into the *clair-obscur* of surrealism to tell our tales in a new and overwhelming way. [*Note:* he does not mean Surrealism, the film form, but a kind of surreality.] At the risk of stating one more something that I cannot prove, I would like to say that, in my opinion, we who make films, we use only a minuscule part of a frightening power—we move no more than the little finger of a giant who is nothing if not dangerous.

But it is equally possible that I am wrong. It may be that film has attained the highest point in its evolution, that this instrument, by its own nature, is not able to conquer new ground, that we are brought up short with our noses to the wall, the road ending in a cul-de-sac. Many are of this opinion, and it is a fact that we are standing in a swamp, nose just above the water's surface, paralyzed by economic cares, conventions, foolishness, fear, uncertainty, and disorder.

I am sometimes asked what I am looking for in my films, what is my *goal*. The question is difficult and dangerous, and I usually reply with a lie or an evasion: "I am

43

trying to say the truth about the human condition, the truth as I see it." This response satisfies them, and I often ask myself why nobody notices my bluff, because the real response should be: "I feel an irrepressible need to express in film that which, completely subjectively, is part of my consciousness. In this case I have therefore no other goal but *myself*, my daily bread, the amusement and respect of the public, a sort of truth that I find to be right at that particular moment. And if I try to sum up my second response, the final formula is a not very enthusiastic: "An activity of no great significance."

I will not say that this conclusion overly embarrasses me. I am in the same position as the majority of the artists of my generation: Our activity has in the end no great meaning. Art for art's sake. My personal truth, or perhaps three-fourths of the truth or none at all, except that it has value for me. THE ARTISTS MISTAKE.

I know that this way of looking at things is very unpopular, especially these days. Thus I will make haste to put my position more precisely by formulating the question in another way: "What would you like to have as a goal in making your films?"

They say that in the old days the cathedral of Chartres, struck by lightning, burned to the ground. Then, they say, thousands of people hurried from all the corners of the world, people in every walk of life; they crossed Europe like migrating lemmings and began, all together, to rebuild the cathedral on its ancient foundations. They lived there until the immense building was completed, architects, workmen, artists, jugglers, nobles, prelates, and ordinary middle-class people, but their names were unknown, and even today no one knows who built Chartres Cathedral.

Without saying that this should cause you to prejudge my beliefs or my doubts—which in this context are not important—I think that art lost its significance to life at the moment when it separated itself from worship (religion). It broke the umbilical cord, and it lives its own separate life, surprisingly sterile, dulled and degenerated. Collective creativity, the humble anonymous man are relics, forgotten and buried, destitute of value. My little griefs and moral stomach aches are examined with a microscope *sub specie aeternitatis*. The fear of the dark that characterizes subjectivism and the scrupulous conscience has become the great thing, and we run finally into the dead end where we argue with each other on the subject

44

of our solitude, without any of us listening to the others or even noticing that we have pressed so close to one another as almost to die of suffocation. It is thus that the individualists see themselves in their own eyes, denying the existence of what they see and invoking the omnipotent obscurity, never testing, even once, the saving grace of the joys of community (working together). We are truly imprisoned in our vicious circles, so enclosed in our own anguish that we have become incapable of distinguishing the real from the false, the ideals of gangsters from sincere abandon.

To the question asked about the goal of my film, I would be able thus to reply: "I want to be one of the artists of the cathedral that rises on the plain. I want to occupy myself by carving out of stone the head of a dragon, an angel or a demon, or perhaps a saint; it doesn't matter; I will find the same joy in any case. Whether I am a believer or an unbeliever, Christian or pagan, I work with all the world to build a cathedral because I am artist and artisan, and because I have learned to draw faces, limbs, and bodies out of stone. I will never worry about the judgment of posterity or of my contemporaries; my name is carved nowhere and will disappear with me. But a little part of myself will survive in the anonymous and triumphant totality. A dragon or a demon, or perhaps a saint, it doesn't matter!" *PRIDE AS AN ARTISAN — AGAINST ALL OF MANKIND*

Ingmar Bergman (1918–   ):
Filmography:
1945—Kris. 1946–Det Regnar Pa Var Karlek. 1947—Boat for the Indies, Night Is My Future. 1948—Port of Call, Prison. 1949—Three Strange Loves, Till Joy. 1950—Illicit Interlude, High Tension. 1952—Waiting Women, Monika. 1953—The Naked Night. 1954—A Lesson in Love. 1955—Dreams, Smiles of a Summer Night. 1956—The Seventh Seal. 1957—Wild Strawberries, Brink of Life. 1958—The Magician. 1959—The Virgin Spring. 1960—The Devil's Eye. 1961—Through a Glass Darkly. 1962—Winter Light. 1963—The Silence. 1964—All These Women. 1966—Persona. 1968—Hour of the Wolf, Shame. *SCENES FROM A MARRIAGE. CRIES + WHISPERS 1969 PASSION OF ANNA*

45

Robert Bresson

Robert Bresson represents the principle of repression in cinematic art. His players are strictly controlled, his images rigidly framed, his timing painfully precise, his tone awesomely austere. His films reflect the spiritual severity of the Jansenist tradition in French Catholicism. Bresson's philosophy might be summed up in the last line of Bernanos from Diary of a Country Priest: *"What does it matter? All is Grace."*

Bresson's films have never been particularly popular at the box-office, but the seriousness of the director's art has never been questioned even by his severest detractors. Richard Roud has most aptly described Bresson's movies as the chamber music of the cinema. His procession of saints and sinners, exalted and expressionless, leads the viewer toward one contemporary Calvary after another, toward Grace without Joy.*—A.S.

This interview with Robert Bresson was recorded at the 1962 Cannes Film Festival. Originally intended for broadcasting, the interview was conducted in English. As he wished to avoid any chance of inaccuracies (although he speaks English very well), he insisted on half-an-hour's preparation to jot down any words that he might need and forget during the recording session. We settled down in the lounge of the largest hotel in Cannes to discuss the questions over a whisky (mine) and a tonic water (his). Three hours later, many of the questions had been discarded and others completely altered to the questions which Bresson

* Ian Cameron's interview with Robert Bresson originally appeared in Movie, No. 7, February 1963.

wished to answer. As the whole interview was thus written out before it was recorded, the questions and answers became very terse, and without any of the usual interplay of conversation. Predictably, it was considered unsuitable for broadcasting, as it now lacked even the appearance of spontaneity. It sounded not so much like an interview as a Bressonian dialogue.—Ian Cameron

Why did you wish to add yet another to the number of films made about Joan of Arc?

To make her real and immediate.

What was your principal aim in the film? Was it to show history?

That's the privilege of the cinema—to bring things of the past into the present, providing you avoid the style of the historical films in general. I think the only way to reach the public with historical characters is to show them as if they lived at the present with us. So that was my principal aim.

You never show Joan in the same shot as her accusers. Why?

First, I couldn't do it. The natural decors made it impossible to show them together. But I believe that it is good to create obstacles. For my part I don't work very well without obstacles. Anyway, perhaps even without this difficulty, I would have shown Joan and her accusers in the same way. Because there is only one way of shooting people: from near and in front of them, when you want to know what is happening inside.

Often you seem to place Joan on a light background when her interrogator is on a light background, or to place them both on dark.

That's because it gives a shock to the eye; . . . you can't have white in one shot and black in the following one.

The shooting so that each character has his or her shot in the trial sequences gives a feeling not of conflict between Joan and her judges, but of a ritual in which all the participants have their parts to play, parts which they accept.

I don't agree. For me it is a duel between the Bishop Cauchon and Joan. From the beginning to the end, the English and the priests have only the role of witnesses.

47

You haven't allowed it to become a drama in the normal sense.

My idea is to suggest the things and the feelings also.

What do you expect the audience to bring to your film?

Not their brains but their capacity for feeling.

Do you expect them to know the facts of the trial? Is that why you don't explain who the various participants are?

I never explain anything, as it is done in the theatre.

Or is it that you want the audience to look upon the trial as spectators at a ceremony that is new to them?

This is a good motivation.

Are all your characters in the film those referred to in the historical account of the trial?

They are.

You never show the crowd at the execution except for a couple of shots including their legs. You never show the audience at the trial. Why?

It's a necessity. The sight of a mediaeval crowd would break up the film.

At the beginning of the film we're shown the back of Joan's mother, with a hand on each of her shoulders. Why do you just show her back?

Because I didn't want her to be a character. Besides, it is not in the film itself. It appears before the title.

At the end of the film you stress the tightness of the garment in which she's burnt, that it prevents her from walking properly.

Her garment makes her walk ridiculously, like a little girl. It seems that she's running to the stake.

What's the significance of the gesture when the stone is thrown through the window of her cell? She picks it up and looks at it, at the window and then back at the stone.

She's astonished, but she doesn't care. She's sure till the end that she's to be delivered.

At one point in the trial, the judges make Joan kneel. Then you dissolve away to her standing again afterwards.

The moment of cutting has the same function as that of movement in other films. Shakespeare also cuts at strange times. His cutting is like a door through which the poetry enters.

Why is there so much emphasis placed in the film on Joan being a virgin? Particularly on the attitude of the English to this?

I have shown exactly what I have found in the real account.

There are many shots of doors, open doors. Do these relate to Joan's speech "If I see a door open," etc.?

When one is in prison, the most important thing is the door.

The photography is often unusually dark. Is this to establish a sombre mood?

Well, it's important for me to establish the real proportions of light between outside and inside. Outside is very light. Inside more or less dark. The truth about the light takes its part in the general truth of the film.

Why are there a large number of shots of the English peering at Joan through the crack in the cell wall?

There are not as many as you say—as few as possible.

The crack is low down on the wall. You show this by holding the shot on the crack as the observers stand up.

They are sitting down on the other side, which I of course never show. But you may guess that the observers sit down and get up.

When Joan is ill in prison, you show a detail shot first of a priest's hand—the doctor's hand—holding hers when she's ill. Why this detail?

I want to make the public want to see her face before showing it.

Why is it not the Bishop but the two monks in white who inform Joan that she is to die?

One is her confessor. The other is Brother Martin, who tried to help her by signs during the trial. The two who have been the closest to her.

There are a number of detailed shots of pens writing the account of the trial. Why have you put these in when she says "You're writing against me, not for me"?

Because there is a dramatic significance in it. All that is said is written down, and will be taken in general against her. The scratching of the pen is dramatically significant for me.

Why is the garment she wears at her death brought at the moment when she is receiving the bread at her communion?

The quickness of the end, which is my invention, is for me a dramatic point.

One hardly notices in this film that it is the English sol-

49

dier who gives Joàn the cross. Shaw made quite a lot of this.

This detail is so well known to everybody here in France that I only wanted to suggest it by the sight of his helmet.

Nothing at all is made in the film of the roles of the English nobleman Warwick and the English priest. Effectively the action involves only Joan and the French priests.

I didn't want to introduce the psychology of Warwick.

Why do you have a shot with a dog in the open as she's about to be burnt?

There's always a dog walking across in the open during a ceremony. The animals feel it when there is something unusual.

Why the details of her clothes being thrown on the fire?

That is very important. They don't want to leave relics.

You show Joan's feet as she's tripped by one of the crowd. Why do you do this?

That has a certain connection with what happened to Christ when he went to be crucified. I mean the way Christ was mocked and molested.

And the doves which land on the gauze roof of the pavilion?

There is no symbolism in this. I don't like symbolism. It is only to show that life is going on.

Why do you treat the burning partly as a subjective shot of the cross being obscured by smoke?

I think you want me too much to explain what I did.

And, if I could ask you one more question, the reason for the very long held shot at the end just of the stake with chains hanging from it?

Well, it's for me like a miraculous disappearance of Joan.

Your next film I believe will be Lancelot du Lac. What in particular interests you about Arthurian legends?

I think it is our mythology as well as yours.

Robert Bresson (1911–   ):
Filmography:
1943—Les Anges du Pêché. 1944—Les Dames Du Bois de Boulogne. 1950—Diary of a Country Priest. 1956—A Man Escaped. 1959—Pickpocket. 1962—Trial of Joan of Arc. 1966—Balthazar. 1967—Mouchette. 1969—La Femme Douce.

Peter Brook

Peter Brook is interesting mainly as an emissary traveling freely and frequently between the modern theatre and the modern cinema. His films serve as extensions of his ideas about the ultimate direction and destination the cinema must follow. Moderato Cantabile is an exercise in languorous introspection of the Resnais-Hiroshima, Mon Amour school. The Lord of the Flies is an expedition in search of inspired improvisation. Brook himself remains a stimulating and articulate spokesman for the growing interdependence of the theatre and the motion picture. As we go to press, Marat/Sade is still in production; thus, it remains to be seen whether Brook will on this occasion succeed in transposing the theater of cruelty into cinema without any formal or intellectual erosion.*—A.S.

Although Peter Brook has directed only three feature films, his work in the cinema extends over a remarkable range of production conditions. He made an amateur film from Sterne's A Sentimental Journey while still an undergraduate at Oxford during the war. In 1953 he made his one British picture in orthodox studio conditions: The Beggar's Opera, starring Laurence Olivier and produced by Herbert Wilcox. In 1960 he went to France to direct Moderato Cantabile, with Jeanne Moreau and Jean-Paul Belmondo. His Lord of the Flies, one of the two British en-

* The interview with Peter Brook by Penelope Houston and Tom Milne appeared in Sight Sound, No. 3, vol. 32, Summer 1963.

tries at this year's Cannes Festival, was shot on an island off Puerto Rico, edited in Paris, and financed (like The Connection) by a number of independent backers. The rights in William Golding's novel, originally purchased by Sir Michael Balcon, had passed from him to Sam Spiegel, for whom Brook originally intended to direct the picture, before Spiegel gave up the idea after any number of scripts had been tried and found wanting.

In talking to Peter Brook, we want to approach his ideas about the cinema through these three films and the experiences of making them. We began, consequently, with the British cinema, and by an inevitable extension the theatre in Britain.

Do you think that critics, and perhaps audiences as well, have become too self-conscious about the British cinema? For the last three or four years we have been talking about a breakthrough, questioning each new film as it comes along about how far it measures up to expectations, pulling the cinema up by the roots to see how it's getting on. Does this attitude perhaps put an unfair burden on British film-makers?

No, I don't think so, because there is a real mystery here. We all talk about England's terrible heritage, about how impossible everything is in this country. But at the same time we know, by a piece of double-think, that this is really completely untrue, and that there's a tremendous tradition and fund of intelligence and imagination and originality which has always been there, and which has suddenly come out in a certain form in the theatre. There doesn't seem any reason why it shouldn't take the British cinema way out into all sorts of exciting directions. But in fact it doesn't; and so we have, I think, to go on hoping and praying and nudging and wondering.

But it happens for no apparent reason, doesn't it? In the theatre, for instance, one reached the point at which a number of playwrights seemed to be going further and further into the logical conclusion of Look Back in Anger. And then suddenly everyone said, "Now I'm writing a historical play." In fact I believe no one except John Osborne did write a historical play, but instead we find any number of plays which are going off on entirely different tracks— things like David Rudkin's Afore Night Come, Henry Livings' work, Spike Milligan's The Bed-Sitting Room. All of these are far out, if you like. Do you think the same thing could happen, just as suddenly, in the cinema?

The fact that the breakthrough has come in France in the cinema and in England in the theatre is partly practical—certain sums of money and certain production conditions existed in the cinema in France and in the theatre here. The wish to break through being there, the break simply came at another point in the dam. But the question here, it seems to me, is whether the amount of talent and energy is limited or unlimited. If it's limited, then maybe the cinema in France represents an almost complete outlet for the x per cent of people in a certain age group who have the desire to express themselves in one way or another, and it may take the French theatre fifteen years before it finds a form that corresponds to its times. Here, on the other hand, the fact that the breakthrough in the theatre has worked so widely and so well—that more and more people are writing plays, and finding this tremendous freedom in the playwriting form—may actually be doing something to hold back the cinema.

Fashion, in the deepest sense of the word, has such a lot to do with it. Take someone of a certain age, walking through the streets of a town and deciding to go into a cinema or a theatre—does he do that because he wants to, or does he feel a bit self-conscious about it? In this country it's now a very exciting thing for young people to be able to say "I'm working in a theatre," or "I want to get a job in the theatre." There is all that feeling of current life about it. Whereas in France almost everyone I know of any degree of intelligence really dreads the theatre. If I say that I'm going to see a play, people look at me and say "Well, I suppose you have to: after all, it's your job. . . ." There couldn't possibly be any reason why one should *want* to go. But going to a screening or a late night projection, or rushing over in the morning to catch the first show of somebody's re-edited version of a film—all that is really part of life. . . .

But the big question for all of us, it seems to me, concerns our relationship to what one must call reality. This is the eternal question, and in the theatre it has recently been opened up in a very interesting way. The reason everyone suddenly rejected a certain type of naturalistic play—the three act drawing-room drama—was not because we didn't any longer believe in naturalism. We now see that, through breaking away from certain conventions of plot-making and so on, the new drama was actually more naturalistic than the previous one. And it's no sort of coincidence that there has been this recent re-emergence of Shakespeare in the theatre; no accident that the English have become aware that the only valid tradition in our theatre is this one, which is more realistic than any form of writing before or since because it can give you simultaneously the surface image in a context, and also tremendously dense information about things unseen and unspoken.

This can't be done any longer through language, through verse, which means that writers are consciously or instinctively beginning to look towards ways of introducing into the naturalistic pattern, the greater surface truths, all those cracks through which you can simultaneously penetrate in other directions. The use of a dated device, surrealism, in a play like *The Bed-Sitting Room* is very interesting in this context. On one level the audience can follow the situation through like a story—even if the action does happen to involve a man changing into a room. And all this is made complex and glittering, partly serious and partly touching and partly disturbing, by a possibility of spinning other ideas around it which is created not through language but through the use of surrealism as a theatre technique. Perhaps the pointers of this, of Rudkin's *Afore Night Come,* of the Theatre of the Absurd, are towards a possible coming together of these separate strands; so that a writer will find his way towards developing an action which is as photographic on the surface as, say, *Look Back in Anger* seemed at the time, and yet as disturbing on a mythological level as Rudkin's work, and as open to shifting viewpoints as *The Bed-Sitting Room.*

Isn't something like this happening in the cinema as well, although not yet in England?

It's blocked here because no writer in the British cinema has sufficient freedom, and no director has sufficient freedom in relation to his story. You should be able to make a film without a script, off the cuff, with three sheets of paper the way Godard worked. At least you ought in principle to be able to do this, and it's enough for the possibility to be there, open to one man, for it to affect other people. Without it, the first destructive factor of auto-censorship comes in. This is not the fear that some front office man is actually going to change what you write, and some damage has been done to our understanding of the real facts by all those naïve over-simplifications—the old story of the villain in the front office sending for the honest writer and demanding cuts in his script. Auto-censorship works very much more subtly, through the writer knowing that all sorts of practical decisions are going to be made on his document, and the director knowing whenever he writes something into a script that this is going to be typed, budgeted and put into a shooting schedule.

In the theatre, at rehearsal, one may have an idea, something one wants to try out and work on, and by the end of the morning as likely as not one has discarded it. Stage managements are driven mad trying to catch up with this sort of thing, but a good stage manager usually knows by instinct when rehearsal talk really means that something has to be done, some set built, or when it's an idea you are just playing around with. But when you are dealing with the full machinery of the conventional big film production, as I was with *The Beggar's Opera,* it's terrifying to find that all manner of things one has scribbled into the script as local colour, notes one has made as a reader for oneself, possibilities to try out, have been taken deadly seriously and that months later someone will hold you to them. Unless there are orders to the contrary, the director's whim on that sort of thing is law and must be carried through by each department, while his deeper intentions are not law at all.

All this means that you are put in the position of taking conscious, final and responsible decisions at a point where you really shouldn't and can't. There are all manner of ways of writing scripts, of preparing your intentions in advance, which don't involve this. During the period I was working with Sam Spiegel on *Lord of the Flies,* for instance, there were altogether about seven screenplays. In the end we had one which wasn't to my mind the picture I was going to make; but it also seemed to me we'd reached a point where the only thing I could do was to accept it, and then trust to the fact that we were going to be far away on an awkward island and might cheat another script on the spot. I emerged from this period with a 140-page document into which I'd put meaningless but fantastically impressive camera directions. . . . "The camera tracks slowly back, and as it begins to rise it discloses over the top of the palm, left of screen. . . ." This document was hardly touched or seen again, and of course it bears no relation to the finished film. It did come in very useful, though, as something to show people when we were raising money privately to make the picture; and because of the way we were doing *Lord of the Flies,* entirely independent of any production set-up, I was then able to go ahead and make the film actually without a script.

If I had been doing this in England, however, working with a regular production set-up, I couldn't possibly have played the same trick. I might have tried it, but by that time the script would have been broken down into days and budgeted, so much screen time would have been allotted to each day's shooting, and however hard I tried to sabotage my own script and find the freedom I wanted, it wouldn't have been possible. It's rather like an actor trying to resist the director during rehearsals: he can never get away with it, because by the first night he's hemmed in, trapped by all the details around him. In the same way, once you have got on the floor with a schedule and a completion guarantee (something we mercifully avoided on *Lord of the Flies*), then your possibility of finding new things is drastically reduced. And that is why so many directors seem to end up by going about things the same way. Take *Lawrence of Arabia*, for instance. In spite of David Lean's reputation, the film's Academy Awards and all the rest of it, it seems to me there is nothing of him in that film, nothing that couldn't be the work of eight other top men. Looking at those great desert long shots, one realises that the position of the camera must have been charted by a team, that the operation of simply getting the camera up must have been conditioned by so many fixed factors that the director's possibility of choice could scarcely have existed.

British films are financed and planned and controlled in such a way that everything goes into this crippling concept of screenplay. And a breakthrough can only come about thoroughly and satisfactorily if the working conditions can be freed, so that smaller crews and lower budgets give people the opportunity to take more time, and to go back on their tracks if necessary, without anyone worrying them.

This whole question of advance planning seems one of the key aspects of the cinema at the moment. Apart from the Lawrence of Arabia *type of film, the really big commercial undertaking in which everything must be worked out long before shooting begins, you have the distinction between directors such as Antonioni and Bresson, very much in control of every aspect of their material, and the whole* cinéma-vérité *movement, the films of Jean Rouch, the Maysles' film about Joseph Levine, the Drew-Leacock films, in which decisions are taken at the moment of shooting and the subject of the film itself virtually takes charge. No one feels that these two kinds of cinema cancel each other out, or that if you want one you can't also have the other. Do you think, though, that the second line of development is more interesting?*

This, I feel, is a crucial question. The film director is still in a tradition that goes right back to the nineteenth century: the tradition of the maestro, the boss, the orchestra conductor, the myth of the man who takes charge. The greatest effect of debunking introduced by *cinéma-vérité*—and like any major event of that sort, there is no going back on it—is that continually one sees that the result of a man who knows his own mind imposing his own will is often considerably less effective than what can happen by itself. This is where the problem really begins; and in the theatre one sees it all very clearly. I don't think there is a director left in the world in that old high tradition of shouting from the stalls and telling the actor how to do it. The idea of the actor saying "Mr. Reinhardt, I put myself in your hands," and the director pulling up his riding boots and saying "You will play this, and you will play it in this way"—all that has gone. And this means, in effect, that directors have repeatedly learnt, to their cost, that the result isn't as rich and lively when you impose yourself consciously on an actor, as when by some other means he manages to achieve the effect for himself. The director still eventually imposes himself, as of course he cannot but do, but in another way.

What one tends to resent in films is the top cameraman's view of reality, since one knows that his notion of what, say, a bar looks like is almost always less good than the real thing. Do I, as a director looking for a particular expressive effect, go into a studio or into a real bar? Do I trust that top cameraman's interpretation of reality, or if I stick the camera in the corner of the real bar and switch it on, may the result come closer to achieving my purpose? Is my direction of Orson Welles playing a film director actually going to give certain moments as extraordinarily telling and expressive as Joe Levine playing himself in *Showman*, the Maysles' film? From a standpoint of strict story-telling, and in order to get a certain result in a certain space of time, I'm mad if I don't use some technical aids, including having a time-table, getting what I'm going to shoot that day down on paper, and using a man with a

57

couple of lights when the sun goes in. And yet, by experience, one knows continually that this very thing one is straining after is not going to be as good as something achieved in another way.

I've had an extraordinary case of this on *Lord of the Flies*, where we used two cameramen as a consistent technique right through the picture. If this particular story were to be caught on celluloid in the time and conditions available, I realised that I must put every penny we had into an unlimited supply of film stock. This meant that I could stop the gaps of time and money and children and everything else running out by keeping on shooting, speaking through shots, going back without cutting the camera. And at the same time there was a second cameraman, Gerry Feil, a man who had worked for *Life* and was used to the routine of the morning story conference, who knew exactly what we were doing on the picture, down to the intention of every shot, but who worked with as much freedom as a newsreel cameraman. Through the official cameraman I would set up, say, a tracking shot; and without trying to go in for conscious compositions, all those futile bits of vanities that you will regret in the end, I would still be working to a precise pattern. This was, in other words, controlled shooting. At the same time this second cameraman would be scouting around, taking a set-up which had been brought into existence by the director but trying to find other aspects of it which would fit. And the really interesting thing is that about a third of the picture, I suppose, comes from his material. You'd have said on the spot, while you were filming, that the fellow who's stuck away behind a tree, shooting from the back, couldn't possibly have got the really expressive moment. Then in the rushes you see that some particular hunch of the shoulders he's caught with his camera may be expressive enough; and in the cutting you realise that the situation preceding the shot makes it so clear that the jerk of a shoulder is all you need at that moment.

So one comes back to this disquieting question: is the conscious language the most living one? There is no doubt, after all, that there are animate and inanimate stretches of film, and that a living stretch of film is related to the apparent spontaneity of what's going on in the frame.

Isn't there a further distinction to be made here between cinéma-vérité, *in which the action is caught as it happens and the work of a director like Jean-Luc Godard, who may use the same kind of realistic setting, as in* Vivre sa Vie, *but for his own particular artistic purposes?*

To me there's no question about it: Godard is far and away the most interesting film director working today—and *Marienbad* is the worst film. In a way, naturally, this is a question of taste. But it does seem there is something here one can define: that there is always an artistic balance in every form between artifice and spontaneity. *Hiroshima, Mon Amour* was a very different kettle of fish from *Marienbad,* because within its very formal structure every element—the mixture of newsreel shots, real locations, fiction within a realistic context, the consciously selected realism of the French scenes—had a flexible pulse of life of its own. The formal structure was illuminated by living detail. But the formal structure of *Marienbad* was filled by details all consistently and equally dead, so that the total effect was of artifice piled on artifice.

Godard has not yet accepted the challenge of a really taxing subject, so that we haven't yet seen the application of what he can do when subjected to rigorous demands. But I'm sure the truth is in his method; that it's not entirely with Antonioni, and certainly not in the *Marienbad* way, and eventually can't be with the hand-held camera under the arm either, because of the lack of subject matter. The quality of *Showman* was that it did get beneath the surface. It did it in a time-wasting, undisciplined and inartistic way, and the statement the film made didn't balance the energy put into it and the time taken. Still, something vital was caught. But *cinéma-vérité* eventually leads to an impasse, I would have thought, in relation to the narrative film. There comes a point when certain things can't be told, and you can't finally accept as valid a style which prevents you at a certain moment from doing something you want to do.

This leads to the problem of the actor, because it's here that the limitations of this style make themselves felt. Objects, I suppose, betray their inner quality most completely when photographed in their natural state. To put it less pretentiously, a real wall has something about it that no art director could predict in all its detail, and therefore must be more meaningful than a beautifully built studio wall. But with human beings this doesn't happen. An actual craftsman at work can seem very moving on the screen, very telling, but he is then a mobile object; and it's the man-as-an-object that the non-actor can best

59

portray. The inner emotional life of a person can only be switched on, ready for photographing at a given moment, by an actor. Bresson's *Pickpocket* shows this very clearly: you had here the actual gestures of the pickpocket at work, more expressive of the real thing than anything any choreographer could have devised; but the man called on by Bresson to play the leading part was a real non-actor, incapable of simulating emotions which he had no earthly reason to be feeling at that moment. In Robbe-Grillet's *L'Immortelle* we see a startling example of this.

You can, of course, go out into the street and pick a man off it who can act—but that doesn't prove anything except that you have made a good choice. Some of the children in *Lord of the Flies* act very well indeed, and no doubt this will help to perpetuate the myth that all children can act. I certainly don't want to take the credit for this. Where I can take the credit, though, is for all the 3,000 children I rejected, because when a child *can't* act he is worse than any bad professional actor. And the same thing goes for taking people off the streets in the old Italian tradition: if the director has the flair to find the right man and if he gives a good performance, that only means he is a natural actor, even though not a professional one.

Eventually, however, to reproduce a narrative situation you are compelled to pick on the freak people who are like mediums, who have that particular power of doing it to order. Jeanne Moreau is for me the ideal contemporary film actress, because she doesn't characterise. She acts in the way Godard films, and with her you are as close as you can be to making a document of an emotion. The average trained actor's approach to a part is based on good Stanislavsky principles: he rationalises, he prepares, he composes his characterisation. He has some conscious direction of what he is doing, so that in a way he is like the classic film director setting up his camera: the actor is setting himself up and directing himself, beautifully or otherwise. But Jeanne Moreau works like a medium, through her instincts. She gets a hunch about the character and then some part of her watches the improvisation of that and lets it happen, occasionally intervening a bit like a good technician when, for instance, she wants to be facing the camera, to be at the right angle. But she is guiding the flow of improvisation rather than stating ahead of time what hurdle she wants herself to leap, and the result is that her performance gives you an endless series of tiny surprises. On each take neither you nor she knows exactly what is going to happen.

The great criticism of *Moderato Cantabile* was that I didn't move the camera enough, that I set it up and allowed things to happen in front of it, and it was assumed I did this because I came from the theatre and didn't know any better. In fact, there was a lot of conscious thinking behind it. The narrative we were trying to capture in that particular film was neither an external one nor entirely an inner one—you can't say that the characters behave as they do because they live by a river in a dull town, but you can't ignore the way these things relate to them either. So, having found the landscape and these particular actors, my task seemed to be to set up a camera that didn't comment; to let you watch, as it were, a documentary record of something so intangible that you could feel it was really happening. Those long silences, like that close-up of Jeanne Moreau standing against a white sky, might have been turned by Shakespeare into fifty extraordinarily precise images which would have described in narrative form what we were trying to communicate with that weight of silence. And it wasn't actually silence that one was photographing, or a Japanese composition of an empty white screen, but a look on her face and a tiny movement of her cheek, which to me were valid because she was actually *and at that moment* experiencing something which therefore became interesting to look at as an object. The particular documentary aspect of filming, the catching of something as it happens, relates in this way to acting: the aim is always to capture that look in someone's eye.

How much of Moderato Cantabile *was actually planned in detail in advance? I'm thinking particularly of the dinner party sequence just before the heroine leaves her husband. The camera is on her, and you hear some casual question asked from just off screen. As the question is asked, as I recall it, you cut to the tracking shot along the railings with the musical phrase accompanying it on the sound-track. Then you cut back to her face again, and she's saying "I'm sorry, what did you say?" The question is repeated and answered. Then another question comes in, and you repeat the same movement. In each case it's almost mathematically worked out. Was this done in the editing, or were the tracking shots, for instance, already there in the script?*

Moderato was made possible by French working conditions, and I did the film with a script which no self-respecting English producer would have considered for a moment. I'm lazy about writing and also don't like committing myself in advance, so I sat down with the book (as I did with *Lord of the Flies*) and just went through it arbitrarily giving a series of numbers—close shot; mid shot; long shot: close shot; mid shot; long shot. There was no detailed description, nothing more than an identification of the location. The producer, Raoul Levy, yelled at me in horror, but I yelled back at him "You're very old-fashioned!" and that seemed to work as an argument. The film was under way already, and it was left like that without a real script. But the whole mood of the dinner party scene was already there very clearly in the book, and I did actually think of the two tracking shots and put down that idea at script stage. After that, everything happened more or less in the proper order; we found the house and got permission to use the dining-room; my French assistant director went around locally finding these people to invite; and after that it was really a very simple scene to do. We sat them down, served them salmon, and went around photographing the scene, doing a considerable coverage of a very formal sort, with symmetrical shots up the table one way, then down it the other. Then we made a pattern in the cutting.

Moderato Cantabile *looks as though it were a very carefully shot film, as though you couldn't possibly have got the same results with the kind of two-camera method you used on* Lord of the Flies. *Have your own attitudes to the cinema changed at all during the last few years, or are the different methods the result of working on two such very different subjects?*

It's really a result of the subjects. And although they are at opposite poles, they do have something in common which attracted me to them. Deep down, both are rituals: *Moderato* is a little death ritual; and *Lord of the Flies* is, I suppose, a little death ritual . . . of another sort. But the only reason I had for wanting to make *Moderato*, and the only value that could come out of it, was such a fine and fragile one that the least jar would have smashed it. So it seemed the technique really had to be one of stillness, and the pre-arranging, all the formal work of putting things into what seemed precisely the right position, was really an act of elimination. The particular effect I was after seemed so slight that it could only be seen in the eyes of

Jeanne Moreau. And this meant that I started from a total conviction that the camera just out of range, getting her from the back, couldn't in the circumstances catch anything as valid as I could myself by staring at her from the best possible viewpoint.

The qualities of *Lord of the Flies* aren't fragile at all. In fact, there is an element of fragility, in the paradise state at the beginning of the story, which unhappily the actual physical conditions of shooting made it impossible for us to catch. The best moments in the film really come when we were charging among the children at night with our flares and hand-held cameras, since group behaviour can always be caught most interestingly when it's loosely approached. Ideally, though, I'd really like to combine the two methods much more. I wouldn't choose to make another film as formalised as *Moderato Cantabile,* but I would like to use the things we discovered with our improvised methods on *Lord of the Flies* and be able to apply them more strictly, in a more controlled way.

It all leads back to the central problem, which is that of finding ways of giving a denser impression of reality. We've been prisoners for years of a naïve simplification of what realism means—hence the British cinema view that it is all a matter of art direction, something to be achieved by being more honest than the Americans in the amount of rain that beats upon your heroine. We've touched on some of the problems here. Part of the fiction that has to be exploded concerns the myth that the director's hand must be permanently visible. This becomes an unreality, as in *Marienbad,* and then a consistent style becomes an unreality. Now all the methods of freeing camerawork have brought us closer to a surface realism, and the next thing that comes up is the question of why *cinéme-vérité* also is in the end false, why it too gives us only another two-dimensional version. It's related to the film view of time, that logic by which anyone who has begun to move his hand to the right in one frame will consistently, each twenty-fourth of a second later, still be moving his hand to the right, that cinema world of perfect logic and order. None of this, though, corresponds to our own hunch of a much stranger and more complex reality.

What the French have begun to do, it seems to me, is to introduce into the direct narrative all sorts of other elements—outside references, surreal behaviour, like those odd things in *Jules et Jim,* bits of theatre and so on, which

63

by breaking through the conventions increase the opportunity for a denser expression of reality. What Godard has done in editing, in destroying the logic between two shots, has been equally valid. So has the use of subliminal references, like the extraordinary subliminal effect in the opening titles of *Cuba Si*. And while it may seem false, unrealistic, and therefore meaningless to put a star face into a realistically shot background—Anna Karina, say, against the background of Paris in *Vivre sa Vie*—the very fact that this antagonism of styles can create a sort of comment and question mark within a shot can make that shot denser, because it makes you as a spectator more intelligent. I am a spectator at a film, caught up in its action, and at the same time the actress has just done something so curious that I am pulled out of the scene, forced to ask myself what she is doing and why. The answer that I find makes that scene as three-dimensional as it once was made —to go back to the Elizabethans—through the technical device of having people stop talking conversationally and begin talking in . . . really in images.

Peter Brook (1912–   ):
Filmography:
1953—The Beggar's Opera. 1960—Moderato Cantabile. 1962—Lord of the Flies. 1967—Marat/Sade. 1968—Please Tell Me Lies.

Luis Bunuel

When Luis Bunuel's Viridiana finally materialized in the
dreary twilight of the 1961 Cannes Film Festival, many of
those present were surprised to discover not merely a great
film but, indeed, a really good movie. Some of the more
modern critics still rotating around the Resnais-Antonioni
axis were a bit suspicious of Bunuel's archaic technique,
and the Festival Jury hedged its bets by jointly honouring
Bunuel's rousing entertainment in Viridiana and Henri
Colpi's tedious coupling of amnesia and ambiguity in Une
Aussi Longue Absence. For once, the international box-
office barometer has more accurately recorded the relative
merits of the two works. Of course, every film is liked and
disliked for both right and wrong reasons, and Viridiana is
particularly susceptible to partisan critiques. Bunuel's personal triumph has been used to chastise everything from
Marienbad to the Vatican, with the predictable counter-
reactions. However, when one attempts to place Bunuel in
apposition or opposition to other directors, his remarkable
isolation becomes apparent. On the most obvious level of
identification, he is the only great Spanish-language director, and his career is one of the most bizarre in film history.

For a long time before Viridiana Bunuel had been
treated as a victim of the world's repressions and inhibitions,
variously represented by French censorship, Spanish fascism, Hollywood commercialism and Mexican mediocrity.
The Bunuel cult, at least in the Anglo-Saxon countries, had become an exercise less in cinema than in meta-
cinema, that is, the study of cinema which might have or
should have evolved under the proper social conditions.

65

This cult assumed the mannerisms of privileged scholarship by exploiting the director's underground reputation as the creator of Un Chien Andalou *(1928) and* L'Age d'Or *(1930), banned works carrying the cultural prestige of surrealism but generally unavailable to the lay public. Bunuel himself was gradually fossilized in the swamp of his legend by the reluctance of his defenders to confront the uneven quality of his career as a whole. Consequently, many of us at Cannes had to readjust to a new conception of Bunuel as a master instead of a martyr. Realizing that he had become a creature of festivals and film societies, and that his efforts held no interest for the distributors with the big cigars, most of us were quite willing to go along with the Bunuel claque in awarding him another sympathy prize as for* The Young One. *Then, almost miraculously, the old surrealist crossed everyone up with a resounding commercial success.*

Viridiana *has a plot which is almost too lurid to synopsize even in these enlightened times. The heroine is summoned from a convent by her uncle, Don Jaime, an old Spanish* hidalgo *living on a neglected estate (Spain?) in obsessive mourning for his dead wife (The Republic?). The novice arrives on the thirtieth anniversary of Don Jaime's marriage. Viridiana's resemblance to the* hidalgo's *wife introduces the theme of substitution so dear to Hitchcock, but Bunuel is less concerned with the illusion of the substitution than with the sexual drives aroused by it. Failing to persuade his niece to marry him, Don Jaime orders a compliant maid to drug her. He carries her upstairs to the accompaniment of* The Messiah, *while Bunuel intensifies the outrageous eroticism of the situation by photographing the choreography of abduction through the prying eyes of the maid's little girl. Almost inexplicably, Don Jaime desists from his attempted rape. The morning after, in progressive stages of desperation, he tells his outraged niece that she has been violated, then denies the violation, outraging her even more with his mendacity, and after watching her departure, hangs himself. Viridiana returns to atone for her guilt and the second movement of the film begins with the maid's little girl skipping with the rope that has been the instrument of the* hidalgo's *deliverance.*

The incestuous texture of the film is maintained with the entrance of the novice's virile cousin, Jorge, a pragmatist of the most ruthless kind. He discards his mistress to pursue Viridiana more efficiently, but willingly seduces the adoring maid in the interim. While Jorge is patching up the estate in slapdash Spanish fashion, Viridiana is pursuing the Franciscan ethic by adopting the most revolting beggars in the area. Bunuel intercuts the Angelus recited by Viridiana and her scabrous flock with detail shots of Jorge's rebuilding. Bunuel's despair for Spain leads him to dismiss reform as a possibility; Jorge is moved by humane feelings to purchase a dog which is chained under a cart and forced to trot along at a horse's pace. No sooner is the "liberal" purchase consummated, than another dog comes trotting by under another cart going in the opposite direction, reversing the pattern of futility, on the same Spanish road. The demolition of Viridiana's principles is reserved for the film's remarkable climax.

The beggars' orgy is set up dramatically by the departure of Viridiana, Jorge, the maid and her little girl on business in the town. For the first time the beggars move into the house itself, and assault every sacred feeling of property that any audience could be presumed to possess. Wine and food smear fancy tapestries, antique furniture is smashed, ornate dishes and glasses are broken. But unlike their colleagues in depravity from La Dolce Vita, *the beggars enjoy themselves, and suddenly with* The Messiah *blaring on the gramophone, the screen reverberates with a hymn to liberation. These vile creatures (and Bunuel leaves no doubt of their vileness, their cruelty, even their mean hypocrisy), these blind, halt, leprous, syphilitic dregs, become gloriously human.*

When Viridiana and Jorge return, they are assaulted, and Viridiana's slowly vanishing purity is saved only when her cousin bribes one of the beggars to murder the would-be rapist. Deciding that two lives are too high a price to pay for her chastity, Viridiana casts her cross and her crown of thorns into the flames, and prepares to surrender to Jorge. The production's government supervisor, who must have been dozing until this point, finally intervened. Viridiana and Jorge must not be left alone in a room after this, he ordered. Bunuel dutifully complied with a ménage-à-trois *ending in which Jorge, Viridiana and the maid play cards together in the long Spanish evening while the camera recedes on the hellish tableau to the accompaniment of some appropriate American juke box slop.*

How Bunuel managed to realize Viridiana *at all under the supervision of the Spanish censor may never be fully explained. The intangibles of national prestige may have*

WHAT ALTERS TRISTANA'S PERCEPTION?

played a part. Also, the myopic vision of the bureaucratic mind may not have fully grasped the almost magical transformation of images into ideas between shooting and screening. It would be naive to think that Bunuel was without guile in this undertaking. The deviousness of his subsequent interviews was worthy of Hitchcock, and there is enough ambiguity in the film itself to confound the most perverse critics. For example, there seems to be some controversy about the fate of the beleaguered heroine. To put it bluntly, is Viridiana, the chaste novice in the film, actually raped by the syphilitic beggar who murders her first attacker? If so, does she then renounce her vows of chastity as result of a D. H. Lawrence awakening? The argument for this interpretation depends upon the time gap assumed in the editing of the action. The fact that Bunuel compels normally fastidious critics to ponder such lurid questions reflects the dark humour of his conceptions. And it is this dark humour which rescues Bunuel from the absurdities of Ichikawa. UNEXPLAINED IN BUNUEL

Whether or not Bunuel has circumvented the censor with suggestive elisions, the plot of Viridiana gives one pause. The modern cinema, such as it is presumed to be, is supposed to have supplanted plot with mood. Then suddenly, Bunuel bursts in like a resurrected Victorian novelist steeped in violent depravity and unashamedly flourishing the most obvious symbols. The spectacle of a contemporary director cutting away metaphorically from a brutal seduction to a cat pouncing on a mouse jolts the critic who has finally adjusted to the languorous introspection of an Antonioni. Then, too, the flagrant display of eroticism, sadism and fetishism reveals the director's personality with the embarrassing Krafft-Ebing frankness one recalls in the films of Stroheim and Lang. Bunuel may have been more shocking in the past, but never before have his shock effects seemed so much the warp and woof of his philosophy. Un Chien Andalou and L'Age d'Or have their moments, of course, but audiences are usually cushioned for "avant-garde" cinema where anything goes. Las Hurdes (Land Without Bread) and Los Olvidados mask details of horror with a socially conscious narration. Even though it is hard to imagine any other director conceiving of a mountain goat falling off a mountain or a legless beggar being rolled down a hill, the spectator can console himself with the thought that this is not the best of all possible worlds, and that the next election or the next rev-

olution may improve conditions. There is no such consolation in Viridiana, *Bunuel's despairing allegory of the Spanish condition. For the first time in his career, Bunuel ends his action in an existential enclosure in which hell, in Sartre's phrase, is other people.* ✓

If every director must be assigned a political station, Bunuel is unmistakably a man of the left. He actively supported the Spanish Republic against Franco's insurgents, and he has been highly critical of the Establishments in Mexico, America and France. A story is told about Bunuel, perhaps apocryphal but still relevant. It seems that Jean Epstein, with whom Bunuel began his career in 1926, once offered his Spanish assistant an opportunity to work with Abel Gance. Bunuel reportedly refused because of what he considered Gance's fascist leanings. Epstein, a Gallic product of apolitical amitié, *was outraged, but Bunuel stood his ground. Later, Bunuel had a falling out with Salvador Dali over the sacrilegious treatment of* L'Age d'Or.

The point is that Bunuel has been more intransigent over the years than most of his colleagues, and he has had more than his share of problems, but where one sometimes suspects the temptation of martyrdom in a Stroheim or a Welles, one is struck mainly by Bunuel's tenacity. During the long drought between 1932 and 1947 without any directorial opportunities, he remained on the fringes of the industry in New York and Hollywood. Despite several cancelled projects in Mexico and France since 1947, he has managed to direct twenty films, about half of which are meaningful projections of his ideas and personality. Even in a potboiler like Susana, *released in 1950, the year of* Los Olvidados, *there are one or two passages which foreshadow* Viridiana.

There is a danger in attaching an explicitly political moral to Bunuel's career. For a director of the left, Bunuel has evidenced almost no interest in the mechanics of reform or revolution. The superimposed narrations in Land Without Bread *and* Los Olvidados *suggest amelioration, but the images of the films operate autonomously in terms of a fatalistic Spanish temperament. Even in his Mexican films, there is no trace of the theory of progress through technology, and one could never imagine his making a tractor film behind the Iron Curtain. He has never concerned himself with the mystiques of peasant and worker; nor has he dramatized the injustices of economic exploita-*

69

tion in any detail. As the late André Bazin observed, Bunuel lacks the Manichean tendencies of a propagandist. As cruel as his world may be, its characters are never divided into villains and victims. His obsession with mental and physical deformities generally deprives his plots of any sociological plausibility. Even his handling of the racial issue in Robinson Crusoe and The Young One is too perverse to serve as a respectably liberal blueprint.

Ado Kyrou's recently published book on Bunuel sheds some new light on the paradoxes of the director's personality. Particularly interesting is some of the director's own film criticism in the late twenties, when, like many critics today, he tried to establish polar relationships. Where Truffaut has invented the Lumiere-Delluc and Sagan-Queneau games, Bunuel pioneered in the Keaton-Jannings game. Bunuel preferred Keaton, with all the hostility to German expressionism such a preference implies. He frankly admired the American cinema for its emptyheaded grace and rhythm, qualities which he attributed to a Jungian sense of racial instinct. Conversely, he understood his own limitations, and his perceptive humility is still one of his greatest virtues. Bunuel is not and never has been a stylist of the first rank. He would have been lost in the Hollywood shuffle on commissioned projects even though he functioned creditably and efficiently on impossible Mexican assignments. To Bunuel, the cinema is just a vehicle for his ideas. Once these ideas have taken the appropriate plastic form, he shoots very quickly, and any additional values are either incidental or accidental. One of his Mexican producers has reported that Bunuel seems bored by the actual shooting of a film.

Even though one may treat Dali's accusations of atheism as malicious slander to get Bunuel fired from the Museum of Modern Art in New York, Bunuel's films are clearly not intended to win friends and influence people for the Church. As a director who began his career by throwing live priests and dead jackasses out the window, and then compounding his sacrilege by confusing Christ with the Marquis de Sade, he has been almost exclusively identified in terms of these and subsequent impieties. By titillating anticlerical audiences with glimpses of forbidden frankness, Bunuel has found it difficult to convey the full dimensions of his metaphysical rebellion. As soon as he introduces the theme of sexual liberation into the argument, the latent puritanism of the organized left reacts against the degeneration of protest into anarchy. Yet even Bunuel's anarchy is unusually individualistic. Where Vigo is concerned with the disavowal and destruction of social institutions, Bunuel invokes the biological anarchy of nature to reconstruct humanity. Bunuel finds it quite natural for the protagonist of El to notice the legs of a pretty girl while he is washing a priest's feet for a Catholic ceremony. Bunuel's defiance of the Church for excluding nature from the altar thus takes on a mystical quality. The pleasure Bunuel takes in the beggar's orgy in Viridiana is almost indistinguishable from the religious ecstasy of self-denial one finds in Bresson. It is perhaps appropriate that Bunuel lacks Bresson's sensibility while Bresson lacks Bunuel's force.

The odd circumstances of Bunuel's career preclude an analysis of periods and stylistic progression. More than most other directors of comparable stature, the man is inseparable from his art. His camera has always viewed his characters from a middle distance, too close for cosmic groupings and too far away for self-identification. Normally, this would make his films cold and his point of view detached, but by focusing on the abnormality of life, Bunuel forces his audience to accept man unconditionally. When we look at the monstrous long enough and hard enough, we realize, in Truffaut's phrase, that there are no monsters. The drawback to Bunuel's choice of distance is that he creates horror without terror, and pity without catharsis. In short, he lacks the sense of tragedy his ideas demand. TRUFFAUT - SYMBOL OF SENSE. SLICKNESS.

How a director who seems so disconcertingly obvious can turn out to be so complex is one of the mysteries of the cinema. For example, it seems too symmetrically ironic to synchronize a beggar's orgy with Handel's Messiah. However, Bunuel has never been a champion of background music. He simply does not care enough about his score to seek something more subtle. Yet, his indifference to details that cleverer directors have mastered only reminds us that ingenuity is no substitute for genius. Bunuel's blend of the real and the surreal, the grotesque and the erotic, the scabrous and the sublime never quite fits into any critical theory. The triumph of Viridiana leaves us just about where we were before, but henceforth we shall have to allow Bunuel to tailor his own strait-jacket.*

* The Editor's article on Luis Bunuel appeared in Movie, No. 1, June 1962.

The young Japanese film critic Kenji Kanesaka visited Luis Bunuel at his home in Mexico City, where he recorded the following interview:*

KANESAKA: *Congratulations on your success with* Viridiana. *I caught up with* The Young One *last night.*

BUNUEL: I would like you to see *Viridiana.*

KANESAKA: *In Japan, unfortunately, we could only see two of your films,* Un Chien Andalou *and* Los Olvidados. *But even so, I know that movie people with progressive ideas value your achievements very highly. You have made over twenty pictures. Which among them do you most recommend us to see,* El *and* Robinson Crusoe?

BUNUEL: El *and* Nazarin. About *Robinson Crusoe* I am not so sure. Also you may not find a proper print. Among others, when one makes 21 or 22 pictures, there are some that are not at all good.

KANESAKA: Un Chien Andalou *came to Japan very recently for the first time. Every book says that you and Salvador Dali wrote the script together and you directed it. Can you say which particular ideas were yours and which were Dali's? Would you say you were influenced by Dali? Do you have anything to say about Dali since?*

BUNUEL: It is true—that story was written by both of us. I was director, producer and owner. But now I'm not so sure because it seems that everybody has rights to the film. The film was made 32 years ago and I do not remember much about the details regarding our collaboration. What I know about Dali and me is that now we belong to a totally different world. For Dali has gone to a world of men who make money. *DALI - HIP*.

KANESAKA: *I think the dream sequence in* Los Olvidados, *for instance, is more genuinely surrealistic than surrealism. Some hold a view that you synthesize different approaches of the documentary and avantgarde cinema.*

BUNUEL: I always try to be free of avantgarde affectations. On the other hand, although I had observed the situations of the slums for 18 months before shooting *Los Olvidados,* I would hesitate to call it a documentary film, as I have reflected my own ideas in the film. There is not much sense in attaching labels. In essence, we make films the

PELLINI.

* Kenji Kanesaka's interview with Luis Bunuel appeared in Film Culture, *Spring 1962.*

72

way we please and some can make good ones. Some cannot.

KANESAKA: *I think our style is imitated a great deal by young directors. Especially your images of "violence."*

BUNUEL: If I employ "violence" it is not violence for its own sake. It is to express something else—perhaps something in the world of ideas. In this sense there has been no real influence of me on the world of films. But of course I do not see many films lately unless they are strongly recommended by my friends.

KANESAKA: *Have you seen any Nouvelle Vague films?*

BUNUEL: I saw *Hiroshima, Mon Amour* and *400 Blows*. I like them.

KANESAKA: *Do you think these two are much different from each other? Will they both remain in the history of film art like* Los Olvidados *does?*

BUNUEL: They are quite different from each other. *400 Blows* is something like the vogue. It pursues the momentary, private truth, while *Hiroshima, Mon Amour* intends to deal with a universal problem. Perhaps the latter has a better chance to remain in the film repertory. I think I heard that Resnais said he liked my work.

KANESAKA: *Is the intention to study people's inner problems in order to finally reach social and universal problems, the one that most corresponds between your work and Resnais?*

BUNUEL: It may be so. But I think in my own terms. *Hiroshima, Mon Amour* has a bad narration. It has old-fashioned music. And the last part—where the man and the woman are finding it hard to break away from each other—is endlessly repetitious. But still I value the first three reels very highly. I may say they convey the anguish of our time. But essentially this feeling is unexplainable. Something like an aura that surrounds the film.

KANESAKA: *How about Japanese films? Do you find Kurosawa interesting?*

BUNUEL: I only saw *Rashomon* and *Gate of Hell*. I like them in a different way from *Hiroshima, Mon Amour*. I like Resnais' film from the viewpoint of ideas and politics, and the Japanese films from that of lyricism and exoticism.

KANESAKA: *By lyricism do you mean visual beauty? Have you seen* Ikiru?

BUNUEL: I have not seen enough Japanese films to pass any judgment. Oh, yes, I saw *Seven Samurai* too. Kuro-

73

sawa is superficial but an extraordinary master of spectacle. I like his films very much. *Gate of Hell* contains something more universal in that it has "love" as a central theme. I was a member of the jury at the Cannes Film Festival the year it won the prize. I may have missed it if I hadn't been. But anyway, the Japanese films I saw are a lot better than Hollywood films today. I want to go to Japan but I'm horrified by planes. It is not logical but I'm more horrified by propelled flights than by jets. Travelling is for young men like you.

KANESAKA: *I have just made a survey of Hollywood and the independent film-making in America, and I think that the film-making in America is coming into a new era. What advice would you give to the young film-maker? Should he concentrate on expressing himself or on pleasing the audience?*

BUNUEL: There have always been two kinds of cinema, the "commercial" and the "artistic." There are always some men who will try to express their inner world, to convey it to others through the medium of the film, which is above all a marvelous tool for artistic creation. At the same time, films are made to please the culturally inferior masses, who are so either for social or economic reasons. Thus such films are apt to be superficial, stereotyped, easy to understand, and usually kowtow to the morals and politics of the different governments. This could be a good definition of the "commercial" film. Sometimes, very seldom, a creative film is also commercial but then this quality of commerciality is the predicate whereas the subject is art.

Luis Bunuel (1900–   ):
Filmography:
1928—The Fall of the House of Usher, Un Chien Andalou. 1930—L'Age d'Or. 1932—Land Without Bread. 1947—Gran Casino. 1949—El Gran Calavera. 1950—Los Olvidados (The Young and the Damned), Susana. 1951—Daughter of Deceit, A Woman Without Love, Ascent to Heaven. 1952—El Bruto, Robinson Crusoe, El. 1953—Wuthering Heights, Illusion Travels by Streetcar. 1954—The River and Death. 1955—The Criminal Life of Archibaldo Cruz. 1956—La Mort en Ce Jardin. 1958—Nazarin. 1959—La Fièvre Monte à El Pao. 1960—The Young One. 1961—Viridiana. 1962—The Exterminating Angel. 1965—Simon of the Desert. 1967—Belle de Jour. 1969—La Voie Lactée. 1970 TRISTANA –

DISCREET CHARM OF THE BOURGEOUISIE
CET OBSCUR OBJET DU DESIR

74

First of all, there was the village which I knew well, and I liked the people there very much. That part of it I enjoyed doing a lot. But at the same time I was learning the technical side, and that lost us lots of time!

Haven't a lot of documentary things about the village been cut out during the montage?

At the outset, the film was at least two and a half hours long. Luckily I showed it to some people and they said "Aië, aië!" so I cut three quarters of an hour. And in comparison with the original scenario I'd *already* cut half an hour. So it *could* have lasted three hours. It was cut mainly in the transitions, and then there were two things which took up a hell of a lot of time. The cutting was done so that the film could be more successful commercially, but I took care to make sure that the topography of the village was respected. So in order to get from one place to another, even if it meant going right across the village, one went right across following the guy or whoever it might be. That took plenty of time!

Then there were things like the baking of bread and scenes in the bistro with people talking among themselves that had nothing to do with the subject of the film but seemed to me to be indispensable at the time. You see, even the tables of the bistro were of very old wood, and so much wine had been spilt on them that they had a unique colour. Henri (Decaë) had rendered this colour so well that I would have liked to have it in the film. But then everything would have been interminable.

Had you ever worked with actors before? Rivette began, for instance, with actors in a short film.

No, I hadn't done anything interesting. Short films aren't really the same. But for *Le Beau Serge* I mainly chose friends and old hams. In using these people, I realised that I liked barnstormers and actors who exaggerated a little. I always encourage them to grimace. If you are afraid you go (*makes expression of horror by shrinking back with eyes popping*), if you are happy you go (*throws up hands in glee*)! It's because of this taste of mine that from time to time the actors grimace. The ones I used in *Le Beau Serge* were good, but not good at that.

Do you prefer to use their natural mannerisms?

Yes, there was the way in which Jean-Claude (Brialy) runs. That was very useful to me. It was when I saw him run like that I made him wear the scarf, because it suited him. That was nowhere in the script. Gerard Blain rolls his shoulders like this . . . when he walks, so I told him to walk faster to accentuate the fact. Little guys with complexes about their size often do things like this to make them look bigger. Hawks must have noticed this too in *Hatari!* On top of all this rolling motion, he was often supposed to be drunk as well, seeming to lean on one leg first and then on the other.

Did you have more technical than acting problems?

I had my main problems with that infernal device they call the camera-blimp! That was dreadful. All the same, there are one or two things I like. In the camera movements there are some that don't serve any purpose: when a man walks across the main square, I put down all the tracking rails I had, maybe four hundred, five hundred metres of rail! I had already intended to do lots of camera movement—travellings which started here and ended there, crossing the main square, ending by going through a door into a house! Fantastic! As the camera followed the actor through the door, he was obliged to walk on the rails —clack, clack, and you could see them too! Then we had to go through little doors inside which there was no room for anything much more than the camera. Poor Rabier, he had a hell of a time working on the framing.

What was it about the subject of Les Cousins *that interested you particularly?*

I had both *Les Cousins* and *Le Beau Serge* prepared at the same time, in fact; I had the idea for *Les Cousins* but I couldn't do it because it would have been too expensive. Construction-wise *Le Beau Serge* was at once too long and without enough incident for its length. The pieces about the father-in-law were added later. *Les Cousins* was just three pages long when written down. The situations were more compact. It has more construction. *Le Beau Serge* was economical and it was good on the village, but the story was rather tricked up. The people in *Les Cousins* are real.

What do you like especially in Les Cousins?

I'm very fond of the tomates à la Provencale, and I quite like the second surprise-party. The man who breaks the chains—things like that. The background to the party . . . nothing quite like it on the screen for twenty years . . . I think I broke all records there! Madness. There's everything there—Wagner, girls with bare feet, the lot!

Weren't there repercussions from that film?

Not particularly. There was a little. People didn't think

there were any Fascists in France then: they were that stupid. Now they can see that it was true.

The characters?

I like the character played by Brialy, and Carolus (Blain), quite well. It's sad that a chap as frank as he ends up a victim of his own foolishness.

Is Gegauff's part in it mainly concerned with the characters or with the construction of the script?

It's not the construction which is Paul's part, but the dialogue, which is real Gegauff dialogue. It succeeds in saying in two pages what would have taken me four to say. That's very useful because it allows you to do a lot more in the same amount of time. And also by Gegauff are one or two little things such as the scene where they talk about the erotic quality of their skin. The whole story depends on this, he would say: it's a story about skin texture. He wrote that scene in about half an hour.

Didn't he have any ideas as a scenarist?

No, no, no ideas of construction.

So the symmetrical construction of the film is your work?

Yes, I like symmetry. I like it when everything comes together at the end, but one mustn't strive for symmetry. It annoys me to strive for "rhymes." It's good working with Gegauff because he takes a delight in destroying casuistry. I like what Paul does.

What was it that appealed in the subject of A Double Tour?

I read Stanley Ellin's book when I was doing my military service and there was one thing which I found very remarkable then: a chap who's very conformist and then suddenly takes off rejoicing into nature. The subject was impossible. There was one thing in it about a key which locks a granary. I have *never* understood whether the important thing was that it was locked or that it was unlocked! So I cut that out. And I amused myself with the mythological aspects of the story: Leda, and there were swan references in the house! Then there was the scene of the row between the man, Dacqumine, and his wife, the first version of which was refused by the Hakims who were producing the film: it was much more horrible than the scene we eventually shot. It was entirely physical with the bloke saying to his wife "You look a mess, your armpits smell bad," and other nasty things. Finally there was the character of the Hungarian, Laszlo (Jean-Paul Belmondo). He interested me. But at the same time, this was a mistake because the film would have done better at the box-office without him. It didn't do badly, but without this bizarre guy, spectators would have been less upset by the film. He was a worrying element, spending his time saying and doing outrageous things to offend people.

In A Double Tour *André Jocelyn plays the role of a person who excludes or destroys beauty, a person who seems to crop up quite a lot in your films—*L'Oeil du Malin *and* Ophelia *as well*.

Joycelyn represents a certain type in French society— the son of a good family, rather degenerate, a bit queer. Jocelyn is good at portraying that kind of character.

But let's imagine a young chap who's intelligent, sensitive, kind, handsome, who lives in a milieu which is unintelligent, insensitive, ugly, hard, and yet he cannot abandon the milieu because his roots, his family are in it. When he comes face to face with something that contradicts what he has been brought up to, it's inevitable and normal that he will try to destroy it. In *L'Oeil du Malin* it's a bit different: the wish for destruction comes more from the man's mediocrity than from anything else. The reaction is to turn their destruction outwards, preferring to fire on others. One finds the same sort of thing in present day politics—the young people who have become *plastiqueurs*. I'm sure their origins aren't so different from those of the Jocelyn character in *A Double Tour:* they're people who have problems inside themselves, inside their families. That sort of character interests me a great deal.

It's the opposite in Ophelia, *isn't it, a bit like* Vertigo, *where the character wants to make his dream concrete and thus destroys the real thing?*

It's very much like *Vertigo*, and that's a film which I admire very much. I saw it again when I was making *Ophelia* and I found it totally unbearable. I found ridiculous arguments so that I could say to myself "What is all this driveling nonsense?"! But the arguments that I used to myself when I was making *Ophelia* were ridiculous.

Vertigo *certainly had its influence, because there were things in* L'Oeil du Malin; *there were very similar shots.*

Oh yes.

And the colour in A Double Tour . . . *the field of poppies. You said the main problems were Decaë's.*

There's one thing which I hate about colour films . . . people who use up a lot of their despairing producer's money by working on the colour in the laboratory to bring out the dominant hues, or to make colour films where there isn't any colour. The hell with that! I like to have the screen full of colour, twenty colours on the screen at once, fifty colours. There are no dominants despite what people have said.

It must have been awful for Decaë . . .

Yes, but the result was very faithful . . . and it was horribly complicated. I mean the golds and the interiors, with the windows with the coloured glass giving the faces three colours at once. The relationship between the interiors and the Provence exteriors was very important, and co-ordinating the ideas of the decorator and costumier, the cameraman and director, are specially important in colour movies, and much more difficult than for a black and white film. I like making black and white films in natural surroundings, but I much prefer shooting a colour film inside a studio where the colours are easier to control. Some colours are very difficult to render, and you must compensate to get the colour you want on the screen. It's pretty complicated, but not so much for me as for the cameraman. I say to him, "You see this, you see that. I want that exactly rendered as it is. Is that possible?" In the studio there are no troubles about the sun going in!

A Double Tour is very exact on the colourings of the south of France.

It was also very important to get the decors right for the South. There were family photos in the house we used, and the paternal grandfather of the house looked exactly like Dacqumine.

Were you happy with the actors there?

That was rather complicated. Everything was prepared, the locations were chosen and all that. My first choice for Leda was Suzy Parker but she didn't fit in with the decor at all. So Antonella Lualdi was chosen. The plot had to be modified a bit . . . she became an Italian who had known a Hungarian in Japan. Rather remarkable! I also wanted Charles Boyer for the Dacqumine part. On the other hand Madeleine (Robinson) was just what I had wanted.

Jean-Paul Belmondo's gastronomic orgy was quite something . . .

Yes, I've often noticed that in films people don't really stuff themselves full when they're eating. So now I work on the principle of having at least one meal in all my films. After all one must eat. And after all, again, it's very scenic. It's difficult to put across on film, to get everyone in the shot without cutting to and fro. I've often thought of having a table made with a hole in the middle for the camera to film meal scenes!

Les Bonnes Femmes *is perhaps your most "symmetrical" film.*

Symmetrical? From the symmetrical point of view it's symmetrical!

In the montage or what?

In my last version there was a final quarter of an hour of flashes of people in the street leaving their work between six and seven. That was cut. At the outset it was more symmetrical. The whole thing came full circle. *Most people either think that* Les Bonnes Femmes *is a masterpiece or they're violently against it.*

I wanted to make a film about stupid people that was very vulgar and deeply stupid. From that moment on I can hardly be reproached for making a film that is about stupid people. I don't think that it's a pessimistic film. I'm not pessimistic about people in general, but only about the way they live. When we wrote the film the people were, for Gegauff, fools. It was a film about fools. But at the same time we could see little by little that if they were foolish, it was mainly because they were unable to express themselves, establish contact with each other. The result of naïvety, or a too great vulgarity.

People have said that I didn't like the people I was showing, because they believe that you have to ennoble them to like them. That's not true. Quite the opposite: only the types who don't like their fellows have to ennoble them.

But the cinema is an art of identification and that makes it annoying for the spectator. And that is perhaps the reason for the film's failure commercially.

As the film shows vulgar people, who explain themselves instinctively without any kind of mask, so spectators and critics talk about "excess." But the girls aren't shown as idiots. They're just brutalized by the way they live. They're simple girls who are impressed by *savior-faire,* by people who *do* things, tricks and conjurors for example. Maids and shop girls love this sort of thing. The poetical side doesn't really interest them. You see much more grotesque things going on every day than you do in *Les Bonnes Femmes.* Actually it wasn't a *group* of girls in the film. In effect it was one.

Les Bonnes Femmes is the one I like best of all my films. I like *Ophelia* too, but I prefer *Les Bonnes Femmes*.

Ophelia was not quite what we wanted. I think it was shot too late. It should have been made sooner and nearer the time when I had the idea. And then it wasn't shot just *where* I would have liked: the chateau I had wanted had been sold and that was annoying. And we had changed the scenario around too much by the time the film was made. But I like *Ophelia* very much.

I have the impression that you aren't very fond of Les Godelureaux.

It's a failure. From the start it was of an unfathomable idiocy. It was about uselessness, and its lack of success came from the fact that it too was useless. It should never have been started. Gegauff wrote a scenario of extraordinary uselessness! There are things in it I like well . . . the charity party. The film would only have made any sort of sense if it had lasted five hours and people had walked out all the way through so that there was no one left at the end. If the film had been a complete success there would have been three hundred people in the cinema at the beginning and only three at the end. But you can't make films on that principle, so it should never have been made at all.

The film is very close to absurdity, and what I really wanted can best be seen in a scene which was cut of Ambroisine and the bottle of cognac. Ambroisine (Bernadette Lafont) takes a bottle of cognac and hides it behind a curtain. Then she says, "I'd like a glass of cognac. I can't find it. Go and get it." Her idea is to mess Brialy about. They go off to the kitchen for it, but a third man, who's reading some kind of Latin at the same time, follows them and finds them kissing in the kitchen. So they pretend to be looking for the cognac. They are unable to find it, and continue their useless game all over the house, in all the rooms. In the end they give up and go back to the first room. Of course, nobody liked that scene, and there was no reason why they should have been happy with it. But then the whole film was about uselessness, about nothingness.

L'Oeil du Malin was a bit the same. It was about a pitiful man and the story was seen from his point of view. And so the film was, in a way, also pitiful, mean.

Did the film cost a lot to make?

No, very little, but it lost a lot!

Did you enjoy shooting the scenes of the beer festival?

I had to shoot it very quickly in one day only. And then I had 200,000 people on the screen all at once. More than *Ben Hur!*

What did you think of the character played by Charrier? Are you against him?

Charrier knew he was playing an unsympathetic character and did his best to make him sympathetic. Charrier is very usable as an actor.

L'Avarice—the sketch from The Seven Capital Sins?

Ah yes, that meant a fortnight in St. Tropez for me. The producers liked the sketch and the public liked it too. Making it helped me a lot. But I made it too quickly in six days and nights and got very tired doing it. I'm very happy about the girl who played the young prostitute. She's very gifted, very true, very gentle. She was a virgin then. Still is, I hope.

What is the difference between the projected version of Ophelia *and the present one when finally made?*

I pushed it more towards having fun. And then the origginal version was more serious. I had the film *Hamlet* interposed in it. I put the guards back in and a bit where they chase Jocelyn, who puts on a cap and scarf to make them think he's breaking into the grounds of the chateau. I was obliged to change some of the scenes between Ivan (Jocelyn) and the girl (Mayniel). I'm very fond of Juliette, but she wasn't quite what I had in mind at the outset for the part. I wanted a girl with a sort of angelic quality, more ethereal, so that one should understand the impossibility of any erotic quality there. I like the little film within the film and the reception that goes with it because it's more normal than the rest of the film. The hero is normal in comparison with the rest of them. He's not at all mad. In the context of all the other monstrous people around, the relationship of Jocelyn and Mayniel is not at all strange.

Landru! That's something else again! . . . The women? There are two sorts of women in *Landru:* victims and non-victims! I must be careful but . . . there are sixteen victims I think . . . one, two, three, four, five important ones. Some one sees rapidly, their heads, then the smoking chimney. The last one he brings back. He doesn't kill her because the circumstances are unfavourable.

I didn't realise that Landru's first words would be so surprising. You see him going about his business, looking for furniture, as is his job, trying to make some money to take home to his family; he goes home, takes the paper from his wife, everything is quiet and then he roars "I would like a small cup of chocolate" and I tell you that is very frightening! He says it in a very savage voice.

He's very fastidious about his work. He's very sweet from time to time. Landru is a good father, though. He doesn't let his family go wanting.

The colours and the decors are pastel, but from time to time there are colours which are acid—worrying colours. Everything is pretty, pastel, and then suddenly there's a colour which has nothing to do with the rest, expressing anguish. When he goes for the replies to his advertisement for lonely women, there's a little set which is an entresol so that you only see the women's hats and heads as they walk along the pavement outside. And those you see through a red window. On a screen of 25 or 20 square metres there are 16 square metres of red. The red shocks because it is out of place there.

I don't like stories which attempt to demythify a myth. But Landru . . . is he a myth or is he a man? A man transformed into myth. So when one makes a film about Landru does one transform the myth into a man, or must one transform the man into myth? That's the question! So there are both in this film. For the first time in World Cinema, we see Before Our Very Eyes the metamorphosis from man into myth!

After *Landru* I have a sketch in *Les Plus Bells Escroqueries du Monde,* a farce about a guy who sells the Eiffel Tower in Germany to scrap merchants for the value of the iron. He has a small Eiffel Tower in his garden. Very beautiful. First shot is the Eiffel Tower covered in snow. Then an enormous nose of a watering can appears and pours water over it. And you see that it's not snow but soap and the man is washing down his Eiffel Tower. After that he puts a cover over it! He sells it at a false price because the iron has a sort of myth attached to it, even though the myth is not saleable to a scrap-merchant. I have to make it in CinemaScope. The Eiffel Tower fits into that shape of screen so beautifully.

Claude Chabrol (1930–   ):
Filmography:
1958—Le Beau Serge, Les Cousins. 1959—Léda. 1960—Les Bonnes Femmes, Les Godelureaux. 1961—The Third Lover. 1962—Ophélia, Landru. 1964—Le Tigre Aime La Chair Fraîche. 1965—Marie-Chantal Contre le Docteur Kah, Le Tigre Se Parfume à la Dyna-

mite. 1966—La Ligne de Démarcation. 1961—Seven Capital Sins (L'Avarice). 1965—Paris vu par . . . Chabrol. 1967—The Champagne Murders. 1968—The Route to Corinth, Les Biches. 1969—La Femme Infidèle.

LE BOUCHER

THE NADA GANG

WEDDING IN BLOOD

LA RUPTURE

Charles Chaplin

Charles Chaplin has now been an international movie celebrity for more than fifty years. Even to anti-movie scholars from other disciplines, Chaplin is accepted as a full and genuine artist. There are those within the cinema who feel that his reputation has been gained at the expense of other directors who have not been blessed with his popularity. Be that as it may, Chaplin's importance and influence are incontestable. The apparent simplicity of Chaplin's directorial style has been confused with lack of technique. For Chaplin, his other self on the screen has always been a supreme object of contemplation, and the style that logically followed from this assumption represents the antithesis to Sergei Eisenstein's early formulations on montage. The late André Bazin brilliantly analyzed this fundamental opposition between montage and the one scene sequence thusly: "If burlesque triumphed before Griffith and montage, it is because most of the gags came out of a comedy of space, of the relation of man to objects and to the exterior world. Chaplin, in The Circus, *is actually in the lion's cage, and both are enclosed in a single frame on the screen." However, Chaplin, unlike Keaton, eventually subordinated his physical ties to the exterior world to the interior, almost schizophrenic relationship between director and actor. The physical objects that remained mechanical props in Keaton's cinema became universal symbols in Chaplin's. The breathtaking anal ballet, the globular and global balloon in* The Great Dictator, *derives its effect not from the physical property of balloons, but from a symbolic extension of megalomania. The circle Chaplin traces on the ground in* The Circus *is less an image in space than an image in time and* life. The loss of plasticity and specificity in Chaplin's films coincided with the loss of humor and a gain of meaning. Ultimately, Chaplin lost most of his audience, and in Limelight, he celebrated the occasion by imagining his own death, a conception of sublime egoism unparalleled in the world cinema. To imagine one's own death, one must imagine the death of the world, that world which has always dangled so helplessly from the tips of Chaplin's eloquent fingers. Chaplin dabbled in Marxian (Modern Times) and Brechtian (Monsieur Verdoux) analysis, but the solipsism of his personality negated the social implications of his program. The idea of the actor has always contradicted the idea of the masses, just as the close-up has always distorted the long view of history. What is the final close-up of City Lights, after all, but the definitive image of a man who feels tragically unworthy of his beloved? Chaplin has been criticized for abandoning the tramp, a creature who had engulfed his creator in the public's mind. Chaplin might be criticized with equal justice for having grown old and reflective. The bitter melancholy of Limelight carries over into A King in New York, a film widely misunderstood as an anti-American tract. For Chaplin, however, America is like Dawn Addams, a fantasy and a delusion, a marvelous world that he may yet revisit, but never reconquer. Viewed as a whole, Chaplin's career is a cinematic biography on the highest level of artistic expression.*—A.S.

Almost as soon as we arrived, the bronzed swimming instructor at the hotel in Cap Ferrat cornered us. "You are here to see Mr. Chaplin? What luck! I want to see him more than any other man in the world. I teach his son Michael water-skiing. One day I went up to the villa; I could just see the top of Mr. Chaplin's head through a window. But the secretary told me 'Please don't look at Mr. Chaplin. He doesn't like to be stared at. . . '" He sighed, adjusted a dazzling smile and went off to give a lesson.

But the slight chill he left behind him was catching. "Of course," explained the publicist, "it all depends on Mr. Chaplin's mood. Maybe he'll spend the whole day with you—or maybe you'll just get ten minutes. You never can

* Margaret Hinxman's interview with Charles Chaplin appeared in Sight and Sound, No. 2, Vol. 27, Autumn 1957

tell." Suddenly this interview with Chaplin, that had started as a job, began to assume the proportions of an Experience—and maybe not of the pleasantest kind.

And then at last we were shaking hands with a wiry, white-haired man, who greeted us as though we were the first welcome visitors from the outside world. He cocked his head on one side and smiled that ridiculous, coy smile. We breathed again. Obviously the mood was right.

Anxiously, he wanted to know what we thought of *A King in New York*. "Did you think it was so anti-American, as they all say it is? *Did* you?" For a while he gave a fair imitation of a man who didn't care that it had been ignored by America. "Of course; it will never be shown there." But from the way he worried the point you felt that he did care, desperately. No matter how Europe honours him, he is still deeply hurt at the manner in which America rejected him. He gives the impression of a man who is trying to conceal a wound that will never entirely heal.

"I'm not a politician. I'm not a Communist. I told them at the Press Conference when *Monsieur Verdoux* was shown, 'I've lived in the United States for forty years. I haven't started a revolution yet, I'm certainly not planning to start one and I don't think I ever shall, I told them," he repeated.

Reverting to *A King in New York* and its jibes at America: "Americans have no sense of humour about themselves, not like the British," he shrugged. At the end of the film, he had implied that this American witch-hunting hysteria was just a passing phase: did he think it had passed now, we asked. But he wouldn't commit himself. "Everything has to change—everything, in time."

Through the window that looked on to the terrace, we could see various Chaplin children, slim, brown and all like diminutive copies of his wife, Oona, flitting nimbly around. "They're such wonderful mimics, they inhibit *me* —and I thought I was a pretty good mimic." The switch from anxious film-maker to proud father was revealing. He related with obvious pleasure his son Michael's remark on seeing himself in *A King in New York;* "it makes me look so young." He is apparently a solemn boy, given to deep meditations and poetry reading in the early morning.

His daughter Josephine, Chaplin told us, was in the throes of wanting to become a Catholic. "There was a time when I'd have liked to turn Catholic. That was when I was just a boy, one of the Lancashire Lads. All the other

Lancashire Lads were Catholics, and how I envied them with their beads and crosses and religious statues. It all looked so mysterious and exciting. I never did change my religion, though—it would have hurt my mother too much."

When Chaplin remembers the past he becomes a different person. And, at sixty-eight, the past seems to be frequently and vividly in his thoughts. "Smells, you know, smells bring it back more than anything else. That's what I discovered when I returned to England. As you get older the far-off past becomes clearer; the recent past you can't remember so well." And for the first time we were conscious that Chaplin wasn't a young man any more. Occasionally, he brings out a pair of serviceable spectacles to peer at some document. Even so, he can only read when the paper is an inch from his nose.

The people he talks of most vividly—all "very dear friends of mine"—are the colleagues of the past, some of them long dead. "Jolson—he had the kind of projection none of the young people have today. He was a silly man—always 'let's go to the races,' that sort of thing. And he sang the most terrible songs. But he *believed* them and he made the audience believe them."

"Pavlova—such perfection, it made me cry."

Only when he was searching for a contemporary name did his memory desert him. "There is one young actor . . . he played in—what was that film?—something to do with a streetcar. M . . . M . . . Marlon Brando"—he produced the name triumphantly—"I saw him in a film about paraplegics" (*The Men,* we volunteered) "and there was a moment in that when he'd been given some bad news. I watched the way he handled that scene and I thought 'this man has something.'"

Discussing his own films, he reveals an eager enthusiasm that easily transfers itself to the listener. "My greatest success? Well, financially, *The Great Dictator.* I may revive it," he decided. "Almost everyone warned me not to make it. You know who gave me the idea for it—Alexander Korda. I was looking for a subject and he suggested I try a mistaken identity story."

Divertingly, he considered the subject of where drama ends and comedy begins. "Who knows where you draw a line between comedy and tragedy? Take a funeral, for instance: the most solemn occasion. Everyone in black; tears, flowers, handkerchiefs. And then a little man arrives

89

rather late, very breathless. He sneaks into church and sits down beside a very fat mourner who gives him a perishing look. Nervously, he moves up a seat and sits on somebody's hat. In no time, it's an hilarious comedy." He jumped up promptly and mimed the absurd episode for us.

"There's one joke that I've always wanted to use. I thought of it as long ago as *The Kid,* but I couldn't find a spot for it in that film. It's a man with a flea circus. He goes into a doss house . . . they still call them that, don't they? And the fleas get loose. He runs around searching for the fleas, calling them by name. Everyone is scratching furiously. Finally, he manages to round up all the fleas but one. There's a big man with a great straggling beard. He spots a flea in the beard, picks it out, studies it intently, then says 'Sorry, wrong one' and puts it back. And the pay-off is when a scrawny old dog starts scratching itself. The flea trainer sees it, makes a grab for the dog; and it races off down the street with the little man, calling his lost fleas, chasing after. I used a little of that in *Limelight,* but I've never been able to fit the whole episode in anywhere.

"Then there's the gag about the man who goes to a very pompous dinner party. Everything goes wrong for him. The butler gets his name wrong; his neighbour at table drops butter on his coat; the serving maid pours soup down his neck. He suffers it all with a smile and polite reassurances: 'Oh, please don't bother—it's quite all right.' Then, finally, after the last indignity, he goes beserk, runs wildly round the room, breaking the china, scaring the guests, and at last, setting fire to the place." For a moment, Chaplin was lost in visions of happy anarchy.

It was a vengeance, you felt, that he'd like to have wreaked on the hapless cinema manager in America who ran a sneak preview of his *City Lights.* "Hate the things. I went to this one with Professor Einstein and his wife. I sat there waiting for the film to begin. When it did, I held my breath until the first laugh. And I knew I'd done it. But then, after half an hour, the houselights went up, in the middle of the film, and a voice over the loud-speaker started extolling the virtues of this magnificent new cinema that had just been opened. I got up furiously and went in search of the manager . . ." It isn't on record whether the manager recovered from the encounter.

It was getting late. But the Chaplin stream of reminiscence was still in full flow. He had to be reminded that he was dining with a friend. "Very wealthy. He has a beautiful villa. Always asking us to stay there. *Very* dear friend."

When we got back to the hotel, the swimming instructor was waiting for us. "Well—what was he like?" "He was like—Charlie Chaplin," we told him, lamely. You couldn't say fairer than that.

Charles Chaplin (1889–   ):
Filmography:
1914—Making a Living, Kid Auto Races at Venice, Mabel's Strange Predicament, Between Showers, A Film Johnnie, Tango Tangles, His Favorite Pastime; Cruel, Cruel Love; The Star Boarder, Mabel at the Wheel, Twenty Minutes of Love; Caught in a Cabaret, Caught in the Rain, A Busy Day, The Fatal Mallet, Her Friend the Bandit, The Knockout, Mabel's Busy Day, Mabel's Married Life, Laughing Gas, The Property Man, The Face on the Barroom Floor, Recreation, The Masquerader, His New Profession, The Rounders, The New Janitors, Those Love Pangs, Dough and Dynamite, Gentleman of Nerve, His Musical Career, His Trysting Place, Tillie's Punctured Romance, Getting Acquainted, His Prehistoric Past. 1915—His New Job, A Night Out, the Champion, In the Park, The Jitney Elopement, The Tramp, By the Sea, Work, A Woman, The Bank, Shanghaied, A Night in the Show. 1916—Carmen, Police, The Floorwalker, The Fireman, The Vagabond, One A.M., The Count, The Pawnshop, Behind the Screen, The Rink. 1917—Easy Street, The Cure, The Immigrant, The Adventurer. 1918—Triple Trouble, A Dog's Life, The Bond, Shoulder Arms. 1919—Sunnyside, A Day's Pleasure. 1920—The Kid. 1921—The Idle Class. 1922—Pay Day. 1923—The Pilgrim, A Woman of Paris. 1925—The Gold Rush. 1928—The Circus. 1931—City Lights. 1936—Modern Times. 1940—The Great Dictator. 1947—Monsieur Verdoux. 1952—Limelight. 1957—A King in New York. 1967—The Countess from Hong Kong.

George Cukor

Even George Cukor's detractors concede his taste and style, but it has become fashionable to dismiss him as a woman's director because of his skill in directing actresses, a skill he shares with Griffith, Chaplin, Renoir, Ophuls, Von Sternberg, Welles, Dreyer, Rossellini, Mizoguchi—ad infinitum, ad gloriam. Another argument against Cukor is that he relies heavily on adaptations from the stage, that his cinema consequently lacks the purity of the Odessa Steps. This argument was refuted in principle by the late André Bazin. There is an honorable place in the cinema for both adaptations and the non-writer director, and Cukor, like Lubitsch, is one of the best examples of the non-writer director, and Cukor, like Lubitsch, is one of the best examples of the non-writer author, a creature literary film critics seem unable to comprehend. The thematic consistency of Cukor's career has been achieved through a judicious mixture of selection and emphasis. The director's theme is imagination, with the focus on the imaginer rather than on the thing imagined. Cukor's cinema is a subjective cinema without an objective correlative. The husbands never appeared in The Women, *and Edward never appears in* Edward, My Son. *Most critics would argue that this merely proves Cukor's slavish fidelity to his playwrights, but the fact remains that most directors attempt to make plays more "cinematic" by moving outdoors and adding characters and extras. Not Cukor.* Bhowani Junction *and* Heller in Pink Tights *demonstrate that Cukor is fully capable of exploiting exteriors when they serve his purposes. The opening Central Park sequence in* The Marrying Kind, *is one of the most graceful exercises in open-air film-making in the history of the cinema, and the corresponding sequence in* It Should Happen to You *is not far behind. Yet, when characters have to thrash out their illusions and problems across the kitchen table, Cukor glides through his interiors without self-conscious reservations about what is "cinematic" and what is not. It is no accident that many of Cukor's characters are thespians of one form or another. John Barrymore and Marie Dressler in* Dinner at Eight, *Ina Claire in* Royal Family of Broadway, *Katharine Hepburn and Cary Grant in* Sylvia Scarlett, *Judy Garland and James Mason in* A Star Is Born, *Jean Simmons in* The Actress, *Marilyn Monroe in* Let's Make Love, *and even Sophia Loren, De Sica's alleged earth mother, in* Heller in Pink Tights. *Even when Cukor's characters do not appear formally behind the footlights, they project an imaginative existence. W. C. Fields is pure ham in* David Copperfield, *and Katharine Hepburn is pure egoism in* The Philadelphia Story. *Cukor is equally sympathetic to the absurdities of both.* Les Girls *is Cukor's* Rashomon, *but where Kurosawa argues that all people are liars, Cukor suggests that all people tell the truth in their fashion. Even when imagination extends to transvestism in* Adam's Rib *and* Sylvia Scarlett, *Cukor retains an indulgent affection for the misguided brashness of Katharine Hepburn. The theme is consistent; the pattern is established. Cukor is committed to the dreamer, if not to the content of the dream. He is a genuine artist.**—A.S.

GEORGE CUKOR: You know, there's nothing worse than making excuses. For example, saying when a picture hasn't gone well or when you've been badly reviewed that it was so-and-so's fault. What I do is just make a blanket statement: it was just an unfortunate thing and let's forget it. But since you're going into detail I will tell you about something. Curiously enough, some of the best scenes I've ever had anything to do with are in pictures that did not succeed. That is odd. But unless the story line carries the scenes the scenes really don't mean anything. I believe the story is frightfully important. Simple story telling. Without it you get a most beautiful production, most beautiful act-

---

* *Richard Overstreet's interview with George Cukor appeared originally in* Film Culture, *No. 34, Fall 1964.*

ing . . . but it's all ineffective because you don't arrest the attention of the audience.

RICHARD OVERSTREET: *Do you feel that* The Chapman Report *was a success in this respect?*

GC: I must tell you about that. It was the story of three women and their problems. With Jane Fonda the problem was frigidity . . . well, the basic problem was that it was a rather lurid book and I believe the author, after a while, threw caution to the wind at the request of the publisher. So the whole ending is very hectic. But the book diverted me, nevertheless.

RO: *Did you read it before they asked you to do the picture?*

GC: I read it before . . . and I will say that I was influenced by one thing: I had an obligation to Fox. They were planning to sue me or some damn thing so I thought: let's just get this over with. But the story did interest me. It amused me greatly.

RO: *It must have . . . for, after all, it is a story about women.*

GC: Yes . . . about women. Sort of a cheapish story, really, but I thought it could be filmed without any vulgarity, you see. The book is full of it . . .

The Jane Fonda episode was extremely interesting and much more complete than the others. You saw her run the gamut of experiences. You saw her try all these things: she goes into a motel with a man and draws back when he approaches her. And the Shelley Winters thing: she performed it well but she was rather vulgar. I was especially careful with the Claire Bloom part. There were moments when she had aspirations of some kind and you should have felt that she was a rather noble woman doing ignoble things.

RO: *Of the four actresses, were you most content with her performance?*

GC: Well, it was certainly the most complete. When the thing was all put together we took it up to San Francisco for a sneak preview and it went very well. It was quite interesting because the screening was in a theatre on Market Street and there was a rather nondescript crowd there. But I felt that the crowd was actually ahead of us. They had heard of the book. Thought it was very sexy. We could have gone even farther with the audience—not hedged at all with the touchy parts. I don't mean we should have been erotic, just more frank.

The preview was a very good one . . . but before I go

on I should give you a little background. The picture was to be released by Warners but it was produced by Zanuck. Zanuck, however, was here in Europe shooting *The Longest Day*. He was a friend of mine, Zanuck. We got on very well together and his son was acting as producer. I was very nice to the son.

After the preview I made some minor suggestions about recutting, just reworking it a little. Then with these suggestions we shipped the print over to Zanuck. He then, as usual, cut the damned thing, completely re-cut it so that it no longer made any sense at all. He emasculated it.

RO: *What are the major changes that he made?*

GC: He just cut everything every sort of mad way, that's all. When he brought it back to Warners it was absolutely incoherent. He did all this revising while he had *Longest Day* going. He was cutting the poor *Chapman Report* to bits and at the same time sending me ecstatic wires declaring how great it was. Then I learned that he was "fixing it up." At that point I refused to see the cut version. Warners were appalled at what he had done. Finally, I spoke to him, told him what I thought and he replied: "Let's preview it just once my way to see how it goes." I agreed—what else could I do? Warners restored certain things after Zanuck's re-working and while they were doing this I said to them: "You know, if you cut out the high-minded parts of this thing the censors will jump down your throat because of the book's bad reputation. That is why we cast Claire Bloom. The part had to be played on a high level."

Zanuck said, "I promise you on my word of honor . . . here's my son to bear me out . . . we'll preview it once with the re-cut version that I did, then we'll preview it your way." That was that. There was to be no nonsense. The next thing I knew I was holding a wire in my hands: "I find there is a clause in the contract. We don't have time for the previews. The picture must be released immediately so the last cut print will have to go out." I wrote Zanuck a very indignant wire, then he sent me one back, very long and very nasty. He said that some ex-prizefighter friend of his had seen his version and thought it was great.

Then the censors jumped on our backs, made us cut the hell out of the picture . . .

RO: *Was Glynis Johns' part cut up by the censors—the erotic implications here being of a comic sort?*

GC: Her episode was completely different from the book—and surprisingly enough the only one which was very little hurt by the censors. So this pushed the whole thing out of proportion. Originally, she had a comic-minor role and coming out of the ordeal unscathed she was the only one who remained coherent . . . but much too important. The other girls absolutely unbelievable, incoherent. At best, the film was not a masterpiece but in its original form it was amusing and slick and would have done well. But every quality it ever had was ripped out. It was ruined. RUINED.

RO: *Even though it was cut and desecrated your tasteful handling of the subject still came through.*

GC: Yes, it was in "good taste."

We had three . . . two very appetizing girls. Shelley Winters was, well, all right. We decided that her hair was to be dark in the picture, then she gradually snuck this peroxide effect in. Before we knew it she had made herself into a brassy blond. It was too late to do anything about it . . . a stupid move. She did play some scenes with a great deal of feeling . . .

The picture really was ruined. They said they made a lot of money. There would have been a lot of money in their pockets if they would have left the picture as it was. As you know it was received with the greatest contempt in England. There is this man there by the name of Trevelyan who is the czar of what people see and what they don't see. He said it was vulgar . . . so that was the end of *The Chapman Report* in England. I think the man's nose is out of joint. After all, he turned down *A Kind Of Loving*.

The whole thing was a complete disaster from beginning to end.

RO: *With all these cutting problems—and they weren't the first such run-ins you've had with producers—why didn't you produce sooner?*

GC: For many years I was under contract to Metro. There were hang-overs from old commitments which I had made and I just wasn't free. Then when *My Fair Lady* came along I took that because I thought it was a great *coup*. I liked the idea of doing it even if I wasn't producing. But now I definitely will produce on my own.

In the past there have been pictures marred by disagreements. For instance, there was *The Actress* with a scenario by Ruth Gordon based on her play *Years Ago*. The producer made some minor cuts and they had an *enormous* effect on the picture. Ruth was very pained by it because they changed the whole sense of the film. Jean Simmons, playing Ruth as a girl, had the willfulness, the slight ruthlessness of an actress. But in the cutting, slight as it was, her strength was mitigated—her character was completely changed. Ruth was very pained by the slices and I agree with her.

The curious thing is when you're making a picture there's damn little help from others on the set. You've got this piece of paper in front of you . . . and the actors . . . and that's all. There's no one there with the clever advice but when the thing's all over there are hundreds of stooges all around telling you to cut this and that. Actually, they don't know a thing, those people, and I would hate any picture to have to go through the emasculation that this poor *Chapman Report* went through.

RO: *But* The Chapman Report *wasn't as butchered as* A Star Is Born, *was it?*

GC: No . . . no. They just hacked into that one. Junked it completely. Bits were cut and lost . . . very painful, indeed. Bosley Crowther wrote an article called "A Star Is Shorn" . . . and it was, in fact! Things were taken out and the negative corresponding to them were lost. A complete disaster.

There were some terribly funny scenes that fell out. At the beginning when Judy Garland and James Mason go out to the oil wells in a Los Angeles suburb—she's still unknown then and he's the great star. It's night, they have a little conversation, he's in love with her, she's moved . . . very moved by him, but the smell of the oil is just too much and she gets sick; she's so humiliated.

The picture was, in fact, too long. But while I wasn't there they produced a big production number right in the middle—"Born in a Trunk." It went on and on and in the context of the final cut version was way too long. If they thought it was too long there were other ways of shortening it besides chopping and hacking out vital bits. Had we been allowed, Moss Hart and I could have sweated out twenty minutes which would have been imperceptible to the audience. That's something which I can't understand. Producers spend millions of dollars to do pictures and then suddenly, right out of the blue, they say: "Let's chop this out, then that. . . ." In what other business does this happen? I'm sure at Ford they don't make models of some car and then just throw them out.

It's very painful, all this. Fanny Brice, who was a wonderful woman and a great friend of mine, once said, "The older we get, kid, the less you can brush off them knocks." And she was right. The older you get the less you can. But there are some things I won't stand for, old or not. For example, when you're filming and there comes a moment of indecision—the people around you say: "O.K., let's do it both ways . . . do the scene both ways and you can't go wrong." I refuse point blank and say that there is only one way to do it: let's decide what is the correct way and after there will be no alternatives. There is a right way and a wrong way—that's all. Mind you, I'm not always right, don't think that by any means. I've miscalculated a great many things. Very often you imagine certain things and then the audience tells you differently. You must never underestimate the audience. The audience is, after all, always right. Sometimse they react the way you don't want them to and sometimes there are a lot of kids in the house and they laugh at the wrong place. But the audience is always right. You must not be hysterical, though; you must interpret their reactions calmly and correctly. You must know cause and effect. If you had a bad laugh in the fourth reel that doesn't mean the line is bad. It simply means that what preceded, what came before the line, is all off . . . that the preparation for the line is wrong. You must be detached and look at your children from a distance . . . you must be patient and loving.

RO: *When you are filming are you often thinking of audience reactions?*

GC: No, not at all. I'm thinking of myself . . . just me and what I like. I'm not trying to guess what the audience does.

RO: *You're not trying to gauge a certain type of public then? Filming for a particular type of audience?*

GC: No. That is the kiss of death. You must please yourself. You must profoundly please yourself hoping that the audience will like it as well. If you're trying to outguess the audience or trying to be "popular" only one sort of product can come out: a synthetic one—and it's not really you. It's false.

RO: *Of all your pictures which one did you most enjoy filming? It certainly wasn't* The Chapman Report . . .

GC: No, it wasn't that one! I must tell you that when I work the atmosphere has to be happy, cheerful . . . amusing and funny. That doesn't mean that there aren't all sorts of *crises*, but I will not put up with strain—I can't think, I'm distracted. And I will not have unpleasant pressures on the set. Unless I'm sympathetic with people I cannot function. All the pictures I've done have been joyous experiences . . . there must be this happiness while we work—it must be enjoyable. This doesn't necessarily mean that the picture will be good, though. As a matter of fact, one film where every day was Christmas on the set and where presents were exchanged right and left was a complete disaster: *Sylvia Scarlett*.

Here was a picture where Cary Grant first felt an audience liked him. Up to then he had been a rather handsome, rather wooden leading man . . . somewhat inexperienced, too. But suddenly during the shooting he felt all his talents coming into being—maybe because it was the first part which really suited his background. He suddenly burst into bloom. Quite a blooming—it produced a wonderful performance.

It is an interesting moment when people come into their own. Now take Joan Fontaine, for instance. I always thought she was a talented girl and one day I requested to test her out in a few scenes. We began working together and she was completely petrified—couldn't move. The test was still interesting, though, and when it came time to do *The Women* I said, "Let's get that girl, she's very pretty and she'll be good for the part of the young wife." Up to that point she had been at R.K.O. playing not too interesting leading women and she wasn't terribly good, especially in a picture she did with Fred Astaire.

There is a scene in *The Women* where she is in Reno with a lot of other women waiting to get a divorce. Suddenly her husband calls her, there is a long conversation and she realizes that she is still in love with him. Joan did the scene, talking on the phone, and all at once everything fell into place. All the things she ever dreamed of happening to her as an actress, actually happened. She did this scene with the most tremendous force and feeling. It was a thrilling moment when she realized that she was an actress and after the take she looked at me and said, "I really am an actress." She had been acting for four years and not very successfully. Suddenly there was this breakthrough. It was a thrilling moment.

I try to make every picture the best. It's the only way to work. There must be a climate of amiability and fun and excitement. Every picture I do is the first one I've ever done . . . and it's the last. Making a picture is enormously important to me and the experience is a joyous one.

RO: *Are you ever a little worried about starting a film —scared on the first day of shooting?*

GC: Yes. The older you get the more scared you get. You see, the older and wiser you are the better you see the pitfalls. The first three or four days on the set I'm rather shaky but I plunge into my work just the same. On those shaky first days people look at me and say: "So, you're going to start all over again?" I reply "Yes . . . yes. . . ." I'm not absolutely confident but my nerves get better. Well, everyone's nervous at first I suppose.

RO: *Do you take extra precautions on your first day of shooting—over covering shots, for example?*

GC: Sometimes yes, sometimes no. I do take the precaution of usually starting out with scenes that aren't too complicated so I can break things in slowly. As a matter of fact, I started *My Fair Lady* two days earlier than planned—we did all sorts of experimenting with the rain scenes to help the crew limber up, to help me break myself in. When we started with the principals a few days later we were all over our jitters.

RO: *I wonder if we could take a scene from one of your pictures and discuss it inside and out; how it was conceived, put together, filmed, edited and so on.*

GC: All right. You pick one.

RO: *What about the "Somewhere There's a Someone" number from* Star Is Born—*where Judy Garland improvises a whole musical comedy production number in her front room?*

GC: That's not quite fair because it's a musical number. They are always so well planned out ahead of time— and most of the work there was done by the choreographer.

RO: *Toward the end of* Star Is Born, *perhaps. James Mason is in bed and Garland is out on the porch facing the ocean with Charles Bickford. Mason hears that his wife is planning to give up her career and spend the rest of her life nursing him. He cries—the camera stays on him for some time sobbing in bed. When Bickford has gone he tells his wife to make a sandwich for him while he goes down to the ocean for a swim—she sings in the kitchen while he walks into the water . . . but maybe I should let you choose a scene yourself.*

GC: I liked that scene, too. But it didn't require anything special . . . it all happened so naturally. Moss Hart wrote it and I believe it was very moving . . . mainly because of James Mason. He is a complete actor. He is a man who has the greatest discretion . . . rather reserved by nature . . . a mysterious creature. To see that man break down was very moving. But all the credit for that goes to James. He did it all himself. What I did was to let him do it and let it go on and on—let it run for a long time, let the camera stay on him for an eternity. He became so involved that he couldn't stop . . . and I let him do what he felt.

Let me think . . . what scene can I tell you about which required a kind of conception or a kind of direction. It's hard. There are so many of them . . .

RO: *Maybe something from* The Philadelphia Story?

GC: Perhaps . . . no, no. Here is a scene. In a picture I did a long time ago called *Dinner at Eight* which was taken from a stage play. Jack Barrymore gave an extraordinary performance as an untalented, fourth-rate actor. He did it with the greatest subtlety. If you remember he was in his hotel room talking on the phone. This society woman was asking him to come to dinner and he was saying: "Yes, I'd love to come." Well, Jack asked me if he could put something in and I told him he could do whatever he liked. So he added something to the line and it came out: "Yes, I'd love to come, dear lady." This little addition painted the whole character: a rather cheapish actor, slightly old-fashioned. He created all sorts of wonderful *nuances* that way.

He always spoke in a rather actorish way in the film but when the bell hop would come in he tried to be tough, always in this rather over-elegant voice: "I gotta have a drink, see?"

He was on the skids but always hoped there was a part somewhere for him. Finally, when all his plans fell through and he learned that the part he hoped to get had been given to an English actor he cried out: "English, English . . . I can be as English as anybody!!" Remember that?

There was something he did with enormous wit. Still trying to convince those around him that he would play anything he declared: "Ibsen. I can play Ibsen." Then he leaned up against the mantel piece and proceeded to do a scene from Ibsen—a scene which never existed and which he invented all the way. It was all so obvious—he had

101

never heard of Ibsen. "Mother, mother dear, give me the sun . . ." he went on, not quite knowing what the hell he was saying. But he did it all with the greatest truth.

In the scene where he was going to kill himself one had to feel that he wanted to die beautifully, like Greta Garbo. We started the scene, he crossed the room to plug up the chimney and turn on the gas . . . and I said to him: "Jack, he should not even be able to commit suicide. He has always bungled everything and now some awful indignity should happen to him." Then Jack walked across the room again . . . right in the middle of the carpet was a stool and he tripped on it, went spilling all over the floor —an awful middleaged, ungraceful sprawl which was so sad and so marvelous in the picture. Even in arranging his death he blundered—the touch was just right. So unconventional.

. . . Mrs. Patrick Campbell once made an exit and later when she referred to it she said: "I walked through a chair." Well, Jack did that. The character he was playing thought he should die in as romantic a way as possible— imagining all sorts of dramatic things as he turned the gas on. I thought this awful kind of note right in the middle of it all was quite good. It was so pathetic that way.

RO: *Did something "just happen" like that while you were filming* The Chapman Report?

GC: *The Chapman Report* . . . let me think.

RO: *What about the scene in the doctor's office where he is questioning Claire Bloom? Tension builds up in her to such a point that at last she looks behind the screen which has been shielding her interrogator.*

GC: That was a very simple scene . . . all done in one take, by the way. We did it all in one take.

RO: *It was just a simple office—but remarkably well lighted. The colors were beautiful.*

GC: That is largely due to a good cameraman, Harold Lipstein, who was very influenced by George Hoyningen-Huene and Gene Allen.

In that scene there is a whole exposé, a whole gamut of human feelings . . . a complete human experience: defiance, lying, defenses breaking down. It is a whole long betrayal.

RO: *What about the scene where Claire Bloom, in final degradation, comes to the room where the men are playing cards?*

102

GC: That was rather moving . . . she came in coyly, slowly, but very distinguished, and he was awful to her.

RO: *She was distinguished but she couldn't control herself.*

GC: This was very interesting. I'll tell you what we did there. The problem was to show all these men raping her. I thought it would be interesting to start it off as a game . . . the men playing around with her, laughing with her and at her, but all the time being terribly disrespectful. It all started out as a joke with the men pushing her from one place to another . . . then they did, in fact, rape her. Then the fascinating thing is that she responded to it—she was horrified but she responded to it. A fast fast series of cuts of pushing, shoving, grabbing, falling, grasping, arms, legs . . . the men holding her down.

RO: *In the released version we never saw any of this —just the very beginning where she is shoved down. Was this scene shown in its entirety at the San Francisco preview?*

GC: Yes, and the audience thought it was marvelous. It was very effective: the men putting their hands on her brutally, jumping on top of her . . . she got a big kick out of being indignant. And in *our* scenario, not the Zanuck final cut, she left the men, was driven away . . . went right home and killed herself. When all those people got through with it it didn't make sense any more. I particularly liked the scene where she came into the room, her bedroom, locked the door behind her, took the bottle of pills and killed herself.

The scene with the men was of an extraordinary violence. They manhandled her, climbed on top of her and laughed. Her head moved from side to side . . . the men's gestures . . . her movements . . . a marvelous scene cut out by Zanuck. It was a long thing to shoot and we did many, many takes. The actors did it all with the greatest of delicacy. Claire was pushed around in the most violent way—her dress was ripped and torn. An agonizing experience . . . a big, heavy fellow lying on top of her . . . but the actors did it all with such delicacy, the greatest gallantry.

RO: *This was the first time you worked with Clair Bloom.*

GC: Yes, it was, and she was marvelous to work with. She's a most accomplished actress. She's played all the great parts and can do almost anything.

I asked her in one scene—where she was drunk in her bedroom—to remove her blouse. She moved across the room, slowly, like a cat . . . you saw her breasts. But all that was cut out, completely sliced to bits. Had we been able to make this picture say, in France, it would have remained intact . . . and made a sensation. As it was, we were the victims of stupid censorship, lack of courage and lack of taste. As I conceived it *and filmed it* the picture would have gone over. It would have been a sensation.

RO: *Now that you are producing your own pictures do you think you would ever come to France to do one—to be at complete liberty and to escape just such restrictions?*

GC: It depends. It depends on the kind of picture . . . it's not an impossibility. In any case, on the next film I do I don't plan to pull any punches—there is only one way to do it and next time it will be done that way.

This isn't the first time censorship has hacked away. There were scenes in *Bhowani Junction* where Ava Gardner is taking a shower . . . where she uses her lover's toothbrush and washes her mouth out with whiskey. You know the scene in *Les Amants* where the man is making love to Jeanne Moreau . . . he is on her and then all of a sudden his head disappears and the camera remains on her face, her ecstasy. I did exactly the same thing in *Bhowani Junction* with Ava and Bill Travers . . . years before Louis Malle. But it all went onto the cutting room floor.

All those things are very interesting to do, if you're allowed to do them. I sincerely believe that *The Chapman Report* had no vulgarity whatever, but after they re-arranged things . . . all the time you felt that Claire Bloom was a rather noble creature doing ignoble things. That was very important.

RO: *It was supposed to be a picture about sex, but after the cuts one hardly knew what the basic idea behind the whole thing was.*

GC: Disgraceful thing—just as well to forget it.

But we're getting away from your question about how I work. I haven't answered that very satisfactorily.

RO: *Do you work a lot with your writers?*

CG: Yes, I do. But I don't write myself.

You know, I didn't realize until I saw the *Ten Commandments* just what De Mille's strength was. A long time ago I thought what he did was a big joke, just preposterous, and I couldn't understand why the audience went for it in such a big way. There were always all sorts of orgies with belly dancers, veils and all the trappings. The eroticism was a joke. Then I saw *The Ten Commandments* . . . it was preposterous from the word go but I suddenly saw something new there, something which had escaped me before: the story telling was wonderful. The way that man could tell a story was fascinating—you were riveted to your seat. That's exactly what he was: a great, great story teller. It was often ridiculous with all those excesses and froth but the man did *tell a story*. That was De Mille's great talent and the secret behind his popular success.

RO: *When everything is ready for shooting, the text written, preliminary rehearsals done, do you ever come onto the set and at the last minute change something . . . at the last minute decide to take out 15 lines, remove a big chair from the living room, a lamp here, a pillow there?*

GC: Maybe I will the day before—very rarely just before the cameras roll. I try to think everything out ahead of time. I feel my way around a long time ahead to see how things can be managed. For example, in *My Fair Lady* everything was planned ahead—you have to do that for big super-spectacles.

RO: *In the* Cahiers du Cinema *interview a few years back, you talked a little bit about how you conceive the framing of shots. You cited several examples from A* Star Is Born—*which was the first true cinemascope film, conceived expressly for the wide screen.*

GC: On this subject I should tell you that I have working with me one of the most talented art directors in the world: Gene Allen. He has been the greatest help to me and has worked on all the pictures since *Star Is Born*. And then there's George Hoyningen-Huene who is my color consultant—he was, as you know, a great photographer. So, you see, it's not all me—these men are responsible to a great degree.

RO: *You did many original things in framing shots in this picture. For instance, when Charles Bickford comes to console Judy Garland in her dressing room. During that conversation you see their heads cut off on opposite sides of the screen. Just their profiles are visible with this great empty space in between.*

GC: Well . . . I don't remember that. Someplace else, though, we pushed all the action to one side and one third . . . two thirds of the screen was blank.

You realize, of course, that Cinemascope is the most unfortunate shape.

RO: *You don't like working in Cinemascope?*

GC: No. No. It's the most terrible shape. The old shape was the best. The old square. 70 mm. is much better. Cinemascope is such an unfortunate shape.

RO: *You certainly did some very beautiful things with it.*

GC: The problem is, you can't get any height in the thing. That makes it very difficult. All I did with my Scope pictures . . . all we did . . . was simply refuse to buckle under to the things they said you can't do. The technical people said that everything had to be played on the same plane—if someone were too much up-stage they would be out of focus. I paid no attention to that.

RO: *You said in the* Cahiers *interview that for certain framings you were inspired by sections of David's* Sacre de Napoleon *reproduced in a book.*

GC: Yes, I was. You're used to seeing the whole of a thing—then suddenly you see a section, arbitrarily, not composed. Just a section of something cut off. In the David painting you see a head to one side, bits of other heads cut off here and there when the detail is reproduced in the art book. And I thought why not do that in a movie? We made use of this especially when Judy Garland sang "The Man That Got Away." In the little night club after hours the camera followed her always in front . . . sometimes she went to the side and almost disappeared out of the frame . . . she was rarely right in the middle. It was all done in one long take, the whole musical number.

RO: *You often emphasize "simplicity" in your pictures —color, movement . . . and the one take. Do you especially like these no-cut sequences? Do you try to get them in whenever possible?*

GC: I do it whenever I can, for you get a very complete sort of result. I did it with Judy Garland because she could sustain it. It isn't easy for an actor or actress to carry a long take—you have to be strong.

In a picture called *Adam's Rib* we did almost a reel— that's about 900 feet . . . no, more than 900 feet—with no cuts. It was a scene with Katharine Hepburn in the house of detention, a woman's house of detention where Judy Holliday was being interviewed by the lawyer Katharine Hepburn. It was an extremely well written sequence with Hepburn facing away from the camera for the whole thing. She had her back to the camera almost the whole time but that had a meaning: she indicated to the audience that they should look at Judy Holliday. We did that whole thing without a cut.

These long shots, prolonged sequences . . . they just happen when the scene is right. It just happens.

RO: *I notice in most of your musical numbers that there are very few cuts.*

GC: Really?

RO: *For instance in* Les Girls *where the girls do their first dance number—not the "Ladies in Waiting" but the first one. It was extremely simple—only a few cuts which were hardly perceptible.*

GC: I don't really remember. I hate to say this, but the reason a lot of this comes out the way it does is because I always set up at least two cameras for the musical numbers. You do it with an "A" camera and some supplementary ones just to see what happens. When it's all over you see that the "B" camera, the one you had there for fun, is the really interesting one. It turns out to be the most fascinating. It's not always in perfect focus, it's not in perfect composition but it's very exciting, very dynamic. Sometimes you plan a scene for a series of close-ups, you know that is the only way to do it—then when the "B" camera result comes up you realize that you were all wrong. You say to hell with the close-ups and decide to keep the long shots. But you usually realize that when the picture is all done.

RO: *Of the "before and after" stages of film making— scenario, cutting—which do you prefer? Do you like to monkey around with a moviola?*

GC: Not so much the moviola . . . but I'm fascinated with what can be done with cutting. For example, in this wretched *Chapman Report,* I never cut to the interrogator in the interviews with the woman. You never saw the doctor asking questions—just the woman, her facial expressions, her movements, her reactions. You were on her the entire time. It was very interesting because you just heard the man's voice off and caught the woman's reaction.

RO: *So you're not like Hitchcock then who feels that once the scenario and dialogues are written the film is all wrapped up—that the actual filming is mere mechanics.*

GC: Well, Hitchcock is an absolute master. An absolute master. And what you say is very much his style. He's a master of well thought out effects. But between you and me I'm not quite sure that he is telling the complete truth. He must improvise with performances sometimes. There was a picture of his called *Suspicion* where Joan Fontaine gave the most extraordinary performance. Now, I can't believe that that was all mechanical—all planned out ahead of time. Very often it is, especially in his case . . . but not always. He is hiding things from you; he doesn't say how he works, how he achieves effects—easier to say it was all planned in the script and the rest is mechanics.

Sometimes the actor feels that he is being directed by someone with taste who will automatically bring out the best in them . . . who will not have to tell them a great deal. The actor just *feels* the director's presence, his will, what he wants. I don't know what Hitchcock says . . . all I know is that he is an absolute master. I like Hitchcock. I think he's a very original man, a great man . . . very talented. He's left his mark. The very word "Hitchcock" means "mystery story"—it's become synonymous with "suspense." His name has become a word with a rich meaning.

RO: *So has yours.*

GC: No. Not quite . . . no, no.

RO: *Maybe not entirely in America, but certainly here in Europe.*

GC: Maybe I'll come here and spend my declining days then. And they're fast approaching.

I'm very touched at the *real* interest in my films here.

RO: *You knew, of course, that the Cinémathèque Française organized a "hommage" to you last summer and over a three week period showed practically all of your films?*

GC: I had heard something about that. There was a man in New York last year who said "We should have a George Cukor festival," but he was just making a joke. I was going to answer him with a joke, answer his snide remark . . . but I thought, what the hell!

Yes, I did hear something about the Cinémathèque. It's a film library, isn't it?

RO: *Yes, and every day they have showings of six different films.*

GC: Howard Hawks. He's one of the sacred cows, isn't he?

RO: *And Hitchcock, too . . . with the* Cahiers *crowd.*

GC: Well, they should admire him. They certainly should. They like Nicholas Ray, too. He's pretty hot stuff.

RO: *How do you have all this inside dope on film tastes in France?*

GC: Because I read the *Cahiers du Cinema*. Sometimes I'm very amused at reading these very nice articles about my work . . . and then I read what they think of other gentlemen and I think . . . Well, I don't know what to think. I'm not so sure, then, that their judgment is all that . . .

RO: *I'd like to ask you two very superficial questions.*

GC: And I'll give you two very superficial answers.

RO: *This is the "Aurore-type" question: What are your favorite pictures, Mr. Cukor? (Cukor was interviewed the day before by a reporter from the Paris daily,* Aurore. *Consequently, he now refers to all chit-chatty-type questions as* Aurorish.)

GC: I really haven't any. I have favorite pictures which other people have made, though.

RO: *What are they?*

GC: I loved a picture called, *Lady With A Dog.* It was Russian. A most ravishing, marvelous film.

It's a very peculiar thing to ask. There are so many pictures which I have enjoyed but I have no particular favorite—of my own.

You cannot look back. When you reach my age you must look forward. You can't say: This was awfully nice, and I did this and that and it was pretty good . . .

RO: *There must be some which you like for certain reasons. Maybe* Camille?

GC: Well, I cherish that one because it was a success.

I'll tell you something very interesting about that film. A bit of Aurore talk . . . When *Camille* was previewed it was shown with two other Metro pictures the same evening. The picture was dismissed. Garbo was dismissed—the whole thing was dismissed as no good. I was given a rather bad notice—and it was all because I didn't want to advertise in a trade paper. They cut the hell out of me and the film because I did not wish to advertise. You know the type of advertising I mean—your name in a trade paper, put there regularly and heavily paid for. The treatment of *Camille* had the most extraordinary effect on me. From then on, I said, about advertising: "finita!" They heckle you about advertising and it's always embarrassed me to advertise because when I was very young, before I ever went into "show biz," the only advertising you got was with vaudeville acts. Someone would come out on the stage and say: "At liberty . . ." and then sell the bill of goods. And that sticks in my craw as something terribly cheap about the whole thing.

So now when they come to me and say: "Would·you advertise?" I reply: "Well, let me see the review first." I have not advertised my name in a trade paper since 1936. And nothing will get me to do it. When President Wilson died everyone put their name in the papers . . . surrounded by a black band. Advertising just the same. I never do it. Never! Not in the *Reporter, Variety, The Year Book* . . .

RO: *I'd like to ask you a few questions about your cameramen, the directors of photography, as they say over here.*

Why haven't you used Daniels or Ruttenburg lately?

GC: These men were under contract to M.G.M. And some of them . . . not Ruttenburg . . . are great stars in their own right and refuse to listen, refuse to be influenced. Now that I've worked with Gene Allen and Hoyningen-Huene I've become spoiled—I must have cameramen who will listen. Lipstein is very good and so is a man called Danny Fap who did *Let's Make Love*, the Marilyn Monroe picture. He is a wonderful technician who knows a great deal and he will listen. With him you don't have all the boring things that cameramen do—you put your foot down and you don't have it.

For example, we started out with Harry Stradlin, who is, by the way, a very talented man. I said to him, "Harry, these sets are very well painted, the colors are perfect as they are and we don't want any more color of any kind . . . no filters!" He's rather tough and said that he wouldn't put any color in. Well, when I saw the rushes I discovered that he had snuck a little color in—some little nuances way in the back. So I said to him again, "No color, Harry. No color!" He finally got the idea that I meant business. The set was beautiful and there was no need to jazz it up with any more color.

RO: *What picture was this?*

GC: *My Fair Lady.* But he was very good about this finally. Cameramen get into all kinds of habits and one has to watch them very carefully. It's best to have someone with an open mind who won't put in all sorts of boring shadows and things like that. You have to give these men their head because they're artists—you have to stimulate them, not let them fall back on habits.

RO: *In the old Metro days, whom did you like best to work with, Daniels or Ruttenburg?*

GC: I only did black and white pictures with them. I don't know. I like them both.

RO: *What is the difference between the two men?*

GC: I think Daniels was a much more original and daring innovator. Now he plays it safe . . . what is he doing now . . . a great photographer of Lollobrigida, I think.

We were going to do *Lady L* . . . based on the novel of Romain Gary, and Lollobrigida had the lead. We were doing make-up tests and I said to her, "Gina, you can't have the Cinecitta look . . . all that heavy orange crust on your face." "My eyes," she replied. And all the time Daniels was trying to tell me that he was going to put some color in the thing, change the color of her face.

I tried to tell them that this was a period picture, that the women had white skin and pink cheeks and did not have any god damned Italian sunburn on! Well, Lollobrigida looked like the rice fields . . . or whatever the hell. And Daniels was with her a little bit. I got out of patience with him a little bit. He never used to be that way—I thought he was more independent. I do not like people who ingratiate themselves with the stars.

There used to be a wonderful cameraman who died . . . Franz Planer . . .

He started to do the Marilyn Monroe picture and years ago he did *Holiday*. He was *very* modern, very sensitive. He didn't use key lights and things like that. He was simple and direct and did the most marvelous things.

RO: *You did some pictures with Robert Planck as cameraman, didn't you?*

GC: Yes. He's dead now . . . I liked him very much. We did a picture together with Joan Crawford called *A Woman's Face*.

RO: *I particularly liked the snow scene at the end.*

GC: That was all done by the second unit, you know. It was brilliantly photographed and put together—technically. Technically . . . that was the whole thing. It was pure fabrication. There wasn't really snow, there wasn't really a waterfall, there wasn't really an aerial railroad. It was all achieved with such dazzling tricks, marvelous technique.

RO: *What do you think of Milton Krasner?*

GC: I think Krasner is very good. I did *A Double Life*

and *The Model and the Marriage Broker* with him. He's worked a lot with Minnelli, I think. I'm not so sure that I like his color work that much, though.

But Surtees . . . Robert Surtees . . . is a master. He is very easily stimulated. He did *Les Girls*.

RO: *The color in that was superb.*

GC: That is not Surtees. That is Huene.

Surtees is so sensitive. You give him pictures of things and say, "Look at this painting. Isn't it great!" And he'll reply, "I can't wait to get to the studio tomorrow morning and try that." You have to stimulate these people and he was stimulated—he loved it, having new ideas.

RO: *What about Frederick Young with whom you did* Bhowani Junction *and* Edward, My Son?

GC: Freddy Young? I think he's a very, very talented man.

RO: *Did you see* Lawrence Of Arabia? *What did you think of the photography?*

GC: I thought it was a wonderful picture, a wonderful picture . . . but I don't think it was a satisfying picture. You mustn't say this to anyone, but I think there was a sort of *folie de grandeur* in *Lawrence.* You know, they all took themselves so frightfully serious and it was much too long . . . and too grandiose. I think the real *core* of the story escaped them. After I came out I really couldn't say what they were trying to tell me. The *story* wasn't there. Mind you, he was a curious creature, Lawrence, but I didn't know what their point was. It was lost in all those surging masses. It was just too much. That's what happens when someone has a hit. The next time it has to be bigger and better. They get terrified and forget tradition.

Young is a very talented man . . . not easily influenced, though. He is rather nervous and he makes me a little nervous although I like him very much.

RO: *Can you tell me a little bit about Hoyningen-Huene? Who is he? How did he start working with you?*

GC: He is half-Russian, half-American. A man who has enormous taste about everything . . . a photographer for *Vogue, Harper's Bazaar,* and he did some wonderful books on Greece, Palmyra and Baalbec. The first picture I did with him was *A Star Is Born* and he influenced everything.

RO: *How does he work—what is his function on one of your pictures?*

GC: He works on the overall design of the picture and is there when it's being photographed. He knows everything about film and influences so many things . . . from sets to color effects, to costumes . . . he works in close collaboration with Gene Allen.

While we were preparing *Lady L* . . . they were assisted by Leslie Blanche (Mrs. Romain Gary) and Orry Kelly was doing the clothes. The combination was thrilling. The sets were ravishing. It would have been one of the most extraordinary films—what they produced was unbelievable. From no other people could you have gotten such beautiful results.

George works on the sets, the general design, the use of color . . . he does all that. He selects every bit of material. For example, if we need a grey on a wall or on a chair, anywhere, he looks it over, scrutinizes it, and if it's the wrong grey, too blue perhaps, he changes it. He edits color and nothing escapes him.

For example, he does the most unconventional things. We were doing a scene in *Les Girls,* a London exterior, and he said, "The whole thing should be this one color— the dresses, the room later on, the exterior walls, the sidewalk, the sky, the fences." Everything was the color of clay and I said, "Isn't that going to be awfully dull and drab?" He assured me that it wouldn't. He was right and the effect was wonderful. He used this same "uniformity of color" in *Let's Make Love.* Everything in Yves Montand's office was beige and brown. The effect was one of great beauty.

If you notice in *Les Girls* the color comes in "packages." Sometimes the girls are in red, sometimes in blue, sometimes in black. It's not a mélange but wonderfully edited.

In *Heller in Pink Tights* do you remember those clothes for the wild west productions of *Mazeppa* and *La Belle Helene* with Sophia Loren, Anthony Quinn and their company? George went down into the basement of the studio, to the wardrobe storage place where nobody ever goes, and he came back with old costumes of the crusades, the Revolution . . . all sorts of incorrect things falling apart and he put them all together. It was so real on the screen, all the actors in the far west with this incredible mélange.

RO: *The color in the cabaret-saloon was wonderful . . . all deep red, rich green . . .*

GC: Yes . . . that was Gene Allen there. Wasn't that

wonderful the color of the walls—intense red. Do you remember where she was in black and then when she was all in white and the men were all in black . . . she wanders through the saloon, exploring it, opening windows, sticking her head through, framing herself by the red walls . . . It was clean and bold.

In *Les Girls* one girl wore one color all the way through and another wore another color.

Take the office scene in *The Chapman Report*. Gene Allen and Hoyningen-Huene influenced the lighting. It was logical lighting. The outside was lighter than the inside. There were none of the clichés that you usually have. I insist that lighting be logical—light should be where it would normally be in a real setting. You see, look over there at the window. It's dark inside this room and when you look in the direction of the window the light source is all burnt up. You don't tone down outside light just to get artificial balance. The sky is not blue all the time—sometimes it's grey. It could be any color. Cameramen, of necessity, put lights in the wrong places . . . to be pretty. They jazz things up with key lights that are very old-fashioned: it's photography of the past; a slight shadow on the eye, the eyelash throwing a shadow. It's a lot of work watching out for all these things, establishing the composition, establishing the position of the camera.

RO: *What is Gene Allen's role?*

GC: Gene Allen is a very talented set designer—an art director who does everything. He also writes and did some of the scenes in *The Chapman Report*. He will be a brilliant producer some day. He started out as a detective because his father was a police captain. On his vacations he worked in the studio as a print boy and taught art. When I first met him he was a sketch artist and I found him very talented—so I hired him. He writes scenarios and hopes to be a producer or maybe even a director.

He did some wonderful sets for *A Star Is Born* and for *My Fair Lady*. Although the sets were supposed to be done in collaboration with Cecil Beaton, he, in fact, did most of the work while Beaton concentrated on the clothes.

RO: *How did you like working with Beaton for the first time?*

GC: I don't like Beaton. He was the only sour note in the whole picture.

RO: *But he certainly brought his great talent to the service of the picture.*

GC: Yes, he did. He's enormously clever. He knows everything there is to know about Edwardian costumes but I dislike him. I think he's publicity seeking and ungenerous . . . and terribly pretentious.

RO: *Did Hoyningen-Huene work on* My Fair Lady?

GC: No. Beaton was engaged before I had anything to do with the picture.

RO: *How is* My Fair Lady *different from your other pictures—have you tried anything new or different here?*

GC: No, it is not different from the other films . . . no great revolution in style, that is. I thought that *My Fair Lady* was such a perfect work . . . the combination of Shaw and music . . . a minor masterpiece. All I could do was bring it to the screen with as much style and truth as I could. And that's what I did.

RO: *From the stills I have seen, the sets appear to be very stylized. This appears to be a little innovation because in your other pictures sets are usually so real right down to the little details.*

GC: This is somewhat out of necessity. We couldn't do Ascot realistically. Everything is in its own world—Covent Garden is a reproduction of Covent Garden. We've worked for a poetic stylization.

I'll tell you something about the conception. When Audrey sings "Wouldn't It Be Loverly" she dances with people of 70 and 80 who had never appeared on the screen before. We went all over the place to find them. When Audrey dances with them it is fresh and charming. Then when you go to Wimpole Street it isn't really Wimpole Street. Of course, you can't sing on a real Wimpole Street so we put together a composite of things. Ascot is probably the most stylized, though.

This is the first time I've worked in 70 mm. and also for the first time with a six track sound system.

RO: *After the unpleasant experience with one producer on the previous picture, how did you get along with Jack Warner?*

GC: Jack Warner? He's tough but he's a showman. Quite a remarkable showman, I might add. He's very intelligent. This picture is sort of the apotheosis of his career and he did everything. He is a perfect gentleman. Everything depended on him and he behaved wonderfully . . . generously and courageously.

I think *My Fair Lady* is a charming picture. If you liked the play . . . it is exactly like it, but it's a movie. Audrey plays with a great deal of power in it. She's a hard worker . . . extremely intelligent, inventive, modest . . . and funny. To work with her you wouldn't think she was this great star. She's tactful . . . the most endearing creature in the world. Rex Harrison is magnificent, too. He gives a great performance, just as he did on the stage.

RO: *One has the impression that you do quite a bit of documenting before starting a picture. You certainly did for* My Fair Lady, *in any case.*

GC: Yes, the ground work must be well gone over. You must be familiar with the climate of your subject down to the smallest details. When I am going to do a picture on New York I go to New York and look all around, all around. I look at locales with different eyes because when you know you are going to do a film you see things altogether differently, with different eyes. I delve into the texture of life and reality.

For instance, when we were preparing *The Actress* we went to see an old house that served as a model for the one in the film. It was a wonderful house and had a kitchen with six doors. We used that kitchen . . . not *exactly* the same way, but almost. Reality must be observed then transmuted. If I were going to film this hotel room I would begin to see it with new eyes. I would look all around, see that newspaper over there, those books. Mind you, I couldn't film it just as it is—I would make notes in my mind about the casual bits of reality and then re-create the whole thing.

RO: *What about your historical pictures . . . how do you research and "observe reality" here?*

GC: I look at photographs of the time, paintings, read books, look at old engravings. For one picture I looked at an old photograph of my grandfather . . . no, it was a picture which my grandfather had given me of the Civil War. I am very influenced by paintings and old photographs.

When we were preparing *Lady L* . . . I looked at numerous paintings by Boldini, Sargent. Lollobrigida was supposed to do this picture but she was too stupid. She doesn't know anything and is a very ignorant woman. I also looked at portraits by Van Dongen . . . to get a smell of the period.

When I filmed *David Copperfield* I went to the actual

places where the action was to take place. The slightest things gave me ideas.

In *My Fair Lady* there is a scene where Eliza's father sings "With a Little Bit of Luck." He leaves a bar and, slightly drunk, wanders along in some trenches with a group of workmen. I was inspired to do this because I had once seen a painting of the period representing some workmen.

It was fun working with all the technical phonetic inventions. We had a technical advisor come over from U.C.L.A. and he brought all sorts of period phonetic machines. For instance, for the breathing, they used a candle on the stage but we found a marvelous contraption . . . it was a complicated thing with all sorts of mirrors that turned and revolved and indicated if your breathing was right or not.

Mrs. Higgins was an *art nouveau*, intellectual sort of lady so we dressed her all in modern style. There was considerable research done for this picture over a long period of time.

RO: *What sort of research went into* Camille?

GC: The same . . . I looked at many paintings of the period, many obscure ones.

One of the first shots of *Camille* is when she is walking through the glittering halls of the Opéra. There are a lot of men standing around smoking, with their hats on, top hats. There was a problem: how should Garbo walk through this group of arrogant men? She was a courtesan, had a certain reputation and couldn't walk through the crowd like a "respectable" woman would. Garbo moved through them marvelously—she carried herself proudly. Almost slipped through as if to avoid their glances. Garbo invented this. But if I had it to do all over again I would do it differently—she wouldn't "slip" through. She would be much more proud and aloof . . . haughty.

RO: *Faulkner said when working on Hawk's* Land of the Pharaohs *he had trouble with the dialogue because he had no idea how Egyptians talked. How do you solve this problem . . . how do you know how people in the mid-1800's talked?*

GC: In the first place, Faulkner was much too practical minded. I'm not saying this in a derogatory way, but when you do dialogues you have to have a free mind, create, make things up which have the ring of truth. Faulkner found it difficult to create things which he himself had not experienced . . . in part. Right now I am planning a picture on mediums around 1874. Every century has its own flavor and color and you have to catch that. It may not be perfectly accurate right down the line but if it manages to catch the "flavor" that's what counts.

This is what we did for *Les Girls*. The set was not an exact slice of reality but a combination of things. We came to Paris and climbed up six and seven flights of stairs and took stills of this room and that room. The set was a composite of all sorts of elements. It was filmed in Hollywood and done in Cinemascope proportion. The scenes, the sets, had to be especially designed for the Cinemascope proportion.

There was a scene where the girls are eating. Usually food in a scene is left to the last minute to the property man who rushes off to the studio commissary to get a few pieces of ham, some bread . . . and spreads them all over the table. But in *Les Girls* we had the most wonderful, real French food . . . down to the smallest details. We even looked at Cézanne's still lifes . . . the great Impressionist. On the table were wine and cheeses and with the girls all around it was pure Cézanne. There was quite a bit of loving thought put into it and it paid off—scenes must be done this way, with no slap-dash about them. I do them with a great deal of affection and detail.

RO: *There seems to me, that there is always a certain logic in the way you put musical numbers together . . . the way you introduce music and singing into the dramatic action. Songs never seem to come at unnatural places—the placement of the "number" is much less "stylized" than in Minnelli's musicals. In* A Star Is Born, *for instance, one doesn't stop and say: Now the music starts and the dialogue stops. One flows into the other in a most natural way.*

GC: I am not a musical comedy director, you know. I just don't have the experience. I am not very skillful about putting songs in, I suppose. It has to be *natural;* I can't seem to get them in really clever spots. The screen is terribly logical—and once you establish your logic, anything can be fit into it, anything can happen. Like all those prisoners singing in René Clair's *A Nous la Liberté.* The screen is so logical . . . I don't know enough about music to put songs in more cleverly, more skillfully.

It's important not to have any real rules, solid do's and don't's. Nothing should be sung arbitrarily . . . this idea has always stuck in my crane. We started doing the Rex Harrison number, "Why Can't the English" but somehow the thing was robbed of all its vitality. We tried it every way to make it work but to no avail. Finally Rex got mad and started singing in indignation. That worked! It was perfect.

I must be very logical about music. I don't have the assurance of Donen or Minnelli. They are born musical directors.

There's one big thing to keep in mind. . . . Garson Kanin once said a propos of one of his plays which he was just opening, "The audience will not stand for any bull shit." That is true . . . the audience is right and they will not take any bull shit.

RO: *What stage musical have you enjoyed?*

GC: I adored *How To Succeed in Business Without Really Trying*. It has tremendous style and wit.

RO: *Minnelli's* Gigi?

GC: I really didn't care for it too much. It was trying to be too typically French—o-o-o-o-o la la, and all that.

RO: *What about your association with Lubitsch on* One Hour With You?

GC: Lubitsch was the producer but he didn't have time to shoot the picture. He was an extremely busy man. I did the shooting and Lubitsch didn't like what I did. It was an awkward time of my life. . . . I sued Paramount because they wanted to take my name off the picture. I went right into the head office and said: "All right, give me 100,000 dollars!" Well, maybe it wasn't that much but it was quite a bit.

At that time David Selznick had gone to R.K.O. and wanted me to come over there with him. Paramount wouldn't let me go—so I agreed to drop my law suit if they would release me. They did and that's how I left.

When I came to Hollywood it was just at the time when talkies were coming in. Everyone thought I was a New York sophisticate. They immediately typed me. For a while I did nothing but costume pictures . . . then this kind, that. . . .

RO: *While we're on the subject of musicals, can we talk a little about* A Star Is Born? *I think it's one of the greatest musicals of all time*

GC: Did you see it in its entire version, the uncut one?

RO: *Many years ago, when it first came out in America. Recently I've see the version here in France.*

GC: That's very badly cut. That's the foreign version . . . all cut and trimmed with some very important parts missing.

RO: *The big dance number towards the end, "Somewhere There's a Someone," seems casual. Judy Garland improvises a musical production number in the living room in front of her husband. Was that number in any way improvised?*

GC: No, not at all. It was carefully rehearsed. Very carefully rehearsed. She gave it the effect of improvisation but it was created to give that impression . . . very carefully rehearsed. I don't know whether you saw a picture I did with Jack Lemmon and Judy Holliday called *It Should Happen to You*. They are in a bar and Jack is playing the piano. He was very happy singing and she just happened to be singing along with him and they "just happened" to do the whole bit. Well, that was all very carefully rehearsed. Judy's such a good musician and so is he. The scene was so casual and they were singing and talking. They started out by saying, "Let's fall in love . . ." then he started playing. You had the impression that it was evolving for the first time before your eyes . . . but it was very carefully prepared.

RO: *When you work with an actress, do you like to establish a personal or emotional rapport with her before you start working—or can you just start out cold?*

GC: You can do all sorts of preparation but nothing can be planned out perfectly ahead of time. The proof of the pudding is the eating. You know, you can make proportions, you can talk and you can establish a sort of friendly relationship. But when you're before the cameras with your actress you're sort of alone with your god. There you are. When the cameras start to purr it really happens. Up to then it's very polite and hopeful and cordial. You establish a relationship before but the real "working relationship" doesn't happen until you're working.

RO: *I asked you this because you seem to have a way of getting under an actress' hide—of coaxing extraordinary performances from any woman.*

GC: Well, I think that most of these ladies are very practical minded and expect you to deliver the goods. They have to feel that what you're telling them makes sense. This is very important. After you establish a rapport with them you can tell them the most devastating things. They

120

don't care as long as they trust your judgment and have confidence in you. They don't care as long as they feel that you are watching them very sharply and sympathetically. You can say anything to them as long as you make them feel that they will eventually get it. You don't treat them like hopeless cases, you see. You can say awful things to them because you believe they will eventually get it . . . and they know that you believe.

RO: *It's a quirk of fate that you made* My Fair Lady—*in a way you yourself are a Pygmalion. You seem to specialize in bringing movie "idols" to life, or at least into "being."* . . .

GC: Well, all directors do that to some extent . . . but there are so many who are not really interested in making their actors come alive before the camera. There are some wonderful directors who are not terribly interested in performances—who are much more intrigued by the picture as a whole. They will build up an effect of a door knob turning rather than concentrating on the actor's face. I think human values are more important. Human behavior, to me, is what makes things go.

RO: *Most of your pictures have been with actresses who are big stars. What do you think of doing pictures with people who are totally unknown? Do you feel more in your element with the "sacred beasts"?*

GC: I've done more picture than you think with unknowns and a great many people started out with me. Let me think off hand . . . there was Angela Lansbury in *Gaslight*. Jack Lemmon . . . and Aldo Ray.

RO: *Was the* Marrying Kind *his first picture?*

GC: No, he played a taxi driver, just a bit part, the time before and then in the *Marrying Kind* he had a long, leading part. He was a constable in Crockett, California and he really didn't want to become an actor. His brother heard that they were going to do a picture up there, something about football, and Aldo went to do a test. I saw that test. We were preparing the *Marrying Kind* and Garson Kanin and Ruth Gordon had their hearts set on Sid Caesar for the lead. He turned it down . . . wasn't good enough for him.

Anyway, here was Aldo . . . in the test I saw he did something very interesting. He was sitting on the floor playing cards, just throwing them out in all directions. I thought he would be great for the part. By this time, though, the boy had gone back to Crockett—but he was still under option, so I asked the producer to bring him down for another test.

He came to Hollywood but he was too fat. I told him to lose weight and he did, in fact, he lost 30 pounds. Some incredible amount. I began making tests and we worked very hard on them. He was a natural sort of actor with enormous individuality. When we were through I sent the tests out to Ruth Gordon and Garson Kanin and they thought he was marvelous. So we signed him up.

When we began shooting the first day he froze up. I knew it was dead terror—the same thing happened to Shelley Winters on the first picture she did with me. It was the Coleman film, *A Double Life*. She too made a very good test and then was absolutely frozen, didn't know what the hell she was doing and completely terrified.

Aldo was scared to death and he lost everything. After a day or two he relaxed and about the third or fourth day he did a scene with Judy Holliday—a silent scene—where he lay on the bed and did some silent acting which is very difficult to do. Judy was lost in admiration for him. . . . He has a great advantage: the way his eyes are made. The light comes into them. There are certain people who have opaque eyes which refuse to catch the light. But his eyes had a certain glow and gave quite well in the photographed result. He did this silent scene very well lying there on the bed in the same room with Judy. Then later he did comedy scenes with her and alone—very difficult ones—and there were also emotional sequences where he broke down and cried. They were brilliant.

He did his next picture with me . . . with Spencer Tracy and Katharine Hepburn. That was *Pat and Mike* and he played the role of a punchy prize-fighter. Then I don't know what happened to him. I haven't seen him play for quite some time now and it's a shame for he's a very talented actor . . .

RO: *Perhaps you could tell me something about the actual direction of your actors and actresses—do you have a technique? . . . Was there any influence from Lubitsch?*

GC: Lubitsch, you know, wrote everything out beforehand. Everything was so carefully calculated in advance. He worked night and day with his writers, supervised everything—everything was down pat, perfect. He knew exactly what was to be said and done. I'm not that rigid. In places I allow room for improvisation. I feel my way more . . .

You can rehearse up to a certain point, but not too far. For example, Rex Harrison . . . I would not let him rehearse. During rehearsals he had a tendency to give too much of himself and there wasn't enough left for the real thing. Rehearsals are just meant for going through the mechanics of the thing. In the actual being before the camera something must be discovered; there must be an electricity there that can only come the first time something is done. Before, you just go through the motions and let yourself go when your time comes. . . . When you are before the camera things should "happen." Good people will vary it every time, for every take . . . make it fresh, give little changes each time. You know how some dumb actresses will say: "I can't do it unless I believe it." Well, there's truth in that. If you have too much rehearsal it becomes mechanical.

I never tell them what they should do. I coax, persuade, push sometimes. But it's important to let them discover reactions and feelings in the character they're playing. Everything is not perfectly laid out ahead of time and on the set I'm not a dictator. There must be a pleasant happy atmosphere.

RO: *Perhaps you could give me a few thumb-nail sketches . . . thumb-nail impressions, rather, on some of the actresses you've worked with.*

GC: Who? You name them.

RO: *Joan Crawford.*

GC: She was and is a great movie personality. You can photograph her from any angle, from any side, anywhere, under any conditions . . . she always looks good. But her real talent is the way she moves. All she has to do is walk across the room, from one side to the other, and you notice that something very special is happening. The way she carries herself, the way her arms move . . . the position of the head . . . she attracts attention simply by moving and she arrests you. She wouldn't have to open her mouth —just walk—and she would be superb. But look, she did that in the silent films, didn't she? Albert Finney has the same talent for "moving."

RO: *Ava Gardner.*

GC: She interferes with herself. She's extremely intelligent. A fatalistic woman. A creature of great fascination . . . and of desperation. An extraordinary beauty. You know, she doesn't think a hell of a lot of herself as an actress. That's too bad.

123

In *Bhowani Junction* she did some marvelous erotic scenes, as I told you. She used his tooth brush in a very special way, brushed her teeth with whiskey. Very low class and exciting. But this was all cut by the censors.

RO: *Lana Turner*.

GC: I directed her in *A Life of Her Own*. All I can remember about that one is that I hated it. It was an awful story. When we went to the first story conference, I couldn't believe my ears. It was terrible. At the beginning she was supposed to kill herself and then they wouldn't even let her do that.

RO: *In closing, maybe a few words about Garbo*.

GC: I directed her in her picture, *Two Faced Woman*, in 1941. We started doing it without a script and this is always dangerous. Garbo was extremely well behaved and disciplined. She made many, many requests but they were always practical and reasonable.

She had great self possession. She requested that no one come on the set while she was filming. She had an idea, a notion of illusion that went very far and she didn't want to break it. People around shattered this illusion—and then she didn't want gawkers to see her "unguarded" while she worked. Thought if they wanted to see her they should go to her pictures. She never saw rushes because they always fell short of what she thought she could do . . . of what she imagined. A great perfectionist . . . to the extreme.

She often had to quit working early to calm down—when she acted she put her whole self into it and it wore her down, exhausted her.

She liked to work the way I do: very sketchy rehearsals and real acting done for the first time before the cameras.

She had a talent that few actresses or actors possess. In close-ups she gave the impression, the illusion of great movement. She would move her head just a little bit and the whole screen would come alive—like a strong breeze that made itself felt. Wonderful movement. Technically, she was enormously resourceful. She always had great trust in the people she worked for—most of the time.

She knew how to act for the camera . . . for the camera.

Irving Thalberg died after the first week of shooting on *Two Faced Woman* but saw the first rushes. He was amazed and said to me, "She's never been so good. She is unguarded or the first time." The picture was bad but he was right when he said that she was unguarded for the first time. She was never so fragile and unprotected. . . . It was already the end.

It was an interesting idea to have her play twin sisters but the script wasn't written—we did it as we went along and it just went bad. It was too bad for Garbo . . .

It is hard to talk about Garbo, really, for she says everything when she appears on the screen. That is GARBO . . . and all you say is just so much chit-chat. There she is on the screen. How she achieves those effects may or may not be interesting. She is what she is; and that is a very creative actress who *thinks* about things a great deal and has a very personal way of acting.

You have to give her her head—let her do what she feels. If you remember in *Camille* when the father comes in to tell her to leave his son, she falls to the ground and puts her hand on the table. That's a very original thing to do. One must let her do these things and they happen marvelously.

Also, do you remember in *Camille* when the man made her pick up her fan—he just stood there, the Baron de Varville. When she reached down she did the most unforgettable thing. Sweeping down, like a dancer . . . Isadora Duncan . . . she swept it up—the whole motion was done without bending her knees. It was so unexpected for it is not a natural gesture. Yet, it was pure grace when she did it—just that way, for some peculiar reason.

(At this point Cukor rises and tries to imitate the movement.)

I can't do it. Impossible. The *plastique* of her body was marvelous. She doesn't move like a ballerina acting—but like an actress acting. It is not dance but acting. This is an important point. She moves like an actress. Margot Fonteyn is an actress in this scene. There was a bit of Garbo in her performance of *La Dame aux Camellias*.

I think all you have to know about Garbo is what you see on the screen. How she achives what she does is a mystique . . .

RO: *In* Camille *I particularly liked the scene where she wakes up for the first time in the country. Sitting up in bed with the morning light streaming in it is as though she is re-born.*

GC: She is primitive, in fact. She's basically like an animal. She likes the smell of the ground . . .

125

George Cukor (1899–   ):
Filmography:
1930—The Royal Family of Broadway (with Cyril Gardner), Grumpy (with Cyril Gardner), Virtuous Sin (with Louis Gasnier). 1931—Tarnished Lady, Girls About Town. 1932—One Hour With You (directed by Cukor from Lubitsch plan, signed by Lubitsch), A Bill of Divorcement, What Price Hollywood, Rockabye. 1933—Dinner at Eight, Little Women, Our Betters. 1935—David Copperfield, Sylvia Scarlett. 1936—Romeo and Juliet. 1937—Camille. 1938—Holiday, Zaza. 1939—The Women. 1940—The Philadelphia Story, Susan and God. 1941—A Woman's Face, Two-Faced Woman. 1942—Her Cardboard Lover. 1943—Keeper of the Flame. 1944—Gaslight, Winged Victory. 1948—A Double Life. 1949—Adam's Rib, Edward, My Son. 1950—A Life of Her Own, Born Yesterday. 1952—The Model and the Marriage Broker, The Marrying Kind, Pat and Mike. 1953—The Actress. 1954—A Star Is Born, It Should Happen to You. 1956—Bhowani Junction. 1957—Les Girls, Wild Is the Wind. 1960—Heller in Pink Tights, Let's Make Love, Song Without End (begun and signed by Charles Vidor). 1962—The Chapman Report. 1964—My Fair Lady. 1969—Justine.

been monkeying around with, for a leading role for Warren Beatty. One day Warren Beatty and Shirley Maclaine had walked into the Hungry i or Bitter End, or somewhere, and Shirley had said "Why don't you use Woody Allen." Woody had worked for a year on the script long before it came into my ken, and then got fed up and said "Look, this is the script I want to write, if you don't want to do it, let's forget it." That was what Charlie came over and showed me. I read it; I went back to the States, and the idea at that time was that it would be Warren Beatty, Woody Allen and a lot of beautiful girls. Woody and I got on very well, and we decided that we shared enough of an outlook to be able to do the picture together. So we worked on the script there for a couple of months, and came back to Europe to start setting it up. Warren dropped out for complicated reasons, and we were going to do it totally with unknowns. Then Feldman said to me "How do you feel about O'Toole playing the part?" and I thought that would be marvellous. Thereafter we had a long talk about the girls, and still went on trying to find unknowns, but it became very much a conflict between Charlie and myself, with Charlie wanting pretty little girls who had personality and on whom we could get a lot of publicity. I was not averse to this in any way at all, as long as they had talent and could play these quite difficult roles. In the end I feel I came off well because I got people who, whether you like them or not, at least are actresses and can play it, and haven't ended up with four schleppers off the Via Veneto. Then we got Peter Sellers, which was something I had been working on, and so, as the thing accumulated, it became evident that shooting in Paris was not going to be done cheaply; you couldn't just nip out and whisk round with a hand-held Arriflex, so the thing enlarged. But, I must say that, although it enlarged from the period when it was going to be done totally with unknowns, I don't think the way in which the cast and myself handled the *material* became enlarged. In other words, we never at any point felt ourselves saying "Why can't we make this more of an *impressive* scene, why can't we make this have more scope or size?" We took the situations and the comedy within the given situations and just made them as funny as we possibly could.

I imagine you see it as a very moral picture.
Yes, I believe it's a very moral picture. Highly moral.
It seems to me you've tried to use comedy to be serious

128

about sex, which is something you can't yet do in a "serious" movie.

I don't know. I hadn't thought about doing it that way, and I hadn't particularly *wanted* to do it that way. I don't agree with you that this attitude to sex *can't* be treated seriously, in terms of direct drama. I think it's more *difficult* because one has to fight the repressions and inhibitions. It's much easier to blow off that sense of embarrassment, which comes out of touching one's repressed sexuality, by doing it with a joke. In direct dramatic terms you have no release given you. In other words you can say "That's a smashing bit of stuff" (nudge, nudge) but if you say "What a beautiful girl, I'd very much like to sleep with her" or "She's somebody with whom I'd like to have a deep and perhaps short, but hopefully satisfactory, relationship," people say "Well, do you want to screw her or not?" They immediately have to use words which have a humorous meaning in order to cover up the embarrassment which arises out of the fact that we are repressed about speaking directly in serious terms. I prefer to use the crutch of comedy to express something that we feel very, very deeply. That's why I work in comedy anyway.

The film should have a U certificate, shouldn't it?

I don't say it *should* have; there's just no reason why it *shouldn't* have. The *only* reason I think it shouldn't have is that it's all very well to say that we are, or should be, moving into a period where sex is having the bogeyman trappings removed from it. But I think there are an enormous number of people who are not *that* emancipated and who are bringing up their children in a repressive atmosphere. They are not yet ready to be able themselves to cope with it and to cope with it in relation to their children. Therefore you have a situation where (though whatever happens to *them* I don't mind too much) their feelings about it, their own guilt and sense of discomfort in front of their children would reflect on the *children* and might make life uncomfortable. The children might start saying things for which they would be quite wrongly and repressively punished, or the parents would create an atmosphere about the film in the house which would give it a sort of furtiveness and a disgusting quality which I think would be wrong and bad and immoral. So I don't mind there being this degree of control on it in terms of censorship; but only for that reason, not because of the actual film itself but because there may be some people who are not yet ready to deal with it. They may be *more* able to deal with it if it's in comic terms than if it were not, but I still think they're not *necessarily* free enough from repression. Everybody thinks more, plays more, talks more about sex, sexuality and in sexual terms than they ever admit to themselves in public. They never relate the way they do it to the way anybody else does it. Everybody else does it and they say "They're more smutty than we are," or something like that. I've heard people say a dozen times "After all, I don't mind a blue joke every now and again," but that's all it is. It's only a matter of degree, but I think that they're not really yet able to admit the fact that sex is very powerful and its power has been repressed for a very long time, so that as soon as it's unrepressed, it either tends to bubble up in a great burp, in unhappy conflict, or else it comes up in little iddy bits and pieces. Dirty jokes have always been an outlet. I think that younger people today just talk about it and don't really bother with dirty jokes.

It seems to me that the revolutionary thing about the film is not that the hero goes around screwing everything in sight, but that after an evening out with, of all people, the girl's parents he suddenly decides of his own accord to marry her.

I approached that particular piece of construction which, to me, is absolutely valid, on very simple emotional terms. This is *why* I don't worry about what people say about the film in these terms—because my own feeling is that everything in it is based on a truthful and honest emotional response. That's what this scene is; they've had a flaming row a little while ago and they haven't been seeing each other, and they're choked off with each other. He has had a big barney with her and knows that there is nothing he can say; there's no little gift he can give, no argument that he can make that will win her back. He's miserable. So he thinks "Well, there's nothing I can do about it," and he's a reasonably sensible character, so he says to himself "Forget it. I still feel the way I do about her, but there's nothing I can do about it" and then coincidentally the parents arrive and—flash—they spend the evening out. They don't really get close or anything like that and he says "It's been some time," and she says "I still feel the same way about him" and they can play and coquette a bit while the parents are around. As soon as the parents are gone, they're terribly nervous and ill at ease, and he, because he's bright, thinks about it and says "I've

130

been bloody unhappy, and I've been thoughtless, and here she is and her parents are married and they begat her. And the way I feel about her, this is the moment to say if I want her any more, and I *do* want her some more because, since I've been with her again, I've been sort of aroused by her. The only way to do it is to say 'Will you marry me?'" It's a simple emotional scene with honest attitudes in contemporary terms. No, that's a lot of balls: it's been true at *any* time.

When they're married, they go off and start arguing again. Another honest way of looking at it. . . .

Of course. But this doesn't mean they won't have a happy marriage together. The very words they use when they argue are half-hurtful and yet half-protective. In other words they're saying "I'm not quite sure about you. Maybe you're going to hurt me some more. Therefore I'm having this discussion, but at the same time I don't want to really hurt you because then you may say 'I'm going off with another girl.'" So there's a very ambivalent thing there of "Don't touch me," "Touch you? I've just *been* touching you." Oh, they cut that out of the film! But . . . it's all "in jokes." It's a serious argument, because if she said "Let's sit down calmly. Look, are you biologically capable of being the man I want?" then she knows she'd lose him, but at the same time she can't bear, shouldn't bear, just to be permissive about his going off elsewhere if he is indeed going to. So even *that* conversation has an attitude.

This harks back to the Peter Sellers suggestion "Why don't you just get married and cheat?" And O'Toole obviously does not want to do that; he wants to get married in his own sweet time when he doesn't want to cheat any longer.

Yes, but Peter Sellers' suggestion is a more primitive and deceitful and traditional way of dealing with the subject; the way that O'Toole and Romy Schneider deal with it is much more open and healthy, I think. In other words Sellers lies. He says "I'm going off to an analysts' convention." O'Toole doesn't lie.

One of the interesting things about the relationship is that Romy never ever says, "You play around with other girls." All she ever says is, "Stop playing around with other girls and marry me." In other words she has moved on from the nineteenth century attitude towards marriage which says "I know men are bastards, but we must pretend they're not, otherwise we'll lose them." We've now

131

got to the stage where she says "I know men are bastards, all right just *stop* being a bastard and come to me." This is the question mark of the film; where do we go from there? And, in terms of dealing with that subject, where do I, the person watching it?

There seems to be a link between the evening out with the parents and the sequence with Paula Prentiss earlier on, where there's also lots of dancing and hand-clapping and sinking to the floor.

If this is true, and there's no reason why it shouldn't be, it's certainly not a conscious device. And if it's true, that's because it's the nature of our social pattern today. Her parents come to Paris and they say "Where do we go in Paris?" and because the parents are rather swinging, not at all the sort for the Brasserie Lipp and huge plates of sauerkraut, they go to the swinging place. And to that it's a reflection, but no more.

In Paris, those dances like the bostella are done today, and if this situation were to happen (and there's absolutely no reason why it couldn't and shouldn't, and probably has, give or take a few minor discrepancies) that's where it would happen. There's another point, that when the parents come and he says "Yes, I adore this city," this is really an outside sort of comment and one which I would never have put in deliberately but I somehow felt it was true of the parents of *that* girl. They wouldn't have the traditional German outlook on Paris, but they would, in a sense, vicariously want to re-identify themselves with youth, because they would have been bright, gay swingers in the twenties and thirties. This is evident because of what their daughter is.

This is what O'Toole sees in them, and as a result in Romy, and what he and she could become together.

Yes, that's right. He says "I adore your parents." The reason he adores them is because he sees what they were. He doesn't intellectualise it like that, but he sees it.

The character of the parents makes it more believable for them to go off to the hotel at the end.

Oh, you *could* have had Emil Jannings and Lola-Lola going off to that hotel; you *could* have turned up with a real couple of weirdies, and he would say "Your parents are odd" and she'd say "Yes, I know, they're *weird*, aren't they?" No, I don't think that's true.

O'Toole is more honest throughout than Sellers. Finding the truth about yourself in psychoanalysis tends in Sellers

132

to be a sort of wish-fulfillment, an excuse to live vicariously.

The film is a great big send up of psychoanalysis and phoney psychoanalysts. This is not to say that psychoanalysis and psychoanalysts in themselves are bad, harmful, wrong and shouldn't be encouraged, because I think they are none of those things and *should* be encouraged. The attitude in the film is a total send up of all the barmy, quack values of psychoanalysis. An absolute, total, complete spoof. Sellers is a man who's dead randy and who gets vicarious satisfaction, which is almost the only sort of sexual satisfaction he *can* get, by listening to his patients' fantasies. I think Peter gives a brilliant performance because on the face of it, with that red velvet suit, the Carnaby Street collar, the wig, the accent and the general behaviour, it is the most bizarre character role that he's ever adopted. But I think it is the most moving, rounded, consistent and true, with the possible exception of the man in *I'm All Right Jack*. I think it's a major bloody performance. *Acting* performance as distinct from Peter Sellers-type funny performance.

How did it grow? How was this get-up arrived at?

It evolved a little from discussions we had, but that was Peter's idea. It evolved gradually. He would keep coming with ideas, and I'd say, "Are you sure, Peter?" And he'd say, "Don't worry, it'll be all right." And then he came up with this idea, and we had a long talk about it, and we decided to go ahead. The character was trying to be young again. He was trying to be a mod, to keep up with it all. It's a search for youth.

But to get back to the earlier part of the question, as to whether the O'Toole character was more honest than Sellers; of course this is true. O'Toole is an innocent throughout. The fact that he makes love to girls has got absolutely nothing to do with it. There's nothing about that which means that you aren't a person who has purity and innocence. He loves girls; he enjoys sexual satisfaction; he enjoys the thrill of the chase. These are not things he enjoys in a depraved or pornographic way. He just enjoys them, and he finds a variety of opportunities where he *can* enjoy them. Soceity gives him no firm indication that he *must* enjoy them with only one woman for the rest of his life and *will* enjoy them should he commit himself to bother with only one woman. Society doesn't tell him that at all; it does the very opposite. Society says marriage is in a

133

state of chaos, so he says "All I'm doing is following my instincts, by my own morality." He never does anything vicious; he always behaves with courtesy to people; he never perverts or depraves people at all. He's a very passive character in many ways, but he behaves to people entirely in terms of the way everybody is behaving to him.

The film in a way is a provision of reasons why he should want to change from being a general consumer to staying with one particular girl.

I think that's a question of time. I think it's in the chemical nature of people that eventually they grow out of it, and he resists it for various psychological reasons. But he is also very confused as to exactly what it is he *does* want. And when he opts for what he wants, he senses that it's no more perfect than he ever thought it was going to be. It's just that that's where he goes next.

Let's move off sex for a moment on to another aspect of things—you seem to be going flat out to make this the chicest looking and sounding film ever made . . .

Since my last one!

. . . it's much more chic than the last one!

I don't know what you mean when you say that.

Chic, in the sense of fashionable-looking, if you like.

In terms of the *à la mode* today, maybe, but *Nothing but the Best* was, I think, intensely elegant.

. . . but it was elegant in a sort of British interior-decorating way.

Oh yes. You may be at the present moment looking down your nose at that, but it doesn't mean to say that in absolute terms it isn't elegant.

Why did you choose Art Nouveau *as the style, or rather, if there had been a great gothic craze going on at the moment, would you have chosen that style?*

No. Because, in spite of your injunction that we should get away from sex, there's no sex in gothic. No, I chose *Art Nouveau* for a simple reason. Because it seemed to me to reflect in fashion a psychological attitude of the people in the film; this, without being idiotic about it, is a mod film. It's a film about people who, wherever they are in Europe, have come under the cultural influence of the mid-1960s; they are mods to a lesser or greater degree. Part of mod culture is something that is intensely decorative, erotic, harkens back to the styles, shapes and designs and many techniques of that era. I think that it's tradition. Then it was a reaction against restriction—Isadora Duncan and all that—and *Art Nouveau* did that for another era. This is clearly why it's happening today, as a reaction to what we had here in the fifties and forties. So to that extent it seemed to me to be significant, because the picture is related to what's going on in the world today in terms of its primary points.

Gothic *couldn't* be fashionable today. So I *did* use *Art Nouveau* because it was fashionable in that sense, not fashionable merely, but because it's part of the world that we're in today. Secondly, it seemed right for the picture in every possible way; it's intensely decorative, it's intensely erotic and, further, because we were in Paris where there's some of the finest *Art Nouveau* in the world lying about waiting to be picked up. And I thought, what do you do with Paris? Here it is, why are these people in Paris, why aren't they in Lyon or somewhere?

Why in fact were they in Paris?

That's a very long and complex question, and you know jolly well that I can't answer it. The point is this: you couldn't make the picture in Rome this way. Someone once said when we were talking about it that the difference is garlic and gallic. Seriously!

Another point. I didn't have a great deal of time to prepare it. I was looking for a unit of style and this one had so much going for it anyway that once I'd unearthed it, it gave the picture a unity of style.

Some of the things which were evidently real looked terribly unreal; this is probably a property of Art Nouveau, particularly in the scene at the Square Rapp?

I would have liked it to look real. I think that in concept anyway that's an hilariously funny sequence, but I'm not sure that I couldn't improve on it. It's acted pretty damn well, but it's one of the few sequences I've ever done in which I could make a few improvements in the shooting and the editing.

This sequence brought out the total lack of any contact with reality in the Sellers character. "Your face is like a pale autumn moon . . . you must be joking."

I know what you mean but I think that would be an overstatement. I think he *has* contact with reality, but it's a part of reality which doesn't amuse or satisfy him; he is in fact obsessed by another aspect of reality which he can't reach. He doesn't know how to reach it. He goes out of his way to try and do things to help him, like wearing his hair long and going to the Crazy Horse, but he doesn't

135

really know how to reach it. And one of the manifestations of his not knowing how to is falling back on love poems, which are pathetically ill-suited to achieve what he wants.

And what he wants is a nymphomaniac who doesn't want him.

Yes, but really the trouble is that he's unhappily married, sexually unfulfilled; he's randy, he's been turned in all sorts of different directions, but he's basically not unhealthy, he's muddled.

In fact the least real-looking thing in his life is his wife.

I don't think she's unreal looking.

It's just that she's so impossibly huge and impossibly blonde, but this is, I suppose, going back to Freud, Vienna, large German women and all that sort of thing.

The whole film is conceived in very broad strokes, but within those broad strokes I like to think there's a great deal of subtlety. If you take a man who has a wife he does not love, you make her a grotesque. That is not to say that she is unreal. She is just The Most, the wife with whom, in the most extreme way, he is unsatisfied. Now Woody would approach this another way. He'd say he put her in there entirely for a laugh, but Woody is motivated by exactly the same sort of sense of reality that we're talking about at the moment. I don't think she's an unreal person at all.

Even when changing into a Valkyrie at the end?

She behaves in an eccentric way and you can't actually claim that the end scene is an absolutely logical, realistic scene evolving from what's gone before, but I think the characters by then should be well enough established and also sufficiently flexible in the way they have been established to do quite a lot of things. But there are certain things they can't do. This is true of all farce: you can make a man lose his trousers, but you can't make him lose his jockstrap. A modest metaphor.

How much of the dialogue is improvised?

I turn round on the set to Woody and say, "It says here 'Is your husband upstairs?' We need a joke at that point." Woody says, "Suppose we say, 'Is that great fat slob upstairs?'" Then I say to the actor "How about that?" and he says "Suppose I say 'Is that charming, elegant, tiny slip of a woman upstairs?'" I say "Yes, fine." Now in a sense, that's one form of improvisation. Another form is giving people a basic skeleton for a scene in which they know backwards its inherent dramatic and narrative demands, the characters that they're playing, in all their diversity, and they know they have to make two or three points. I say "go to it and see what happens." Now all these are valid techniques, but people talk about improvisation as though it were like the Method, something you lay on to a scene. As though, if you improvised a scene, and this was a technique which you used well, it would come out as something that was evident and good, creatively viable. I don't think improvisation is that. I think it's just a technique. It depends a lot on the actors concerned, on how flexible they are, on how uninhibited they are, on the nature of the scene, on how important the scene is. There may be a scene in which I want to make certain plot points and character establishment points very carefully. In that case, I might very well not want to use those sorts of improvisation techniques; they might lead me into something which would blur the necessary clarity of the points that I believe ought to be made in the scene.

In fact one of the scenes which was very clear—the drunk scene—had this feeling of improvisation.

There's a line that I adore in that scene. Peter Sellers was talking about when he went to school—I understood this so well because he and I both went to the same sort of school—and he wasn't the popular type. The most popular boy had a new bike—marvellous Sturmey Archer three-speed gear, 24-inch wheels with hub caps—and the favourite boys were being allowed a ride on it: there was this funny little boy who said to the chap with the bike "Can I be the bloke who sees no one touches it for you?" and this was the line that Sellers put in to the scene where they're talking about Paula Prentiss. Sellers says to O'Toole "Why don't you introduce me to her? I could be the man who sees no one touches her." That was not improvised on the set, but in rehearsals. I suppose it's a bit sentimental, but I like it.

How much rehearsal did you have time for?

Not enough. I was supposed to get the basic three weeks before we started shooting, but with that cast it was a bit impossible, with everyone flying round the world. O'Toole was there for three weeks, and I rehearsed with him and the girls at different times. Peter Sellers didn't come in till quite late on. So I didn't get the full three weeks, but I worked a lot with them in the hotel in the evenings.

The picture was, for various complicated reasons, put on terribly quickly. We were going to shoot locations in Paris and studio in Rome, which was barmy, and then thank God, quite late on in production and preparation, we moved the whole thing to Paris and shot it all there, and this did leave me rather exposed in terms of preparation. There were certain things there which the art director would come along and say "Do you like this?" and I would say "Yes, it seems right to me." That was another reason I chose *Art Nouveau*, because any time I didn't know quite what was wrong about something, I could say "But it isn't *Art Nouveau*." It gave me a sort of lodestone. It was of great value.

Whose idea was it to have Dick Williams do the credits?

Mine. I think they're marvellous, so inventive. We started that from *Art Nouveau*. Some of the designs have slipped over a bit into *Belle Epoque* but the lettering is very *Art Nouveau*. The clothes—exactly the same—Fonssa-grives and Tiel, who did Prentiss's clothes and Ursula's clothes and all the others except the other principals, are walking *Art Nouveau* themselves. They're divine. Bright as buttons, well informed, very intelligent, sweet and marvellous. Cap, who loved what they did but was scared (she's an elegant Paris couture lady) shot off to some chum on the Faubourg St. Honoré. In any case I only wanted her in very severe black and white except at the end. Romy should not have been in this sort of thing, but something simple, and off she went to Chanel, as usual.

The music was originally going to be by Dudley Moore, wasn't it?

Yes; I'm very happy with the present music indeed, but I'm sorry Dudley didn't do it, because he could have produced a very witty score, although not necessarily as "fat" a score as Burt and certainly not as box-office. It's all on the charts now in the States. Dudley, taking into account how time was passing—though it's more complicated than this; one was just simply getting twitchy. He had his show to finish, and one thing and another; he had done a few sketches and things but he never really got to the stage of things where he was working. And so Burt coincidentally blew into town and we got hold of him through social contacts—not mine but Feldman's. Through Angie Dickinson. She and Charlie were old friends, and he ran into her in the Dorchester and he said "Hello love, what are you doing here?" She said "I'm here with my new boyfriend." "Who's that?" "Burt Bacharach." He said, "What does he do?" and she said, "He writes music." "Is he any good as a composer?" And she says "Best there is." So Charlie came upstairs and rang me and said, "Have you ever heard of Burt Bacharach?" so I said "Yes." In many ways the sun shone on the making of this picture. The one thing in the casting I'm pleased about is that nobody comes out really below the others. Everybody has favourites and some are higher than others, but there isn't anybody way behind.

And no one comes on and does their routine number except possibly Ursula Andress, which is obviously very suitable.

Even *that* is the way it's written. Actually Ursula was the most pleasant surprise to me, because although she has no confidence in herself as an actress, she has quite a lot of qualities. I wouldn't mind working with her again.

Clive Donner (1926–   ):
Filmography:
1956—The Secret Place. 1958—Heart of a Child. 1962—Some People. 1964—The Guest, Nothing but the Best. 1965—What's New Pussycat? 1967—Luv. 1968—Here We Go Round the Mulberry Bush. 1970—Alfred the Great.

Carl Dreyer

September 17, 1965

Dear Mr. Dreyer,

I am preparing a book from interviews directors have given concerning their art. The book will be published this winter, and I would be honored to include your words in this collection, particularly since by common consensus, you are one of the world's greatest directors. I therefore humbly submit the following questions which you may answer in any way you please, at your leisure.

1. How and why did you first enter motion-picture production?

Dreyer (written with red ink): In the silent films as a text writer.

2. What are the themes, feelings, and ideas you have wanted to express?

Dreyer:All kinds of intolerance.

3. Of what influences are you most conscious?

Dreyer: From David Griffith and Seastrom.

4. You have been criticized in some quarters as being too "slow." What is your reaction to this criticism?

Dreyer: The rhythm of a film depends on the rhythm of milieu and epoch.

5. Most of your films are shadowed by the spectre of death, and in Gertrud the poetic statement is made that all that matters is love and death. Would you care to state your own attitude to the problems of religious faith your films imply from The Parson's Widow to Gertrud.

Dreyer: To Gertrud it is stated that all that matters is love: Love Is All.

6. Through your career you have evolved a style of

140

subtle camera movement, careful composition, and expressive lighting, a style that sets you apart from directors of the montage school. Could you discuss the evolution of this style, which, in my opinion, finds its ultimately sublime expression in Gertrud.

Dreyer: Camera movement gives a fine soft rhythm.*
—A. S.

Dreyer's last film, Gertrud, *and the circumstances surrounding its opening (the sad welcome given it—since compensated by the work's ever growing prestige) render the publication of an interview with Dreyer, which has been called for for a long time, still more urgent. But Dreyer, beyond his natural repugnance for the worst, is one of those who, knowing how to say everything in their art, have little to add in words. However (and he set himself, in addition, the duty of speaking French, a language he knows well—you will be able to judge this—but which he has little occasion to use), Dreyer lent himself with immense gracefulness to the game of the interview, and did it with a suppleness and vicacity that youth may well envy. The result is this commentary on his work, in which Dreyer knows so well how to utilize anecdotes in order to illustrate the profound sense of its course, to define it as well, thus giving in a few words a quintessence of lessons to be drawn from art and from life. Let us add that this interview took place at Silkeborg, near Aarhus (Jutland), in a rest home where Dreyer, who has gone to take his wife there, realizes that it would do him good to spend several weeks, if only in order to recover from his Parisian misadventure. This took place then not far from Himmelsbjerget and on the shore of the Gusena, that is to say the Mountain of Heaven and the River of God.*

CAHIERS: *It seems that your films represent, above all, an agreement with life, a progress towards joy* . . .

CARL DREYER: Perhaps this is because, quite simply, I do not at all involve myself with beings—men or women —who do not personally interest me. I can only work with people who allow me to realize a certain agreement.

* *Michael Delahaye's interview with Carl Dreyer originally appeared in* Cahiers du Cinema, *No. 170, September 1965, and was reprinted in* Cahiers du Cinema in English, *No. 4, 1966, translated by Rose Kaplin.*

What interests me—and this comes before technique—is reproducing the feelings of the characters in my films. That is, to reproduce, as sincerely as possible, the most sincere feelings possible.

The important thing, for me, is not only to catch hold of the words they say, but also the thoughts behind the words. What I seek in my films, what I want to obtain, is a penetration to my actors' profound thoughts by means of their most subtle expressions. For these are the expressions that reveal the character of the person, his unconscious feelings, the secrets that live in the depths of his soul. This is what interests me above all, not the technique of the cinema. *Gertrud* is a film that I made with my heart.

CAHIERS: *In order to arrive at what you want to obtain, I don't think there are precise rules . . .*

DREYER: No. You must discover what there is at the bottom of each being. That is why I always look for actors who are capable of responding to this quest, who are interested in it, who can help me with it. They must be capable of giving me, or allowing me to take, what I seek to obtain from them. But it is difficult for me to express this the way it should be—and besides, is it possible?

CAHIERS: *You choose your actors, therefore, from amongst those who can give?*

DREYER: That is to say that I choose them from amongst those who I hope will be able to give. And, in general, they verify my choices as being correct. Having real characters for real roles is for me the first thing, the first condition for agreement.

CAHIERS: *But from time to time perhaps it happens that an actor cannot give you what he is capable of giving?*

DREYER: Then we do it over! We start over and we do everything again! Until he arrives at it. For if he is capable of giving he will always end up giving. It's a question of time and patience.

With Falconetti, it often happened that, after having worked all afternoon, we hadn't succeeded in getting exactly what was required. We said to ourselves then: Tomorrow we will begin again. And the next day, we would have the bad take from the day before, projected, we would examine it, we would search and we always ended by finding, in that bad take, some little fragments, some little light that rendered the exact expression, the tonality we had been looking for.

It is from there that we would set out again, taking the

142

best and abandoning the remainder. It is from there that we took off, in order to begin again . . . and succeed.

CAHIERS: *How did you discover that Falconetti had something to give?*

DREYER: I went to see her one afternoon and we spoke together for an hour or two. I had seen her at the theatre. A little boulevard theatre whose name I have forgotten. She was playing there in a light, modern comedy and she was very elegant in it, a bit giddy, but charming. She didn't conquer me at once and I didn't have confidence in her immediately. I simply asked her if I could come to see her the next day. And, during that visit, we talked. That is when I sensed that there was something in her to which one could make an appeal. Something that she could give; something, therefore, that I could take.

For, behind the make-up, the pose, behind that modern and ravishing appearance, there was something. There was a soul behind that facade. If I could see her remove the facade it would suffice me. So I told her that I would very much like, starting the next day, to do a screen test with her. "But without make-up," I added, "with your face completely naked."

She came, therefore, the next day ready and willing. She had taken off her make-up, we made the tests, and I found on her face exactly what I had been seeking for Joan of Arc: a rustic woman, very sincere, who was also a woman who had suffered. But even so, this discovery did not represent a total surprise for me, for, from our first meeting, this woman was very frank and, always, very surprising.

I therefore took her for the film, we always understood each other very well, we constantly worked very well. It has been said that it was I who squeezed the lemon.

I have never squeezed the lemon. I never squeezed anything. She always gave freely, with all her heart. For her heart was always committed to what she was doing.

CAHIERS: *This way of proceeding seems revelatory of what is constantly found in your films: the beauty of the soul and the body as revealed one by the other. This is also perhaps what you have in common with Kaj Munk, who, for a pastor, eulogizes the body as well as the soul of woman, both creations of God. You do not separate them either.*

DREYER: I was so much happier doing *Ordet* when I felt myself very close to the conceptions of Kaj Munk. He always spoke well of love. I mean to say, of love in general, between people, as well as love in marriage, true marriage. For Kaj Munk, love was not only the beautiful and good thoughts that can link man and woman, but also a very profound link. And for him there was no difference between sacred and profane love. Look at *Ordet*. The father is saying, "She is dead . . . she is no longer here. She is in heaven . . ." and the son answers, "Yes, but I loved her body too. . . ."

What is beautiful, in Kaj Munk, is that he understood that God did not separate these two forms of love. That is why he didn't separate them either. But this form of Christianity is opposed by another form, a somber and fanatic faith.

CAHIERS: *The first form relates, I believe, in Denmark, to the reform of Grundtvig, and the second to the ideas of the Interior Mission, born of the teachings of Kierkegaard. These are the two forms that define—or defines—the Danish faith. Did you experience this opposition?*

DREYER: The latter form of Christianity, severe, often fanatic, which establishes a divorce between thought and action, is above all the faith of western Jutland. Me, I'm from Seeland. . . . But I remember certain cases. . . . Yes: one time in particular, an affair made quite a stir, born of the intransigence of a priest of the Interior Mission. He had given proof, in his church, of a particularly outrageous violence and harshness. The entire country was shocked by it. Everyone rose against this black Christianity. Everyone opposed him with the other form of Christianity: clear, joyous, illuminated. . . . This is the antagonism incarnated by the rich farmer and the poor tailor.

But Kaj Munk, who obviously had sympathy for that bright form of Christianity (which, in the play, is that of the farmer), also had some for the other. He understood that there was much good faith among them, that they sincerely believed, acting as they did, they were living up to the mission of Jesus, which for them excluded indulgence. There was the same problem with this priest I spoke of, who was more Christian than Jesus himself; who burned, or believed he burned, with the same fire as he.

CAHIERS: *I believe that a large part of Danish literature at the end of the 19th century and the beginning of the 20th was influenced by this struggle.*

DREYER: Yes. Denmark was marked by a schism. In France you had something analogous at the time of Jansenism. For me, that also relates to a question I have always posed myself: that of tolerance and intolerance. That intolerance between two religious parties is a thing I did not like, for never, in any case, have I accepted intolerance.

In *Day of Wrath*, for example, Christians show their intolerance for those who are attached to remnants of ancient religions, to superstitions. Even in *Gertrud*, you can also feel the presence of intolerance. Here it is Gertrud's, for she cannot accept anything she herself does not feel, which, in a sense, requires everyone to bow to her.

CAHIERS: *How was* Gertrud *received in Denmark?*

DREYER: The critics didn't like *Gertrud* very much. But they didn't like *Day of Wrath* either. However, after a few years, they ended up accepting that film. I hope it will be the same with *Gertrud*.

CAHIERS: *How did your other films fare?*

DREYER: *Ordet* was well received. So was *Joan of Arc*. But, personally, I think that *Ordet* is more successful than *Joan of Arc*, although in *Joan of Arc* there are certain greater possibilities in the heart of the film that can open a way. Other directors could take it up again, pursue this path and do better than I in this style of close-ups and very intimate acting.

If I were to remake the film today, perhaps I would do it in another way. Although. . . . No. After all, I am not sure I would re-do it any differently. *Joan of Arc* was a big thing for me. Previous to that I had never undertaken such a big film. Nevertheless, I had a free hand, I did absolutely what I wanted and, at that time, I was very satisfied with what I had done. Actually, I see the film a bit differently, but, in spite of everything, perhaps today I couldn't do it any other way.

For me, it was, before all else, the technique of the official report that governed. There was, to start with, this trial, with its ways, its own techniques, and that technique is what I tried to transpose to the film. There were the questions, there were the answers—very short, very crisp. There was, therefore, no other solution than to place close-ups behind these replies. Each question, each answer, quite naturally called for a close-up. It was the only possibility. All of that stemmed from the technique of the official report. In addition, the result of the close-ups was that the spectator was shocked as Joan was, receiving the questions, tortured by them. And, in fact, it was my intention to get this result.

CAHIERS: *The thing that the heroines of* Day of Wrath *and* Joan of Arc *had in common is that they were both accused of sorcery....*

DREYER: Yes. And both ended on the stake. ... Except that Lisbeth Movin didn't come to it in the same fashion. ... Moreover, I envisaged another ending for *Day of Wrath* that I found nicer. You didn't see the sorceress going to the stake. You only heard a young choir boy singing the Dies Irae and from this you understood that she, too, was destined for the flames. However, the actual ending, in certain respects, appeared to me to be necessary. It was necessary to give a material form to the consequences of this intolerance.

CAHIERS: *This idea of intolerance—that you recognize as having put in your films—is found in a very noticeable fashion in, for example,* Master of the House.

DREYER: Yes. The husband treats his wife like a sort of inferior, a slave, and that is why he must be taught to show a little more understanding.

CAHIERS: *But this idea of intolerance is, it seems to me, less obvious with* Gertrud *whom one has a tendency to see as a more absolute woman, but also richer and freer than the men she meets.*

DREYER: Yes, but even so, there is a certain form of intolerance at the bottom of her character. This is less marked than with Hjalmar Sjoderberg (Gertrud recognizes that the man must also live for what interests him, for his work), but all the same she is jealous of his metier, she doesn't want that to have the place she believes is coming to her. She doesn't want to be an accessory in the man's life. She wants to be number one, have the first place. After that, he may pursue his work ...

CAHIERS: *Let us go back now to your beginnings. Are there cineastes who have influenced you?*

DREYER: Griffith. And, above all, Sjostrom.

CAHIERS: *When you started in the cinema, had you seen many films?*

DREYER: No, not many. I was above all interested in the Swedish cinema: Sjostrom and also Stiller. Then I discovered Griffith. When I saw *Intolerance* I was, above all, impressed by the modern episode, but all of his films have moved me: *Way Down East,* and the others. ...

CAHIERS: *Isn't the principle of* Intolerance *(in which your theme is found again) rather similar to that of* Pages from the Book of Satan?

DREYER: It was not I who did the scenario for the film. It was by a Danish playwright, Edgar Hoyer, after a novel by Marie Corelli. After having written this scenario he gave it to the Nordisk Company. They submitted the scenario to me. I spoke with the author and he said he would be very pleased if I were to make the film.

CAHIERS: *But if you interested yourself in this scenario it was doubtless because it related to certain preoccupations of yours.*

DREYER: It was only after having seen *Intolerance* that the idea came to me that I might, in fact, attempt to do something analogous. But Griffith mixed his four stories, while as for me, I treated them separately.

CAHIERS: *And didn't you collaborate on the scenario?*

DREYER: Gradually as I studied it, certain ideas came to me on which I reflected and took notes. Afterwards I asked for, and obtained, the right to change it a little bit. Above all, concerning the modern episode, which unfolds in Finland at the time of the revolution of 1918: the war between the Whites, sons of the bourgeoisie, and the Reds, Russian revolutionaries.

CAHIERS: *And doesn't the inquisition episode have some relationship with* Joan of Arc *and* Day of Wrath?

DREYER: Doubtless, but in any case do not forget that I was above all, at that time, the disciple who has everything to learn and who must, before all else, learn. I was happy to make this relatively important film, for this gave me the possibility of having new experiences.

CAHIERS: *There is a great proportion of adaptations in your work. Especially of plays.*

DREYER: Yes. I know that I am not a poet. I know that I am not a great playwright. That is why I prefer to collaborate with a true poet and with a true playwright. The last, to date, is Sjoderberg, author of the play *Gertrud*. Sjoderberg is a great author who was not highly enough esteemed when he was alive but whose qualities are beginning to be discovered. Up to now, he has always been in Strindberg's shadow, for which he was reproached, as he was considered much the inferior.

CAHIERS: *What rules or what intuitions guide you when you adapt a play or a novel?*

DREYER: In the theatre, you have time to write, time to linger on words and feelings, and the spectator has time to perceive these things. In the cinema it is different. This is why I have always concentrated on the purification of the

147

text, which I compress to the minimum. I did this as early as *Master of the House,* for example, which was also originally a play. We compressed it, cleaned it, purified it, and the story became very clear, very clean. That was the first time I employed this method. Later, I employed it for *Day of Wrath, Ordet, Gertrud,* which are also plays.

"Day of Wrath" was a play I saw in 1920. But, at that time, it was still too soon to make the film. Therefore I put the play in a drawer and, later, in 1943-1944, I took it up again and began thinking about how one might transpose it, as cinematically as possible. For that, I was obliged to proceed exactly as I had already previously done, but to a further extent: I had to clean the text as much as possible to the maximum.

If I proceed in this way, it is because I believe that in the cinema, one may not permit what is permissible in the theatre. In the theatre, you have words. And the words fill the space, hang in the air. You can hear them, feel them, experience their weight. But in the cinema the words are very quickly relegated to a background which absorbs them and that is why you may retain only what words are absolutely necessary. The essential is sufficient.

CAHIERS: *The way you have of illustrating this problem of adaptation by passing from* Master of the House *to* Joan of Arc, Ordet *and* Gertrud *is also very revelatory: you do not separate the different forms of cinema any more than you separate the soul from the body. The same problem is posed by the limitations of silent films and those of sound films and you have resolved it in an analogous fashion.*

DREYER: I seek before all else, and in all cases, to work in such a way that what I must express becomes cinema. For me, *Gertrud* is no longer theatre at all, it has become a film. Obviously, a talking film . . . therefore with dialogue, but a minimum of dialogue. Just what is required. The essential.

CAHIERS: *The greatest part of critical misunderstanding comes from the fact that, too often, critics see things in a disassociated way. Thus, for them, in your case there is* Joan of Arc *which is made of images and* Gertrud *with words, while . . .*

DREYER: Oh! but . . . *Joan of Arc* is also words! And it is even more of a tragedy, more theatrical than *Gertrud!* And then, there is also something I always say to myself: it hardly matters what appears on the screen, provided it is interesting. Whether the text predominates, or the image

—it is all the same. In addition, it is a proof of stupidity not to recognize the very important role of the dialogue. Each subject implies a certain voice. And that must be paid attention. And it is necessary to find a possibility for expressing the voice as much as one can. It is very dangerous to limit oneself to a certain form, a certain style.

A Danish critic said to me one day, "I have the impression that there are at least six of your films that are stylistically completely different, one from the other." This moved me, for that is something I really tried to do: to find a style that has value for only a single film, for *this* milieu, *this* action, *this* character, *this* subject.

Vampyr, Joan of Arc, Day of Wrath, Gertrud, are completely different, one from the other, in the sense that they each have their style. If something links them it is the fact that, little by little, I am approaching closer and closer to tragedy. That, I have become conscious of, but at the beginning I didn't do it on purpose. It came by degrees.

CAHIERS: *And now, you would doubtless like to get close enough to tragedy to coincide with it?*

DREYER: Yes, I would like to. And I hope to arrive at it with the film about Christ, and with *Medea. Medea* is a very cinematic thing and I will treat it very freely. For I asked Mr. Euripides to give me a free hand and he made no trouble. Briefly, I have tried to make a cinematic tragedy out of this theatrical tragedy. We'll see whether I have succeeded.

CAHIERS: *Are you very far along with the project?*

DREYER: The scenario is worked out, along its major lines, but I have not yet finished the dialogue. Now I need someone to help me.

CAHIERS: *Do you have other projects in the same realm?*

DREYER: Yes. There is Faulkner's *Light in August.* And *Orestes.* . . . But I won't be able to do *Orestes,* because I met Mr. Jules Dassin and Mr. Jules Dassin has sort of reserved *Orestes* for himself. So we came to an agreement by which he will do *Orestes* and I will do *Medea.* In any case I have been thinking of *Medea* for years and I believe I'll be able to make a good film from it.

CAHIERS: *And* Light in August?

DREYER: It is a very beautiful subject, but very difficult. However, I am set on doing it, all the more so because it is tragedy. An American tragedy and, obviously, it should be made in America.

CAHIERS: *Do you have other American projects?*

DREYER: I would like very much to adapt O'Neill. Particularly *Mourning Becomes Electra,* which I find a very fine play.

CAHIERS: *These are adaptations which you will again approach from the standpoint of the purification of the text . . .*

DREYER: Yes. Always the same thing. But I will try to go farther, to do it in depth. In a theatre play, there are always so many little inessential things. Well, everything that is not absolutely necessary is a stumbling block. Things that block the way must be removed. The path must be clear, and lead towards what is essential, which is at the end of the road. When you take a theatrical dialogue there are too many accessory possibilities in it. And there is too much risk, in an adaptation, that the words, the sentences will be lost. It calls for pruning in such a way that what remains has an importance. By purification I want to make it possible for the spectator, who is following the images, the words and the intrigue, to have an open path so that he may get to the end of the road. It is for him that the dialogue must, so to speak, be put in close-ups.

CAHIERS: *During the shooting, do you continue the work of purification?*

DREYER: Yes, but in terms of the continuity. I mean to say that I eliminate anything that may cause fragmentation of the continuity that I am seeking to obtain. Continuity within the shot is for me a very important thing, for I like the actors to be involved with their dialogue and I respect the love they have for scenes that work.

I also take into consideration their way of working. When an actor makes it apparent to me that it is difficult for him to say something, then we discuss the problem and I modify the thing in question somewhat. And if, while they are working, I notice that the actors are cheating on the idea of a scene, or that it is difficult for them to respect certain movements that they find too complicated, well, then too, we discuss and often I rectify, that is to say, I continue to purify. . . . The work of purification is a work that must be pursued constantly.

CAHIERS: *Do you always collaborate in this way with the actors?*

DREYER: Always. Because it is they who speak, who must feel the importance of what they are saying. That is why we have rehearsals. Above all for the dialogue. And that is how we come to feel, from time to time, that the dialogue must be concentrated. Sometimes it is the actors who come to an agreement, amongst themselves, to ask me to delete several words or a few lines.

CAHIERS: *But you don't rehearse only for dialogue?*

DREYER: No. Everything must be rehearsed in such a way that everyone feels the movement and perfectly understands what he is doing. For *Gertrud*, we rehearsed a great deal. And I was very happy with the result. All the more so because all the work was done during the shooting so that the editing no longer posed any problem at all. In three days, the editing was completed. Terminated. Definitive. I thus realized a progress, for *Ordet* was edited in five days and *Day of Wrath* in twelve. Before that, I spent a month, or even longer, on the editing of my films.

Yes, I very much believe in long takes. You gain on all levels. And the work with the actors becomes much more interesting, for it creates a sort of ensemble, a unity, for each scene which inspires them and allows them to live the relationships more intensely and more accurately.

CAHIERS: *Have you always used direct sound?*

DREYER: Not absolutely, but as a general rule, yes. For *Day of Wrath*, I added much of the sound after the shooting. With *Ordet*, much less, and with *Gertrud*, none at all. Except, obviously, for the music. Another thing I like, in *Gertrud*, is that it is a modern subject and I attempted somewhat to draw it towards tragedy. That is what I wanted to approach. I do not like big effects. I like to approach gently.

CAHIERS: Gertrud, *a very modern subject that tends toward tragedy, reveals, on another level, your sense of totality . . .*

DREYER: Yes. But in this case it is the rhythm, above all, that makes the tragedy. As for the style . . . everyone always believes that I wanted such and such a style. And everyone sets himself to look for the style—here, there and everywhere. But it is much more simple, for, basically, everything in the film is always natural. The actors act in a completely natural way. They walk, they talk, in a natural rhythm, and they behave completely naturally in all the situations. What is curious is that there is a journalist, in Aarhus, who liked the film very much and wrote to me: "There is something I admire very much, and that is that you have Gertrud wear a cape, on the bottom of which is found a *Greek* motif. This is a sign that reveals that you were thinking of tragedy." I liked that thought a great deal, although this motif was in no way a function of my idea of tragedy: it was there purely by chance.

CAHIERS: *It is perhaps a chance revelation of your preoccupation . . .*

DREYER: In any case, this motif is the work of the film's couturière—who is, by the way, Anna Karina's mother—and I accepted it without thinking much about it. Therefore it is really by chance. But this relationship worked out by the journalist pleases me all the same . . .

CAHIERS: *I met a Dane one day who said to me that the dialogue in* Gertrud *is false because spoken in a very artificial way. As for me, I am absolutely persuaded of the contrary but I absolutely could not discuss this with my Dane who could always answer: "You—you don't know Danish . . ."*

DREYER: Obviously, the dialogue is not artificial! Simply, I wanted to make a film that is set in a certain period —the turn of the century—and that unfolds in a well-defined milieu. It is therefore certain that the language reflects something of this time and this milieu, that it possesses a special coloration. Perhaps that is what got your interlocutor off the track.

CAHIERS: *Did you demand certain intonations, certain rhythms, certain vocal forms, of the actors?*

DREYER: Yes. But with good actors, that is generally an easy thing to achieve, and we always arrive at an understanding of what we are to do. Good actors understand the necessity for this work. They know that poetic phrases must be brought out in a certain fashion, with a certain rhythm, and everyday speech in another fashion. And it is not only the tone that is concerned.

If you are in front of a screen, at the cinema, you have the tendency to follow everything that unfolds on it, which is different from the theatre, where the words move through space and exist there, hanging in the air. At the cinema, as soon as they have left the screen, the words die. Therefore I tried to make little pauses in order to give the spectator the possibility of assimilating what he hears, of thinking about it. That gives the dialogue a certain rhythm, a certain style.

CAHIERS: *Doubtless, you would also like to have the possibility of working in color? Do you envisage it for your next films?*

DREYER: Yes. For all of them.

CAHIERS: *Do you envisage color in, for example,* Medea?

DREYER: I have an idea, very simple. But I prefer not to talk about it now. I think it is better this way.

CAHIERS: *Among the films you have made, are there any you would have liked to do in color?*

DREYER: I would very much like to have made *Gertrud* in color. I even had a certain Swedish painter in mind who has studied the period in which the film takes place and who has made many drawings and paintings in which he utilizes very special colors.

CAHIERS: *More exactly, what would you have wanted to obtain?*

DREYER: That is very difficult to describe. The painter of whom I speak, whose name is Halman, above all does drawings for newspapers. You know, these big colored pages for the Sunday edition. It is very pretty and done with very few colors. Four or five at the most. It is in that spirit that I would have wanted to do *Gertrud*. Soft colors, few in number, that go well together.

CAHIERS: *Did you also see* Ordet *in color?*

DREYER: No. At that time the problem did not interest me. It was with *Gertrud* that I thought about it and, of course, I am thinking about it now for my coming films.

CAHIERS: Gertrud *was recently shown on French television. What do you think, in general, of televison?*

DREYER: I don't like television. I need the big screen. I need the communal feeling of the hall. A thing made to be moving must move a crowd.

CAHIERS: *What do you like in today's cinema?*

DREYER: I should tell you first of all that I see very few films. I am always afraid of being influenced. I have, however, seen, among the French films, *Hiroshima, Mon Amour* and *Jules et Jim*. I liked *Jules et Jim* very much. *Hiroshima* too, especially the second half. Briefly, I like Jean-Luc Godard, Truffaut, Clouzot and Chabrol.

CAHIERS: *Have you seen Robert Bresson's films?*

DREYER: I've never seen any of them.

CAHIERS: *What do you think of Bergman's films? I believe you don't like them . . .*

DREYER: Well, if you believe that, that's a mistake. For I saw one film of his that I liked very much: *The Silence*. I find that this film is a success, for he had the courage to take a subject that is very delicate and very difficult to treat, and by making the film, he found a good solution. I

153

saw the film in Stockholm at a large movie theatre, and during the screening, and even afterwards, the most complete silence held sway. It was impressive. It also proves that he achieved his end, in spite of the subject's danger, and he really did what was called for. But I have seen very few of his films and that is because people were beginning to say that he has imitated Dreyer's films.

CAHIERS: *Do you think that is true?*

DREYER: No, I do not think there is imitation involved. Bergman has a strong enough personality to dispense with imitating other people's films. But I have seen very few of his films, I must repeat. I know his work hardly at all. All I can say is that *The Silence* is truly a masterpiece.

CAHIERS: *Independently of the question of imitation, it is certain that there are many cineastes who have been led to the cinema by your films, who have acquired, thanks to you, a taste for the cinema.*

DREYER: That is why I rarely go to the movies. I want to see neither films that have been influenced by me—if there are any—nor those that might influence me.

CAHIERS: *Let's go back now, to the beginning. What did you do before making films?*

DREYER: I was a journalist. There was also a period during which I worked in journalism in the mornings and the cinema in the afternoon. I began in the cinema by doing titles for silent films. At that time, Nordisk was making about a hundred films a year. There were five or six directors who worked the four summer months and who did not edit their films themselves. They sent them to the laboratory. Well, that's where I was, together with someone who was the director of the laboratory. We worked together, and put in the necessary texts. This was a genre of work that constituted a marvelous school. Following that, I wrote some scenarios and then I began to film novels. But before that I "went to school" for five years. Today, when I work, the film edits itself in my head, gradually, during the shooting. It is part of the *mise en scène.*

CAHIERS: *At the time when you were doing journalism and "going to school," were you already thinking of directing films?*

DREYER: I did a few reviews, a little theatre criticism but mostly I covered trials. Every day I gave a complete account of what had happened at the Court House. This work also gave me the opportunity of studying many middle class personalities. It was as a theatre critic that I saw the play from which *Day of Wrath* was taken. It was in this way as well that I saw *Ordet*, out of which I was to make a film in 1954. I also did a little cinema criticism.

CAHIERS: . . . *and* Pages from the Book of Satan, Joan of Arc, Day of Wrath: *there you are, plunging into stories about trials . . .*

DREYER: Yes, but *Joan of Arc* also came to me in another way. When I arrived in France, in order to make a film for the *Societe Generale de Films,* I proposed three subjects. One on Marie Antoinette, another on Catherine de Medici, and the third on Joan of Arc. I had several interviews with the people at the *Societe Generale* but we couldn't arrive at a choice of subject. Then someone said, "Let's take three matches, and draw." I agreed. We drew. I got the headless match: it was *Joan of Arc.*

CAHIERS: Joan of Arc *was your eighth film. We might perhaps go back to the first one now. It was* The President . . .

DREYER: I made this film somewhat as a study and for the experience. What was pleasing to me was the flash back, which at that time was something new. But even then I was beginning to do my own decors, and I also tried to simplify them. As for the actors, at that time there were very few. There were, notably, at Nordisk, two or three actors who absolutely played all the parts that called for old people, who specialized in it and who were always called whenever you needed someone old. For the first time, I took, to play old people, *old* men and *old* women. Today, this is a completely normal thing but at that time I was breaking with a tradition. I also took, for bit parts, instead of certain other actors who were proposed to me, people I met on the street. I chose two second rank actors as well, who were better than the famous but routine actors who were offered to me. I did the scenario for the film but it was an adaptation of a novel by an Austrian, Karl Emil Franzos.

CAHIERS: *Don't you find, even in this early film, a struggle between rigidity and tolerance?*

DREYER: Perhaps that is saying too much. In any case what is dramatic, in the case of *The President,* is that it's about a very fine and very upright man who one day learns that a girl, imprisoned for having killed her baby, is his own daughter, a thing he was ignorant of. Henceforth, there is a battle, inside of him, between the father and the President. Finally the father gets his daughter out of the prison and flees with her and later commits suicide. But the novel I started with was mediocre enough. A bit melodramatic. My film was also a film of apprenticeship.

After that, I made *Pages from the Book of Satan,* of which you have already spoken. All I can add is that I worked on the scenario, that I did not do the decors, but that I discussed the question with the head of that department at Nordisk, who also did decors for the theatre.

CAHIERS: *The first episode was about Jesus . . . which you will take up again, when you make your life of Christ.*

DREYER: But in that episode, it was uniquely concerned with Jesus and Judas. In any case, my film on Christ will be very different from that, all the more so as I do not see things as I saw them during that period. I did the episode on Christ as a sort of iconographic image. All I can say is that my Life of Christ will not be a spectacle. Cecil B. DeMille is dead. . . . But I am not at all speaking contemptuously of Cecil B. DeMille, far from it. He expressed himself with what he had inside of him. And it must be admitted that, had this not been the case, he would not have been the great success that he was. In addition, at that time no one had ever done what he did. Today, it is easy to belittle him, but he was a great director in his genre.

CAHIERS: *Coming back to* Pages from the Book of Satan, *the second episode . . .*

DREYER: . . . was about the Spanish Inquisition. The third, about Marie Antoinette.

CAHIERS: *. . . That you all but remade later.*

DREYER: . . . And the fourth, about the revolution in Finland.

CAHIERS: *Do you have a favorite among these episodes?*

DREYER: Yes, the last. It was there that, for the first time, I used a close-up of the principal actress, in which she did what I asked of her and rendered a whole range of feelings, with a long succession of changing expressions.

CAHIERS: *That was Clara Pontopiddan. Was she related to the writer, Henrik Pontopiddan?*

DREYER: She was not a blood relation, but her husband, a doctor, was a nephew of Henrik Pontopiddan.

CAHIERS: *In the Finnish episode, we find one of those young women who appear again constantly in your films and around whom it seems your work is organized.*

DREYER: It wasn't willful. Each time, it is the subject that attracted me. Here, in this Finnish story, the subject

156

was very pleasing to me: This story of a woman who sacrifices her life for her husband and her country, in spite of everything that rises against her and the threat of her children being killed. In the end, she commits suicide.

CAHIERS: *You then made* The Parson's Widow.

DREYER: That is a film I like very much. Not too long ago, in Copenhagen, there was a gathering of Danish students. On that occasion, one of my films was to be presented and I proposed that they show this one. They appreciated it a great deal; they laughed heartily the whole time. I was very surprised.

CAHIERS: *How did you choose the subject for this film?*

DREYER: It was a question of finding a little subject that could be made very quickly. So I found that story—a Norwegian story—which was very nice, and which was transposed nearly intact to the film. It was also a question of finding a role for the old woman, who was 76 years old, who died immediately after the shooting. Before starting she was already very sick, but she said to me, "Don't worry, I won't die before having finished the film." I had confidence in her. She kept her promise. Yes . . . I very much like this story of three young pastors, one of whom is obliged to marry the old woman. It was a very original subject.

CAHIERS: *It was both grave and gay.*

DREYER: Yes! Joy on a background of gravity.

CAHIERS: *Then, you made a film in Germany:* Die Gezeichneten, Love One Another.

DREYER: A print of this was found again, about a year ago. Mr. Ib Monty, the director of the Danish *Cinematheque,* went on a trip to Russia and someone there told him that a print of the film had been found. He asked to see it, as that interested him, and he was given that print, which is now in the Cinema Museum, where you could have seen it. Mr. Monty was told, in Moscow, that the film—which takes place in Russia during the revolution of 1905—was exceptionally successful concerning the style and the milieu.

CAHIERS: *Didn't you have Russian actors for this film?*

DREYER: Yes. Bolevslavski and Gadarov, the two principal actors, as well as Polina Piekovska, were Russian. Duvan was also known. He had been the director of the Russian cabaret "The Bluebird." As for the others, they were Russian, Danish, German and Norwegian. Besides that, the film was made in Berlin. But the film was adapted from an enormous novel ("Die Gezeichneten," which sort of means "The Stigmatized Ones"), which we had to compress a great deal. Perhaps it was wrong to want to condense this big work in order to make a film out of it. It was necessary to cut, to prune, endlessly. . . . This proves that novels shouldn't be filmed. It's too hard. I prefer to film theatre. There is also another of my films that was recently found again: my other German film, *Mikael*, which I made in 1923 or 1924.

CAHIERS: *Did you have a free hand with these two films? Were they successful?*

DREYER: For *The Stigmatized Ones*, I was very free. For *Mikael*, I had a practically free hand. As for their success, the first was well enough received by the public, but it was, above all, *Mikael* that was a big critical success in Germany. It was called the first *Kammerspiel* (chamber music) film, and I was very flattered by that, for this film was very important for me. The subject for *Mikael* came from a Danish author, Herman Bang. It is the story of a young man who finds himself torn between his "protector" and the woman he loves. The "protector," Zoret, is a celebrated master, a sculptor and painter (a little along the lines of Rodin) who has adopted the young boy and who cherishes him as a son. Well, the young man betrays him, and for the woman: a worldly woman, a princess. And the old master, at the end, dies in solitude. The action takes place during a period when passion and exaggeration were in fashion, when feelings were willfully exacerbated; a period with a certain very false manner, which is seen in its decoration with all its outrageously supercharged interiors. The author of the novel, Herman Bang, belonged to the same period as Hjalmar Sjoderberg, the author of *Gertrud*, and it was even said of Sjoderberg that he imitated Bang, although it was Bang who imitated Sjoderberg . . .

CAHIERS: *Don't you think there is a very profound relationship between* Mikael *and* Gertrud?

DREYER: Yes. That is certain. There is, basically, a certain resemblance. In the tone, in the way the actors act, in the lighting. . . . These are also two films that are set in periods that are very close: the end of the 19th century, for *Mikael*, and the beginning of the 20th, for *Gertrud*. There is also, in both of them, the same sweetness, the same bitterness . . . I just spoke to you of the relationship between the works of Bang and Sjoderberg. Well, it turns out that they knew each other and were even very friendly.

For me, this film counts a lot, even though I see it differently, through somewhat different eyes. It is one of my first films to clearly show a specific style.

CAHIERS: *How would you define this style?*

DREYER: That's not easy to explain . . . but what I just told you also refers to this style and is part of it: a certain reflection of the period. It was, for example, the period when, in France, the monasteries were expropriated by the government. Piles of accessories that came from churches and monasteries were put up for sale, and many people bought sacerdotal ornaments, chairs, benches and other furniture. For example, I knew a Danish actress—she lived in France and was married to the composer, Bereny —who, when she moved back to Copenhagen, set herself up in an apartment filled with horrible things of this genre, all lighted by a bunch of chandeliers. Well, all that was also part of the film's atmosphere which reflects this rich taste . . . which was in bad taste but which, obviously, was considered excellent at that time.

I collaborated on the decors but they were done by an architect who understood my intentions very well and who was absolutely amazing. This was Hugo Haring. He had never done decors for the cinema, and after that he never did any again, for, following *Mikael,* he went back to his true metier, to being an architect. For him, it was an *entracte* in his career (and the period was not so much one for the construction of new houses), an amusement, a fantasy that offered itself . . .

CAHIERS: *The name Thea von Harbon appears on the credits . . .*

DREYER: Ah yes! . . . This was the protegee of Mr. Erich Pommer, so . . . and, with Mr. Pommer, Thea von Harbon was an authority. In any case, whatever intervention there was, I was authorized to consider it as an intervention on principle and to make the film in conformity with my own scenario.

CAHIERS: *Do you have any remarks about the actors?*

DREYER: As principal actor in the role of Zoret, I took a Danish film director: Benjamin Christensen, the director of *Sorcery Through the Ages.* In the role of Michael, there was young Walter Slezak, whom you must know for his American films. It was in this film that he made his debut. It was also the debut for the cameraman, Rudolf

Mate, and our first meeting. Before that, he had done only one short. In fact, Mate did not work on the whole film. Karl Freund was the cameraman who actually was supposed to do the film but he was obliged to leave, as he had other work to do. That is when it was proposed that Mate do the last takes, which consisted principally of interiors. I was very satisfied with him and took him for my following film: *Joan of Arc.*

CAHIERS: *Between* The Stigmatized Ones *and* Mikael, *there was* Once Upon a Time . . .

DREYER: Ah yes! . . . But it's a complete loss. A complete failure. I was not given what I was promised. I was left in the most complete confusion concerning the actors, the places and the shooting time. I worked with a crew of actors from the Royal Theatre in Copenhagen who were free for only one month, in the summer. It was therefore necessary for me to organize myself as much as possible, but at the last moment I learned that the studios would not be free for the necessary time. Therefore I had to do it in haste, with neither any support nor any organization.

As a film it is a loss. There are things one misses in life. And it is necessary at times to miss them. Many detours must be made, to the right and to the left, in order to finally discover the true path. And it is straight ahead.

CAHIERS: *This film is a failure? I am not entirely in agreement with you, but let's go on to* Master of the House, *about which you have already said a few words, when you were talking about adaptation. Now can you talk to us a bit about making this film?*

DREYER: We were absolutely set on shooting this film with real decors, in a real apartment. We found one, a workman's apartment, that corresponded exactly to what we desired. Unfortunately the work would have been too difficult for the crew, so we built an exact copy of that apartment at the studio. This permitted a great deal of verisimilitude.

After this film, I made *The Bride of Glomdale*, in Sweden. It was a little folk tale. I have nothing special to say about it. Then came *Joan of Arc*, which I have already talked about, then *Vampyr. Vampyr* is an original subject that my friend Christen Jul drew from our imagination, starting from several pre-existing elements. What attracted me to begin with, in this subject, was an image I had: something in black and white. But that was not yet defined

160

as a style, and this style was what Mate and I sought to find.

Generally, you find the definitive style for a film at the end of a few days. Here, we found it right away. We started to shoot the film—starting with the beginning—and, at one of the first screenings of rushes, noticed that one of the takes was grey. We asked ourselves why, until we became aware of the fact that it came from a false light that had been projected on the lens.

The producer of the film, Rudolf Mate and I thought about that take, in relation to the style we were looking for. Finally, we said that all we had to do was to repeat, on purpose, every day, the little accident that had happened. Henceforth, for each take, we directed a false light on the lens by projecting it through a veil, which sent the light back to the camera.

After that we had to look for an ending: our first idea was to have the old doctor disappear in the earth, swallowed up by quicksand. But we couldn't utilize that idea, as it was too dangerous for the actor. Therefore we had to find something else. One day, on the way back to Paris after a day of shooting, all the while talking about what we might do, we passed a little house that looked as if it were full of white flames. As we were unoccupied, not yet having found anything, we went into the little house and, once inside, understood that it was a little factory where they worked at reclaiming plaster. The whole interior was white, all the objects were bathed in a white dust and the workmen, too, were all white. Everything partook of that extraordinary white atmosphere. This was utilized by us as a point of departure for another stylistic element of the film.

The grey photography, the white light: this became, definitively, the tonality of the film. For, out of each of these styles we made a third style: that of the film itself.

CAHIERS: *In order to realize this style, a great suppleness was required of the cameraman. In general, do you collaborate with your cameramen?*

DREYER: I have always had the good luck to find someone who loves to work and knows how to, and who does not refuse to collaborate, or to open himself to certain research. I also believe that I am very easy. When someone knows how to work.

CAHIERS: *Now, let's talk about your documentaries.*

DREYER: Oh! They're little things . . .

161

CAHIERS: *When you say about these films, "They're little things," not having seen them, I am disarmed and cannot contradict you as, perhaps, I should. . . . Therefore, let's go on to another film:* Tva Manniskor (Two Beings).

DREYER: That doesn't exist.

CAHIERS: *But I've seen it. I am thus in the position of having a point of view. It exists.*

DREYER: You know, for this film, I was placed in a precarious situation. It was in 1944. I was told that perhaps I was in danger, because of the Germans. Therefore I left for Stockholm, with *Day of Wrath,* for the official reason of selling the film. Then I stayed in Stockholm and wanted to make this little film. Unfortunately, the producer decided to choose the actors himself. He wanted a great career. Well, the actors in question represented the exact opposite of what I would have wanted. And, for me, the actors are extremely important. Thus, I wanted the woman to be a bit theatrical, a little hysterical, and, as for the actor for the part of the savant, I wanted a man with blue eyes, naive but completely honest, who was interested in nothing but his work. Well, they gave me an actress who was the personification of a little bourgeoise, and for the man, instead of a blue-eyed idealist, I was given an intriguing demoniac with brown eyes . . .

CAHIERS: *Don't you think that this film also has a certain relationship to* Gertrud?

DREYER: Oh no! There is absolutely no comparison. And it is a film that was doomed from the start, completely.

CAHIERS: *Here now is a list of some of your shorts:* De Gamle, Shakespeare and Kroneborg, They Caught the Ferry, Storstrom Bridge, Reconstruction of Ronne and Nexos, Thorvaldsen, the Rural Church . . . *Have you something to mention about their subject?*

DREYER: *De Gamle, the Old Men,* is a film about social changes in favor of old people. *They Caught the Ferry* is a little film about the dangers of traffic. It is one of my best shorts. There is another I like very much: *Shakespeare and Kroneborg,* a documentary on the castle where the action in "Hamlet" takes place. I also made another documentary on this castle, more purely historical and archeological, on the remains of the old castle of Kroneborg, of which there still exist some ruins.

Storstrom Bridge is a documentary on the three kilometer long (1.8639 miles) bridge that links the two Danish islands. *Thorvaldsen* is a documentary on the work of the Danish sculptor, a contemporary of Canova. As for *Reconstruction of Ronne and Nexos*, this is a document of the reconstruction of two towns, on the island of Bornholm, that were bombarded by the Russians . . .

CAHIERS: *If we add* The Rural Church *and your other film on* Kroneborg, *we note that your shorts are, above all, based on architecture, old or modern . . .*

DREYER: They're little things.

CAHIERS: *Among all the films on which you collaborated, as scenarist or editor, before becoming a director, there must be some that owe a lot to you, which are, to some extent, by you?*

DREYER: There were many films made from scenarios I wrote, alone or in collaboration, or from ideas I suggested, but these are films I do not recognize. All that is my period of apprenticeship, including *L'Argent,* after Zola, whose scenario I did. But I collaborated more on *Hotel Paradise* (whose subject must have been re-used later): that is somewhat mine. You see, all that was apprenticeship, school. For one must learn and sometimes that takes a long time. Then, you have to make a few mistakes. I told you this a little while ago: You must make many detours before discovering the true path.

Carl Dreyer (1899–1968):
Filmography:
1919–1920—The President. 1920—Leaves From Satan's Book, The Parson's Widow. 1921–1922—Love One Another. 1922—Once Upon a Time. 1924—Mikael: 1925—Master of the House. 1925–1926—The Bride of Glomdale. 1928—The Passion of Joan of Arc. 1932—Vampyr. 1943—Day of Wrath. 1945—Two People. 1955—Ordet. 1964—Gertrud. Documentaries: 1942—Good Mothers. 1947—The Danish Village Church. 1948—They Caught the Ferry. 1949—Thorvaldsen. 1949—Storstrom Bridge.

Sergei Eisenstein

Sergei Eisenstein represents one of the terms by which the cinema is defined. When one thinks of the somewhat mystical term "montage," one is usually thinking of the spectacular effects obtained by Sergei Eisenstein. Originally Eisenstein defined the cinema largely as a function of dialectical montage, that is, by the new meaning derived from the collision of two images. There has been for many years an Anglo-Russian school of film criticism that has denounced the cinema for abandoning the theories of Eisenstein. The coming of sound saw a decline in dialectical montage even in Soviet productions. Stalin, notorious philistine that he was, insisted on dramatic stories at least formally very much like those being turned out by Hollywood. Dwight MacDonald, one of Eisenstein's earliest admirers, accused the Russian director of selling out to Stalin with Alexander Nevsky. *Certainly, Eisenstein's later writings seemed to qualify some of his earlier enthusiasm for montage. Eisenstein's last works,* Ivan the Terrible, Parts I and II, *can be viewed as a virtual repudiation of the fundamental montage theory. Throughout Eisenstein's work, however, runs a single personality often overlooked by those obsessed with pure theory. Ultimately, Sergei Eisenstein's career suggests that a genuinely individual artist will pass beyond ideological considerations whether of form or of politics. The following essay represents the director's effort to reconcile the often conflicting demands of personal expression and social policy.**—A.S.

* *Sergei Eisenstein's article originally appeared in* Cahiers du Cinema, *No. 82, April 1958, and was reprinted in* Cahiers du Cinema in English, *No. 3, with an English translation by Rose Kaplin.*

164

When one speaks of *Potemkin,* one generally notes two qualities: the organic harmony of the composition as a whole and the pathos.

Let us take these two most striking qualities of *Potemkin* and endeavor to show by what means they have been achieved, above all in the realm of composition. We shall examine the organic unity of the composition of the film as a whole. We shall study pathos in the episode in which it attains its maximum tragic intensity, in the "Odessa Steps" sequence, in order to derive thereby analogous conclusions about the remainder of the work.

Our study shall be devoted also to determining how the processes of composition have contributed to the organic unity and pathos of the theme. We could as well study, chapter by chapter, how these elements are realized in the play of the actors, in the development of the subject, in the gamut of lights and colors, in the treatment of the landscape, in the treatment of crowd scenes, etc. Also, we are concerned here only with the specifically delineated problem of the *structure of the work;* we would hardly pretend therefore that what follows is an exhaustive analysis of the film.

But in a work this is organically one, the elements that nourish the whole penetrate each detail. One and the same law pervades, not only the ensemble and all of its elements, but each sphere called upon to participate in the creation of the whole. The same basic principles give life to all the spheres, coloring each one of their own qualitative particuliarities. And it is in this sense alone that one may speak of the work's organic unity, for organism is understood here, as Engels defined it in the "Dialectic of Nature," as *superior unity*.

These considerations lead us, at the outset, to the first theme of our study: the question of organic unity of structure in *Potemkin*.

Let us try to approach the question starting from the hypothesis that the work's organic unity, as well as the sensation of organic unity given by the work, must be apparent where the compositional law of the work conforms to the structural laws of natural organic phenomena as presented by Lenin: *"The specific exists only as a function*

165

of the general. The general does not exist except in the specific, for the specific."

In a first example, we shall examine this law from a static point of view, and in a second example, from a dynamic point of view. In the first example, we shall speak of the terms and of the *proportions* of the film's order. In the second, of the *development* of its construction.

Potemkin is offered as a chronicle of happenings, and it operates as a drama.

The secret of this resides also in the fact that the development of that chronicle is ruled by the laws of tragic composition in its most strictly codified form, that of the tragedy in five acts.

Taken as naked facts, the events develop in five acts of tragedy. And these facts were chosen and logically assorted in such a way as to correspond to the exigency of classical tragedy that Act III differ from Act II, Act V differ from Act I, etc.

This form of composition, which has proven itself in the course of the centuries, is found to be underlined again in our drama in which each act has its title.

Let us briefly recall these five acts.

ACT I: Men and Verses

Exposition. Situation on the battleship. The rotten meat. Fermentation of spirits in the crew.

Act II: The Drama of the Quarterdeck
"Everyone on the bridge!" The sailors refuse to eat the soup. The tarpaulin scene. "Brothers!" Refusal to shoot. The revolt. The officers overboard.

Act III: The Blood Cries Vengeance
The fog. Vakoulintchouk's body at the Port of Odessa. Funeral lamentation. Meeting. The red flag is raised.

Act IV: The Odessa Steps
The population fraternizes with the battleship. The yawls filled with provisions. The fusillade on the Odessa steps.

Act V: The Passing of the Fleet
Night of waiting. The fleet in view. In the engine room. "Brothers!" The fleet refuses to fire.

From the point of view of the action, the episodes of each part of the drama differ absolutely, but a double refrain runs through them and, so to speak, cements them.

In "the drama of the quarterdeck," the little group of rebel sailors, a minuscule part of the battleship, cries "Brothers!" when faced with the rifles of the firing squad. The rifles are lowered. Organically, the whole battleship is with them, it is with the rebel sailors.

In "the passing of the fleet," the whole rebel battleship, a minuscule part of the fleet, hurls the same apostrophe, "Brothers!", faced with the maws of the cannons of the fleet that has been sent out against the mutinous vessel. The cannons are lowered. Organically, the whole fleet is with the *Potemkin*.

From an organic cell of the battleship to the organic whole of the battleship; from an organic cell of the fleet to the organic whole of the fleet: thus the sentiment of revolutionary brotherhood is developed as a crescendo in the theme. And we find it again in the order of the work, which has for its theme the brotherhood of workers and the revolution.

Just as, in the interior of the film, this sentiment of brotherhood flies from the rebel battleship to the coast, in the same way the work, above the head of bourgeois censors, carries the theme of the brotherhood of workers and shouts its fraternal "hurrah!"

As for the rapport of theme and emotion, this could suffice to show organic unity. But we are going to show the composition of *Potemkin* with more formal strictness.

Linked only by the guide-wire of the theme, the five acts, on the exterior, resemble each other not at all. But, seen in a certain relationship, they are absolutely *identical:* each act is found to be cleanly articulated in two nearly equal parts, above all starting with the second act:

The tarpaulin scene—the revolt.

Vakoulintchouk's funeral—the meeting.

The fraternization idyll—the fusillade.

The anguished wait—the triumph.

Even more, the hinge between the two parts is found to be always marked by a sort of stop, a caesura, so to speak.

Sometimes it is several shots of clenched fists that serve as transition between the funeral theme and that of rage (Act III).

Sometimes it is a sub-title—"and suddenly . . ."—cutting the fraternization scene in order to pass to the scene of the fusillade (Act IV).

Or again the immobile rifles of Act II, the gaping maws of the cannons in Act V, and the apostrophe "Brothers!"

that cause the stopping-point of the wait to teeter to an explosion of brotherhood.

It is necessary to remark that the hinge not only marks the passage to another state of soul, to *another* rhythm, to *another* event, but each time, to a violently inverse movement. Not contrasting but truly inverse because each time it gives *the image of the same theme from the angle of the opposite view,* at the same time that it is *born out of this theme.*

The explosion of the rebellion after the atrocious wait in front of the cocked rifles (second act).

The explosion of anger that gushes organically from the theme of Vakoulintchouk's peasant funeral (third act).

The salvos on the stairway, organic "conclusion" drawn by reaction from the fraternal embraces of the *Potemkin* mutineers and the Odessa population (fourth act).

The constancy of this rule of the action's development, of this rule that is repeated in each act of the drama, is in itself already significant.

Thus this constant rule constitutes the distinctive character of the *composition as a whole* of Potemkin.

Also the entire film, in effect, found to be cut in two, towards its middle, by a full stop, a caesura by which the movement that carries the whole beginning stops completely in order to start again with élan for what follows.

The episode of Vakoulintchouk, assassinated, and Odessa under the fog plays the role of this caesura in relation to the film as a whole.

From this moment on, the theme of revolution, going beyond the mutinous battleship, embraces the entire city with its deflagration, a city that, *topographically,* is *opposed to the ship,* but is one with it in terms of sentiment, and will find itself nevertheless cut off from it by the troops (Odessa steps episode) while the theme passes once more to the drama in the larger sense.

We see to what point the development of the theme is organic. We see, at the same time, that the *structure of Potemkin,* which issues entirely out of this development of the theme, *is one in terms of the ensemble, in the same way that it is one with its basic terms, no matter how fractional.*

The law of organic unity is thus found to be observed to the end.

Organic unity in the realm of proportions is the relationship known in aesthetics as the "golden section."

Works of art constructed on the golden section possess an absolutely unique power.

The question has been studied in depth, particularly in the plastic arts.

As applied to the arts that have time as a dimension, the golden section is less popular, although here it possesses perhaps an even vaster field of action.

In the cinema the "golden section test" has apparently never been attempted. It is even more curious to note that *Potemkin,* a film empirically known for its organic unity of composition, is found to be built according to the rule of the golden section throughout.

We have already said that the binary cut through the film as a whole, as well as what happens in each part of the film, occurs *approximately* at the halfway point.

In reality, it comes closer to the ratio of 2:3, which represents the closest schematic approximation of the golden section.

Well, it is at the 2:3 cut, that is to say between the end of the second act and the beginning of the third, that the principal caesura is found, the zero when the action pauses.

Let us be even more precise: the theme of Vakoulintchouk's funeral comes into play not at all at the beginning of the third act, but *at the end of the second,* adding, after a fashion, the .18 missing from the six units in the remainder of the film. (If you calculate the ten demi-acts of the film according to the golden section, 1 and 1.618, you get, to two decimals, 3.82 for the first part and 6.18 for the second.) And the caesuras are found to be placed according to an analogous rule in the interior of each part.

But, without a doubt, the most curious thing is that in *Potemkin* the golden section is observed not only when the movement is at zero, when the action reached its lowest point, but we find it again at the point of apogee as well. This point of apogee is the moment when the red flag is hoisted on the ship. And the red flag is placed at the exact point determined by the golden section! But, this time, you must calculate *starting from the end,* using the ratio 3:2, going towards the cleavage shot that separates the first three parts from the last two, *at the end of the third act,* the red flag figuring in this way at the beginning of the fourth part.

Thus, not only each part considered separately, but the film as a whole with its two points of culmination, that of the total arrest of movement and that of the most frenzied flight, rigorously follows the rule of proportionality, the rule of the golden section.

Now let us study the second key element in *Potemkin:* pathos and the compositional processes by which the pathos of the theme becomes the pathos of the film.

We shall not be stopped here by the nature of what constitutes pathos "as such." We shall restrain ourselves and consider the work's pathos in terms of its perception by the spectator, more exactly its effect on the spectator.

Pathos is what most profoundly awakes in the spectator a sentiment of impassioned enthusiasm.

A work of pathos must observe throughout in the way it is ordered, the condition of violent explosions of action and that of continuous passage to new qualities.

It is self-evident that, in a work of art, one and the same fact may be treated in all manner of forms: from the cold official report to the authentic hymn of pathos. What interests us here are the particuliarities of the processes that allow an event to be raised to the level of pathos.

Incontestably, this is conditioned at the beginning by the comportment of the *auteur* with regard to the material to be treated. But the composition, in the sense that we understand it, is an architecture that equally defines the comportment of the auteur with respect to the material treated and the degree of the work's effect on the spectator.

Also, in the present article, we shall not interest ourselves in the "nature" of pathos in this or that phenomenon "in itself," nature being always socially relative. And no more shall we stop at the nature of pathos *in the comportment of the auteur* in relation to this or that phenomenon, this being no less socially conditioned. What interests us is a very limited problem: how this "comportment" with respect to "the nature of phenomena" is realized by the composition within the conditions of an architecture of pathos.

When one wants to obtain the maximum emotional élan from the spectator, when one wants to make him "step outside of himself," the work must present an "outline" that he has only to follow in order to arrive at the desired state.

The simplest "prototype" for obtaining this imitative reaction will be, of course, a character who, on the screen, acts in a state of ecstasy; in other words a character in the grip of pathos, a character who, in one sense or another, "has stepped outside of himself."

More complex, but also more efficacious, are those cases where the fundamental condition for pathos in the work—the continual passage to a new quality *reinforcing* the *effect*—goes "beyond the limits" of the man in order to extend to the milieu and to the character's entourage, that is to say those cases when the milieu itself is presented in a state of what we may call "trance." The classic example is that of *King Lear*, in which the protagonist's frenzy is transfigured as the frenzy of nature.

Let us come back, however, to our example, to the "Odessa Steps" sequence.

How are the events presented and grouped in this scene?

Leaving aside the exaltation of the masses and the beings represented, we are going to study the development of pathos in one particular aspect, that of the structure and composition: the curve *of the movement*.

First you have a chaos (close-up) of bodies rushing forward. Then a *general shot* of bodies still rushing about chaotically. Then this *chaos* becomes the *rhythmic* hammering of the soldiers' boots as they descend the steps.

The movement accelerates. The rhythm becomes precipitous!

At the apogee, the *descending* movement is suddenly reversed and becomes an *ascending* movement: the rush of the masses (going down) gives way to the *slow solemn* walk of the mother, *all alone*, carrying her dead child (going up).

The mass. The rushing of a lava flow. *Going down.*

And, suddenly:

A figure, *all alone.* Solemn slowness. *Going up.* This lasts only a second. And, again, an *inverse leap of descent.*

The rhythm is precipitous. The movement accelerates.

Abruptly, *the flight of the crowd* gives way to the falling baby carriage. It is not only an acceleration of the movement. We *jump to a new mode of exposition:* from the figurative, we pass to the physical, which modifies the representation of snowballing.

Also, from *close-ups* we jump to *general shots.* From chaotic movement (the crowd) to *rhythmic* movement (the soldiers). From one form of movement (men who run, who fall, who gallop) to the following stage of this

171

theme of movement (the rolling baby carriage). From *descending* movement to *ascending* movement. From *numerous* salvos fired by *numerous* rifles to *one* shot from *one* of the battleship's guns.

We leap continuously from one dimension to another, from one quality to another, and, in the final analysis, it is not an isolated episode (the baby carriage) but the method as a whole of showing the complete event that changes all in all: from a *narrative style,* we leap with the roaring (bounding) lions to an allegorical mode of composition.

These passages by successive bounds from one quality to another, that mount in intensity as well as dimension, rigorously reproduce the angle of the steps on which the action is carried by successive rebounds, towards the bottom.

The theme of pathos that is developed impetuously on the steps gives pathos to the fusillade, also inspires the ordering of the plastic composition and the rhythm of events from end to end.

Is the "Odessa steps" sequence in this respect organic? Doesn't it clash with the general style of the architecture? Not at all. The characteristic traits of the work of pathos are here merely carried to their point of culmination; the episode as well, with its tragic aspect, constitutes a point of culmination of the film as a whole.

This is the place to recall what we have just said about the nature of the two sections into which the five acts of *Potemkin* are divided, in conformity with the golden section. We have noted that, throughout, once past the caesura there is a "rebounding" of the action, that we "leap" to a new quality, because the change to a new quality is, in each case, the maximum *of possible change:* it is, in each case, *an inverse leap*.

Thus it becomes apparent that in all of the key elements of the composition we continually meet the fundamental formula of ecstasy: a leap of the action "outside of itself," which is a change of quality and, most often, an inverse leap.

Here too—as with our recent discussion of the golden section, of the establishment of proportions—it is in the *movement* itself of the work that the "secret" of its organic unity is discovered. The passage by successive bounds from one quality to another is not only the formula for *increase* but also the formula for *progress,* which

172

leads us not as isolated "vegetables" enslaved by the *natural laws of evolution* but as individuals in a collective, in a society, consciously participating in its progress, for we know that such leaps occur in the social scheme also. It is *revolutions* that make for social progress.

We might say that here, underlined for the third time, is *Potemkin*'s organic unit. The jump that characterizes the structure of each link of the composition, as well as the composition of the film as a whole, translates as the key element of the theme: revolutionary explosion. And this is one of the leaps by which the continuous chain of social progress is maintained.

The order of any work, as well as the order of all works of pathos, may be defined in this way: the order of pathos makes us *intensely relive the becoming and the accomplishment of development* as it unfolds in conformity with the dialectic laws.

We, and we alone of all the inhabitants of the globe, have received a share in the happiness of living step by step, in its real accomplishment, each moment of irrepressible becoming of the greatest achievements in the realm of world social progress. And more, we have received a share in collectively cooperating in the building of a new history of humanity.

To live a moment of history is the most sublime pathos in the sense of our being welded to this becoming, in the sense of our progression as a bloc and of our collective participation in the struggle.

Such is pathos in life. And such is its reflection in works of pathos. Born of the pathos of the theme, the arrangement of the composition repeats here the single, fundamental law, in conformity to which all organic, social and other development is achieved in the universal becoming. And it is by our communion with this law, of which our consciousness constitutes the reflection, that we arrive at experiencing the flame of the highest emotion: pathos.

One question still remains: by what practical means can the artist arrive at these formulas of composition?

These formulas are found again unmistakably in each successful work of pathos. But they cannot be arrived at by *a priori* arrangement. Knowledge and facility are not sufficient.

A work will become organically one and be saturated with pathos only when its theme, its material and its idea

173

Federico Fellini

Federico Fellini has come to be known and admired as the director's director since the release of 8½, the first film in history concerned exclusively with the creative anguish of a film director. The title itself, referring as it does to the number of works directed by Fellini, imparts to the cinema some of the dignity and grandeur formerly reserved for the older and presumably wiser arts. Fellini began his career as a close collaborator of Roberto Rossellini and even acted the part of the bogus Saint Joseph in the controversial Rossellini-Magnani tour de force, The Miracle. *Fellini's first features,* Variety Lights (*co-directed with Alberto Lattuada) and* The White Sheik, *revealed a flair for satiric comedy leavened by general pathos. At this point in his career, Fellini was considered, mainly in Italy, one of the more promising of the new comedy directors. The worldwide release of* La Strada *not only lifted him above most of his contemporaries, but also marked a poetic point of departure for Italian neo-realism which had been slowly suffocated from unimaginative literalism. In retrospect* I Vitelloni, La Strada, Il Bidone, *and* Cabiria *comprise a tetralogy of tender nostalgia for lost innocence and lost idealism. These four films are based on a tragic-comic lyricism that is intensely personal and reflects Fellini's compassion for the rejects of the modern world. Subsequently, Fellini undertook in* La Dolce Vita *to provide a Dantean vision of the modern world as viewed from the top instead of the bottom.* La Dolce Vita *marked a magnification of Fellini's stature as a director of international influence. There were those who have felt that there is more to a great film than a great conception, that Fellini*

175

has enlarged his material without expanding his ideas, and that, consequently, La Dolce Vita *is as bloated as the dead fish which terminates the orgy sequence. Nonetheless, even Fellini's severest critics cannot deny the forcefulness with which the director expresses his feeling and insights on film. It could even be argued that in terms of social impact,* La Dolce Vita *is the most important film ever made. This does not necessarily imply a correlation with artistic merit, since, by the standard of impact,* Uncle Tom's Cabin *is superior to* Moby Dick. *The fantastic popularity of* La Dolce Vita *can be summed up by the beggar's comment in Luis Bunuel's* Viridiana: "One must sin before one can repent." *Without being consciously hypocritical, Fellini has dramatized the fundamental injustice of social morality. The poor creatures abandoned by Antonioni to their lives of necessity flock to* La Dolce Vita *to share Fellini's disgust with the sweet life, but the spectacle of corruption fills them with envy for the options of the hero. Confident of their ultimate righteousness, many spectators would like to slide along the infernal surfaces of fur and chrome before regaining their moral footing. In some ways Fellini has become a harsh satirist of modern man's sensual orientation.* La Dolce Vita, 8½, *Giulietta of the Spirits and especially the Fellini–Anita Ekberg episode in* Boccaccio 70 *all reflect a disenchantment with desire as the end-all of human aspiration. For Fellini, libertinism is not genuine liberty, but an unfortunate reaction to repression. Controversy over Fellini continues as his films become more and more visually extravagant and intellectually ambitious.**— A.S.

Monday, July 6th, 1964. I accompany my friend Guido Alberti, with whom I have just been shooting, to the little studio on Palatine Hill. There, Fellini is beginning his first color film, *Giulietta of the Spirits*. We find, not a film crew but another universe, light-years away from what one thinks of as a first day of shooting. Or an Italian Renaissance principality. An interview is spoken of.

Six months go by. This universe has grown. On Decem-

* *Pierre Kast's interview with Federico Fellini appeared originally in* Cahiers du Cinema, *No. 164, March 1965, and then in* Cahiers du Cinema *in English, No. 5, 1966, with English translation by Rose Kaplin.*

ber 6th, passing through Rome, I find myself in the heart
of the film. An immense set at Cinecitta, in sparkling colors. Sandra Milo's salon, where a sort of reception is being
given. Dozens of vividly beautiful women, practically
nude, incredible apparitions, groups of strange characters
augment this impression of an entirely other planet.

And, for all that, in this excessive and gigantic enterprise, there is a feeling of freedom. And of a group that is
quasi-family. You walk through a production on a colossal
scale where everything is done according to the methods
of spontaneity, improvisation, if you will, as in a little
workmanlike film. You know that at the eye of the cy-
clone there is a miraculously calm zone. This whole cy-
clone is run as if it were all eye.

Fellini is in the throes of a formidable amusement. He
pulls a scrap of paper out of his pocket, in order to give
the actors their dialog, as a sleight of hand artist would
pull a dove out of his sleeve. Everyone is enchanted, under
a spell. CIRCUS PRODUCTION

In the midst of this fabulous agitation, Fellini, four days
in a row, will find at least an hour to come and sit down
at the tape recorder that belongs to the film, run by a
sound engineer who belongs to the film, in order to talk,
to answer, to banter.

A month later, a few days ago, he will again find the
time, like a general of the Imperial Wars dictating his dis-
patches while in the distance the battle continues, to re-
read and to correct, to cut and establish order out of
everything that has been taped.

Meanwhile, during lunches, between shots, he still talks,
as much as one wants. My memory is flooded. I shall try,
as well as I can, to give a feeble echo of these conversations. Thus you will find, first of all, the text as taped, and
corrected by Fellini, and secondly, a few fragments that I
was able to gather, filtered through the prism of my doubtless unfaithful memory.

A *film*, says Fellini, *is made, not told about*. Its impetuous course modifies any pre-established scheme. Its face
appears only gradually, as it is made. Basically, the paradox is that Fellini, the maker, can speak of nothing else
and that, however, since he makes it, he is able to tell
nothing about it. If I had wanted to speak with him of his
career, of his films, it would have been necessary to
choose an interlude.

Giulietta of the Spirits seems to me to be an attempt to

177

reconstruct in its totality, beyond all traditional realistic process, the mental world of becoming of a woman, herself captured in full movement. Memories, the events of the present, fears, obsessions, apparitions or representations of presentiments, premonitions, the materialization of fantasms in which obscure terrors are totally mixed. The will to escape the dry limits of reality (what is improperly baptized reality), the national, congealed as it is, the explainable in the Aristotelian sense, is obvious. The story appears to be that of the slow conquest, by a woman, of freedom, from a course that escapes into conventions, into rules, in order to arrive at a sort of other, superior morality, beyond the ruins of conventional morality. In order to arrive at an undefined, rich, multiple zone, which Fellini calls sincerity. A powerful machine crashes the barriers and the limits of human, conjugal, sentimental relations imposed by the current organization of the world. A *fantasy*, says Fellini. The fantasy of the Greek gods, doubtless, free and laughing—gay, as Nietzsche said, and tragic. Something else. Beyond. Neither magic nor spiritualism: moreover, the pseudo-images have not finished shouting. Decidedly: another sanity.

Twelve days, at three different times, therefore, I came to see and look at that dreadful mechanism in operation, to watch a fabulously alive spirit at work, a spirit curious about everything, impetuous, delirious, passionately seeking a way to get beyond excess. Baroque is a limited weak word to describe it. Abundance is the law, generosity without limit, without precaution. One day I hear Jean Renoir say, "How contemptuous I am of good taste, how fed up I am with it." I thought constantly of that little remark in this tumult of noise and colors, in this delirium that seemed to invent to measure other laws on its scale.

I reread a few lines that touch me to the quick. My greatest hope is that from these visits these few lines are communicated.

KAST: *If, now, you were to look back at the films you have made, what in your opinion would be the result of the curve described by your work? Do you think there is, for your films, an image in the rug, a motif in the tapestry?*

FELLINI: This is precisely the type of operation I avoid doing . . . I don't want to look back. . . . An ideological motif, do you mean? I don't know. Doubtless a motif returns incessantly in my films, and it is the attempt to create an emancipation from conventional schemes, a liberation from moral rules; that is to say the attempt to retrieve an authenticity of life rhythms, of life modes, of vital cadences, which is opposed to an inauthentic form of life. There, I believe, is the idea that is found in all of my films, from *The White Sheik* to the film I am making at the moment: *Giulietta of the Spirits.* *A REALIST MODE*

KAST: *Do you think that having recourse to color for this latest film will enable you to go further than 8½?*

FELLINI: This problem of color has obsessed me all through the shooting. . . . Making films in color is, I believe, an impossible operation; cinema in movement, color immobility; to try to blend these two artistic expressions is a desperate ambition, like wanting to breathe under water. In order to truly express the chromatic values of a face, a landscape, some scene or other, it is necessary to light it according to certain criteria, in function of both personal taste and technical exigencies. And all goes well so long as the camera doesn't move. But as soon as the camera moves in on the faces or objects so lighted, the intensity of the light is heightened or deadened; and, depending on whether the light is heightened or deadened, all the chromatic values are intensified or deadened; the camera moves, the light changes.

There is also an infinitude of contingencies that condition the color (even aside from those very grave things that happen at the laboratory: the negative, once it is in the hands of the specialists who are not seeking to interpret but processing according to a daily routine of scales and figures, and staying within certain safe limits, can be totally transformed and conditioned by its development and printing): these are the innumerable and continual traps that have to be dealt with, every day, when shooting in color. For example, colors interfere, set up echoes, are conditioned by one another. Lighted, color runs over the outline that holds it, emanates a sort of luminous aureola around neighboring objects. Thus there is an incessant game of tennis between the colors. Sometimes it even happens that the result of these changes is agreeable, better than what one had imagined; but it's always a somewhat chancy, uncontrollable result. Finally, the human eye selects and in this way already does artist's work, because the human eye, the eye of man, sees chromatic reality through the prisms of nostalgia, of memory, of presentiment or imagination. This is not the case with the lens,

179

and it happens that you believe you are bringing out certain values in a face, a set, a costume, while the lens brings out others. In this way, writing becomes very difficult; it is as if, while writing, a modifying word escapes your pen in capital letters or, still worse, one adjective appears instead of another, or some form of punctuation that completely changes the sense of the line. However, in spite of these pessimistic considerations, the film I am working on is in color, because it was born in color in my imagination.

KAST: *I have the impression that* Giulietta of the Spirits *is a film in which time does not exist: the past, the present, the future and the imaginary are mixed* . . .

FELLINI: Yes, that's quite so. The color is part of the ideas, the concepts, in the same fashion as, in a dream, red or green have this or that significance. The color participates not only in the language but in the plot itself of the film. This is why, in spite of deceptions or fears that attend shooting in color, I believe that color is an enrichment, with the disquieting, sinister, carnivalesque, in a certain sense lugubrious, tone that it brings with it.

Obviously, in order to be able to foresee the photographic result, much effort and attention are necessary. In a black and white film there is already—if only on the mechanical level—an artistic interpretation of reality in the sense that when photographing the sea or a meadow one allows the spectator to give this sea or this meadow the blue or green of his memory of the sea and his memory of the meadow. But, when the blue of the sea, the green of the meadow are already chosen and fixed, they lose a large part of their evocative power and their force of allusion; they may be refused by the spectator or appear false to him. This is why trying to do a film in which the color can remain both evocative and evoked, open to the individual's receptivity, is not simple: each time one tries to pin down artistic reality, it becomes less poetic because it comes to lack just that margin of indefiniteness, the unexpressed that truly makes the charm of an artistic evocation . . .

KAST: *The part played by reality becomes greater* . . .

FELLINI: . . . of the *convention* of reality.

KAST: *But isn't the problem in* Giulietta of the Spirits *that of attempting to fix the imaginary world, a woman's mental world?*

FELLINI: Yes. . . . But I should make a preliminary

180

confession: speaking about a film before having finished it is nearly impossible for me, to the extent that since I haven't fully materialized it I don't really know either what it is or what it will be. In this there is neither coquetry nor humor on my part: it is completely impossible for me to explain my film. Everything I say before making a film, or even during the shooting, I say only in order to satisfy those who get me to speak of it; to be honest, it would be better if I kept quiet, because I have found that I always regret what I say before beginning a film—and, in any case, when I don't regret what I have said, once the film is finished it always contradicts me. Intentions, projects, represent for me only instruments of a psychological nature that put me in a condition to realize the film.

The long preparation for my films does not correspond to a desire I might have to be precise about each detail, to foresee very exactly and meticulously who the actors and actresses will be, to fix the architecture of a decor or the choice of a character. No. It's not that. For me, the principal effort is to create an <u>atmosphere in</u> which the film can be born with the greatest <u>spontaneity,</u> without its being forced to remain within the limits or in the paths of the imagination that has given birth to it. I am accused of being an improvisor. It's not true. I should say, rather, that there is in me a constant openness to ideas, to changes, to improvements that may be born less out of myself than out of the situation that is created around the film and in which the film lives and takes form. For example, to remain faithful to ten pages of dialog written three months previous before anything was known about either the actors or the psychological atmosphere that will reign over the troupe, what does that signify, when one perceives on arriving on the set that some object or other, the color of a pillow or a shadow on a wall can perfectly replace these ten pages of dialog?

KAST: *In this way you reserve for yourself the possibility of utilizing everything that presents itself . . .*

FELLINI: Absolutely.

KAST: *In sum, you make a film as one writes a novel, and you are the only director, perhaps, to be able to do that, with the possibility of changing whatever you want to change. . . . What is striking about watching you shoot is the extreme pleasure you take in it—it is the same pleasure as the writer's . . .*

FELLINI: Such as it is, I can work only in this fashion.

181

This is why, as I already said, when the film is finished it is never the film I said I wanted to make.

KAST: *It's a different object* . . .

FELLINI: It's another thing, another creature, born of certain stimulations and initial conditions, but which has taken on bit by bit a completely different physiognomy. If you want me to speak of my intentions a propos this film, I can talk about them, ready however to deny them when the film is finished . . .

KAST: *What is difficult, I believe, is talking about the film while in the process of making it and, at the same time, having a clear enough vision of the past course of your films. I believe there is something very important in your films, in particular in 8½ : a reflection on the current contour of the moral sense. What is sin, for example. This sin whose frontiers have become particularly soft, changing. But it is I who say that: I see your film once it is finished. For you, now, it is more difficult to talk about it.*

FELLINI: I can say, *grasso modo*, what I have started from; I can also say what I imagine the film will represent or suggest. It concerns, once again, the emancipation of certain conditions of education or of psychology, of certain myths, of certain aberrant structures. This try for freedom is made by a woman, and not a man as was the case in 8½, although *Giulietta of the Spirits* has nothing to do with 8½ on a figurative or stylistic level. It is completely different—at least that is what I hope. It is the story of the struggle taken up by a woman against certain monsters in herself, which are certain psychic components in her deformed by educational taboos, moral conventions, false idealisms. All this is not told in terms of literary or romantic psychology, or in psychoanalytical (scientifically psychoanalytical) terms, but in terms of fable. The film takes all of its meaning, finds its true justification on the level of imagination. And then, each one will appropriate it to himself according to his own sensitivity and his own intelligence.

KAST: *Isn't the ensemble of your films as well this depiction of the moral trouble of our times?*

FELLINI: It is always a little difficult for me to superimpose my voice on my films. But this thread, this motif that reappears in my films, is, I believe, the effect of a certain ethical point of view. At bottom, I am always making the same film, to the extent that what arouses my curiosity, what interests me definitively, what unlatches my inspira-

182

tion, is that, each time, I am telling the story of characters in quest of themselves, in search of a more authentic source of life, of conduct, of behavior, that will more closely relate to the true roots of their individuality.

KAST: *With something that is not* against, *but* beyond *conventions . . .*

FELLINI: The stories of my films are always articulated and take their dimension in the course of episodes that also go against conventions; but their most profound, most essential aspect seems to me, as you have said, to go beyond these conventions, in search of something more purely individual.

KAST: *I believe that remaining in this way on the side of the individual allows, in fact, for general understanding . . .*

FELLINI: Yes, in the sense that a person who really finds himself can insert himself into the collectivity with more freedom, more force and confidence, precisely because he has found his individuality.

KAST: *It has at times been said that there is a certain mysticism in your films. . . . But I believe that this aspect is secondary in relation to this general intention of retrieving something that escapes the social, mental, even political, limits of life . . . One cannot separate* the whole, *with your films. When I think of your films, I can't consider them one by one: it is as if, each time, there were a supplementary stone in the whole that is being constructed. And I return to this feeling of freedom your work gives, even in the most practical sense . . .*

FELLINI: I believe I have already answered you on the subject of this openness to *follow* a film, while trying to conserve it in its potential for spontaneity, for spontaneous growth. Obviously I must take into account the principal stages of the story I am doing. However, I believe I can say with a certain honesty that, very often, I have modified the story itself when I realized that certain essential prefabricated, preconstructed points of the story no longer relate to the new exigencies of the characters, exigencies that have ripened in the course of the shooting.

KAST: *It seems to me that your way of working can be defined as a sort of synthesis of two very different ways of working: that of Resnais and that of Godard . . .*

FELLINI: That's possible, but I don't know how Resnais works, or even how Godard works.

KAST: *Have you seen their films?*

183

FELLINI: No. I rarely go to the cinema.

KAST: *That is because your world is, I believe, some-what apart from others: it seeks its own laws . . .*

FELLINI: I am making this confession reluctantly and I don't want it to be interpreted in the wrong way, but going to the movies is a diversion that has no part in the things that interest me. I prefer to go for a walk or to blab with a friend. I lost the habit of going out and buying a ticket, going into a hall and sitting down to watch a film with other spectators. At least that is how I justify it to myself: perhaps it's an unconscious way of defending myself.

KAST: *There is a universe that you are in, and which is in search of its own laws, that has no need of knowing how other things evolve .* NONSENSE INTERVIEWER

FELLINI: What you are telling me is flattering . . . and it makes me uneasy to accept it as a justification for my laziness. I used to go to the movies often when I was young and then, when I started to make my own, I com-pletely detached myself from it. Yes, I've seen a few films. I saw two films by Bergman, almost all of Rossellini's, a few Japanese films, by Kurosawa and Mizoguchi . . .

KAST: *Have you seen Francesco Rosi's films, which ap-pear to me very interesting within the scheme of the Ital-ian cinema?*

FELLINI: I saw *Salvatore Giuliano*. I haven't seen *Le mani sulla citta*. But, a few days ago, I saw a few scenes on the moviola from the film Rosi shot in Spain: it seems very fine to me. I have much esteem for Rosi: he is a thoroughbred novelist-journalist, a true cineaste . . .

KAST: *In a certain direction, that of naturalism—that rises above naturalism—it is the strongest thing that can be done, I believe. For there is a kind of barrier with na-turalism that doesn't permit one to go any further . . .*

FELLINI: Certainly: this somewhat fanatic aspect of sensory reality stands in the way of greater depth—a depth that can even be dangerous, because it can easily de-generate into divagation. In any case, a journalist's eye is a journalist's eye. That is to say that he is held to give an account, with a certain objective scrupulousness, of what the eye—in the physical sense—registers, with no subjec-tive interpretation at all.

KAST: *Alexandre Astruc says that the cinema is not the thing shown but the eye of the director.*

FELLINI: This definition seems very right to me—in what concerns my cinema. On the other hand, I would like to try—if only to the end of experimentation—to make some short films that would humbly reproduce reality, on the level of the most objective material reality. I think this would be useful to me.

KAST: *In any case, style and expression are so alive that, even when one does* cinema-verite, *they reappear.*

FELLINI: That is a very profound contradiction. Always the same. There is already in the fact of choosing one episode instead of another, one face in place of another face, as well as the fact of photographing, a very relative objectivity, since precisely here intervenes a choice, a selection, thus an interpretation.

KAST: *Are you interested in the whole science fiction movement, in the literature of fantasy, by everything that tries to arrive at a new mode of reasoning, that aspires, despite conflicts and contradictions, to another way of thinking, as if the rules of logic for another thought were not yet found?*

FELLINI: All the products of the intelligence, and particularly of the imagination, of human nature, fascinate me, interest me to the highest degree. The literature of science fiction interests me very deeply, doubtless because I, too, am trying to restore a dimension that would be more free, perhaps catastrophic, perhaps deadly and menacing, but which would for all that go beyond ethics and morality that are somewhat congealed, paralyzed by certain taboos. I am profoundly attracted by anything that tends to restore man to a stature that is more vast, more mysterious even, and more anguished, but in any case neither pacifying nor consoling. I prefer a dimension whose contours are lost in obscurity, but which is more vast, to a little well lighted construction that is a prisoner of very rigid walls. It seems to me that today it is no longer possible to remain there, protected by a type of thought that considers all things as organized and established.

KAST: *Do you think the cinema should espouse this ambition, or reject it?*

FELLINI: It seems necessary for me to maintain this ambition, this conception, within certain limits of modesty. That is why I am a little uneasy about the turn this interview is taking: in order to answer you, I would have to have a particularly defined culture and philosophy of life . . .

KAST: *Let's come back to* Giulietta of the Spirits: *when*

you came to grips with the subject of the film, had you already chosen the characters?

FELLINI: In fact, I acknowledge no fixed system of work at all for myself. . . . However, if I had to be precise about the phases of my work, I would say that at the start there is always a manuscript, very approximate in structure, because to push for precision in the scenario corresponds, for me, to a halt, a period of stagnation that, far from clarifying my ideas, confuses them. The richest part of this preparation is the choice of faces, heads, that is to say the film's human landscape. The nutritive milieu which will give the film its own physiognomy is elaborated from these meetings, these interviews, these bantering conversations, the irruption of this crowd of looks and smiles. Today, I no longer know whether this way of working is suggested to me by my laziness or whether I superstitiously remain faithful to it as a sort of ritual apt to bring the film to its proper incandescence. During this period, I am capable of seeing up to five or six thousand faces, and it is just these faces that suggest the comportment of my characters to me, their personalities, and even the narrative cadences of the film; I would be tempted to say that this is the most serious phase of my preparative work. Then, there is the research of exteriors and, in this case as for the faces, I pin nothing down. I am somewhat lazy about deciding.

KAST: *You speak often of your laziness, but it's a fiction . . .*

FELLINI: It's true! When, for the same character, I have a choice of five or six faces, this incertitude nearly tears me to pieces: each one of these faces, these types, could give an equally valuable originality or weight to my character.

KAST: *For example, when you take Rougeul to play the intellectual in 8½ . . .*

FELLINI: But before Rougeul, I had four or five faces that would have been equally appropriate. . . . So, I make some test shots. But this uncertainty may last up to the last hour before shooting. At the last minute, I place myself almost superstitiously in the hands of destiny, that is to say that this "choice" is never definitively motivated; it is guided by something irrational that pushes me to take the one who, because of some ineffable, undefinable element, suddenly appears to me to be not only the most appropriate but the unique choice. Sometimes this choice,

UNLIKE B. MAN — 186 *NOT*
CHARACTERS PRECONCEIVED),

having been irrational, proves to be unfortunate. Then, I try to take advantage of this mistake. I abandon the character I had in mind, and I seek the character in the chosen actor or person.

KAST: *That corresponds naturally to the pleasure you yourself take in being free . . . one has the impression that the margin of freedom at the disposal of a character is very large . . .*

FELLINI: Very often, it is the actors themselves who suggest the action to me when they tell me their own stories, or when I see how they live off the set, during breaks. It is very important to me to permit the whole troupe, actors or not, to live spontaneously, in order to create a very comfortable atmosphere, a playful ambience in which each one finds himself completely at ease, without ever having the feeling—paralyzing for me—that he is accomplishing a professional duty, but breathing, living, moving in a way that is most familiar to him, most congenial.

KAST: *Doesn't that also correspond to an extreme curiosity in you about other people?*

FELLINI: Yes, but I believe that curiosity is essential to anyone who wants to express himself visually. The eye must be stimulated by this curiosity to look and discover around it the multiple aspects of reality.

For the fourth time, I arrive at Cinecitta, still a bit stupefied by what I have seen on the preceding days, and by the fabulous niceness of Fellini, by his availability, incredible, if you really think about what tension and effort of concentration is represented in the direction of such a mechanism. On another stage, another set, the studio of a sculptor, a woman, another of Giulietta's friends.

Twenty meters of glazed bay give on to a lively ochre beach. The disc of a red sun, in iron, is above the horizon. In half an hour, during which we will walk around on the set, Fellini will show me a clockwork mechanism that, with real timing, will move off and make this disc sink below the horizon, for the entire duration of a shot that is being set up.

White statue-people, giants. Stupefying. These are exact copies of statues by an English sculptor, who died a few years ago, that Fellini saw by chance. They are beyond all possible judgement. Figures out of a dream mythology. A winged spirit descends from the sky and kisses a man who is on tip-toe. The whole thing a good ten meters high. It is this statue that Silvana Jachino, who was the most marvelous ingenue in the Italian cinema of the forties, is finishing at the moment Giulietta comes to pay her a visit.

The marvelous little crane that is already in place is the one I had already seen on the other set. It rolls on a ply-wood path that gives it an immense trajectory, from the human group that serves as model to a group shot (long shot?). Meter by meter, Fellini establishes his shot with an extreme attention to detail. I ask myself what I am doing in this factory that is making a sort of precision chronometer, I ask myself how I can dare to disturb the man who is there, sitting on a little plastic-covered seat, playing with his winches. I remember that Orson Welles said that the cinema is the finest set of electric trains. I had already noticed, on the preceding days, that part of Fellini's passion is also that of the game, the grave, serious passion that concentrates the whole exterior world in one point and one second. The gravity of childhood, the spirit and heart that are not yet bent to the routine and convention of the adult world. BERGMAN-THE GAME,

It's finished. The shot is established. Gianni Di Venanzo begins to light it. Fellini sees me and approaches. I am paralyzed by the idea that someone is going to bring out the tape recorder again, mobilize the sound engineer once more, so charming for all that, and even more attentive than I to what is said. I propose to Fellini that we finish talking while at lunch. I will try to remember what is said. I cannot bring myself to break this attention, by a few questions that are so removed from what is happening. All right. Some laughs. Then Fellini explains the function of the crane to me at length. Its advantage over others. All that it allows for doing. All that he is doing with it. Then, abruptly: *You can do very bad things marvelously with this,* he says. And he bursts into laughter.

With no continuity problem, the set follows along, re-solves itself, if you will, as another, a sort of imaginary vision of the children's theatre that Giulietta went to as a child. One passes naturally, from one to the other; from what is perhaps reality, the studio, to a memory, itself profoundly modified by imagination. I begin to understand that *Giulietta of the Spirits* will also be a meditative fantasy on the real and the imaginary, an exploration of the paths of realism.

We go to lunch. My first question is ready; I have been turning it over in my mind for an hour, seeking a way to formulate it, in order to try to pin down what I have glimpsed.

I have no vocation for theories, says Fellini. *I detest the world of labels, the world that confuses the label with the thing labelled.*

Realism is a bad word. In a sense, everything is realistic. I see no line between the imaginary and the real. I see much reality in the imaginary. I do not feel myself responsible for setting all that in order, on a national level. I am indefinitely capable of wonder, and I do not see why I should set a pseudo-rational screen in front of this wonder.

He talks, he eats, he laughs all the time. Everyone laughs. The set is not a cathedral in which you can hear a pin drop. But a very special silence, mostly sonorous. This was not a scene of tiptoeing around a genius at work. But a noisy affection, touched, attentive, a thousand exuberant liberties, that became another silence. Like at that table, where everyone listens without listening. *Any shot at all,* continues Fellini, *expresses the totality of a world. It totally implies the conception of a world. There is no need to even say it.*

We talk again about *Giulietta.* I fully understand, at the same time, that it is nearly impossible for him to talk about it, for fear perhaps of spoiling an inspiration that is fluidity and suppleness itself, for fear of enclosing within a definition a film that is perhaps a weapon against definitions. One has seen too many valiant relativisms become dogmatic in their attack against all dogmatism. General semantics itself has its sects, doubtless paradoxical, but tearing itself apart with heresies.

Thought, says Fellini, *encloses itself within limits, which are its negation, and beyond which it has a hard time going. One should use thought as a point of departure for going beyond thought, in order to attain to something that would be more itself. . . . To get out of prison without inventing the walls of another prison.*

There is a contradiction, apparent, out of which one can get only by a certain humility, by means of a certain humble recognition of one's self, one's limits or one's weaknesses. . . . There is a certain confusion, a collapse of myths, which is in a sense a farce. . . . But a farce that leads to freedom, whose contours one does not see. One cannot see them. With difficulty divine them. But morals, the conventions of morality, the order that flows

189

from them, all that is of another time. Terminated, even if the professional moralist mourn them.

Something else is appearing, still in a mist, in the midst of masks and of monsters, in an infernal din. I see clearly that *Giulietta* also turns, as if on tip-toe, on an idea of sin . . .

. . . whose frontiers are soft, variable, says Fellini. *The paths of morality are confused, variable. The feeling of guilt is the suffering one experiences on passing these new frontiers.*

The story of a woman's slow progress towards her freedom, her independence. I do not see why a woman must wait for everything to come from a man, or from the convention of the relationship between men and women. One can imagine that she may succeed in discovering a unified interior world, an individual richness. Beyond the sense of propriety, the use of recipes for life in pairs, defined by the couple, or by the man.

Good, grace, if you will. One can surely relieve oneself of outdated slaveries. Above all by a complete transformation of morals and mores. I am not charged with being a master of thought, or with thinking for others. Obliging them to think about what happens to them.

It seems to me that freedom, especially a woman's freedom, is a conquest to be made, not a gift to be received. It isn't granted. It must be taken.

It is dangerous, obscure. The unhappiness of a thousand faces. . . . But there is perhaps a kind of felicity beyond it. And, above all, beyond imposed limits. Limits that are changing, without knowing it, and above all without saying it.

Then, there is the danger and the taste for mortification, suffering as a means of redemption, or everything that can mask the ravings of the sense of propriety, or of vanity. Everything that a cunning and avid ego can transfer on to the level of more elegant moral values. More noble. That call themselves more noble. That are charmed to be more noble.

All this obviously turns on a certain institution, let us say marriage. On a delirium of jealousy, visibly provoked by Giulietta as one would an infected tooth, with the same secret pleasure that is hidden behind worrying an infected tooth.

It seems to me that it is more worthwhile to look directly at what is happening, says Fellini, *instead of hiding behind morality. Of course, in a sense, Giulietta is a film about marriage. A fable, a serious pleasantry on morality. The limits and the overthrowing of a moral convention. The vanity of words like cheating, jealousy, possession. An attempt to explore what they conceal. A slow and confused approach to another freedom, another morality that is emerging from the old. Remorse, suffering, cradled in complacence. And the search for another faithfulness to oneself, for example. Of Giulietta to herself, to her profound exigencies, unknown, perhaps. A superior faithfulness.*

And then the idea that something will come out of this confusion. Beyond the word clarity. A more free, and bigger, means of knowing oneself.

I recognize themes, words, that are a constant in Fellini's universe. The universe that he describes, it seems, in a manner that is more and more free, more and more apparent, more and more open.

My turn to worry at my infected tooth. Won't people say, which would be comical, that Fellini is making literary films? That he had from all evidence a high ambition? I tell about how the French critics, the licensed ones, I mean to say, those of the weeklies, those of the dailies, shout with rage, speak of pretension, of aberration, of ridiculous will to accede to a form of culture in which the cinema has no place. There is much laughter. Fellini has the good humor of the old Greek gods, who knew themselves to be the butt of things and of men.

Of course the cinema may say everything, says Fellini. If people refuse it this, that means that it is themselves, cleverly, that are refused. Out of pride, or out of vanity. They treat others as pretentious, above all because that is what they themselves are, primarily. When one shows a world that is open, baroque, delirious, demanding, clamorous, multiple, contradictory, a farce and a tragedy, there is no reason at all to suppose that it must be less accessible, immediately, than a world enclosed in conventions by force or by usage. . . .

Generosity is better; let us say that I like that better than restriction or precaution.

More laughter. We have talked for hours. For all that, I have the impression of having just started. Of having forgotten everything that I wanted to ask. Several weeks later, today, my pen runs across the page, trying to force my uncertain memory, trying to give, even weakly, an idea

191

of the richness of this vocabulary. Not to mention its charm. Multiplied by the charm of the Italian language, the divine Italian volubility. Generosity, openness of spirit, attention to others, all this no doubt explains those stupefying working conditions, that fanatically faithful, fanatically seduced, crew. I was abruptly intimidated, at the end of that meal. All the more curious to know everything, to understand everything. As if I found myself faced with the open road of a new humanism, not yet daring to venture along it.

I can no longer remember the exact words. Only the general tone taken by the discussion. Fascinated by the agility, the richness and high speed of this spirit. The first day, I believe, Fellini said: *I am always making the same film.* I see the outlines of this total film being drawn, I see the profound intention becoming clarified, and at the same time the true modesty of the work persisted in.

It is time. It is finished. We get up. Arm in arm, we tell jokes, we speak of projects. I leave. Full of melancholy. Giddy, fanatically charmed. And then the lights of Rome.

Federico Fellini (1920–):
Filmography:
1950—Variety Lights (Co-directed with Lattuada). 1952—The White Sheik. 1953—I Vitelloni, Love in the City (Matrimonial Agency Episode). 1954—La Strada. 1955—Il Bidone. 1957—Nights of Cabiria. 1959—La Dolce Vita. 1962—Boccaccio 70 (Temptation of Doctor Antonio Episode), 8½. 1965—Giulietta of the Spirits. 1967—Tony Dammit (sketch from Histoires Extraordinaires). 1969 —Satyricon. AMARCORD

THE ORCHESTRA REHEARSAL

John Ford

John Ford is the American cinema's Field Marshal in charge of retreats and last stands. In the work of no other director is the pastness of experience so vivid and the force of tradition so compelling. No other director has ranged so far across the landscape of the American past, the worlds of Lincoln, Lee, Twain, O'Neill, the three great wars, the Western and trans-Atlantic migrations, the horseless Indians of the Mohawk Valley, and the Sioux and Comanche cavalries of the West, the Irish and Spanish incursions, and the delicately balanced politics of polyglot cities and border states. Ironically, Ford was adopted by the Critical Establishment at the wrong time for the wrong films for the wrong reasons and abandoned when his work attained new summits of personal expression. The Informer *and* The Grapes of Wrath, *his official classics, are among his lesser works.* The Informer, *like* The Fugitive, *runs counter to Ford's sense of order. Liam O'Flaherty's renegade informer and Graham Greene's renegade priest are clearly beyond Ford's comprehension, and in both instances, Ford's casual Catholicism cannot encompass the authors' causal Catholicism.* The Grapes of Wrath *involves a conservative director with liberal material just as* Advise and Consent *involves a liberal director with conservative material. In both films, the tensions between director and subject are more compelling than the subjects themselves. Ford's personal style was particularly inimical to Steinbeck's biological conception of his characters. Where Steinbeck depicted oppression by dehumanizing his characters into creatures of abject necessity, Ford evoked nostalgia by humanizing Steinbeck's economic insects into heroic champions of an agrarian order of family and community.*

Ford's major works can be traced in a rising parabola from Steamboat 'Round the Bend *and* Judge Priest *in the mid-Thirties to the extraordinary American trilogy in 1939—*Stagecoach, Young Mr. Lincoln, *and* Drums Along the Mohawk—*and then on to the postwar classics beginning with* My Darling Clementine *and culminating with* The Man Who Shot Liberty Valance. *How Green Was My Valley established Maureen O'Hara as the definitive Ford heroine, just as* Stagecoach *established John Wayne as the definitive Ford hero. The extraordinary rapport of the Wayne-O'Hara team through* Rio Grande, The Quiet Man, *and* Wings of Eagles *adds a sexual dimension to Ford's invocation of tradition in human experience. How Green Was My Valley is also notable for introducing Ford's visual treatment of the past as a luminous memory more real than the present, and presumably more heroic than the future. Ford and Hawks, the directors closest to the Griffith tradition, project different aspects of Griffith's personality: Ford, the historical perspective and unified vision of the world: Hawks, the psychological complexity and innate nobility of characterization. Of course, Ford can never become fashionable for the rigidly ideological critics of the Left. Too many of his characters wear uniforms without any tortuous reasoning why. Even the originally pacifistic* What Price Glory *is transformed by Ford into a nostaglic celebration of military camaraderie with the once raucous Charmaine emerging from the dim shadows as an idealization of the Chivalric Code. As a director, Ford developed his craft in the Twenties, achieved dramatic force in the Thirties, epic sweep in the Forties, and symbolic evocation in the Fifties. His style has evolved almost miraculously into a double vision of an event in all its vital immediacy and also in its ultimate memory-image on the horizon of history.*—A.S.*

Just as my slim volume on John Ford came off the press, I learned quite by chance that Ford had just arrived in Paris. It was an unprecedented stroke of fortune.

* *Jean Mitry's interview with John Ford appeared originally in* Cahiers du Cinema, *No. 45, March 1955, and was translated for this book by the editor.*

Beyond the pleasures of meeting someone whose work I had long admired, I looked forward to learning at first hand whether Ford agreed with what I had written, especially whether he agreed with what I call the Fordian theme, specifically the revelation of character, by action and gesture, of a handful of men gathered together at a particular place by fortuitous circumstances or fate. Would Ford be as ironic as Hitchcock about such an involved interpretation of his work?

My lack of facility in English turned out to be a painful handicap, particularly when I tried to elicit Ford's views on film esthetics. Furthermore, Ford is reluctant to talk about his career or himself.

I found he was vacationing—convalescing from a gall-bladder operation. He started off by talking about cigars, travel, and his obligations as a retired U.S. admiral. He was well aware of his fame, but expressed surprise that I had treated the movies and his own pictures with a seriousness usually reserved for works of art.

He then remarked that though a director is naturally pleased when his work is seriously analyzed and found to contain the elements he had hoped he had put in his pictures, it is fatal for a director to consider only the aesthetic side. It is equally fatal, he continued, for a director to be preoccupied with doctrinaire theories about technique. "Directing is a craft," he said bluntly. "If a director's films do not make money, he cannot expect to retain the confidence and good will of the men who put up the wherewithal."

Ford said he made films because it was his trade, which he liked. "But for producers," he continued, "there are other considerations, commercial ones, which must be respected. You see directors disappear, or make nothing but mediocre pictures. It is not that they have less talent, or that they have lost their ability. It is that they have turned out one film after another without box-office appeal, with the result that they lose their prestige and wind up on the beach. They must start again from the bottom to regain the confidence of producers. That can take a long time, and sometimes they are restricted to mediocre projects."

The best directors can be defeated by this process of aesthetic attrition, and after enough setbacks they lose their ambition.

According to Ford's calculations, directors who want to make only artistic films get a chance to do so about once every ten years. If the film is a commercial success, they get another chance, but otherwise they are through. "Only rarely," Ford added, "does the opportunity arise to make such films two or three times in a row."

The secret, Ford said with the utmost seriousness, is to turn out films that please the public, but that also reveal the personality of the director. "That isn't easy," he added.

I asked if he didn't always do what he wanted.

"What I want, yes, but what I would like to do, certainly not."

"Do you choose your scripts or are they chosen for you?"

It depends, he explained, on the studio that employs him and on the kind of contract he signs. In rare exceptions Ford has what amounts to a choice—from among a dozen possible projects he may choose the one he likes best. In all his films, he said, he tries to maintain a certain feeling, a unity, and to retain in the script only that which contributes to this unity and sets forth his personality.

"But that isn't always possible," he exclaimed, "and I must make films whose success is assured in advance in order to have the right, and the opportunity, to make others that are commercial risks but more worthwhile. On their success hangs my freedom of action. In this way I have been able to make some films I wanted to make, and to make them according to my tastes and weaknesses. But I haven't been able to make ten such films.

"I waited four years to do *The Informer* and got the chance only after every sort of hesitation. Then I had a little more luck and was able to choose films which left me a certain leeway in which to express myself."

"But are you not also a producer?"

"Yes, but like all producers, I am subject to the demands of the distributors. There's not much freedom in being a producer. In fact, one takes on more worries—the financial ones. One is doubly responsible—for the film, and for the money. Like other producers, I hesitate to throw myself into an attractive but risky project.

"At the moment I want to make in Ireland, for very little money, a picture for my pleasure, to be called *The Three Leaf Clover*. I hope it will express some of the poetry of my native land. After that I shall undertake a big Western with a subject that interests me—one that corresponds to what you call 'my world.' It is called *The Search* and is set in the Rocky Mountains and concerns some pioneers who seek a little girl taken away by Indians. It's a kind of psychological epic."

I then ventured the opinion that he seemed in almost all his films to have this theme of a small group of people thrust by chance into dramatic or tragic circumstances. "On purpose?" I asked.

"It seems so to me," he replied. "It enables me to make individuals aware of each other by bringing them face to face with something bigger than themselves. The situation, the tragic moment, forces men to reveal themselves, and to become aware of what they truly are. The device allows me to find the exceptional in the commonplace. I also like to discover humor in the midst of tragedy, for tragedy is never wholly tragic. Sometimes tragedy is ridiculous. I should like to do a tragedy, the most serious in the world, that turned into the ridiculous."

"Your penchant for unity of time and place," I asked, "does it tempt you to play down the story in order to make a film more universal, more abstract?"

"Not at all!" Ford said quickly. "That may be the result, but it certainly is not the end. Unity of time and place is solely a means of defining the drama and individuals, a way of getting there more directly and quickly. I look, before all else, for simplicity, for the naked truth in the midst of rapid, even brutal, action. To be as selective about time and place as one is about the action is to get rid of useless complications. When the circumstances are clearly comprehended, the force of the conflict is increased, since its effects are more completely understood. Time is important only when one follows individuals through all their lives.

"I suppose everybody pursues one idea in many guises. In any event, everybody tends to emphasize those aspects of life he finds the most interesting. Movie directors certainly do. What interests me are the consequences of a tragic moment—how the individual acts before a crucial act, or in an exceptional circumstance. That is everything.

"However, a situation must never limit a director. It must never be more than a point of departure."

"How do you work?" I asked. "Do you just shoot a scenario finalized by others, or do you collaborate on the cutting?"

"*The cutting!* I do it myself. And I plan the film. When a subject interests me, I also take part in the scripting. If the subject doesn't interest me, I am satisfied to do my job to everybody's best interest. When I work with a scriptwriter, he outlines the situations, develops the continuity, writes the dialogue. The shooting arrangements, and the cutting, I do myself. We have numerous conferences with the camerman, the set designer, and sometimes the actors. Each one knows what he has to do and understands the picture before starting to work it. A well-prepared film is shot quickly."

I then remarked that some of my colleagues were surprised that American directors remain seated during the shooting of a scene. Ford was astonished.

"What do you want them to do?" he asked. "They observe, they control, they direct. Everything is arranged beforehand. There are assistants who rehearse the actors, who set the scene. It is quickly done. There is nothing more to do than to integrate it into a whole, to make it flexible. If everything goes well there's no reason to be nervous."

"Do you determine what the camera shall see?"

"With the cameraman. It's done in advance. A good cameraman knows how a shot should be framed. I have always had excellent cameramen. Sometimes, when the composition is very detailed, I may take over, but usually a few suggestions are enough."

"You never improvise?"

"Oh certainly—but strictly within the predetermined framework. You can change cue, modify an incident, but the movement of the camera, like its position, is determined in advance. A director who changes his mind is a director who loses time. You should make your decisions before, not during the shooting."

"But if a movement of the camera proves impossible?"

"The director doesn't know his job. You should know in advance what is and isn't possible. I sometimes make a film in three weeks—after six months of preparation.

"What would you think of an architect who arrived at his building wondering where to put the staircase? You don't 'compose' a film on the set; you put a predesigned composition on film. It is wrong to liken a director to an author. He is more like an architect, if he is creative. An architect conceives his plans from given premises—the purpose of the building, its size, the terrain. If he is clever, he can do something creative within these limitations. Architects do not only create monuments and palaces. They also build houses. How many houses are there in Paris for every monument? It's the same with movies. When a director creates a little gem from time to time, an Arc de Triomphe, he certainly has the right to make some run-of-the-mill pictures."

"And your Arcs de Triomphe—your favorite films—what are they?"

"*Stagecoach; The Long Voyage Home; The Informer; Prisoner of Shark Island*. Also *The Sun Shines Bright*—it's a very simple story, the kind I like."

"And *My Darling Clementine?*"

"Yes, if you like. My children liked it a lot. But I—you know."

I then asked Ford about Henry Fonda, but I gathered from his manner there had been a falling out, so I did not pursue the subject. Ford's great favorite is John Wayne. I asked him about *The Quiet Man*. Did he like it?

"Yes, most certainly, especially because of the Irish setting. I shot it on my native heath. The actors were old family friends—they worked on it as pals. That is how I like to work."

"And *Mogambo?*"

"I don't know a thing about it. I haven't even seen it. But why should I have deprived myself of a trip to Air ca and the chance to make one more film? One does one's job. The film of really personal interest is the exception."

John Ford was kind enough to draw my attention to two mistakes in my book about him. I had said his daughter Barbara was married to John S. Nugent, the screenwriter who frequently collaborates with her father. She is married to the actor, Frank Curtiss. My mistake came from the fact that she calls herself by her maiden name—Barbara Nugent Ford.

And I neglected to mention the presence of Peter Lorre in *Four Men and a Prayer*.

I have come to the conclusion—although I did not verify this from Ford himself—that Ford was not born at Cape Elizabeth, near Portland, Maine, on February 1, 1895, as I say in my book, and as all the American biographies indicate. I think he must have been born four or five years before in Ireland, in the neighborhood in which *The Quiet Man* was shot. I think February 1, 1895, may have been the date of his parents' naturalization. But I say this parenthetically.

John Ford (1895–   ):
Filmography:
1917: The Tornado, The Trail of Hate, The Scrapper, The Soul Herder, Cheyenne's Pal, Straight Shooting, The Secret Man, A Marked Man, Bucking Broadway.
1918: Phantom Riders, Wild Women, Thieves' Gold, The Scarlet Drop, Hell Bent, Delirium, A Woman's Fool, Three Mounted Men.
1919: Roped, A Fight for Love, The Fighting Brothers, Bare Fists, The Gun Packers, Riders of Vengeance, The Last Outlaw, The Outcasts of Poker Flat, Ace of the Saddle, Rider of the Law, A Gun Fightin' Gentleman, Marked Men.
1920: The Prince of Avenue A, The Girl in Number 29, Hitchin' Posts, Just Pals.
1921: The Big Punch, The Freeze-Out, The Wallop, Desperate Trails, Action, Sure Fire, Jackie.
1922: Little Miss Smiles, Silver Wings, The Village Blacksmith.
1923: The Face on the Bar-Room Floor, Three Jumps Ahead, Cameo Kirby.
1924: Hoodman Blind, North of Hudson Bay, The Iron Horse, Hearts of Oak.
1925: Lightnin', Kentucky Pride, The Fighting Heart, Thank You.
1926: The Blue Eagle, The Shamrock Handicap, Three Bad Men.
1927: Upstream.
1928: Four Sons, Mother Machree, Napoleon's Barber, Riley the Cop.
1929: Strong Boy, Black Watch, Salute.
1930: Men Without Women, Born Reckless, Up the River.
1931: The Seas Beneath, The Brat, Arrowsmith.
1932: Air Mail, Flesh.
1933: Pilgrimage, Doctor Bull.
1934: The Lost Patrol, The World Moves On, Judge Priest.
1935: The Whole Town's Talking, The Informer, Steamboat Round the Bend.
1936: The Prisoner of Shark Island, Mary of Scotland, The Plough and the Stars.
1937: Wee Willie Winkie, The Hurricane.
1938: Four Men and a Prayer, Submarine Patrol.
1939: Stagecoach, Young Mr. Lincoln, Drums Along the Mohawk.
1940: The Grapes of Wrath, The Long Voyage Home.
1941: Tobacco Road, Sex Hygiene, How Green Was My Valley.
1942: The Battle of Midway.
1943: December 7th, We Sail at Midnight.
1945: They Were Expendable.
1946: My Darling Clementine.
1947: The Fugitive.
1948: Fort Apache, Three Godfathers.
1949: She Wore a Yellow Ribbon.
1950: When Willie Comes Marching Home, Wagonmaster, Rio Grande.
1951: This Is Korea.
1952: What Price Glory, The Quiet Man.
1953: The Sun Shines Bright, Mogambo.
1955: The Long Gray Line, Mister Roberts.
1956: The Searchers.
1957: The Wings of Eagles, The Rising of the Moon.

1958: The Last Hurrah.
1959: Gideon of Scotland Yard, Korea, The Horse Soldiers.
1960: Sergeant Rutledge.
1961: Two Rode Together, The Man Who Shot Liberty Valance.
1963: How the West Was Won, Donovan's Reef.
1964: Cheyenne Autumn.
1965: Young Cassidy (completed by Jack Cardiff).
1966: Seven Women.

Jean-Luc Godard

According to the latest unconfirmed reports, Jean-Luc Godard's latest film, La Femme Mariée, *already entered in this year's Venice Film Festival, has been completely suppressed by the French Government. The problem is not so much the artful nudity, but the director's allegedly subversive attitude toward the modern French married woman. This is not Godard's first brush with the censors. In his first feature film,* Breathless, *Godard displeased Generalissimo De Gaulle by linking a shot of De Gaulle following Eisenhower on the streets of the Champs-Elysees to a shot of Jean-Paul Belmondo chasing Jean Seberg along the sidewalk. This mocking linkage was never seen by American audiences, but technically it was worthy of the Eisenstein of* October. *Only just try to imagine Eisenstein mocking Stalin instead of Kerensky, and you get some idea of Godard's audacity.*

Godard's second film Le Petit Soldat, *described some of the intrigues of the Algerian War without resolving the issues. The story is told from the point of view of an uncommitted intellectual, who, in many ways, resembles Godard. The film was completely suppressed for two years. When you add provincial and international inhibitions over Godard's penchant for nudity, recurring controversies with other critics and film-makers, and wildly varying reactions from audiences, Godard would seem to be eternally embattled, trapped between the steady crossfire of his defenders and his detractors.*

It is strange, however, that film-makers who consider themselves far more engagé *or committed than Godard never seem to have as much trouble with the authorities.*

The explanation is simple. Most left-wing directors, despite an occasional exception like Francesco Rosi, prefer to deal in universals rather than specifics. Their concern is Man in general, not men in particular. The Bicycle Thief *is their model, and who would dare call such an abstractly humanistic tract Communist or even Marxist in orientation? After all, we are all brothers, and every man should have his own bicycle. It would be difficult even for Franco to argue the contrary. The fact remains that Jean-Luc Godard is the only French director who has ever indicated on the screen that* Humanité *is a Communist paper read and published in Paris. Not only that, but Godard's male protagonist in* Une Femme est une Femme *reads it casually while he is listening to the soccer match. Two policemen invade his apartment to investigate a bomb incident, snoop around a bit, and then sarcastically congratulate him for reading* Humanité *and advise him to continue.* Une Femme est une Femme *is ostensibly a frivolous musical comedy, but I cannot recall when an Italian film has shown me anyone reading a Communist paper on the screen. Nor have any left-wing French directors bothered to indicate that there is any such thing as a Communist party in France. Even Jean-Paul Sartre's* Dirty Hands *is set in an imaginary Iron Curtain country.*

This is one of the many fascinating paradoxes in the cinema of Jean-Luc Godard. Although Godard is the most self-conscious film-maker in the world, the most addicted to inside jokes for the initiates and to internal aesthetic judgments for himself, he is also in many ways the most realistic director of all time. Obviously, however, to call Godard realistic is to re-examine what we mean by realism, a term which has acquired a pejorative connotation over the years because of its association with too many dull movies. We are all familiar with some of the mannerisms of realism. No background music. Unprofessional actors. Bad sound recording. An emphasis on exteriors. A concern with the social problems of the lower classes. Black and white, small screen and oodles of montage. Above all, realistic movies must pretend not to be movies at all, but impersonal documents of reality. Godard has broken most of these rules at one time or another. His characters are liable to look at the audience (and the camera) from time to time just to remind us that we are watching a staged illusion. Godard's Galatea, Anna Karina, is most guilty of this mannerism, and we are thus un-

able to avoid the conclusion that Godard is making love with his camera. Yet, as Godard would argue, what could be more realistic than the visual assertion that a movie is a movie? And more modern as well. After all, why should Godard be condemned for allowing Karina to look confidentially at the audience when Tony Richardson is praised for doing the same thing with Albert Finney and Joyce Redmon in Tom Jones, not to mention Jules Dassin's indulgence of Melina Mercouri in Topkapi? The irony is that Godard did it first and took the blame, only to see imitators Richardson and Dassin take all the credit.

However, looking at the camera is not the sole index of Godard's realism. What Godard acknowledges in every foot of film he shows is his own point of view and moral responsibility. Look, he says. This film did not just happen. I made it happen, and I made it happen here and now. Each of my films is an entry in my diary, the diary of an artist, a critic and a journalist. Each film, no matter how fictional and far-fetched the plot, is a documentary on my state of mind at the time I made the film. In a sense, this has always been true, but it is Godard's contention that film-making is now entering a new era of self-awareness. For the first time, there are film-makers with a sense of film history, and as audiences shrink, they become more specialized and sophisticated. Godard, unlike Truffaut, is not hedging his bets with anything resembling the conventionally well-made film. His films are searching for a new audience, an audience willing to break with the comfortably illusionist past.

Although Godard has always admired American movies, he has never imitated their pragmatic virtues. He has always been much closer to Rossellini, for example, than to Hitchcock. Like Renoir, Godard will always sacrifice form to truth. He admires the classical confidence of the American movie storytellers, but he is too racked by intellectual self-questioning to follow in their footsteps. This is what makes his films so modern, and I insist, so realistic. He is speaking to a new generation of moviegoers, and it is significant that most of his admirers grew up in the Fifties when the idealistic momentum of the Depression and World War II had largely spent its force. The American and European critical establishment still believes in the moral conventions and cliches of the Thirties and Forties, *and, quite logically, has singled out Godard as its most dangerous antagonist. The cinema, allegedly the most modern of the arts, has lagged far behind the other arts in its naive conceptions of form, content and the social benefits of mass communication. Consequently, Godard's allegedly revolutionary position is comparable to the positions of Stravinsky, Picasso, Joyce and Eliot. It is not that Godard is superior to classical masters like Renoir and Dreyer any more than Stravinsky is superior to Mozart or Picasso to Rembrandt or Beckett to Shakespeare, but that Godard is more symptomatic and representative of our time than his would-be neo-classical colleagues.*

Godard's career has undeniably been shaped to some extent by necessity. If he had had the chance, he would have preferred to make lavish technicolor films with Kim Novak and Tony Curtis, but dire economies have driven him to the very edge of the 16 millimeter abyss. He has made do, however, with eight features and four shorts in less than five years. He has even managed to work twice with wide-screen and color (A Woman Is a Woman *and* Contempt). *He has rendered the reality not only of Paris* (Breathless, A Woman Is a Woman, My Life to Live, Band of Outsiders, La Femme Mariée), *but of Switzerland* (The Little Soldier) *and Italy* (Contempt). *The photography of Coutard and the musical scores of Legrand and Delerue have contributed to the stylistic consistency of Godard's career, and the faces of Jean Seberg, Anna Karina, Brigitte Bardot and Macha Meril constitute a uniquely Godardian gallery. Nevertheless, Godard's cinema is defined mainly by the extraordinary treatment of reality as a volatile mixture of the subjective and the objective, fact and fiction, logic and improbability, plausibility and actuality. Godard's characters often read the newspapers aloud on the screen, and what they read from the authentic journalism of our time is infinitely more bizarre than anything Godard could invent. Truth is stranger than fiction, and history is hysterical. This is Godard's narrative aesthetic, and he accepts full responsibility for it. He is not saying that this is life, but that it is life as it is filtered through the camera. To accept one's responsibility as a director is to deny an impersonal objectivity to the camera. Every nuance of technique is a personal expression since it is Godard himself who once said that tracking was a moral* statement. This acceptance of responsibility is the ultimate source of Godard's personal brand of realism. By standing between us and his characters, Godard forces us once and for all to accept the director as a creative force. For those of us who realize that films do not materialize miraculously on the screen, Godard becomes the foremost realist of the modern cinema.

Some confusion has been caused by erroneous assumptions about Godard's attachment to the ethos of Hollywood. Godard is a hopelessly European director who admires American movies, but can only comment on them without ever capturing the directness of Hollywood decoupage. Breathless renders the gestures of the gangster movie without providing the gestation of motivations. Belmondo is not Bogart, but a stylistic elaboration of Bogart, replacing American necessity with French nihilism. The hero of Le Petit Soldat is too aesthetically political to suggest any transposition to the American landscape. The clumsiness with which the rival agents of the Arab FLN and the ultra-French OAS dispose of each other reflects the chasm Godard senses between the theoretical and the practical. On the physical level, Godard seems to assert, European reflection is no substitute for American reflexes, but Godard himself is irrevocably a European, and like all Swiss intellectuals, an instinctive Bohemian.

A Woman Is a Woman pays its homage to the American musical, but Godard's token choreography is about as graceful as Donald Duck attempting Swan Lake. Out of the six left feet of Karina, Belmondo and Brialy, Godard almost achieves a charming effect of anti-rhythm. A Woman Is a Woman reflects the admiration of a director who can't dance for those elfin sprites who can. It is the director's admiration reflected in spasmodic twitches of melodiousness which makes A Woman Is a Woman such a beautiful movie. With My Life to Live, Godard passes irrevocably into that European cinema which can never return to the classical past. He is now not commenting on the Monogram quickie or the Metro musical, but on the sublime art of Carl Dreyer. In a series of twelve tableaux, Godard dissects a human soul in terms of the full range of cinematic vocabulary. Godard alienates once and for all those of his American admirers who misinterpreted Breathless as a serious tract on juvenile delinquency.

Les Carabiniers *is too rigorously intellectual in its conception even for Europeans, and too historically erudite even for the most fanatical films buffs. Godard moves here into the cinema of the absurd with a form of storytelling, cluttered frame by cluttered frame, which seems unconscionably primitive. He ridicules both war and the glossy illusionism of anti-war movies. There is one brilliantly comic moment when a soldier sees his first movie, and keeps trying to invade the screen where a nude girl is bathing. First, he keeps shifting from one side of the auditorium to the other to get a better camera viewpoint. (The impiety of innocence.) Finally, he rushes up to the screen to assault it only to find that the illusion has vanished.*

No other film has so aptly rendered the banality of war, and yet Les Carabiniers *seems wilfully inaccessible to audiences. Godard has labored mightily to truncate the emotions of both war and pacifism so that the entire spectacle will be devoid of facile moralizing. This degree of intellectual integrity could be commercially fatal.*

Contempt *may go down in history as the classical contretemps of international co-production. Delerue's curious score reflects the peculiar tension in the film caused by an intellectual austerity in the midst of scenic luxuriance. Delerue's score resembles a Bach melody orchestrated by Stokowsky, and Coutard's color photography intoxicates a spare scenario in which human emotions break under the weight of the words needed to express them. Brigitte Bardot, Fritz Lang, Jack Palance and Michel Piccoli float through a deterministic dream in which the unity of the world of Homer, like that of Lang, disintegrates before our eyes. The marriage of Bardot and Piccoli dissolves in a climactic tracking scene of classical interiors and robes reducing the resiliency of living flesh. By merely expressing the idea of contempt, Bardot comes to feel the emotion. Modern relationships, Godard argues, are destroyed by the words we use to define them. The act of definition becomes the act of dissolution. By contrast, the art of a Homer or a Lang consists of a faith in the world as it appears. Godard appears in the film as Lang's assistant, but it is clear nevertheless that Godard agrees with Moravia on the dissolution of modern personality through excessive analysis. It is to Godard's credit in* Contempt *that he realizes he would like to be an integral artist like Lang, but* *that he cannot be anything but what he is, the analytical conscience of the modern cinema.**

Q. Jean-Luc Godard, you came to the cinema by way of film criticism. What do you owe to this background?

A. All of us at *Cahiers* considered ourselves as future directors. Frequenting film societies and the Cinematheque, we were already thinking in strictly cinematic terms. For us, it meant working at cinema, for between writing and shooting there is a quantitative difference—not a qualitative one. The only critic who was one completely was André Bazin. The others—Sadoul, Balazs or Pasinetti—are historians or sociologists, not critics.

While I was a critic, I considered myself already a cineaste. Today I still consider myself a critic, and, in a sense, I am one more than before. Instead of writing a critique I direct a film. I consider myself an essayist; I do essays in the form of novels and novels in the form of essays: simply, I film them instead of writing them. If the cinema were to disappear, I'd go back to pencil and paper. For me, the continuity of all the different forms of expression is very important. It all makes one block. The thing to know is how to approach this block from the site most appropriate to you.

I think, too, that it's very possible for a person to become a cineaste without first being a critic. It happened that, for us, it went as I said, but it's not a rule. Rivette and Rohmer made films in 16mm. But if criticism was the first echelon of a vocation, it was not so much a means. It is said: they availed themselves of criticism. No—we were thinking cinema and, at a certain moment, we felt the need to deepen that thought.

Criticism taught us to love Rouch and Eisenstein at the same time. To criticism we owe not excluding one aspect of the cinema in the name of another aspect of the cinema.

* *The Editor's article on Jean-Luc Godard appeared originally in* NY Film Bulletin, *No. 46, 1964.*

The following interviews with Godard appeared in NY Film Bulletin, *No. 46, 1964. The first interview appeared originally in* Cahiers du Cinema, *No. 138, and was translated by Rose Kaplin for inclusion in* NY Film Bulletin. *The second interview appeared originally in* NY Film Bulletin *and was conducted by Warren Sonbert and transcribed by Gretchen Weinberg.*

We owe it also the possibility of making films with more distance and of knowing that if such and such a thing has already been done it is useless to do it again. A young writer writing today knows that Moliere and Shakespeare exist. We are the first cineastes to know that Griffith exists. Even Carne, Delluc, or Rene Clair, when they made their first films, had no true critical or historical formation. Even Renoir had very little. (It *is* true that he had genius.)

Q. This cultural basis exists only in a fraction of the new wave.

A. Yes, in those from *Cahiers,* but for me that fraction is the whole thing. There is the group from *Cahiers* (and also Astruc, Kast—and Leenhart, who are somewhat apart) to which must be added what we might call the Left Bank Group: Resnais, Colpi, Varda, Marker. Also Demy. These had their own cultural basis, but there are not thirty-six others. *Cahiers* was the nucleus.

They say that now we can no longer write about our colleagues. Obviously, it has become difficult to have coffee with someone if, that afternoon, you have to write that he's made an idiotic film, but what has always differentiated us from others is that we take a stand for a criticism of praise: we speak of a film if we like it. If we don't like it, we exempt ourselves from breaking its back. All one has to do is hold to this principle.

Q. Your critical attitude seems to contradict the idea of improvisation which is attached to your name.

A. I improvise, without doubt, but with material that dates from way back. One gathers, over the years, piles of things and then suddenly puts them in what one is doing. My first shorts had a lot of preparation and were shot very quickly. *Breathless* was started in this way. I had written the first scene (Jean Seberg on the Champs Elysees) and, for the rest, I had an enormous amount of notes corresponding to each scene. I said to myself, this is very distracting. I stopped everything. Then I reflected: in one day, if one knows what one is doing, one should be able to shoot a dozen sequences. Only, instead of having the material for a long time, I'll get it just before. When one knows where he is going, this must be possible. This is not improvisation, it's decision-making at the last minute. Obviously, you have to have and maintain a view of the ensemble; you can modify a certain part of it, but after the shooting starts keep the changes to a minimum—otherwise it's catastrophic.

I read in *Sight and Sound* that I was improvising in the Actors' Studio style, with actors to whom one says: you are such and such, take it from there. But Belmondo's dialogue was never invented by him. It was written: only, the actors didn't learn it—the film was shot silent and I whispered the cues.

Q. When you started the film, what did it represent for you?

A. Our first films were purely films by cinephiles. One may avail oneself of something already seen in the cinema in order to make deliberate references. This was the case for me. Actually, I was reasoning according to purely cinematographic attitudes. I worked out certain images, schemes with relation to others I knew from Preminger, Cukor, etc. . . . In any case Jean Seberg's character is a follow-up of the one in *Bonjour Tristesse*. I could have taken the last frame of that and linked it with a title: "three years later." . . . This is to reconcile my taste for quotation, which I have always kept. Why reproach us for it? People, in life, quote what pleases them. We have therefore the right to quote what pleases us. I show people "quoting"—only I arrange it so that the quote pleases me. In the notes I keep of what might be useful to me in a film I also put a sentence from Dostoievsky, if I like it. Why be constrained? If you want to say something, there is only one solution: say it.

Moreover, the genre of *Breathless* was such that all was permitted, that was its nature. Whatever people might do —all this could be integrated into the film. This was even my point of departure. I said to myself: there has already been Bresson, we just had *Hiroshima*, a certain kind of cinema has just ended—well, then, let's put the final period to it: let's show that anything goes. What I wanted to do was to depart from the conventional story and remake, but differently, everything that had already been done in the cinema. I also wanted to give the impression of just finding or experiencing the processes of cinema for the first time. The iris-shot showed that it was permissible to return to the sources of cinema, and the linking-shot came along, by itself, as if one had just invented it. If there weren't other processes, this was in reaction to a certain cinema, but this doesn't have to be a rule. There are films where they are necessary: from time to time one could do more with them.

What is hardest on me is the ending. Is the hero going to die? At first, I was thinking of doing the opposite of, for example, *The Killing*. The gangster would succeed and leave for Italy with his money. But this would have been a very conventional anti-convention, like having Nana succeed in *My Life to Live*. I finally told myself that since, after all, all my avowed ambitions were to make a normal gangster film I couldn't systematically contradict the genre: the guy had to die. If the descendants of Atreus don't massacre each other any more, they are no longer descendants of Atreus.

But improvisation is fatiguing. I am always telling myself: this is the last time! It's not possible any more! It's too fatiguing to go to sleep every night asking oneself, "What am I going to do tomorrow morning?" It's like writing an article at twenty-to-twelve at a cafe table when it has to be delivered to the paper at noon. What is curious is that one always arrives at writing it, but working like this month after month is killing. At the same time there is a certain amount of premeditation. You say to yourself that if you are honest and sincere and in a corner and have to do something, the result will necessarily be honest and sincere.

Only, you never do exactly what you believe you're doing. Sometimes you even arrive at the exact opposite. This is true for me, in any case, but at the same time I lay claim to everything I've done. I realized, at a certain point, that *Breathless* was not at all what I believed it to be. I believed I'd made a realistic film and it wasn't that at all. First of all, I didn't possess sufficient technical skill, then I discovered that I wasn't made for this genre of film. There are also a great number of things I'd like to do and don't do. For example, I'd like to be like Fritz Lang and have frames which are extraordinary in themselves, but I don't arrive at that. So I do something else. I like *Breathless* enormously—for a certain period I was ashamed of it, but now I place it where it belongs: with *"Alice in Wonderland."* I thought it was *Scarface*.

Breathless is a story, not a subject. A subject is something simple and vast about which one can make a resume in twenty seconds: revenge, pleasure . . . a story takes twenty minutes to recapitulate. *The Little Soldier* has a subject: a young man is confused, realizes it and tries to

211

find clarity. In *A Woman Is a Woman* a girl wants a baby at any cost and right away. In *Breathless*, I was looking for a subject all during the shooting; finally I became interested in Belmondo. I saw him as a sort of facade which it was necessary to film in order to know what was behind it. Seberg, on the contrary, was an actress whom I wanted to make do many little things that pleased me—this came from the cinephile side I no longer have.

Q. How do you think of actors now?

A. My position with regard to them has always been somewhat like the interviewer and the interviewed—I run behind someone and ask him something. At the same time it is I who have organized the race.

Q. What led you to The Little Soldier?

A. I wanted to catch up with the realism I had missed in *Breathless*; the concrete. The film takes off from an old idea: I wanted to speak of brainwashing. One would say to a prisoner, "If it takes 20 minutes or 20 years, we always make someone say something." The happenings in Algeria made me replace brainwashing with torture, which had become the big question. My prisoner is someone who is asked to do something he doesn't want to do; simply doesn't want to do it, and he resists on principle. This is liberty as I see it: from a practical point of view. To be free is to be able to do what pleases you when it pleases you.

The film is witness to an epoch. People speak of politics but it is not *politically* oriented. My style of commitment was to say to myself: they reproach the *new wave* for showing nothing but people in beds—I'm going to show some who are politically involved and have no time to go to bed. Well, politics was Algeria. But I had to show that from the angle I knew and in the way I felt it. If Kyron or the people from *L'Observateur* wanted it to be spoken of otherwise, very well—all they had to do was to go with a camera to the F.L.N. If Dupont wanted another point of view he had only to film Algiers from the point of view of the paratroopers. It's a shame about the things that are never done. Me—I spoke of the things that concerned me insofar as I was a Parisian in 1960, a member of no party. What concerned me was the problem of war and its moral repercussions. Therefore I showed a guy who poses himself a great many problems. He doesn't know how to resolve them, but posing them, even with confusion, is already an attempt. It is more valuable perhaps to pose questions than to refuse to question or to believe oneself capable of resolving everything.

Q. How did the experience of Breathless *serve you?*

A. It served me, but I had a great deal of trouble shooting *The Little Soldier.* We could have shot it in two weeks. With stops, it took us two months. I reflected; I hesitated. Quite the opposite of *Breathless,* I couldn't say everything. I could only say certain things, but which ones? Finally, it was already something to know what not to say—by elimination what remained was what had to be said.

Also I came back to improvisation. Well, after *The Little Soldier,* I said to myself: it's finished! Therefore I started from a very preconceived scenario: *A Woman Is a Woman.* But there was more improvisation. For *Breathless,* I was staying up nights, writing, all during the shooting; for *The Little Soldier*—in the morning; and with *A Woman Is a Woman* I was writing in the studio while the actors were making up. But once more, you only hit upon the things you've thought of for a long time. In *My Life to Live* I worked out the scene of the *Oval Portrait* that morning but I knew the story. At the moment I hit upon it I had forgotten it, I said to myself: I'll use that. But I was at a point where in any case I would have found something. If the solution hadn't come then it would have the next day.

With me it's a method: since I make films on small budgets, I can ask the producer for five weeks knowing that there will be about two weeks of actual shooting. The big difficulty is that I have to have people at my disposal all the time. Sometimes they have to wait an entire day before knowing what I can make them do. I have to ask them not to leave the place of shooting, we might start working again any minute. They suffer for it. That's why anyone who works with me is always well paid. The actors suffer, from another point of view: an actor likes to have the impression of being in control of his character, even if it's not true, and with me they rarely get that impression. What is terrible is that it is very difficult to do in the cinema what the painter does naturally: he stops, steps back, is disheartened, starts again, modifies . . . all goes well.

But this method is not valuable for everyone. There are two major classes of cineastes. In the Eisenstein-Hitchcock group, there are those who write out their film in the most complete fashion possible. They know what they want,

213

they have everything in their heads, they put everything down on paper. The shooting is only a practical application, a construction of some sort resembling as much as possible what was imagined. Resnais is in this category, and Demy. The others, in the Rouch class, don't have a very clear idea of what they're going to do and they are searching. The film is this search. They know that they're going to arrive somewhere, and they have the means for that, but where exactly? The first group makes circle-films, the others—films in a straight line. Renoir is one of the rare people who do both together; this is what makes his charm.

Rossellini is still another thing. He is the only one who has an exact vision and sees things as a totality. He films them, therefore, in the only way possible. No one can film one of Rossellini's scenarios. His vision of the world is so exact that his way of seeing detail, formal or not, is exact also. With him, a frame is beautiful because it is correct; with most other people, a frame becomes right because it is beautiful. They try to construct an extraordinary thing, and in relation to how effective it becomes, we see that there were reasons for doing it. Rossellini, however, does things he had reasons for doing in the first place. It is beautiful because it is.

Beauty and the splendor of truth are two poles. There are cineastes who seek truth, and if they find it, it will necessarily be beautiful. We find these two poles in the documentary and in fiction. Certain people start with a documentary and arrive at fiction, like Flaherty who ended by making very carefully composed films; others start with fiction and arrive at the documentary: Eisenstein, coming from montage, finished by making *Que Viva Mexico.*

The cinema is the only art which, as Cocteau says (in *Orpheus,* I believe) "films death at work." The person one films is growing older and will die. We film, therefore, a moment when death is working. Painting is immobile; the cinema is interesting because it seizes life and the mortal aspect of life.

Q. And you—from which pole do you start?

A. I believe I start more from the documentary, in order to give truth to fiction. That's why I've always worked with excellent, professional actors—without them, my films would not be as good.

I am also interested in the theatrical aspect. In *The Little Soldier,* when I was seeking to arrive at the concrete, I saw that the closer I drew to the concrete the more theatrical my work became. *My Life to Live* is both very concrete and very theatrical. I would like to film a play by Sacha Guitry; I would like to film "Six Characters in Search of an Author" to show, cinematically, what theatre is. By being a realist one discovers the theatre, and by being theatrical. . . . As in *The Golden Coach:* behind the theatre is life and behind life, the theatre. My point of departure was the imaginary and I discovered the real; but, behind the real there was the imaginary.

According to Truffaut, the cinema consists of the spectacle (Melies) and research (Lumiere). If I analyze myself today I see that I have always wanted, basically, to make a research film in spectacle form. The documentary side is this: a man is in such and such a situation. The spectacle side comes from making the man a gangster or a secret agent. The spectacle side comes, in *A Woman Is a Woman,* out of the fact that the woman is a comedienne; in *My Life to Live,* she is a prostitute.

The producers say: Godard—he talks about Joyce, metaphysics, or painting, but he will always have with him a commercial side. I don't say this at all—I don't see two things, I only see one.

Q. How do you rank A Woman Is a Woman *in your work?*

A. As with *Jules and Jim* for Truffaut, it is my first real film.

Q. Is this the film that resembles you most?

A. I don't believe so, but it's the film I love the most. It's like *Lady Windermere's Fan* for Preminger: one's sick children are the most loved.

For me, the film also represents the discovery of color and direct sound, since my other films were post-synchronized. The subject, like that of my two previous films, is how a character resolves a certain situation. But I conceived this subject as the interior of a neo-realist musical. This is an absolute contradiction, but it is exactly that which interested me in the film. An error, perhaps, but a seductive error. And it fit the subject well, since we are showing a woman who wants a baby in an absurd manner when it's the most natural thing in the world. But the film is not a musical comedy. It's the *idea* of the musical comedy.

Moreover, I hesitated for a long time about doing scenes that were truly musical. Finally, I preferred to suggest the idea that the characters are singing, thanks to the utilization of music while having them speak normally. Nevertheless, the musical comedy is dead. *Adieu Philippine,* in a certain way, is also a musical comedy, but the genre itself is dead. Even for the Americans, there's no longer any sense in doing re-makes of *Singin' in the Rain.* Something else is necessary. This is also what my film is saying: it is nostalgia for the musical comedy, as *The Little Soldier* is nostalgia for the Spanish Civil War.

What people must not have liked was the discontinuity, the changes of rhythm or the breaks in tone. Perhaps also the theatrical aspect, *cinema dell'arte.* The people in the film play and bow at the same time; they know and we know that they are playing, that they are laughing and, at the same time, that they are crying. In sum, it's an exhibition, but that's what I wanted to do. The characters are always playing to the camera: it's a parade. I wanted people to be able to cry for Columbine, even when she's on parade. In *My Life to Live,* on the contrary, we should have the impression that the people are fleeing the camera.

I also discovered 'scope with *A Woman Is a Woman.* I believe that that's a normal format and that 1.33 is an arbitrary ratio. You can shoot everything in 'scope. Not in 1.33—but it is extraordinary. 1.66 is nothing at all. I don't like intermediate ratios. I hesitated about 'scope for *My Life to Live,* then I didn't use it—it's too sentimental as a ratio. 1.33 is harder, more severe. On the other hand, I regret not having used 'scope for *Breathless.* That's my only regret. *The Little Soldier* is in the right ratio. But these things can be seen more clearly after the fact. These are the surprises and I like being surprised. If you know in advance exactly what you're going to do, it's no longer worth the trouble of doing it. If a spectacle is all written out, what's the point of filming it? What's the use of cinema, if it follows literature? When I write a scenario, I also want to put everything on paper but I don't arrive at it. I am not a writer. To make a film is to superimpose three operations: thinking, shooting, editing. Everything can't be in the scenario; or if it is—if people cry or laugh when they read it, the only thing to be done is to print it and sell it in a bookstore.

What bores me is that when you sign with a producer he wants to know what you're signing for. A producer likes to engage a director about whom he thinks that when he finishes his film it will look like the idea he started out with.

Q. Is this what has led you to refuse certain projects?

A. The Hakim brothers proposed that I do *Eva*. To start with, I didn't like the actors they had in mind. I wanted Richard Burton. They thought it was a good idea. They said, "We'll telephone him." I said, "There's the telephone." They said, "Oh, yes—but you know—maybe he's not home!" So I understood that they weren't willing. For the female lead, I saw someone like the Rita Hayworth of five or six years ago. In any case, I wanted only American actors. Film people, if they're not American, I don't know what to do with them. If a Frenchman says, "I am a scenarist," what does that mean? That doesn't exist. Whereas for an American if it doesn't exist it doesn't matter: what is "American" has a mythical side that makes something exist.

Eva caused me pain, also, because it was too much like *La Chienne*. And there was no subject. I did, however, propose this: the story of a guy who is approached by a producer to write a scenario about a woman in order to prove that he is really a writer. This becomes the story of a man who tries to write about a woman but does not succeed. Or maybe he does, I don't know. In any case, what happens is what it is necessary to tell about. I wanted to show the poem he writes and the analysis of the poem. For example, he writes: "I went out; the weather was fine; I met her; she had blue eyes." Then, he asks himself why he wrote that. Finally, I think he doesn't arrive at anything . . . it's a little like the story of the end of Porthos.

The producers didn't want it. The Hakim brothers aren't stupid, but, like all the big post-war producers, they no longer knew what to do. Before, a producer knew what genre of films he ought to do. There were three or four directions and each producer had his own. Braunberger already existed and he knew his direction and it was different from the others. Today, there are ten thousand directions. Braunberger isn't lost, for he always has his own little way, and those who make films like *Ben Hur*—they, too, always have their own way. But eighty per cent of the producers are completely lost. At one time they could say, "I'm going to do a film with Duvivier," but today? They can't succeed with either big films or little intellectual films. Everything is mixed up.

So they say to themselves, "There's Antonioni. Two

217

hundred thousand people went to see *La Notte* . . . let's do a film with him." What loses them is that they don't really know why they're doing it. Losey, and Antonioni, when utilized in this fashion and at the wrong moment, no longer bring in anything at all. After following a certain path in cinema for forty years, these people can't adapt. In my contract with the Hakim brothers it was specified that they could, if they so judged, re-edit the film in accordance with their ideas. I was disillusioned. They said to me, "Duvivier, Carne, all the others have this kind of contract."

They no longer know. Also, the public baffles them. At one time, they didn't know that they knew nothing. Today they know it. But I shouldn't speak too negatively about producers, because the exhibitors and distributors are much worse. The producers, basically, are like us: these are people who don't have money and who need to make films. They're on the same side we are. They want to work without anyone's interference and they are, like us, against censorship. The distributors and exhibitors are not in love with what they're doing. I have never seen a producer who didn't have a love for his metier. Compared to an exhibitor, the worst producer is a poet. Mad, imbecilic, innocent or stupid—they are sympathetic. They put their money on things that are uncertain and, often, follow their own pleasure. A producer is often a guy who buys a book and suddenly wants to build a whole production on it. It might or might not go well, but he must push on. The annoying part is that, since most of the time he doesn't have good taste, he buys worthless books. But, whatever he may be, he is sympathetic. And he works. Distributors and exhibitors are functionaries and that's what is terrible. The functionary's ideal is this: that every day at the same hour a film should make the same number of spectators come in.

The public is neither stupid nor intelligent. No one knows what it is. It is sometimes surprising and generally deceiving. You can't count on it. And in a sense that's good. In any case, it's changing. The old average-cinema-public has become the television public. When producers speak about the public I say to them, "I know what it is, because I go to the movies and pay for my seat; and you —you never go anywhere—you don't know what's happening."

Q. Well, let's talk about My Life to Live. *Was that hard or easy to make?*

A. This film was at the same time very simple and . . . it was as if it were necessary to extract the images from the night, as if they were at the bottom of a pit and had to be attracted to the light. When I extricated the frame, I said to myself, "Everything is there, nothing to retouch, but I mustn't make a mistake about what I'm bringing out, about what should be brought out first." I didn't want to search for effects. I had to risk each stroke. In *A Woman Is a Woman*, it was different. I wanted to obtain certain things; for example, the theatrical aspect. This aspect, I had it in *My Life to Live* but without saying to myself that I must do *this* or *that* to get it. I knew, however, that I would have it. It was a little like *theatre-verite*.

This way of getting shots does away with editing. All you have to do is put them end to end. The rushes seen by the crew are pretty close to what the public saw. Not only that. I shot the scenes in order. Neither was there any mixing. The film is a series of blocks. It is sufficient to make the stones and place them one after the other, side by side. The whole thing is to pick up good stones in the first place. The ideal, for me, is to obtain right away what will work—and without retouches. If they are necessary, it falls short of the mark. The immediate is chance. At the same time it is definitive. What I want is the definitive by chance.

I obtain a theatrical realism. The theatre is also a block which cannot be retouched. Realism, in any case, is never exactly the truth and the realism of the cinema is obligatorily faked. I am close to the theatre also by my use of words: in my film you have to listen to the people talking, so much the more because they are often seen from behind and one isn't distracted by the faces. The sound is as realistic as possible. It makes me think of the first talkies. I have always loved the sound of those films; they had a great truth, for it was the first time one heard people speaking.

In a general way, we are coming back now to more authentic sound and dialogue. People have made use of this to reproach us for our grossness. In *Monkey in Winter* the word *merde* occurs dozens of times; in *Les Bonnes Femmes,* two or three times—but there people call it grossness since Audiard remains conventional. If a girl says to a boy, "Poor bastard, I detest you" in life, that hurts. Thus, in the cinema, it should hurt as much as in life. That's what people don't accept. That's why they refused *Les Bonnes Femmes,* which told the truth and had an effect on them. There we really had a case of a theatre full of people who saw themselves in a mirror.

Q. When you made My Life to Live, what was your point of departure?

A. I didn't know exactly what I was going to do. I prefer searching for something I don't know to doing well something I already know. In fact the film was realized right off the bat, as if I were carried away. *My Life to Live* was the equilibrium that makes one suddenly feel good about life, for an hour, a day, or a week. Anna, who is in 60% of the film, was a little unhappy never knowing much in advance what she would have to do. But she was so sincere in her will to act for something that it is finally that sincerity which acted. For my part, without knowing exactly what I was going to do, I was so sincere in my desire to make the film that, the two of us together, we succeeded. I like very much to change actors, but, with her, working represents something else. I believe it is the first time that she is absolutely conscious of her means and is utilizing them. Thus, the interrogation scene in *The Little Soldier* is made in the Rouch way: she didn't know in advance the questions I would ask her. Here, in *My Life to Live,* she acted with a text as if she didn't know the questions. Finally one arrives at spontaneity and naturalness.

The film was made in a special state, and Anna is not the only one to have given the best of herself. Coutard achieved his best photography. What astonishes me, on seeing the film again, is that it seems to be the most composed of those I've made when it really wasn't. I took raw material, perfectly round pebbles which I placed one next to the other, and it's organized. And then—this strikes me now—I had a habit of paying attention to the colors of things, even in black and white. In this case—no; what was black was black and what was white was white. And the shooting was done with people wearing their own clothes, except Anna for whom we bought a skirt and a jersey.

Q. Why the division into twelve tableaux?

A. Why twelve? I don't know, but as for the tableaux themselves—that accentuates the theatrical aspect, the Brechtian side. I wanted the idea of "the adventures of Miss Nana Untel." The end of the film, that too is very theatrical: the last tableau had to be more theatrical than all the others. Also, this division corresponds to the exterior side of things, to permit me to show the sentiment of the inside to a greater extent, the exact opposite of *Pickpocket* in which the character is seen from inside. How to render the inside? Well, that's it—by wisely staying outside.

In any case, something happens. This is why Antonioni's cinema, with its aspect of non-communication, is not mine. Rossellini said to me that I grazed Antonioni's sin in passing but that I correctly avoided it. I think that with this kind of problem it is sufficient to be of good faith. To say that the more you look at someone the less you understand him—I believe that that's false. But obviously, if you look at people too much you end by asking yourself what's the use; that's inevitable. If you look at a wall for ten hours in a row you end up by posing it questions—when it's a wall. One creates useless problems for oneself. This is another reason for the film's being a series of sketches: it is necessary to let people live their lives, not look at them for too long, or else you'll end by no longer understanding anything about them.

Q. One of your projects is The Riflemen. *Will you make the film in color?*

A. Yes, but what color exactly? It's all the same to me. I would be happy to obtain the color of Bunuel's *Robinson Crusoe* or of Rossellini's *Jeanne d'Arc*. And I shall make the film in 16mm. Blown up to 35mm., the image will be somewhat washed out but I see nothing wrong with that. Maybe that'll even make it better. Shooting in 16mm. is in the spirit of this film. The big Mitchell is another spirit. For *My Life to Live* I held absolutely to a big camera. If there had been a bigger one than the Mitchell I'd have taken it. I very much like the shape of the Mitchell: it really looks like a camera. I was very unhappy doing *Sloth* because the producer had everyone using a Debrie. This is a square camera which doesn't have the camera spirit, not at all. Maybe it's foolish but I attach importance to these things.

Also, I am going to do a sketch. A man goes out on the street, everything seems normal, but two or three little details reveal to him that people, his fiancee, are no longer reasoning normally. He discovers for example that a cafe is no longer called a cafe. And if his fiancee doesn't come to a rendezvous, it's not that she doesn't love him any more—it's simply that she reasons in a different way. They no longer have the same logic. One day he reads a newspaper and finds out that there has been an atomic explosion somewhere; then he tells himself that he is without doubt the only person on earth who is reasoning normally. Things are the same, but everything is different. It's anti-Rossellini, but that's the way it is.

The Riflemen would be more like the old Rossellini, when he made *La Machine a Tuer Les Mechants* and *Ou Est La Liberte?* The scenario is so strong that all I have to do is film it without posing problems for myself. The solutions will impose themselves. It's the story of two peasants who see riflemen arrive. They are not there to arrest them but to bring them a letter from the king. In fact it's an order of mobilization. They are annoyed but the riflemen say to them, "War is great; you can do anything, have everything!" They want to know what. Leave a restaurant without paying? Of course! And they continue to ask questions, enumerating things from the most trifling larcenies to the greatest atrocities. May one massacre children? Of course! Steal old men's watches? Why yes! Break people's glasses? That too! Burn women? Obviously! When the enumeration is finished, they leave for the war. The film will be nasty, because each time an idea emerges from their stupidity it is a wicked idea.

They write to their wives: "We have taken the Arc de Triomphe, the Lido, the Pyramids, raped lots of women and burned things; everything is going well!" At the end they come home, happy but mutilated, with a small valise, saying, "We have brought back all the treasures of the world." And they take out heaps of post cards representing the monuments of every land: for them, this is as much as having titles to the property; they believe that as soon as the war ends they will be given all of it. The riflemen say to them, "When you hear shouts and noises in the valley, that will mean the war is over and that the king is coming to reward everyone; go there and you will have everything." Some time later, they hear cries and explosions—they go there, but there is shooting (the scenes are analogous to those of the Liberation). The king has not won the war, but he has signed a peace treaty with the enemy and those who have fought for him are considered war criminals. Instead of gaining riches, the two peasants are shot. Everything will be very realistic, in a purely theatrical perspective—we will see war scenes, commando style, as in Fuller's films, with some newsreel footage. But now that I've told all about it I'm suddenly less anxious to do it.

Q. You also want to do Ubu Roi.

A. Yes, in somewhat the same style. Ubu, for cinema, should be very gangsterish—with raincoat and soft hat—and we should see Ubu and his clique get in their cars and go to cafes.

What annoys me is that the tone of Ubu already exists in *Shoot the Piano Player* and the realistic side was very successful, not to speak of the text, which was very fine. The film, from this point of view, was extraordinary.

I should also like to shoot *Pour Lucrece* by Giraudoux. There I will have theatre in a pure state, for I'd like to specifically record a text, record the voices that speak it. I should also like to make an immense film about France. Everything would be in it. It would last two or three days. The film would be in episodes and each episode would be screened for a week or two. If one were to rent a theatre for a year it would be feasible. Anything is possible. To show everything has always been the temptation of novelists in their big books. I'd show people going to the movies and you'd see the film they see. You would see an intellectual with the job of interviewing people and you'd see the interviews. We could interview everyone, from Sartre to the Minister of War including the peasants of Chantal or workers. We'd also see sports, racing, etc. It would have to be organized on principle and then go in all directions. The shooting would last three or four years.

Q. Do you like television?

A. Television is the State and the State is functionaries, and functionaries . . . that's the contrary of television. Of what it should be, I mean. But I'd like very much to do something in it. Not make films *for* television, in the sense of making them for cinema, but do *reportage,* for example. I'd like to do some programs in the form of essays, interviews or travelogs—to speak about a painter or a writer whom I like. Or, quite plainly, some "dramatics." But directly. Television is not a means of expression. The proof is that the more idiotic it is the more it fascinates and the longer people stay hypnotized in their chairs. That's what television is but we may hope that this will change. The annoying thing is that if you start watching T.V. you can't get away from it. The thing to do is not to watch it.

Television should be considered as a means not of

expression but of transmission. It has to be taken as such. If this is the only remaining way to speak about art to people it should be used. For, even with films like *Lola Montes* or *Alexander Nevsky,* something remains in spite of the distortion, the rounded screen, the greyness of the image, or the absence of color. The spirit remains. In *Lola Montes* what you lose of the images you gain by the dialogue since you pay more attention. The film can hold you simply by the dialogue: its spirit comes to you through that. The same is true of all good films: it suffices that one part came through and that part suffices to indicate the whole film. Thus television in spite of everything transmits the spirit of things and that's very important.

And newsreels? That could be extraordinary. And why not make reconstructed newsreels, like Melies did? Today, we should show Castro and Johnson, played by actors: "this is the sad story of Castro and Johnson . . ." We would add real footage and people would love all that, I'm sure of it.

And miscellaneous "human interest" stories? They should be shown in the same way that we see them in *France-Soir.* In this genre, the only extraordinary things you can see are the reconstructions of crimes. First of all, it's really "real life" and then the reconstituted part of it is fascinating. In a general fashion, *reportage* is only interesting when it's inserted in fiction, but fiction is interesting only when it is verified by reality.

The *nouvelle vague* is defined, in part, by this new rapport between fiction and reality. It is defined also by regret, by nostalgia for a cinema which no longer exists. As soon as you can make films—you can no longer make films like the ones that made you want to make them. The dream of the *new wave,* which will never be realized, is to shoot—*Spartacus* in Hollywood with ten million dollars. Yet I am not bothered by making small inexpensive films —but people like Demy are very unhappy.

People have always believed that the *nouvelle vague* means cheap films as opposed to expensive ones. It is, simply, good film as opposed to bad film. Only it was found that the only way was to make inexpensive films. It is true that certain films are better for being made on small budgets but you have to think of the films that are better for having cost a great deal.

Q. And if someone had offered you a hundred million (francs) to make My Life to Live *with?*

A. I would never have accepted. What would the film have gained? The only thing I could have done would have been to pay more to the people who worked with me, that's all. At the same time I'd refuse to do a film for one hundred million (francs) if I thought it would cost four hundred.

Definitively, it is only in France that the producer recognizes, at least on principle, the notion of the *auteur*. (Hitchcock is one exception: as soon as the directors have their names outside the theatre, he has his photograph!) The best of the Italian producers consider the director as an employee. The difference is that the Italian system isn't worth much while the Americans are very strong. They are doubtless less so since the organization of the big studio has disappeared, but before they were the strongest in the world. Ben Hecht is the strongest scenarist I have ever seen. The Americans, who are much more stupid when it's a question of analysis, instinctively succeed in constructing things. They also have the gift of a simplicity which gives profundity: take the little western, *Ride the High Country*.

In France, if you want to do things like that you seem to be an intellectual.

Q. We come back to the idea of compartmentalization.

A. France is made of compartments. Well, in expression everything is linked and all the means of expression are linked. And life is one. Shooting and not shooting, for me, are not two different lives. Making films should be part of life and should be a natural and normal thing. Shooting hasn't changed my life much, for I was already shooting while doing criticism, and if I were to go back to being a critic it would still be, for me, a way of making films.

The only interesting film of Clouzot's is the one in which he searched, improvised, experimented and lived something: *The Mystery of Picasso*. Clement or the others don't live their cinema. It is a separate compartment.

In France, as I have already said, you must not mix genres. In America, a murder mystery can also be political and have gags. It is accepted here, of course, because it is American, but do the same thing in France and they shout.

It is true that now people reproach us less because they finally saw that we were arriving at talking about something other than "surprise parties." The only one who hasn't done anything is Vadim and he isn't reproached.

225

Him—he's the worst. He has betrayed everything he could have betrayed, even himself. The public adores that: Vadim is comfortable. He gives people the impression that they are seeing Shakespeare when he presents them with *Confidences* and *A Tout Coeur*. People say to themselves, "This is Shakespeare? Great! Why didn't anyone tell us before?"

I don't believe that a person can feel that he's doing something stupid and nasty and still continue doing it. Vadim must not be aware of what he's doing. Neither did he know what he was doing in the beginning, when he was spontaneous and sincere. Simply, he was on time. The fact of being on time when the rest of the world is behind gives the impression of being ahead. Since then he's stayed in the same place while the rest of the people have come to be on time—which makes him behind.

Having a *metier* is something that has always counted in France. Before the war, a director wasn't compared to a musician or to a writer but to a carpenter, an artisan. It turned out that among these artisans there were artists—like Renoir, Ophuls. Today the director is considered an artist but most of them have remained artisans. The *metier* exists, but not in the way they think. Carne has a *metier:* that's what makes him make bad films. When he was inventing his *metier* he made extraordinary films. Now he no longer invents. Chabrol, today, has more of a *metier* than Carne and it makes him search. It's a good *metier*.

Q. The nouvelle vague cineastes, *in criticism as in cinema—have they in common the will to search?*

A. We have many things in common. As for Rivette, Rohmer, Truffaut—obviously I feel different from them, but we have basically the same ideas about cinema. We have more things in common than we have differences—the details are quite different but on a profound level the differences are tiny.

We don't make the same films, that's true, but the more I see of so-called normal films and the more I see our films the more I am struck by the difference. And it must be a big one, because I have a general tendency to see what things have in common. Before the war, for example, there was a difference between Duvivier's *La Belle Equipe* and Renoir's *La Bete Humaine,* but only one of quality. Whereas now, between our films and a film by Verneuil, Delannoy, Duvivier or Carne, there is truly a difference in kind.

There were two sorts of values: the true and the false. *Cahiers* said that the true were false and the false were true. But today, there is neither true nor false and everything has become more difficult. The people at *Cahiers* were commandos: today they are an army in time of peace, going off on war games. But I think this is a temporary situation. For the moment, as in any peace-time army, *Cahiers* is divided into clans. It's like when Protestantism divided into an incredible number of sects. If you like one director you have to detest the other.

In other countries *Cahiers* has an enormous influence. People wonder if we're serious. It was bad enough to admit that guys like Ray and Aldrich have genius, but when they see interviews with someone like Ulmer—I am for the *Politique des Auteurs,* but not just anybody—I find that opening the door to absolutely everyone is a very dangerous thing. Inflation is menacing.

The important thing is not to want to discover someone at all cost. The snob aspect of the game of discovery should be left to *L'Express.* What is important is to know how to discern who has genius and who doesn't and to try, if you can, to define the genius or to explain it. There aren't many who try.

It is true that for today's critics everything has become very difficult and that many of *Cahiers* faults are old ones. In any case, we have in common the fact that we are searching: those who do not cannot for very long give the illusion of doing so; things end by clarifying themselves.

Jean-Luc Godard (1930–   ):
Filmography:
Short Subjects: 1954—Opération Béton. 1955—Une Femme Coquette. 1957—Tous les garçons s'appellent Patrick. 1958—Charlotte et son Jules, Une Histoire d'eau (with Truffaut). 1959—Breathless. 1960—Le Petit Soldat. 1961—Une Femme est une femme. 1961—The Seven Capital Sins (Sloth episode with Eddie Constantine). 1962—My Life to Live. 1962—RoGoPaG (Alexandra Stewart episode). 1963—Les Carabiniers, Les Plus Grands Escroqueries du monde (Jean Seberg episode). Contempt. 1964—Band of Outsiders, The Married Woman, Six From Paris (Joanne Shimkus episode). 1965—Alphaville, Pierrot le fou. 1966—Masculin-Féminin. 1967—Deux ou trois chose que je sais d'elle, Made in U.S.A., Le plus vieux metier (Futuristic sketch), La Chinoise. 1968—Weekend. 1969—One Plus One.

Howard Hawks

Howard Hawks has been the subject of much critical controversy over the years, perhaps as a compensation for decades of neglect by the "serious" film historians. Hawks' unyielding eye-level point of view is his distinguishing stylistic characteristic and represents a total commitment to the subjective over the objective. A director of parts as well as a unified whole, Hawks has stamped his distinctively bitter view of life on adventure, gangster and private-eye melodramas, westerns, musicals and screwball comedies, the genres Americans do best and appreciate least.*—A. S.

"The evidence on the screen is the proof of Hawks's genius," we had recently written. It would have been an exaggeration to pretend that this evidence was accessible to everyone; and critical unanimity is happily far from being settled on the genius of one of the great American cineastes: it is clear enough that our own evaluation has not changed.

It was not a question of interrogating Hawks on his "genius"; no metaphysical speculations; nothing that could distress the champions of clarity or common sense; at least, let us hope that each will find here his own account, and that includes the "Hitchcocko-Hawksians" of pure obedience.

When we arrived for our interview, we found Hawks

* *The interview of Jacques Becker, Jacques Rivette, and François Truffaut appeared originally in* Cahiers du Cinema, *No. 56, Vol. X, February 1956. The English translation was provided by the editor.*

*conversing with whom? Jacques Becker, one of our old
friends. The* auteur *of* Casque d'Or *courteously took his
leave of the* auteur *of* Sergeant York *when we protested
his departure: since Jacques Becker was a friend of Howard
Hawks, the interview could only gain in interest. Furthermore, Becker's fluency in the language of Griffith made him
more than an interpreter, a valuable collaborator.*

*Since our interview transpired a few days before the re-
lease of* The Land of the Pharaohs, *our first questions quite
naturally dealt with that film.*

HOWARD HAWKS—I made this film for one simple reason: Cinemascope. At the time I was approached to direct
a film in this new screen size, I was considering as a project the story of an astonishing feat of construction in
China during the war. The American Army wanted an airfield which the engineers estimated would take eight
months to construct. The Chinese supplied twenty thousand men and women, who carried stone in little baskets
on their heads, and this huge airfield was completed in
three weeks. I was about to abandon this project because
the political situation made cooperation with Red China
impossible; the producers then considered shooting the
film in Thailand. It then occurred to me that the building
of the pyramids was the same kind of story—it too demonstrated what man is able to create with his bare hands
from sand to stone. This kind of story appeals to me tremendously. We thus wrote our script on this one theme:
the construction of a pyramid.

CAHIERS—*What part did William Faulkner play in the
development of the scenario?*

HAWKS—He collaborated with Harry Kurnitz in the
writing of both story and screenplay. As always, he contributed enormously. He's a great writer; we are very old
friends and work easily together. We understand each
other very well, and any time I need any sort of help, I
call on Faulkner. He has done three or four scenarios for
me, but he has also helped me on many others. The story
of *The Land of the Pharaohs* because his imagination was
challenged by these men, their conversations, the reasons
for their belief in a second life, how they happened to
achieve these tasks for beliefs we would find it difficult to
understand today, such as the slight importance attached
to the present life in comparison with the future life, the
rest that was to be assured to the Pharaoh in a place
where his body would be secure . . .

229

CAHIERS—*For ages, or even . . .*

HAWKS—For eternity, for eternity. For all these reasons, Faulkner was the man for the assignment: he has an affinity for these ideas. They are what he is made for.

CAHIERS—*We would like to know how you transported your imagination back to an age so remote as the ancient Egyptian.*

HAWKS—We were assisted by several historians in Egypt's Department of Antiquities, and above all by a Frenchman who has lived and written numerous books on Egyptian history in a little house in the shadow of the great Pyramid—the exact spot on which we shot the picture. He and the other authorities instructed us in the ways and customs of the Egyptians. I'm afraid we paid attention only to what best suited our picture. It is possible to reconstruct the furniture and dress, and even some of the ritual, of the Pharaohs from the hieroglyphics and drawings on the tombs. We know what the soldiers' uniforms looked like, what musical instruments were played, and what utensils were used. As for the architecture, Trauner did a great piece of work. He is, without doubt, one of the greatest scene designers in the world. We tried to reproduce Trauner's visual conceptions exactly.

CAHIERS—*Did that French Egyptologist see what you shot each day?*

HAWKS—He saw some of the rushes, I think. He was very interested in some of the schemes we concocted for moving and transporting the blocks of stone. According to him, it was quite possible the Egyptians had thought of the same stratagems. For example, we were in agreement about the use of a ramp to get the stones to the summit, and the subsequent dismantling of the ramp once it was no longer needed. The method by which stones are raised from the ground and lowered onto the boat in the film is our invention. So is the way the pyramid is sealed after its construction. The scholars were quite intrigued. We employed a hydraulic process which is quite modern, but instead of water or oil, we used sand. Thus, we had a huge stone rest upon enormous wooden pilings. Each pile was sunk in a hole, and each hole was filled with sand. For each block of rock to fall into place it was necessary merely to open a small hole which allowed the sand to run out. As the sand did so, the huge block settled down slowly into its final position. This is probably the method the Egyptians used. We don't know for sure.

CAHIERS—*Then you have tried to make a realistic film?*

HAWKS—As realistic as possible, but that didn't stop us from using camels, even though very few camels were in Egypt at the time of our story. Our justification, shaky on purely historical grounds, was that camels did seem integral to our image of Egypt. There were many other things we could only guess about. That's why we had the workers be free at the start of the pyramid and slaves at the end. We reasoned that the employment of 10,000 men on a pyramid for 30 years would drain the country economically and that after the first few years of exaltation, discontent would smolder into collective rage and the workers would have to be enslaved to make them continue. This thesis is an integral part of our film.

CAHIERS—*You ordinarily avoid stories with a long time span, and the notion of continuity plays a great role in almost all your films. Were you bothered by the fact that this story extended over thirty years?*

HAWKS—Bothered, no, but handicapped. It was difficult to devise a story that lasted thirty years while maintaining an acceptable continuity.

CAHIERS—*What have you concluded from your experience with Cinemascope?*

HAWKS—We have spent a lifetime learning how to compel the public to concentrate on one single thing. Now we have something that works in exactly the opposite way, and I don't like it very much. I like Cinemascope for a picture such as *The Land of the Pharaohs,* where it can show things impossible otherwise, but I don't like it at all for the average story. Contrary to what some think, it is easier to shoot in Cinemascope—you don't have to bother about what you should show—everything's on the screen. I find that a bit clumsy. Above all, in a motion picture, is the story. You cannot shoot a scene as quickly in Cinemascope, because if you develop a situation quickly, the characters jump all over the wide screen—which in a way makes them invisible. Thus you lose speed as a means of exciting or augmenting a scene's dramatic tension. You have to proceed differently. What you lose on the dramatic plane, however, you gain on the visual plane. The result can be very pleasing to the eye. You have to decide what seems best. Have you seen a film entitled *The Tall Men* with Gable?

CAHIERS—*No, not yet.*

HAWKS—My brother produced it. It's *Red River,* but in

color and in Cinemascope. and it's a very pleasant film to watch. It's not a great film, but a good film. It made me regret not having Cinemascope when I made *Red River*. John Ford and I made some anamorphic attempts around 1926, but we didn't care for the results. I always think that the artist who paints a scene in a certain manner must, in changing his manner, change his scene.

CAHIERS—*And Africa?*

HAWKS—For this film we must use portable cameras. For certain scenes even hand-held cameras; the Cinemascope gear would be too difficult.

CAHIERS—*Will this be your next film?*

HAWKS—I don't really know We can start shooting. the scenario is finished. but I must make another film before; we won't go down into Africa before next September.

CAHIERS—*Could you tell us a little about this other film?*

HAWKS—It's difficult, we are only beginning to work on it. I can't tell you very much. because we haven't even decided on the main plot line. I don't know what form it is going to take. I don't even know what genre of film it will be. Its point of departure is a true incident that I've heard about. but it might never become a film. It depends.

CAHIERS—*All your films are based on events which tend to show a man in action. his effort and struggle. Even considering the wide variety of your projects. these themes keep recurring in almost all your films. Do you think this is so?*

HAWKS—That may be true but I am not really aware of it. I make movies on subjects that interest me: That could be automobile racing. airplanes. a western or a comedy. but the best drama for me is the one which shows a man in danger. There is no action when there is no danger. It follows that if you achieve real action. there must be danger. To live or to die' What drama is greater? Therefore I have probably chosen this direction because I have gradually come to believe that it matters more than anything else. It's very easy to make a movie knowing that everyone will love it. but that doesn't count for much. What one should do. what one must do. is try to anticipate what the public is going to like. I don't think that these people are producers: they make a picture because somebody makes a picture that is successful, so they make one like it. you know?

CAHIERS—*Yes, too many films exist only as imitations of others.*

HAWKS—That's true. We made *Scarface* because the violence of this particular era was interesting. *Scarface* is still being copied—and hence still lives. There were fifteen murders in *Scarface*, and people said I was crazy to have so many. But I knew that was the story: violence made the story. Also, in practice, all the gangster movies that have followed *Scarface* only reiterated the same material. Similarly, when I made *Red River,* I thought an adult western could be made for mature audiences, and now everyone is making "intelligent" westerns. And a film like *Twentieth Century* . . . have you seen *Twentieth Century?*

CAHIERS—Hélas non!

HAWKS—It was the first time the dramatic leads, instead of secondary comics, played for laughs. I mean we got the fun out of John Barrymore and Carole Lombard. It was two or three years ahead of its time.

CAHIERS—*We think that a film like* Monkey Business *has renewed American comedy, and is undoubtedly more ambitious than it seems* . . .

HAWKS—Oh, probably, yes. Because of its general theme: the laughs are born out of the inhibitions that restrict each of us and are here abruptly removed by rejuvenation. It was a good story. Perhaps we pushed the point a bit too far for the public. From this point of view, it is less amusing than *Male War Bride* or *Bringing Up Baby. Monkey Business* went too far, became too fanciful and not funny enough: this is my opinion.

CAHIERS—*And* Gentlemen Prefer Blondes?

HAWKS—Oh, that was just . . . fun! In other movies, you have two men who go out looking for pretty girls to have fun with. We pulled a switch by taking two girls who went out looking for men to amuse them: a perfectly modern story. It delighted me. It was funny. The two girls, Jane Russell and Marilyn Monroe, were so good together that any time I had trouble figuring out any business, I simply had them walk back and forth, and the audiences adored it. I had a staircase built so that they could go up and down, and since they are well built . . . This type of movie lets you sleep at night without a care in the world; five or six weeks were all we needed to shoot the musical numbers, the dances and the rest.

CAHIERS—*What period of work do you prefer? Script, shooting, editing?*

HAWKS—I hate the editing.

CAHIERS—*But you do the editing of your films?*

233

HAWKS—Oh, yes! Simultaneously with the shooting, if possible. When I started out in this profession, the producers were all afraid that I made a film too short because I didn't give them enough film for editing. And I said: "I don't want you to make the movie in the cutting room, I want to make it myself on the set, and if that doesn't suit you, too bad." That's not to say that editing isn't a chore, particularly when you haven't done a good job with the shooting. Editing is a horror for me because I look at my work for a second time and say that's pretty bad, and that, and also that— The difficult work is the preparation: finding the story, deciding how to tell it, what to show and what not to show. Once you begin shooting you see everything in the best light, develop certain details, and improve the whole. I never follow a script literally and I don't hesitate to change a script completely if I see a chance to do something interesting. I like to work on the scenarios. Some of my best movies were written in very little time. *Scarface* took only eleven days, story and scenario.

CAHIERS—*Does that include the dialogues?*

HAWKS—Everything. The whole thing took eleven days. I know because I paid the writers who worked for me by the day.

CAHIERS—*Who gave you the material, the basic facts?*

HAWKS—The facts came from several reporters in Chicago, many books, and magazine articles. The outline was done by Ben Hecht. He didn't have to do any research. All he had to do was ask me about this or that detail, and I would rattle off the information because I had read a lot on the subject. For example, I don't know if you recall George Raft flipping a "nickel" in his hand? There had actually been a large number of murders in Chicago, where, as a mark of disrespect, the killer stuck a nickel into the hand of the corpse. Raft's character being that of a killer, he always had a coin in his hand. We also exploited another little known fact: The papers that published the photos of a murder indicated "X marks the spot where the body was found." So we designed fifteen or twenty scenes around the X, finding all sorts of ways to use the X when a murder occurred.

CAHIERS—*Each time someone was killed, there was an X?*

HAWKS—Yes. X.

CAHIERS—*Did that have something to do with the scar on Muni's face?*

HAWKS—Yes. Once you start off on that path, why not go all the way? Do you remember the scene in which Boris Karloff is bowling? As he lets the ball go, he's hit; the pins all go down. An X for a strike is marked on the scorecard.

CAHIERS—*And the cloud in* Red River, *was it intentional or accidental?*

HAWKS—We saw it coming just as Wayne began reading the prayer over the grave. We told him to hurry his reading so that we could catch it at the right moment. This was a case of seizing an opportunity as it presented itself. I don't think we would have held up the scene to wait for a cloud.

CAHIERS—*You were the producer of* The Thing *without getting credit as a director, but you undoubtedly supervised the production very closely.*

HAWKS—Oh, yes. The direction was handled by my editor, but I was on the set for all the important scenes. It was a very pleasant assignment. We wrote the script in four and a half days. I had read the story in Germany, in Heidelberg, where we shot *Male War Bride*. We only used four pages from it. I bought the rights and hired two good screenwriters. The story interested me because I thought it was an adult treatment of an often infantile subject.

CAHIERS—*Many critics have complained about the big differences that existed between the Hemingway story* To Have and Have Not, *and the film you shot from it. Why did you change it so much?*

HAWKS—Hemingway and I are good friends, but whenever I tried to persuade Hemingway to write for the movies, Hemingway insisted that he could be a good writer of books, but he didn't know whether he could be a good writer of movies. Once when Hemingway and I were hunting together, I told him that I could take his worst story and make a movie out of it. Hemingway asked me what was his worst story. *"To Have and Have Not,"* I said. Hemingway explained that he had written the story in one sitting when he needed money, and that I couldn't make a movie out of it. I said I'd try, and while we hunted, we discussed it. We decided that the best way to tell the story was not to show the hero growing old, but show how he had met the girl, and, in short, show everything that had happened before the beginning of the novel. After four or five days of discussion I left. Faulkner and Jules Furthman then wrote a script incorporating the ideas

Hemingway and I had evolved on our hunting trip. In fact, there was enough material left over for another movie (Michael Curtiz' *The Breaking Point*) which was pretty good.

CAHIERS—*Your career has been divided equally between adventure films and comedies. The adventure films seemed optimistic and the comedies pessimistic, but there always seemed a lesson to be drawn from the humor in both genres. Are you more interested in the mixture of genres within your subject or in the clash of genres?*

HAWKS—Perhaps I can best answer in the following manner. Life is very simple for most people. It becomes so routine that everybody wants to escape his environment. Adventure stories reveal how people behave in the face of death—what they do, say, feel, and even think. I have always liked the scene in *Only Angels Have Wings* in which a man says "I feel funny," and his best friend says "your neck is broken," and the injured man then says "I have always wondered how I would die if I knew I was going to die. I would rather you didn't watch me." And the friend goes out and stands in the rain. I have personally encountered this experience, and the public found it very convincing.

But a comedy is virtually the same as an adventure story. The difference is in the situation—dangerous in an adventure story, embarrassing in a comedy. But in both we observe our fellow beings in unusual situations. You merely emphasize the dramatic or the comical aspects of the hero's reactions. Sometimes you can mix them up a bit. My serious pictures usually have their comic sides. You've seen *The Big Sky?* You remember the scene where they amputate Kirk Douglas' finger; it was really funny. I had already wanted to do that scene in *Red River*, but John Wayne had said that I was crazy to want such a scene played for comedy. I said okay, I would do it in my next picture instead. When Wayne saw it, he phoned me and said he'd do whatever I wanted to in our next picture together.

It's possible to do comedy scenes even at very tragic moments. I once told a Spaniard I was thinking of doing *Don Quixote* with Cary Grant and Cantinflas, and the Spaniard said it was impossible to make a comedy out of a tragedy. I asked the Spaniard to tell me the story of *Don Quixote,* and after the Spaniard had done so, I said,

"You've just told me the story of three of Chaplin's best pictures." He looked at me and said, "You're right. Let's go make a comedy." And that's pretty much the way I see it. The only difference between comedy and tragedy is the point of view. That's the only way I know how to answer your question.

CAHIERS—*The question has been answered.*

HAWKS—You know the story of *The African Queen*? I turned down an invitation to direct it because I couldn't see any humor in the situation. It pleased me to see how they made it a comedy. There were some silly things in it, but it went. Whenever I hear a story my first thought is how to make it into a comedy, and I think of how to make it into a drama only as a last resort. Do you remember the story about the man who wanted to commit suicide and stayed on a window ledge—*Fourteen Hours*? They wanted me to do it, and I said no. "Why not?" they asked me. "It's a great story." I told them I didn't like suicides, and I told my friend Henry Hathaway that I didn't like the film he had directed. The public didn't like it either, and Zanuck told me I had been right. I told Zanuck: "I might have done it if it had been Cary Grant getting from the bedroom of a woman whose husband had come back unexpectedly and after he was found on the ledge he pretended he was contemplating suicide." Zanuck asked me if I wanted to start on that one the next day.

CAHIERS—*You're not interested in abnormal characters?*

HAWKS—Sometimes I get interested in the encounter of a normal person and an abnormal person. Almost all my caprices, my manias (like the way I am playing with key chain while I talk to you), I like to think that these are abnormal things. To see the difference in the way of thinking makes good scenes, but to tell a long story about a nut isn't easy. Besides, I don't like theoretical situations. I like stories like *Viva Villa!* which I wrote and half of which I directed. The Villa in that film, like the Villa in real life, was a quite bizarre man. So was Scarface. Ben Hecht agreed to write *Scarface* only after I told him that I wanted to make the Capone-like character a Caesar Borgia and Capone's sister like Lucretia Borgia. This analogy permeates that script, and every intelligent person senses something unusual, something that can't be brought out into the open, but affects all the scenes.

Pancho Villa had a very complex personality—that's

what made him interesting—but these subjects are rare. Fox wanted me to do Zapata, but the script was all wrong about the character. Zapata was the worst murderer Mexico had ever seen. Had Fox been willing to tell the true story of Zapata, I would have been interested. But they made a sort of Santa Claus of him and had him riding around the country giving presents to poor peons.

CAHIERS—*In short, you're guided in your work by an intentional reaction to what is going on around you.*

HAWKS—Exactly. I've already said that it's easy, when one sees crowds rushing off to see a movie, to make another movie almost exactly like it. What is more fun is trying something new, and hoping it will work. That's how I hit upon the tempo of my movies. I made a film called *His Girl Friday* in which the characters spoke so fast that the characters kept stepping on each other's lines. The public liked it. Moreover, the tempo in *Scarface* was faster than usual in that period. I generally work with a faster tempo than that of most of my colleagues. It seems more natural to me, less forced. I personally speak slowly, but people generally talk, talk, talk without even waiting for other people to finish. Also, if a scene is a bit weak, the more rapidly you shoot it, the better it will be on the screen. Moreover, if the tempo is fast you can emphasize a point by slowing the rhythm. Similarly, when you have a scene with two characters, don't always use a close-up. When you use close-ups sparingly, the public realizes that they are important. I hate movies which, without any reason, are composed completely of close-ups. I don't like them. I don't want to say that they're necessarily bad movies, but I don't like that particular style of film-making.

CAHIERS—*Have any particular directors influenced you?*

HAWKS—In the beginning, I was very much impressed by Murnau's *Sunrise,* particularly for its camera movements. I once made a film in this style—*Paid to Love*—with a great many camera effects, but I have never used such trickery since that time. I try to tell a story as simply as possible with the camera at eye level. Since I had directed *Paid to Love* at a time when the public was easy to impress, the result was well-received. But I don't believe the future is in that direction. The other directors who have most impressed me are John Ford, Ernst Lubitsch, and Leo McCarey; these are the men who, in my opinion, have been the best.

CAHIERS—*What do you think of the young directors: Nicholas Ray, for example.*

HAWKS—I've seen several of Ray's films, and find them very promising. He is one of those directors of whom it is said: "I will go see everything he does because he is a good story-teller." But the actual situation in Hollywood is hard for young directors. They don't get the freedom we older directors enjoy. Young directors are told what to direct, where to shoot it, on what day to be finished. It's hard. However, the more successful a young director's movies, the more freedom he will be given.

CAHIERS—*What would be your ideal film, that which you would make for yourself alone?*

HAWKS—I have no desire to make a picture for myself. There has never been a picture so good the public didn't care to see it. I like to make comedies because I like to go into a theater and hear people laughing—the more laughter the better I feel. I have no desire to make a picture for my own pleasure. Fortunately, I have found that what I like, most people also like, so I only have to let myself go and do what interests me.

I am actually thinking about a subject for a movie. For four-fifths of the picture there is only one person on the screen. A girl, cut off from all contact with humanity by avalanches and melting ice, bears a child and cares for it for three months before she is found.

CAHIERS—*Do you always work on your scripts?*

HAWKS—From the beginning and for all my films.

CAHIERS—*If you had to choose three or four of your films to be saved, which ones would they be?*

HAWKS—For sentimental reasons, my first talking film, *Dawn Patrol,* then *Scarface* and probably *Twentieth Century*; but . . . there are many others I would like to save. *Dawn Patrol* was very interesting because it was my first experience with sound. I had not worked since the coming of sound because the producers didn't know if I could work with dialogue. I had never had any theatrical experience. I myself wrote almost the entire scenario, and during the shooting, everyone kept telling me: "It's not good dialogue, it's not dramatic. Everything is flat. Everything you're doing is going to be flat." No one liked the film because none of the characters cried or screamed. When the editing was finished, the studio had so little confidence in the movie, they dispensed with the premiere. They preferred to release it discreetly, and then it turned out to be the best film of the year, and then they got into the habit of screening it for other directors and saying: "That's what good dialogue is like."

Howard Hawks (1896–   ):
Filmography:
1926—The Road to Glory, Fig Leaves. 1927—The Cradle Snatchers, Paid to Love. 1928—A Girl in Every Port, Fazil, The Air Circus. 1929—Trent's Last Case. 1930—The Dawn Patrol. 1931—The Criminal Code. 1932—The Crowd Roars, Scarface, Tiger Shark. 1933—Today We Live. 1934—Twentieth Century, Viva Villa (with and signed by Jack Conway). 1935—Barbary Coast. 1936—Ceiling Zero, The Road to Glory, Come and Get It (with William Wyler). 1938—Bringing Up Baby. 1939—Only Angels Have Wings. 1940—His Girl Friday. 1941—Sergeant York, Ball of Fire. 1943—Air Force. 1944—To Have and Have Not. 1946—The Big Sleep. 1948—Red River, A Song Is Born. 1949—I Was a Male War Bride. 1952—The Big Sky, Monkey Business, O'Henry's Full House (The Ransom of Red Chief Episode). 1953—Gentlemen Prefer Blondes. 1955—The Land of the Pharaohs. 1959—Rio Bravo. 1962—Hatari! 1964—Man's Favorite Sport. 1965—Redline 7000. 1967—El Dorado.

Alfred Hitchcock

Alfred Hitchcock is the supreme technician of the American Cinema. Like Ford, Hitchcock cuts in his mind, and not in the cutting room with five different set-ups for every scene. His is the only contemporary style that unites the divergent classical traditions of Murnau (camera movement) and Eisenstein (montage). (Welles, for example, owes more to Murnau, while Resnais is closer to Eisenstein.) However, Hitchcock seldom receives the visual analysis he deserves in the learned Anglo-American periodicals devoted ostensibly to the art of the cinema. Pages and pages will be expended on Resnais' synchronized tracks in Last Year at Marienbad, *but the subtler diminuendo of Hitchcock's cross-tracking in the American remake of* The Man Who Knew Too Much *will pass by unnoticed. Resnais, Truffaut, and Chabrol can pay homage to Hitchcock, but the Anglo-American admirers of Resnais, Truffaut, and Chabrol will continue to pass off Hitchcock as a Continental aberration. "The Master of Suspense" is thus virtually without honor in his own countries.*

Hitchcock's art is full of paradoxes. The Birds, *for example, reveals a rigorous morality coupled with a dark humor, but the theme of complacency that runs through all his work is now so explicit that it is generally misunderstood. Hitchcock requires a situation of normality, however dull it may seem on the surface, to emphasize the evil abnormality that lurks beneath the surface. Hitchcock understands, as his detractors do not, the crucial function of counterpoint in the cinema. You cannot commit a murder in a haunted house or dark alley and make a meaning-*

ful statement to the audience. *The spectators simply with-draw from these bizarre settings and let the decor dictate the action. It is not Us up there on the screen, but some play actors trying to be sinister. However, when murder is committed in a gleamingly sanitary motel bathroom dur-ing a cleansing shower, the incursion of evil into our well-laundered existence becomes intolerable. We may laugh nervously or snort disgustedly, but we will never be quite as complacent again. Hitchcock's repeated invasions of ev-eryday life with the most outrageous melodramatic devices have shaken the foundations of that facile humanism that insists that people are good, and only systems evil, as if the systems themselves are not functions of human experi-ence. Much of the sick, perverse, anti-humanistic humor sweeping through America today is an inevitable reaction to the sickening sentimentality of totalitarianism masquer-ading as all-encompassing humanism. Hitchcock has never been accepted as part of this fashionable sickness, and that is all to his credit. He insists, almost intolerantly, upon a moral reckoning for his characters and for his audience. We can violate the Commandments at our own psychic peril, but we must pay the price in guilt at the end. Hitch-cock can be devious, but he is never dishonest.*—A.S.*

Can you tell us something about The Birds?

It's taken from a well-known short story by Daphne Du Maurier. It concerns the attack by domestic birds on a group of people living in a community; the film is laid in northern California, northern San Francisco. The series of attacks start very mildly and increase in seriousness as it goes on.

What would you say was the theme of the film?

If you like you can make it the theme of too much complacency in the world: that people are unaware that catastrophe surrounds us all.

The people are unwilling to believe that the birds are going to take over?

That's true, yes.

What particularly attracted you to science fiction?

This isn't science fiction at all, not at all. It's treated

* *The interview by Ian Cameron and V. F. Perkins with Alfred Hitchcock originally appeared in* Movie, *No. 6, January 1963.*

quite naturally and quite straightforwardly. Many of the incidents in the film are based on actual fact. Birds have attacked and do attack, all the time. As a matter of fact, one of the incidents we have in the film was based on an actual incident which occurred at La Jolla, California, on April 30, 1960. A thousand swifts came down a chimney into the living room of some people. These are birds that nest in masonry rather than in trees, in roofs and chimneys and so forth. And the people were completely swamped with them for half an hour. Another incident occurred in the very place we were working, in Bodega Bay in northern San Francisco, where a farmer reported to the *San Francisco Chronicle* that he was losing a lot of lambs due to crows diving and pecking at their eyes and then killing them. So there are precedents for all these things. That's what makes it more or less accurate, in terms of facts rather than science-fiction.

There are also precedents in your films for birds, aren't there? Particularly in Psycho.

Oh yes.

Is this any particular fondness for birds?

Not particularly, no.

Do you find them threatening in some way?

No. No, not at all. I'm personally not interested in that side of content. I'm more interested in the technique of story telling by means of film rather than in what the film contains.

As far as telling this particular story goes, had you a lot of problems?

Oh, I wasn't meaning technical problems. I was meaning the technique of story telling on film *per se*. Oh no, the technical problems are prodigious. I mean films like *Ben Hur* or *Cleopatra* are child's play compared with this. After all we had to train birds for every shot practically.

You had some trouble with the American version of the R.S.P.C.A. . . .

Not really; that was a technicality. You're allowed to catch so many birds. I think the bird-trainer had about four over his quota, really.

Did you restrict yourself in the bird kingdom, or did every sort of bird take over?

Oh no. No birds of prey at all. Purely domestic birds. Seagulls. Birds you see every day. Seagulls, crows, ravens, finches, and canaries and that sort of bird.

You're not using music?

No music at all, no. We're using electronic sound, all the way through. A simulated sound of actual things. For example the sound of birds' wings and birds' cries will be stylised to some extent. And that will occur all the way through the picture.

You have used music a lot in your previous films. This is going to fulfill exactly the role of music?

Oh, it should do, yes. After all, when you put music to film, it's really sound, it isn't music *per se*. I mean there's an abstract approach. The music serves as either a counterpoint or a comment on whatever scene is being played. I mean we don't have what you call "tunes" in it at all.

The shrilling in Psycho *is rather of that sort.*

Yes, you see you have the screaming violins. It was a motif that went through the murder scenes.

You will use your strange sounds as motifs in that way?

Yes.

I hear Psycho *made a lot of money.*

Yes, that was a secondary consideration. *Psycho* is probably one of the most cinematic films I've made and there you get a clear example of the use of film to cause an audience to respond emotionally.

It was primarily an emotional response you were after from your audience?

Entirely. That's the whole device. After all, the showing of a violent murder at the beginning was intended purely to instil into the minds of the audience a certain degree of fear of what is to come. Actually in the film, as it goes on, there's less and less violence because it has been transferred to the minds of the audience.

The use of Janet Leigh to be killed early in the film is to upset one's sense of security because the star is expected to survive to the end.

Oh, no question about it. The ordinary person would have said "Janet Leigh, she's the leading lady, she must play the lead." But that was not the intention at all. The intention in that early part was to portray average people and in this particular case to deliberately divert the audience's attention into a character in trouble, you see. And you follow the adventures of a girl deliberately detailed to keep you away from anything that's going to turn up later on, you see.

North by Northwest. *Near the beginning, in the mad car chase, one knows that Cary Grant can't be killed this early. So why is one excited?*

That again is purely the use of film in terms of the substitution of the language of the camera for words. That is the most important function of film. As a substitute for words. I wouldn't say substitute. I don't think that does film even sufficient justice. It's the mode of expression. And the use of the size of the image. And the juxtaposition of different pieces of film to create emotion in a person. And you can make it strong enough even to make them forget reason. You see when you say that Cary Grant can't possibly be killed so early in the film, that's the application of reason. But you're not permitted to reason. Because the film should be stronger than reason.

Above all of your films the one that seems stronger than reason is Vertigo.

There you get, in a sense, a remote fantasy. In *Vertigo* you have a feeling of remoteness from ordinary worldly things. You see the attitude of the man, the woman's behaviour. Of course behind it lies some kind of plot, which I think is quite secondary. I don't bother about plot, or all that kind of thing.

You got rid of it very early in the film.

Yes, that's, what shall I call it? That's a necessary evil. But that's why I'm always surprised at people and even critics who place so much reliance on logic and all that sort of thing. I have a little phrase to myself. I always say logic is dull.

You seem rather to distrust the psychiatrist's explanation of Norman Bates in Psycho. *It isn't given all that much weight.*

Possibly the details would have been too unpleasant. I think that there perhaps we're skimming over . . . You have to remember that *Psycho* is a film made with quite a sense of amusement on my part. To me it's a *fun* picture. The processes through which we take the audience, you see, it's rather like taking them through the haunted house at the fairground or the roller-coaster, you know. After all it stands to reason that if one were seriously doing the *Psycho* story, it would be a case history. You would never present it in forms of mystery or the juxtaposition of characters, as they were placed in the film. They were all designed in a certain way to create this audience emotion. Probably the real *Psycho* story wouldn't have been emotional at all; it would've been terribly clinical.

Psycho *is, though, very honestly presented. There is a very striking shot of Norman Bates swinging his hips as he goes upstairs. When one sees the film for the second time, one realises one could have solved the mystery the first time.*

Well, I'm a great believer in making sure that if people see the film a second time they don't feel cheated. That is a *must.* You must be honest about it and not merely keep things away from an audience. I'd call that *cheating.* You should never do that.

Was this shot meant deliberately as a clue?

Well, you might as well say that the basic clue was in the feminine nature of the character altogether.

The very complex montage of the murder of Janet Leigh was not just intended to avoid showing some things you couldn't show . . .

Well, I did photograph a nude girl all the way through. In other words I covered in the shooting every aspect of the killing. Actually some of it was shot in slow motion. I had the camera slow and the girl moving slowly so that I could measure out the movements and the covering of awkward parts of the body, the arm movement, gesture and so forth. I was actually seven days on that little thing; it's only forty-five seconds really.

Is there a sexual reference in the compositions? It seemed that you were consciously cutting between soft round shapes and the hard, phallic shape of the knife to suggest copulation.

Well, I mean you would get that in any case, with any sense of intimate nudity those thoughts would emerge naturally. But the most obvious example of that is in *North by Northwest,* the last shot with the train going into the tunnel.

One feels of your later films that you have got much less interested in the mystery thriller element, much more interested in broadening things out.

Well, I think it's a natural tendency to be less superficial, that's Truffaut's opinion—he's been examining all these films. And he feels that the American period is much stronger than the English period. It's a much stronger development. For example, I think it's necessary to get a little deeper into these things as one goes along. For example *The Birds*—you see usually in these films, which I call an "event film"—you know, like *On The Beach,* or one of those things—I felt it was much more necessary to intensify the personal story so that you get, as a result, a greater identification with the people, and therefore the fire through which you put them is much stronger.

In Psycho *you presumably intended the audience to identify with Janet Leigh.*

I wouldn't say *Psycho* was necessarily the best example. Because I felt there that the characters in the second part were merely figures. I was concentrating much more on the effect of the murder and the menace and the background of the boy/mother situation, rather than the other people. But in the case of *The Birds*, I think three of the four characters do go through a process which ties them directly in to the bird attacks.

In The Birds *you have worked without stars—or without big stars. Why?*

I felt that one should have anonymous people, not too familiar, because the subject matter itself is not quite so facetious as that of other films: although the Birds do attack, it is treated quite realistically. One of the most—to me—satisfying scenes in *The Birds* is where there are no birds seen at all. You have a room which is boarded up —it comes toward the end of the picture—there are four people in the room: a child, young man and woman, and a mother, mother of the young man, sitting there in silence just waiting for them. I just keep that silence going for quite a bit until the first sounds come, then you begin to hear the attack outside and you don't see the mass of birds at all. And it's that kind of thing which permitted one to have comparatively unknown people because the thing belonged as a whole. It wouldn't have looked good to have had a familiar film star sitting there waiting, you know; it's hard to describe why; but this is quite an interesting sequence; to me it's really satisfying because there I threw everything to the audience to use their imagination; to help them along a little bit, I had one shutter blow open. The young man has to pull the shutter to and then you see just the close-up attack on his hand and the seagulls biting and drawing blood.

The atmosphere sounds similar to that of the sequence in North by Northwest *where Cary Grant waits at the road-side for Kaplan.*

That was, I would say, an amusing approach. This thing in *The Birds* is not. We've shown the audience sufficient samples—I had one sequence where 300 crows wait outside the schoolhouse for the children, and when the kids come out they are chased down the road: montage sequence of individual crows attacking each child on the back, pecking at them and so forth.

Little menacing bits of dialogue—do you write these yourself: "Crop-dusting where there ain't no crops" in North by Northwest?

Oh that's my line, yes.

How much of your scripts do you in fact write yourself?

Oh, quite a bit. You see I used to be a writer myself years ago. The difficulty is that one is working in the visual so much—that's why I so rarely use film writers—I always use novelists or playwrights, definitely not people working in the mystery field. They're no use to me at all. In *The Birds,* I opened the film with the shot of birds in their nicest—what *we* think are their nicest—surroundings: in their cages. They're chirruping away, and they're all beautifully set—all very happy, ostensibly, and there's a little light-hearted sequence. I treat the film in the beginning as a light comedy and there's some byplay with the girl and the young man where a canary gets out of a cage, and the girl is a rather rich society girl, and she is not aware that the young man knows her identity—when he gets the bird from under his hat he says, "Let's put Melanie Daniels back into her gilded cage, shall we," and that's his way of telling the girl he knows who she is. The pay-off on that one line comes much later in the story when the centre of the town is attacked by seagulls and the girl seeks refuge in a phone booth—it's glass-walled—and she can't get out. I take high shots and you see birds beating all around. The gulls are the people now you see and she's the bird. So I have to write these lines in myself because I know it's going to help appreciably later on. There's no comment made about it, but it's very clear that she's in a cage but it's no longer gilded.

You expect quite a lot of your audience.

For those who want it. I don't think films should be looked at *once.* I think they go by too fast. But the critics sit in there at their 10:30 a.m. sitting, and they see a film through once and that seems to be sufficient. But I don't really think it is. Most films should be seen through more than once.

Why is The Trouble with Harry *a comedy rather than a thriller?*

I think it was a nice little *pastorale,* you know. A typically English piece of humour, though it was set in America. It was an English novel and we followed it pretty closely. I laid it in the autumnal setting to counterpoint the macabre of the body, but I even tried to photograph that in an amusing way.

How do you choose your subjects?

I don't probe particularly deeply. If something appeals to me . . . I think instinctively one would go for a subject very often that would lend itself to one's treatment. I'm not terribly keen on just taking a stage play. As far back as when I made *Juno and the Paycock* I felt very frustrated about it and kind of rather ashamed when it got terrific notices. It wasn't anything to do with me. It belonged to Sean O'Casey. My job was just to put it on the screen. I think that's the job of any craftsman, setting the camera up and photographing people acting. That's what I call most films today: photographs of people talking. It's no effort to me to make a film like *Dial M for Murder* because there's nothing there to do. On the other hand, you say to me: why do you make a film like *Dial M for Murder?* Because I run for cover when the batteries are running dry. You know, I might be engaged in a subject which is abortive—I've done that many times, I've been half way through a subject and found it didn't work out after all—so immediately, instead of waiting, to keep one's hand in you go for something which is fairly routine while the batteries are recharging.

In North by Northwest, *Grant seems to want Eva Marie Saint dead: he's happier when she's an enemy or in danger than when she seems to be an available wife or lover.*

What's that old Oscar Wilde thing? "Each man kills the thing he loves . . ." That I think is a very natural phenomenon, really.

You don't find it somewhat perverted?

Well, everything's perverted in a different way, isn't it?

Was the falling body at the end of North by Northwest *a superimposition?*

Yes, that's a double printing job. You photograph your background first and then you get a white backing and a large arm sticking out of the backing and you strap the middle of the torso to the arm and then with a side worm gear men can take that body and do *that* (twisting gesture) with it—Jimmy Stewart's done it as well. Now you take the camera close and whip it back on rails and then also by making the movement slow you can undercrank it too, so that your whip back can be taken care of that way. Then it's superimposed on the background. We're working in *The Birds* on the sodium light system. We're having to double-print a lot of birds over existing birds, where we have a small quantity of birds, trained ones, moving in and out, or whatever they're doing, then you print over that scene a lot of other birds. And we're using a sodium light process, which is a background which is lit by sodium—those yellow fog lights, you know—so that the camera picks up just the images, the background goes back, you get your colour image. And in the camera is a prism and that prism also makes the silhouette matte at the same time on a regular b/w film so that it doesn't register colour. The filter in the prism turns the image black and the sodium background plain. So you make your travelling matte at the same time as you're photographing: we use an old technicolour camera for that.

You must have been very thrilled with your Vertigo *effect.*

I've been trying for fifteen, twenty years to get that effect. I first tried it in *Rebecca.* I wanted to get, in an inquest scene, Joan Fontaine to start to faint and see everything receding from her. I tried everything—I even thought of printing a photograph on rubber and stretching the middle.

You obtained the stretching of the perspective by simultaneously tracking in and zooming out, didn't you?

Yes.

We have an argument about Rear Window. *One of us says that a good deal of the suspense comes from one's not being sure whether James Stewart is right, whether he's making a fool of himself. The other says that you're meant to be certain that he's right and the suspense comes from whether he will prove it in time.*

I would say that it's the latter, because it's frustration you see. The audience *are* with Stewart, the identification is direct and therefore they must feel superior to the other characters with him, but the frustration is there all the same. The interesting thing I think about *Rear Window* is that there's more pure film there, even though it's static, than in many films I've made. After all you get the famous examples that Pudovkin experimented with—where you get Stewart looking, what he sees, and his reaction to it. And there, after all, is the most powerful thing of film. You've got three pieces of film. Let's assume, for example,

Stewart looks, you see a mother and child; then you go back to Stewart and he smiles. Now you see he's rather benevolent or benign, call it what you like. Take the middle piece away and put a nude girl in there and he's a dirty old man.

Would you say that your films now are rather more thought out than instinctive, and were more instinctive in the thirties?

I would say so, yes. Well, I think you can have a bit of both really. But I think I got that (*i.e. more intellectual*) when I was aware of the *global* implications of audiences. That's one thing that you do learn in America, because America is a polyglot country. I often tell people, there are no Americans, it's full of foreigners. You become very audience-conscious because there are so many different types of people. Axiomatically you're appealing to your Japanese audience and your Latin-American audience as well.

The idea of Stage Fright *intrigues us a great deal. Do you like it?*

No. It wasn't well done. You remember I said I liked to work with playwrights and novelists preferably. I went a bit overboard—I had James Bridie and he was too careless for me, structurally. He used to say, "Well, what does it matter?"

Whose was the basic idea of the flash-back that wasn't true?

That was mine, but that was probably an error. That was going a bit too far because I suppose people are so accustomed to flash-backs being true that it was just confusing when it was untrue. It's like the boy with the bomb in *Sabotage*. I should never have let that bomb go off. It was a cardinal error to let that bomb go off. If you work an audience up, it's obligatory to relieve them, to release them from that.

Having built them up, the explosion didn't release them?

No, of course not. It got them mad.

What next?

I'm going to do the *Marnie* picture next. The story of the compulsive thief that I was going to do with Grace Kelly.

Who's taking the Grace Kelly part?

I've got a girl in mind, but we're not letting on yet.

You're going back to big stars?

Not necessarily. Sometimes I think big stars are useful but today they don't help a picture any more. They help it if it's good, but if it's not good the public won't go.

And Psycho *showed you could get along without them . . .*

Yes.

Alfred Hitchcock (1899–   ):
Filmography:
1925—The Pleasure Garden. 1926—The Mountain Eagle, The Lodger. 1927—Downhill, Easy Virtue, The Ring. 1928—The Farmer's Wife, Champagne, The Manxman. 1929—Blackmail. 1930—Juno and the Paycock, Murder. 1931—The Skin Game. 1932—East of Shanghai, Number Seventeen. 1935—The 39 Steps, The Man Who Knew Too Much, Strauss' Great Waltz. 1936—Secret Agent. 1937—Sabotage. 1938—The Lady Vanishes, A Girl Was Young. 1939—Jamaica Inn. 1940—Rebecca, Foreign Correspondent. 1941—Mr. and Mrs. Smith, Suspicion. 1942—Saboteur. 1943—Shadow of a Doubt. 1944—Lifeboat. 1945—Spellbound. 1946—Notorious. 1947—The Paradine Case. 1948—Rope. 1949—Under Capicorn. 1950—Stage Fright. 1951—Strangers on a Train. 1952—I Confess. 1954—Dial M for Murder, Rear Window. 1955—To Catch a Thief, The Trouble with Harry. 1956—The Man Who Knew Too Much, The Wrong Man. 1958—Vertigo. 1959—North by Northwest. 1960—Psycho. 1963—The Birds. 1964—Marnie. 1966—The Torn Curtain. 1969—Topaz. FRENZY   FAMILY PLOT

director I had ever interviewed. The day after I moved into a new apartment in Rome, people began calling me on the phone and asking for Huston. It turned out that I had accidentally moved into the apartment that he had vacated when he went to Egypt to shoot exteriors. I called up the studio and said I had some messages for Mr. Huston. He invited me out to the set to watch him shoot the sequence of Noah's Ark.

The De Laurentiis studios are the biggest in Europe today, and they are brand new. When I got there, I found myself in the center of a circus—a typical travelling circus with caravans and cage carts, with animal noises and smells all around, and with a whole stationary zoo that had been constructed near the studios to supply the 200 land animals and 1,000 birds that were participating in the shooting of the ark sequence. The ark itself was inescapable —it wasn't just there once, but five times, in various sizes and in various stages of completion. Huston—who had less time than Noah—needed five arks to shoot the various stages of development of the vessel and in order to be able to shoot interiors or exteriors at will in any kind of weather.

Our actual meeting took place at the enclosure of the hippopotamus. Huston himself plays Noah in this sequence, and he was busy trying to convince the hippo to follow the requirements of the script. For an entire morning, while the cameras turned, the lights blazed, and Huston in his sackcloth costume endlessly repeated his biblical words, the animal refused to cooperate. Finally, in exasperation, Huston said to me: Let's give the poor beast a rest. What was it that you wanted to talk to me about?

And so right there, among the giraffes and the peacocks, the lions and the Himalayan goats, I asked Huston how he made films.

BACHMANN: I think this is one of those rare times when I can start an interview [for radio use also] without any introductions. You're the kind of person who creates around him not only the normal fame as a director of the kind of films everybody has seen, but also a kind of personal aura, a sort of romantic halo, which means that you are as known as your work, and I don't have to go into a lot of explicatory remarks. And in any case, all I am interested in at this time is how you make films.

HUSTON: I wish you had a better reason for omitting the introductions. On the other hand I am really happy that you go straight to the heart of the matter. This also corresponds to my method of working—it never seems to me that my films start with much preparation. In fact, I often get the feeling that my films make themselves. By this I don't mean that I don't take part in the production process, but very often I couldn't tell you exactly how ideas start to crystallize. For example, I never start off by saying "I'm going to make a specific film," but some idea, some novel, some play suggests itself—very often it's something I read 25 or 30 years ago, or when I was a child, and have played around with in my thoughts for a long time. That was the case with pictures like *Moby Dick, The Red Badge of Courage,* and several others. Suddenly, surprisingly, I discover that I am actually making it. There's a film that I am going to make after I finish *The Bible* that has the same background: *The Man Who Would Be King,* the Kipling story. The first script on this film was written about ten years ago, but it was based on my reading of the story at age 12 or 15, and my impressions of it, that have remained with me. Most of the time my pictures begin with this kind of inbred idea, something that lives in me from long ago. Sometimes it's more erratic, though; someone has a picture they want you to make and if you think it's good enough to take a shot at, you step in as a sort of surgeon or practitioner. The only safe thing I can say is that there are no rules.

How does the script get written? Do you do it alone? And how long does it take you?

Again, there are no rules. I've written scripts and made pictures out of them in two weeks. At other times I've worked a year and a half just on a script. *The Maltese Falcon* was done in a very short time, because it was based on a very fine book and there was very little for me to invent. It was a matter of sticking to the ideas of the book, of making a film out of a book. On *Treasure of Sierra Madre,* I wrote the script in about 3-4 months, but I had had quite a long time to think about it before. The actual making of the film didn't take very long, but I had had the idea of making it since before the war. It was the first film I made after the war.

You wrote that one alone, and got an Oscar for writing it. But don't you sometimes write together with other people? Or, when other people write for you, do you take a very active part or do you leave them pretty much alone?

When I do not write alone—and of course you must remember that I began my film career as a writer, not as a

255

director—I work very closely with the writer. Almost always I share in the writing. The writer will do a scene and then I'll work it over, or I'll write a scene and then the other writer will make adjustments later. Often we trade scenes back and forth until we're both satisfied.

You don't like to work with more than one other writer?

Not really. But sometimes other people make additions. For example, the writer of a play or a book on which I am basing a film. Tennessee Williams, for example, came and worked with Anthony Vay and myself on the script for *Night of the Iguana*. He didn't come there to write, but once he was there he did do some writing, and actually he did some rather important writing for the film. But such cases are the exception.

Could you put into words some principles you employ in order to put ideas into film form? Do you feel there are any rules a writer for the cinema must follow?

Each idea calls for a different treatment, really. I am not aware of any ready formula, except the obvious one that films fall into a certain number of scenes, and that you have to pay attention to certain limitations that have to do with time, according to subject. Depending on what you are writing about, you have to decide the time balance between words and action. It seems to me, for example, that the word contains as much action as a purely visual scene, and that dialogue should have as much action in it as physical motion. The sense of activity that your audience gets is derived equally from what they see and from what they hear. The fascination, the attention of the man who looks at what you have put together, must be for the thoughts as much as for the happenings in your film. In fact, when I write I can't really separate the words from the actions. The final action—the combined activity of the film, the sum of the words and the visuals—is really going on only in the mind of the beholder. So in writing I have to convey a sense of overall progression with all the means at my command: words and images and sounds and everything else that makes film.

This brings up one of the basic questions about films that adapt literary works: in a book there are many things that you can't see or hear, but which in reading you translate directly into your own interior images and feelings. Emotions that are created in you neither through dialogue nor action. How do you get these into film? The monologues from Moby Dick, *for example?*

Well, first of all, I try to beware of literal transfers to film of what a writer has created initially for a different form. Instead I try to penetrate first to the basic idea of the book or the play, and then work with those ideas in cinematic terms. For example, to see what Melville wanted to say in the dialogues, what emotions he wanted to convey. I always thought *Moby Dick* was a great blasphemy. Here was a man who shook his fist at God. The thematic line in *Moby Dick* seemed to me, always, to have been: who's to judge when the judge himself is dragged before the bar? Who's to condemn, but he, Ahab! This was, to me, the point at which I tried to aim the whole picture, because I think that's what Melville was essentially concerned with, and this is, at the same time, the point that makes *Moby Dick* so extremely timely in our age. And if I may be allowed the side-observation: I don't think any of the critics who wrote about the film ever mentioned this.

I suppose you are speaking about the problem of taking personal responsibility in an age where the group has largely attempted to make decisions for the individual. This is an interpretation of Melville, or perhaps I should say ONE interpretation of Melville. And so in the attempt to understand the basic idea of a work (in order to translate those ideas into film) you are really doing more than that: you add your own interpretation, you don't just put into images what the original author wanted to say.

I don't think we can avoid interpretation. Even just pointing a camera at a certain reality means an interpretation of that reality. By the same token, I don't *seek* to interpret, to put my own stamp on the material. I try to be as faithful to the original material as I can. This applies equally to Melville as it applies to the Bible, for example. In fact, it's the fascination that I feel for the original that makes me want to make it into a film.

What about original material, where you are not adapting a play or a book? Are there any ideas of yours, basic ideas, which you try to express in your work? Do you feel that there is a continuity in your work in terms of a consistent ideology? In short, do you feel you are trying to say something coherent to mankind?

There probably is. I am not consciously aware of anything. But even the choice of material indicates a preference, a turn of mind. You could draw a portrait of a mind through that mind's preferences.

Well, let me do that for a minute, and see if what I see as a unifying idea in your work is indeed a coherent feeling on your part. I see that in your films there is always a man pitched against odds, an individual who seeks to retain a sense of his own individuality in the face of a culture that surrounds and tends to submerge him. I would call the style of your films the style of the frontier, or what the frontier has come to symbolize in American culture: a sense of rebellion against being put into a system, into a form of life and into a mode of thinking rigidly decided by others.

Yes, I think there is something there. I do come from a frontier background. My people were that. And I always feel constrained in the presence of too many rules, severe rules; they distress me. I like the sense of freedom. I don't particularly seek that ultimate freedom of the anarchist, but I'm impatient of rules that result from prejudice.

In any case, you believe that at the basis of every film of yours there is a basic idea, whether an idea of yours or one of another author. But how do you proceed to put that idea into film form? In writing, what do you do first, for example?

I don't envisage the whole thing at the beginning. I go a little bit at a time, always asking myself whether I am on the track of the basic thought. Within that, I try to make each scene as good as I can. This applies both to the writing and to the directing—to the whole process of preparation and production, in fact—which are only extensions of the process of writing. It's hard to break down into details.

Do you mean to say that you do not write the whole script in the beginning?

Oh yes, oh sure. I am speaking about the making of the film. I try to make it in sequence as much as possible, to develop the making of the film along with the development of the story within the film. I try, for example, to give my actors a sense of development not only within the troupe, but also a sense of development within the story of the film. And I improvise if necessary. This is not a luxury; when one shoots as much on location as I do, improvisation is a necessity. Everything that happens in the process of making the film can contribute to the development of that film's story. But of course one always tries to remain within the bounds of the controllable as much as one can, to stay within the bounds of the script. But one must be open to take advantage of the terrain, of the things that the setting can give you.

Do you write your scripts with the idea of change and improvisation already in mind?

Improvisation is used more today than it used to be. Partly this is caused by a new, less rigid approach to film-making, and also partly by the decentralization of the production process. Actors have become producers, they have commitments of conflicting sorts, and it is no longer possible to prepare a script in great detail in a major studio set-up, and then call in your contract actors, whose time you control completely, and make the film in exact accordance to plan. It has simply become essential today to be more flexible, to adjust to new conditions, both practical and aesthetic.

Do you see this as a positive or a negative development?

It has certainly helped some directors to come into their own, people who could never have succeeded under the old, less independent system. Some French and Italian directors—Fellini in the vanguard—have found it possible to tell much more subjective stories, often their own, in a valid cinematographic way. Like 8½ for example.

What is the technical process of your scriptwriting?

Usually I write in longhand first, and then dictate a later version. I use a standard script form: action on the left and dialogue on the right. When it's finished it's mimeographed and distributed to the people who need to see it. I often change again later. Sometimes I finish the final version on the set itself, or change again something I've written as a final version the day before. Mostly these changes come to me when I hear the words first spoken by an actor. It's always different once it comes out of a living person's mouth. By this I do not mean that I try to adjust to an actor's personality—I try to do that as little as possible. When I write, I don't have in mind an actor, but a character. I don't conceive this character with a specific star in my mind. I guess what I am trying to do with this constant changing, is to try to put to work more than my own imagination, or at least allow my imagination the liberty of play, the liberty of coming out of its cage—which is me, my body, when I am alone and writing—and in this way it begins to live and to flower and gives me better service than when I put it to work abstractly, alone, in a room with paper and pencil, without the living presence of

259

the material. Then, when the character has been born out of this extended imagination, I have to look for someone to play the role, and this someone isn't always necessarily the person who I thought could play it originally, because often it no longer is the same character. In fact, I've often —at least, sometimes—delayed the making of a film because I couldn't find anybody to play the new and adjusted character that I had finally arrived at construing. Although in my experience you usually find someone; there are enough good actors if you are willing to wait a little.

Is it possible for you to tell how much of your writing comes from inside you, at the start, and how much is written in adjustment to a situation or to hearing your words spoken? And do you also adjust to location, for example? I mean, when you write about Sodom, do you write for Vesuvius, for the landscape where you decided to shoot those sequences?

It's the same thing as trying to interpret Melville. You write for an ideal. Then when you make the film, you try to live up to that ideal. Casting, locating, shooting: you try to stick to what you start with. Sometimes there are problems when the material changes in my hands, sometimes I have even miscast my own films. But generally these adjustment problems can be overcome. I've been pretty lucky that way. In fact, I can usually do pretty much exactly what I set out to do. I've been lucky.

Is that what gives you this tremendous peace that you seem to have on the set? I have watched perhaps a hundred directors shooting, and nobody is as calm. And you have this kooky set: this silly ark with all these animals, peacocks flying among the long necks of giraffes, hippos who refuse to act the scenes written for them, a hundred breakdowns a day with technical things caused by the animals, and you just stride through the whole thing in your Noah costume, feeding the giraffes, smiling and taking it easy . . .

I am astonished myself. And I marvel at the patience of everybody, especially the animals, who are among the best actors I've ever worked with . . .

All typecast, too. . . . But, is that an answer?

In a way, yes. You see, in working with actors, I try to direct as little as possible. The more one directs, the more there is a tendency to monotony. If one is telling each person what to do, one ends up with a host of little replicas of oneself. So, when I start a scene, I always let the actor show me for the start how he imagines the scene himself. This applies not only to actors; as I tried to indicate before, I try to let the whole thing work on me, show me. The actors, the set, the location, the sounds, all help to show me what the correct movement could be. So what I said about the animals wasn't only a joke. Because, you see, the animals have one great advantage as actors; they know exactly what they want to do, no self-doubts, no hesitations. If you watch them, quite extraordinary opportunities present themselves, but you must see them. Here in the Noah's Ark sequence of *The Bible* this has happened a number of times. Animals do remarkable things. The hippo opened his mouth and let me pet him inside.

Is that when you wrote the line, which you say to Noah's wife at that point: "There is no evil in him, wife. Do not fear him!"

Exactly. And very fine actors are as much themselves as animals are. I would rather have someone whose personality lends itself to the role than a good actor who can simulate the illusion of being the character. I do not like to see the mechanics of acting. The best you can get, of course, is when the personality lends itself exquisitely to the part and when that personality has the added attribute of being technically a fine actor so he can control his performance. That is the ideal.

What do you consider to be the attributes of a fine actor?

The shading he can give a line, his timing, his control, his knowledge of the camera, his relationship to the camera—of course, I'm talking about film acting.

What should an actor's relationship to the camera be?

He must have an awareness of the size of his gesture, his motion, in relation to the size that his image will be on the screen. It isn't absolutely an essential quality, but it is very useful. I don't mean that I tell him the focal length of the lens I'm using and expect him to adapt himself accordingly, but a good actor has an almost instinctual awareness of these things. When an actor comes from the stage, he usually has to make adjustments of this kind. He doesn't need to project, he doesn't need to make his voice heard over a distance. He can speak very quietly. He can be more economical in every way before the camera than he could be on the stage. And he can work with the small details of his face.

Does a good actor, one with all the best technical attri-butes, make a star?

Oh, no. One doesn't have much to do with the other. Of course, the star must know how to act, and a good actor can become a star, but what a star really is, is hard to describe. There are many fine and beautiful actors who would never be stars. I don't think that's a lack in their personalities, because it's beyond that—something very mysterious happens. Some personalities seem to take on another dimension on the screen. They become bigger than life. When that happens, there is a star. Some stars are not good actors, but a lot of good actors aren't stars.

Can you recognize this star quality when you meet a person, or do you have to see the person on the screen first?

I recognize it more or less. For instance, I had Marilyn Monroe in her first real film role [in *The Asphalt Jungle*] and I can't claim to have had any notion of where she was headed, but I could feel that she was going to be good in this film and I chose her over a number of others. But still I didn't dream of the places she would go.

How did you meet her?

She was brought in by an agent in Hollywood.

Did you have one of those ideal characters ready in mind when you saw her?

Yes, and she was it. I guess it was an interesting moment, but I didn't know it at the time.

How do you—even more or less—recognize the star quality?

In certain instances, it stands out all over the individual, just as it stands out in certain horses now and then. You look at an animal and you know it is top class. It's the same with certain persons—with an Ava Gardner, with a Humphrey Bogart, with a Katharine Hepburn. There's no mistaking that quality when you see it any more than there is a chance of mistaking the looks of a great horse in the paddock. It's hard to put it in other words, and it varies from person to person.

In any case, you are speaking of something that isn't just a flamboyance of bearing?

On the contrary. Flamboyance is something that people assume when they feel a lack of structure in their own characters. But this, too, is not invariably the case. I've known some flamboyant people who were extraordinary too. Flamboyance is all right when it is a natural expression of something that is really that person. It's like every other characteristic that a person has: it's good only if it's real. I don't like it if people put on false surfaces, and I think by now I can tell when they do. And it always works against my choosing a certain person to play in a film.

Let's see if we can follow your film-making method through logically and go to a description of the process of turning the script into film.

Actually I don't separate the elements of film-making in such an abstract manner. For example, the directing of a film, to me, is simply an extension of the process of writing. It's the process of rendering the thing you have written. You're still writing when you're directing. Of course you're not composing words, but a gesture, the way you make somebody raise his eyes or shake his head is also writing for films. Nor can I answer precisely what the relative importance, to me, of the various aspects of film-making is, I mean, whether I pay more attention to writing, directing, editing, or what-have-you. The most important element to me is always the idea that I'm trying to express, and everything technical is only a method to make the idea into clear form. I'm always working on the idea: whether I am writing, directing, choosing music or cutting. Everything must revert back to the idea; when it gets away from the idea it becomes a labyrinth of rococo. Occasionally one tends to forget the idea, but I have always had reason to regret this whenever it happened. Sometimes you fall in love with a shot, for example. Maybe it is a tour de force as a shot. This is one of the great dangers of directing: to let the camera take over. Audiences very often do not understand this danger, and it is not unusual that camera-work is appreciated in cases where it really has no business in the film, simply because it is decorative or in itself exhibitionistic. I would say that there are maybe half a dozen directors who really know their camera—how to move their camera. It's a pity that critics often do not appreciate this. On the other hand I think it's OK that audiences should not be aware of this. In fact, when the camera is in motion, in the best-directed scenes, the audiences should not be aware of what the camera is doing. They should be following the action and the road of the idea so closely that they shouldn't be aware of what's going on technically.

Am I right in assuming, then, that you do not share the modern view that the form of a film can be as important as its content? I take it, from what you say, that you are interested more in what is being said than in how it is being said.

When you become aware of *how* things are being said, you get separated from the idea. This doesn't mean that an original rendering isn't to be sought after, but that rendering must be so close to the idea itself that you aren't aware of it.

If the optimum is to stay close to the original idea without imposing one's individuality upon it, then the old Thalberg-Ince system of having a script written by one man and then farming it out to another to shoot, wouldn't appear to be so bad.

That's carrying a principle to an extreme. Let's be sure to have enough regard for *style*. I am not saying that the director who is carrying onto film the idea created by another man should obliterate his individuality. After all, there are many ways—as many as there are people—to do any one thing, including the direction of a film. One sticks to an idea within one's own ability and with the means that are native to oneself, and not through employing means that are so commonplace that anybody could use them. What goes for film also goes for literature, for any form of art; the originality of Joyce is in no way to be divorced from what he was saying. There's no separation between style and subject matter, between style and intention, between style and—again—the idea. I do not mean to indicate, in anything I say, that the work of a man shouldn't bear witness to the personality of that man, beyond the fact that he expresses a specific idea in that work. It's the combination of his personality and the idea he expresses which creates his style.

How do you define style?

As the adaptation of the word or the action to the idea. I remember when I was a kid this question of style puzzled me. I didn't know what they meant by the style of a certain writer. One day Plato's *Apology* fell into my hands. It was an accident, but it was an eye-opener for me as far as style was concerned. I understood that the words of Socrates were in keeping with the monumentality of his conceptions.

Do you adjust your style to what you consider the intelligence level of your public to be? In other words, if you made a film today about Socrates in the style of Socrates (if I may oversimplify for a moment), this style itself would stand between the ideas you are trying to express and the person in some small town who might see your film.

I don't adjust to what they call the level of the audience. The mentality of an audience is something I consider as quite extraordinary. Audiences can feel and think with a celerity and a unison perhaps beyond the power of its most intelligent members. They laugh instantly if something is funny, and in other ways, too, they react in the most extraordinarily perceptive way. So I think it's nonsense to listen to the producers who tell you "they won't understand you." When I make a picture I go under the assumption that if I like something, there are enough people like me who will like it too, to make it worth doing.

Does that mean that to make something worthwhile it must be accepted by a major number of other people?

Yes, there's that requirement.

I mean, beyond the financial requirement that films be sold.

Well, you can't go beyond that.

I mean in terms of your own personal satisfaction. Is it very important to you that your films be seen by many people, and understood by many people?

I don't make pictures for myself. And I do believe that if I like a film, others will like it too. I make films with the intention that they be seen. I make a picture for others. It's not just a personal satisfaction that I'm seeking. On the other hand I don't try to imagine the reactions or to figure out, ahead of time, the minds of others. It's hard enough for me to understand my own mind and to understand myself. I couldn't possibly speculate on what fifty million people might like or not like. I can only hope that among those fifty million there are enough who resemble me in taste.

Do you think that a film is better if more people like it?

Sometimes. But this is quite a question that you've asked me there. We're getting into quite an abstract area. Films are not always immediately popular. Sometimes films acquire popularity slowly over the years, as has happened with some of mine. For example *The Red Badge of Courage*. And also *Beat the Devil*, which was a complete bust when it came out, and now it has a sort of cult following. Over the years these two pictures have probably had bigger audiences than *Moulin Rouge*, which was immediately successful.

265

Let's get back to the film-making process. You've assembled, changed, and rewritten your script and chosen your actors. Do you give them the script to read before they come on the set?

Yes, of course. They read the script before they ever get any instructions from me. Sometimes they then like to talk about the role before they appear on the set in make-up. But I try to tell them as little as possible, because I want to see what they can give me. There's always time later to give them what I've thought about. In the beginning I want them not to be influenced by my pre-determinations, because that would close up their individual creativity, it would eliminate their ability to give me something new, something I might not have thought of myself. The best illustration of this is the story of my first film, the first one I directed. I made drawings. I wanted to be very sure. I was uncertain of myself as far as the camera was concerned and I wanted to be sure not to fumble, not to get lost in the mechanical aspects of the film. So I made drawings of every set-up, but didn't show the drawings to anyone. I discovered that about 50% of the time the actors themselves automatically fell into the drawings, and about 25% of the time I had to pull them into the drawings, which were, in fact, set-up designs. But another 25% of the time they did something better than I had thought of myself.

That means you work through the actor's intellectual comprehension of your material?

Of course, and I benefit from this comprehension very often. In fact, even before Stanislavski I think actors always functioned this way. The only reason it became such a fad was that so many young people were marching out onto the screen without any preparation, so suddenly the emphasis shifted strongly towards preparation and it was made into something of a religion; I mean "the method" and the Actor's Studio, etc. And of course many good actors came out of that school. Personally I don't prefer conscious actors, or actors with that particular training, nor do I reject them, because I believe that every good actor prepares, maybe not always so consciously.

Do you let them rehearse a lot on the set?

It depends on the scene. I don't let them rehearse too much, as a rule, but some scenes call for more rehearsal than others.

What kind of instructions are you likely to give an actor?

Anything that will give him a sense of security. In the initial conversations, I may talk about the idea of the role, what its relation to the whole picture is, the background of the character. Some actors like to talk a lot. It helps them.

Do you, yourself, like to talk a lot?

Not very much. But I find it my job to do anything I can to help the actor, to make him feel at ease, to give him a sense of independence, of importance, if you will. I'll do anything for this, even talk. But I always keep hoping that it will be the actor who will show me, rather than the other way around.

What then do you tell them, in precise terms, when they get on the set? Do you tell them where to stand . . .

Not even that. I let them stand where they please. Sometimes they wait to be told, and I always try to get them to take the reins themselves. I say, let's rehearse the scene, you show me. Mostly they do this of their own accord. I'd say four out of five times the actors—especially if they are very good actors—take over right away. I don't have to say a word. If they are talented and intelligent they expect to be let alone. For example, working with George Scott, I seldom even gave a clue of direction, and he did exactly what I wanted without any of us ever saying a word, practically. Only occasionally I would have to ask him to move a bit to the left or the right. His approach to the scene would be so real and true that I couldn't add anything, except those mechanical camera directions. Not all actors are that good, and some you have to work a lot with. Sometimes very good actors need a lot of direction, too, but if they are gifted and intelligent one is on the same wavelength anyway and one can talk in a kind of code. They catch immediately what you want, and they fit right in. They catch what you want, use it, and it comes back to you stronger, better than you gave it to them, because they have digested it and are using their talents to put it into reality. Sometimes I have directed people in ways which disappointed me, and have later discovered that when I left them alone to do what they wanted, it came out better. I suppose it's because a good actor knows what he can do well and how, and through this self-knowledge he can produce something I couldn't abstractly imagine. Sometimes I shoot a scene both ways: mine and his, and often—like for example with Clark Gable—I find that his version is better on the screen.

Do you consider the actor raw material for your manip-

ulation or an alive organism that you must adjust to? Does he retain his personality in what you make him do or is he only a means to your end?

He's a means to my end only insofar as he retains his personality.

You try not to impose yourself on him at all?

I try not to. He must be a very bad actor for me to try to do this. And, by the way, on the part of the director there is as much work in concealing bad performances as there is in developing good ones.

What else, besides controlling the actors, does your job of directing include? How much control do you exercise over the camera, the light, the sets, the other mechanics?

Lighting is almost completely up to the cameraman, who of course must be in complete sympathy with the director. The set-up is something else. There you're telling the story, the composition will appear on the screen, also the movement of the camera. The variety of material to be included in the shot, and its displacement, those are things I try to control. Again, when I decide about these things, I go by the rules that are imposed upon me by the central idea, by what I'm trying to say, and how I've decided to say it. And I choose set-ups and camera angles that will tell my story as quickly and as strongly and as surely as possible.

Do you have the precise set-up in mind when you write the script?

No. I write first, then seek the set-up that demonstrates. And I find that if the set-up is chosen well, I hardly ever have to change a line for a set-up or a set-up for a line. The fact that I write the words first doesn't mean the words have precedence. I find that dialogue and camera set-up are not at war. I don't seek a set-up to carry a certain word; I seek a certain word and a certain set-up to carry a certain idea. Sometimes one single word is enough for this, or even complete silence, if the image is right.

Do you think the fewer words spoken in a film, the better film it is?

Depends on the film. Some films depend on words. Take *Night of the Iguana.* Take the spoken words out of that, and you won't have very much.

Is that only because that particular script was based on a play? Or do you feel that scripts that are very word-oriented could also be read as literature as a play can?

I don't think you can make rules. In the case of *Iguana*

the words were important because they carried Tennessee Williams' thoughts. But I think a good screenplay could be read as literature, too. It simply depends on the particular material.

You are not taking sides, then, in the perennial controversy over what's more important in film, the word or the image?

I don't see that they are in conflict. Depending on what is being said, they complement each other in the hands of a good craftsman.

Well, there's a difference in impact, of course. I'm thinking of the aesthetic problems of the intake of stimuli by a man sitting in a dark hall. If you put words and images on the same level, certain problems arise. Sitting there in the dark, his ears can be unbusy for some length of time, so you can introduce silence on the sound track. But there's got to be something on the screen to see all the time.

The problem of the attention of the audience to the screen has occupied me quite a lot. Because of the dark tunnel in which he sits, the spectator in a film has nothing else to fix his attention onto, only that oblong of light which is the screen. This causes a whole different *time factor* to operate in his process of perception, than in other forms of spectacle, like plays. Two or three seconds of delay in a scene in a film can immediately cause a dull and laborious effect, and the viewer can begin to behold himself, rather than the screen. He shifts in his seat and coughs and scratches and feels his internal organs at work. So you must work to this different time factor when directing a film. Film isn't like most arts, where you can stop watching for a while—you can put a book aside, stop watching a wall with pictures while taking a cup of coffee —but in film all the viewer can do is watch, watch constantly, and the film-maker has to fill the screen for him all the time. It's a requirement of film-making that the viewer's attention be held all the time. It's a requirement, unfortunately, that's not often lived up to. I only know of very few instances in my own experience of film-going where this requirement was constantly being met. On the other hand, making films where something is constantly happening, also imposes greater demands on the viewer than is the case in any other medium. But there are many things inherent in the medium that work for you; the whole immediacy of the experience, and the subjectivity of the emotions that can derive from a good film. The ideal film, it seems to me, is when it's as though the projector were behind the beholder's eyes, and he throws onto the screen that which he *wants* to see. Films are usually very good for their first two or three minutes. The audience is completely taken outside of itself. They are not aware of themselves. And then comes that awful moment when they become self-aware once more. It's the film that allows this to happen, of course. I think that one of the problems of the people who make films is that they have not realized that most of the devices of film are inherent in the physiology of man. I mean, all the things we have laboriously learned to do with film, were already part of the daily physiological and psychological experience of man before film was invented, and if we only knew how to make a bridge between these natural experiences and that which we put on the screens, we would be able to eliminate those dead moments, those dull and laborious times, when the human being begins to feel the distance between his real experience and that which is suggested to him *via* the screen. Let me make an experiment—maybe you will understand better what I mean. Move your eyes, quickly, from an object on one side of this room to an object on the other side. In a film you would use the cut. Watch! There—you did exactly what I expected: in moving your head from one side of the room to the other, you briefly closed your eyes. Try it again, in the other direction. There! You see, you do it automatically. Once you know the distance between the two objects, you blink instinctively. That's a cut. If you were to pan, as we could do with the camera or as you could do with your eyes, from one side to the other, passing all the objects on the way, and then back again, it would become tedious beyond endurance. This does it for you. In the same way, almost all the devices of film have a physiological counterpart. It's a matter of learning—again—to use it.

And you can look at most other filmic devices with this point of view. Take the dissolve. Your thoughts are changing. There's that moment of impingement of thoughts and images where you are aware of your surroundings, or perhaps looking at something else, outside your direct field of vision. Thoughts change while the things you see intermingle. And take the fade-out: that corresponds to sleep. It's an opportunity to rest, to change completely. Exactly as we use it in film.

I'm particularly intrigued by what you said about the time factor. Film is the only graphic medium in which the intake period, the time it takes to receive the stimulus, on the part of the spectator, is controlled not by that spectator, but by the maker of the film. You control how long he looks. In fact, it has always seemed to me that this possibility of controlling the time element is much more important, is a more basic aesthetic element in film, than the fact that it moves. Movement is simply one of the functions of time. Film is the only art form in which you can manipulate time. In fact, I would say one could make a film in which nothing moved, which would be composed entirely of stills, but which would still be entirely "filmic" because it controls the psychological experience of time in an artificial way. Sometimes I wonder how many film-makers are aware of the power they possess through this capacity to change man's concepts of time.

Most film-makers are aware of the time element in the sense that they are worried about the lagging attention of the viewer. That means they are aware of the problem of time manipulation, but not consciously. They know they've got to speed up a scene, for example. They don't know why—they don't know what they're doing. But then I don't necessarily believe that complete consciousness makes better artists.

What other elements of film-making do you try to control as part of the creative process?

One of the most important elements is to control the producer. Artistically, I am most concerned with controlling the color. Some films would suffer from being in color. Color, like camera acrobatics, can be a distraction unless it's functional in the film. But both are important, black-and-white and color film. Artists have pigments, but they continue to draw. Certain subjects are better in one and others in the other medium. I would never have made *Freud* in color. There was a certain projection of a unilateral thought, the development of a logic. Color would only have distracted. I wanted the audience to follow the logic that was as real as a detective's pursuit of a criminal, without distraction by visual elements. And by the same token, I would never have made *Moulin Rouge* in black-and-white. And in *Moby Dick* I tried to combine both by inventing a technique of printing both types of film together.

Do you always try to experiment with new ideas? Do

you feel that there is a continuity, in this sense, in your work?

As far as I can say, talking about myself, I think there is a certain uniformity in my work from the beginning up till now. And the one thing I always try to experiment with is accepting suggestions from the people who work with me. I don't like to dictate, I like to receive stimuli from all: not only the cameraman and the actors, but the grips and the script girl, or the animal trainers as in the case of *The Bible*. I try to create an atmosphere on the set where everyone feels they can participate. I guess this is as much as I can say in terms of having a basic theory of directing: letting the material have complete freedom, and imposing myself only where necessary. That's what I meant when I was guilty of that original cliché by remarking that I let my films make themselves.

How do you finish your films?

I shoot very economically, sometimes not enough, even. I shoot as if I were editing in the camera. Then there's usually only one way to cut the film. I look at the rushes every day, again allowing for my collaborators' views in choosing the final takes to use. Then, when the film is cut, I choose the music with the idea that it has to have a dramatic purpose. I hate decorative music. I want the music to help tell the story, illustrate the idea, not just to emphasize the images. That means that it must have a certain autonomy. And there should be economy.

Would you say that your principle of making films, and your principle of using the various elements, like music, for example, is this economy?

Everything must serve the idea—I must say this again and again. The means used to convey the idea should be the simplest and the most direct and clear. I don't believe in overdressing anything. Just what is required. No extra words, no extra images, no extra music. But it seems to me that this is a universal principle of art. To say as much as possible with a minimum of means. And to be always clear about what you are trying to say. That means, of course, that you must know what you are trying to say. So I guess my first principle is to understand myself, and then to find the simplest way to make others understand it, too.

John Huston (1906–   ):
Filmography:
1941—The Maltese Falcon. 1942—In This Our Life, Across the Pa-

cific, Report from the Aleutians. 1944—The Battle of San Pietro. 1945—Let There Be Light. 1948—The Treasure of the Sierra Madre, Key Largo. 1949—We Were Strangers. 1950—The Asphalt Jungle. 1951—The Red Badge of Courage. 1952—The African Queen. 1953—Moulin Rouge. 1954—Beat the Devil. 1956—Moby Dick. 1957—Heaven Knows, Mr. Allison. 1958—The Barbarian and the Geisha, The Roots of Heaven. 1960—The Unforgiven. 1961—The Misfits. 1962—Freud. 1963—The List of Adrian Messenger. 1964—The Night of the Iguana. 1966—The Bible. 1967—Casino Royale, Reflections in a Golden Eye. 1969—Sinful Davey, A Walk with Love and Death.

Buster Keaton

That Buster Keaton had regained a certain critical eminence before his death is due largely to the tireless efforts of the film cultists in the little magazines. What the late James Agee described as the "Golden Age of Comedy" (and Silence) now boils down to Chaplin and Keaton or Keaton and Chaplin. The difference between Keaton and Chaplin is the difference between poise and poetry, between the aristocrat and the tramp, between adaptability and dislocation, between the function of things and the meaning of things, between eccentricity and mysticism, between man as machine and man as angel, between the girl as a convention and the girl as an ideal, between life as farce and life as fantasy. Keaton is now generally acknowledged as the superior director and inventor of visual forms. There are those who would go further and claim Keaton as pure cinema as opposed to Chaplin's essentially theatrical cinema. Keaton's cerebral tradition of comedy was continued by Clair and Tati, but Keaton the actor, like Chaplin the actor, has proved to be inimitable. Ultimately, Keaton and Chaplin complement each other all the way down the line to that memorably ghostly moment in Limelight when they share the same tawdry dressing room preparing to face their lost audience.*—A.S.

Our readers would be very interested to know how you got into motion pictures.

* Christopher Bishop's interview with Buster Keaton originally appeared in Film Quarterly, No. 1, Vol. XII, Fall 1958.

Well, I was born with a show. My parents were already in vaudeville. When I was four years old I became a regular. When I was twenty-one we decided to try another branch of show business and told our representative to see what he could do and he immediately got me signed to the Winter Garden in New York, which was the Schubert's Theater for "The Passing Show of 1917."

This was an annual show?

Yes, it always started in the summer and generally ran for, oh, about six months in New York and a year and a half on the road. The Winter Garden was Al Jolson's home, and the show I was supposed to go in would have starred the Howard Brothers. But anyhow, they signed me for that show and I was walking down Broadway—down along Eighth or some place—and I met an old vaudevillian, and he was with Roscoe (Fatty) Arbuckle and he told me that he took his make-up off for a while and was going to try running a motion picture company for Joe Schenck, who was producing pictures with Norma Talmadge and Constance Talmadge at the Colony Studio on 48th Street in New York, and that he had just signed Arbuckle from Sennett. And Roscoe asked me if I had ever been in a motion picture, and I said no I hadn't even been in a studio. And he said, well come on down to the studio Monday and do a scene with me or two and see how you like it. I said, well, rehearsals don't start for another week or so, so I'll be down. I went down there and I worked in it. The first time I ever walked in front of a motion picture camera—that scene is in the finished motion picture and instead of doing just a bit he carried me all the way through it.

This was The Butcher Boy?

Yes, *The Butcher Boy*. So I was very interested in it—the mechanics of it. I wanted to know how that picture got put together through the cutting room, and the mechanics of the camera, which fascinated me the most.

What part did you play?

Oh, in those two-reelers, they didn't bother to give you any character or name or anything, things just started happening.

Where was the studio at that time?

Forty-eighth Street between Second and Third Avenues in New York.

They were shooting this in a studio—not on location?

Yes, but we did in good weather sneak out and shoot

275

exteriors. Well, we stayed there and shot pictures until October—I went in in May—and altogether I think we made six pictures there—in the East. Then Arbuckle persuaded Joe Schenck that the East was no place for our type of motion picture—we needed too many exteriors and changes of scenery, while in New York in that neighborhood you were kind of helpless.

How many were there in the Arbuckle company at that time?

Oh, there'd be a standard troupe. Your cast were always your leading lady, your villain, and you always carried a handful of bit people—they were cops or whatever you wanted them to be—you certainly had two to three in the scenario department helping you lay out pictures, you had a cutter, you had a cameraman—two cameramen. It's just done on a bigger scale today, that's all.

Did all these films star Arbuckle?

At that time, yes. I was just one of his feature players. I stayed with him until the spring of '18 when I went into the Army, into the Infantry, the 40th Infantry Division. I was in France seven months. I was released the following May, 1919, and went back and made just two more pictures with Arbuckle, when Joe Schenck sold Arbuckle to Paramount and then turned Arbuckle's company over to me and got me a studio of my own in Hollywood called The Keaton Studio. Then I started there on my own.

I understand you made a feature in 1920 called The Saphead.

Yes, that's right. It was before I made one of my own two-reelers. Loew's Incorporated bought the Metro studio and its exchanges, and one of the first Broadway shows that they bought to make a special feature was called *The Henrietta,* and it had starred Douglas Fairbanks.

That was his first film, wasn't it?

He took the character but he didn't tell the story of "Henrietta." He took the character called "Berty." I made that special feature for Metro. This was quite a while before it ever became Metro-Goldwyn-Mayer, because when I made my two-reelers then I released through Metro. I did, for two years, make shorts, and then I went into features in '22, in *Three Ages.* Wally Beery was the villain in it. It told a simple story laid in the stone age; the same thing happened in the Roman age and then in the modern age. Every sequence of this script was repeated, one after the other—just doing the same thing, only doing it three different ways.

Which of the two-reel shorts was your favorite?

A picture called *Hard Luck*. It was the biggest laughing two-reeler I ever made, but I had two other pets. One was called *The Boat*, where I had a wife and two small boys and I built a family cruiser in the cellar of my house and had to knock the end of the house out to get the boat out, and when I launched the boat it sank.

Of the features, which is your favorite?

I have two—*The Navigator* and *The General*.

How do you rate Sherlock Jr. *now?*

I like *Sherlock*. It was a good picture for me. It was the trickiest of all the pictures I ever made because there were so many camera tricks and illusions. We spent an awful lot of time getting those scenes.

How did you ever do the scene on the motorcycle? Is that a camera trick, or were you actually—

No, there's no camera trick there.

There is one shot where you can see the motorcycle from a distance and see that it isn't attached to anything. How did you manage to learn to do that?

I'd just go out and learn to handle a motorcycle on the handlebars. It wasn't easy to keep a balance. I got some nice spills though, from that thing.

How did the scripts for these features evolve?

Well, now we will go back to our type of pictures. Now when I say "our type" you've got three people who were making them at that time: Chaplin, Harold Lloyd, and myself. Until I left my own studio and went to MGM—where it was a different proposition—we never had a script.

You never had any kind of shooting script?

We never had a script. We didn't work by one. We just got to talking about a story and laying out all the material that we could think of, and then got it all put together—everybody connected with our company knew what we were going to shoot, anyway, and we didn't have a schedule.

How long did it take you to shoot a feature in the mid-20s?

We averaged about eight weeks of shooting.

And how much did a feature cost?

Our pictures cost, on the average, about twenty or thirty

per cent more than the average feature—dramatic feature.

How much would that be as of about 1925?

Oh, I'd be spending around $210,000—$220,000 to a feature. At the same time Harold Lloyd would go higher —he would probably be going closer to $300,000. And Chaplin—you had no way of telling at all because he was liable to quit in the middle of a picture and go to Europe, take a trip, start and get lazy and only turn out about one picture every two years, so I never knew what his costs would run.

About the dream sequence in Sherlock Jr., *was this something that you thought of on the spur of the moment, or something that had been planned out ahead?*

No, it was planned out ahead because we had to build a set for that one.

How was that done—did you have an actual screen beforehand on which the characters were appearing?

No. We built what looked like a motion picture screen and actually built a stage into that frame but lit it in such a way that it looked like a motion picture being projected on a screen. But it was real actors and the lighting effect gave us the illusion, so I could go out of semi-darkness into that well-lit screen right from the front row of the theater right into the picture. Then when it came to the scene changing on me when I got up there, that was a case of timing and on every one of those things we would measure the distance to the fraction of an inch from the camera to where I was standing, also with a surveying outfit to get the exact height and angle so that there wouldn't be a fraction of an inch missing on me, and then we changed the setting to what we wanted it to be and I got back into that same spot and it overlapped the action to get the effect of the scene changing. . . .

The illusion is perfect.

I know it was. I've seen it with many an audience.

Speaking of Chaplin and Lloyd and your other contemporaries, I wonder if you would care to express an opinion of their work as fellow comedians, or tell us which among the other comedians were your favorites?

Well, my favorites—I guess Chaplin, of course, was number one. But I liked Harry Langdon very much, and I liked an old one called Lloyd Hamilton. I liked W. C. Fields. Those were my pets, and then probably Lloyd.

Lloyd actually made the most films, didn't he?

Yes, he did. He turned out quite a list. He was doing

the same as I was, he'd make a spring release and a fall release—two pictures a year.

How did you pick up the acrobatic skills that turn up in such films as Sherlock Jr.?

Well, I was just a harebrained kid that was raised backstage. He tries everything as he grows up. If there is a wire-walker this week, well, he tries walking a wire when nobody's looking. If there's a juggler, he tries to juggle—he tries to do acrobatics—there's nothing he don't try. He tries to be a ventriloquist—he tries to be a juggling fool, a magician—Harry Houdini, I tried to get out of handcuffs and strait jackets.

Do you look at your early films—have you seen them recently?

Every now and then I see one. Somebody else gets them; I don't have any prints of them any more.

How did you feel about the coming of sound?

It didn't bother me at all.

You felt that you could function just as well in sound?

Why, sure. The only thing we did in laying out our material was to deliberately look for action laughs, not dialogue laughs. That has always been my fight with the brass. There were all these writers, and all these writers could think about was funny sayings and puns. I'd try to fight those down.

How do you feel about the comedians who have come up since sound? Do you have any favorites among people like the Marx Brothers, Fields, and Red Skelton?

Skelton I like very much. Lou Costello I like very much.

Did you like the Marx Brothers' films?

Some of them—when they didn't get too ridiculous.

Well, there you've got a good many verbal gags and sometimes—

That's Groucho.

The gags don't develop as they did in the silent comedies and as they certainly did in your films—where you get one gag and you keep thinking it is going to end, but it turns into something else.

Oh, yes, we deliberately tried to keep something rolling.

Have you seen any of the work of Jacques Tati, the French pantomimist?

I've seen very little of it, only what's been on television.

How do you feel about him?

Well, he's—I don't know what you'd call him. He is just out to be artistic.

Well, of course I bring him up because he is the one person recently who has made a conscious effort to make comedies almost entirely without dialogue. I wonder how you feel about making a sound comedy—whether they are silent comedies with music and sound effects added.

I wouldn't want to do that today. I still would look at it just the same as I looked at it when television first got a good hold and they put me out to doing half-hour shows. Well, I said, here's what I'm going to do. We go ahead and talk—put all the dialogue in the first fifteen minutes —let 'em try for little laughs as we go—but for that second fifteen minutes deliberately go for places that just don't call for dialogue. In other words, we don't go out of our way to avoid them, but it is just a natural thing that two people busy building something—there's no reason to talk, you just go ahead and build. Well, that's the type of material I looked for.

If you were making a feature at this time, what sort of film would it be?

I'd go back to my old format—that's the way I made 'em before. But I have no intentions of doing it. I just don't think it is worth while any more. I think in making a program picture today you're just asking for trouble. You can't get your money back. You've got to make an *Around the World in Eighty Days, The King and I,* you've got to get into one of those big things in order to get your money back. I'm anxious to see the day when television and the motion picture industry marry and set out a system, because it can't continue the way it is. I see only one solution to it. There should be paid television, and they could keep the costs so low that the poorest man in the world could have a television; they can keep the entertainment that low priced. And in that way you'd make pictures exactly the way you used to make them before television —I mean you'd think nothing of spending a million and a half for a program picture.

What kind of future do you think screen comedy has— what would you expect a really good screen comedy of the future would be like?

There won't be any change. Everything seems to travel in cycles—it always did. Some fellow comes along like Jerry Lewis who gets all his laughs talking fast, screaming and making faces and things like that—and he is sure top box office for a while; I don't know but what he is still up there. Then along about this time when our back is turned, someone like W. C. Fields will come along—the funny character type of comic—and he'll be the rage—and you'll find nine more like him working. Then along will come another type and he'll be the rage for the next five or six years, and everybody will try to work like him.

Did you have imitators yourself?

Oh, yes.

Which was the most popular of your features?

My biggest money-maker was *The Navigator*. And next to that was *The General*.

How did Sherlock Jr. *stand up?*

Hospitality outgrossed it, *Battling Butler* outgrossed it, *College* outgrossed it, *Steamboat Bill* outgrossed it. And then at MGM both *The Cameraman* and *Spite Marriage* outgrossed it. It was all right, it was a money-maker, but it wasn't one of the big ones. Maybe it was because at the time it was released the audience didn't pay so much attention to the trick stunts that were in the picture.

Was there any single film, perhaps one of the shorts, that you think did the most for your reputation?

Perhaps the first short I made, called *One Week*.

What decided you to go into feature films instead of continuing with the shorts?

Well, because the exhibitor would buy two pictures—he'd buy a feature-length picture and a short, and he would advertise one of my shorts, or Lloyd's, or Chaplin's above the feature he bought, and of course the feature he bought with us was always a second-rater. We didn't get William S. Hart, Mary Pickford, or Douglas Fairbanks on the same bill with us. We had the second- and third-rate stars on the bill with us. Well, for instance if the theater, a first-run theater here in Los Angeles, was paying us $500 a week rental for our short, he was probably paying only $500 for the feature.

So it was mainly a financial decision?

As long as they were going to advertise us above it anyhow—we're the drawing card, we might as well get into the feature field and instead of getting $500 for the picture we take $1,500. It makes a difference.

Do you feel that there is anyone that you learned most from in your early days—perhaps your father?

Arbuckle. From the stage it was my father.

He was quite an acrobat himself?

Not exactly an acrobat, just a—he was a very funny man.

He appeared in some of your films?

Yes, I used him. He was the girl's father in *Sherlock Jr.*

And then you feel that you learned most from Arbuckle later?

Picture technique I learned from Arbuckle. But not from an audience standpoint—I learned that for myself and from my father, 'cause I had all that experience. See by the time I'm 21 years old I'm a vet.

Was it your father who persuaded you never to smile?

No. Nobody did that. I just simply worked that way, because I learned as a kid growing up with an audience that I just had to be that type of comedian—if I laughed at what I did, the audience didn't.

So you stopped laughing?

Sure. The more serious I turned the bigger laugh I could get. So at the time I went into pictures, that was automatic—I didn't even know I was doing it.

Have you ever smiled on the screen?

I did it for somebody once—just to prove a point—that an audience wouldn't like it—and they didn't. We actually went in the projecting room when I started to get a reputation from film magazines and critics of being a frozen-face, a blank pan. We ran our first few pictures to see if I had smiled—I was unconscious of it and didn't know it. I hadn't, so everything was fine.

When you worked with Arbuckle in the shorts, was your screen character essentially what it was in the later features?

I worked the same way. I always stayed the same way.

Do you feel that American or European audiences appreciated your films more?

I did a bigger business in Europe than I did in the United States. I was a box-office draw in the darndest country in the world.

Which was that?

Russia. I was a bigger box-office attraction than Chaplin in Russia. And it was the one country we couldn't get any money out of.

You mean you never got any money out of Russia?

No. The limit was $5,000. That went for Doug Fairbanks, Mary Pickford, Chaplin—anybody—$5,000 was the most you could get. The reason for this is that they bought from the Berlin Exchange. They rented a picture just to play one week in Moscow, and while it was there they made a dupe negative and made as many prints as they wanted, and they sent them all over the country. They paid you $5,000 for that one week.

How about the total gross on an average silent feature of yours?

We'd average between a million and a half and two million.

Were you much aware of what the critics were saying about you during the '20s? Did you pay much attention to them?

I hadn't because I'd been reading house notices since I was born, and was used to that. This critic likes you and this one don't, so that's that. I've had some good friends. One of the best critics I think I had was when Bob Sherwood was editor of *Life*. He was always on my side. I could do no wrong for him. The majority thought that I was going to develop good. The biggest mistake I made in my career was leaving my own studio and going to MGM. Chaplin warned me, so did Lloyd—but Joe Schenck talked me into it. And it wasn't that they didn't try, but those types of pictures and those little independent companies working—you could do better. There was an old-fashioned expression that explains the whole thing—too many cooks. When they turned me loose at MGM, they gave me the entire scenario department—there must have been 300— all the brass turned gag men for me—and just too much help. And I guess it's silly to say, but it is a fact, they warp your judgment in the role you're working.

On the features that you made independently, you usually co-directed these—

Yes. And the majority of them I did alone.

On the co-direction, did this mean that you were directing the scenes in which you yourself didn't appear, or—

When I did appear.

The Navigator is co-directed with Donald Crisp?

Yes, that's right.

How did the responsibility for the direction break down in a case like that?

Well, when we first laid out the story of *The Navigator* ahead, a few dramatic scenes at the start of it were legitimate and not done in a comedy way, and I had mobs stuffed in there, such as the cannibal island we got onto, and things like that—you get a good dramatic director to take care of those sequences in the picture. We won't worry about the comedy part of it, we take care of that. We do that. The only one mistake we made there, and that was Donald Crisp—he was strictly from the D. W. Griffith school, a topnotch dramatic man—he had just made one of the best pictures for Paramount that year called *The Goose Woman*. But when he joined us, he turned into a gag man. He wasn't interested in the dramatic scenes, he was only interested in the comedy scenes with me. Well, that we didn't want. But we did manage to pull through the picture all right.

When did you start cutting your own films?

When I started to shoot my own pictures. I had learned to cut from Arbuckle.

He did his own cutting, also?

Yes.

Some of your films have more melodramatic situations than, say, the Chaplin films—you get into very dangerous situations and then get out of them. Was this something that you were particularly working on?

Our best format for our type of pictures was to start out with the normal situation, maybe some little trouble—not enough to handicap us for getting little laughs—and introducing our characters if we wanted to, getting into situations and out of them, but when we got down to around about that fourth or fifth reel, we would get into something serious and start getting laughs. And then get out of that situation and end up getting our biggest laughs in that last reel. That was always the perfect format for this type of picture.

How did you conceive of the screen character you usually played?

That's not easy. In laying out *The Navigator*, for instance, we're going to end by putting two people adrift on an ocean liner and it's a dead ship—there are no lights on it, no water, nobody to wait on them. Well, all right. Now you go back to your first part to establish your character. Well, if I was a laborer or a poor guy, or something like that—it would be no hardship for me to be on that ocean liner. But if I started out with a Rolls Royce, a chauffeur, a footman, a valet, and a couple of cooks and everything else to wait on me—and the same thing with the girl—in other words, the audience knows we were born rich, and never had to lift a finger to do anything. Now you turn those two people adrift on a dead ship, they're helpless. The same thing as going into the Army in making *Dough-*

boys. We start in the office with a very rich character, well dressed and everything else. Now when you give me an Army outfit that I was too small for—everything was big that they gave me in the Army—I'm a misfit, and come to living in the barracks and eating in the mess hall, that was a hardship to me. But if I'd have been a bum in the first place, it would have been an improvement. Well, then you lay out your character according to the situations you're going to get into.

Of course this is very different from Chaplin's character.

Well, he starts and stays a bum at all times. He was handicapped there. He is always a bum.

He was always a bum and Harold Lloyd was usually the country boy.

Who went to the big city to make good.

There is a consistent character in all your films who, for instance, seems to be quite helpless with machinery.

Well, as a rule—I'll take two different comics. You took Harold Lloyd off of the farm and you put him into the Ford Motor plant in Detroit. He would be afraid to touch anything, unless he was forced to by one of the foremen or something. With me, I would be just as scared of it but I would take it for granted that I ought to know what I'm doing and to set out immediately to try and do it. And of course I'd gum it up—that's what would happen to me, because I don't know what I'm doing but I'd make the attempt.

Could you tell of some of your experiences in stunting for the films? I understood you broke your neck at one point.

They found a fracture—years later—I didn't even know it. I was doing a scene in *Sherlock*. I was running along the top of a freight train, and I grabbed the rope of a water tower to get on the other train, and of course all my full weight pulls on the rope and of course I pull the spout down and it drenches me with the water. Well, when you're up on top of a freight car you're up there twelve feet high and that water spout is a ten-inch pipe. I didn't know how strong that water pressure was. Well, it just tore my grip loose as if I had no grip at all and dropped me the minute it hit me. And I lit on my back, with my head right across the rail—the rail right on my neck. It was a pretty hard fall, and that water pushed me down. I'm pretty sure that's when I did it.

285

*All the comedians of that time did their own stunts,
didn't they?*

Yes.

Did you ever use a double?

Only for special things—such as one of a pole vault into
a second-story window. That's in *College*. I went and got
Lee Barnes from USC—he was the Olympic champion.
When it comes to pole vaulting into a window—I mean,
you've got to get somebody who knows what they're
doing. But you know the cop that falls off the motorcycle
—that was me.

Oh, that was you too—your assistant?

Well, I doubled him because he couldn't fall off the motorcycle, so I took my assistant prop man, Ernie Rossetti,
and put my clothes on him to be on the handlebars and I
put Gillette's things on on the back seat and of course fell
off. I doubled him. There's a pretty good beating in *Steamboat Bill*—working in front of those wind machines is
tough. We had six of those machines and they were those
big Liberty motor babies. One of them—in the course of a
shot of running a truck full of paper boxes—about the
size of shoe boxes—between me and the camera, that
wind just emptied all the shoe boxes off onto me—just for
one shot. We took a truck past there once and that one
machine blew it off the bank, and it rolled into the Sacra-
mento River. That's how powerful those wind machines
are.

Buster Keaton (1896–1966):
Filmography:
1919–1923—Shorts: One Week, Convict 13, The Scarecrow, Neigh-
bors, The Haunted House, Hard Luck, The High Sign, The Sap-
head, The Playhouse, The Paleface, Cops, The Electric House, My
Wife's Relations, The Blacksmith, Frozen North, Day Dreams, Bal-
loonatics, The Love Nest. 1923—The Three Ages (with Eddie
Cline), Our Hospitality (with Jack Blystone). 1924—Sherlock Jr.
(with Eddie Cline), The Navigator (with Donald Crisp). 1925—
Seven Chances, Go West. 1926—Battling Butler, The General (with
Clyde Bruckman). 1927—College (with James W. Horne). 1928—
Steamboat Bill Junior (with Charles F. Riesner).

Akira Kurosawa

*Akira Kurosawa is the only Japanese director with any
consistent distribution and long-range reputation in the
West. A man of all genres, Kurosawa represents the evolution of Japanese Art away from the decorative facility of
its national past toward the expressionistic anguish of its
international future. East and West, Old and New are in
constant conflict in Kurosawa's films. The director, in fact,
has been criticized for not being Japanese enough. In both
form and content, however, Kurosawa reveals a restless
spirit and a civilized taste.*—A. S.*

*Kurosawa does not like to talk about his films, nor is he
fond of discussing film theory. Once, when I asked him
about the meaning of one of his pictures, he said: "If I
could have said it in words, I would have—then I wouldn't
have needed to make the picture."*

*Recently, however, Kurosawa expressed an interest in
looking back over the body of his work, and these are the
results. I have deleted nothing and have only added to the
material when it seemed relevant.*

SUGATA SANSHIRO (Sanshiro Sugata/Judo Saga/ La Lègende de judo), 1943, Toho

I remember the first time I said *cut*—it was as though it

* *Akira Kurosawa's notes on his films were edited and compiled
by Donald Richie in* Sight and Sound, *Nos. 3–4, Vol. 33, Summer
and Autumn 1964.*

was not my own voice at all. From the second time on it was me all right. When I think of this first picture I remember most that I had a good time making it. And at this period it was hard to have a good time making films because it was war-time and you weren't allowed to say anything worth saying. Back then everyone thought that the real Japanese-style film should be as simple as possible. I disagreed and got away with disagreeing—that much I could say. Still, I was anything but sure of myself. I remember doing a scene with the heroine, Yukiko Todoriki, and we decided together how it should be done. I remember when I saw an advertisement for the novel this film was based on, I intuitively thought it would be right for me. When it came out I went to the producer's house and asked him to buy the rights. He did so and two days later every major studio was wanting it. It was ideal for an entertainment film and that was about all we were allowed to make back in 1943.

I remember the first day I met Shimura [Takashi Shimura was later the woodcutter in *Rashomon*, the hero of *Ikiru*, and early became a member of the Kurosawa "group"] he was standing on the lawn of the studio and I didn't recognise him. He was wearing a very old and very shabby hat and I remember thinking that the hat suited him extraordinarily well. At the same time I met Fujita [Susumu Fujita was the hero of this film, and later appeared in *The Hidden Fortress* and other Kurosawa films] and Ryunosuke Tsunagata, who was playing the villain. I remember that the critics said he overacted and stole the show. That is not true. He did not overact. He certainly stole the show, however. I told him to. I was much more interested in his character than in the hero.

ICHIBAN UTSUKUSHIKU (Most Beautifully/ Le Plus Doux), 1943, Toho

This is one of Kinoshita's favourite films. [Keisuke Kinoshita is known abroad mainly for *The Legend of Narayama*.] He has always liked it best and I still like it myself. It was my own story and in it I wanted to portray women in a group—a kind of everyday documentary of their lives. All the actresses were told not to use their personal idiosyncrasies and I told them to play it like amateurs. I made all the girls live together in a dormitory during the filming, and I made them run a lot to get them tired—to show themselves on the screen. It is interesting that, after the film, one after the other got married and all became exemplary wives. It was rumoured that I was in love with my star but that was not true. I too got married after it was over, however. I married Yoko Yaguchi.

SUGATA SANSHIRO ZOKU (Sanshiro Sugata—Part two), 1944, Toho

This film did not interest me in the slightest. I had already done it once before. All I remember is that I took Masayuki Mori off the stage for it. [Mori was the husband in *Rashomon*, and also appeared in *The Idiot* and *The Bad Sleep Well;* he still maintains a career in the theatre.] Again what interested me was not the hero but his opponent. It was an odd film.

TORA NO O O FUMU OTOKOTACHI (The Men Who Tread on the Tiger's Tail/Walkers on Tigers' Tails/Sur la Piste du Tigre/Die Tigerfährte), 1944, Toho, released 1953

I had originally wanted to make a costume picture to be called *Doko Kono Yari* [the film—title untranslatable—was never made] and the script was ready but we couldn't make it. No horses. So we made *Kanjincho* instead. [*Toro no O* is based on the Kabuki play *Kanjincho*.] I wrote the script in one night. There was only one stage-set. All the rest was location. This was an order. But, even so, it was much easier to shoot this way. Enoken was very easy to work with [Enoken played the stupid porter who almost gives the plot away: this character is not in the original play; Kurosawa used him to give the reactions of the contemporary Japanese and it was he who contributed all of the comedy in this short film] and this was because he had, after all, had a long career on the stage, and had been trained by Kajiro Yamamoto. [Yamamoto also trained Kurosawa, who was his assistant for the 1941 *Uma* (Horses); together they made the 1946 *Those Who Make Tomorrow*.] It was later shown to, among others, Michael Powell, who expressed himself as pleased. I wanted to remake this film with more sets, lots more technique. Hayasaka and I talked about this project, but never did anything about it. Then he died. His death ruined that as well.

[One of Kurosawa's closest friends was Fumio Hayasaka, the composer who contributed all of the film scores up to and including *Seven Samurai*. Kurosawa has said that the reason for the "failure" of *Ikimono no Kiroku* was because he was deprived of Hayasaka's help, which was much more than that which a composer usually gives a director. They used to think up story ideas together and Hayasaka often helped with the script as well. It is unfortunate that the West is mostly familiar with his music for *Rashomon*, which is quite untypical. He had prepared a Japanese score for the picture and it was Kurosawa who insisted that he wanted something else, something more like the *Boléro*—which is just what he received.

I knew Hayasaka very well during this early Occupation period, though I did not know Kurosawa at that time. He was an extremely gentle, extremely intelligent man with thick glasses and wild hair. He used to come to listen to new records I would get from America and I remember his excitement when he first heard the Berg Violin Concerto. His own music was highly adventurous and I remember the première of his Piano Concerto which stunned the 1946 audience. Later, he took me to Toho one afternoon and we watched them make a film and I talked with the young director. The film was *Drunken Angel* and the director was Kurosawa.]

ASU O TSUKURU HITOBITO (Those Who Make Tomorrow/Ceux qui font les lendemains), co-directed with Kajiro Yamamoto and Hideo Sekigawa, 1946, Toho

This film is not really mine. Not the other directors' either. It was really made by the labour union and is an excellent example of why a committee-made film is no good. I did my part in a week. Even today when I hear the band music on May Day I feel very, very sleepy. Still, it wasn't too bad for just a week's work.

WAGA SEISHUN NI KOINASHI (No Regrets for My Youth/Je ne regrette pas ma jeunesse), 1946, Toho

The original script was a lot better than the one we had to use. Eijiro Saita wrote it and told what really happened to Hidemi Ozaki, how he was suspected of spying, how he died in prison. The trouble was that there was another script which Kiyoshi Kusuda wanted to use and there was a certain amount of resemblance. The scenario committee told me that I was "standing in the way of a young director." This I didn't want to be doing, but I told them that simply because two directors were involved the films would be different. That is the way movies are: the difference comes from the director, not the story. In fact, I said, I wanted to make a better film than he would. This they did not like and so I had to change the whole second half of my script. Saita refused, I begged, and somehow we started shooting.

The critics were ferocious about the character of the woman in this picture [the heroine, Setsuko Hara, goes to work on a farm, to forget what has happened, turning her back upon social "responsibilities"], but it was only here and in *Rashomon* that I ever fully and fairly portrayed a woman. Of course, all my women are rather strange, I agree. But this woman I wanted to show as the new Japan. I was right, I still think, to show a woman who lived by her own feelings. The critics hated her as though she were a man. But she wasn't—that was the point.

At any rate, it wasn't much of a production—the labour union got in the way. Still, it was the first film in which *I* had something to say and in which *my* feelings were used. Everyone disagreed. They said I should go back to the style of *Sugata*. Look, I said, if I could have made anything better than *Sugata* at the time I would have done it —what do I have to go back to? Then they said it was technically more proficient. It wasn't. Besides, techniques are there only to support a director's intentions. If he relies on techniques his original thought cannot help but be cramped. Techniques do not enlarge a director, they limit him and they tend to undermine the basic idea which should prevail.

SUBARSHIKI NICHIYOBI (One Wonderful Sunday/ Un Splendide Dimanche), 1946, Toho

I got the idea for this film from an old Griffith picture about a couple after the first war who plant potatoes. Someone steals the crop but they don't give up; they try again. [Naturally, the "idea" was not literal. Kurosawa, always interested in people trying again and again, made it into the story of a young couple who, despite everything, manage to enjoy themselves on Sunday—their one day

off.] Though this film won me the prize for the best director of the year, I think I did not make it nearly freely
enough. It is certainly by no means my favourite picture. I
had a lot of things to say and I got them all mixed up. I
remembered this in *Drunken Angel* and kept my eyes
open.

YOIDORE TENSHI (Drunken Angel/L'Ange ivre/ Der trunkene Engel), 1948, Toho

In this picture I finally discovered myself. It was *my*
picture: I was doing it and no one else. Part of this was
thanks to Mifune. [Though Toshiro Mifune had been in
several films this was his first starring role and it resulted
in almost instant fame.] Shimura played the doctor beautifully but I found that I could not control Mifune. When I
saw this, I let him do as he wanted, let him play the part
freely. At the same time I was worried because, if I did
not control him, the picture would be quite different from
what I had wanted. It was a real dilemma. Still, I did not
want to smother that vitality. In the end, although the title
refers to the doctor, it is Mifune that everyone remembers.

I had seen him in Taniguchi's *To the End of the Silver
Mountains* but had no idea that he would be like this. His
reactions are extraordinarily swift. If I say one thing, he
understands ten. He reacts very quickly to the director's
intentions. Most Japanese actors are the opposite of this
and so I wanted Mifune to cultivate this gift.

It was from here on that the critics started calling me a
"journalistic" director, meaning that I interested myself in
"topical themes." Actually, I have always thought of films
as a kind of journalism, if journalism means a series of
happenings, usually contemporary, which can be shaped
into a film. At the same time I know that a timely subject
does not make an interesting film, if that is all the film
has. One ought to make a film in such a way that the original idea, no matter where it comes from, remains the
most important thing; and the feeling that one had at that
moment of having the idea is important. Timely then, in
my sense, is the opposite of sensational.

One of the reasons for the extreme popularity of this
film at the time was that there was no competition—no
other films showed an equal interest in people. We had
difficulty with one of the characters: that of the doctor
himself. Jin Uekusa and I rewrote his part over and over
again. Still, he wasn't interesting. We had almost given up

when it occurred to me that he was just too good to be true, he needed a defect, a vice. This is why we made him an alcoholic. At that time most film characters were shining white or blackest black. We made the doctor grey.

For this film I had originally wanted to use the *Dreigroschenoper* music but we could not get the rights, so we used cheap guitar music as a substitute. This was the first picture on which Hayasaka worked with me; and from the first we agreed on everything. Like using the vapid *Cuckoo Waltz* for the saddest part of the film. We thought of it separately but together, and after inspiration had struck us both, I remember, we shook hands. It was until that time music *and* pictures. We wanted both to contribute to each other. It is easy to talk about this but extremely difficult to do.

SHIZUKA NARU KETTO (The Silent Duel/ Le duel silencieux), 1949, Toho

Originally, I saw the stage play, done by Chiaki Minoaru, and I thought it would be good for Mifune. He had been a gangster, now he could be the doctor. This was also the first production of an independent unit I had formed, and it was the kind of film that a young production company could more easily do. Still, the people who work in movie studios are pretty much the same, and I have certainly never had any lack of confidence.

Yet, when I remember it, it seems to me that only the early scenes in the field hospital have any validity. This is because I didn't *describe* things too well in this picture. When the locale moved back to Japan somehow the drama left the film.

I am the kind of person who works violently, throwing myself into it. I also like hot summers, cold winters, heavy rains and snows, and I think my pictures show this. I like extremes because I find them most alive. I have always found that men who think like men, who act like men, who most *are* themselves, are always better . . . certainly they work better.

The synopsis of the film was sent to CIE [this was during the American Occupation and all film scripts were supervised by the Civil Information and Education Section, lest "feudal content" be included] and was then sent to the Medical Section, where the doctor in charge informed me that I would absolutely terrify the people of syphilis and they would not come for aid. [In the film the doctor acci-

dentally contracts syphilis while operating. In the original
version of the film the tertiary stages of the disease were
to be shown.] In addition a number of Japanese doctors
agreed that it was "un-medical." If you show a man going
insane from syphilis, they said, it would not be true. Anyway, the script was approved up to that point and so it
could not be helped—Mifune did not go insane in the end.
Because of this, however, there were many script problems. I decided to make it a tragic love story and that, tell-
ingly, was the most difficult part of the picture to film.

NORA INU (Stray Dog/Chien enragé), 1949, Shintoho.

I am very fond of George Simenon and I wanted to do
a film in his manner. I wanted to, but I failed. Everyone
liked the picture, but I do not. It is too *technical*—all that
technique and I had not one real thought in it. Shimura is
quite good in it but I had not seen very deeply into his
character; nor anyone else's for that matter. If I saw into
anyone at all it was the murderer. This part was played by
Ko Kimura and it was his first part in a film. [Kurosawa
used him later in both *Seven Samurai*—the love-struck
warrior—and *High and Low*.]

I remember the difficulties we had with the music. Hayasaka and I went from one used record store to the next
trying to find just the right music for the scene with the
showgirl where the radio is playing. The record had to be
old and scratched and the music had to be right. I remember we were so happy when we finally found that ancient
rendering of *La Paloma*. During the scene the dubbing
was so difficult that I remember my sound man actually
cried with rage and frustration.

Other troubles were in shooting. There is the scene
where the detective is wandering around looking for his
pistol (this story is true, by the way; the original idea for
the film came when I heard about a real detective who
was so unfortunate during those days of shortages as to
lose his pistol), and originally he was to wander through
four sections of the city: Shinjuku, Asakusa, Shibuya, and
Ueno. It was to be shot in sections on consecutive days. At
this point a typhoon descended upon us, the producers
asked us to hurry, we did, and all of this interesting material never got filmed.

I made this film in an unusual way. After hearing the
original anecdote I wrote a novel (unpublished) about it.

From this I had thought it would be easy to make the script. Not at all. Writing the script took just as much time as it usually does. Time was a problem in another way. Movies have their own internal time—motion-time. In writing a scenario one is always surprised at how much longer it takes than the actual filming does, but this is the way it is. You write a scenario with a different part of your mind, as it were. And you have to remember the context of each shot and make use of it. I remember that the first scene in the film was to have been the opening scene in the police station. We saw the rushes and it was just no good for the opening. I re-read my novel and finally understood why. In the novel it explained itself; in the film there was no context for it to exist in. The novel had begun with a number of details—for example, that it was the hottest day of the year. I filmed these hot-day details, then put in the station scene and the talk about the gun which follows; and it all worked.

SHUBUN (Scandal), 1950, Shochiku

This is a protest film. It is directly connected with the rise of the press in Japan and their habitual confusion of freedom with licence. Personal privacy is never respected and the scandal sheets are the worst offenders. I felt outrage that this should be so. [Though Kurosawa's protest had no personal involvement. He has for so long remained cool to the press that even simple details about his home life are not published. He has never appeared on TV, from which no Japanese celebrity is ever entirely immune; and he dislikes reading even favourable criticism of his work.] Still, the script wouldn't work right, and no matter how hard we worked it did not satisfy us. Then I thought of the character that became the lawyer in the film and this solved the problem. It is interesting how I thought of it. About ten years earlier I had been drinking in a bar in Shibuya and got talking to the man next to me. He was an older man and he was taking some food to his daughter in the hospital and had stopped off for a drink on the way. We talked about her. He adored her, said there was no one in the world like her. For some reason or other this apparently impressed me. In making this picture I thought, all of a sudden, of the character needed for the lawyer, and went on and made the film. When I looked at it, I found what I had done. The lawyer was the very image of this old man: he talked like him, acted like him.

The part was played by Shimura and was a much more interesting character than that he had played in *Drunken Angel*. I think this was because the doctor was someone I had thought up; but the lawyer had been living in the back of my head, waiting to come out.

In the film we have the daughter die. At that point Hayasaka insisted we use the trumpet. The trumpet? I wondered. And until I saw it I did not know how right he was. I still remember that scene—music and image were one. It taught me an enormous amount.

RASHOMON, 1950, Daiei

I was supposed to make a film for Daiei. At that time Shinobu Hashimono [with whom Kurosawa later worked on *Ikiru* and many other films] had a number of available scenarios. One of them appealed to me but it was too short and had only three episodes in it. All my friends liked it very much, but Daiei did not understand it. They asked: What is it about? I made it longer, put on a beginning and ending—and eventually they agreed to make it. Thus Daiei joined those—Shochiku for *The Idiot,* Toho for *I Live in Fear*—who were brave enough to try something different. [This is charitable of Kurosawa. Actually Daiei was fairly adamant in its reluctance to understand. The head of the studio walked out on the first screening and, until the picture began winning prizes abroad, was fond of telling the press how little he understood; Shochiku, of course, butchered *The Idiot*.]

I think Machiko Kyo was marvellous in the film . . . so forceful. And it took about a month of work to get that. After we had finished I wanted to work with her again but never had the opportunity. [Until recently Miss Kyo was exclusively contracted by Daiei, and Daiei never invited Kurosawa to make another film.] We were staying in Kyoto, waiting for the set to be finished. While there we ran off some 16 mm. prints to amuse ourselves. One of them was a Martin Johnson jungle film in which there was a shot of a lion roaming around. I noticed the shot and told Mifune that that was just what I wanted him to be. At the same time Mori had seen downtown a jungle picture in which a black leopard was shown. We all went to see it. When the leopard came on Machiko was so upset

296

that she hid her face. I saw and recognised the gesture—it was just what I wanted for the young wife.

Another thing about this film, I like silent pictures and always have. They are often so much more beautiful than sound pictures are. Perhaps they have to be. At any rate, I wanted to restore some of this beauty. I thought of it, I remember, this way: one of the techniques of modern painting is simplification. I must therefore simplify this film.

We had our share of troubles in making the picture. After one reel was edited there was a studio fire, and another one during the dubbing. I'm not happy when I think back to those times. Also, I did not know that the film was being sent to Venice. And it certainly would not have been sent if Giuliana Stramigioli (then head of Unitalia Film) had not seen and liked it.

The Japanese are always terribly critical of Japanese films, so it is not too surprising that a foreigner should be responsible for this film having been sent. It was the same way with Japanese woodcuts; foreigners first appreciated them. We always think too little of our own things. Actually, *Rashomon* wasn't all that good. When I say this then people say to me: You Japanese always think too little of your own things. Why don't you stand up for your film? What are you so afraid of?

The thing that most surprised me about the film was the camerawork. Kazuo Miyagawa [photographer of *Ugetsu, Kagi,* and, later, *Yojimbo*] was worrying about whether it was good enough. Shimura had known him from way back and told me about his fears. I saw the first day's rushes and I knew. He was absolutely perfect.

HAKUCHI (The Idiot), 1951, Shochiku

I had wanted to make this film since before *Rashomon.* Since I was little I'd read Dostoievsky and had thought this book would make a wonderful film. Naturally you cannot compare me to him, but he is still my favourite author, he is the one who writes most honestly about human existence. And I think that when I made this picture I really understood him He seems terribly subjective, but then you come to the resolution that there is no more objective author writing.

I tried something like this in one of the scenes, when the Prince (in the original) tells Anastasia how good she is. She laughed. I had Setsuko Hara do it just as Dostoievsky had written it. Mori was watching and he was surprised. He liked it but it surprised him. This is just what I wanted.

Making the film was very hard work—it was difficult to make. At times I felt as though I wanted to die. Dostoievsky is heavy enough, and now I was under him—I knew just how those enormous *sumi* wrestlers feel. All the same it was marvellous experience for me.

People have said the film is a failure. I don't think so. At least, as entertainment, I don't think it is a failure. Of all my films, people wrote me most about this one. If it had been as bad as all that, they wouldn't have written. I trust my audience. They understood what I was saying. It was a new kind of melodrama [in Japan the word *melodrama* has no nuance of the derogatory; we should perhaps use the term psychological-drama, with the understanding that psychology is shown by action] and this the audience understood. That is why I wanted to make it at Shochiku. [That is, Shochiku had a reputation for making action-films of the *melodrama* variety. Even so, perhaps this company was not the best choice. Kurosawa neglects to note that the company asked him to cut the film by half and he made his famous reply: If you want to cut it, you had better cut it lengthwise.] If a director does not make a habit of lying to his audience, he can trust them.

The reviews were terrible [and those from America when it was shown, more or less uncut, in 1963 were equally bad] and if I had not made this film perhaps critics would not have had it so in for me. But, on thinking it over, I suppose that any director ought at least once to have been roundly attacked and embarrassed. One should be brave enough to risk this kind of "mistake." Nowadays no one does. Directors are too smart. They avoid this kind of failure. Yet, to make a failure surely is no disgrace. Still, I would have been happy if at least one critic had admired something about it. Certainly Mifune and Yoshiko Kuga were fine enough.

IKIRU (Living/To Live/Doomed/Vivre/Vivre enfin un seul jour/Leben!), 1952, Toho

What I remember best here is the long wake sequence that ends the film, where—from time to time—we see scenes in the hero's later life. Originally I wanted music all under this long section. I talked it over with Hayasaka and we decided on it and he wrote the score. Yet when it came time to dub, no matter how we did it, the scenes and music simply did not fit. So I thought about it for a long time and then took all the music out. I remember how disappointed Hayasaka was. He just sat there not saying anything, and the rest of the day he tried to be cheerful. I was sorry I had to do it, yet I had to. There is no way now of telling him how I felt—he is gone.

He was a fine man. It was as though he (with his glasses) were blind and I was deaf. We worked so well together because one's weakness was the other's strength. We had been together ten years and then he died. It was not only my own loss—it was music's loss as well. You don't meet a person like that twice in your life.

[Kurosawa has mentioned elsewhere the genesis of the idea that resulted in *Ikiru*: Occasionally I think of my death . . . then I think, how could I ever bear to take a final breath, while living a life like this, how could I leave it? There is, I feel, so much more for me to do—I keep feeling I have lived so little yet. Then I become thoughtful, but not sad. It was from such a feeling that *Ikiru* arose.]

The first part of this article, in which Akiro Kurosawa looks back on his own films, was published in the Summer SIGHT AND SOUND. *Donald Richie writes: "I have deleted nothing, and have only added to the material when it seemed relevant." His comments appear in the text in square brackets.*

SHICHININ NO SAMURAI (Seven Samurai/ The Magnificent Seven/Die sieben Samurai/ Les Sept samourais), 1954, Toho

Japanese films all tend to be *assari shite iru* [light, plain, simple but wholesome] just like *ochazuke* [green tea over rice, a dish whose *assari* connotations are so celebrated that Ozu once used it in a film title], but I think we ought to have richer foods, richer films. And so I thought I would make this kind of film, entertaining enough to eat, as it were. Of course, I've felt that way from the beginning —still, the labour of doing just that in Japan! Something always comes up. We didn't have enough horses; it rained all the time. It was just the kind of picture that is impossible to make in this country.

And then when it was finished it was too long, but they released it uncut in Japan anyway. [The original was over three hours long and was shown only in 1954 and then only in key cities. A shortened version played second and third runs. A second shortened version was made for export and this is the version most people have seen. A third was made for the Venice Festival—upon which Kurosawa remarks below. There are no prints of the original in Japan, and even negatives of the cut-outs seem to have disappeared.] But we had to shorten it for Venice. Naturally none of the critics understood it. They all complained about the first half being confused. It certainly was—that was the half that was so cut. I know what a good film it was. The second half, which went to Venice without major cuts, they understood and liked; as a matter of fact minor cuts helped it.

It was difficult making that film. [Kurosawa does not mention that part of the difficulty was occasioned by the producers who, understandably disturbed that an expensive production should be over a year in production and that half of that time should be spent at a distant location site, sent a number of telegrams telling the director to come back at once. These the director answered with other telegrams saying that they had the alternative of allowing him to continue or firing him.] But it was wonderful work too. My own staff, those people who always work with me . . . well, there are no better people in the world to work with. And I don't mean only those who worked on the script or the design or the production—I mean the carpenters, the electricians, the grips. Even if I didn't tell them how to do a single thing, they would know just what I wanted. It is due to people like this that I have been able to make films such as this one.

IKIMONO NO KIROKU (Record of a Living Being/ I Live in Fear/What the Birds Knew/ Si les Oiseaux savaient/Vivre dans le Peur/ Bilanz eines Lebens/Ein Leben in Angst), 1955, Toho

While I was making *Seven Samurai* I went to see Hayasaka, who was sick, and we were talking and he said that if a person was in danger of dying he couldn't work very well. He was quite ill at the time, very weak, and we did not know when he might die. And he knew this too. Just before this we had had word of the Bikini experiments.

When he had said a person dying could not work I thought he meant himself—but he didn't, it turned out. He meant everyone: all of us. Next time I met him I suggested we do a film on just that subject. He was pleased. The film was begun. Together and through asking other people we decided that a satire would be best. This followed my idea: I wanted to do a satire, but I didn't know how to make a satire on something like the H-bomb. And this was the problem I kept running up against while trying to write the script. It was difficult to keep it satirical.

As we [Shinobu Hashimoto, Hideo Oguni, and Kurosawa himself] worked on the script we more and more felt that we were really making the kind of picture with which, after it was all over and the last judgment was upon us, we could stand up and account for our past lives by saying proudly: We made *Ikimono no Kiroku*. And that is the kind of film it turned into.

Perhaps that is the reason it might be thought incoherent or even chaotic [i.e. turning a satire into a tragedy]. Still, it was good we made it. Anyhow, the way we felt how could we have made a satire? This time the entire staff knew how we felt, sensed our confusion. No one said very much, everyone worked very hard. And it was very hard work indeed. After it was all over we had a party to celebrate and Noriko Sengoku [who had a part in the film] said to me: "Well, we worked hard, didn't we? But from now on our parts will be all the more difficult." I agreed with her, and would still agree. Still, after I had made the film, I felt as though I had put down a heavy load, I felt as though I had got rid of lots of things.

It was during the filming of the scenes after the fire in the factory, it was just then that Hayasaka died. This was a great shock. I didn't even have the strength to work, to work well at any rate, and that is why these scenes are so weak. And the ending too [where the hero, gone mad, looks at the sun and says: The earth—at last it is on fire, it is burning up], that is weak. After *Seven Samurai* was over we were all tired out but happy; after *Ikimono* we were exhausted.

The turn-out for this film was very bad, few people came, and it was my biggest box-office failure. After having put so much of myself into this film, after having seriously treated a serious theme, this lack of interest disappointed me. When I think of it, however, I see now that

301

we made the film too soon. At that time no one was thinking seriously of atomic extinction. It was only later that people got frightened, and that a number of films on the subject appeared, among them *On the Beach*.

KUMONOSUJO (The Castle of the Spider's Web/ The Throne of Blood/Kumonosu-Djo/Macbeth/ Das Schloss im Spinnennetz/Château d'Araignées/ Le Trône de Sang), 1957, Toho

With this film, *The Lower Depths,* and *The Hidden Fortress,* I seem to have made a *jidai-geki* trilogy. [Almost all Japanese, and Kurosawa is no exception, think of films as being divided into period-pictures *(jidai-geki)* and modern-story pictures *(gendai-mono),* as though these were the only two alternatives. The West has something like this in its attitudes toward Westerns (i.e. the "adult Western" etc.) and the crime film.] I have long thought that the Japanese *jidai* picture is very often historically uninformed, and, beyond this, has never really availed itself of modern film-making techniques. In *Seven Samurai* we tried to do something about that, and *Kumonosujo* had the same general feeling behind it.

Originally I had wanted to produce this film and let a younger director direct it. But when the script was finished and Toho saw how expensive it would be, they asked me to direct it. So I did—my contract expired after these three films.

I also had another idea about the film, and that was simply that I wanted to make *Macbeth*. [Kurosawa had seen none of the other film versions, though much later he saw Orson Welles' on television.] The problem was: how to adapt the story to Japanese thinking. The story is understandable enough but the Japanese tend to think differently about such things as witches and ghosts. [Though ghosts tend to be vengeful, as in the innumerable *kaidan* films, the idea of a gratuitously malevolent trio of witches is far from the Japanese imagination.] I decided upon the techniques of the Noh, because in Noh style and story are one. I wanted to use the way Noh actors have of moving their bodies, the way they have of walking, and the general composition which the Noh stage provides. [In the film the most successful examples of this are usually associated with "Macbeth's" wife, who uses slightly accelerated Noh movements, and the scene where she tries to wash

302

her hands clean is pure Noh; also the asymmetrical composition of Noh is much seen, particularly in the long conversation scenes between "Macbeth" and his wife before the initial murder. The appearance of Banquo's ghost, on the other hand, uses very little Noh technique.]

This is one of the reasons why there are so very few close-ups in the picture. I tried to show everything using the full-shot. Japanese almost never make films in this way and I remember I confused my staff thoroughly with my instructions. They were so used to moving up for moments of emotion, and I told them to move farther back. In this way I suppose you could call the film experimental.

It was a very hard film to make. We decided that the main castle set had to be built on the slope of Mount Fuji, not because I wanted to show this mountain but because it has precisely the stunted landscape that I wanted. And it is usually foggy. I had decided I wanted lots of fog for this film. [Kurosawa has said elsewhere that since he was very young the idea of samurai galloping out of the fog much appealed to him. At the beginning of the original version of this film, Mifune and Minoru gallop in and out of the fog eight times.] Also I wanted a low, squat castle. Kohei Ezaki, who was the art director, wanted a towering castle, but I had my way. Making the set was very difficult because we didn't have enough people and the location was so far from Tokyo. Fortunately, there was a US Marine Corps base nearby and they helped a great deal; also a whole MP battalion helped us out. We all worked very hard indeed, clearing the ground, building the set. Our labour on this steep fog-bound slope, I remember, absolutely exhausted us—we almost got sick.

DONZOKO (The Lower Depths/Les Bas-fonds/Nachtasyl), 1957, Toho

Gorky's setting was Imperial Russia but I changed it to Japan, the Edo period. [Kurosawa's choice of period was intended ironically. Most Japanese look back romantically to the Edo period—age of the great courtesans, great Kabuki, great woodcut artists, great literature—with extreme nostalgia. Kurosawa thinks of life at that time as comparable to the miseries in 19th-century Russia.] Also I used *bakabayashi*. [This is the kind of music—flute, drums clappers—traditionally associated with travelling entertainments, with shrine fairs, with the annual *matsuri*.] We always think of this music as being joyous and festive. I used it for precisely the opposite reason. I wanted to suggest something tragic and dark. [In the choice of "La Paloma" in *Stray Dog,* the "Cuckoo Waltz" in *Drunken Angel,* and in his deep appreciation for the music of Kurt Weill, Kurosawa has often demonstrated that the use of innocent, unsophisticated music, or at least unsophisticated-sounding music, heightens the tragic suggestion.]

In Edo during this period the Shogunate was falling to pieces and thousands were living almost unendurable lives. Their resentment we can still feel in *senryu* and *rakushu* [satirical poems and entertainments] of the period. I wanted to show this atmosphere, to reveal it, though whether I really did or not, I don't yet know.

This film was easy to make. We worked steadily and well, and shooting did not take long. We had only one closed set, and one open set. We also had many rehearsals, and worked out all the choreography, movements, camera, etc., well in advance. Once, to get everyone in the proper mood, I invited on to the set one of the few remaining practitioners of the old Edo *rakugo* [humorous but highly satiric stories]—and we never had more fun than on that day. Also I wanted Mifune to play his part (the gambler) in the style of Nezumi-Kozo. [A fictitious and romantic robber who saves maidens and only steals from the rich, the hero of a hundred films. Naturally, he is a figure much looked down on by the intelligentsia, and only children, farmers, and labourers crowd into his frequent film appearances. A bit like Robin Hood, he is too near in time to have acquired any antique patina, and Kurosawa's idea was personal, highly interesting and almost dogmatically unfashionable.] That did not work though. Mifune is simply too well-built, he has too much presence, he cannot help but bring his own identity to his roles.

KAKUSHI TORIDE NO SAN-AKUNIN (Three Bad Men in a Hidden Fortress/The Hidden Fortress/ Die verborgene Festung/La Fortresse Cachée), 1958, Toho

The first half of this film was made in Arima in Hyogo [not far from Kobe] and the second half was done around Gotemba at the base of Fuji. I remember there was good weather at Arima and we worked fast, but Fuji!—the weather changes so rapidly that it is cloudy one minute and bright sun the next. Making it there was difficult enough, but just then a big typhoon came and tore up all our scenery. I remember, at one point, we waited over one hundred days for good weather, and so our film was considerably over its three-month production schedule.

And there was always a strong wind, blowing all the time. Come to think of it, there has always been a gale whenever I wanted to make a picture. There was even one during the location scenes for *Sugata*. People have occasionally called me *kaze-otoko* [lit. wind-man] as a joke. On the *Kakushi* set everyone called me that. [Other nicknames for Kurosawa have included *Kurosawa-tenno* or "the Emperor Kurosawa" because of his presumed directorial ways. It is telling, however, that only the newspapers use it, never his own staff.]

Anyway, no matter how hard it was to make this film, it was an enormous hit [and remained Kurosawa's biggest financial success until *Yojimbo*] and the company was delighted. It was very expensive but the books balanced out most comfortably in the black.

WARUI YATSU HODO YOKU NEMURU (The Bad Sleep Well/The Worse You Are the Better You Sleep/ The Rose in the Mud), 1960, Kurosawa Productions (Independent), Toho (Distribution)

This was the first film of Kurosawa Productions, my own unit which I run and finance myself. From this film on, everything was my own responsibility. Consequently I wondered about what kind of film to make. Making a film just to make money did not appeal to me—one should not take advantage of an audience. Instead, I wanted to make a film of some social significance. At last I decided to do something about corruption, because it has always seemed to me that graft, bribery, etc., on a public level is the worst crime that there is. These people hide behind the façade of some great organisation like a company or a corporation—and consequently no one ever really knows how dreadful they are, what awful things they do. Exposing them I thought of as a socially significant act—and so I started the film.

But even while we were making it, I knew that it wasn't working out as I had planned, and this was because I was simply not telling and showing enough. Like the final scene with Mori on the telephone. That suggests, but it is not explicit enough. An even worse man is at the other end of that telephone line, but in Japan you cannot go further than that. [Kurosawa's comment means the above but is almost untranslatable. In Japanese it reads: *Sodo made tsukondeiku to hobo ni sashisawari ga dete duru* or "if you go (too) far you (might) make trouble come to someone (else?)"—but the inference here, as in the final telephone scene where the villainous Mori calls someone and tells them that the matter (Mifune's murder) is taken care of, is that the greatest corruption of all in Japan is governmental. Kurosawa had suggested this in *Ikiru*, but there he was only dealing with a single ward office in the city government. In *Warui Yatsu* he was, ostensibly, incriminating big business, but if he had tried to show a corrupt government, trouble would indeed have come to someone. The revelations of the film, even so, were considered quite sensational in Japan, though in Europe and America they seemed tame indeed.] At any rate it was too bad I didn't go further. Maybe I could have in, say, America, a big country. Japan, however, cannot be this free and this makes me sad.

YOJIMBO (The Bodyguard/Die Leibwache/Le Garde du Corps), 1961, Kurosawa Productions, Toho (Distribution)

For a long time I had wanted to make a really interesting film—and it finally turned into this picture. The story is so ideally interesting that it's surprising no one else ever thought of it. The idea is about rivalry on both sides, and both sides are equally bad. We all know what this is like. Here we are, weakly caught in the middle, and it is impossible to choose between the evils. [I doubt that Kurosawa intended any political implication. He is not interested in politics. The moral aspects of the problem—of any problem—appeal to him most.] Myself, I've always wanted somehow or other to stop such senseless battles of bad against bad, but we are all more or less weak: I've never been able to. And that is why the hero of this film is different from us. He is capable of standing squarely in the middle and stopping the fight. At any rate, this was the beginning of the film in my mind.

It was truly an enormous popular hit. Everyone at the company said it was because of the sword-fighting. But that is not so; the reason was the character of the hero and what he does. He is a real hero, he has a real reason for fighting. He doesn't just stand by and wave his sword around.

TSUBAKI SANJURO (Sanjuro Tsubaki/Sanjuro), 1962, Kurosawa Productions, Toho (Distribution)

Originally this was a story by Shugoro Yamamoto [who also wrote the novel upon which Kurosawa's latest, *Aka-Hige (Red Beard)*, is based]. I'd changed it around and finished the script before doing *Yojimbo*. In the original version the hero is not very good with the sword but he is smart and he fights with his head. After *Yojimbo* was such a success, however, our company decided to make something like it and so this not-so-strong samurai became the hero, Sanjuro. [Though Kurosawa takes full responsibility for all of his films, the new company naturally has a board, numerous advisers, holds committee meetings, etc. —naturally, since it is a Japanese company—and Kurosawa usually listens to the wishes of these people.] I rewrote the script and was going to give it to Horimichi Horikawa to direct, but again the company decided that I would have to. So, I wrote the script over again and Sanjuro became more athletic, better with the sword. Eventually we only used a third of the original script but we included lots of action not in the original.

From this original we only kept two characters, that played by Kobayashi Keiju [the comic spy who is treated so well by his captors] and by Takako Irie [the winning and funny lady who insists upon observing proprieties in the midst of emergencies], and among the things sacrificed was my original idea of using colour just for the section where the white and red camellias are floated down the stream.

Personally, I think it very different from *Yojimbo*—in Japan the audiences do too. The youngsters loved *Yojimbo,* but it was the adults who liked *Sanjuro*. I think they liked it because it was the funnier and really the more attractive of the two films.

Kurosawa did not want to talk about his two latest films. Of the 1963 *Tengoku to Jigoku (Heaven and Hell/High and Low/The Ransom)* he only wanted to say that he liked it better than *Stray Dog*—thus stressing a connection which has been noticed by reviewers in countries where the film has played. About *Red Beard* (about a late Tokugawa Period doctor—Mifune—and a younger medical student; a story perhaps aligned to that of *Drunken Angel*) Kurosawa did not want to say anything. "After all, I don't know—it isn't finished yet. It has been difficult enough talking about all my past films without trying to decide what I think of this new one."

Akira Kurosawa (1910–   ):
Filmography:
1943—Sanshiro Sugata. 1944—The Most Beautiful. 1945—Sanshiro Sugata—Part Two, They Who Step on the Tiger's Tail. 1946—Those Who Make Tomorrow, No Regrets for Our Youth. 1947—One Wonderful Sunday. 1948—Drunken Angel. 1949—The Quiet Duel, Stray Dog. 1950—Scandal, Rashomon. 1951—The Idiot. 1952—Ikiru. 1954—Seven Samurai. 1955—Record of a Living Being. 1957—The Throne of Blood, The Lower Depths. 1958—The Hidden Fortress. 1960—The Bad Sleep Well. 1961—Yojimbo. 1962—Sanjuro. 1963—High and Low. 1965—Red Beard.

DERSU UZALA

Fritz Lang

Fritz Lang's cinema is the cinema of the nightmare, the fable, and the philosophical dissertation. Long before Adolf Hitler and James Bond, Lang had conceived a world trembling with terror and bedeviled by diabolically designed gadgets. If there has been some critical controversy about Lang, it has centered on the relative level of Lang's melodramatic genres as cinematic art. Since most film histories have been written by critics with an orientation toward realism and documentary, Lang's film fantasies have been somewhat down-graded. Lang's long American period (1936–1956) has generally been treated in terms of decline and downfall, and only the French critics, particularly those of Cahiers du Cinema, have attempted to keep Lang's total career in some sort of personal perspective. Lang himself seems to prefer his earlier work in Germany, and he has gone on record to that effect in Jean-Luc Godard's Contempt. Yet throughout his career, Lang has been remarkably consistent in projecting a world in which innocent people are pursued and persecuted. If this vision be called paranoid, Lang's films might be said to recall the century of Hitler and Hiroshima with the post-Freudian punch-line: "I'm not paranoid. I am being persecuted." *—A. S.

Against a back-projected background of moving traffic, we see a white car which is on the move. As the camera

* Mark Shivas' interview with Fritz Lang appeared originally in Movie, No. 2, September 1962.

draws back, a black car eases alongside the white one and blocks it from view. In the rear of the black car sits a man in dark glasses, his hands drumming on a violin case.

Cut to a door with a notice marked HOMICIDE. Behind it a police inspector is reluctantly persuaded to talk on the phone to a Doctor Cornelius. Cut to a white-haired man, also in dark glasses, sitting in a room which is decorated with zodiac signs. "Someone's life is threatened by a deadly foe," he breathes. "Danger approaches. An evil plan. Murder!"

Cut back to the cars stopping at traffic lights. The man in the black car opens the violin case, takes out a strange gun, aims and noiselessly fires at the white car. Its driver slumps over the wheel. A policeman waves the cars on, and from above we see the white car left behind as the others drive past.

In the first shots of The Thousand Eyes of Dr. Mabuse, the film's method, plain absurdity and weird complexity are revealed. The white car, driven by a man who knows Mabuse's secret, is blotted out by the black of Mabuse's car. The immediate juxtaposition of the word HOMICIDE surprises the audience, since so far there has been no "action." The "action" is announced by Dr. Cornelius, sitting far away in a darkened room. As he shouts "Murder!" the cars stop and the man shoots, as though ordered by the clairvoyant's voice. The white car remains and the black one disappears anonymously with the others.

In the clearest terms of black and white, Lang starts to build his story. On the face of it the story is simple to the point of naïvety. There is little characterisation, the décor is cheap and stark, there is no decoration in the images. But then all fables are simple, and out of their apparent simplicity comes something complex. Each shot in the film leads on to the next, not logically, but with the force of the director's will, and the content of each one affects the next. Lang's style is completely functional. There are very few dissolves and fades, and each scene leads into the next, giving a sense of driving force.

Though it is never stated in words, Lang can thus suggest that Cornelius is connected with Mabuse. The cut from his warning to the actual murder; the cut from the chauffeur, who wants to see the face of his unknown master, to a close-up of Cornelius; the cut from Cornelius, who has just been told that an informer has contacted the police, to the chauffeur being shot for "using the telephone too much"—all these suggest the power of Cornelius.

Cornelius equals Mabuse, it is hinted. Jordan also. Cornelius refers to "a frightened female," and Lang cuts at once to Dawn Addams: a connection between these two characters is suggested by the immediate juxtaposition. This method of cutting is used throughout the film, so that almost all the protagonists appear to be in some way connected with Mabuse. The Mabuse idea thus becomes a demonic force, an overriding power, an evil which threatens them all.

The mechanical devices which we are shown in the course of the film serve to further this impression of omnipotence. The one-way mirror allows a woman to be watched, her movements surveyed, although she does not know it. If movements can be surveyed, they can probably be regulated.

The television cameras which survey each room and corridor of the Luxor hotel further suggest that this overriding power organises the life of those it looks down upon. Their images are captured on its screens, albeit imperfectly. Lang here throws in a joke with the appearance of sudden electrical interference on one of the screens. The sight of the police inspector arriving outside the hotel, passing some of Mabuse's henchmen, entering the hotel lobby, on three different screens next to one another, gives us an impression of superhuman power, the ability to be in three places at once, to see three sets of happenings at once. We never have this impression from the quick cutting of a film from shot to shot.

But the power which Mabuse feels from this ability to "capture" his victims on these screens is illusory, as is the rest of his power. In capturing their likeness, he does not capture their essence. When, as Doctor Jordan, the psychoanalyst, Mabuse hypnotises Mrs. Menil (Dawn Addams), he has regulated her outward behaviour, but he has been unable to stop her falling in love. As Cornelius, he can only prophesy events that he has himself put in motion. Although, through the person of Cornelius, he can confuse and terrorise the people around him, this ruse does not always work. His love of the flashy effect, the appearance of omniscience, his wish "to gamble with people and the lives of people" (to quote from Dr. Mabuse, the Gambler) is dangerous to his cause.

When the man is eventually revealed to us, he loses his

311

menace as he removes his false beard. He is rat-like and insignificant. Only in the disguises, only in the mechanics of his hotel Luxor, is there power. And these can be defeated by the Love of a Good Woman for a Good Man and by clever use of an over-faithful dog. The mechanics can produce hysteria and an atmosphere of oppression, but behind the massive façade, there is a small man who can be overcome by simple means. Behind the intricacies of the film's plot, the scientific devices which play such a large part—the gun with the steel needles, the lift with the secret door, the one way mirror—there is a simple fable to be found.

Fritz Lang's most recent film opened in the West End a few weeks ago to undeservedly bad reviews, and closed after ten days. We hope that it has not vanished forever as it is among Lang's best films.

To tell you why I went back to Mabuse in the sixties is a long story. The original Mabuse was a book written by Norbert Jacques. He is now dead. I came very close to him, and I made one film which runs for two evenings in Germany, which was the big fashion then. This was *Dr. Mabuse, the Gambler*. At the end of this Dr. Mabuse became insane. For me the sonofabitch was dead, out of my life. That was in 1924. In '32, I guess, someone came to me and said, "Look, Mr. Lang, we have made so much money with *Mabuse*. . . ." I said, "Yes, much more than I did. . . ." He said, "Can't you give us another *Mabuse*?" So I started thinking about it and I said, "All right, what shall I do? This guy is insane and in an asylum—I cannot make him healthy again. It is impossible."

So I invented, with the help of Mrs. von Harbou, the next Mabuse—*The Testament of Dr. Mabuse*—and then said, "Now I am finished. Now I am killing him." I had been able to put into the mouth of an insane criminal all the Nazi slogans. When the picture was finished, some henchmen of Dr. Goebbels came to the office and threatened to forbid it. I was very short with them and said, "If you think you can forbid a picture of Fritz Lang in Germany, go ahead." They did so.

Then I was ordered to go to see Dr. Goebbels. I put on striped trousers and my cutaway jacket, stiff collar. I didn't feel very agreeable. It was in the new Ministry of Propaganda. You go down long, wide corridors, with stone flags and so on, and your steps echo, and as you come round the corridor, there are two guys there carrying guns. It was not very agreeable. You come to another desk, a third desk, and finally to a little room and they say, "You wait here." So now you are perspiring a little. The door opens on a long, long office, and at the end of the office, there is Dr. Goebbels. He says, "Come in, Mr. Lang," and he is the most charming man that you can imagine.

I was sitting opposite Dr. Goebbels and he said to me, "Look, I am terribly sorry, but we had to confiscate this picture. It was just the ending we didn't like." He didn't say anything about the real reason—the Nazi slogans in the mouth of an insane criminal. And he said, "With this picture as it is, it must have another ending. That such a criminal is insane, that's not punishment. He must be destroyed by the people." I could only think, "How do you get out of here?" I wanted to get some money out of the bank. Outside the window there was a big clock, and the hands went slowly round.

So finally he said to me, "The Fuehrer has seen your pictures, and he has said, 'This is the man who will give us the big Nazi pictures.'" I said, "I am tickled pink, Herr Minister." What else could I say? And this was the moment where I said to myself, "This evening is the last moment you can be sure of getting out of Germany." I looked at the clock again. At two-thirty the banks close and how can I get out of here? I didn't get out. He was very nice. I said "Yes" to everything.

When I got out, it was too late. I couldn't get my money out. I went home and said to my butler, "Look, I have to go to Paris. Put out the things necessary for a few days," because by now I didn't dare tell anybody the truth. And when he wasn't looking, I put in all the things which a man has—a golden cigarette case, a gold chain, buttons for your shirt, a little money which you have in your house, and said, "You will take this to the bahnhof, you take the ticket and I will be there."

Because I was afraid that I was now tailed by someone, I came just one minute before the train left. I looked around over my shoulder. It was like a very bad moving picture. Next morning I was in Paris, and things were quiet for a bit. Then came a letter from the income tax people, saying, "There is a slight difference in income tax of the year 1927. I think you should come back as fast as possible." I was intelligent enough by now to know what that was about, so I wrote a very polite letter saying, "It cannot be very important, but I will come back, but not at the time you want me. I am just here trying to get a job which cannot be got in Germany; I will be back in eight or ten days." Eight days later I got a letter saying that they had confiscated all my money. Then they confiscated *M* and took everything.

When I came back to Germany after I was in India (1958), I was offered a remake of the *Niebelungs*. I said "No." The man had written to the United States. I gave him certain reasons; I didn't want to give him the real reasons. I didn't want to hurt his feelings. I came back to Germany and he had already announced the *Niebelungs*. I said, "I am sorry, but I will have to go to the press and tell them that you are a goddamned liar, I will not make the *Niebelungs*." He said, "Let's do it a nice way and say that I wanted Brando and you didn't." I said "No" again. So now he said, "What do you want to do?" I said, "I want to make *Faust*," which would have been a tremendous business. So he pondered and pondered and asked, naturally, other people, and they couldn't see it. He offered me certain things which I turned down, then he finally came and said, "Look, I don't know if you know, but I bought the rights to the name of Mabuse from the widow of Norbert Jacques, and I would like to remake *The Testament of Dr. Mabuse*." I said, "Look, do it—I will not do it. I'm not doing remakes of my own pictures." So finally he said, "Can't you make me a new Mabuse?" I said, "Look, for me the sonofabitch is dead. Buried." Finally he talked me into it, and I now had an idea that it might be interesting to show a similar criminal twenty or almost thirty years later with the new possibilities of technique and create some new thing where again you can say certain things about our time: the danger that our civilisation can be blown up, and that on the rubble of our civilisation some realm of crime could be built up. So I put this again into the picture and I did it. And then he wanted to do other Mabuse pictures. I said, "No, I am not doing another." He has already made two more, and I cannot stop it.

Fritz Lang (1890–   ):
Filmography:
1919—Halb-Blut; Der Herr der Liebe; Die Spinnen: Der Goldene See; Hara Kiri; Die Spinnen: Das Brillante Schiff. Das Wandernde Bild. 1921—Vier um die Frau, Der Müde Tod. 1922—Dr. Mabuse,

Der Spieler. 1924—Die Niebelungen. 1926—Metropolis. 1928—Spione, Frau im Mond. 1932—M; Das Testament Von Dr. Mabuse. 1933—Liliom. 1936—Fury. 1937—You Only Live Once. 1938—You and Me. 1940—The Return of Frank James. 1941—Western Union, Manhunt. 1943-Hangmen Also Die. 1945—Ministry of Fear, The Woman in the Window, Scarlet Street. 1946—Cloak and Dagger. 1948—Secret Beyond the Door. 1950—House by the River, American Guerrilla in the Philippines. 1952—Rancho Notorious, Clash by Night. 1953—The Blue Gardenia, The Big Heat. 1954—Human Desire. 1955—Moonfleet. 1956—While the City Sleeps, Beyond a Reasonable Doubt. 1960—Journey to the Lost City. 1961—The Thousand Eyes of Dr. Mabuse.

David Lean

David Lean began his film career in close association with Noel Coward on such memorable adaptations as Blithe Spirit, In Which We Serve, Brief Encounter *and* This Happy Breed. *Lean continued to specialize in the well-made adaptation, particularly the works of Charles Dickens. Indeed,* Great Expectations *and* Oliver Twist *are considered the finest screen renderings of Dickens. Lean has been particularly adept at obtaining precise performances from such players as Cecilia Johnson and Trevor Howard* (Brief Encounter), *Ralph Richardson* (Breaking the Sound Barrier), *John Mills and Brenda de Banzie* (Hobson's Choice), *and Katharine Hepburn* (Summertime). *During the past decade, Lean has devoted his energies to three super-productions:* Bridge on the River Kwai, Lawrence of Arabia, *and* Doctor Zhivago. *Lean is admired by many critics for his professional discipline in an era when self-expression has too often degenerated into self-indulgence.*—A. S.*

PRATLEY: *Mr. Lean, you were saying about the difficulties of getting one's film projected correctly these days since screen sizes changed. It seems most theatres have their own idea as to what shape it should be.*

LEAN: Yes. That's true. We take a tremendous lot of trouble over composition, and very often, I go to a theatre

* Gerald Pratley's interview with David Lean was conducted in Madrid in March 1965 for the Canadian Broadcasting Company.

and the screen is quite a different shape. Quite unnecessarily so. It just takes the theatre manager's fancy, I suppose. Or the projectionist's, I don't know. And very often the tops of heads are cut off, or the feet are cut off or . . . and the whole composition altered. And it's an awful pity. They also find it very hard to keep it in focus. It always drives me mad to see stuff out of focus. You can't really see it. You know, it's particularly painful in long shots.

PRATLEY: *Yes.* Dr. Zhivago *is a very dramatic subject and yet most directors and cinematographers I've spoken to claim that colour works against getting drama in a film. You are making* Dr. Zhivago *in colour. What are you doing in order to prevent it from seeming, say, too bright or too technicoloured in the usual way?*

LEAN: Well, we're using colour in certain scenes in order to emphasize colour in the same way as one wants to emphasize silence. We have made a lot of the scenes in grays, whites, and blacks. In fact, things on the set which, in life, would be coloured, we have blown down with a spray gun to a gray. It's completely unnoticeable, when you see it on the screen. And I think when we really do use colour in some scenes, it will be that much more effective. So that, in other words, if you were going to make a great noise on sound it's very good to have a great silence before it. Contrast.

PRATLEY: Dr. Zhivago *would have seemed, at first sight, to be a completely unfilmable book. To most people, it's also unreadable. What was there about it which made you feel it would make a good film? Or what was it rather that attracted you to it?*

LEAN: Well first of all, I suppose, I have done . . . let's see, I have done two films, *River Kwai* and *Lawrence,* that only had men in them, and I'm rather sick of having men. I want to get back to the ladies. And this has got a first rate love story. And I think it's got a marvellous story altogether. The book is very, very long. It's in the great Russian tradition. And it is tough . . . reading. But we have been, I think, faithful to the book but have condensed it and dramatized it. And I think Robert Bolt, who wrote the script, has really got a good dramatic structure out of it and I think it will be a very exciting movie. At least, I hope so.

PRATLEY: *Did you have to make many changes or introduce anything new?*

LEAN: Yes, in a sense. I mean, this writing of a film script of these great big long novels. I mean, years and years ago I did two Dickens films: one, *Great Expectations;* and the other, *Oliver Twist.* And people who hadn't read the book for some time thought they were seeing the book. In fact, they weren't. They were seeing, as it were, a synopsis of the book. And it's rather the same with *Dr. Zhivago.* We have had to take great lumps of the book out and condense it into one scene, which, nevertheless, says what the book says, but it's done in a different way. That's not very well explained, but that's roughly what it is.

PRATLEY: *Do you feel that there are too many films being adapted from novels and plays these days? Would you like to get back to an original story?*

LEAN: Yes. If I had the brain to be original I'd love to be original. But I haven't. Every now and again one gets an idea that it's mighty difficult. Well, *Lawrence* was pretty well original, I must say, because anybody faced with *Seven Pillars of Wisdom* would find it quite a tough job to make a film of, I think. And so, it is original in that way, in the same way, I think, that *Dr. Zhivago* is.

PRATLEY: *Do any ideas ever come to you . . . into your mind about, say, life as it is, or as you see it, that you feel perhaps even if you couldn't write it yourself that you could work with someone like Robert Bolt and develop it?*

LEAN: I'm not mad about messages. I think that belongs to the philosophers. I think I consider myself an entertainer.

PRATLEY: *I mean, entertainment means different things to different people. I . . . some of them think it's just musicals . . . or anything completely empty. I think that to be absorbed is the right word. And you can be absorbed, not necessarily by heavy, sad chronicles but by things done lightly, as, say,* The Americanization of Emily, *which have a great deal under the surface.*

LEAN: Yes. I agree with you. But we've got this in *Zhivago.* I mean . . . I think that the film industry term for it is "identification." I think lots of people will identify with the characters. They happened to be Russians in the Revolution, but I think they speak for most of us human beings. I think that's the greatness of the book.

PRATLEY: *We talk a great deal and we hear a great deal about the director being the creator of a film. But if you have taken a story from a novel, and it's been adapted by someone else, what can you bring to it? What will you do as the creator and how much of yourself will be in it?*

LEAN: This is a difficult question. Well first of all, I take such a long time doing . . . making films because I spend a lot of time on the script. I work with the writer. I sometimes, not in this case, but in some of the movies I have made, I have written quite a lot of it myself. But in the early stages I suppose the director is, as it were, a shaper of the film. And then, of course, as the shooting gets nearer he . . . he takes more and more responsibility. I mean, he's responsible for the casting, if he's powerful enough to have that control. That makes quite a lot of difference. I mean, whether one plays well known stars or takes a risk with unknowns, as indeed we're doing with this, in several cases. And then one comes to shoot it. I've often wondered . . . I'd love to see a script shot by three directors. The identical script shot by three directors. I think you'd find the finished results very different. Because it's a matter of taste, I suppose. Most of the time I'm encouraging certain things and suppressing certain things in the people around me. In the photography, the sound, perhaps. Yes, quite a bit and certainly in the actors. One tends to put one's own point of view over through the actors. And so, a kind of personal taste or touch, if you like, will probably come out. I'm not quite sure. Above all, the director chooses what the audience sees, and when. He decides whether you shall see it in close-up or long shot, on their backs, on their faces; whether it's dark; whether it's light; whether it's fast or slow. So that, in itself, has quite an effect, of course. When I was a boy, I never thought of becoming a director, I think, because I thought it was over some vast distant horizon. And then, when you become a director, you wish you were a better director, and so forth and so on. But this question of freedom, it's a question of one's record, I suppose. If a large company is going to put a vast amount of money into a film project, I suppose they naturally entrust that money to people who have proved things in the past. And I suppose I've had a fairly good record that way, I don't know. And, I mean, on the films, it's costing a fortune and um . . . I must say, the first time I've worked with MGM. And I've not had quarrels with them at all. They've let me do just as I like. Fantastic freedom. And for instance, we've got two very juicy parts for two women. And we've got Julie Christie who's not all that well known, and Geraldine Chaplin, who's only done

319

one film. And that's quite a gamble. I mean, they really are big parts. And then we've got Omar Sharif playing the leading role, and the first time he was on the western screen at any rate was in *Lawrence*.

PRATLEY: *Are we going to have any of these problems after the film is finished, Mr. Lean, which seem to have beset* Lawrence *in some places, I think, and* Cleopatra, *and several other of the long films. I gather this is going to run how long? Three, three and a half hours?*

LEAN: Well, I think it's going to run about three and a quarter. Three hours, ten minutes, I hope.

PRATLEY: *Because it's so discouraging that a film opens, it runs four hours, or three and a half or whatever it is, and then we hear these stories starting that somebody at the studio has decided to take out ten minutes and someone else is going to take out ten minutes and then by the time the film gets around . . . indeed, they may even change the print if it is being shown on a reserved seat basis and then again later on it's a cut-down version.*

LEAN: Well, I tell you. I'll tell you what happens. I have a certain amount of sympathy because it's a question . . . it all boils down to the last bus. If the film is four hours long, they have to go in at seven o'clock, which is a bit early to be out by eleven and perhaps the last bus goes at five minutes to eleven. And so they beg one to cut it down. And then, of course, the critics, I think, have had a great influence here because they get pretty bored, I suppose. They see too many films, and they always complain about the length of films. Any film over two hours you're liable to get a kick for it. And I think that's the danger of every artist. I mean it must have been so throughout the ages. And we're a very, very young art. I'm flattered that you say it's an art. I think it's coming up that way a little . . . pieces of certain films are, I suppose, art, but I think we've got quite a way to go. We're a very young toddler at the moment.

PRATLEY: *I realize you have to go but I would like to ask you one last thing. You mentioned the critics, and I wonder what you think of critical opinions and influences? I think the critics have much to answer for, especially in cinema. Especially in these days where the obscure is so fashionable. And critics who elevate the work of unknown young film-makers who have been totally unclear as to what they're doing. And they elevate this far above the*

*work of someone, such as yourself, who goes to a great
deal of trouble to make himself explicit.*

LEAN: Well, I don't really . . . I don't think it's true
perhaps for the rest of the world, but I know the English
critics are highly suspicious of anything that costs a lot of
money. While, if you're a dentist or a doctor or a school
teacher and you save up your pocket money, buy a lot of
junk film, put it together, and make a film over three years
on weekends and it's an appalling film, I think they tend
to give it good notices. While if you spend a lot of money
and you've got big star actors, I think they tend to sharpen
up their razor blades and dive in. But I agree with you. I
agree with what you say about some of these young directors and the obscure. I, personally, often worry about being
old-fashioned. But I like a good strong story. I like a beginning, a middle and an end. And I find a lot of these
new films are rather like diaries. "I got up in the morning
with a headache and my mother, whom I was rather bored
with, was making tea and we sat down and had a dreary
conversation about what she said to her aunt yesterday
and I then went to the office where there were another lot
of dreary people and so forth and so on." . . . And there's
no end to it. There's no dramatic construction. And I must
say I like a good dramatic construction. And I like to be
excited when I go to the movies. I like to be touched. And
I like a good yarn, I suppose.

David Lean (1908–   ):
Filmography:
1942—In Which We Serve (with Noel Coward). 1945—Blithe
Spirit. 1946—Brief Encounter. 1947—This Happy Breed, Great Expectations.   1949—One   Woman's   Story.   1950—Madeleine.
1951—Oliver Twist. 1952—Breaking Through the Sound Barrier.
1954—Hobson's Choice. 1955—Summertime. 1957—Bridge on the
River Kwai. 1962—Lawrence of Arabia. 1966—Dr. Zhivago.

Joseph Losey and Nicholas Ray

La Crosse, Wisconsin; population about 50,000; birthplace of Nicholas Ray and Joseph Losey. As an entry for a cineaste's guide-book, this one must take a little beating. Add that they both went, if not quite simultaneously, to the same school (Losey was born in January, 1909; Ray in August, 1911) and this is only the second link in the careers of two film-makers whom chance, and later the critics, seem determined to bracket together.

Ray was thirty-six when he made his first feature, They Live by Night; *Losey, at thirty-nine, followed him with* The Boy with Green Hair. *Both pictures were made for R.K.O.; but coincidence doesn't enter into it here, since this was the time when Dore Schary was strenuously reminding R.K.O. that it was, after all, the studio that had let Welles make* Citizen Kane. *Both men arrived at the cinema via theatre and radio, Losey in particular having pursued a pyrotechnic course through the theatre of the Thirties. He was writing book and theatre reviews in his early twenties, worked on some of the first stage shows at Radio City Music Hall, and after a tour of Scandinavia and Russia came back in 1936 to put on the celebrated* Living Newspaper *production, in which Nicholas Ray acted. He edged his way towards the cinema by way of a marionette film sponsored by the petroleum industry for the New York World's Fair, followed by several educational shorts. In 1942 he was working in radio; in 1945, after military service, he made an Oscar-winning short in M-G-M's* Crime Doesn't Pay *series. Then came the famous Hollywood production of Brecht's* Galileo, *with Charles Laughton. Of his work with Brecht, Losey has*

322

been quoted as saying: "My own experience was that he didn't follow his own theories too rigidly. When dealing with actors, for instance, he used whatever means produced the best results. If the Stanislavsky method worked, that was fine; but he was always ready to try other approaches."

Nicholas Ray, meanwhile, had been a slower starter in the theatre, though a precociously successful radio script, at the age of sixteen, had won him a scholarship to study under Frank Lloyd Wright. In the theatre he worked with the producer John Houseman, went with him to the Office of War Information, and in the early Forties was engaged on propaganda radio programmes. In 1943 he directed Lute Song on Broadway, with Yul Brynner and Mary Martin; in 1946 Beggar's Song, with Alfred Drake. Sandwiched between, however, had been a trip to Hollywood as assistant to Kazan on A Tree Grows in Brooklyn. He arrived in Hollywood as a feature director in 1947, shooting They Live by Night in a brisk seven weeks. The producer was his old associate John Houseman, who was also one of the men behind the production of Galileo.

Ray made fourteen Hollywood films in ten years, working for most of the major companies. He came to Europe in 1957 for Bitter Victory, went back again for Wind Across the Everglades and Party Girl, then returned to Europe to make The Savage Innocents (shot at Pinewood and elsewhere) and King of Kings (shot in Spain). Losey's career, meanwhile, had been abruptly checked after five American pictures. He was in Italy, working on a co-production variously known as Stranger on the Prowl and Encounter, when he learnt that he had been called before the Un-American Activities Committee. Threatened with blacklisting in Hollywood, he settled in England but at first could take no credit for the films he made here. The Sleeping Tiger and The Intimate Stranger were both made under pseudonyms. Time Without Pity (1958) broke the enforced silence; since then Losey has made four more British films, all correctly credited.

Including pictures to be released this autumn, Ray has now directed nineteen features and Losey thirteen. Both scored the same kind of critical success early on (Ray with They Live by Night, Losey with The Dividing Line); both then lost some ground with the critics, though Ray made a spectacular come-back with Rebel Without a Cause; and both now find themselves labelled as cult directors, a dis-

tinction hard to win and even harder to shake off. Cahiers du Cinéma, *which has long admired Ray, caught up with Losey only last year. The lead has been quickly followed, in Britain and elsewhere. M. Hoveyda says that* Party Girl *gives him "a glimpse of the kingdom of heaven"; Losey has been compared, for reasons not immediately apparent, to Klee and Stravinsky. The game of critical cross-references is in full cry. Adulation can scarcely go further than the case of one over-eager French journalist who contrived to publish an interview with Ray, without actually meeting him, in which he generously ascribed to his hero many of his own opinions.*

Something less than enthusiasm for the Ray-Losey cult, however, does not imply lack of interest in the film-makers themselves. We hope, at least, that we managed to communicate this to both Nicholas Ray and Joseph Losey, when a group of us were able to talk with them, separately and at length, last August. The interviews published here are based on these conversations.—*Penelope Houston and John Gillett

Nicholas Ray

Nicholas Ray is tall, eager, communicative, an improbably young-looking fifty. He speaks slowly, as though he were chipping his sentences off some rough block of ideas, knocking his thoughts into shape as he goes. Talking about his own work, he is self-critical, absorbed; he is concerned about what people think, concerned especially about clarity, the way an idea communicates itself on the screen. Looking back recently at his early films, shown *en bloc* a few months ago in Paris, he said he was disconcerted to find how often he repeated himself, took pains to emphasise a point already clearly enough made. Talking to him, one feels the same pressure towards lucidity, together with an undiminished fascination with the mechanics and possibilities of his craft. His image of the cinema—"the biggest, most expensive electric train anyone could be given to play with"—is a young enthusiast's.

* The conversations of Penelope Houston and John Gillett with Nicholas Ray and Joseph Losey appeared in Sight and Sound, No. 4, Vol. 30, Autumn 1961.

As a film-maker with rather more experience than most of critical snakes and ladders, Ray might be expected to be interested in what—or how—critics think. Clearly he is; and equally clearly he finds the existing critic-director relationship rather less than ideal. He would like greater definition of terms, would like the critic to set out the standards he applies in evaluating a film, then to meet the director on the ground of a specific picture which could be analysed by critic and director according to their separate lights. This would be a fascinating laboratory exercise, and one hopes it can be realised. A critic's possible answer—that he knows what he's looking for on the screen when he finds it—is not as evasive as it might appear. Critical "standards" are set up to be knocked down by film-makers demanding new responses. But Ray is right in pressing towards a firmer, sharper definition of terms.

He's disturbed, in fact, by simple ignorance, the failure of so many reviewers to know basic technical facts of the thing they're writing about. One of us mentioned a reviewer's reference to "slow cuts" as a case in point: we knew what was meant, but the way it was put revealed depths of disinterest. Talking of the French critics, Ray readily concedes that some of his admirers are "pretty far out" in their wilder judgments. It was disconcerting, he said, to resee one of his own films, to point out where he felt he had gone wrong, and to hear all around the murmurs of *formidable, merveilleux* from an audience which would not admit the possibility of error. At the same time, he feels, the young French critics *do* know more. "They make it their business to know." And they have proved their point in action: one test of a critic is the sort of films he makes when he stops being a critic.

Generally speaking, Ray clearly feels that critics are too resistant to innovation. (How many of us, for instance, would hold now to the opinions we first expressed about Cinema-Scope?) Screens, he says, had to get bigger; and he regards *How the West Was Won,* the first story film in Cinerama, as a test case, and perhaps also a test for the critics. Are we prejudiced, he asks, against size itself? We try to assure him, not perhaps successfully, that if very big films usually get unenthusiastic reviews it's not because of a critical resistance movement but because they impose problems few film-makers have proved equipped to tackle. Ray himself likes to work in CinemaScope, though not always. Pointing across to the high trees of Green Park, he commented that a story set there should never make a CinemaScope subject. He's also deeply interested in colour, and the cinema's failure to explore it imaginatively, to know how and what to select. He felt, he said, that the black-and-white 35mm. picture had more or less had its day, then saw Jean-Luc Godard's *Breathless* and slightly revised his opinion.

He also liked Godard's Berlin Festival film *Une Femme Est une Femme:* "It's really inventive; it's got some bounce." Not surprising, perhaps, that Ray should enjoy Godard's work, or that he should prefer Fellini's talent as a film-maker to Antonioni's, while willingly conceding his respect for Antonioni's quality of mind. *L'Avventura* he finds attenuated and fragile; *La Dolce Vita* he admires, though thinking the whole Steiner episode, from organ playing to suicide, much too predictable. He sees, he says, too few films—an almost universal complaint among film-makers. But his admirations are firmly positive: Buñuel, Jean Renoir, Bergman, and, from Hollywood, Billy Wilder.

Ray's capacity for self-criticism and appraisal goes well beyond anything usually encountered among directors. His best film, he feels, is *Rebel Without a Cause* (most of us would probably agree); he has solid affection for *The Lusty Men,* a story about rodeo people, starring Robert Mitchum and Susan Hayward, which has hardly been revived since its first appearance in 1952, and a reminiscent interest, slightly tinged with scepticism, about *In a Lonely Place,* his Hollywood murder story. Of his first film, *They Live by Night,* he said that he suddenly thought about it again a year or so ago, walking down a dark, draughty corridor in a house in Maine, and wished that he'd been able to manage "just one more angle in the car scene." Otherwise, he felt it got about as close as could be expected to what he wanted it to express. He's also satisfied with *Bigger Than Life,* with one major reservation. This was the story of a man who reached the edge of insanity after taking cortisone; and Ray argues that he made a bad mistake in actually naming the drug, involving his audience in the pros and cons of one particular medical discussion, rather than letting the miracle drug theme carry his point about the fallacy of believing in *any* magical solution to a human problem.

All these films have an element of violence, and there's no doubt that violence fascinates Ray as the unpredictable factor in human personality. He's equally concerned, though, with the precise placing of a story, its degree of documentary truth. The rodeo world of *The Lusty Men;* the intelligent suburbia of *Bigger Than Life;* the Eskimo settlement of *The Savage Innocents;* the gypsy life of *Hot Blood:* these several settings he sees as a series of explorations. One of his early films, *On Dangerous Ground* (1950, with Robert Ryan and Ida Lupino), was a not very successful attempt to link two kinds of violence—the brutality of the hard city cop, confronted with the raw winter countryside which was the scene of murder. Some moments in cars (Ray, like Antonioni, has an eye for a car scene) and some snow-and-ice landscapes were about all we, or Ray, felt like recalling from the film. But he emphasised that he had driven out with police squad cars in the toughest district of Boston for weeks before making it, just as he studied endless photographs of gypsy ceremonial before embarking on *Hot Blood.*

Ray is absorbed by fact, details of the way people conduct themselves, as the anecdotes he tells reveal. While making a Western, *Run for Cover* (1955, with James Cagney), he wanted to get away from the standard Indian scenes. "What do they do," he says, "when they're *not* being Indians?" He devised a game, a sort of polo played with a hat instead of a ball; but the episode, characteristically, was cut before the film reached the public. Of Cagney, intriguingly, he said that he tried "to bring out a kind of serenity in his personality." Among the actors he has directed, he cited James Dean as one of the most stimulating to work with.

With Dean he was able freely to improvise, something he regards as an essential element in his style. He quoted the quarrel scene in *Rebel Without a Cause,* when the boy comes home after the chicken run. The sequence was causing trouble, and Ray one evening asked James Dean to come to his house and work on it there. He himself would play the father; and he stationed himself before a television set, switched to a blank screen, so that he could watch Dean unobtrusively as he roamed around, snatched up a bottle of milk from the refrigerator, thought himself slowly into the situation. When the scene was right, in Dean's and the director's understanding of it, he got the set designer to come over to his house so that the living-room set could be replanned on the lines of his own room.

327

The point, essentially, was the working out of a mood in terms of a particular setting.

Twenty-five per cent of his work is probably as much as the average film-maker (certainly the average Hollywood film-maker) expects to be able wholly to endorse. Ray now has as much independence as most directors. But he's had in the past the usual experiences of making films not from choice but necessity, to work out a contract or get a friend "off the hook." His second film, *A Woman's Secret* (1948, from a Vicki Baum novel), was made, he implies, because Dore Schary caught him when his resistance was low and his spirits high after a holiday. He expected little from this, or from *Flying Leathernecks* (1951, John Wayne as a tough air force pilot) or *Born To Be Bad* (1950, Joan Fontaine as a tough girl on the make). He talks, as not all directors are ready to do, of the strain of gearing yourself up to a day's work on a project you suspect from the start to be hopelessly wrong.

In other cases, the project had its possibilities, or the dissatisfactions came at a later stage. *Johnny Guitar* (1954), in which Joan Crawford plays Vienna, the saloon owner who sits at the grand piano, dazzling in a white evening dress, while she waits for the lynching party, amuses him in recollection. It was "baroque—very baroque." If you're filming anything as bizarre as this story, of rivalry between Crawford and Mercedes McCambridge (her performance as leader of the posse, he admiringly says, was "straight sulphuric acid"), then there's no point in going less than all out. Much more seriously, Ray regards both *Bitter Victory* (1957, Curt Jurgens and Richard Burton in the desert war) and *The Savage Innocents* (1960) as flawed films; ambitious undertakings whose themes somehow became muffled in the making

The problems of *Savage Innocents* were the kind likely to crop up in co-productions, particularly when the subject is as tricky to cast as this one. Ray did not want his Eskimos to be noble savages, conversing in pidgin English. But somehow, as the film developed, his more fluent, literary dialogue was sacrificed. He regrets, too, that the version seen internationally had to be the one originally cut for the Italian market. The score had an Italian flavour; the jokes were a bit broader than they need be, to meet the Italian sense of humour; there was rather more emphasis on blood and slaughter in the cutting. He wasn't attempting a second *Nanook,* which wasn't in any case practicable, but a film which would make a particular moral point. The Eskimo and the mountie, he says, have established a human contact; but this, when it comes to the test, is not enough. The gap between cultures and civilisations cannot be jumped by good will alone.

This, at least, was the intention; and Ray feels the film blurs it, that there's a failure in clarity. Back one comes, in fact, to clarity, and his concern with it. One particular project, which Nicholas Ray first mentioned to me four years ago and which remains unfilmed, seems to sum up a lot about him. It was to be a story called *Passport,* about an American whose passport is stolen, and who finds that the loss of a piece of paper is also a loss of identity. Searching for it, he would come one day upon a thief: a child, sitting by the sea, tearing up the passport pages and throwing them into the water. The child's question: "Where does the tide become national?" It's the sort of question, one feels, which Ray feels a need to keep asking, in however many different forms he puts it.

Joseph Losey

Conversation with Joseph Losey is restless, stimulating, abrupt. We lead him off the track, he leads us off; one anecdote sparks another, unrelated and probably off the record; he counters a question with another question; he twists in his chair as he develops a point, then relaxes and smiles widely. Deeply concerned about problems of communication, he has no difficulty in establishing an immediate, personal contact with the people he's talking to. On the screen, one imagines, he finds communication as such not much more difficult, though he repeatedly stresses its fundamental importance. Talking of Resnais' *L'Année Dernière à Marienbad,* which he has recently seen, he emphasises its technical mastery but is convinced that it will be all but incomprehensible to most audiences. And he clearly finds it a little shocking that a film-maker should spend this kind of money on anything so indulgent. At the same time, he asserts, audiences are probably rather ahead of distributors in their appreciation and understanding. This need to get a point across to an audience is a recurring theme. Of *The Criminal,* he says that his primary purpose was to bring home something about prison conditions to the general public; and he measures the film's success partly in these terms.

329

More has been written about *The Criminal* than about any other film he has made; and most of the comments he regards as really perceptive come from France—this not only because the film had the bad luck in England to clash with *Saturday Night and Sunday Morning,* but because of the level of critical consideration. Losey was a friend of the late Richard Winnington, whom he still regards as unequalled among daily press critics. "He just had this feeling for films." He also respects Paul Dehn's enthusiasm. Shared with Ray, however, are doubts about just how much critics really know and care; and it's enthusiasm he also misses at some levels of the industry in Britain.

In Hollywood he says, "relations between director and executive can be strained and full of misunderstandings, but even the most commercial people really do care about pictures. Over here, I sometimes get the impression that they just don't like films." He's quick to qualify this with unstinting praise for British lighting cameramen ("you have some of the best in the world") and operators, for producers such as Anthony Havelock-Allan, for individual technicians and executives. But he cites an assistant director's comment—"why kill yourself, it's only a film?"— which is clearly incomprehensible to a man whose involvement in his own work is total. "I direct everything in the films I make," he says, "including second units." On another level, he tells an anecdote of a British production executive who would not be convinced that audience tastes were moving in the direction of downbeat films. Losey quoted *Room at the Top* as an example, to be greeted with a surprised, "but *Room at the Top* has a *happy* ending."

Losey's own films, both here and in America, have mainly been made for independent producers. In America he worked very fast on *M* (20 days), *The Prowler* (17 days) and *The Dividing Line* (23 days). This, of course, was nothing out of the way by Hollywood standards and was possible because of the amount of pre-planning and rehearsal. In Britain it's more difficult to find rehearsal time and our studios are not geared to such rapid operation. In the case of *The Criminal,* for instance, he had to leave three scenes unshot because they couldn't be fitted into the schedule. In particular, a key one was to have established the character played by Jill Bennett as a drug addict, an omission which makes her first appearance in the film as it stands unintentionally bizarre.

In whatever country he's worked, Losey, like many directors, has hardly yet been in a position to film entirely on his own terms, initiating a project from scratch and developing it exactly as he wants. "A director doesn't choose his subjects," he says, "they're offered to him." But this is said without bitterness: it is one of the facts of a film-maker's life. He has planned productions which have never reached the screen—Brecht's *Galileo*, Strindberg's *The Father*, with Wilfrid Lawson, whom he directed on the stage in *The Wooden Dish* and regards as one of our great actors. *The Wild One* and *The Four Poster* were both films he might have made had he stayed in Hollywood.

Looking back to the Hollywood years, Losey names *The Prowler*, with its integration of decor and camera style into the narrative, as his favourite film from this period. He likes to co-operate with a production designer, someone whose function goes considerably beyond that usually taken by the art director; and, just as he has worked here with Richard Macdonald, a man who combines the unusual triple career of painter, advertising agency art director and (on Losey's British films) production designer, so on *The Prowler* his collaborator was John Hubley. *The Prowler* is a film about pressure on character, the pressure of a violent action; and so, in a different sense, is *M*. "I don't think of this as a remake of Lang's film, though I did use a couple of his ideas. I wanted the man to be more sympathetic, for one thing. The main trouble was the establishing of this kind of subject in an American setting—I couldn't believe myself in the idea of the whole underworld ganging up against the killer." The film was so heavily cut in this country that we have never had a chance to see it as he intended.

He is not entirely satisfied now with *The Dividing Line*, on which there were casting problems, or *The Boy with Green Hair*, which he regards as a bit too sentimental. He accepts, tentatively, a criticism that it's the liberal characters and the way their attitudes are expressed which now date *The Dividing Line*, while its feeling for latent violence remains as strong as ever.

On these films Losey was working within the socially critical framework of the postwar American cinema, in a tradition allowing for a kind of mental toughness that has never been part of British film-making. On the whole, we protect our institutions. "You have the most successful

331

class system in the world," he comments. Coming to terms with British life, to the point where he felt he could give it valid expression on the screen, would be a problem for any director of this temperament; and in Losey's case it must have been accentuated by the hole-and-corner conditions in which he had to work during his first years here. But he has never, he affirms, taken on a project he thought had nothing to offer him, and prefers television commercials to unrewarding feature work—"Though I have turned down one or two commercials as well." The efforts to re-establish himself, the breach with Hollywood, must have been accompanied by deep frustrations, though any scars are kept well hidden. Return to Hollywood is not impossible: but Losey has never been prepared to pay the price of turning informer.

To date, Losey regards *The Criminal* as by far the most successful of his British films. From *The Sleeping Tiger,* in which psychiatrist Alexander Knox became hazardously involved with Dirk Bogarde as a psychotic adolescent, he looks back with affection only to two of the love scenes between Bogarde and Alexis Smith. *The Gypsy and the Gentleman,* his solitary period film, was elaborately designed to give the effect of a series of Rowlandson prints. He took on this fanciful Regency novelette, with its wild gypsy heroine (Melina Mercouri) and story of a stolen inheritance, largely for what he thought could be done with it visually. But the film was overlaid with a sentimental score, cancelling out the much more robust visual style. *Blind Date,* again, was not a subject he would necessarily have chosen; and was in fact taken on after another and more attractive project had fallen through. A problem here was to get over the initial improbability of the plot, which all hinges on the fact that a man who discovers a corpse doesn't really look at it properly. To counteract this, Losey worked for maximum credibility in the characters and, again with Richard Macdonald, in the settings of police station and artist's studio.

Losey's picture of the police in *Blind Date* met strong opposition, and his view of prison life in *The Criminal* has been similarly challenged. "But everything I showed in the film has since been reported in the press," he insists. It was the prison scenes that really concerned him, and again he found himself accepting a subject because he was attracted by some aspects rather than by the whole. He took advice from someone he would identify only as "the head of the underworld in London" as well as from prison officials, and the film reflects the life of professional crime as he encountered it. We raised the question of his attitude to brutality, the apparent fascination with the facts and face of violence. "People who say I'm fascinated by violence are fascinated by it themselves," was the crisp retort. Someone, with Buñuel in mind, suggested that there was no real reason why an artist shouldn't build his work around an obsessive violence, and Losey pounced on the point. "De Sade, after all, produced a great deal that was psychologically and socially valuable." For his own part, however: "I hate violence. I don't consider that I exploit it on the screen. But I'll tell you of a director who does . . ." And he named an eminent American film-maker usually thought to be above such considerations. The standard criticism of his work, Losey says, is not that he enjoys violence but that he encourages overacting. "I am interested in larger-than-life characters, not overacted ones. I like to work with actors like Patrick Magee who have a really creative contribution to make."

He should be doing this on his next picture, which stars the explosive combination of Jeanne Moreau and Stanley Baker. The film is *Eva*, adapted from a James Hadley Chase story about a hack writer and a high-priced call-girl; the producers are French, and the picture is to be shot in Italy. After this, there are plans for *Holiday*, to be filmed in Greece for Carl Foreman's company, a possible collaboration with Marguerite Duras, and a version, if the production can be set up, of Alun Owen's *No Trams to Lime Street*.

The first requirement Losey makes of a film-maker is that he should have a "signature," an immediately recognisable style. His off-the-cuff list of British directors who have, have had, or could have it: Carol Reed, Alexander Mackendrick, Lindsay Anderson, Seth Holt, John Guillermin. *Saturday Night and Sunday Morning*, for all its qualities, misses out on this point, as does *Room at the Top* ("Clayton's signature here is Signoret"). He finds the indispensable signature in *L'Avventura*, which he greatly admires, and, with reservations, in *Breathless* ("But aren't they more kids playing at film-making than kids in the film playing at life?") There's a craftsman's impatience with some of the *nouvelle vague* "innovations" which, he says, are only old tricks refurbished.

His own craftsmanship is not in doubt, however violently critics disagree about the uses to which it's put. A glance through the British and French press comments on *The Criminal* makes instructive reading. "Losey's thought has never been more lucid, nor its expression more rigorous"; this is "a style of admirable elegance, and a hard, violent, passionate style"; he creates "a pitiless world, into which only intelligence throws a sharp, dazzling, necessary light." "A phoney film it may be, but it is one for the students"; it is "all done in sawmill style, a high-pitched buzz interrupted by shrieks"; it "never properly establishes its own level of shock and conscience." The nationalities proclaim themselves, though if anyone should be in doubt the second three quotations are British. Are these irreconcilable differences? Losey, one feels, would like to prove they are not; and the greater freedom in choice of subjects that he's now acquiring may give him the opportunity.

Joseph Losey (1909–   ):
Filmography:
1948—The Boy with Green Hair. 1950—The Lawless. 1951—The Prowler; M; The Big Night. 1953—Stranger on the Prowl. 1954—The Sleeping Tiger. 1956—Finger of Guilt. 1957—Time Without Pity. 1958—The Gypsy and the Gentleman. 1960—Chance Meeting. 1962—The Concrete Jungle. 1964—The Servant. 1965—These Are the Damned, Eva. 1966—King and Country, Modesty Blaise. 1967—Accident. 1968—Boom!, Secret Ceremony.

Nicholas Ray (1911–   ):
Filmography:
1949—They Live by Night, Knock on Any Door, A Woman's Secret. 1950—In a Lonely Place, Born To Be Bad. 1951—Flying Leathernecks, On Dangerous Ground. 1952—The Lusty Men. 1954—Johnny Guitar. 1955—Run for Cover, Rebel Without a Cause. 1956—Hot Blood, Bigger Than Life. 1957—The True Story of Jesse James. 1958—Bitter Victory, Wind Across the Everglades, Party Girl. 1961—The Savage Innocents, King of Kings. 1963—55 Days to Peking.

Ernst Lubitsch

The range of Lubitsch's art is without parallel on the screen. Comedy, drama, satire, fantasy, tragedy, farce, spectacle—he has mastered them all. Yet even such astonishing versatility would not have given his work so wide an appeal had it not been for his quasi-Shakespearean concern with people, the multi-colored characters who populate and quicken his films. They are a raffish lot and he has delineated them with an acidity that makes them as real to us as our closest friends. He has subordinated everything to them, frequently even the stories of his films. In a Lubitsch film, the play is not the thing—it is but a device wherewith he can reveal people to us—their petty bickerings, their foibles and weaknesses, vanities, desires, dreams, disillusionments, in the "human-all-too-human" comedy of life. But perhaps it is as a farceur *that he is best known. Most of the time he is content not to scratch the surface of his characters too deeply but just to show us how thin the veneer of their "respectability" usually is. After that, he lets them go with a wink or a leer, and we laugh with him, recognizing these all-too-familiar traits in ourselves. It is all good-natured fun and the world is at least that much better off for having had it.*

Critics have marked his blending of Gallic zest with Attic wit, albeit it would seem that the culture of Gaul and Hellas are not the well-springs of his inspiration so much as a considerably more latter-day Hungary and the Balkans. Lubitsch (a Balkan name, incidentally) employs a Central European harshness and irony of attack in achieving his effects—it is the repartee of the cafés and clubs, as in that exclusive Budapest club with its sign, "Members may not bring their mistresses as guests unless they are the wives of other members."

Touché!

"Lubitsch touch!" *—Herman G. Weinberg.

Dear Mr. Weinberg:

Enclosed I am sending you a copy of a letter which I sent to Mr. Theodore Huff. I should like to repeat that I think Mr. Huff's criticism is sincere and very good, but there are some points on which I might differ, but that is only natural. The purpose of this letter is not to contradict his criticism, but to point out as impartially as possible (if that is possible at all) what in my opinion are the most important phases of my career.

In speaking of the pictures which I have made in the past, I naturally judged them from memory and the effect they had at the time they were produced, and not by present standards.

The well-known actor, the late Victor Arnold who is mentioned in your Index, was my teacher. He had a great influence on my entire career and my future. Not only did he introduce me to Max Reinhardt, but he also was responsible for my first success in pictures in getting me the part of the apprentice in *Die Firma Heiratet*.

Although being starred in the next picture, *Der Stolz der Firma,* and despite its success, my picture career came to a standstill. I was typed, and no one seemed to write any part which would have fitted me. After two successes, I found myself completely left out of pictures, and as I was unwilling to give up I found it necessary that I had to create parts for myself. Together with an actor friend of mine, the late Erich Schoenfelder, I wrote a series of one-reelers which I sold to the Union Company. I directed and starred in them. And that is how I became a director. If my acting career had progressed more smoothly I wonder if I ever would have become a director.

After having completed this series of one-reel comedies, I decided to switch to feature pictures again. Like every comedian, I longed to play a straight leading man, a sort of "bonvivant" role. So together with my collaborators I wrote a screenplay, called *Als ich tot War* ("When I Was Dead"). This picture was a complete failure because the

---

* *Herman G. Weinberg's tribute to Ernst Lubitsch appeared in* Film Culture, *No. 25, Summer 1962.*

Ernst Lubitsch's letter to Herman G. Weinberg was printed in Film Culture, *No. 25, Summer 1962.*

audiences were unwilling to accept me as a straight l
ing man.

I decided to switch back again to the kind of p
which had brought me my first success in the pic
Schuhpalast Pinkus. This picture was a great success,
I made a new contract with the Union Company for a
ries of that kind of pictures. I like to mention that tl
time these pictures were considered feature pictures a
were the main attraction.

It was during this period that I discovered Ossi O
walda, and gave her the leading part in one of my pi
tures. She became so successful that I decided to star he
in her own pictures and just direct her. Eventually I be
came more and more interested in directing than in act
ing, and after making my first dramatic film with Pola
Negri and Jannings I completely lost interest in being an
actor. Only in 1919, I believe, when I acted in *Sumurun*,
or Arabian Nights as it was called in America, did I ap
pear before the camera again. My last stage appearance
was in 1918 in a revue, *Die Welt Geht Unter*, at the
Apollo Theatre in Berlin.

I would say that the three most outstanding comedies I
made as a director in Germany were *Die Austernprinzessin*, *Die Puppe* and *Kohlhiesels Toechter*. *Die Austernprinzessin* was my first comedy which showed something
of a definite style. I remember a piece of business which
caused a lot of comment at the time. A poor man had to
wait in the magnificent entrance hall of the home of a
multi-millionaire. The parquet floor of the multi-millionaire's home was of a most complicated design. The poor
man in order to overcome his impatience and his humili
ation after having waited for hours walked along the ou
lines of the very intricate pattern on the floor. It is ver
difficult to describe this nuance and I don't know if I su
ceeded, but it was the first time I turned from comedy
satire.

In a completely different style was *Die Puppe*. It w
like *Die Austernprinzessin*, a great success from eve
angle. It was pure fantasy; most of the sets were made
cardboard, some even out of paper. Even to this day I s
consider it one of the most imaginative pictures I e
made.

However, the most popular of all the comedies I m
in Germany was *Kohlhiesels Toechter*. It was *The Tam
of the Shrew* transferred to the Bavarian mountains. It

typical German. This picture has since been remade or four times.

Of the historical and costume period of my pictures, I would say that *Carmen, Madame Dubarry* (Passion) and *Anne Boleyn* (Deception) were the three outstanding pictures. The importance of these pictures, in my opinion, was the fact that they differed completely from the Italian school, then very much en vogue, which had a kind of grand-opera-like quality. I tried to deoperatize my pictures and to humanize my historical characters—I treated the intimate nuances just as important as the mass movements, and tried to blend them both together. In this connection I might mention *Sumurun* (Arabian Nights), which was a playful fantasy, based on the Max Reinhardt production. It was successful, but not up to the standard of the three aforementioned pictures.

The picture *Die Bergkatze* was a complete failure, and yet this picture had more inventiveness and satirical pictorial wit than many of my other pictures. Released shortly after the war, I found the German audiences in no mood to accept a picture which satirized militarism and war.

There were two other pictures during my German period which I believe did not get the right evaluation, *Rausch* and *Die Flamme* (Montmartre). As an antidote against the great big historical canvases, I felt the necessity of making some small intimate "Kammerspiele." Both pictures were very successful. Naturally the acting of Asta Nielsen, Alfred Abel and Carl Meinhard and the rest of the cast in *Rausch* was outstanding and was recognized at the time as an example of a "Kammerspiel" tone.

The same applied to *Montmartre* with Pola Negri. The version which was released in America had a different finish and was cut to pieces and did not give the slightest idea of the dramatic value and the impact this picture had in its original version.

In my silent period in Germany as well as in America I tried to use fewer and fewer subtitles. It was my aim to tell the story through pictorial nuances and the facial expressions of my actors. There were very often long scenes in which people were talking without being interrupted by subtitles. The lip movement was used as a kind of pantomime. Not that I wanted the audience to become lip readers, but I tried to time the speech in such a way that the audience could listen with their eyes.

About my American period you are naturally fully in-

338

formed, and therefore I can be much briefer. I again should like to point out what in my opinion were the most essential pictures of my American period.

Of the silent days I would like to name *The Marriage Circle, Lady Windermere's Fan* and *The Patriot,* and also *Kiss Me Again.*

The talking-picture period is too well-known to you and Mr. Huff for me to go into it at length, and I will right away jump to the period which in the Index is described as my "downhill" period.

It might be true that my career is moving downward, and I will not try to dispute it. Nevertheless, I would like to point out that during that very period I have made four outstanding pictures, three of which were in the opinion of many people the three best picturss of my entire career: *Trouble in Paradise, Ninotchka* and *Shop Around the Corner.*

As for pure style I think I have done nothing better or as good as *Trouble in Paradise.*

As to satire, I believe I probably was never sharper than in *Ninotchka,* and I feel that I succeeded in the very difficult task of blending a political satire with a romantic story.

As for human comedy, I think I never was as good as in *Shop Around the Corner.* Never did I make a picture in which the atmosphere and the characters were truer than in this picture. The picture, produced in twenty-six days at a very modest cost, was not a sensational, but a good success.

Heaven Can Wait—I consider it one of my major productions, because I tried to break away in several respects from the established moving picture formula. I encountered partly great resistance before I made this picture because it had no message and made no point whatsoever. The hero was a man only interested in good living with no aim of accomplishing anything, or of doing anything noble. Being asked by the studio why I wanted to make such a pointless picture, I answered that I hoped to introduce to a motion picture audience a number of people, and if the audience should find them likable—that would be sufficient for its success. And as it turned out, I was fortunately right. Besides, I showed the happy marriage in a truer light than it is usually done in moving pictures where a happy marriage is only too often portrayed as a very dull and unexciting by-the-fireplace affair.

To Be or Not to Be has caused a lot of controversy and in my opinion has been unjustly attacked. This picture never made fun of Poles, it only satirized actors and the Nazi spirit and the foul Nazi humor. Despite being farcical, it was a truer picture of Naziism than was shown in most novels, magazine stories and pictures which dealt with the same subject. In those stories the Germans were pictured as a people who were beleaguered by the Nazi gang and tried to fight this menace through the underground whenever they could. I never believed in that and it is now definitely proven that this so-called underground-spirit among the German people never existed.

In the last few years my activities were unfortunately greatly curtailed due to long and repeated illnesses, but I hope to start *The Lady in Ermine* in the near future, my first musical picture in fifteen years.

I agree with Mr. Huff whole-heartedly that I made sometimes pictures which were not up to my standard, but then it can only be said about a mediocrity that all his works live up to his standard.

Attached you will find a list of corrected data. I should like to make the same suggestion to you that I made to Mr. Huff: if you do not agree with my comments, throw them in the waste basket. But I would very much appreciate it if you would let me know which corrections, if any, you are going to make and when the Index is going to be published in England.

Sincerely yours,
Ernst Lubitsch

Ernst Lubitsch (1892–1947):
Filmography:
1915–1918—12 comedy shorts. 1918—Die Augen der Mumie Ma (The Eyes of the Mummy), The Ballet Girl, Carmen. 1919—Meyer from Berlin; My Wife, the Movie Star; The Schwab Maiden, The Oyster Princess, Rausch (Intoxication), Madame Dubarry (Passion), Die Puppe (The Doll). 1920—Kohlhiesel's Daughters, Romeo and Juliet in the Snow, Sumurun (One Arabian Night), Anne Boleyn (Deception). 1921—The Wildcat. 1922—The Loves of Pharaoh. 1923—Die Flamme (Montmartre). 1923—Rosita. 1924—The Marriage Circle, Three Women, Forbidden Paradise. 1925—Kiss Me Again, Lady Windermere's Fan. 1926—So This Is Paris. 1927—The Student Prince. 1928—The Patriot, Eternal Love. 1929—The Love Parade. 1930—Paramount on Parade (with Edmund Goulding, Victor Schertzinger, Rowland V. Lee, Edward Sutherland, Lothar Mendes, Frank Tuttle, Dorothy Arzner, Edwin H. Knopf, Victor Heerman, Otto Brower), Monte Carlo. 1931—The Smiling

Lieutenant. 1932—The Man I Killed, One Hour With You (Cukor directed from Lubitsch plan, signed by Lubitsch), Trouble in Paradise, If I Had a Million (with King Vidor, James Cruze, Norman Z. McLeod, Stephen S. Roberts, William A. Seiter, Norman Taurog, Bruce Humberstone). 1933—Design for Living. 1934—The Merry Widow. 1937—Angel. 1938—Bluebeard's Eighth Wife. 1939—Ninotchka. 1940—The Shop Around the Corner. 1941—That Uncertain Feeling. 1942—To Be or Not to Be. 1943—Heaven Can Wait. 1946—Cluny Brown. 1948—That Lady in Ermine (completed by Otto Preminger after Lubitsch's death, signed by Lubitsch).

Rouben Mamoulian

Rouben Mamoulian holds court at the Drake Hotel in New York when he is away from his home in Beverly Hills, California. Among film and stage directors, he is extraordinarily precise in his interviews. He has lectured at many universities and museums and has written such articles as "The World's Latest Fine Art"; "Use of Color on the Screen"; "Colors Are Emotions"; "Use and Abuse of Camera Perambulation"; "George Gershwin"; "D. W. Griffith, Director"; "Stage and Screen"; "Eleanora Duse vs. Sarah Bernhardt"; "Colour and Lighting in Films from 1946 to 1956"; "Hollywood Needs a Laboratory"; and "The Function of Motion Picture Criticism." He is also the author of two books: Abigayil, Story of the Cat at the Manger (New York Graphic Society, Publishers—1964) and Shakespeare's Hamlet, A New Version (Bobbs-Merrill, Publishers—1966).

Rouben Mamoulian's theoretical formulations are, however, only the footnotes to a career of extraordinary innovations on stage and screen. Applause and City Streets have been honored in their time and after for helping break the sound barrier, and Becky Sharp was the first feature film in Technicolor, and is usually cited in any tract on the color film. Yet this is the same man who directed such landmarks of the American theater as Porgy, Porgy and Bess, Marco Millions, R.U.R., Wings Over Europe, Oklahoma!, Carousel, St. Louis Woman, Lost in the Stars. This is a man who has directed Greta Garbo, Marlene Dietrich, Helen Morgan, Irene Dunne, Sylvia Sidney, Alla Nazimova, Pearl Bailey, Miriam Hopkins, Ida Lupino, Jeanette MacDonald, Rita Hayworth, Gene Tierney,

Cyd Charisse, Alfred Lunt, Richard Bennett, Gary Cooper, Fredric March, Walter Huston, William Holden, Tyrone Power, Henry Fonda, Brian Aherne, Mickey Rooney, Maurice Chevalier and Fred Astaire, not to mention one year's tryst on the Thames (which stood-in for Tiber) with Elizabeth Taylor in something called Cleopatra. Henry Fonda and Clifford Odets were extras in one play he directed; Katharine Hepburn made her first professional appearance in another. Bette Davis and Charlton Heston played their first important young leads in two others, and Myrna Loy changed type in still, still another. Mamoulian brought Elissa Landi to America and Claude Rains, Sylvia Sidney, William Holden, and Rita Hayworth to stardom. And so on, and so forth. Consequently, with Mamoulian, it is no longer a question of finding his way, but of retracing his steps and reviewing his grand strategies.

It all began in Tiflis on October 8, 1899. Mamoulian was virtually born into the theater on his mother's side. She was President of the Armenian Theatre in Tiflis. As a child, Mamoulian went to school at the Lycée Montaigne in Paris, where his family lived for several years. At that time he had two heroes: Napoleon and Buffalo Bill. Later he was graduated from high school in Tiflis and proceeded to the University of Moscow to study criminal law. Before long, he joined the Second Studio Theatre of the Moscow Art Theatre which held its sessions in the evenings under the direction of Eugene Vachtangov. After an interlude of functioning as drama critic on a newspaper in Tiflis, Mamoulian went to London. It was there that he began his professional career by directing The Beating on the Door, a play by Austin Page, which opened at the St. James Theatre in November, 1922, with an all-star cast.*—A. S.

MAMOULIAN—To direct a professional production in London at that early age was unprecedented. The management put into my contract a clause saying that whenever I was asked, in public or in print, as to how old I was, my answer should be: "Around thirty." A London paper carrying the first release of my engagement had a photograph

---

* The editor conducted the following interview with Rouben Mamoulian at the Drake Hotel in New York City in December 1966.

of me with the caption: "Mamoulian thirty but has tasted life." How did this happen? I don't know; even now I find it hard to believe. It was a concatenation of unexpected circumstances, accidents, luck, destiny—whatever you choose to call it. It was not a time for encouraging youth, believe me.

In the direction of *The Beating on the Door*, I was totally under the influence of the Stanislavski method of the Moscow Art Theatre. You know, utter realism—chopping wood, real wood, naturalistic action, and all that. This was the first and last production that I directed in this manner. I discovered I had no affinity for naturalism on the stage. In my subsequent work, my aim always was rhythm and poetic stylization.

Anyway, I made one crucial choice at that time. Jacques Herbertot of the Théâtre de Champs-Élysées had offered me a post at his theatre as part of the trinity, which included Louis Jouvet and Theodor Komissarjevsky. At almost the same time, George Eastman (of Kodak) asked me to come to Rochester, New York, to help organize and direct the American Opera Company. I have never regretted the decision I made in choosing the land of Buffalo Bill. To me, the appeal of the "New World" was irresistible.

While at Rochester, I directed in English such operas as *Carmen, Boris Godunov, Faust, Tannhauser, Rigoletto, Pelleas & Melisande* and others, as well as Viennese operettas and Gilbert & Sullivan. Then came Maurice Maeterlinck's *Sister Beatrice* in English, the first production in which I tried to integrate dialogue, music, and dance. I felt strongly that theater at its fullest should utilize all forms of expression that come within its scope by harmoniously combining in one production dialogue, dramatic action, dance, song, and music.

From Rochester I went to New York, where I directed several "straight" plays at the Theatre Guild School of Acting *(Seven Keys to Baldpate, He Who Gets Slapped, Enter Madame*, etc.). I "arrived," you might say, on October 10th, 1927, with *Porgy*, a play by Dubose and Dorothy Heyward. This was my first production for the Theatre Guild in New York. The New York drama critics of that time—Percy Hammond, Alexander Woolcott, Brooks Atkinson, Heywood Broun, and others—gave it rave reviews. It ran for two and half years in the United States, then was sent to London. Max Reinhardt referred to it, in a published letter to Alexander Woolcott, as one of his greatest experiences in the theater and a perfect example of utter stylization combined with psychological realism. Maurice Ravel, the composer, called it "the best opera" he had ever seen. Among the unusual high spots in the production were: the 4-minute-long scene of Catfish Row awakening in the morning, which consisted of gradual rhythmic progression of household noises (it became known as the "symphony of noises"), and the lighting of the Negro wake scene resulting in a kind of ballet of huge shadows on the wall. The latter has been widely copied ever since. Reinhardt himself used it in Berlin in the production of *Burlesque*. In direction and staging, I used my favorite principle of integrating all theatrical elements into one stylized rhythmic pattern. I had developed this method during 1924, 1925, 1926 in Rochester, and later applied it to such Broadway productions as *Porgy and Bess*, 1935; *Oklahoma!*, 1943; *Carousel*, 1945; *St. Louis Woman*, 1946; *Lost in the Stars*, 1949; and such movies as *Love Me Tonight*, 1932; *The Gay Desperado*, 1936; *Summer Holiday* (musical version of Eugene O'Neill's *Ah, Wilderness)*, 1948; *Silk Stockings*, 1957.

QUESTION—*How did you get into the movies?*

MAMOULIAN—Jesse Lasky and Walter Wanger of Paramount engaged me for *Applause*. Actually, if I had had to go to Hollywood, it might have taken me years to leave Broadway, but Paramount was still making movies in its Astoria studio in 1929, so I broke into the movies without leaving New York, something you couldn't do later on. Anyway, I was one of those stage specialists they were hiring in those days to help the silent directors make sound movies. From the beginning of my career, I made it a policy never to sign a long-term contract with options. I hung around the set when Herbert Brenon made *Cinderella* and Jean Limur made a film with Jeanne Eagels. George Folsey, my cameraman on *Applause*, the sound engineer, even the head of the wardrobe department, all kept telling me what couldn't be done. It's curious really. Here I had been recruited as a stage expert on dialogue, and all I could think of was the marvelous things one could do with the camera and the exciting new potentials of sound recording. The camera fascinated me. Some theorists talk about the camera as a means of rendering reality. This is true; but the camera's greater and more glorious power is in its capacity of conveying truth through stylization and poetic rhythm.

QUESTION—*Had you been influenced by any particular movies in the Twenties?*

MAMOULIAN—That's a hard question to answer. As often as not, I was influenced negatively. That is to say that I would see something and think that's *not* the way to do it. I remember among the films that impressed me most favorably were Ernst Lubitsch's *The Marriage Circle* and F. W. Murnau's *The Last Laugh*.

QUESTION—*You certainly didn't have any precedents to follow when you made* Applause?

MAMOULIAN—Indeed not. Everyone was against change, against rocking the boat, or rather, moving the camera or jiggling the sound. You have no idea how cumbersome sound and camera equipment was in the beginning. It was like walking around with a bungalow on your back. The camera had to be enclosed in a booth so that the whirring of the motor didn't get on the sound track, and the sound technicians kept telling you that "mixing" was impossible. For a certain scene in *Applause,* I insisted on using two separate channels for recording two sounds: one, soft whispering; the other, loud singing; which later would be mixed, so that the audience could hear both simultaneously. It seems funny today when we use a multitude of channels that this was a revolutionary break- through. I had to fight for every innovation, for every camera movement. In those days, a scene was shot with three cameras, two for close-ups, one for long-shot. And then into the cutting room to intercut the three. I insisted on a fluid camera which would pan freely, as well as move in and out of a scene. George Folsey kept telling me that it couldn't be done, but we did it, and he was very proud of it. I also had trouble keeping Helen Morgan in character as a blowsy burlesque queen. They kept wanting to pretty up everything—glamour, you know.

QUESTION—*Did you have any trouble with* City Streets?

MAMOULIAN—Not as much, but some. For instance, I was convinced that sound on the screen should not be constantly shackled by naturalism. The magic of sound recording enabled one to achieve effects that would be impossible and unnatural on the stage or in real life, yet meaningful and eloquent on the screen. I conceived the idea of running an audible sound track over a silent close- up of Sylvia Sidney which would express her thoughts and memories. No one thought audiences would be able to accept this kind of audible inner monologues and reminiscences combined with a silent face. The audiences understood and accepted it quite easily. Here again, the filmmakers were underestimating the public. Subsequently, of course, it became an important and frequently used device in film-making.

QUESTION—*How did you achieve that fantastic final close-up of Garbo in* Queen Christina?

MAMOULIAN—That's a quaint story. I had quite an argument with L. B. Mayer on the ending of the film. He wanted a happy ending. This, to me, was unthinkable. Mr. Mayer and his associates felt that the tragic ending would be depressing to the audience. I told him that I was as much against depressing audiences as he was but that tragedy in the theatre does not produce depression. I insisted on shooting the ending as I had conceived it. Then I would show it to Mr. Mayer, and his other producers, and see if they still felt the ending was depressing. As you remember, the whole last sequence in *Queen Christina* is practically silent. It consists of a rhythmic progression of graphic images (ship sails, faces, pantomimic action) ending with Garbo's close-up. I was sure that the dramatic effect of this silent sequence would produce a feeling of exaltation, the classical catharsis. When Mr. Mayer and all the big brass were shown the film in the projection room, nary a one of them mentioned depression; in fact, they were all exhilarated. My trump in this was the final close-up of Garbo's face, which began with a long view and ended with an enormous close-up that ran for 85 feet. I gambled much on this last shot. Again, the technicians said it couldn't be done. The dilemma was that the long shot at the start required a wide-angle lens, while the close-up at the end called for a 4- or 6-inch lens. It was obvious that I had to use a wide-angle lens which would have to come within a few inches of Garbo's face to achieve the final close-up. For this, I needed a device which would progressively modify the degrees of diffusion as the camera rolled in. There was the rub—no such device existed at that time. (Today, of course, it is child's play.) We were stuck. Suddenly an early childhood memory popped into my mind when my parents gave me a magic lantern for Christmas. I thought of that long glass slide on which there were four separate pictures that could be projected on a white sheet or a wall by gradually moving the glass slide in front of the lens. That was it—all we needed was a similar piece of glass on which, instead of pictures, there would be graduated diffusions. The laboratory went to work and the new gadget was ready by 5 o'clock. Garbo always stopped shooting at 5; this time, however, she stayed until 7. We made two takes: one was no good; the other was perfect. The rest, as we say, is history.

QUESTION—*What did you tell her to think of when she was staring into the camera?*

MAMOULIAN—Ah, that is precisely the question she asked me: "What do I express in this last shot?" My answer was: "Nothing; absolutely nothing. You must make your mind and your heart a complete blank. Make your face into a mask; do not even blink your eyes while the camera is on you." You see, with a tragic ending like this, no matter what feelings are portrayed by the actress, and these could range from hysterical sobs to a smile, some of the audience would disagree, find them wrong. This was one of those marvelous spots where a film could turn every spectator into a creator. If the face is blank, just like John Locke's *Tabula Rasa*, then every member of the audience inevitably will write in his own emotions. Thus, the "expression" would be true for every spectator because it is created by him. Incidentally, some of the scenes in *Queen Christina* were shot to a metronome—to achieve a rhythmic quality akin to a dance. You may recall the scene of Miss Garbo saying goodbye to her room at the inn—that was a graphic poem.

QUESTION—*What do you think of current trends in movies and the theater?*

MAMOULIAN—Theatre of the Absurd, The Nouvelle Vague, Improvisation, Avant Garde, etc?

QUESTION—*Yes.*

MAMOULIAN—Actually, there is little new about all this. Avant garde has existed in every generation. It starts out with much sound and fury, but before you know it, its iconoclastic passions settle into a conformism of their own. One good thing has been achieved: the breaking down of rigid, conventional forms of movie-making.

I think today films, not unlike other arts, suffer from psychic depression. Ours is a peculiar age—while scientists are lifting man into space, most artists keep shoving him into the gutter. Too many film-makers seem obsessed with human foibles, illnesses, and frustrations. Also, the crowning absurdity: After millions of years of evolution we are "discovering" sex, violence, cruelty. The claim is that this is life, this is truth. Not so; half-truths at best. Noble impulses and "immortal longings" are also a part of human nature. Art must be concerned with the whole truth, not just its sickly fragments. Also, too frequently people tend to confuse novelty with originality, fad with achievement, slogans with principles.

The future? I am optimistic about it. The screen is the most powerful, exciting and contemporary medium. One of these days we will learn to do it full justice.

Rouben Mamoulian (1899–   ):
Filmography:
1929—Applause. 1931—City Streets. 1932—Dr. Jekyll and Mr. Hyde, Love Me Tonight. 1933—Queen Christina, Song of Songs. 1934—We Live Again. 1935—Becky Sharp. 1936—The Gay Desperado. 1937—High, Wide and Handsome. 1939—Golden Boy. 1940—The Mark of Zorro. 1941—Blood and Sand. 1942—Rings on Her Fingers. 1948—Summer Holiday. 1957—Silk Stockings.

Max Ophuls

"Je n'ai pas la prétention d'être un réalisateur d'-
avantgarde. C'est un mot dont j'ai horreur. Il laisse
supposer un mépris de la masse des spectateurs. Je
suis seulement persuadé que, même dans un film commercial, on peut essayer de faire quelque chose de
neuf . . ."

Max Ophuls, 1935

"I think I know the reason why
Producers tend to make him cry.
Inevitably they demand
Some stationary set-ups, and
A shot that does not call for tracks
Is agony for poor dear Max,
Who, separated from his dolly,
Is wrapped in deepest melancholy.
Once, when they took away his crane,
I thought he'd never smile again . . ."

James Mason

*I have been brooding for some years over the fact that little
has been written in English on Max Ophuls beyond obligatory reviews, Eugene Archer's remarkably sympathetic
essay entitled "Ophuls and the Romantic Tradition" in the
Summer 1956, Yale French Studies, and Richard Roud's
comprehensive British Film Institute Index on Max
Ophuls, first published in 1958. The preponderance of
lucid Ophulsiana, as of Mizoguchiana and Rosselliniana
and directoriana generally, has been written in French,
and a French, incidentally, more coherent and contextual*

than the fractured French excerpts of the British Film Institute would indicate.

On this occasion, however, I will merely acknowledge without amplification the contributions of Claude Beylie and his colleagues toward the apprehension and comprehension of the Ophulsian œuvre. For one thing, the sheer geniality of the late director's genius discourages any renewal of Anglo-Franco aesthetic hostilities. For another, the individual works of Ophuls have never required the rationalization of auteur analysis. From Liebelei to Lola Montès, the director's dominant concern has been more to please his audience than to punish it, and somehow pleasure seems less amenable to analysis than pain.

Also, the director himself had always remained discretely in the wings until his death in 1957 amid a Vigo-like scandal unbefitting a career so consecrated to entertainment and enchantment. Max Ophuls, who had always spurned the temptations of martyrdom, ultimately had martyrdom thrust upon him. The fact that his career ended with a bang instead of a whimper was simply an accident of film history, but if the coda of Montparnasse 19, which Ophuls was scheduled to direct before his death, had followed the climactic summation of Lola Montès, it would still be through Lola's filters brightly that the director's entire career would be focused. Yet even Lola Montès can be enjoyed as much as a self-contained spectacle as it can as a creative synthesis of Ophulsiana. Max Ophuls, like most directors, always made one film at a time, and anti-auteur moviegoers are free to pick and choose, but when Ophuls had concluded, he had constructed at least for some of us a vertiginous whirl of elegance and splendor around a world seen and felt in terms of memory and mortality. This is not simply a matter of waxing profound over the Dance-Fools-Dance dirge, currently updated to take in the Twist, nor a facile evocation of the pathos of pastness so fashionable in contemporary memory-lane movie reviewing. The Ophulsian sensibility was always too precise for period sentimentality. In fact, Ophuls invented his own pastness, with the result that his films can never be dated in the superficial contexts of costumes and coiffures which make up so much of the content of camp.

Pending the long overdue Ophuls retrospective in America, a consummation of this article devoutly to be desired,

I would like to propose some paradoxes in the art of Ophuls, and, in the process, explain why Max rhymes with tracks. Years ago, it would have been unthinkable to talk about films in terms of the expressive meaning of camera movements. And particularly in America. After the elementary montage theorizing on Potemkin, lesson two was the need for Human Brotherhood, World Peace, Social Reform, Class Struggle, and all sorts of related Big Themes. Realism—Poetic, Social, or Neo—was all that separated us from the convulsions of Caligari and the horrors of Hitler. By these dubious standards, Ophuls seemed too frivolous for serious discussion. His plots were concerned excessively, almost exclusively, with the love affairs of women, most often in an atmosphere of luxury, far from the madding crowd of peasants and proletarians. Ophuls was always basically a set director, and when he did go outdoors in Lola Montès, he painted the trees gold as opposed to Antonioni's painting the trees gray in The Red Desert. However, the old chestnuts about Form and Content, Escapism and Edification, Art for Art's Sake and Social Significance have been roasted beyond recognition, and it is unlikely that anyone would criticize Ophuls these days for not promoting the class struggle. In fact, if anything has come into intellectual fashion, it is non-significance, and the result is that instead of drowning in dogmas, we are transfixed by trivialities, and Ophuls is still "out" because of the force of his gravity.

No, the argument has shifted somewhat. Even in America, critics and audiences have become more aware of the permutations of film techniques. I can tell the difference by comparing the letters I get nowadays with the letters I used to get only four or five years ago. For example, Ronald Caro wrote me just recently on a stylistic matter which would have been of little concern five years ago: "I saw Lola Montès on TV some time ago and, even though it was a cut version, I don't think I've ever seen such graceful camera movements. The film completely floored me; it was like one long sublime dream. Then I saw Caught and Letter from an Unknown Woman. I watched the latter carefully and here is my question: for what reason does Ophuls use the track? It is not, I think, to convey a state of mind, i.e., track equals euphoria, happiness, etc. (very crude equation) because he tracks Fontaine with Jourdan and with the soldier. The first long track with the soldier is when he is trying to woo her after Jourdan has left her.

*Surely this is not a pleasant moment for her! And I don't
think he uses tracking to simulate reality and/or unreality,
although I admit this would be extremely difficult to
prove. In* Lola Montès, *some of his tracks are fairly evident in meaning, such as the 360 degree around Lola.
Here she is being trapped both literally and cinematically.
But I can't seem to pin down the technique in* Letter From
an Unknown Woman. *Can you help me?"*

Mr. Caro is quite correct in not ascribing a specific
mood or meaning to the tracks in Letter From an Unknown Woman. *Nevertheless, the meaning of the scene
with the young officer is quite clear. It is a curious scene
in many ways. Joan Fontaine is obviously not in love with
the officer. How does Ophuls show this? Certainly not by
caricaturing the officer into a feeble substitute for the romantic pianist played by Louis Jourdan back in Ophulsian
Vienna. Ophuls never resorts to caricature to make life's
choices look easier. The young officer is attractive and dignified and reasonable. What he lacks for Fontaine is the
aura of romantic illusion. We know at this point that our
heroine will be deceived, but we know also that she can
make no other choice. As the camera follows her walk
with the officer, passing horse-drawn traffic in the streets
masks the couple from time to time. The clanging bells of
the town's churches are a cacophonous contrast to the
Liszt etude that obliterates the street noises when the heroine is thinking of the pianist. By objectifying the scene,
mainly through the sound track, Ophuls expresses the subjective void in his heroine's heart. It is her destiny never to
accept a world she can sense in all its concreteness and
immediacy. She is too enmeshed in the trap of time, too
paralyzed by the numbness of nostalgia.*

For Ophuls, the track is less a method of treating individual scenes than the instinctive expression of a personal
vision. The Ophulsian style is neither dramatic nor dialectical. He usually tells his stories from the woman's point
of view, and the fluidity of his camera serves to hasten his
heroines to their disillusioning rendezvous with reality.
From Magda Schneider in Liebelei to Martine Carol in
Lola Montès, the Ophulsian woman triumphs over reality
only through a supreme act of will. For Magda Schneider,
it is suicide. For Martine Carol, it is jumping into the circus tank without a net, and then offering her soul to the
public. For Barbara Bel Geddes in Caught, it is cleansing
her body of the child of one man so that she can be re-

deemed by another. For Paule Croset in The Exile *and Danielle Darrieux in* Madame de, *it is a question of renunciation.*

Of course, anyone can track. In recent years such otherwise disparate directors as Stanley Kubrick, Jacques Demy, and Valerio Zurlini have tended to transport their scenarios on the conveyor belt of camera movement, but though Kubrick has acknowledged a debt to Ophuls, and Demy even dedicated his first film (Lola) to the director of Lola Montès, none of the three directors can be termed Ophulsian. Kubrick is essentially a satirist with a habit of putting his players through their paces. His elaborate track in the gymnasium dance scene in Lolita is designed to exaggerate the milieu with the sustained satire of incongruity. If he cut back and forth, Kubrick would imply a logical relationship between images and individuals while, in fact, he finds this relationship grotesque. In Paths of Glory, Kubrick forces Menjou and Macready to follow the camera's chalk lines over an ironically tiled floor. The difference between Kubrick and Ophuls is that Kubrick makes the players follow the camera and Ophuls makes the camera follow the players.

Jacques Demy bears only the most superficial resemblance to Ophuls. A combination self-conscious stylist and Left Bank intellectual, Demy emphasizes the artifice involved in both camera movement and fortuitous plot construction. If Kubrick creates satirical caricatures rather than characters, Demy is content with sentimental constructs which he can manipulate with calculating condescension. There is no feeling of mortality in Demy's world because there is no genuine life. Zurlini is quite simply flamboyant in his use of tracks as lyrical sweeps of emotion. Though there is less meaning than mannerism in his camera movements, he does achieve his emotional effects on occasion by suggesting momentary liberation from conventions.

The main point is that Ophuls is much more than the sum of all his camera movements. What elementary aestheticians overlook in Ophuls is the preciseness of his sensibility. His women may dominate subjectively, but his men are never degraded objectively. James Mason in Caught does not know what Barbara Bel Geddes is feeling when he proposes to her, but Ophuls conveys through the acting sensibility of Mason that a man need not understand what a woman feels to be capable of providing love. The Bergman-Antonioni problem of communication between the sexes does not arise in Ophuls simply because the director recognizes the two separate spheres of men and women. The Ophulsian view is never feminist, like Mizoguchi's, nor feminine like Bergman's and Antonioni's. No Ophulsian male, for example, is ever caught with his pants down like Gunnar Bjornstrand in Smiles of a Summer Night or Gabrielle Ferzetti in L'Avventura, and no Ophulsian female ever displays the smug complacency toward her own moral superiority evidenced in the superior expressions of Eva Dahlbeck and Monica Vitti. We have instead the desperate effort of Wolfgang Liebeneiner in Liebelei to recapture his lost innocence with Magda Schneider on a sleigh ride that is mystically reprised by the camera after they both have died. It is not merely the moving camera that expresses the tragedy of lost illusions, but the preciseness of the playing. There is a direct link between Liebeneiner and Gerard Philipe's jaded count in La Ronde looking deep into Simone Signoret's eyes to find something he has forgotten forever. There is the same delicacy of regret nearly twenty years apart.

Some critics, particularly in England, have objected to the softening of Schnitzler's cynicism in the Ophuls versions of Liebelei and La Ronde, not to mention the Ophulsian rendering of de Maupassant in Le Plaisir. Ophuls himself observed that Schnitzler wrote Liebelei after Reigen, and not before. The implication is clear. It is cynicism, and not idealism, that is generally the mark of youthful immaturity, or rather it is the cynic who is generally the most foolish romantic. A cynic delights in the trivial deceptions lovers practice on each other, and his attitude is particularly fashionable in a culture dedicated to the happy ending. There is a time in every film critic's life when he thinks that Billy Wilder is more profound than John Ford, and that nastiness is more profound than nobility. However, the acquiring of moral wisdom comes with moral awareness, and vice begins paying back all its youthful debts to virtue. At such a moment, Ophuls becomes more profound than Schnitzler and de Maupassant, and Madame de becomes infinitely more tragic than The Bicycle Thief. By showing man in his direst material straits, De Sica and Zavattini imply a solution to his problems. Ophuls offers no such comforting consolation. His elegant characters lack nothing and lose everything.

There is no escape from the trap of time. Not even the deepest and sincerest love can deter the now from its rendezvous with the then, and no amount of self-sacrifice can prevent desire from becoming embalmed in memory. "Quelle heure est-il?" ask the characters in La Ronde, *but it is always too late and the moment has always passed.*

This is the ultimate meaning of Ophulsian camera movement: time has no stop. Montage tends to suspend time in the limbo of abstract images, but the moving camera records inexorably the passage of time, moment by moment. As we follow the Ophulsian characters, step by step, up and down stairs, up and down streets, and round and round the ballroom, we realize their imprisonment in time. We know that they can never escape, but we know also that they will never lose their poise and grace for the sake of futile desperation. They will dance beautifully, they will walk purposively, they will love deeply, and they will die gallantly, and they will never whine or whimper or even discard their vanity. It will all end in a circus with Lola Montès selling her presence to the multitudes, redeeming all men both as a woman and as an artistic creation, expressing in one long receding shot the cumulative explosion of the romantic ego for the past two centuries.*

Letter to the editor-in-chief: . . . and believe me, I know from experience that I am neither an essay writer nor a professional literary man. If you feel you absolutely must have an article about *my experience,* for your Easter edition, I ask you to be content with these notes that have no pretension to being a coherent ensemble.

Thoughts without definite form, pell-mell notes, reflections in fits and starts—for people like me, these things signify a kind of relaxation. The brain goes on vacation, on a cure, and wants to gather, instead of a red thread, a multitude of vari-colored ones. That's good because with a film everything is completely opposite; you must construct, calculate, you need a general view since film is an indus-

* *The Editor's article on Max Ophuls appeared originally in* Moviegoer, *No. 3, 1966.*

The statement of Max Ophuls appeared originally in Cahiers du Cinema, *No. 81, March 1958, and was reprinted in* Cahiers du Cinema in English, *No. 1, January 1966, and was translated by Rose Kaplin.*

trial product, and as I am in this industry up to my neck, my experience has been . . . but that's what I'm going to tell you about now.

"Indeed! You'll end up having your experience!" (Prophetic words of 1922.) My uncle was right. All uncles are right when they prudently give such pessimistic advice to young people at the beginning of their career. Experience —one only learns this late—means losing the ignorance and dreams of childhood. One exchanges illusion for reality; one passes from things divined, desired, inaccessible, to the world of limitations. A man of experience is a broken child. We like to place our destiny in the hands of politicians, pilots and dentists.

In Darmstadt, I once met a bankrupt theatre director. It was winter, during the occupations after the first World War. Having come from Aix-la-Chapelle, I was obliged, in order to visit him, to cross the Mayence bridge on foot in a snow storm. My small valise was full of publicity brochures and hope. He was at home, lying on a sofa and he looked grey in the daylight. He had an ice-bag on his head and dirty handkerchiefs spread over his chest. A performance under his direction (I believe it was *Egmont*) had been a complete fiasco because of defections, strikes, the theatre crisis, a row and the reviews after opening night. "All this—these aren't men," he groaned, "excuse me if I can't listen to you today . . . even the musicians in the orchestra, even the chief designers, not to mention the actors: they're all big babies."

Thirty-five years later, the day before yesterday to be exact, I paid a visit to a Parisian studio. A colleague, a director, had a very resigned air: "I'm fed up. All this— it's kid stuff and nothing else." But as for me, I like children. I don't like little children, not at all, but big ones. Unfortunately, in my *métier*, it appears that the time of the adults has begun, the time of broken children. The cinema was taking its first steps, barely forty years ago, when my uncle prophesied, "You'll end up having your experience!" Was he right? If we have truly entered the era of the *experienced* cinema, we can only hope that this stability will be short lived.

"Seek qualified engineers; no experience necessary." If I were in iron-and-steel following an ad like that I would go and present myself immediately. But they don't look for directors in this fashion. That's why, these last few years, before each film I place this ad in my imaginary newspaper and then I answer it myself.

In order to illustrate what I mean, Paris traffic is the best example. There are laws. Many people know these laws. Many hardly know them. Some people pay attention to them, others hardly at all. The police know that they are taken seriously and also made light of. That's why they change continually. Result: everyone knows how to drive. The traffic in Paris is a work of art. The police commissioners are marvelous directors. When they have proven their capacities, they have to go away. To Morocco, even. The traffic in Paris should be studied by all aspiring directors. Not from manuals or diagrams, but nonchalantly, just glancing at it, from the terrace of a cafe. In any case, that's the reason my friends give in order to justify the long hours they spend at the café terraces.

If one gave the commissioners—or their lieutenants or the patrolmen at the Place de la Concorde—a free hand with the problems of production or distribution, it would result in a gigantic mish-mash. The film wouldn't obey them. Film demands a rigorous order. Today it wants to be sure of itself, and there is its drama. Once, when it lacked assurance, it was not yet menaced. Today, it tries to be a divertissement that has proved itself, that is constructed on conventions it can rely on, hanging desperately on to proven recipes instead of going on a search for the marvelous and mysterious. Perhaps it's the fault of the financiers, who are now rich and fashionable people. The big banks and the Ministry of Finance have taken the place of the speculators and they are responsible for the savings that have been entrusted to them. It is necessary to understand them.

There is a man in the history of the cinema that I like very much without ever having made his acquaintance, and for whom I would have liked to work. He is the merchant who founded this profession and who was nearly an artist. This man is the Laskys, the Samuels, the Mayers, the Loews. Today he has practically disappeared. Such a man must have been an impetuous lasso-thrower of the cinematographic adventure. I see him in front of me with a large cowboy hat, boots, cartridge pouch and a revolver. But this uniform is worn only for me, for, experienced spectator that I am, I can imagine a pioneer in no other way. In reality, perhaps he wore a monocle and a cutaway. This magic merchant, with no experience, saw little strips of celluloid on which little things jumped around for two minutes—an acrobatic cyclist or a monkey—and the merchant cowboy believed one could put long stories on this celluloid, with a beginning, a middle, and an end and a dramatic action.

And then these cowboys left in a caravan or on horseback or perhaps by express train, towards California, for the desert. There, there was nothing—except the sun. And that's a lot. There, on the sand, they built studios, laboratories and production houses. The money that was gathered wasn't "invested"; it was risked. They were the first adventurers of the imagination. What they photographed were the first dreams, the first kisses, the first fires and the first waters, the first war and the first peace, the first birth and the first death. What they shot was the first shooting.

Today, the adventure has become a commercial branch on which are installed the successors to these pioneers: the presidents, the employers, the advisors. So that no one will saw their branch off, they only let go of their money for a sure thing. I fear that this is the illness from which all industrial trees suffer. For when we make films we are building castles in the clouds. But there are no castles in the clouds that are solid. When you want to consolidate them you must bring them down to earth.

Extract from a discourse (to be delivered to the students of some university or other around 1969): ". . . With that, I wouldn't want, for the love of God, to venerate chaos, to give the cue to the iconoclasts who didn't even have the time to learn to paint, by dint of destroying. The self-styled avant-gardists grow old quickly because they want to stay young forever. The make-up on their interior face doesn't efface the wrinkles of years. There is a knowledge that, in my opinion, escapes explanation, a miraculous knowledge. I don't know why, but it has always obliged me to stop, to mark a classic and refreshing pause. When you meet with it, your heart starts to pound. You mustn't copy it but, more humbly, try to follow it on its path. Honoring masterpieces is an experience that must be preserved living. The golden number of this knowledge must be transmitted across the ages with infinite precautions, from the hands of the master to the heart of the disciple. For, whoever has not been touched by the healing breath of what was made before him will never meet with the benedictions of tradition. Full of respect and admiration, we look at the films of Murnau, Lubitsch, Griffith,

Eisenstein and Podovkin. We feel them, like the last echoes of a divine music; they prevent us from taking ourselves too seriously in the concert of time and we . . ." Student's remark, to his neighbor: "Ahh! How solemn he is! The professor is beginning to act like an old man!"

Extract from a speech I gave January 15th, 1956, in Hamburg: ". . . and then, Ladies and Gentlemen, your president gave me to understand that he would like to have a speech entitled: *experience of a creator of films*. I didn't refuse this title, I simply changed it to *experience*. For I don't believe there *is* a creator in a film: I think, and this is nearly an axiom with me, that there are as many creators to a film as there are people who work on it. My job as director consists of making, out of this choir of people, a creator of films. A film cannot live with the aid of one man alone. I can only—and as far as I'm concerned my colleagues can only—awaken the creative drive in each person, whether he be an electrician or an actor, a musician, an editor or a decorator. (I haven't the time to enumerate everyone in this little world that I love). It is necessary to discover in them the creator, nurse them until they come to life—and then we have a good film. But how to arrive: Ladies and Gentlemen, at having my costumer design prettier costumes for me than I myself could ever have imagined? How attain to—this word is often abused but here it is used in the proper sense—this "freedom"? By not clinging to experience. For, I fear, when you are hooked on your experience, routine awaits you at the next day's shooting. The door must stay open. Although we generally liked closed doors—at the studio or at home, when someone from the gas company or a cousin is always dropping in—but the door, in a profession, must always stay wide open for the unknown, the unexperienced. When we have open house, guests do not fail to arrive.

In the history of the cinema, as I see it, a very peculiar thing happens. The *métier* advances only when there is an opening, when experience can no longer help us. These "holes" are the keynotes of evolution. It is at these times that Chaplin is born, fully grown, at the beginning. When, after the war, Roberto Rossellini made *Open City* in Italy, the same thing happened, with no precedent at all. Until that time, there had been no example of someone's going out with a camera under his arm, with damaged materials and no floodlights, and setting it up in entrance-ways, in

360

order to extract a drama out of daily life and make a poem out of it—without permission, almost clandestinely. A marvelous moment, full of magic and surprise. A lack of experience is an important factor in the health of our *métier:* for it is quite simply appalling to think that a dramatic means of expression, dating from only forty years ago, already has the temerity to pretend to establish laws.

If you come, as I do, from the theatre, which is more than a thousand years old, you find that the pride taken by the *cinéaste* in his professional experience is a bit precocious. The technicians, above all, try to forge a system out of their new technical discoveries. Beware the technicians! They can be our friends, when they set themselves to it, but they can be tyrants when they decide that technique comes first. They are nice people, but they have no idea how dangerous they can be, when they welcome us with open arms, declaring, "This or that must be like that and you can't do this or that because, for example, when it's developed, the print will lose clarity. . . ." And then they whisper a thousand things in our ear that sound like crytograms from the middle ages. I lose my head and can hardly follow them. I no longer understand about it. Only one thing persists in my thoughts: at this moment they are in the process of leading the soul of our profession astray.

It's very serious, for the consequences are far reaching. Already, they are beginning to contaminate the actor. Today, all over the world, we see actors involved with technique, even before being actors.

In Berlin, in the Thirties, there was a great lady who taught me many things. She was old and her name was Rosa Valetti. I saw her, for the first time, at the studio. She had to do a scene and someone was hammering nails. She got up and said, "Where I act, people do not drive nails." And she went home. Today, all the actors are ready to accept an uproar without batting an eyelash. There is no longer any true respect for creation in the proper sense of the word. They allow themselves to be intimidated by technique, they come out of the guts of technique. They no longer have the courage to avoid it. And technique becomes insolent.

Several weeks ago, I went to a laboratory. There, they had come up with some very clean prints, with the help of chemical preparations, of some sonorous passages in my film that I had wanted to be very confused. I didn't want to allow it. The gentleman who had directed this operation declared to me: "The policy of our laboratories is this: people must always understand what one is saying." I tried to explain to him what it was all about. He cut me off with: "You must consider, Mister Ophuls, that you are working in an entertainment industry." I answered: "That's true. That's why I try to do what gives me pleasure."

Extract from my private journal (April 1st, 1956): "Today I met a financier. He had an air of being sort of new to the *métier*. It wasn't I who telephoned him, but the contrary. I know from experience that it's better that way.

Financier: Will you make films for your pleasure?

Director (me): Not entirely. More exactly, because it gives me pleasure.

F: That means you amuse yourself continually?

D: No, but one's sorrows procure pleasure.

F: And who, permit me to use harsh words, guarantees me that what gives you pleasure will give the spectators pleasure?

D (stealing away): Well, one believes that one has a heart that beats for them, feelings that see for them, in brief, after all, a nose.

F: Aside from that, there are other guarantees?

D: None.

F: None?

D: None (Silence).

F: And your experience?

D: In this domain, nothing. You cannot calculate success in advance. Yesterday I went for a walk with Henri Jeanson down that Champs-Elysées. The Champs-Elysées is a good place to talk. Maybe that's where it gets its name. Well, he said, "When Julien Duvivier and I were finished with *Pépé Le Moko* (and *Pépé*, as you know, Sir, was one of the most successful films ever made in France) and when we saw the first print, we were convinced that it had been a catastrophe. We left for London before the premiere so as not to be present at this disaster." So much for guarantees!

F: You please me enormously, you know, because you don't tell stories. I will give you all the necessary capital for the film.

D: . . .

F. At least if it doesn't require too much. Of course, it would be on condition that you employ, beyond your talent, all of your experience. Not only a good film, but an economically good one. (He looks in his portfolio, in which is found my *curriculum vitae*). You have experience, that is correct?

D: Yes, I've done some small things.

F: Many?

D: Many small things.

F (bluntly): And color, for example? What do you think of color?

D: If you aim to be in the black, it isn't too necessary to show it.

F: And the camera, sound, the cutting, the décor, the costumes, the scenario—you know how to handle all that?

D (in a peremptory tone): Like a surgeon his instruments, a pilot his log book, a painter his brushes. One learns that.

F: And the actors?

D (bantering): You must liberate their desire to express themselves, by trying to do everything to make them believe in it. It's a bagatelle. Aside from that, there isn't much to do.

F: And the time?

D (for the first time, truly, serious, conscientious and desirous of convincing): Look, everything is made of a multitude of little experiences. And this is the real core of the subject. Obviously one can make plans. There is so much of it. You go around the world, from "Time is money" to "Stakhanov.'" There are many people who can be bought. They are strong and take care that an established time-table is respected: the production director, the stage manager, the propertyman. In the United States, they particularly knuckle down. It's guaranteed that the film's director won't be late: he is taken there by plane, nothing is unforeseen, he arrives on time. I have never understood how. When these specialists are intelligent, they adapt their plan to the subject. An adagio is directed more slowly than a polka.

One might well shoot a detective story at a very accelerated pace but *Tristan and Isolde* will be arrived at more rapidly if it unfolds slowly. Obviously, Sir, these little experiences are perhaps in contradiction to the big ones, the essentials. May I read you something without presuming on your time?

The Financier indicates "Yes." The Director puts on his glasses:

"The artist is everything to his subject. He communi-

363

cates with it with love. He carries the best of his spirit and his heart to it. He makes it be born again. In this act of rebirth, time doesn't count, for it is love that accomplishes it. What lover feels the passage of time in the presence of the object of his adoration? What true artist pays heed to time when he is working? (Silence). . . . The author of this truth without guarantee, Sir, is called Johann Wolfgang. His family name is undecipherable. As you see, Sir, it can't be Goethe."

I raised my head. My financier had disappeared on tiptoe. It was no loss. Since, in any case, he was only imaginary." End of extract.

In spite of everything, I do not feel abandoned if I shoot or if I write—private journal or article—if I pace in my room or walk down the street, head full of projects, but without a film to make. In Hollywood, I spent four years without work, but I never felt myself abandoned, for I believe in a certain current. There is a certain current that carries the ship of our life, an immense boat on which actors and directors are giving a performance. This is neither an electric nor an atomic current, but poets live on its banks. It is the current of the imagination. It runs across all the arts and if, from time to time, it sprinkles the cinema a little, we should feel joy and contentment. At the moment, this current is menaced by an excess of intelligence. It was Musset, I believe, who said one day, "Whoever abuses his intelligence, in order to stop the imagination's flow, would have been better born stupid." To keep this current from drying up is our duty, the duty of people of the cinema and guardians of the flow—this current of poetry that was ahead of us, that is around us or will be born tomorrow. It is up to us to detect it, to stay with it on its course, even when it runs underground, to let ourselves be carried along.

As long as we do that, in spite of crisis, our *métier*, I believe, will continue to exist. To be able, one day, to say to oneself that one was lucky enough to help keep it alive, should be the most beautiful and essential experience one could have.

Max Ophuls (1902–1957):
Filmography:
1930—Dann schon lieber Lebertran. 1931—Die Lachende Erben, Die verliebte Firma. 1932—Die verkaufte Braut, Liebelei. 1933—

Une Histoire d'Amour, On a Volé un Homme. 1934—La Signora di Tutti. 1935—Divine. 1936—Komedie um Geld, Ave Maria of Schubert (short), La Valse Brilliante (short), La Tendre Ennemie. 1937—Yoshiwara. 1938—Werther. 1939—Sans Lendemain. 1940— De Mayerling à Sarajevo. 1947—The Exile. 1948—Letter From an Unknown Woman. 1949—Caught, The Reckless Moment. 1950—La Ronde. 1951—Le Plaisir. 1953—Madame de. . .1955—Lola Montès.

MEMORY OF JUSTICE

Pier Paolo Pasolini

Pier Paolo Pasolini comes to the cinema from literature, and his films tend to follow a literary schema. Nonetheless, Pasolini has emerged as one of the most articulate and erudite theoreticians of the cinema. Consciously a classicist and a humanist, Pasolini is nonetheless sensitive to the achievements of the formalists in the cinema. His career thus far demonstrates the path a literary artist can follow in the cinema. In addition, Pasolini has evolved a unique blend of Marxist historical consciousness and Christian compassion.*—A. S.

It seems to me the difference between cinema and literature as means of expression can be found in metaphor. Literature is almost exclusively made up of metaphor, whereas in cinema metaphor is almost totally absent.

Technically speaking, the creation of a literary work always requires the usage of rhetoric, however liberally, sparsely or even unconsciously it may be used. I believe it would be impossible to find any piece of literature, no matter how simple or elementary, based entirely on grammar and syntax alone. Even speech cannot be strictly confined to the grammatical and syntactical; it will always contain at least some small shred of metaphorical expression, which is an aspect of style that we call "natural."

Metaphor is the most outstanding of all the various ele-

* *Pier Paolo Pasolini's statement appeared in English in* Film Culture, *No. 24, 1962.*

ments of rhetoric. In fact, no piece of literature exists that is not somehow shaped, formed and characterized by some kind of metaphoric design. It might also be said that metaphor represents the fundamental uniqueness of words, the possible reduction of all words in their infinite variety to one single word, i.e., the archetype: the Word of man. Considering the endless possibilities of metaphor, one might even be able to make an analogy between hot and cold, between light and dark, between good and evil. . . . Nothing can resist the unifying power of the metaphor; anything conceivable by the human mind can be compared with something else. For example, let us consider the following written or spoken statement: "Gennarino* looked like a hyena" or "Gennarino was a hyena" or even "Gennarino the hyena" or simply "the hyena." Now, if shortly preceding this statement, we had written or said that Gennarino looks like a hyena, then no reader or listener who comes upon the word "hyena" would have any doubt that the person we are referring to is Gennarino.

In certain avantgarde films, the attempt has been made to juxtapose a hyena with Gennarino by joining two frames: one showing Gennarino grinding his teeth and the other showing an actual hyena with its teeth bared. Now, I won't say that something like this could never be done legitimately. But it would be inconceivable to think of a film proceeding along these lines for a period of two solid hours. Whereas in a novel, one could easily go on piling up metaphor after metaphor for two hundred pages; as a matter of fact, if one didn't do so, there would hardly be a novel.

Nevertheless, if cinema cannot express directly the metaphor "Gennarino is a hyena," it can still create such an impression in the viewer's mind by forcing the images. If the film-maker wants to represent Gennarino as having the characteristics of a hyena, he can show the image of Gennarino grinding his teeth in such a way that the viewer can form his own mental picture of the corresponding metaphor, i.e., the hyena, or if not exactly a hyena, then perhaps a panther or a jackal.

Cinema is often compared with theatre. But such a comparison is ridiculous. The two forms of expression have nothing in common. It is more appropriate to compare cinema with the narrative, although, as we have seen,

* *The name of one of the lead characters in* Accattone.

the problem of metaphor makes even this comparison somewhat negligible. However, though cinema cannot take full advantage of those stylistic figures of speech which benefit the narrative much in the same way that an eldest son benefits from his father's estate by virtue of his having been born first, it is not excluded entirely from such. It may seem strange but the stylistic figures of speech which could benefit both cinema and literature classified as juvenile, religious or archaic, and, on the other hand, those which are generally used in a third art form, namely, music. I refer specifically to anaphora and reiteration.

When a writer resorts to anaphora ("He said . . . he said . . . he said . . .") or to reiteration (litany), it usually means he is in a very excited state of mind, approaching that of the irrational, the collective unconscious. In a thoughtful, serious writer, therefore, anaphora and reiteration are quite rare. But in cinema these techniques can be exploited to their fullest. The repetition of an image, especially for comic purposes, or the anaphoric recall of an image to set off a chain reaction of phrases or short sequences, are stylistic devices which all film-makers use, and they do so with the utmost facility, almost automatically. . . .

But the question of anaphora and reiteration presents us with a problem that by its very nature is quite substantial. . . . In literature, anaphora and reiteration serve as building blocks which are neatly and securely held in place by "words," but in cinema, what do they represent? Let's take an example of a cinematic anaphora: here is a scene being observed by Gennarino. The camera moves from his face to the scene he is observing, back and forth, several times. (In literature, this might be written thus: "Gennarino looked . . . Gennarino looked . . . Gennarino looked"). Now, in cinema, what is the anaphora? Gennarino's face itself, or Gennarino's face as framed within the camera (which can frame that hyena-like face from several angles, from above, below, frontally or in profile, CU or MS, with 75, 50 or 35 lens, tilted or fixed position)? Evidently, both things at once, providing that Gennarino's face has not been picked at random but has first been chosen by the film-maker out of a thousand possible faces (like choosing one noun among the thousand possible nouns available in the lexicon), then lighted, and finally obliged, for better or worse, with or without an awareness on his part, to grind his teeth. Not only this, but other things as well form part of the anaphora, such as the sound of voices heard off-screen which causes Gennarino to grind his teeth, and finally the insertion of some musical comment. In short, where literature is concerned, the stylistic figures of speech are simple, and involve nothing more than a single linguistic act of writing them out. In cinema, however, these same figures of speech are complex; they require at least two concomitant and supplementary acts, or in other words, they are produced on two separate levels, one on top of the other. First there is Gennarino's face, and all the rest, which has to be set up for the shot; then there is the camera, which does the shooting. Before anything else, there is a specific job to be done on each of these two levels. As I select the right expression for Gennarino's face, prepare it, mask it as a hyena, and search for a depth of field in which to shoot it, I could very easily overlook the fact that I will then have to decide what to do with the camera.

Apparently, this schism between two separate operations, which ultimately wind up as a single operation, in itself is something monstrously complicated, especially when compared with its literary counterpart. We might say that the selection of actors, of expressions, of clothing, of place, of lighting—all these are the various components of the overall vocabulary; they are, so to speak, the nouns, the verbs, the adjectives, the adverbs, while the choice of camera movements, of framing, etc., is the syntax itself, the rhythmical arrangement of the various components into one complete sentence.

In speaking or writing, this can be done with extreme rapidity—the words and the syntax, or the meter, spring forward almost simultaneously. But in cinematic expression, a kind of interruption takes place, a pause. The "words" pile up in front of you unmercifully, almost brutally, then wait there to be formed into a complete "sentence" by the mind behind the camera that sets up the particular shot (syntax).

I realize, of course, that I am dealing here with two kinds of creativity (one uses words and the other images) as if they were the same things and as if words or images were indiscriminate "symbols" to be selected and inserted like so many pieces in a jig-saw puzzle. In effect, however, what I am saying is that a word, within certain limits, could be pure image; and an image, also within certain limits, could be as logical as a word. But this is not really

Sam Peckinpah

*Sam Peckinpah burst out of the virtual anonymity with his
second film,* Ride the High Country, *a Joel McCrea-Ran-
dolph Scott Western that combined realistic details and heroic legends. Peckinpah has since suffered excessively from
producer interference in the execution of* Major Dundee
and The Cincinnati Kid. *Peckinpah's trouble suggests that
a director with a very personal vision still has problems
functioning in Hollywood. It is to be hoped that the
uniquely personal vision evident in* Ride the High Country
*will find further expression. Ironically, Peckinpah found
himself on the firing line at a time when the Hollywood
Western itself was so much in disrepute that there was no
particular need to encourage even the most inspired innovator in the genre. Peckinpah served his directorial apprenticeship, as have so many of his contemporaries, on
television. A native-born Westerner, he remains determined to rejuvenate the Western.*—A. S.*

Ride the High Country, which was Sam Peckinpah's second film, was a Western, and in some ways a conventional
Western at that. But it was a leisurely and beautiful film,
and something about it began to attract attention: its sense
of space, its complete control in setting forth the moral dilemma at its center; perhaps most intriguingly, its occasional bursts into almost surrealist uproar and its lively eye

* *Ernest Callenbach's interview with Sam Peckinpah appeared
originally in* Film Quarterly, *No. 2, Vol. XVII, Winter 1963–64.*

for character. When it appeared, no one took it terribly seriously. But as time wore on, its unobtrusive virtues began to seem more appealing, and by now it is hard to see what American picture of 1962 could be rated above it. If it was a conventional film, it was a masterful one.

The story has a neat balance. Steve Judd (Joel McCrea) is an ex-marshal who seeks to recoup his fortunes, and in a way to re-establish his own character after some mysterious reversals, by getting a job transporting a shipment of gold from a mining camp across the Sierra to the bank. To help him, he hires an old friend, Gil Westrom (Randolph Scott), who has a young and slightly sinister sidekick. It is a long ride through the mountains. On the way they stop at a ranch where a plain but appealing girl (Mariette Hartley) is tyrannized by her father, and they carry her with them, taking her to her fiancé in the camp. This much is filmed straightforwardly. At the camp the scale begins to alter. The fiancé has a pack of brothers, wild and wolfish men. The marriage takes place in the brothel: and this scene, with its interplay of the frightened girl, the whores, the brothers already itching to get their hands on the girl, is an extraordinary evocation of milieu and character.

Then comes the trip back across the mountains, with the gold and with the girl too, running from the impossible "marriage." It develops, little by little, that Westrom's life has hardened and corrupted him, and that in fact he is intent on making away with the gold—by persuading Judd to join them if possible, but by force if necessary. In a long, Faustian sequence, he tempts Judd and argues with him. Judd wavers, for all the obvious arguments are on the other side, but he holds out. Westrom and the kid try to jump him.

Judd escapes, however, and his outrage at the deception, the betrayal of what he had taken to be bonds of long friendship, together with his disgust at Westrom's moral position, leads him to rope him up and take him along captive. It turns out that the brothers are also after the party to retrieve the girl. Another shift has been going on, however, which makes this virtually impossible situation tenable: the boy, callow and defiant and sullen at the outset, has learned something from Judd; and in the showdown he is with Judd rather than with Westrom. In the terminal gun-battle with the brothers, Judd is killed; but the gold goes on to the bank, with both Westrom and the boy wiser men.

There is no social or psychiatric stuff in this fable; it is a purely moral tale. It employs no ironies, at the expense either of characters, story, or audience. Nor are its characters epic heroes: they are clearly real men, with notable weaknesses and confusions, and if they are "symbolic" (of the difficulties of being good, in a world where the customary forms of goodness tend to be suicidal), this is on a remote level where it must be dredged up analytically rather than seen. Yet the film has a remarkable size and scope to it, perhaps because, in the Western form, so much that is confining and demeaning in ordinary contemporary characters can be omitted. It is enough that we grasp the moral nature of the men; we take them in a stylized context so that we are not bothered about their "reality"—though Peckinpah insists, and it is clearly a matter of prime importance to him, that the virtues of the film spring from his actual knowledge of the scene and of similar real persons.

His first film, *The Deadly Companions,* bears certain similarities to *Ride the High Country,* and these may have led to his being brought to Metro when the latter film was proposed. It vanished without trace, but is now to be reissued under the title *Trigger Happy.* It is worth seeing, if only for the study of the later film. The basic situation and the characters were both deficient in many respects (see below), but the film uses the forbidding desert terrain ingeniously, and some of the dialogue exchanges—when they manage to get around the inanities of the script—foreshadow the kind of moral tension, the confrontation of two men measuring each other's values as well as their strength, which is one of Peckinpah's special achievements.

His television work is extensive, and I have only seen two examples of it. His favorite in the "Westerner" series, *Jeff,* is the story of a whore who does *not* have a heart of gold. She is a rather plain girl who once was innocent; now Brian Keith rides to rescue her from her bondage to a boxer-turned-tavern-keeper who seems to be modeled on Gentleman Jim Corbett. Keith wants to bring her back to his ranch and marry her; he takes on the boxer and, by some ungentlemanly tactics ("This isn't a game!" he snarls) beats him. The boxer says they are both fools to be concerned with her, and gives permission to take her

373

away. But she does not go; for better or worse she is beyond that simple redemption. Keith must ride away again, with his dog, past a street revivalist who asks if he has found salvation. This tale is handled with a pleasant sincerity. It shows technical flaws inevitable with a three-day shooting schedule, but the performances are first-class and the rather delicate point conveyed with restraint. (I asked an experienced Hollywood TV writer who saw *Jeff* with me why the series was dropped, and he replied: "Well, you can see it right there. It was good.")

The Losers is quite another type of work—a loosely strung episodic story about two ne'er-do-wells (Lee Marvin as the relatively straight man and Keenan Wynn as the sharpie gambler) who roam about Texas, gambling, fighting, partying, and being chased, in various rattletrap vehicles, by a gang of gambling horse-dealers in a giant white Lincoln convertible. It would be pointless to outline the drift of events; suffice it to say that they involve another oppressed ranch girl and her wiry father, some card-game chippies who do a bored twist, marked cards, the shoveling of a barnful of manure, a supposedly blind gospel singer who plays Spanish songs on his guitar (sometimes accompanied by Rosemary Clooney—the girl), a wild fruitless night chase after a raccoon, and several touching renditions of "I Believe." Marvin and Wynn talk in an ornate, Yale-boy speech and make their footloose existence appallingly attractive. The car chases are pure Sennett, complete with gagooga horn noises and plinkety-plink piano accompaniment. The whole thing is delightful, and one may wonder whether this kind of rambling fun, faintly reminiscent of vaudeville, is not something that television is especially suited for.

Now, with the success of *Ride the High Country* behind him, Peckinpah is able to make his next film as he wishes. He is in an unusually lucky position. Born in Madera County, California, on the side of a mountain which bears the family name and was homesteaded by his grandfather, he gained a firsthand knowledge of the real West. He is equipped, like W. S. Hart before him, with a solid and extensive experience which happens to lie well within the traditions familiar to Hollywood. His personal background and, one gathers, his personal taste and vision of life are reasonably congruent with something the industry is used to. So long as his vision does not become too harsh, too flamboyant, or too unorthodox, he should be able to work freely and successfully.

Peckinpah is a laconic man, as befits a Westerner. But the following conversation gives something of the flavor of his approach, as well as background on the Hollywood scene in which he operates.

He went to Los Angeles in 1949 and attended drama courses at the University of Southern California, where he received an MA in 1950. After that he began working in television . . .

How did you decide to follow that route—was it a conscious thing, when you were at USC?

Mostly economic. I wanted to direct very badly. I did, at USC, in a local community theater, finally in summer stock. When my second daughter was born I had to make a living and went to work at KLAC-TV as a stage hand ($22.50 a week). After two and a half years of sweeping stages I got a job as a dialogue director with Don Siegel.

Was Siegel doing TV at this time?

No, these were theatrical films. As a dialogue director I did 13 pictures at Allied in a little over a year. During that time I realized it was kind of a slow way to get behind a camera myself, so I started writing on my own. Again, Don Siegel, and Walter Wanger, gave me a chance to rewrite a scene—in a picture called *The Invasion of the Body Snatchers.* And because of that scene I did the rewrite on the picture. Shortly thereafter Bill Warren, who started the TV series "Gunsmoke," asked me if I wanted to write one. It took me five months to write the first one. I ended up doing 13, and later wrote five television pilots, three of which sold.

Were these pilots all Westerns?

All Westerns, but good ones. I got two nominations—one for a "Gunsmoke," the other for a 20th Century-Fox Hour. Two years later, I was writing, producing, and doing most of the directing on my own series, "The Westerner," which didn't last very long but turned out critically very well.

How did you set that up? I'm very naive about how these television series are generated. Was this an idea you had and took to the studio or—

No. I had written a series called "The Rifleman," and it was very successful. But I wanted to leave "The Rifleman," because I thought it was getting typed—it was a children's program. And they had a title called "Winchester." It turned out they didn't have the title at all—but from that title I wrote the pilot script which later became "The Westerner." Dave Levy of NBC liked it and bought it. And, thank God, both he and Dick Powell were very explicit in giving me carte blanche.

Incidentally, how fast did you shoot the TV Westerns?

Three days, some of them two and a half days.

You've gone on doing TV work, which isn't usual for a director who has started making films, so evidently you are pretty happy with the way you can work in TV?

Well, after I finished *Ride the High Country* I went back to Four Star to do two Dick Powell anthologies; *Pericles on 34th Street* from a story by Harry Mark Patrakis, which we wrote together, and which I produced and directed; the second was called *The Losers*, by Bruce Geller and myself, which I produced and directed.

Set in contemporary times?

Both of those are contemporary shows.

Could you sketch out briefly your new project, Major Dundee?

It's a story by Harry Julian Fink, who took several historical incidents of the Civil War and the Indian campaigns of the 'eighties, and made a fascinating treatment out of them. Very simply, it's the story of a strong-minded major who takes it upon himself to run down an Apache predator. Actually the chase is subordinate to what happens within the man. It's high adventure, and I hope a little something else.

I still think Ride the High Country *is probably the best US film of 1962. But I had to see it in a drive-in, which is hardly the best place to see a movie, and it didn't get much serious critical attention. Is it still running anywhere?*

Well, in Europe we've had tremendous critical acclaim, particularly from Sweden and France, and from England too. Both *Sight & Sound*, and *Films & Filming* I think, and the papers too. But both here and in New York it was well received. There's a funny story about the release of this picture, which is a little bitter. The producer, Richard Lyon, and the head of the MGM studio at that time, Sol Siegel, brought me in to rewrite the N. B. Stone script and shoot the picture—and they also gave me a free hand. Sol Siegel not only gave me a free hand in shooting the picture but let me cut it—I had a marvelous cutter working with me named Frank Santillo whose enthusiasm had a great deal to do with the success of the picture. However, Mr. Siegel left the studio just as we were beginning to dub, and Mr. Vogel took over. Mr. Vogel hated the picture, and I think that's why it was released as a second feature.

Why didn't he like it?

We had a very brief discussion, and I don't remember his exact words, but he thought that a great deal of it was distasteful, that the brother, for example, were not true to life.

The scenes in the mining camp?

Especially the brothel scene.

That's one of the glories of the movie! I was wondering whether you had any special strategies in mind about that. The film up to the arrival in the mining camp is quiet, natural, nothing pushed at all, calm and matter-of-fact. But when you get into the mining camp, and have met the brothers, and get into the whore-house, everything becomes practically surrealistic. But this switch works smoothly.

Well, a lot had to do with the girl who was playing Elsa, and I mainly wanted to show the difference between her life with her father on a remote ranch, as compared with the vitality of these towns, which I know so well myself. I also know the brothers—like they were my own. Those people *do* exist. I think they're as true to life as anybody in the picture.

It wasn't that they were unrealistic, but the scale suddenly expanded.

I just tried to play that sequence from her point of view.

Mariette Hartley's performance was very good, whereas I thought Maureen O'Hara's in Deadly Companions *was terrible. The only thing she could do right was point a gun and snarl. Or was I missing something?*

I don't think her performance was terrible—she had a very difficult script to work with.

You didn't rewrite that one?

I was forbidden to, by the producer, Miss O'Hara's brother. The picture was done in 19 days under tremendous difficulties.

It looks skimped. I noticed two moving-camera shots in the whole thing—where the camera rises over Serengo, and then—and maybe that was a zoom—in the showdown scene. You must have shot it at a breakneck pace.

Nineteen days, all on location, twelve days of inclement weather.

Why did they use Pathécolor, by the way?

Pathé was financing the picture.

I wondered, because it's kind of nice on the interiors, with this golden quality, but terrible on the outdoors.

The miracle is that we got anything outside at all. You can give Bill Clothier complete credit for that.

It has impossible lines in it—even a great actress couldn't manage some of them. Like "I could never love a man who was a cold-blooded killer—"

It was an unmanageable story.

But there are certain resemblances between this movie and Ride the High Country, *in the central character, who is a maimed man in a certain sense, and trying to re-establish himself with himself. I thought one of the great achievements of* Ride the High Country *was that line that McCrea delivers and gets away with; where Scott has been tempting him, and asks him what he wants anyway, and he replies "I want to enter my own house justified." That's a big line, hard to make stick, but you did it.*

The people in *Ride the High Country* are *real*, the situation was real, even though in some ways it was cliche. The people in *Deadly Companions*, it was all based on gimmicks—the scarred head, the dead boy being carried across the desert for five days. The one thing I *will* take credit for doing, at least I kept off that enough so that you weren't too conscious of the . . . to do it realistically would I suppose have been a lot of fun—you'd have buzzards flying over them and wearing the masks and so on. —That line, by the way, in *Ride the High Country*, was paraphrasing a biblical verse I learned from my father. He was a great student of the Bible, and this is one of the things I remember from my childhood.

Did you have these actors in mind when you were doing the script?

The actors were cast, but they hadn't been set yet. But I knew these were the actors I would have to work with. And I was delighted. These two gentlemen are strong, hard workers.

How about the kid?

Ron Starr. He was new at the time. I think he came off very well.

At the beginning he's callow and by the end he's become a man. It seems to me that the Western is a form in which you can deal with serious moral conflicts on a level where you're not tied down with a lot of narrow realistic considerations—whether a drugstore clerk would really talk like that, and so on. So you can play on a bigger scale and yet have people accept it. But do you want to work in other forms?

I have worked in other forms, and my next picture, in fact my next two, will be non-Westerns.

Do you feel there's any common thread running through your work?

If you mean message, no—leave that to Army Special Services. But up to date it seems that most of my work has been concerned one way or the other with outsiders, losers, loners, misfits, rounders—individuals looking for something besides security.

What did you think of The Ox-Bow Incident—*that was one of the first Westerns to get much "social" stuff into it.*

It was a fine novel, and particularly the first half of the picture was beautifully done, beautifully acted; when they get on the night set the realism suffers.

—That letter.

Exactly right.—One picture that holds up very well is *The Gunfighter,* with Gregory Peck. Another is *Bad Day at Black Rock.*

Tracy is an actor I should think you'd like.

I certainly would.

Who's going to be in your new film?

Charlton Heston. He read Harry's treatment, saw *Ride the High Country,* and committed. So now Oscar Saul and I are doing the script. We'll begin shooting in January, in Mexico—we'll be down there two and a half or three months, the whole picture will be done in Mexico. Jerry Bressler is producing.

Is this the same project that was originally to be shot in Colorado?

No, I did a script for Walt Disney, based on a novel *Little Britches,* which we tried to whip and then just threw out completely because I found that my doing *Little Britches* wouldn't work—but I had some ideas and Disney said go ahead. He was quite enthusiastic about it, and I am too, it's a hell of a good script; it's a family story of the *Shane* genre. The producer on the show wanted a rewrite, to bring more children and dogs into it, so we engaged in some arguments along those lines, but the producer had to go to Greece and I came to Columbia. But I

379

gather they'll do it, and I hope they'll leave it structurally the way it is.

How do you work with actors? I get the impression, from what you've said about McCrea and Scott, that you probably let them pretty much alone—they were doing what they usually do. . . .

No, that's not the case at all. We rehearsed—we only had four days—and I worked very closely with them on the set. They *want* to work, they are looking—I won't say for help, but they give a lot on the set and they expect a lot, which is exactly the way I like to work. Brian Keith, Theo Bikel—these are also dedicated performers.

How much stage direction did you do—you were with the Huntington-Park Civic Theater for a year or two—

Two years, and then I was in summer stock, and did a lot of university work, about 30 plays in all, I think.

A lot of young film-makers coming through documentary films and so on don't seem to be able to work with actors.

I had nothing to do with the Cinema Department at USC. I had nothing to do with films until I was a dialogue director. Except for making my own shows—I did four 16mm monstrosities, for $35 or $168, or—in fact I shot my MA thesis as a film.

Going back to Deadly Companions, *I thought one of the best things about it was the score—what was it, guitar, accordion, organ—*

Something like that, plus some castanets, or a can full of rocks—I didn't like it.

When he makes "When Johnny Comes Marching Home Again" into a fugue—it's full of stuff like that—

Well, after making my first cut I left the organization very abruptly. I didn't like it. So I had nothing to do with that. In fact the whole point of the story was screwed up by the cutting. For example, at the end, where Brian Keith is marching to kill Turkey, the character played by Steve Cochran steps up in front of him, with his particular kind of little-boy bravado, which he does quite well, and Brian pulls his gun and kills him, a brutal, realistic act. But it was cut in such a way that it appears the shot came from Turkey, which changed the whole focus of the thing—we really had everybody riding off into the sunset.—Which wasn't my touch.

I thought the basic problem with it was the psychiatric revelation about his scar. Given the way the first part of

380

the picture goes, this is an unreasonably slight explanation, though Keith was very good in that scene where she says "Aw, I've seen you with your hat off," and he does that slow smile. But it was the best of a bad job.

I couldn't work with it, obviously, so I just kind of went around the edges, trying to bring some life into it. I think I failed. However, it was because of that picture that I was called to Metro.

Do you have anything printable to say about the title change—you know they're going to call it Trigger Happy *now.*

I don't even have any idea of what they're doing with it. Obviously I'm not happy about the picture, though I'm glad the reviews came out as well as they did. It was a great lesson to me, that I would never do a picture again until I had complete story control. So from that standpoint it was quite valuable. I enjoyed working with Miss O'Hara, though I didn't have too much communication with her. We were under such tremendous shooting pressure that I would try to figure out, every night, some way to change the lines, and I think we changed about 20 per cent, Brian and I, because he felt exactly as I did.

Did a lot of this bad dialogue come straight from the novel?—it had a stilted quality that can arise that way.

All I can say is this: you think it's bad dialogue, I think it's bad dialogue, but Mr. Fitzsimons thought it was excellent dialogue. I believe the novel was adapted from the screenplay.

As critics say, there's no accounting for some tastes.

Well, Mr. Fleischman is a clever writer, but I think they just fell in love with the script and couldn't stand to have a word of it changed. Also they were under tremendous pressure from the exhibitors, who had okayed the script with the idea that it wouldn't be changed. So I suppose the ultimate blame must go to the exhibitors.

Some of the money came from one of these exhibitor combines?

Yes, and I think their standpoint was that it must be shot as written, and this put shackles on everybody, including Fitzsimons.

How much did it cost?

Damn little, but nobody really knows exactly.

I wanted to ask if Deadly Companions *and* Ride the High Country *made money?*

Deadly Companions *I am sure broke even—if it played*

in four cities it broke even. *Ride the High Country*, I heard from Dick Lions (the producer), a couple of months ago, is one of the highest-grossing Metro pictures in Europe in five years. It's done very well.

What did it cost?

Their studio figures were $813,000, I believe.

A very modest figure, these days.

Studio costs were very heavy—the picture could have been made for a great deal less. We had 24 days, and went 26, I believe.

It had a marvellous sense of space and leisure to it; it certainly didn't look hasty.

That was the soapsuds we used in the Bronson Canyon in the 115-degree temperatures, to make it look like a mining camp! I give a lot of credit to Leroy Coleman, the art director. He stole old *Bounty* sails to make the tents, and everybody pitched in. Then again I had a marvellous cameraman in Lucien Ballard.

You're lucky to be able to use your own background.

It's very difficult to write about things you don't know. Those mining sequences and the brothel sequence, for instance, took a great deal of research—but it paid off. We've had letters from all over the Western United States, from people who wrote in and said "That's how it was!" And they're right.

It had a very fluid feel, with a lot of moving camera—

I had learned! I insisted. Everybody would say, no you don't need a dolly, and you don't need this, and we'll fix that. It's a lie. You have to worry and fight—until you get what you want.

Though I don't particularly want a fluid camera just to have a fluid camera: sometimes you want to lead or follow someone, sometimes you want them to come to you. That can change.

What did you think of the Budd Boetticher Westerns— Ride Lonesome *and so on?*

He did a great many with Randolph Scott. I saw one. I understand he's in Mexico now.

It's been alleged that Ride the High Country *was a kind of summary of the Boetticher films.*

No, I think it came from N. B. Stone, who did the story and the screenplay. I'd like to be able to make a Western like Kurosawa makes Westerns.

But I notice you didn't include Seven Samurai *in that*

*list of your favorite films. Is this because you didn't like it
for some reason, or just didn't think of it?*

No, it's a highly entertaining film, but can't be compared to *Rashomon*. Did you see *The Bad Sleep Well?*

Yes. That beginning scene I liked.

Marvellous. And the rest of the picture was bad soap opera on the grand scale! Very pretentious—which is what I really resent in a picture more than anything else, that fatal weakness of so many really astonishingly good directors. Speaking of pretentions, there's a motion picture called *The Leopard* . . .

Sam Peckinpah (1926-   ):
Filmography:
1962—The Deadly Companions, Ride the High Country. 1965—
Major Dundee. 1969—The Wild Bunch.

383

Abraham Polonsky

In 1949 a writer, whose experience, with the exception of two previous screenplays and two unmemorable novels, had been primarily in radio, made an adaptation of an unsuccessful journalistic novel to the screen, and directed a film of it. The event would not seem to be a particularly auspicious one nor much of a novelty for Hollywood, where every other day finds one hack adapting the work of another hack. Nor would it have been much more promising to know that the film made use of several elements that were sufficiently familiar—the bad-good guy involved in the rackets who finally goes straight, the ingenue who tries to reform him, etc. Yet, apparently, to have known all this was not to know enough. How else to account for the fact that out of it all was created an original, moving, and even beautiful work whose only tangency with clichés was at the point at which it transformed and transcended them? I think it is accounted for by that phenomenon which never ceases to be somehow both inexplicable and unpredictable: the presence of an artist.

But the event was, perhaps, not quite so unpredictable as I may, somewhat Hollywoodishly, have made it sound. The artist's name was Abraham Polonsky, and his film was Force of Evil; *previously, he had written the original scenario for the film* Body and Soul. Body and Soul *did not lack acclaim; although independently produced, it won an Academy Award, and was financially successful.* Force of Evil *was without acclaim or appreciation; noticed only by the British film periodicals, it was allowed to die its quiet death, a gangster film with only muted violence, a love story without romantic apotheosis, a Hollywood film without the Happy Ending. Both* Sight and Sound *and* Sequence *had cited it as among the most original films of its year, and it still occasionally crops up in catalogues of neglected works. Lindsay Anderson, in his close analysis of the last sequence of* On the Waterfront *which appeared in* Sight and Sound *several years ago, invoked* Force of Evil *as foil to that film's operatic dishonesty. The habitual British reader may have caught the aptness of the comparison; for the American one, it must have been merely a little baffling.*

In theme and meaning, Body and Soul *and* Force of Evil *form an extraordinary unity. In each, the hero, played in both cases with a combination of tough cynicism and urban dreaminess by the late John Garfield at his most characteristic, allows himself to become involved with certain forces of corruption, only, finally, to revolt against them, and attempt to wrench himself free. In both films, the hero is not moved to this final breach without first having caused some irrevocable violence to those most close to him, and both films end not with some cheap and easy redemption, but deep in* Angst *and ambiguity. "What can you do? Kill me? Everybody dies," are the final words of* Body and Soul, *as the fighter says them to the gambler whose fight he has refused to throw. The effect is not entirely pessimistic; there is a certain heroic implication in the fighter's assertion of his moral triumph, inalterable even in death; still, the fact remains that a life is not this casually disposed of, and the audience demands some compensation for the lack of final Uplift. This it got, in* Body and Soul, *in the physical excitement of the prizefight scenes, photographed so dynamically by James Wong Howe on (!) roller skates, and in the reliable familiarity of the fundamental story line: ambitious slum boy battles way up to success. It is the kind of story that allows the audience the illicit thrill of a vicarious participation in the somewhat unscrupulous rise of the hero without the guilt that belongs properly to him. So, despite the frequently rich and even lyrical language of the film, its often striking images of city life, and the sense of flexible and sensitive human relationships which managed to cluster about the success story's rigid central structure, despite, that is to say, the presence of artistry, it was officially recognized by the Academy of Motion Picture Art and Sciences as a work of art.*

Force of Evil *is not so immediately likeable a film; it is* without such direct compensations for its underlying sadness. Unlike the fighter of Body and Soul, Joe Morse, the hero of Force of Evil, is not so simply and understandably the product of social determinations. We first see him as a successful lawyer; he is not fighting to escape poverty, but to annex greater wealth. Nor is he unaware of the nature of his involvement, or without moral understanding. One is never certain that the fighter of Body and Soul is wholly aware of his moral predicament; but Joe Morse acknowledges full responsibility, without even pleading the excuse of weakness. By his own admission, he is "strong enough to get a part of the corruption, but not strong enough to resist it." But this is not so much weakness as a perversion of strength, a defect not in quantity but in kind. The progress of Force of Evil is that of the painfully gradual burgeoning of a moral imagination—if you prefer, a conscience. It is not miraculously achieved by romantic love, but only attained after the death of Joe's older brother, whom he had tried both to advance and to protect within the racket in which they become involved. It is the relationship of the two brothers which is the central love story of the film—the Freudian "family romance"—a love thwarted mutually by guilt, and ending in anguish. In terms of plot, the film ends utterly without stereotypic satisfactions: the older brother is killed; Joe is about to confess to the police, and inevitably to be punished; there is no final, solipsistic kiss. "I decided to help," are Joe's last words as the film concludes, after he has found his dead brother's battered body. It is a moment entirely free from the pieties which customarily attend such a regeneration, nor has it any of that sense of straining to engage some good, gray abstraction like "Society," which hangs so heavily over the last sequence of On the Waterfront. Force of Evil ends in moral awakening, but it reaches out not so much toward society as toward community, even communion; a sense of the oneness of human involvement without any diminution of that involvement's ineluctable guilt.

Were this all, one might have simply a film of the tenderness, sensitivity, and, I believe, somewhat vitiating softness of, say, They Live by Night. Even Sight and Sound tended to relegate Force of Evil to the status of a sympathetic but "minor" film; I think this is other than the case. The film was said to be overly literary, and there is no doubt that it is a work which relies heavily on its language; perhaps, we are still not entirely free of the tyrannical dogma that language is not properly an element of film. To observe that the language of Force of Evil is beautiful in itself may not be quite to the point. The impression of that language is of for the first time really hearing, on the screen, the sound of city speech, with its special repetitions and elisions, cadence and inflection, inarticulateness and crypto-poetry; much as Odets had brought it to the stage. As in Odets, the effect is naturalistic, and, as in Odets, it is achieved by an extreme degree of mannerism, artifice, and stylization. But the astonishing thing about Force of Evil, more obvious now, perhaps, in the light of such more overtly experimental works as Hiroshima, Mon Amour, is the way in which the image works with the word. Nothing is duplicated, or supererogatory. Even in so simple an instance as that of the heroine's face in close-up, as the first person narrative runs "Doris wanted me to make love to her," is the relationship of word to image complementary rather than redundant. The sound track is the image slantwise; refracted through an individual consciousness, and, to that extent, interpreted. Throughout the film, Joe is constantly commenting upon the action, telling us not only what he and the others think, but even describing his own, overt actions as we see him engaging in them. It is this kind of awareness and volition which is alien to the conventional melodramatic hero; and it is interesting to note that it is a departure from the novel which is related in flatly omniscient third person. The effect of all this off-repetition, with its language overlapping image and language overlapping language, is finally quite different from that of the very similar devices of Hiroshima, Mon Amour. In that film, the final effect is merely rhetorical and consequently artistic; in Force of Evil, the language takes on the quality of incantation, and imparts an almost choric resonance to the Cain and Abel myth which lies at the film's center.

The more one sees Force of Evil, the closer one gets to the film's center, the more one becomes aware of that central myth, and the formal means by which it is exposed. The language becomes a kind of insistent music, and the images move congruently with an extraordinary purity and freedom. A brief conversation is composed from a remote angle above a gracefully curving stairway; the moment exists both in and independent of the plot; and, independently, it is startlingly beautiful. Such imagery proliferates *throughout the film, from the simplest of conversational exchanges to the complexly moving vision of Joe running senselessly down a deserted Wall Street at night, knowing that never again will he be able to return to his "fine office up in the clouds."* Force of Evil *is, actually, a very impure film; it is literary and dramatic, but only insofar as the film is a literary and dramatic medium, and no further. Beneath and beyond that, there is the autonomous beauty of poetic diction; the aesthetic paradox that what is harrowing in life may be that and be also beautiful in art. And the final passage of the film, in which, in the pervasive grayness of the early morning, Joe discovers his brother's body at the base of an arching bridge, from the desolate rocks upon which it has been discarded, "like an old rag," is both immensely harrowing and starkly beautiful. It is a descent to "the bottom of the world," to a kind of hell; the symbolic death that must be suffered before regeneration. "Because, if a man can live so long, and have his whole life come out like rubbish, then something was horribly wrong . . . and I decided to help."*

[The "interview" with Abraham Polonsky related below was conducted entirely through correspondence. I have taken the liberty of some slight rearrangement so that there might be a clear relation of answer to question, but the words remain unchanged. Therefore, while the exchanges may occasionally approximate the give and take of conversation, they may be accepted as having the value of written reflection, such as that may be.] *—William Pechter

Would you begin by giving me some idea of your background before you began working in films? Somewhere I picked up the information that you originally wrote for radio, and, if my memory doesn't play tricks, I recall reading a radio script of yours in the old Quarterly of Film, Radio, and Television. *I also seem to remember hearing that you taught for a while at the University of Southern California and even the City College of New York, although I am not sure of the chronology (i.e., before or after film-making), and virtually certain that I must have*

* William Pechter's interview with Abraham Polonsky originally appeared in Film Quarterly, No. 3, Vol. XV, Spring 1962.

dreamed the latter. Would you also refer to your published fiction and film criticism?

I led the usual restless street life: gang (East Side); schoolboy (P.S. 32, 57, De Witt Clinton); teacher (CCNY, A.B.); Law (Columbia); volunteer in politics (Democrat, Anarchist, Radical, Confused). I taught at City College from 1932 to the war; never taught at the University of Southern California. I am familiar with the learned professions (teaching and law), the vagrant ones (sea, farm, factory), and the eternal ones (marriage, fatherhood, art, science). The most extraordinary shock in my life was not the war which I survived, but the films which I did not. I always wrote, produced little motion in life and never stopped talking.

My first novel *(The Discoverers)* was accepted, announced, advertised by Modern Age Books and then withdrawn as unreadable. I retired to silence in art, action in politics, and gibberish in radio (Columbia Workshop, Orson Welles, Goldbergs, and I forget). Two potboilers (Simon and Schuster, Little, Brown). The war (O.S.S.). My blueberry pie was Paramount.

Excluding the movies for the moment, I managed a semiserious return to the novel with *The World Above*, and, after being blacklisted, *The Season of Fear*. These attempts were laced with some short stories, criticism, and genteel scholarly editing *(Hollywood Quarterly, Contemporary Reader)*.

The guerrilla life I pretended to practise in the war I played with some amusement and frequent disgust in the jungle of TV as a blacklisted writer. Likewise in films. Those minor victories and major defeats admit no obituaries at the moment.

How did you begin your work in films?

By accident. I signed with Paramount before going overseas. However appalled as I was by the industry and its product, the medium overwhelmed me with a language I had been trying to speak all my life.

Since I am under the impression that it is not extensive, would you mention all of your screen credits, official and unofficial, if the latter case is such?

Credits. *Golden Earrings:* direction, Mitchel Leisen. Assigned to an incredible romantic melodramatic stew, I painstakingly studied gypsy life under the Nazis (they were incinerated) and very cleverly worked the whole thing around to something else. The film, starring Marlene

Dietrich, appeared as an incredible romantic melodramatic stew. I never could sit through it. I know there isn't a single word or scene of mine in it, but I was instructed to rejoice in the credit which I shared with two old hands, Helen Deutsch and Frank Butler.

Body and Soul: original screenplay; direction, Robert Rossen.

Force of Evil: screenplay with Ira Wolfert from his novel, *Tucker's People;* my direction.

I Can Get It for You Wholesale: screenplay based on Weidman's own treatment which simply kept the title of the novel. A comedy of sorts, directed by Mike Gordon with Dan Dailey, Susan Hayward. It was a stopgap for me to return to Europe to write another book and set up *Mario and the Magician.* Before I left, Thomas Mann told me he felt his exile was beginning all over again since fascism was inevitable in America. The novel I completed years later. No one wanted to finance the film.

I returned to Hollywood and made a deal with Sol Siegel at Twentieth to write and direct a picture, but the blacklist intervened.

Was your scenario for Body and Soul *a wholly original work, or was it derived from some other source?*

It's an original screenplay. A folk tale from the Empire city.

Was Rossen to direct the movie from the time of the script's inception, or did he only come to do it through the contingencies of film production?

Rossen was hired after the script was done.

Did your work on Body and Soul *end with the scenario?*

No.

Were you present on the set during shooting?

Continuously.

Of course, it is easy to look knowing in retrospect, but to judge from Rossen's other work, Body and Soul *would seem to have closer affinities with* Force of Evil *than with the other films of his, even in the elusive matter of visual style. Or am I just second guessing?*

There was a struggle during the shooting to prevent Rossen from rewriting the script and changing the ending. In fact he shot an alternate finish in which the fighter is killed and ends up with his head in a garbage can. I think a comparison of *Body and Soul* with *The Hustler* might

390

indicate not only the uses Rossen made of the former but where his temperament and style inevitably lead him.

Are you satisfied with the realization of Body and Soul *as a film?*

I liked *Body and Soul*. It was a surprise to see something I had written become film. I have an animal faith that survives moral weakness and defeat. To urge this against Rossen's metaphysical identity with everyday cynicism and the journalism of sense and sex indicated the realities of film-making. Our resources on the set were immense: Garfield, James Wong Howe, Robert Aldrich, Lyons and Parrish, Don Weiss, Pevney. A slew of directors emerged from the film. Rossen's talent is force applied everywhere without let-up. My only concern was to save it from parody, except where deliberately I had kidded *Golden Boy* and that dear old violin. However, I'm not so sure any more that the obvious isn't one of the strengths of film language. If so it violates a bias of my nature.

What attracted you about Tucker's People *as an original source?*

Experiment. Garfield and Roberts suggested that I direct. I had already been brooding over this notion. Being a novice didn't prevent me from sharing all the illusions and frustrations of more seasoned writers. I was under fire long before I knew I had volunteered.

I knew *Tucker's People*. It had an allegory, true then and even more bitterly apt today; a milieu and characters familiar as my own habits; a hint of the language of the unconscious I could use as dialogue. In realization, necessities of the medium evaporated the allegory, leaving great uncharted reefs of symbolism to wreck the audience; the people emerged except where I agreed to wrong casting; and the language almost obeyed my intention to play an equal role with the actor and visual image and not run along as illustration, information, and mere verbal gesture (wisecracks, conventional middle class slang, elevated notions drawn from the armory of Longfellow and Hemingway).

In the course of adaptation, you altered the novel rather radically, excising some characters and events, combining and condensing others. What particular problems did you feel were fundamental to your decisions in making the adaptation? I don't mean so much with regard to Tucker's People *in particular as with the question of adapting to the screen in general.*

I no longer remember anything except the days Wolfert and I spent endlessly talking along the beaches. Under the windy sun we didn't reason so much as proclaim discoveries. In effect, we eliminated the discursive power of the book and substituted for it so to speak centers of suggestion. We reimagined the novel as if it were an aborigine again. Then it became obvious that some characters would play larger roles and others disappear. Adapting a book to film is fundamentally a moral crisis. Assuming the intention is serious, the book is not chosen to be translated for non-readers but because still embedded in the conception is a whole unrealized life whose language is a motion of images. Where a book is unfulfilled a frightful problem arises. The film, if successful, is a critique of the author's failures. I am a coward here and prefer my own stories.

Do you have any particular conception of the nature of the medium? One of the original reviewers of Force of Evil *(Robert Hatch in* The Nation, *as I recall) suspected the presence of blank verse, and was duly horrified; but even admirers of the film have characterized it as "literary." Does this have any meaning to you? Do you have any ideas about the relation of word to image in the film; yours, and, perhaps, the film in general?*

I've heard them talk in talking pictures. Might talkies be like the opera? The main thing is the music but O the joy when the singers act and the songs are poetry. Let's pretend, I assumed for *Tucker's People (Force of Evil)* that the three elements, visual image, actor, word, are equals. (After all, the human personality is the medium of total human expressiveness. After all, language has been a medium for an art of two.) I didn't project anything important, just an experiment in which each of my resources was freed of the dominance of the other two. I was too inexperienced to invent novel visual images or evoke great performances. And certainly there was nothing in my literary record to suggest a New Voice. All I tried to do was use the succession of visual images, the appearances of human personality in the actors, and the rhythm of words in unison or counterpoint. I varied the speed, intensity, congruence and conflict for design, emotion and goal, sometimes separating the three elements, Sometimes using two or three together. As for the language, I merely freed it of the burden of literary psychology and the role of crutch to the visual image. Blank verse? No. But the babble of the unconscious, yes, as much as I could, granted the premise that I was committed to a representational film. It was a method I would have tried again and again until solved. After all, we had that big Hollywood machine which the success of *Body and Soul* had delivered into our hands and we didn't mind seeing what we could do with all that horsepower. But the blacklist took the machine away from us. While we had possession, like those bicycle fanatics at Kitty Hawk, we couldn't wait to waken in the morning, knowing that each day would surprise us. We had the right feelings. Only our plane never flew.

Would you say you have been influenced by any other film-makers?

Vigo.

Mention has been made in a way I think might be valid of Odets as a literary influence. What is your opinion of this?

We both derive from Jewish jokes and street quarrels. I live dangled between the formal and argot without solution. I've tried to avoid American Standard Movie dialogue which is a genuine Hollywood convention. But I can write it and have for a living.

What film-makers do you particularly admire?

I like going to the movies.

What Hollywood films have you thought commendable since the late 'forties?

I seem to remember liking some but I can't remember which.

Is there an identity of theme and meaning between Body and Soul *and* Force of Evil?

Yes, but in *Force of Evil* every character and situation is compromised by reality while *Body and Soul* is a folk tale.

Eric Bentley has made the point that in both Elia Kazan's On the Waterfront *and Arthur Miller's* A View from the Bridge *there is, scarcely beneath the surface, an apologetics for each of their respective positions on political informing, a certain acting out of private crises; informing being the crucial act in both works, good in the former and evil in the latter.* Force of Evil *ends with the hero about to confess to the police, and "help" them. I do not mean to suggest that the final act is ever simply this, but do you feel that there is any political parable underlying the conclusion to your film?*

Not a parable, a fact. The hero is about to confess to the police because that was the way we could get a seal.

393

There was an allegory underlying the film. It got lost somewhere and had nothing to do with confession or avoidance. Bentley is certainly right in his estimate of those works although the distinction between good informing and bad escapes me. One informs not only to escape punishment and regain acceptance but to share once again in the authority of the state. It is a hard life outside the pale.

Do you believe or know that you were blacklisted?

I know it and I believe it.

How did you discover this?

I was told by the studio, my agent, the newspapers, Congress, and my landlord.

How is one blacklisted; I mean, what is the typical nature of the process?

One is named in a hearing by an informer, or one is summoned to the hearing in person. The consequences are the same.

Do you know of particular individuals who were behind the blacklist, or was its authority always kept anonymous?

The cold war was behind the blacklist and everyone participated, from those on the political right through those who had no politics. It was like collaboration under the Nazis. And it was like the resistance. The spectrum took in everything human including the inhuman.

Did you ever appear before the House Un-American Activities Committee?

Yes.

Was there any opportunity for compromise in order to "clear" yourself?

Then and now and frequently in between.

John Cogley, in his Report on Blacklisting, *observes that there was virtually no political content in the films of the blacklisted, and when it did exist it was usually in the form of so generalized a commitment to democratic ideals and justifiable revolution as could be subscribed to by any member of the audience but the most avid Hitlerite. Do you agree? Would you ascribe this to lack of intent, or lack of accomplishment? Or lack of talent?*

Hollywood radicals were mainly moral humanists and their films when they reflected anything at all showed a concern for the suppressed elements in human life. Political programming of any sort, left, middle, right, couldn't ever appear because producers wanted to make money. When political programming did appear as in the so called anti-communist pictures they were made in deference to the climate and not from the usual expectation of profits. Cogley's argument that blacklisting radicals is silly because they're too stupid or talentless to use the film for direct Marxist propaganda is jejune. He is talking about journalism, not story telling.

Do you have any thoughts on the career of Edward Dmytryk, who went from the Hollywood Ten to "exoneration," and eventually was to film such a tribute to conformity as The Caine Mutiny?

He probably thought it was capitalist realism.

It has been suggested that John Garfield's political difficulties and debarment from Hollywood work were a considerable influence in accelerating his early death. Do you have any opinion on this?

Yes. He defended his streetboy's honor and they killed him for it.

In the publisher's blurb for The Season of Fear, *it was implied that you left film-making voluntarily in order "to go abroad and devote [yourself] to serious fiction." Aside from the thinly veiled, characteristic cultural snobbery, is there any truth in this?*

No.

Inasmuch as you have any such self-image, do you regard yourself primarily as a novelist or film-maker? Or both?

Neither. If I were younger you might say I had promise.

Were you aware of the sympathetic reception accorded Force of Evil *in* Sight and Sound *and* Sequence?

Yes.

Was their appreciation of any personal importance to you?

Pure oxygen.

Was Body and Soul *a financial success?*

Very much so.

Was Force of Evil *commercially successful?*

No.

Do you have any criticisms of the latter film's distribution?

It got lost in the general dissolution of Enterprise studios. Had we stayed in business we could have rescued it and made some money.

How did you come to use Beatrice Pearson?

She was brought to my attention by Martin Jurow, now a considerable producer himself. He worked for our company at that time.

Where had you seen her previously?

Nowhere.

What became of her?

She was in a few films and disappeared. They didn't know how to use her.

In what work are you engaged at present?

Grub Street.

Have you had any opportunity to make films since Force of Evil?

No.

Have you imagined any new subjects you would have particularly liked to work into a film?

Indeed I have.

Do you see any possibility for your prospective return to work in the film?

No.

What are your plans for the future?

None.

The interviewing of an artist is chancy; the pitfalls are familiar. On one hand, there is the kind of gulling Lindsay Anderson suffered at the hands of John Ford in his well-known Sequence *interview; on the other, those dreary chronologies of how* The Studio *mutilated this film, and how* They *butchered that. Both alternatives may be valuable in their way (and the Anderson piece, I believe, does reveal, even inadvertently, a good deal of Ford's nature as an artist), but I was interested in achieving neither. Existing somewhere in that uncharted area between the put-on and the death toll, I tend immodestly to think that my "encounter" with Abraham Polonsky was something of a success. In anticipating critical intelligence of the artist, one proceeds at one's own risk. In Polonsky, I found this sort of intelligence, and the ability to articulate it.*

Not all of the questions were answered as thoroughly as they might have been, but I conceived my role not as inquisitor; I was not out to "get all the facts"; rather, to open up certain areas for discussion, to that extent which Polonsky was interested in going into them. Politically, for example, it may be observed that, although the specters of the blacklist and the House Un-American Activities Com-

mittee are pointedly raised, no question is put as to Polon-
sky's actual political affiliations. I don't think of this as an
evasion. My own attitude toward the pursuit of this line of
questioning (from an anti-Communist position, it may not
be irrelevant to add) is simply: So what? The fact remains
that Abraham Polonsky, having earned the right to work
in Hollywood on the terms which Hollywood unfailingly
understands, those of having proven the ability to show a
profit, was denied the exercise of that less-than-glorious
right. The fact is that since 1949 a film-maker whom I re-
gard as one of the richest talents to have appeared in Hol-
lywood in the past fifteen years (and, I believe, the richest
literary talent to have appeared in the American film) has
not been able to work in films. One need not respond emo-
tionally to that fact. One need not respond emotionally to
any fact.

Abraham Polonsky:
Filmography:
1949—Force of Evil. 1969—Willie Boy.

Otto Preminger

*The next film Otto Preminger directs will be his thirtieth
in an American career that goes back thirty years. There
are certain ifs, ands and buts in these calculations, however. Preminger refuses to accept any responsibility whatsoever for the films he made before* Laura *in 1944, which
was 21 years ago. These earlier films are* Under Your Spell
(1936), Danger—Love at Work *(1937);* Margin for Error
(1943), and In the Meantime, Darling *(1944). Preminger
is not unique in disdaining the fruits of his early experience.
Fred Zinnemann has never been eager to reminisce about*
Kid Glove Killer, Eyes in the Night, Little Mr. Jim *and*
My Brother Talks to Horses. *George Stevens undoubtedly
prefers to jump straight to* Alice Adams *without pausing
for* Cohens and Kellys in Trouble, Bachelor Bait *and* Kentucky Kernels. *Vincente Minnelli's mystique does not encompass* I Dood it *any more than Robert Aldrich's boasts of*
The Big Leaguer, *and Josef von Sternberg would probably
prefer to forget his close-up of Grace Moore's tonsils in*
The King Steps Out.

*It is only within the past decade that American directors
have been taken seriously* en masse *and* in toto. *Consequently, more than a few feel that they have been caught
with slips showing in their careers. It was so much easier
in those old days, when a director was no better than his
last picture, and no worse. Today, all his films are weighed
on the critical scales, and so his place in film history may
be jeopardized by a piece of hoke he shot to pay off the
mortgage on his Hollywood hacienda.*

*Not that Preminger's pre-*Laura *films are particularly
shameful, and it can be argued that nothing he has done*

since Laura has clicked quite so completely as Laura on every level of evaluation. Nor can it be argued that the director has either soared or sunk since he left Fox in the early Fifties to become his own producer. Ironically, it was only when Preminger began blowing his own horn from The Moon is Blue onward that his earlier films came into focus. His enemies have never forgiven him for being a director with the personality of a producer. His more discerning detractors subconsciously resent him for not ruining himself with the excesses of a creative folly. Culture heroes like Von Sternberg and Von Stroheim and Ophuls and Welles have acquired, rightly or wrongly, a legendary reputation for profligacy. Preminger's legend is that of the cosmic cost-accountant, a ruthless creature who will mangle the muse for the sake of a shooting schedule.

The story is told in the trade of the day Preminger shot the Saint-Newman hilltop scene in Exodus. During the last take, the shadow of the boom fell across the couple. It was too late for a re-take, because the sun was going. Preminger decided to let the shadow stand rather than to return to the location the next day, for a retake, disrupting his shooting schedule. Some finicky aesthetes might write this off as sloppy craftsmanship, but for Preminger it is a question of survival. The fact that he can bring a spectacle in for three million or under, while his colleagues come in for seven or eleven, explains why Preminger is still making his own pictures and why Zinnemann has gone back to work for a studio.

The fact is that Preminger has not had a real critical and commercial smash since Anatomy of a Murder some six years ago. His frugality, and his frugality alone, has kept him from drowning in a sea of red ink. Almost alone of the new tribe of producer-directors, Preminger has accepted the responsibility of freedom, as well as the lesson of a shrinking market.

But what is the artistic point of all these crass production stories? Or as Dwight Macdonald might put it, what's art to Preminger or Preminger to art? Preminger's champions on Movie and Cahiers du Cinema would retort that Preminger's art is of the highest order. I find myself in a dangerous middle position that I would like to explain in some detail. To do so, I must begin with a very personal definition of mise-en-scène.

For me, mise-en-scène is merely the gap between

what we see and feel on the screen and what we can express in words, but it is also the gap between the intention of the director and his effect upon the spectator. Serious film criticism of Hollywood movies is always impaled upon the point that Hollywood directors are not profoundly articulate about their alleged art. How can one possibly compare John Ford to Michelangelo Antonioni, for example? Antonioni talks like an intellectual, albeit a middle-brow intellectual, while Ford talks like an old prospector cut off from civilization. American critics travel abroad bemoaning the fact that American directors are unable to conduct festival seminars on the Pressing Problems of Our Time. Certainly any three Polish directors you might pick up in the street would undoubtedly outpontificate and outparadox the legions of Hollywood directors from time immemorial.

In this respect, Preminger is not a "good" interview. He will freely concede that more is read into his films by some critics than he consciously put there. He neither abuses his detractors nor embraces his defenders. He seems to enjoy the effect he creates with his outrageous personality, a personality that serves also as a mask. To read all sorts of poignant profundities in Preminger's inscrutable urbanity would seem to be the last word in idiocy, and yet there are moments in his films when the evidence on the screen is inconsistent with one's deepest instincts about the director as a man. It is during these moments that one feels the magic powers of mise-en-scène to get more out of a picture than is put in by a director.

However, I would not go as far in this regard as Michel Mourlet of the McMahon Theatre, where Preminger's portrait once occupied a prominent position in the lobby with Fritz Lang, Joseph Losey and Raoul Walsh. (I don't know what has happened to the theater, or to the lobby display, since the McMahonists split into rival Preminger and Losey factions.) It is Mourlet's contention that Preminger must be judged entirely by the effects that the director creates on the screen rather than by any cultural precedents off the screen. To be more exact, Preminger's Saint Joan should be judged entirely by the light patterns on the screen making up the images of Preminger's mise-en-scène rather than by Preminger's fidelity to some interplanetary literary source in the Shavian galaxy. According to Mourlet, the screen creates its own laws independent of the other arts, and the literary and historical Joan of Arc is *less important than the way Preminger renders his Jean of Iowa.*

The trouble with Mourlet's position, tempting as it seems, is that the nature of movies as we have known them, particularly from Hollywood, involves an objective core on which the subjective styles of directors can operate. It is Preminger's manner, rather than his matter, which should concern us most deeply. Otherwise, his extraordinary eclecticism in subject matter would make him a poor choice indeed for a career article. What is one to say of a taste in scripts oscillating between Oscar Wilde and Kathleen Winsor, Bernard Shaw and F. Hugh Herbert, Nelson Algren and Allen Drury, Francoise Sagan and Leon Uris? Some of his defenders argue that he must be commended for tackling the big subjects, but if Preminger is to get a medal for bravely tackling the Big Subject, Stanley Kramer should get a chest-full.

No. It is not a consistent theme we must look for in appraising Preminger's career, but a consistent attitude. One critic has called it fairness, another the ambiguity of objectivity. I would prefer to stress the perversely objective camera viewpoint that keeps his characters in the same frame. Why does Preminger present his spectacle in this way? As he himself explains, he came from the theater where he was accustomed to looking at drama as a spatial whole. Consequently, his deepest instincts are always opposed to montage. Without an inbred instinct for cutting, he is not able to execute the movie gags for which Hollywood has developed an elaborate original cinematographic language. If follows almost logically that Preminger's subjects, more often than not, have a solemn, sombre quality. His melodramas at Fox, particularly Laura, Fallen Angel, Whirlpool, Where the Sidewalk Ends, and his RKO loan-out, Angel Face, are all moodily fluid studies in perverse psychology rather than crackling suspense movies. The characters click even as the action falters. The reviewer in search of crackling melodrama would mark Preminger down as a failure in most of the films, possibly all except Laura. Even his comedies are too fluid to encompass the inevitable reaction shots. The Moon Is Blue comes out being a little sad, and Bonjour Tristesse, far from being a merry Gallic romp, is transformed by Preminger's color/black-and-white duality into a tragedy of time and illusion.

It might be said that where Richard Brooks displays a

401

tendency to transform art into trash, Preminger displays a tendency to transform trash into art. His plots lately have been big, violent and vulgar. Exodus, Advise and Consent, The Cardinal and In Harm's Way have enough holes in their scenarios for a ton of Swiss cheese. Preminger does not entirely transcend his material on any occasion. For one thing, his players are too uneven. John Wayne and Partricia Neal are truly admirable in In Harm's Way, but Paula Prentiss, Tom Tryon and Patrick O'Neal are truly deplorable. For every John Huston in The Cardinal there is unfortunately a Lee J. Cobb in Exodus. Individual scenes can be magnificent—the prison raid in Exodus, the shipboard sequences with the President in Advise and Consent, the Viennese ballroom scene in The Cardinal, and the opening dance scene in In Harm's Way invoking in one slowly moving shot the entire Zeitgeist of the Forties. Too often, however, Preminger seems to destroy what he so lovingly creates. This is part of his ambiguity as an artist, a key perhaps to a cynicism far deeper and infinitely more destructive than Billy Wilder's.

I am not suggesting that Preminger has ever thrown a game or even consciously shaved the points. Every Preminger film, even his most ill-fated, bears the signs of an overall conception and the stigmata of a personal attitude. If a Centennial Summer or a Porgy and Bess fails to come off, it is not because Preminger lacked a discernible approach toward these musicals, but rather because the various elements in the musicals failed to coalesce in terms of Preminger's conception. By contrast, Carmen Jones succeeds on its own questionable terms as the Preminger musical par excellence—drab, austere, unpleasant and completely depoeticized.

In his career Preminger has moved into direct competition or comparison with other directors. A Royal Scandal and The Fan pointed up Preminger's relationship to Lubitsch, as did obviously That Lady in Ermine, which Preminger finished after Lubitsch's death. Lubitsch is generally given the edge in these sectors, and for good reason. However, it is not entirely fair to Preminger to place him out of his time. As Lubitsch was the unobtrusive cutting of the Twenties and Thirties, Preminger is the camera movement and long takes of the Fifties and Sixties. If Lubitsch summed up his time, Preminger was ahead of it in his Fox period. The Lubitsch virtues have disappeared from the cinema, and we are the poorer for it, but Preminger anticipated the conditions that would cause their disappearance. The grace and precision of Lubitsch's sensibility seem out of place in a world consecrated to the most grotesque explosions of the ego. Preminger's impassive gaze—accepting the good with the bad, the beautiful with the ugly, the sublime with the mediocre—is both more appropriate and more merciful.

Preminger himself refuses to allow any comparison between The Thirteenth Letter and the Clouzot original, Le Corbeau (The Raven), but it might be noted parenthetically that Preminger's version is less vicious than the original, and not merely because of the laundered Hollywood script. Preminger has no patience with the virus of suspicion, and he tends to give the show away rather than to degrade his characters with useless doubts.

With In Harm's Way, Preminger invades the realm of John Ford, with curious results. A combination of They Were Expendable and Wings of Eagles, the Preminger film departs from the Ford ethos of the military by dramatizing the conflict over strategy between the aggressive Wayne and the defensive Dana Andrews, that aging Preminger alumnus of Laura, Fallen Angel, Daisy Kenyon, Where the Sidewalk Ends. On the surface, the Wayne side has all the best of it. Andrews and his entourage are virtually caricatured while Wayne is being idealized. Wayne's spoiled rotten Harvard son, Brandon De Wilde, is used as the swing character to indicate the complete collapse of the Andrews arguments. Preminger seems to have succumbed at last to bias, if only the bias in favor of action in the abstract. However, a second look indicates that Wayne wins every argument and loses every battle, and that catastrophe dogs him every step of the way. Once more Preminger has stepped aside from a commitment, and the result is less satisfying intellectually than either Ford's whole-hearted commitment to the institution or Kubrick's giddily anarchistic disrespect for it in Dr. Strangelove.

Where does this all leave us? It leaves us with a director who has made at least three impressive masterpieces of ambiguity and objectivity—Laura, Bonjour Tristesse and Advise and Consent, a director who sees all problems and issues as a single-take two-shot, the stylistic expression of the eternal conflict not between right and wrong but between the right-wrong on one side and the right-wrong on the other, a representation of the right-wrong in all of us as our share of the human condition. In the middle of the *conflict stands Otto Preminger, right-wrong, good-bad and probably sincere-cynical. But don't take my word for it. See the movies and make up your own mind. Whatever your verdict, Preminger will thank you for your patronage and will keep his own counsels.**

Why did you choose to make In Harm's Way?

Why do I ever want to make a film? This book was submitted to me in manuscript. I liked the characters and I liked the story. This is my only reason for making films. It is my profession to make films.

However, there is another reason. Probably the story appealed to me because I felt that so many movies made recently have a terribly pessimistic outlook on our future. It seems that the only way out for us is to give in to almost any kind of demand, or blackmail, or whatever you want to call it—and when I say "us" it goes for both sides, for the West as well as for the Iron Curtain, because both have the Bomb now. And all these films or books seem to feel that any attack would finish the other side, and the world. I don't believe that. I believe that any attack that is executed by weapons invented by people, by human minds, will always find a defence that people can invent. Perhaps this story of an attack—we are attacked, we are unprepared in every way, and manage by sheer guts, character and resourcefulness, to start to work out of it— should remind us and perhaps other people that there is never any reason to give up or to give in to anything that is not right or dignified. I am as much against the war as anyone, and I hope I showed it even in this picture by showing that, of all these courageous people, just two or three are left in the end. I didn't try to make war romantic or particularly attractive, but, on the other hand, I wanted to say, perhaps unlike other people, that war does not necessarily bring the worst out in people always. It often does, but also, for the mere reason that people find themselves in the same predicament, it makes them stick together, work for each other, work together.

* *The editor's article on Preminger appeared originally in* Film Comment, *No. 3, Vol. 3, Summer 1965.*

The interview with Otto Preminger by Ian Cameron, Mark Shivas, and Paul Mayesburg appeared originally in Movie, *No. 13, Summer 1965.*

I don't like to mention other films, but to mention one which I think is a very wonderful film—*Doctor Strangelove*—I do feel that somehow it shows the situation only from one side. Perhaps the director, whom I like very much and admire, didn't want to show it. It cannot be true (and the film seems to imply this), that every military man in the United States is a war-monger or an idiot, or both, or crazy. Nor is it true that the President of the United States is so completely without sense. I don't mind these characters in satire—I think it is very good if there were some *balance* to it. Perhaps it could be told in another film. Let's say I don't tell my story *against* a film like *Strangelove,* I tell it to complement the film. You see, I feel that all films together, or the whole output of literature together, give a mosaic of the thinking and feeling of people. So it doesn't matter whether one film goes all the way one side and another film goes all the way the other side. It might be that people who see my film will wonder why I didn't show a character like the General in *Dr. Strangelove*—although I tried to show that the Navy has not only angels.

When you get a large book like In Harm's Way, *you have to leave out a fair amount of the detail of it.*

Let me say something which I have always wanted to say but never could say quite clearly. Whether I take an original idea and pay for it, or I buy the rights to a book, and an author sells it outright, I consider this raw material and I feel completely free to use it according to my own thinking—to filter it through my own brain, through my talent or whatever I have, in other words, to recreate whatever part of this material I want to. This thing about being faithful or not faithful to a novel should only apply if the author would say: "Look, I don't want to sell you the film rights, I want to be your *partner.* I will sell you the film rights with the condition that I have the final say, because I want to preserve the ideas." I have often been attacked: the author of *Exodus* for instance felt that I didn't do right by his book, and the author of *Anatomy of a Murder* felt that I did better than the book—he admired the film very much. The author of *In Harm's Way* is particularly complimentary about my handling of the son's character, one which didn't really exist in the book. He was a completely innocuous boy, who just met the father and they immediately became friends; he had no feelings about the fact that his father had left his mother 18 years ago, and we changed that in the script. Now, all I want to say is that I consider it material and I use what I want. In the book *In Harm's Way*, there is a lot about command decision and the great responsibility. This is interesting, but very difficult to dramatise and hardly a point that interested me here, because I'm not interested in the military mind really. I did not make a war picture—I don't know anything about the war, and I hope I will never see another war. It was more interesting to see a group of people, characters whom I like, trapped in war, in a difficult situation, and to see how they work out of it.

Why did you use Wendell Mayes?

I think he's a very good writer. We have worked together before and I felt that he could write this very well. You must realise also that I work very closely with writers. Particularly on this picture, we sat together and worked almost every line over. On the other hand, the writer has the advantage that, once I approve a screenplay, I do not change it any more on the set like other directors, or hire other writers to improve it or, as the case may be, to spoil it.

How far did the original book In Harm's Way *delve into the political aspect, which is slightly evident in the film through the Dana Andrews character?*

The Dana Andrews character is unimportant—it is just a question of one group of people wanting to fight, and the other group of people wanting to give up. We all probably forget this (and you are probably even too young to remember), but you know, after Pearl Harbour, there was in America a tremendous group of people of any political affiliation that thought the best thing would be to make peace with Japan and not to enter the war, that we were not prepared and that we would lose. And it seems very crazy today, but at that time people in San Francisco started to move out to the East, because they felt the Japanese might land at San Francisco. I don't think that the Dana Andrews character *is* to do with anything political. But it's typical. It shows the people making use of their power, and you must admit that the fact that I could get character, in spite of Dana Andrews, and in spite of the character of Kirk Douglas, proves a certain liberal attitude. I got all the ships I needed and all the help I needed, otherwise I couldn't have made this picture. We were shooting five days on the high seas between Seattle and Hawaii on a real naval cruiser with an Admiral there—it was his flagship—and he was lying there on his stomach most of the time taking photographs of us because it was his hobby.

How was it that your model shots were so much better than anyone else's model shots?

I will tell you a secret. I had originally hired a famous specialist for these models. You know, they usually make them with ships about two to three feet long, in tanks. When I saw the beginning of his work, which was also quite expensive, I threw the whole thing away because it didn't seem to be right. And I then proceeded to build ships, I did it myself after the picture was finished. I decided to direct it myself without any specialists, and we built ships that were between 35 and 55 feet long—they were really big ships—so that when we photographed them, the detail was very much like on the big ships. And as a matter of fact, the Navy asked us, and we gave them these ships after the picture was finished for their various exhibitions. And we didn't shoot any of these miniatures in a tank. We shot the night miniatures on a lake in Mexico, because we needed the straits with mountains in the background. We shot the day battles on the Gulf of Mexico. I needed the real horizon, you know, and I think that makes a lot of difference.

Is it because of the models that you didn't shoot the picture in colour?

No, I could just as well have shot it in colour. The reason I didn't is because I always feel that a picture like this, a war picture, in colour, has a very unreal feeling. First of all, you cannot possibly avoid the actors using make-up, particularly if they are close to middle age. A soldier in make-up always seems to me somewhat ridiculous. I know that people overlook it, that it is a convention that they accept, but a picture like this has much more impact and you can create more of the feeling, the illusion of reality than when you shoot it in colour. It's the only reason I didn't use any newsreel shots. For Pearl Harbour I got permission and put dynamite all around, and we shot this with real ships and real explosions. We didn't use any of the old stuff, because that was shown in so many pictures that I felt to show the same news clips again (because they're all the same) would be ridiculous.

In the first shot of In Harm's Way, *you start with the notice, then go past the line of caps and along the side of the swimming pool to Barbara Bouchet dancing: I suppose it's possible, in theory, to do this in a number of cut shots, although you get a much smoother idea of getting into the story by doing it in one shot. Is that why you do it in one shot?*

If it were possible, I would do the whole of the film in one shot, because I believe that every cut, no matter how carefully it is done, is disturbing. You may want to emphasise something through the cut (the cut is also a way to point up something), otherwise every cut is only done because you cannot tell something in one shot. You feel a cut subconsciously. There the idea was to show that this was what was going on just before Pearl Harbour: by putting in the sound of some vessels in the background, and the parking space, the announcement of the dance, the Navy hats on the long table, and the dance. Then when she behaves like she does, there are cuts and the story starts. This is already a character in the story. In order not to disturb this, I put the titles at the end, because I felt I wanted to get into the story right away and not to have all the usual clutter. I also wanted to make a point, which I don't know if people get, because they usually get up before the titles are finished: the titles go up to the atom bomb and show the future horror of possible war.

Does it make any difference to you making a film for Paramount as opposed to, say, Columbia or United Artists?

No. They only distribute the film; they have no influence on the making of my films. My contracts give me complete autonomy in the making, the casting and the writing. They can turn down a certain property if they don't want to make it, but once we've agreed on that, they have no more say.

It's good for you to ring the changes among distributors?

Sometimes . . . they are all very nice people!

Bunny Lake is going to be a completely different kind of film?

Bunny Lake is a suspense story. It's the first suspense story I've made in a long, long time, about 20 years. It's the story of the disappearance of a child.

Why are you making it here?

First of all, it seems to me that the farther away from home the mother who loses the child is, the more real the story seems. Every mystery story, you see, naturally has some holes, and it seems more believable that certain facts cannot be checked within the ten hours in which the story

408

takes place. Also the horror of what happens to her seems to be stronger if she's away from home. Even in the original book she is away from home; it takes place in New York. But I felt that this change would be an advantage. I had several scripts on this property. I have had this book for a long time and I never could get the right script out of it. I wanted her to be so lost. Originally, I wanted to do it in Paris, and she didn't speak French. But this problem seemed almost insurmountable because then the police would have to ask everything through an interpreter. That would be too difficult. So I took it here to London. I can probably also get more interesting actors to surround these two young people here than in America. We have a great shortage of really good character actors.

You said you went through several scripts. What were you after that you couldn't get?

The original book has a very weak solution. The solution is OK, but the character who commits the crime is very weak and uninteresting. We did the first script very much like the book. I did this with Ira Levin, a playwright who wrote the play that I did with Henry Fonda, *Critic's Choice*. Then I did another script with Dalton Trumbo. We had analysed it and found that we needed another heavy but he became very theatrical and wrong. When you talk, it is often very different from what happens when you actually write and dramatize it. I gave up this script. Eventually when I wanted to do it here, I sent the book to Penelope Mortimer because she is a novelist, and I told her what the trouble was: she came to New York for conferences and came up with a wonderful character, I think, of a heavy, which gave the whole picture a new dimension. That made me pick it up again. Then she and her husband wrote the present screenplay except for some polishing on American dialogue which I had somebody else do. As a matter of fact, I have had the rights to this story so long that somebody said that Bunny Lake is not missing, Bunny Lake is legally dead!

What will you make after that?

A book that I bought about nine months ago; it was published in America about six or seven weeks ago. It's called *Hurry Sundown,* by B. K. Gilden. They're really two people, married, and they worked for 14 years on this book. And as a matter of fact they were so poor on the way that the husband had to work in a factory in order to support the family. The book has become a very big best seller in the United States. It has a very broad canvas. It takes place in 1946 in Georgia, and shows all the problems of the Negroes and the white people and their relationships. Some critics call it a modern *Gone with the Wind.* And again, while it has no message, no immediate, present political message, it will, I think, show that all the things that happen now—Civil Rights and riots—this whole revolution had to come. It was the only way to solve it.

In The Cardinal *there was a tremendous compression of history into one story. How far was it this aspect rather than the central character that excited you?*

These questions become too specific, because making a film is a complete complex of things. Naturally the background was very interesting. It is the background of history but also the background of an institution like the Church and what was going on in it. I have found that the Catholic Church is really a fabulously interesting institution. It gives its various members much more autonomy than I thought before. I am not a Catholic. I don't know if it comes out in the picture—but I started to understand why the Catholic Church, in spite of always reasserting its moral purpose or at least returning to its principles, is able by compromise to survive almost any other institution and organisation. You see now their willingness to get together with non-Catholics, even with non-believers, which shows that they somehow realise the needs of progressing times. They are not really as conservative or reactionary as most people believe. That interested me very much.

Surely these are last minute changes though?

No. It is clear that any organisation would hang on to its principles as long as it could, just as the monarchy in England has survived all other monarchies, because it is the most liberal monarchy and gives people the right to change their government, under the Crown. The Catholic Church, too, always knows the right moment to compromise.

How much do you rehearse a scene on the floor?

That depends very much on what is necessary, on what kind of actor and what kind of scene. You see certain kinds of pictures—in *Advise and Consent,* for instance, or *Anatomy of a Murder,* there were scenes that I rehearsed several weeks before I started, but other pictures, like for instance *In Harm's Way,* cannot be rehearsed in advance because I cannot go out on the ship, you know, and it doesn't make sense to read these lines in a room. So I rehearse just before I do the scene and I rehearse as long as necessary. There is no limit. Time is expensive and naturally in the back of one's mind; one cannot completely eliminate it, but I've educated myself just to forget it. Otherwise the whole thing becomes hurried and silly. I could make every picture ten days shorter if I slough it. Some actors just need more time and more rehearsal and some don't. Some actors, who are basically picture personalities, cannot rehearse. They become what they call stale. Really it is because they don't quite know what they are doing. You've got to catch them when they are doing it best. Some actors need a lot of rehearsal and those are very good actors.

You use a lot of long takes for dialogue scenes. Do you, as it were, let the actors dictate the length of the shot?

No. The actors don't dictate anything. Sometimes you have an actor who can't remember more than two lines. There comes the moment where you have to compromise and give in, but usually it is not the case, because scenes are not that long. No scene can be longer than nine and a half minutes, because that's how long the film runs in the camera. Six minutes or five minutes most actors are capable of doing. Once in my career I had a difficulty like that with a seasoned actor, but otherwise I don't remember ever having difficulty.

Presumably with actors like Wayne and Douglas who are personalities you didn't have to rehearse much.

No, that isn't true. Wayne turned out—I have not worked with him before—to be the most co-operative actor, willing to rehearse, willing to do anything as long as anybody. I was surprised really how disciplined a professional Wayne is, and he liked this particular part very much. I must say, I am very lucky this way, you know, the actors I work with are not difficult or I am more difficult than they are so that I don't notice!

Otto Preminger (1906–   ):
Filmography:
1936—Under Your Spell. 1937—Danger—Love at Work. 1943—Margin for Error. 1944—In the Meantime Darling, Laura. 1945—A Royal Scandal, Fallen Angel. 1946—Centennial Summer. 1947—Forever Amber, Daisy Kenyon. 1948—That Lady in Ermine (begun and signed by Ernst Lubitsch). 1949—The Fan, Whirlpool. 1950—Where the Sidewalk Ends, The Thirteenth Letter. 1953—Angel Face, The Moon Is Blue. 1954—River of No Return, Carmen

Satyajit Ray

Satyajit Ray virtually introduced Indian cinema to the West with Pather Panchali. *For the most part, Ray has found his most ardent support at Film Festivals round the world. The public has become increasingly reluctant to patronize a cinema completely lacking in lurid sensationalism, and American distribution of Ray's films has actually deteriorated over the years. In India, however, Ray remains a culture hero, and his home base is still secure enough to enable him to mount his aesthetic assaults on the sensibilities of the West. Ray's subjects touch on middle-class domestic life, a realm unknown to Westerners obsessed with the extremes of privilege and poverty in India.*—A. S.*

I shall always carry with me my first impressions of our guest of honor as he arrived at the Flaherty Foundation Seminar this past summer. It was the end of a long road from Bengal to Brattleboro, Vermont. His commanding height, his broad build, the fine head and the probing, wondering, kindly eyes were immediately striking, and he smilingly refused to allow anyone to help him with his heavy bag. Tucked under his free arm was the script of his work in progress, the untitled sequel of *Pather Panchali* and *Aparajito.* In it, as I learned later, was a profusion of neat sketches that seemed to crowd out the sparse Bengali text,

* *Hugh Gray's interview with Satyajit Ray originally appeared in* Film Quarterly, *No. 2, Vol. XII, Winter 1958.*

for Ray had been an artist before he became a director
and was also, among other things, an illustrator of books.
As he explained to me:

"My grandfather was a painter, a poet, and also a scientist who, in addition to editing the first children's magazine
in Bengal, had introduced the half-tone block to India. My
father was equally well known. He it was who wrote,
among other works, Bengal's classic Book of Nonsense—
an Englishman might call him India's Edward Lear. I
myself was attracted first to physics and economics, graduating with honors in those fields from Calcutta University. I went to Shantiniketan, a somewhat unusual school,
one you may never have heard of, founded at the turn of
the century by Rabindranath Tagore. The Tagores and my
own family had been friends down the years, and so it was
natural that I should go there. Anyhow, it was there that I
first developed my aesthetic interests and acquired some
skill in drawing. There is one man in particular to whom I
shall always be grateful—a man named Bose, my teacher
of painting. I think I can truly say that he gave me a deep
insight into creative activity."

"Did you take a degree there?"

"No. I didn't even complete the course. There were no
films there and somehow, I don't know how it happened,
but films appealed to me. With Tagore dead (he died in
1941) and after reading widely in the history of art and
studying in particular Chinese calligraphy, I went back to
Calcutta. Having decided that there was no future for me
in the fine arts, in 1943 I joined an advertising firm there,
as an art director. I stayed with them a long while and
went through every department. When I was in a position
to do so I introduced into their advertisements a fusion of
modern Western and Bengal tradition, to give it a new
look."

Of course, it is easy to be wise after the event, but as
Ray told me the details of his early life I felt a sense of
inevitability about every stage of all this preparatory work.
The decisive moment came when he was asked to illustrate
an edition of *Pather Panchali*. This story had first begun
to appear as a serial in 1931 and had at once become immensely popular. Its authenticity as a story of Bengal village life, much of it autobiographical, was unmistakable;
subsequently it joined the list of best-selling books and
continues there.

Slowly Ray's own instincts and the book worked to-

414

gether, through script after script, to give the right shape in his mind to a tale that called out to him to film it. He knew, however, as he has elsewhere said, that it could not be cast into the usual mold of cut-and-dried film narrative. It had to be true to the world of Bengali village life. But the day of filming was still distant; the final form was still to be found, and there were other seemingly insurmountable difficulties.

"In 1950 I went to England for a while, for my firm, and while I was there, in three months I saw more than 90 films. I was studying everything, ceaselessly. It was *Bicycle Thief* that finally gave me the idea of how to make my own film. No stars, and mainly on location.

"When I got home I started to look about hopefully for finances. For all of 1951 I tried to get backing. But I convinced no one. What I wanted to do had not been done before. Our films are either the conventional ones, modeled on Hollywood, their structure and climaxes derived from theater, or they are devotional, or, again, mythological. The only kind of professional encouragement I got came from one single man: A friend of mine who had worked with Jean Renoir on *The River* had told him of my plans and later, when I met Renoir, he insisted that I shouldn't give up. I didn't, and by 1952 I had scraped together enough to make a beginning. I wanted at least to get a start and then, with that, to convince a backer. So we started, a group of amateurs and one professional—the art director. And only two of our cast were professionals. It would have been foolish for any of us to give up our jobs, so we filmed on Sundays and holidays and in the end we got our footage. But nobody rushed to help. In the end, after more than a year and a half of delays, the Bengal Government came to our rescue. We exposed about 45,000 feet of film and the final cut ran to about 11,000 feet. The music was composed and recorded by a friend of mine, an excellent instrumentalist, in a session of fourteen consecutive hours."

He paused thoughtfully, as if living over that strenuous time. Then he returned once more to the economic problems that had beset him. "Costs have to be held to a minimum in enterprises of this sort. This influences the form and structure of the film itself. It means long takes and the minimum of angles. Then again, in India raw stock is rationed. So you can't afford to waste any. In any case, I don't rehearse much. Especially with nonprofessional actors. I find the first spontaneous actions are usually their best. I averaged about three takes. Of course I was deeply aware that we were all learning as we went along. For that reason we shot in sequence so that we would be a little more sure of what we were doing when we reached the moments of dramatic climax."

"Did you change the story much?"

"Less in *Pather Panchali* than in *Aparajito.* In India *Aparajito* has been criticized on occasion because of the number of departures from the book. People know it so well and expect to see it just as they have read it. Even in *Pather Panchali*, though, I made a number of changes in the order and of course I had to cut down the number of characters throughout. In the book there are three hundred of them!

"In other words, I made whatever changes I felt were demanded by the medium, departing, that is, only from the literary form, not from the truth. Cinema has its own way of telling the truth and it must be left free to function in its own right. I am interested first and last and only in the cinematic way of motion-picture making."

"Did you feel that this story had some sort of moral or message that was essentially Indian, or of Bengal, and for that reason attracted you to it?"

He shook his head. "I don't like morals or messages. This story says true things about India. That was enough for me. It had the quality of truth, the quality that always impresses me, wherever I see it and as I have seen it in films such as *Nanook* and *Louisiana Story, Earth* and *The Southerner.*"

"What about part three of the trilogy?"

"I've started shooting—for three days. But I've halted while my principal actor grows a beard!"

"When do you expect to finish?" He had no final date. But he could not afford to dawdle. Success had made some differences. Already *Aparajito* had got back its negative cost. *Pather Panchali*, delayed because of the business that goes with official associations, was doing well. Ray had had many lucrative offers from the studios. But he wished to go his own way. That meant he must be careful of costs and his pace of work must be economical.

Talk of pace in shooting brought us to story pace, and through this gateway we returned to the world of *Pather Panchali*. "By your standards, my pace is slow—or leisurely, shall we say?" Earlier in our seminar we had agreed that pace was something intrinsic to the subject, and derived from it and not from some external circumstances. He agreed. "It is a matter not just of physical movement but of rhythm, the rhythm of people moving both individually and as a whole, in a pattern." We spoke of the sequence in *Pather Panchali* where the fat confectioner walks through the woods. . . .

Ray continued, "The scenario itself was conceived in terms of seasons and followed their changes of light. As for the day-to-day lighting, when you are outside the studio the morning light is the morning light and the evening, the evening, and there is nothing you can do about that. For the rest, I don't like filters, especially the deep filter. It does something to the Indian skin. In short, I respect natural lighting. Indoors, I don't like multiple shadows. I prefer reflected and not direct light, or light from multiple sources." *LIGHTING*

"We have spoken a little about the music, what of sound effects? Was there any special reason for one use of sound in particular—in the scene in Pather Panchali *when the mother gives way to an outburst of grief."*

"You are asking why I went from a human to an instrumental sound at that particular moment?"

"Precisely."

"There were a number of reasons. First of all, I felt that the impersonal, instrumental sound would give a more universal quality to the expression of grief, and to its effect on the hearer, a quality that the individual personal outburst of the woman could not give. Then again, I felt that my actress, excellent as she was, could never achieve the kind of effect I was after."

Now we passed on to transitions. I noted that he seemed not to favor the traditional cuts, and least of all the standard dissolves.

"I hate conventional time lapses. They draw attention to themselves. I like strong modulations from one thing to another. You see, I am always hopefully concerned to get the feeling of the movement of life itself. There are no neat transitions in life. Things make the transition for me. A traveling train, for example. Again, there is no moment of evident transition, say, from childhood to boyhood, or on to youth." *SCENE IN ADVERSARY — IN OFFICE.*

This brought us to meaning and symbols. Did he intend, as it seemed to me he did, to reach for as many simultaneous meanings as possible?

"Yes. Don't misunderstand me, though. I'm not talking, for example, about composition for composition's sake or anything like that. I shy away from it. It is an aesthetic apart, and not truly cinematic. It is self-conscious, and eventually static. It's too pictorial. I think Sucksdorff falls into that trap, and so, it seems to me, does the Mexican cameraman Figueroa. For surely in cinema we must select everything for the camera according to the richness of its power to reveal."

Satyajit Ray (1921–   ):
Filmography:
1955—Pather Panchali. 1956—Aparajito. 1957—Jalsaghar (The Music Room). 1958—Parash Pathar. 1959—Apur Sansar (The World of Apu). 1960—Devi. 1961—Teen Kanya (Three Daughters), Tagore. 1962—Kanchenjungha, Abhijan. 1963—Mahanagar, Charulata. 1965—The Coward and the Saint. 1966—Nayak.

1971 – ADVERSARY   418
          DAYS + NIGHTS IN THE FOREST
                FAMINE

Jean Renoir

Jean Renoir's career is a river of personal expression. The waters may vary here and there in turbulence and depth, but the flow of personality is consistently directed to its final outlet in the sea of life. In Renoir's films, man's natural surroundings are almost always prominently featured, and it is this emphasis on man in his environment photographed by an unblinking camera that is the true precursor of neo-realism. As Murnau represents the formal antithesis to Eisenstein's montage principles, Renoir represents the thematic alternative to Eisenstein's dialectic. The problem with most conventional critiques of Renoir's films is that humanism is invariably associated with crudity of expression, but there is nothing crude about Renoir's technique once its purposes have been fully understood. Only when style is confused with meaningless flourishes does Renoir's economy of expression seem inadequate for textbook critics.*—A. S.

Can I begin by asking a question about your new film, Caporal Epingle? *What subject have you chosen for it?*

I didn't choose it, someone put it up to me. I didn't know the story, but after reading it I thought it was a subject that suited me very well, one I could feel at home with. It's like *La Grande Illusion* in that it's a story of escape, though naturally with all kinds of differences. The

* *Louis Marcourelles' interview with Jean Renoir appeared originally in* Sight and Sound, *No. 2, Vol. 31, Spring 1962.*

fact that it's an escape story interests me in itself, because one enjoys repeating oneself, returning to the same sort of framework and finding the variations in it. Of course this is an entirely different film from *La Grande Illusion:* the action takes place in 1940 and that means it belongs to another world.

What do you feel the differences really are between the two periods—between 1915 and 1940?

Well, twenty-five years amounts to a generation. And the great turning point, of course, was not the last war but 1914. The people of the last war come after the turning; the people of 1914 were still riding towards it, quite unaware that any turning point was coming. The characters in *La Grande Illusion*—Boieldieu and Maréchal and Rosenthal—would be amazed if anyone told them, "You know, in a few years these ideas about nations will have disappeared. There will be no more nations." They might understand perhaps that there would be social change, a merging of classes—there's enough talk about that in *La Grande Illusion.* But it would never have occurred to them that the world could be politically divided in a different way. . . . And money is shared out differently, so that the people in charge are different people, belong to another race. Europe in 1914 was still in the hands of the politicians, even if they were already servants of the great industrial and financial interests. Now politicians have ceased to count for much: we're in the age of the organisation men, the planners. Wasn't the 1939/45 war above everything one of organisation? It was really organisation —in the factories as much as on the battlefield—that defeated Hitler.

About social themes: in La Grande Illusion, La Règle du Jeu, La Marseillaise, *and I think also in* Diary of a Chambermaid, *you're showing us a society divided "horizontally." Do you think that the attitude in* La Règle du Jeu, *for instance, is already out of date; that there aren't any longer these rigid class divisions?*

Of course nothing is ever fixed or absolute. And I really feel that the distinctions one establishes in one's own mind are only valuable because they help one to understand what's going on around one. I don't think they represent anything final. . . . I often try to work out why I've adopted certain theories which seem fairly arbitrary, and I usually fall back on the comparison with speed. Drive in a donkey cart down a narrow lane, with the trees practically brushing past you, and you can have the illusion of fantastic speed. Record it on film and it looks wonderful. But if you're sitting in an aeroplane, judging your speed by the time it takes the sun to move behind some object on the ground, you might as well be stationary for all the sense of movement you have. You need standards of comparison to measure speed; and I think it's rather like that with theories.

Yes, but I believe you've never cared much for general theories. All I meant, simply, was that if you were to return to La Règle du Jeu *today, you might see it rather differently.*

Well, I don't know about its value as a film, but I do feel that *La Règle du Jeu*, like *La Grande Illusion,* is a sort of reconstructed documentary, a documentary on the condition of society at a given moment. And of course that society is very different now. External reality is often the expression, the symbol, of an interior truth, and I suppose that even in their clothes people are now all pretty much alike. Certainly it's difficult now to distinguish between a Boieldieu going to the theatre on a Saturday and a Maréchal doing the same thing. There are differences, naturally, but they're much more subtle, more interior, and they're gradually being wiped out. It's possible that between Boieldieu's son and Maréchal's there may be no difference. It's extremely possible.

National barriers and class barriers may be breaking down, as you say, but we live in a world with two great divisions—East and West. Do you think we can establish real co-existence? Do you see any breaking down of these barriers?

Yes, up to a point . . . I believe implicitly in the Tower of Babel, and I think all those stories like the one about the Tower of Babel, with which ancient history is dotted, are not meaningless. The stories may be symbolic, things didn't happen just as they've been narrated, but stories like this are all really getting at the same point: the tendency for humanity to come together. Politically, this is the history of the world—the history of the Roman Empire, and of all the later attempts to reconstruct the Roman Empire. At the moment, obviously, the world is split in two; and I suppose that the barriers *are* real ones, though my instinct tells me that they're not. We may be part of an intermediary period, when really big divisions—there are several in the world, after all—are going to replace the old swarm of small nations. But the unifying forces exist too, above all in the way of living and in the coming together of languages. It isn't even always an international thing, after all. It wasn't so long ago, for instance, that when an Italian theatre company from Rome played in Turin the audience couldn't understand the actors. But now, with radio, television, the cinema, they've invented a kind of standard Italian. I must say I regret it. It's just like England, that boring English of their radio and television.

I think there's a movement now in England, though, to get away from this, for actors to use their local accents. Do you know England well?

Not at all well, but what I do know is in a family kind of way; through family connections. I adore England and I'd like to live there: people live there very agreeably.

I've heard some Englishmen say that The River *is one of the most authentically English films ever made. So you must have a certain fellow-feeling with the English.*

Oh, really it's very simple. My sister-in-law is English, so I do know a bit about English family life.

What about the English cinema? The English have no equivalent, for instance, to our own New Wave, the breakthrough of young directors filming independently.

Yes, but things don't happen simultaneously in all countries. After all, the game was really opened by the neorealists in Italy, and it wouldn't surprise me a bit if the English were to come in and give us something absolutely unexpected. . . . Look, for instance, at the way English life and habits are changing. I can't stand the kind of literature which likes to over-simplify national differences—you know, the English are so cold, the Italians are warm, the Germans are heavy. But of course there *are* national characteristics: the climate, the way one eats, the way people move about the streets, the fact that traffic goes on the left—all this does add up to something. A few years ago, English manners depended on tremendous restraint; they didn't break the ice themselves, and they respected the ice that formed around other people. Lately, though, in one hot summer I've seen English journalists behaving more like Neapolitans than the Neapolitans themselves. I remember one session at the Savoy Hotel in London, where in five minutes we were all drinking, shouting, bullying each other. It was a lot of fun, and it wasn't at all like the conventional image of England.

It seems to me a pity that there isn't more of this free-

dom, this letting rip, in English films. The English cinema is so very respectable.

It's very, very respectable, but sometimes it's found in that respectability a kind of genius. . . . The terrible thing about the cinema is the way it uses up everything. It exhausts ideas, stories, brands of stories, and suddenly it finds itself faced with a kind of gulf, a ditch across which it must leap to capture some new and absolutely unforeseen territory. We're not talking, obviously, about eternal masterpieces: clearly Shakespeare always had something to say, and he didn't have to jump any ditch. But it's a situation ordinary film production is likely to run into every five years or so. In France the New Wave has been lucky enough to jump the ditch. In England the same thing could happen.

English cinema has always been best known for its documentarists, people like Grierson and Flaherty. Do you think a move might come from that direction?

Oh, it's all a question of people. New movements come into existence through certain people—in France through the *Cahiers* group, the Cinemathèque. In England the documentary movement was created by a particular group, around Cavalcanti, wasn't it? Cavalcanti played a big part in English documentary.

Well, what do you think about documentary in general, about its importance to cinema?

Of course it's important because it's the only school that exists. If there were any other way for young directors to get a start, well, I don't know. . . . It isn't that documentary is the only possible school theoretically, but in practice it amounts to the only one, and I don't see how a young director can begin in any other way. In any case, it's the way most of our own directors of quality *have* begun. Look at Resnais, for instance: his documentary studies of painters enabled him to enter into direct contact with certain problems.

To get back for a moment to England . . . You probably know about the group who've been called the Angry Young Men, and the importance they attach to the idea of commitment—the feeling that cinema and theatre ought to reflect and criticise the society around them. Last Sunday, for instance, I was talking to an English critic who'd just seen Truffaut's Jules et Jim, *and who said that he found it quite unimportant because "it's not a committed film." This seems to me a bit ridiculous, because from Truffaut's*

*point of view of course the film does have a commitment.
I'd like to know what the word means to you.*

Well, of course it has a meaning. But I feel about this word "commitment" or "engagement" as I do about most general ideas: They take on value only when they move to the particular. You're driving along, and you see a very poorly dressed man limping down the street: do you take him into your car or don't you? This is a commitment, isn't it, of a very precise kind? But as to commitment in a general sense . . . You know I can't believe in the general ideas, really I can't believe in them at all. I try too hard to respect human personality not to feel that, at bottom, there must be a grain of truth in every idea. I can even believe that all the ideas are true in themselves, and that it's the application of them which gives them value or not in particular circumstances. . . . No, I don't believe there are such things as absolute truths; but I do believe in absolute human qualities—generosity, for instance, which is one of the basic ones. Truffaut's film is a good one, in my opinion, because it has this generosity. Of course it has its faults, but these are failings with which I sympathise. I sympathise egotistically, because they are exactly the failings of my own last films, exactly the same . . .

Have you entirely given up your activity in the theatre, or do you still mean to go back to it from time to time?

I haven't given up anything. It's just that things turn out in a certain way, and lately I haven't found anything in the theatre that really catches my imagination.

I seem to remember that about three or four years ago you were quoted as saying "I've said almost everything in the cinema: I find a kind of freedom in the theatre . . ."

In the theatre there is greater freedom because there is discipline. The awful thing about the cinema is the possibility of moving about exactly as one wants. You say, "Well, I must explain this emotion, and I'll do it by going into flashback and showing you what happened to this man when he was two years old." It's very convenient, of course, but it's also enfeebling. If you have to make the emotion understood simply through his behaviour, then the discipline brings a kind of freedom with it. There's really no freedom without discipline, because without it one falls back on the disciplines one constructs for oneself, and they are really formidable. It's much better if the restraints are imposed from outside.

Do you feel that the cinema now—that's to say, with its

424

ultra-mobile cameras, portable sound equipment and all the rest of it—gives you almost the same freedom as the theatre?

For me there's one very interesting demonstration, a kind of open door, and that's François Reichenbach's films. To get the quality of expression, of sound and vision, with the means he employs . . . I think it's tremendously important.

I believe you've worked with a good deal of freedom on your own new film. Was it shot in a studio or on location?

Mostly on location. Very little studio.

Did you work on it alone?

No, because with this kind of subject . . . Isn't there always this old problem of external reality? Of course I'd like to be someone like Chaplin and get away from it completely, but I'm not strong enough for that. I try, quite often, and the attempts usually go adrift; and I know really that if I have some slight contact with external appearances, this helps me to penetrate more deeply to the interior of the characters. I knew something about the lives of prisoners of war, but not directly, not first-hand. It happens that there's a very talented director, Guy Lefranc, who was a prisoner himself and for whom the subject means something very special—like the Bible for a believer. I asked him to help me, and he's given me this sense of first-hand knowledge.

I believe you've kept on with the techniques of your recent films, Dr. Cordelier *and* Le Déjeuner sur l'Herbe. *Does this mean shooting with three or four cameras simultaneously?*

Generally three. And we've mostly recorded direct sound. There's nothing dubbed in the film—oh yes, there is one scene, a short one, where it was raining so hard that you couldn't hear the words.

When you're using this number of cameras, does it make difficulties in the editing, in matching shots? Are there different light levels, for instance?

No, we take all that into account. I'm working with Renée Lichtig, the same cutter who helped me on *Dr. Cordelier* and *Le Déjeuner sur l'Herbe,* and she's used to this sort of juggling about. In fact, with this method of shooting, the editing becomes essentially a matter of selection and assembly. I'm not faced with a mountain of film which can be so reconstructed in the cutting that something which started out as a comedy can end up as a tragedy.

What struck me about Dr. Cordelier *was the extraordinary freedom your methods seemed to give the actors.*

Here too, I hope, here too. I haven't used the identical technique, because the subject doesn't lend itself in the same way. Not all subjects do . . . I can't see Jean Rouch, for instance, going off to make one of his African films with half a dozen cameras. He obviously needs one camera, and needs it in exactly the right place. But there are no theories, no general rules. All one can say is that with some scenes and subjects it's an unbeatable method. You get this freedom for the actors, and you get a kind of emotional progression.

But I suppose you have to rehearse very carefully just the same?

Of course, you always have to rehearse; and you rehearse even more thoroughly when there are several cameras, in order to pin down an emotion and even quite simply to follow through on physical movement. It *is* easy to lose time on this business of matching shots, even when you're just trying to match physical continuity. You take a close-up, and then comes the medium shot which is to follow it in the montage, and which is filmed the next day, and everyone on the set is asking "Was he like this; wasn't his voice sharper; no, not at all, it was less sharp . . . I promise you it was exactly like this . . . I had my elbow bent just this way . . ." And then the cinema finally becomes a job for the continuity girl, and then a job of composition and inspiration. For myself, I'd really rather call a truce to all these problems and shoot the scene in one go.

In A Bout de Souffle *Jean-Luc Godard is trying to get away from the standard editing devices, the artificial linking shots and so on, to use a much more fragmentary kind of montage. What do you feel about this?*

Yes, yes, it's excellent . . . But I must tell you that I don't really bother much about linking shots, physical devices to link action. The thing that counts as far as I'm concerned is the emotional link. I feel that the development of thought and feeling in an actor is indispensable— at least to my kind of film. I don't see how I can expect to establish a relationship with an audience if I don't manage to give it continuity of emotion through a character.

Throughout your career, I suppose, you've always referred back to realism, however many forms it's taken.

426

With constant efforts to escape, since realism annoys me. But it does help me to divine just a little of the interior truth, which is the one vital thing. In effect it has to do with knowing what someone is really like, what stuff he has in him. Then, once one has got at him, one has to make the audience see it too . . . But, you know, everyone really only makes one film in his life, and then he breaks it up into fragments and makes it again, with just a few little variations each time. There's one so-called quality that's more overrated than almost any other: imagination. I've just been writing a book about my father, and I'm delighted to find that he felt this too. He really detested imagination: he thought it was the greatest possible hazard for the artist.

Because it's too capricious . . .

No, not that. It's simply that my father was a modest man who didn't believe that his inventions were important enough or varied enough to concern the public. He thought that the artist's proper function was to absorb material, to digest it and to pass it on. The form didn't matter: it could be Picasso's cubist form, or Mondrian's abstracts, or his own figurative technique. But he didn't believe in the idea of man as God, able to create out of nothing. He really subscribed to that text by Lavoisier which you must know: "In nature nothing is created, nothing is lost, everything is transformed . . ." Well, there you are.

A few years ago, I believe you were quoted as saying that directors ought to be able to make films for art-house distribution, that there should be more of these cinemas throughout the world and that production could be financed through this kind of distribution. Do you still feel like that?

Yes, but it's still an ideal, an intention, rather than a fact. I think something like this will happen, and I'm encouraged by the increasing number of different types of cinema. Cinerama, for instance, clearly doesn't attract the same audience as the one which goes to the Publicis Cinema to see Truffaut's new film. These are two entirely different kinds of enterprise. . . . When I say different audiences, though, I ought to stress that I don't necessarily mean different people: of course every human being is potentially a member of all sorts of audiences, depending on whether he's feeling in the mood for Wagner or for a music-hall.

I was talking recently to Truffaut on this subject, and he said that he didn't want to make films just for specialised audiences, that he wants his films to reach everyone. I think he's a little ahead of his time, because I can't see Jules et Jim *doing the same kind of business a*s The Guns of Navarone. *But I'd like to ask you about this question of contact with the public.*

I can only give you my own opinion, and I rather think I agree with Truffaut. You must make films to reach everyone. If you don't, you split up into your little private groups, you become pretentious, and in my view you lose the sense of what the cinema is really about. It is, essentially, a mass art; and we must accept that, we must take it for what it is. I don't believe that in our age the differences between the various forms of expression are so great that we need to try to bend one form to ends which aren't proper to it. You know, the cinema becomes a mass art simply because of the distribution system: there is a negative, or maybe several negatives, and you take whatever number of prints you want, and there you are. We wouldn't have to talk about a mass art if there were only one copy of each film. Anyhow, if you want to practise something that *isn't* a mass art, heaven knows there are plenty of other ways of expressing yourself!

All the same, as you've said, different films do appeal to different audiences. Do you think this is something for the business men to sort out—to fit the film to the market—or does it mean that directors should consciously make films with certain audiences in mind?

Naturally, it's firstly a matter for the business men. But there's another reason why the situation is quite different from what happens in the theatre. A playwright can write for a certain actor—Giraudoux for Jouvet, say—in the assurance that his work will reach the public. But there's no reason for a film director—for tomorrow's Truffaut—knowing that the Publicis audience has taken kindly to his film, to say to himself, "Well, I'll make another film which will come out at the Publicis. . . ." But why not? It would give the artist a wonderful feeling of security. In fact the only harmful thing about our job is this fact that it's commercial. We are obliged to please too many people, because it's the condition of the job. If you start out with the idea of pleasing everyone, however, of course you end up satisfying no one. One has to start with the idea of achieving a certain objective, uncovering a certain truth, and if the mass public accepts it, so much the better. One makes films for them.

I suppose there are likely to be more and more different kinds of films, and perhaps a more widespread diffusion of films. Do you think there is also going to be more room for individualism?

There will be more specialisation, I suppose. There's no reason why entertainment shouldn't move in the same direction as the rest of life. When I was at college, for instance, one either read science or the humanities; one did Latin or one didn't! The division stopped there. Now there's a frantic kind of forced specialisation, and the subjects which students have to absorb are so complex that they are forced to select, to limit themselves. It will be the same in entertainment, the same in everything.

Do you think that the cinema has absorbed part of the theatre public?

No, I really feel rather the opposite. . . . I see our age as one of great specialisation, as I've just said, particularly in the professions, but in some ways we're moving away from specialisation, for instance in the field of technique. If I have worked in the theatre, it is only because technical development is such that at the moment a director is not exclusively a film director. . . . When I started out in films, you know, the director had to do almost everything himself. He practically developed the film himself; and of course it was tremendously exciting. Then all these technical preoccupations shut us up in our own little world, just as the old-time craftsmen were enclosed in the world of their particular craft. A man who made barrels, for instance, would never have thought of making tables: he had too much to learn about his own craft. Now you make a barrel with a machine, all in a few minutes, and since you can make a table just as easily, why not have a table as well? The New Wave directors know their craft; but there are a tremendous number of directors around who know absolutely nothing about the technical problems of their job. They really haven't the first idea about photography, or about what happens when you develop a film, or about sound recording. The director simply comes along and says "I want such and such a scene," and the technicians do it for him. So people now have their general ideas, their artistic ideas, and the artisan has given way to the artist. And this is something to regret, because great art is made by artisans and not by artists.

Then you can't be very enthusiastic about the Holly-wood tendency towards super-spectacles, bigger and bigger films?

I enjoy watching some of them. But I get far too much pleasure out of doing the odd jobs on a film to want to get tied up in an undertaking where one becomes a kind of general, with a whole staff at one's disposal. The general doesn't have any fun; the really entertaining thing is to be a corporal giving riding lessons to half a dozen men, teaching them how to hang on to a horse. That's where the fun is.

You worked in Hollywood for some time, and might go back there. Were you as free and happy as in France?

But of course!

You obviously like America a lot. What is it that you get from it particularly?

Oh, many things . . . Americans may be less subtle in their attitudes than Europeans, but they're also less bitter. In America you can still sit in a shop and have a chat with the grocer's boy about the development of the local bus service or about pre-Columbian art, or whatever it may be. It isn't so easy in Paris. Try to interrupt your butcher by chatting to him while he's chopping up the cutlets . . .

Are you irritated at all by the American emphasis on technical perfection?

Certainly not, because I have a great regard for good technique. I've spent my time in France bullying the laboratories to get better results, I've always tried for perfect camera movement. . . . The danger for America, as I've said, is that everything becomes so perfect the director doesn't have to know anything about technique at all. But I despise technique—despise it while I'm working, I mean —because I really do know it. And if you don't know it all, I don't see how you can expect to make first class films.

Quite a long time ago, in some interview or other, I be-lieve you mentioned a director called George B. Seitz who had worked with M-G-M on the Andy Hardy pictures. I think you quoted him as a case of an artisan who really knew his job.

Yes, perhaps. I'll try to tell you what I had in mind. I believe that the dangerous thing in a director's career is to make films which earn a lot of money. After a really big box-office success, people turn their backs on you, they don't want to suggest films to you, you're out. But have a good flop which has cost millions, and people love you, they fall over themselves to get you to work for them. . . . It really isn't a paradox: it's true all over the world. Now, I gave as an instance the case of this gentleman who directed the Mickey Rooney pictures, and who kept Metro rich for years. I wanted to know the name of this director, and no one could even tell me who he was. Well, here is this fantastic thing: here is this man who earned more money for the cinema than almost anyone you can think of, and no one even knew his name. Isn't that proof, it you want it, that money doesn't count in the cinema?

I know you've always had a great sympathy for the American cinema. Was Stroheim someone you admired particularly?

Yes, yes. A great character.

You cast him in La Grande Illusion, *and when you were making* Nana *I believe that you were . . .*

Naturally I thought of him. He was a great influence.

And do you feel about Stroheim that he was someone who helped to bring together European and American trends?

Oh, he was like all the Americans: there are very few Americans who are really American and nothing else. Take someone like John Ford, with all his Irish sentimentality. Or take Chaplin, who's an American artist whatever he likes to say, but whose films would have been quite different if he hadn't been born in England. My feeling is that America hasn't yet achieved a complete fusion, that the melting-pot hasn't worked completely. America is still a club for discontented Europeans.

I believe you're now an American citizen.

I'm both French and American. And of course I have an American family: my mother's father was American— at least he emigrated to America—and I have all sorts of American relations.

I'd like to ask you about one last subject: about critics. It seems to me that in a sense criticism is an impossible job.

It's a very difficult one. I try to put myself in the place of the critic.

And being a critic makes you want to make films yourself, because the more you put the questions, the less clearly you see the answers. You want to take a hand in the thing yourself.

That was my father's idea. Given that painting isn't, as Truffaut says of the cinema, a mass art, my father insisted that finally one was painting for other painters.

But what do you expect yourself from a critic? Is there anything he can give you?

That depends on the critic. A man like Bazin, for instance, gave a lot, but probably this was not only through his criticism but through what emerged from his writing as a whole. He had a kind of vision of the world shaped by the cinema, and what he wrote went beyond criticism. In fact the criticism was secondary, and I think this is true of most really good critics. When a critic simply writes that a film is good or bad . . . well, anyone can make mistakes.

Do you think criticism can play a really constructive part? Do you feel, for instance, that the influence of Cahiers du Cinéma *has been a constructive one?*

I believe that modern critics have helped towards the formation of certain trends, certain groups in the cinema. The cinema today isn't the creation of *Cahiers,* but obviously *Cahiers* has done quite a bit towards it. And that's all to the good.

Today we're experiencing a certain reaction after the first enthusiastic response to the new cinema. What do you think about that—is it an unfair reaction?

It's all extremely unimportant. The New Wave came, and after it there was bound to be a counter-reaction. It was inevitable. But it's absurd to suggest the New Wave doesn't represent the cinema of our time: of course it does. One can say that very good films are being made outside the New Wave, but these good films don't give cinematic expression to this world of 1962. In a few years there will be another movement, with another name, or no name, bringing something else with it: so much the better.

I read recently something you were reported as saying . . . I can't quote it exactly, but it seemed to me marvellous. You said something like this: "I'm not ashamed of changing my mind, at least I'm not afraid of setting out, looking for something, without knowing where I'm going . . ."

Well, what matters is the action, not the target. Of course one needs general ideas, but they must be so deep-rooted, so profound, that one hardly knows one has them. You have to start out in a certain direction, and keep to it, but in the way that migratory birds follow a line instinctively, without knowledge. I believe the artist ought to be

432

like that. And then the conscious part of his mind goes into the detail, into action, into doing. An eighteenth or nineteenth century idea which has caused immense trouble is this one of targets. "Do this and you will be rewarded"; "work well and you will have money for your old age." It ought to be done for the pleasure of the moment, the pleasure of working well.

Finally, I'd like to ask whether you believe that there's a return at the moment towards individualism.

Towards individualism? Alas, yes, because we've had quite enough of individualism. The myth of the mass, the myth of the individual . . . I don't believe in them any more. People want to react against the crowd, and so they get the idea that when a young woman writes a book explaining how she makes love, the things that please her, this is exciting. Well, it doesn't excite me. I'm sure she's right to make love, but that's her affair, not mine. . . . I believe in the individual, as I said at the beginning of this conversation, when he reflects the world and tries to explain it. I believe in the individual if he knows how to absorb. It's imagination that we ought to be afraid of.

Jean Renoir (1894–   ):
Filmography:
1924—La Fille de l'eau. 1926—Nana. 1927—Charleston, Marquitta. 1928—La Petite marchande d'allumettes. 1929–Tire au flanc, Le Tournoi, Le Petit chaperon rouge, La P'tite Lili, Le Bled. 1931—On Purge bébé, La Chienne. 1932—La Nuit du Carrefour, Boudu sauve des eaux. 1933—Chotard et Compagnie. 1934—Toni, Madame Bovary. 1935—Le Crime de Monsieur Lange. 1936—La Vie est à nous, Une partie de campagne, The Lower Depths. 1937—La Marseillaise, La Grande Illusion. 1938—The Human Beast. 1939—The Rules of the Game. 1940—La Tosca (with C. Koch and Luchino Visconti). 1941—Swamp Water. 1943—This Land Is Mine. 1944—Salute to France (Allegorical documentary). 1945—The Southerner. 1946—Diary of a Chambermaid. 1947—The Woman on the Beach. 1951—The River. 1954—The Golden Coach. 1956—French Can Can. 1957—Paris Does Strange Things. 1960—Picnic on the Grass. 1961—Dr. Cordelier. 1963—The Elusive Corporal.

Alain Resnais

From Hiroshima, Mon Amour *to* Le Guerre est finie, *Alain Resnais has maintained an uneasy balance between abstract formalism and social specifics. With* Last Year at Marienbad, *the balance teetered toward the formal; with* La Guerre est finie, *the balance has tottered back toward the social. With his synchronized tracks and razor-sharp cuts, Resnais seems gloriously impervious to the content of his scripts. Resnais' materialistic conception of the universe disallows accident and all other appurtenances of causality. There is nothing mystical in his art, no bridges of meaning between what we know and what we suspect. As the camera tracks down streets and corridors, man is imprisoned by the mindless elements of time and space. Everything is present including memory of the past, and nothing exists apart from mental and material impressions. With this method, there can be no unification or development of ideas and emotions. The two films of Resnais end at the beginning and begin at the end with an arbitrary series of phenomena in between. His characters thrash about in abstract time-space patterns and are powerless to alter the relentless rhythm of their experiences. Ultimately, motion and immobility become one.* Marienbad *becomes an optical illusion when the camera rests and reduces three-dimensional landscapes to two. A castle in space becomes a photograph in time; when the camera begins moving again, inanimate sculpture assumes the very life divested* *from animate humanity. The art of Resnais is nothing if not precise and impeccable.**—A.S.

This interview deals almost exclusively with *Last Year at Marienbad,* Alain Resnais' second feature film. After an initial conversation with Resnais, we decided to pursue it together with Alain Robbe-Grillet, scenarist of this film.

And as *Marienbad* is a "sealed" work, without detail, in which all the elements are tightly linked, we have first of all questioned Alain Resnais about one of its most anecdotal aspects: the game—the confrontation of the two male characters, repeated several times.

A. R.: This is the only thing about which I can tell you nothing. I have never played it. It seems to be a very old game: the Chinese played it, 3000 years B.C. It was the game of Nim, of which Robbe-Grillet has invented a variation without knowing its existence.

But it's not a game, actually. It's a trap.

A. R.: Certainly.

The beginning determines everything; if the two players are equally matched, the one who makes the first move loses.

A. R.: As far as I'm concerned, I believe that when Albertazzi loses he does so lucidly and willingly . . . perhaps in an off-hand way. X is, moreover, a very complex character—what I mean is that he has moods of violent wilfullness, of obstinacy, followed without transition by moods of discouragement.

What is the secret relationship of the game to the film?

A. R.: I believe it is the constant necessity of making a decision. And, at the same time, while the characters are playing, it may be that they are taking "time out" before deciding something. Besides, it may all be in the woman's mind; on the verge of making a decision, she gathers together all of the elements in thirty seconds. I don't think there are any other relationships, except insofar as there is a cyclic recurrence of problems—which would rather correspond to the development of a musical theme and to the

* *The conversation of Andre S. Labarthe and Jacques Rivette with Alain Resnais and Alain Robbe-Grillet appeared originally in* Cahiers du Cinema, *No. 123 and was reprinted in* NY Film Bulletin, *No. 2 (Issue 43), Vol. 3, March 1962. English translation by Rose Kaplin. The interview with Henri Colpi by Rudi Franchi and Marshall Lewis appeared in the same issue of* NY Film Bulletin.

obsessive nature of dreams. *Marienbad* is a film which, for my part, presents neither allegory nor symbol.

But there are possibilities for symbols.

A. R.: Yes, of course, we may think of the myth of the Grail or of something else. But the film is open to all myths. If, for example, you set up ten cages for it, based on mythology or realism, you will arrive at a solution that would be true for 60% or 80% of the film, but never for the whole thing. *AMBIGUITY UNTOUCHABLE*

One of the approaches which interests me is the idea of parallel universes. It is very possible that all the characters were right. This isn't something which was deliberately organized . . . here, we should talk about "automatic writing" again. It isn't because Robbe-Grillet has an extremely precise style and exceedingly clear vision that we must reject "automatism." His manner of working often makes me think of the Douanier *HENRI* Rousseau, who used to begin a canvas in the left-hand corner, filling in all the details and finishing-up in the right hand corner. Here's something amusing enough about the film: we had to begin by setting up landmarks, I don't mean without knowing how it was going to end—but, in any case, the last pages were hardly typed when we began shooting. The important thing was to remain faithful at all times to a sort of intuition. It was the genre of film about which you can say, "After the shooting, there are going to be twenty-five montage solutions." Not at all: we fell back, exactly, on the combinations as foreseen.

A. R.: In any case, this is the sense in which I conceived the mise-en-scène. There is also the use of psychoanalytic themes, consciously introduced; for example, the rooms—too large—which indicates a tendency to narcissism. At one point, Albertazzi hears gun shots, which signify sexual impotence; I cut them from the final print, because this didn't correspond to my idea of the character. But perhaps I took them out because I know very well their psychoanalytical implication?

The moments of tension between him and her correspond to moments of tension between the patient and the psychoanalyst.

A. R.: Toward the end, I don't know if you remember that scene in which the man has his hand against the door, after the hypothetical sequence of death, when she imagines that if she were to leave she would be killed, etc. When she says, as if in despair, 'But I have never stayed

436

so long anywhere,' this gives me the feeling, above all by her tone of voice, of a total acquiescence; therefore the thing is real. Now, it is also attractive to make her an invalid. First of all, the hotel itself has a odd look. Moreover, there is a line which has always intrigued me: it's when Sacha Pitoeff says to the woman as she is stretched out on the bed, "You must rest. Don't forget that's what we're here for." I am always reminded of *Caligari*, of the end, when the doctor says, "Yes, he is going to calm down. I shall cure him." It seems to me that this is something on the same order. Perhaps the hotel is only a clinic.

There is another interpretation, with which you seemed to agree: that Albertazzi is Death.

A. R.: At the end, Robbe-Grillet thought of the phrase "granite flagstone," and he realized that, after all, the description of the garden corresponded pretty closely to that of a cemetery. Going on from there, he came to the conclusion that one might very well make a connection between the film and the old Breton legends of Death, who came looking for his victims to whom he had given a year of reprieve. But we never tried to limit the story in a strict sense, always retaining an ambiguity.

There is never an "absolute" real or "absolute" imaginary.

A. R.: It seems that in the first quarter of the film, there are things which have a pretty high degree of reality; we stray further and further from it as the film unfolds, and it is possible that at the end, suddenly, everything is set so as to converge and the end of the film is what is most real. It needs to be studied very closely.

With a big climax in the middle, when she recognizes the statue.

A. R.: Yes, when she discovers the garden and realizes that it is, after all, simply the place where they happen to be—which poses all the problems of the film's chronology.

There is a moment when she feels trapped: when she laces her shoe?

A. R.: Exactly. From this moment on, we may consider her to have remembered. If, by chance, she is sincere at the beginning, if her refusal is truly not pure coquetry or fear, from this moment on, she has recognized it. For her, it is true. But, of course, we never know if the images are in the man's mind or in the woman's. There is always a fluctuation between the two. We may imagine that, basically, everything is told from her point of view. Several spectators have told me that this woman doesn't exist, that she has been dead for a long time, that everything takes place among dead people. But these are things one thinks about after the film is completed, not at all during the shooting, not even during the editing.

What guided you in the organization of this material, which you wanted to keep light and soft? Was it a feeling of affinity between themes, images? Internal rhymes?

A. R.: Interestingly enough, I was not the only one to be guided. During the shooting, there was no discussion, either among the actors or the crew. At several points, we would say, "We may be able to do this or that." We talked a little before shooting a scene; we would say, "This is in the tone of the film; that isn't." And this type of discussion never lasted more than forty seconds. We were all obliged to follow a path from which we couldn't escape. It was a unifying element between the film and the crew. We were in a sense prisoners, not of a logic but of a paralogic which kept us in constant agreement, from the cameraman Philippe Brun to Sacha Vierny (our director of photography) or to Albertazzi. It would be instructive if we had kept a diary of the correspondences in the choice of locations and actors. There was any number of very bizarre things, phenomena which would have delighted Andre Breton or Jean Cocteau and which occurred very frequently. I have the feeling that the form must have pre-existed, I know neither where nor how, and that automatically, when it was written, the story must have slipped into the mould. Each time I've made a film, whether it was in 16mm or in 35mm, I have noticed that it is impossible to insist on any gestures, no matter what character it is, or make them say anything, no matter what it happens to be.

There was a moment, during the preparation for *Marienbad,* when I arrived with my little black notebook and suggested to Robbe-Grillet that we introduce the real world in the form of conversations about an insoluble political problem—at least, insoluble to those who were talking about it. We came to the conclusion that it would be the spectators themselves who, while watching the film, would naturally represent the real world and thus it was impossible to include them in advance. I also wanted, at one point, the woman to be pregnant; I talked to Robbe-Grillet about it, but it was hardly feasible. We weren't free. Moreover, I am convinced that we don't make our own films.

For me the film is also an attempt, still very crude and primitive, to approach the complexity of thought and its mechanism. But I stress the fact that this is only a tiny step forward by comparison with what we should be able to do someday. I find that as soon as we delve into the Unconscious, an emotion may be born. For example, I remember how I felt while watching *Le Jour se Leve,* when there were sudden moments of incertitude, when the image of the wardrobe begins to disappear, then another image materializes. I believe that, in life, we don't think chronologically, that our decisions never correspond to an ordered logic. All of us have "clouds," things which determine us but which are not a logical succession of acts arranged in perfect sequence. I am interested in exploring that universe, from the point of view of truth, if not of morality.

There is the danger of falling into a trap, rather like the one spoken of by Paulhan with respect to language: what we conceive to be the height of liberty risks being received by someone else as the height of arbitrariness.

A. R.: This is the problem in all communication, whether between two people or ten million. One must know to what extent one can share one's subjective reality with "everyone," in the sense that we all have two eyes, hair, a thought, etc. One arrives quite naturally at the notion of a planetary Unconscious. What tempts me and always interests me would be the application of somewhat different disciplines than you find in contemporary films. It's a curiosity I have. There is a notion which pleases me very much, in the cinema, and that is the idea of popularization. A book or a painting, first of all, is seen by a thousand people, while a film reaches millions right away. In this light, it is interesting to recall the experience of a writer in 1880 or a painter known only to a few initiates. I am against sectarianism, and any attempt to shatter its walls seduces me *a priori*. In any case, even if we wanted to redo exactly the same thing which has already been done, the chemistry of the cinema is different. Certainly when Van Gogh amuses himself by copying Delacroix, or Picasso Velasquez, we have a new picture. But the cinema is something of a bull-in-the-china-shop, with its concrete images. Its style is rather pachydermous. The old duality of Lumiere and Melies is still with us. Between these two possibilities, we oscillate and sometimes get stuck. If we take *Lola,* for example, is it Lumiere or is it Melies?

When I see a film, I am more interested in the play of feelings than in the characters. I think we could arrive at a Cinema without psychologically definite characters, in which the feelings would have free play in the way that, in a contemporary canvas, the play of forms becomes stronger than the anecdote.

What is terrifying is the position which Rene Clair pushes to the absurd when he says, "Shooting is only work."

A. R.: For me, shooting is elucidation. I'll admit that I do make sketches beforehand, but it's for my peace of mind.

While shooting, what is your attitude toward these sketches?

A. R.: I keep looking at them. It helps my relationships with the actors, with the photographer, with the camera operator. These sketches save the actors from getting panicky eight or ten days before shooting starts. If he has read the shooting script and has a clear idea of it, and I suddenly, in the midst of shooting, place him in a position or set-up which he hasn't anticipated he is going to worry. And as I like everyone to be as relaxed as possible on set, I prefer arguments to be over before the shooting. I'm in favor of rehearsing the entire film before shooting begins.

For *Marienbad*, we made a complete chronology on graph paper. And we always said, before beginning any scene with the actors: "This scene follows, on the level of the montage, such and such a scene, but in terms of its degree of reality, it follows another scene which will appear much later in the film." Moreover, very often, I would film a bit from the preceding scene, in order to work from the continuity and not from the cue itself. Of course, this chronology was established once the scenario was finished. For example, all costume changes naturally correspond to different pieces of time. This is certainly not the key to the film, if indeed there is one. But it is true that we could re-edit the film so as to restore the chronological order of the scenes. We might imagine, for example, that the film extends over a week, or at least that everything which is in the present takes from Sunday to Sunday inclusive. Which doesn't keep Robbe-Grillet from saying: "Perhaps it happens in five minutes." This is consistent with the dilatation of time in dreams, insofar as we understand the mechanism of dreams.

Your montage is, in a certain sense, the modern version

440

of "montage of attractions." For Pudovkin, the shots were the words of the line; for Eisenstein, each shot remained as a living element in itself.

A. R.: Eisenstein is much closer to the "meeting of the umbrella and the sewing machine on the dissecting table." And, to the extent that I am still very much aware of the Surrealist discipline, I feel much closer to Eisenstein's conceptions. Each shot has its own life.

There is a feeling of great humility before each element, whether it is real or part of an oeuvre, *which must preserve its organic life and at the same time become part of an ensemble.*

A. R.: Even when it concerns an element of the decor, I would prefer not to transform it to suit the camera. It's up to the camera to find the right way to present the decor, it's not for the decor to conform to the camera. The same thing holds true for the actor. I have had an enormous respect for an actor's work. The shooting schedule is never altered to suit an actor's mental state, whereas a sunny or rainy day will call for changes.

We suspect that despite the tightness of the script and the rigidity of the cutting, the filming of Last Year at Marienbad *was not accomplished (if the story be properly told) without "ruses" on the part of its director. It was really a question of grabbing the film by one end, completing it at the other, and, between times, "driving the camera." The previously mentioned complete chronology on graph paper was, precisely, one of those ruses—one of those traps—destined to tame the film in order to lead it in the right direction.*

Questioned on its function, Resnais was, in any case, forced to admit his inability to inform us. And so we just barely understand that it concerns an organization of sequences in terms of their diverse degrees *of reality. If you know how to look you will discover in this picture an essay in chronology and may be tempted to see in it a key to the film or, at the least, a clarifying factor: the playing cards are finally set in order. A patently absurd enterprise, doomed to failure from the start.*

The true interest of the graph is more prosaic and more anecdotal. It is a chart for studio use; today completed, its mission is: to order the choice of costumes and lighting, and above all to facilitate the actors' work while helping them to give their playing a coherence which would be perhaps, without this, missing.

441

*Alain Resnais talked with us about the diversity of in-
terpretations which might intervene in the exegesis of* Last
Year *at* Marienbad. *Now, let us take the film as it
appears: as a set of images in the present.*

Robbe-Grillet: An image is always in the present. I remember a time when the idea of "past" was introduced by
a halo—a halo which often persisted during the entire sequence in the past. But we came back very quickly to retaining the same image for the present and for the past—
that is to say, to admitting that everything is, at any rate,
of the present.

Alain Resnais: You say, "We came back very quickly."
It wasn't so very rapid. The first absolutely typical example of an introduction of the past into the present, with
entirely clean images and without any recourse to the
chain dissolve or to some bit of music to indicate that we
are going backwards, I believe (all the same) is in *Orpheus*, when Roger Blin makes his deposition to the police
commissioner and declares that such-and-such things happened. At this moment, we see an image from this past,
then the conversation in the office picks up again in the
exact same manner. I have a strong feeling that it is Jean
Cocteau who utilized this procedure for the first time in so
precise a way.

—*Already, in* Hiroshima, Mon Amour, *it seemed that
the flashback was no longer used strictly for dramatic
ends. The profusion of images that it engendered considerably submerged its dramatic function.*

A. R. G.: Yes, but in *Hiroshima* the spectator was able,
even so, after the first shock, to place the scene in a chronology of the story. There were certainly images about
which one didn't understand at first that they belonged to
the past. For example, the frame showing the German soldier's corpse. Its shock value is complete but evidently the
spectator, scrupulously looking for "significance," could always say to himself later: oh yes, it's because she was
thinking back to the death of her first lover. It is this spe-
cies of mental realism that we are looking for: she sees
the Japanese on the bed, and then—all at once—she sees
the dead German. There are two images; one is exterior to
her, the other is interior. But at the moment when she sees
them in the same way, so to speak, it is right that the camera be able to render them in the same present tense.

This is why Robbe-Grillet and I both feel very much
outside of the film and look at it as a "thing." We wanted

to set in motion a mechanism different from the traditional spectacle, a kind of a contemplation, a meditation, by hovering around the subject. We wanted to feel somewhat as if we were in front of a piece of sculpture which you look at first from one angle, then from some other, from which you withdraw, to which you come closer again.

But even so, there is a resistance by the material itself, in the film which must be overcome.

A. R.: Yes. For me, the film is an "exploratory" in several ways, in order to know which is a dead-end and which, on the other hand, is a path. It is certain that both are in the film at the same time. Right now, I confess to being still too close to it to see it with any perspective. Every morning, I read what people write to me, and I notice that they speak of a work that is cold, like Mallarme, or else they say it is passionate and tender. Here you have two kinds of diametrically opposed reactions. This doesn't get me very far! It is quite possible that both reactions are real ones, this may be a mirror-film.

It is not a question of making an exegesis of the film, but isn't there a trap in the idea of guiding the spectator, who is in the present, toward the past or the future? Seeing it again, we had the impression that it was concerned with the relationships between the real and the imaginary, rather than with time.

A. R.: It is a film about greater and lesser degrees of reality. There are moments when the "reality" is completely invented, or interior, as when the image corresponds to the conversations. The interior monolog is never on the sound track: it is always in the image, which, even when it represents the past, always corresponds to what is present in the character's mind. What is presented as present or past is thus simply a thing which is unfolded while the character speaks. For instance, I was talking the other day with a girl who had just come back from India, and all of a sudden I saw her in front of the temple at Angkor wearing a blue dress, and yet she had never gone to Angkor and the blue dress was simply the one she was wearing at the time, as I saw her. NOT NECESSARILY REALITY

One aspect of the film is very open to interpretation. For example, when Robbe-Grillet summarizes it, it is from the point of view of the man who suggests a past to the woman . . .

A. R.: That's right. If we take Truffaut's formula, "Any

film must be able to be recapitulated in one word." I want very much for people to say: *Last Year at Marienbad* or "persuasion." It's a solution. But there are others.

You can also look at the film as if the past were real; the woman has a block against it, and the man is somewhat in the position of playing a psychiatrist—forcing the woman to accept a deliberately repressed past.

A. R.: To sum it up, it is a victory for realism. In any case, it is a gain for realism. Certainly the old rhetoric which consisted of introducing the past by means of a "sign" has, in any case, if we can judge it, no more *raison d'etre* than another. Experience it: you talk for a quarter-hour with someone. Then you stop, and you say to him, "You've seen what happened. We are here, in a restaurant, eating. I spoke to you about the sea, about vacations. If I had to describe this 15 minutes out of our lives, what would be the most realistic way?

"Would it be to show the two of us eating in this restaurant, or rather to show the beach with the waves we spoke of? Or even to show all of that, not by the way we spoke of it, but by showing the images that were in our minds at that moment: the ones that corresponded, those which interfered, even the contradictory ones?"

A. R. G.: We can see that this is contrary to an established custom, to a rhetoric accepted by the public; this is not functionally linked to the mechanism of the human spirit. It is linked to an artistic order, to the romantic if you will, but not at all to a mental order. It is not at all to and for reasons of truth—human truth—that we introduced the past with an explicit reference to the past, that we show the restaurant rather than the waves, in the example you evoke. It is strictly a convention; I will say pure formalism.

A. R.: Now, I have scruples. You must not say that this was never done. I am thinking of *Storm Over Asia* which I saw about seventeen years ago. At a certain point you see the big capitalist in a dining-car, thrusting his hands forward. You see a hand with three big fingers and, immediately after, we cut to a frame which shows three submarines which make practically the same movements as the fingers. Then the conversation picks up at the place where it left off.

A. R. G.: Yes, of course, but what is a bit different in *Marienbad* and which risks being disconcerting, is simply generalization: this mechanism was accepted not as an infraction of the rule but, on the contrary, as a general order of thought completely conceivable. When we say that reality is just as much what we have in our minds as what we see before our eyes, we lay the foundation for a cinematographic image which would sometimes show what is in front of us, like this tape recorder we are using now, sometimes what we are talking about, sometimes images which are more or less intermediate, between what we both know, what is in your mind, what I have in mine, etc. In this way, film is still a convention but is to a certain extent more realistic than the convention which would consist in systematically keeping to a single category of reality.

A. R.: Moreover, if we take a very close look at *Marienbad,* we will see that certain images are equivocal, that their degree of reality is doubtful. But there are images whose falseness is much cleaner and lying images which in my opinion are completely evident. You mustn't believe that we amused ourselves by saying while shooting: the spectator will unravel it.

A. R. G.: The use of the decor itself is a good example. At the moment when the room has an extraordinary, complicated-baroque decor, when the walls are laden with incredible pastry volutes, we are probably in the presence of a more "doubtful" image. In the same way, when the heroine takes 300 identical photographs out of a drawer, it is an image which begins to be extremely irrational and which must be much more mental than objective. Perhaps, if we had been obliged to speak of a strictly objective reality, she only took out one photo at that moment; but she saw three hundred. Without our being ourselves always able, moreover, to give a unique and definite interpretation of the intentions of each image.

Certainly what is first of all striking, on seeing Marienbad, *is that the film presents itself to us like an object which requires all of our faculty for comprehension and for seeing the moral of a fable. Like any fragment of reality.*

A. R. G.: It is entirely a question of knowing whether the uncertainty which is attached to the film's images is exaggerated when compared to what surrounds us in daily life, or if it is rather of the same order. For my part, I have the impression that things really happen this way. The question, for these people, is that of an adventure of the passions, and these are exactly the adventures which

445

contain the greatest proportion of contradictions, of doubts, of phantasms. *Marienbad* as a story is as opaque as the way we live our crises of passion, our loves, all of our affective lives. Consequently, to reproach the film for not being clear is to reproach human passions for always being a bit opaque.

The word risks a misunderstanding. For, finally, if Marienbad appears "opaque" to us, it is not because you are willingly using certain fragments which might furnish us with a clear idea of the film.

A. R. G.: Exactly. We show everything, but these are things which are not resolved by a simple explanation. What is amusing is that people very willingly admit to meeting, in their lives, so many irrational and ambiguous real elements and that these same people complain when they meet them in works of art, as well as in novels or films, which supposedly should present something more reassuring than the "real world." As if the work were made to explain the world, in order to reassure man about the world. I do not believe, not at all, that art is made in order to reassure. If the world is really so complex, what is needed is to find its complexity again. Again by attention to realism. But we should go further than that. If we don't, we seem to suppose that reality exists outside of the work and even that isn't all sure. A work is a kind of consciousness. Just as, in life, the world doesn't exist at all without the consciousness which perceives it, the same goes for the work of art. The things told about do not truly exist outside of the tale.

With relation to this, we have heard the reproach of "formalism" made several times about the film.

A. R. G.: Very curiously, the people who reproach *Marienbad* for being "contrived" are those who accept as spontaneous works which respect fixed rules of contrivance, recipes, norms. And these people reason as if there were a previously existent reality and as if it were no more than a question of finding the forms which would make a good understanding of the story available to the public. For us, on the contrary, the anecdote is nothing outside of the fashion in which it is told. Moreover, the genesis of the film clarifies this very well. When I met Alain Resnais and we had our first talk, it turned out that we had cinematographic forms of the same genre in mind. I knew that all the cinema ideas I might have would agree in some manner with what Resnais wanted to do at that moment.

It happened that he wanted to make the kind of film about which I myself was thinking. I didn't really write four scripts in three days for Resnais, but I wrote four page-and-a-half outlines that I'd doubtless had in mind for a long time.

A. R.: When I had finished reading Robbe-Grillet's work, I said to myself: There is already a film which we clearly made together, that is *Toute la Memoire du Monde*.

A. R. G.: Which doesn't keep us from having different views, each of us, of the *ensemble* of his films or of the *ensemble* of my writings. But it happens that there was a world common to the two of us, which was as inhabitable for one as for the other. It was not a question of a compromise between Resnais and me, but of a common form which would function in the same way for both of us, even though we might not attach the same importance to each detail.

A. R.: For example, we don't have the same tastes at all and we would violently oppose each other—about a book, about a film, about a way of life . . .

A. R. G.: At each instant, in spite of that, we had the same intuitions. For example, I was describing a camera movement and Resnais said to me: "It doesn't matter—that's the movement I would have chosen in any case." Moreover, it is still possible that *Marienbad* is not at all the same film for Resnais and for me. In the same way doubtless we each see the real world differently, the same world around us.

We may perhaps shock you, but when we saw Marienbad *we thought of the book by Bioy Casares:* Morel's Invention.

A. R. G.: Not at all. I've practically always been disappointed by the S.F. books I was able to read, but *Morel's Invention* is, on the contrary, an astounding science fiction book. And a curious thing . . . I had a telephone call from Claude Ollier, after *Marienbad* was shown, who said to me, "But it's *Morel's Invention!*"

A. R.: I'm in a bad position for talking about this, because I don't know the book.

It's a novel written in the first person and based on the myth of the total cinema. The narrator finds himself on an island where a machine is running, set up 20 years previously, which reproduces in their three dimensions the events registered by it. You understand, these 3-D images

447

mix with the real world to the point of being impossible to distinguish the one from the other. Like certain frames of Marienbad, *the objects are thus subject to suspicion—they are there, but are they really? That's the whole problem.*

A. R.: The relationship to *Marienbad* is, in effect, striking. But we've often had surprises like this. I remember the first scene we had projected. It was the sequence with the young woman, full sunlight, the length of the balustrade, behind the statue. When the lights were turned on afterward, I said to myself, "It's amusing, we are plainly in Feuillade's feuilletons."

A. R. G.: And I myself described the shot without even knowing these articles. I haven't read the Fantomas stories, or so little . . .

Actually, we thought of Feuillade, too, but at the point when the balustrade collapses.

A. R. G.: This image, however, is one of those which figured in the scenario. And I couldn't have been influenced, as you see.

A. R.: It's a deceitful image. When we were shooting I remember having told Albertazzi to leap over the balustrade "like Arsene Lupin." That was the mood. And, in my opinion, it's justified, for, in the sense that it is a future image projected, doubtless, by the young woman's anguish, it's completely normal that she appeal, in such circumstances, to traditions from popular novels. That sort of happens by itself.

A. R. G.: At that point the young woman says, moreover, "Disappear, I beg of you, if you love me!", which is enough indication of the degree of "theatricality" of the scene!

A. R.: Which makes me regret all the more not having filmed "Fantomas."

These coincidences tend to confirm some ideas clear and dear to Andre Malraux, according to which art would be nourished by and live on art.

A. R. G.: I believe that reality is what nourishes the artist, directly, and that if art interests us deeply it is because we find in it things we want to do under the influence of emotions entirely caused by the real world. I don't believe we really live on art, at the moment of creation.

Then you are opposed to Malraux's theory?

A. R.: Personally, I am for Malraux's theory. I believe that the desire to participate in the universe of art exists very strongly. It is in other respects not incompatible with what Robbe-Grillet says.

A. R. G.: Shock is produced by the world and art is only a recollection. An illumination, perhaps. If I like Kafka's work, for example, it's really because I recognize in it the fashion in which I saw the world around me; it was as if I understood it before reading it. When a film image is striking to me, it is always because I recognize in it an experience as I lived it. If not, communication wouldn't be possible. Every work of art would become uniquely subjective and absolutely without any possible chance for contact with anyone.

A. R.: With respect to this, here is an anecdote which was interesting for me. I received, several years ago, a letter from a woman who said in substance, "Oh, I saw your short film *Van Gogh* . . what a marvelous picture, and what great trips you must have made in order to film all those places." That lady had a memory of the film which was simultaneously Van Gogh's canvases and real landscapes.

Coming back to Marienbad, *there is a curious phenomenon. One might just as well say, "It's a film by Resnais," or, "It's a film by Robbe-Grillet." On the other hand, it's no secret that there are several minimal differences between the very precise cutting scheme of the film and the result.*

A. R. G.: In the scenario as I handed it to Resnais, there were already numerous indications as to the framing, camera movements, montage. But I had no idea of the technical terms which are used in film-making, nor of its real possibilities. I described a film as I saw it in my imagination, and in perfectly naive language.

A. R.: Not at all. In any case, it was very precise. There was even the guile of an old hand!

In any case, the dissolve—insofar as it transforms duration—is indispensable in Marienbad. *Moreover, can we reasonably affirm that the story unfolds in 8 days, in 24 hours, or in the actual running time of the film?*

A. R. G.: We can say that the only time is the film's time . . . that there is no reality outside of the film. You see everything. Nothing is hidden and you mustn't believe that the film lasts an hour-and-a-half and thus recapitulates a longer time—2 hours, 2 days or a week. I wouldn't say that about Clouzot's *The Truth,* for example, where you have the impression that there is another time, more real than the film's. For *Marienbad,* I don't even see another possibility. All other durations depend on the interpretation and only limit it. What leaves it intact is the statement that the story lasts an hour-and-a-half.

There is a shot that surprised us and surprises us still more now that we know that all the sequences of the film and their continuity were anticipated by Robbe-Grillet on paper. This is the over-exposed tracking shot which ends with the repetition of its final portion. It is difficult for us to imagine that such a shot could have been foreseen.

A. R.: That's precisely one of those rare shots which was not foreseen at the beginning.

A. R. G.: There, Resnais knew he wasn't going to shoot what was in the scenario. He told me. That was *the* point of friction between us! Resnais knew that, for several seconds, there would be some other thing.

A. R.: And this other thing, I had the idea of it occur to me a couple of weeks before the shooting, or a little more.

A. R. G.: There is another passage that I didn't anticipate, but this one I should have found by myself, for I recognize it absolutely: it's the series of shots where you see Delphine Seyrig sit down on the bed in diverse ways, on the right and on the left, successively. This is the kind of thing that makes me suffer for having not invented!

What was your feeling on seeing the film for the first time?

A. R. G.: I didn't believe it would be so beautiful. I recognized it completely, of course, but at the same time it had become quite marvelous. Basically, everything had been seen for in advance and everything had to be done. It isn't true that you can describe an image as it will be. It's at the moment that it is realized that you give it an existence.

A. R.: If I was able to prepare the shooting-script for the film in two-and-a-half days, it's really because everything was scrupulously prepared by Robbe-Grillet.

A. R. G.: It is nonetheless true that even if a frame is described beforehand it remains to be realized. It is clear that the film wouldn't have been the same had it been given to another director or to an electronic robot. My descriptions weren't meant to be followed to the letter, but, once more, to be "realized."

A. R.: In the same way that it was necessary to "realize" the statue in the park.

A. R. G.: We can imagine that *Marienbad* is a documentary about a statue. With interpretive take-offs on the gestures and the return, each time, to the gestures themselves, just as they stand, frozen in sculpture. Imagine a documentary that would succeed, with a statue of two people, by uniting a series of views taken from diverse angles and with the help of diverse camera movements, in telling in this way a whole story. And at the end you would see that you had come back to the point of departure, to the statue itself.

In this sense all your books are documentaries, and it is because they are documentaries that they are fantastic. So that the father of the fantastic would not be Melies but Lumiere.

A. R.: The fantastic is thus, in any case, much stronger. The most fantastic moments in *Nosferatu*, for example, are "real" moments. There's no doubt about it.

A. R. G.: But, in *Marienbad,* the important phenomenon is always the basic lack of substance at the heart of this reality. In *Marienbad,* what is chimerical is "last year." What happened—if something did happen once upon a time—constantly produces sort of a gap in the story. In the way that the principal character in *Jealousy* is only a deep emptiness, as the principal act (the murder) is a blank in *Le Voyeur.* Everything, up to the "hole," is told —then told again after the hole—and we try to reconcile the two edges in order to make this annoying emptiness disappear. But what happens is the exact opposite: it's the emptiness that overruns, that fills everything. In *Marienbad,* at first we believe that there was no last year and then we notice that last year has crept in everywhere: there you have it, entirely. In the same way we believe that there was no *Marienbad* (the place, i.e.), and then we realize we're at home there from the beginning. The event refused by the young woman has, at the end, contaminated everything. So much so that she hasn't stopped struggling and believing she won the game, since she always refused all of it; and, at the end, she realizes that it's too late, that in the final analysis she has accepted everything. As if all that *were* true, although it well might not be. But *true* and *false* no longer have any meaning.

A. R.: Of course, it couldn't be a question of "special effects."

A. R. G.: You know the famous line: *"Larvatus pro-deo,"* I present myself masked, but I show my mask. The cinema is a technique that creates a truth. There is no preexistent truth for technique, which alone would serve to capture it. That is why I tend to say that the story un-folds in an hour-and-a-half, and that it has existence nei-ther before nor after. At the end of the film, if the charac-ters go away, they're not going anywhere. They cease to be. There has never been anything but *here* and *now*.

An instance of the way the film exists is the proverb, the beginning of which we hear several times: "From the compass to the ship . . ."

A. R. G.: Yes, if you like. I invented a half-a-proverb. Once again we haven't hidden anything from anyone. What's the good of inventing an entire proverb when you only need the first part? Clearly, by taking-off from this demi-proverb we can imagine many things.

A. R.: It's not necessary to know any more about it. Say it at any cocktail party and everyone will know the proverb. No one will ask for the rest. I know: I've tried it.

Alain Resnais (1922–   ):
Filmography:
Short subjects: 1945–1946—Schéma d'une identification, ouvert pour cause d'inventaire. 1946–1948—Portrait d'Henri Goetz, Visite à Lucien Coutaud, Visite à Félix Labisse, Visite à Hans Hartung, Visite à César Domela, Journée Naturelle, La Bague, visite à Oscar Domínguez. 1948—Van Gogh, Malfray. 1950—Gauguin, L'Alcool tue, Guernica. 1951—Les Statues meurent aussi. 1955—Night and Fog. 1956—Toute la memoire du monde. 1957—Le Mystère de l'a-telier 15. 1958—Le Chant du styrène. 1959—Hiroshima, Mon Amour. 1961—Last Year at Marienbad. 1963—Muriel. 1966—La Guerre est finie. 1968—Je t'aime, Je t'aime.

CAHIERS: *Let us begin at the beginning: how did you enter the cinema?*

RIEFENSTAHL: I must tell you first of all that before entering the cinema, I began as a dancer. I was still a very young girl when I studied ballet, then modern dance, with Mary Wigman, among others. At the same time, I received a certain amount of training at the Berlin Academy of Painting and I set myself to painting. If I mention these things, it is because these two elements, dance and painting, have played a role in forming the style of composing and editing images that became mine.

But, one day, while dancing, I hurt my knee and this was the end of my dancing career.

During that period I saw, quite by chance, in Berlin, a film about mountains: *The Mountain of Destiny*. This film made such a strong impression on me that soon I wanted to know about mountains, and the director of the film as well. This was Doctor Arnold Fanck, who became my professor, and who taught me the fundamentals of my technique of *mise en scène*. This Doctor Fanck was an outsider and if, consequently, perhaps I myself became an outsider, it is doubtless to him that I owe it. Doctor Fanck had his own crew, on the fringe of the normal cinema industry. He was a savant, a geologist, besides being a photographer who, with certain other dreamers, had founded a small company. I was the only girl on the crew. To start with, I had to learn to ski, to climb and, by the press of circumstances, I also found myself somewhat involved in the camera work and at times collaborated with the directoral crew. At any rate, I did not stop watching, observing, and it was not long before I noticed that I often saw things differently than Fanck, although he, too, had come to the cinema by way of nature and, like me, he loved beautiful images. When what he did didn't agree with what I felt, my personal sense of art seemed violated and it was in this way that I came to ask myself how I might give form to this sense. I set about, therefore, seeking a thread, a theme, a style, in the realm of legend and fantasy, something that might allow me to give free rein to my juvenile sense of romanticism and the beautiful image. It was thus, still very young, that I decided to make my first film. And, naturally, I made this first film with myself as producer, scenarist, actress and director, for I had little money. I made it using, as a point of departure, a certain idea that concretized everything I had been seeking for a long time. This idea was "The Blue Light."

CAHIERS: *Where did that idea come from? Perhaps from Heinrich von Ofterdingen's "Blue Flower"?*

RIEFENSTAHL: No. I didn't think of that. However, if I must go back to the origin of the idea, I find a dance. A dance I performed, which was my first success. It was called "The Blue Flower." This idea took on its full meaning only when linked with mountains. I told you: that is how I came to the cinema, although for a long time the idea that I might remain in the cinema never came to me.

Therefore, I was going to make a film. Writing a role, was, for me, the occasion of giving form to some *thing* as well as to myself. This role was that of a strange young Italian girl who, sleepwalking, climbs, at night, towards a blue light which is at the summit of a certain mountain and which is visible only on nights when the moon is full. It is a glimmering emitted by the crystalline rocks of a grotto when the light hits them from a certain angle. But this light has its secret, and this secret, in its profound sense, as described by a legend, is that young beings tend towards a certain light: an ideal.

The young girl, Yunta, is the only one to be able to attain to this light. The others, the people of the village, fail when they try it and evil befalls them. Until the day that a young painter, in love with Yunta, discovers the crystal grotto. Believing that he acts in the interests of his beloved, who he believes is under a spell, he reveals to the people of the village the secret path that leads to the grotto. He is the realist who kills the dream. Who kills his beloved. For, when she discovers that her secret has been violated by the crowd, her heart is broken and she falls from a precipice. But her death brings happiness to the others, to all those who didn't understand her, the peasants and the painter as well, those who accused her of having cast a spell on the village, who pursued her in order to throw stones at her and who would willingly have burned her as a sorceress.

To the above was grafted something that fascinated me, which is the composition of the image ("Bildgestaltung"). I didn't have enough money to work in a studio, so I had to shoot out-of-doors, and in order to render the atmosphere that I wanted, I was forced to stylize the images in default of stylizing the decors. I had to calculate the shadow, the lights and the framing in such a way as to obtain some particular thing that would engender a step back into legend. If I had had to treat of realistic material I would have photographed in a realistic fashion, as I was to do later in my other films, but at any rate, I was then too young for that—I was still at the age when one romanticizes. This style of image played its part, perhaps, in the charm of the film, but the great success it had was doubtless equally due to the fact that by spontaneously expressing what I felt, I must have unconsciously rendered things that profoundly touched on a sensitive point in the public. They felt something authentic in the moral of the fable.

But, in making this very romantic film by instinct, without knowing exactly where I wanted to go, I also found myself expressing the path that would be mine later. For, in a certain fashion, it was my own destiny that I had had a presentiment of and to which I had given form.

CAHIERS: *Don't you think that this juvenile dream of idealism and purity persists in your following films?*

RIEFENSTAHL: Without a doubt, but I didn't know that and wouldn't know it until much later. I knew that in all of my films, whatever they were, whether it concerned *Triumph of the Will, Olympia* or *Tiefland,* there was . . . yes: let us say purity. Yunta was a young girl, intact and innocent, whom fear made retract at any contact with reality, with matter, with sex; and, later, in *Tiefland,* the character of Martha was nearly the same. But I didn't know this. I was searching. When I got somewhere, it was unconsciously.

I only know that I have a great love for beauty. The form taken by beauty, and not only its exterior form but its interior form. I only know how happy it makes me when I meet good men, simple men. But it repulses me so much to find myself faced with false men that it is a thing to which I have never been able to give artistic form.

CAHIERS: *After* The Blue Light, *what was there?*

RIEFENSTAHL: There was *S.O.S. Eisberg,* but I only acted in it. When Dr. Fanck agreed to do the film, for Universal, the company had found no one who could take the role, as it required a great physical effort. At that time, I was beginning to become accustomed to snow and ice. I was able to take the role. I lived in Greenland for several

456

months under the conditions called for by the film. This was the last film in which I was only an actress.

When I returned to Germany, at the end of this very long shooting, I again threw myself into the making of a film. This was in 1934. The film was my first documentary. It was *Triumph of the Will.*

CAHIERS: *At that time, had you seen many films?*

RIEFENSTAHL: Not many. I never went to the cinema much, and when I made films it was always without knowing whether they were going to be good or not, or whether they would have success, as I changed realms each time. I neither believed nor had any presentiments and I had very few references. I had only the joy of working and I always did my work as well as I could. When my films were successful, I was the first to be surprised. There is no doubt that, in their genre, they were new.

CAHIERS: *Did you know, let us say, Lang, Murnau, Sternberg? . . .*

RIEFENSTAHL: The first film of Sternberg's that I saw was *The Docks of New York,* when it opened, and I liked it very much. Sometime after that I visited Sternberg, in Berlin. I experienced great joy on seeing him; he filled me with enthusiasm. We understood each other very well. He and Pabst were the first to believe that I had talent as a cineaste.

One day Sternberg asked me, in an amused tone, "But what pleases you so much about my films?" I answered, "What pleases me is that everything which is interesting, you don't show!" "Ah," he said, "but these are not omissions at all! These are ellipses! . . . That is my way . . ." But my answer had pleased him very much.

During that period I was working, as an actress, on my first film, *The Sacred Mountain.* Sometime after that, *Faust* came out. It was an admirable film. Lang's films struck me by their construction and their composition.

CAHIERS: *Did you see* Potemkin?

RIEFENSTAHL: Yes, of course. I rarely went to the cinema but, all the same, that one I did see. And I also see why you ask me that question: it is because certain people have compared our two films. See here, I am not in agreement. It is difficult to compare a film with *mise en scène* to a documentary. *Triumph of the Will,* a pure documentary, is very different, in spirit and in form, from Eisenstein's film; he directed, himself (and with genius, there is no doubt at all), a film with *mise en scène,* a film with orientation.

CAHIERS: *Don't they at least have in common their being political films?*

RIEFENSTAHL: But my film is only a documentary. I showed what everyone was witness to or had heard about. And everyone was impressed by it. I am the one who fixed that impression, who registered it on film. And that is doubtless why people are angry with me: for having seized it, put it in a box.

CAHIERS: *How did you put it in a box, first of all, technically?*

RIEFENSTAHL: With very primitive means. It was a very cheap film. It cost only 280,000 marks. I had only two cameras at my disposal. As I had, as yet, done nothing in this realm, it was very hard. I still had a great deal to learn about what a camera is, and about cameramen. I had to make many tests, improvise many things. In this way, one day I had a little elevator installed on one of the great masts that carried the oriflammes, that would rise to the top and, thanks to my camera, was able to effect, at any given moment, a movement that I considered rather successful. The trouble was that my installation was considered very inopportune, for it bothered people and threw the harmony of the group into disequilibrium. Therefore my crew was turned out and my elevator dismantled. I was furious about it, for it had been hard work to install all that gear, but at any rate it was one of those occasions that enabled me to discover what may be done with a camera. But the great difficulty resided in the fact the events such as they were repeated themselves constantly, in the same form: there were nothing but speeches, marches, and mobs. It was thus infinitely harder than the Olympics were to be, harder to set the event in a captivating fashion; the nature of the event, itself, sometimes determined the fashion of seizing it. In any case, it was during this film that I acquired the experience that was to serve me for *Olympia.*

Following that, I had great difficulties with the editing, above all with the synchronization. For at that time good sound equipment was still rare. What I had had for filming and what I now had for editing were not among the best, far from it: the better equipment was already at hand, in the hands of cineastes much better known than I. In addition, I had to edit this film absolutely alone. I already had several notions about editing, having done the editing of the French version of *The White Hell of Piz Palu*, but the work I had to do here was enormous: very confining, very exhausting, above all for a girl, and almost all of it had to be done at night. I tried hard to get help but that was a lost cause.

For if I wanted someone, it was to help me. Not to edit the film in my place, not even to do a part of the editing. I had drilled the technical crew, formed it, but I couldn't form anyone to edit this material. Editing, outside of the rules, the current recipes, is not something that is taught.

CAHIERS: *Now I must pose a question, delicate but necessary: what have you to say about the troubles the film brought you and, more generally, about the accusations made against you?*

RIEFENSTAHL: This is not a thing about which I like to speak. Neither is it any longer a thing about which I am afraid to speak. But, doubtless, it was necessary for you to ask me the question . . . and, doubtless, it is necessary that I answer you. Very well.

Among other accusations brought at the beginning, was this: I had been Hitler's mistress. There were many others. I deny all of them, absolutely. All that anyone has ever been able to establish—and God knows after what research!—is that Hitler declared that I was talented. It happens that others also said so . .

What did I do that was political? I was not a Party member. I was someone who was well-known before Hitler came to power. I made infinitely more films before his rise to power than after. I had money. I was self-sufficient. I was, in 1931, already my own producer: "Leni Riefenstahl Studio Films" was founded before *S.O.S. Eisberg* was filmed.

Triumph of the Will brought me innumerable, very hard troubles after the war. It was, effectively, a film made to order, proposed by Hitler. But that was happening, you must remember, in 1934. And, assuredly, it was impossible for the young girl that I was to foresee what was going to come about. At that period, Hitler had acquired a certain credit in the world for himself, and he fascinated a certain number of people—among them Winston Churchill. And I, I alone, I should have been able to foresee that one day things would change?

At that time, one believed in something beautiful. In construction. In peace. The worst was yet to come, but who knew it? Who said it? Where were the prophets? And why should it have to have been me, to be the one? How could I have been better informed than Winston Churchill who was still declaring in '35–'36 that he envied Germany its Fuhrer? Could this be required of me?

Of whom else was it required? Many, many cineastes were shooting films then and many others accepted commissions. But none of them were accused as I was. Not one. Only me. Why? Because I am a woman? Because the film was too successful? I don't know.

Here, however, I could begin my defense. But I have never defended myself in a public fashion and I am not going to begin now. There is also the proverb: Whoever defends himself accuses himself. This remains: a commission was proposed to me. Good. I accepted. Good. I agreed, like so many others, to make a film that so many others, with or without talent, could have made. Well, it is to this film that I am obliged for spending several years, after my arrest by the French, in different camps and prisons. But if you see this film again today you ascertain that it doesn't contain a single reconstructed scene. Everything in it is true. And it contains no tendentious commentary, for the good reason that it contains no commentary at all. It is history. A pure historical film.

CAHIERS: *But don't you think that the impassioned reality espoused by the film (a thing that necessarily is part of its beauty) implies, no less necessarily, a certain significance?*

RIEFENSTAHL: This film is purely historical. I state precisely: it is *film-verite*. It reflects the truth that was then, in 1934, history. It is therefore a documentary. Not a propaganda film. Oh! I know very well what propaganda is. That consists of recreating certain events in order to illustrate a thesis or, in the face of certain events, to let one thing go in order to accentuate another. I found myself, me, at the heart of an event which was the reality of a certain time and a certain place. My film is composed of what stemmed from that.

Moreover, it is difficult for me to think that in 1937, two years before the war, France would have awarded its *grand prix* to a propaganda film . . . That said, it must be recognized that the tribunals of Jews, Americans, Frenchmen admitted, in the end, that they had misunderstood, after the war, an important fact; that it was very comprehensible that one saw things before the war out of different eyes than after.

Be that as it may, we are henceforth sufficiently far from that period to be able to consider the film with a purer eye and see in it, as I said to you, as *film-verite*. From this point of view, the film had, from that time on, such importance that it introduced a certain revolution in the style of newsreels, which were then filmed in a purely static fashion. I had sought to make a striking and moving film. A poetic and dynamic film. But it was while working on the film that I began to feel that I could do that. Previous to that I knew nothing at all about it. Everything came from the rhythm.

If you ask me today what is most important in a documentary film, what makes one see and feel, I believe I can say that there are two things. The first is the skeleton, the construction, briefly: the architecture. The architecture should have a very exact form, for the montage will only make sense and produce its effect when it is wedded, in some fashion, to the principle of this architecture. But that has no value as a general example, for one may also arrive at showing certain things in the opposite way, by making the montage and the architecture discordant. Can one explain everything? Perhaps these things basically come from a gift that one has or does not have.

I told you, just before, that there were two important things. The second is the sense of rhythm.

CAHIERS: *Could you be precise about the nature of the connection between the rhythm and the architecture? What I mean is, are you conscious of the way the work as a whole acquires and maintains this dramatic movement that your films have?*

RIEFENSTAHL: In *Triumph of the Will,* for example, I wanted to bring certain elements into the foreground and put certain others in the background. If things are all at the same level (because one has not known how to establish a hierarchy or chronology of forms) the film is doomed to failure from the start ("Kaput"). There must be movement. Controlled movement of successive highlight and retreat, in both the architecture of the things filmed and in that of the film.

The ensemble must also be very precisely directed to the end that the strong points may be brought out (it should be noted that in many documentary films there is a strong point; not at the end but at the beginning); and, since you ask me how the film, without any pre-existing dramatic treatment, acquired a certain dramatic effect nevertheless, I answer by referring you to what I just said: This dramatization is part of the architecture. This holds true for *Olympia* as well.

CAHIERS: *Here we arrive at what the two films have in common: they both give form to a certain reality, itself based on a certain idea of form. Do you see something particularly German about this care for form?*

RIEFENSTAHL: I can simply say that I feel spontaneously attracted by everything that is beautiful. Yes: beauty, harmony . . . And perhaps this care for composition, this aspiration to form is in effect something very German. But I don't know all these things myself, exactly. It comes from the unconscious and not from my knowledge. I possess, in myself, a certain representation of things and events and seek to express it in images. What do you want me to add? Whatever is purely realistic, slice-of-life, what is average, quotidian, doesn't interest me. Only the unusual, the specific, excites me. I am fascinated by what is beautiful, strong, healthy, but what is living. I seek harmony. When harmony is produced, I am happy. I believe, with this, that I have answered you.

CAHIERS: *A little question now, before coming to* Olympia: *is it correct that you received offers on the part of Moscow?*

RIEFENSTAHL: Yes, that is true. I was asked to go and work in the U.S.S.R. Over there, they liked what I did very much. Only, I did not feel really capable of expressing myself except in my own country. I didn't imagine working anywhere else. I had to live in my country. That's all.

CAHIERS: *We are up to* Olympia. *What was your idea at the beginning?*

RIEFENSTAHL: First of all, it took me a long time before I knew whether or not I was going to make this film. My first interest in it was sports. I had done a lot and was always interested in it. In addition, thanks to *Triumph of the Will,* I knew the cinema. I wanted to make a liaison of sports and the cinema.

Once I had this idea, I started to doubt again, persuaded that this would be too hard. Everything hesitated, vacillated for a long time until, finally, I decided. After that everything went very rapidly. I immediately attacked the problem of the camera work, all the while telling myself that it would be nearly impossible to render the plenitude of the event on film. Thus I came, automatically, to the solution of doing two films, one reserved for gymnastics and the other for other sports.

After I had made up my mind to that, my interest was principally attracted by two things. The title of my book, *The Beauty of the Olympic Contest*, contains both of them. It implies first of all, from an individual point of view, the complete domination of the body and the will; after that, a great tolerance, introduced by the feeling of camaraderie and loyalty which is at the very heart of the contest. For, in such a confrontation, all men and all races must, for themselves and for others, give the best that they have. From this results an extraordinary atmosphere that is lifted well above ordinary life. This is what I sought to render. In the film, the human point of view and the aesthetic point of view are linked, to the extent that they are themselves already linked in the event, by the nature of the Olympic contest. The problems I started with were not resolved so easily. Among other things, it had become evident to me that the film could only be interesting on one condition. It would doubtless be possible for the camera to capture everything that could interest the spectator, but for that, it would have to take on the weight not so much of the event in itself, as in a newsreel, but the form ("Gestaltung") of the event. From that moment on, I began to look at each sport with the eyes of the lens.

Each time, it was necessary that I think about things in order to find the reason behind the camera's position in relation to this or that event. There was no principle at all that demanded that the camera always be one or two meters from the ground, that it always be far from the object or even on the object. Little by little, I discovered that the constraints imposed at times by the event could often serve me as a guide. The whole thing lay in knowing when and how to respect or violate these constraints. Thus, there were some perspectives that had to be respected. There were others that had to be found. At the time of a race, for example, we had installed a hundred meters of track, and the camera ran along it very well, but it seemed to me that the image of the race should be completed with extremely close shots. There was no middle course between extreme proximity and following the movement at a constant distance. As there was no question of getting close to the runner, it called for the use of a telescopic lens. I withdrew to find a vantage point. It was at this moment that

463

we began to employ the gigantic telescopic lenses that were to serve us from then on. It was the fusion of static shots, rhythmic shots and shots animated by technical movement that were to give the film its life, its rhythm. Thus, in the face of each problem, it was necessary to feel one's way, to make tests, and each test resulted in new ideas, some small and some big. For the horses, for example, we tried to attach the camera to the saddle, but in order to keep it from bouncing too much, it was necessary to put it in a rubber bag, full of feathers. While the marathon was in progress, we had a little basket on us, in which was a miniature camera that was set off automatically, by movement—all this was so that the runner wouldn't notice anything. And so it went, from idea to idea, for we always had to find new ones. This also provided us with as much amusement as possible.

I must say that we formed an extraordinary crew. For entertainment, as well as while working, we always stayed together, even on Saturday and Sunday. When we stayed in the tents, we talked, always letting the ideas come, and they always came. That's good practise. There were also nocturnal conversations.

CAHIERS: *It was said that your means were gigantic.*

RIEFENSTAHL: We had less than people said. Look at the photos and documents of the period: they give rather a feeling of improvisation . . . For the most part the effects obtained by our crew were improvisatory coups. Much obliged: people didn't know or it wasn't pointed out, how many things we discovered. The noiseless camera, made so as not to bother the athletes, was brought about by one of my cameramen, and the camera for underwater shots, by another. During this time we were looking for other tricks and even the most modest were made use of. Thus we had the idea of digging trenches (and it was very hard to obtain permission for this) from which we might film the jumpers, in order to give a better rendering of their effort.

The swimming pool, above all, inspired us enormously. We had a little rubber boat, the camera was on a little frame attached to the edge of the boat and we pushed this with a pole—oars being out, because of the motion. In this way we were able, during a shot, to start with a face, seen from close, and move off from it. There were also underwater shots, sometimes followed by emergence, shots made at water level, as well as shots made with the lens half-submerged. Naturally, this required a lot of very hard work on the part of the technicians, given the working conditions and the abrupt changes of light. For the ten meter dive, for example, the cameraman, after having set the focus in order to be able to follow the diver, dove with him, filmed him as he fell, filmed him under the water and came to the surface with him. Obviously, the focus was difficult to hold and the brutal variations of light didn't make things easier. In addition, the operation included, at the bottom of the pool, a change of lens. But everything had been carefully rehearsed in such a way that this could be done as rapidly and as mechanically as possible. Obviously, with these methods, for every 100 meters of exposed, 95 were no good.

CAHIERS: *I return to your great resources.*

RIEFENSTAHL: We didn't have gigantic resources for the good reason that we didn't have gigantic sums of money. Quite simply. And we didn't have gigantic sums for the good reason that no one believed that a reportage on the Olympic games could be a success. I had exactly 750,000 marks at my disposal for each part. A million and a half in all. And it was little enough, when you consider the quantity of film used: 400,000 meters—of which 70% turned out to be unusable. In addition, the tests, tentative procedures and improvisations that I told you about absorbed a lot of money. Beyond that: we had the problem of lack of experience with certain of the cameramen. We had engaged the best that we could, but for the most part the very best cameramen were out of our reach, as the big companies had a monopoly on them. Afterwards, the film's immense success allowed Tobis to recoup the money they had (imprudently, according to some) advanced. Several weeks after the opening the film was reimbursed; six months later, Tobis had taken in 4,210,290 marks and the money continued to come in. . . . But in the beginning no one believed in it and we had to arrange things so as not to go over the budget we had been allotted. Then, the cranes . . . we had, above all, ladders. They went from ordinary ladders to firemen's ladders. But we rapidly eliminated the first because they had an inconvenient way of oscillating. Zcheil, the cameraman who specialized in this type of work, often had a depth of field of no more than 30 cm (12" approx.). It is obvious that with the slightest oscillation everything would be ruined.

To off-set that, we had towers. Steel towers, set in the

middle of the stadium, from the top of which the camera-man could take in, and follow, the total panorama. This type of tower, used for the first time, afterwards appeared at other Olympiads. As for the balloons, yes, from time to time we had some. A balloon, during that period, was as ordinary as a helicopter is now. Except that directors had forgotten to attach cameras to them. We took care of that oversight.

The balloons in question were furnished with automatic cameras, which led to the necessity of running ads in the papers every day so that when they came down in Berlin, people would know they had cameras inside. With this system, out of a thousand meters of exposed film, perhaps ten were good. But they were very good. We had one just above the finish line of the sculls (which was equally assured by a 120 meter travelling shot). Unfortunately, at the last minute the games committee vetoed the whole operation. Sad end to an experiment . . . I cried.

As for the cameras, there was nearly always only one camera for one shot. But I remember that one time we were able to work with two big cameras at the same time: this was the first day of the games, when Hitler gave the opening speech. In the event of mechanical troubles there was no question of retakes for a shot like that. Therefore we had an auxiliary camera.

Here is the way our crew was composed. Six camera-men formed the principal crew—they were the only ones with the right to go into the stadium. Sixteen others (eight cameramen and eight assistants) took care of the trials that took place elsewhere. To which should be added ten non-professionals whom I had asked to mingle with the crowd, with little cameras, to get reaction shots. Thus, there were thirty-three people in all, who had to suffice for the shooting of all the trials, in all the localities in which they took place. Including the sequence in Greece. I can swear to you that my cameramen would have wanted to be a little more numerous! . . .

CAHIERS: *Certain people have said that you were aided, in both your documentary films, by Walter Ruttman.*

RIEFENSTAHL: I have never had either an artistic collaborator or a directoral collaborator. It has been said, in effect, and you have heard, that Mr. Walter Ruttman, who made *Berlin,* collaborated on *Triumph of the Will* as well as *Olympia.* To that I answer that I know—or rather knew—Mr. Ruttman well, but he didn't shoot a single meter of my films *Triumph of the Will* and *Olympia*. During the shooting of these films, quite simply, he wasn't there.

CAHIERS: *On the subject of these two films, exactly what happened between the project and the execution? What I mean is, what guided you in the concretization of your idea? Did you draw up a text? A sketch? A plan? ...*

RIEFENSTAHL: I didn't write a single page of text for either *Triumph of the Will* or *Olympia*. The moment I had a clear picture of the film in my head, the film was born. The structure of the whole imposed itself. It was purely intuitive.

Starting from that idea, I organized, then sent the technical crew out on different tasks, but the true establishment of the form began with the editing. I edited *Olympia* alone, as I had edited *Triumph of the Will* alone. This was necessary, for each editor sets his own stamp on a film. Experience shows that if two or three different people edit a film, it is impossible for any sort of harmony to emerge. The nature of my films demands that they be edited by a single person. And that person must be the one who had the idea for the film, who was looking for precisely such a harmony. Harmony would not be born out of another montage.

For *Olympia* I spent, I lived in the editing room for a year and a half, never getting home before five o'clock in the morning. My life was tied to the material and the film. In my editing rooms, I had glass partitions built, on each side of which I hung filmstrips that went down to the floor. I suspended them one next to the other, very regularly, and I went from one to the other, from one partition to the other, in order to look at them, compare them, so as to verify their harmony in the scale of frames and tones. Thus, in the long run, as a composer composes, I made everything work together in the rhythm.

But I had to make many tests. I made and I unmade. Sometimes I would change a detail in function of the ensemble, sometimes the whole ensemble in function of a detail, for where one left off, the other began. In this way, I was able to establish that with the same material, edited differently, the film wouldn't have worked at all. If the slightest thing were changed, inverted, the effect would be lost. Therefore, I was engaged in a continuous struggle to arrive at what I wanted. I wanted the film to have, silent, a dramatic efficacity. For the rest, I refer you to what I

467

said concerning the relationship between the editing and the architecture of the film.

However, I am going to try to be precise about certain things, although all that is very hard to explain. It's a little like the foundation of a house. There is, first of all, the plan (which is somehow the abstract, the precis of the construction); the rest is the melody. There are valleys, there are heights. Some things have to be sunk down, some have to soar. And now, I am going to be specific about another thing; this is that as soon as the montage takes form, I think of the sound. I always have a representation inside of me and I always take every precaution so that the sound and the image never total more than a hundred percent. Is the image strong? The sound must stay in the background. Is it the sound that is strong? Then the image must take second place to it. This is one of the fundamental rules I have always observed.

CAHIERS: *You said a little while ago that* The Blue Light *foretold your destiny. Do you want to clarify what you meant by that?*

RIEFENSTAHL: I was thinking of this: in *The Blue Light,* I played the role of a child of nature who, on the nights of the full moon, climbed to this blue light, the image of an ideal, an aspiration dreamed of, a thing to which each being, above all when young, ardently desires to attain. Well, when her dream is destroyed Yunta dies. I spoke of that as my destiny. For that is what was accomplished, much later, in me, after the war when everything collapsed on us, when I was deprived of all possibility of creating. For art, creation—this is my life, and I was deprived of it. My life became a tissue of rumors and accusations through which I had to beat a path; they all were revealed to be false, but for twenty years they deprived me of my creation. I tried to write, but what I wanted to do was to make films. I tried to make films, but I couldn't. Everything was reduced to nothingness. Only my vocation was left. Yes, at that moment, I was dead.

But if I was able to be reborn, I must thank the fate that led me, in 1956, to Africa. There, I found my ardor again, and my vital force of times gone by.

CAHIERS: *At the beginning of the war, you had begun a film:* Tiefland.

RIEFENSTAHL: Just before the war, I was preparing "Penthesilea." When the war started, I began *Tiefland.*

Why I made *Tiefland*, why was the shooting so prolonged and finally interrupted: I am going to tell you this.

When the war broke out, I was offered very important political films to do. Dr. Goebbels wanted me to make a film on the press that would have had for title: "Sieg der Grossmacht" ("Victory of Power"), and I was sounded for films on the Western Front as well. I refused. I had good reasons. After that, I made up my mind to escape into the ancient romantic ages. I took an old Spanish play and an opera by Eugen d'Albrecht as pretext for *Tiefland*. But, for this romantic and harmless opera of the highlands, I was absolutely denied the support that would willingly have been granted me for the other films. In any case, everything went for the war. Also, I was obliged to interrupt my work often, once for two years. Then I had to let the people I had with me go. One by one. Soon I no longer had anyone. And in this way the war came to its term before my film came to its term.

CAHIERS: *Since the war, have you seen many films?*

RIEFENSTAHL: I continue to go to the cinema very rarely. Shortly after the war, I saw *Forbidden Games* by René Clement, which pleased me very much. I liked Cayatte's films. But above all I like Clouzot. There is also another film I liked very much: *Diary of a Country Priest,* by Robert Bresson. As for the New Wave, I have hardly seen anything except *Breathless,* which pleased me enormously.

CAHIERS: *Since the war, what have you done?*

RIEFENSTAHL: It's very simple: '45-'48, diverse camps and prisons. From '49 to '53, I was engaged in a struggle for my rehabilitation and I retrieved my films, which had been dispersed, in Paris and in Rome (but in Rome, a misfortune occurred: the negative to *Triumph of the Will* disappeared, as if by magic, on the train). In '51-'52, I established the Italian version of *The Blue Light,* with new editing and new music. In '54, a circuit of Germany and Austria to present *Tiefland*. In 1955, I succeeded in preparing to shoot a mountain film, in color, but the operation failed. In 1956, Africa; in 1957, Spain (where I wrote three scenarios: "Three Stars in the Mantle of the Madonna," "Light and Shade" and "Dance of Death"); in 1958-'59, I did a tour of Germany with *Olympia*. In 1960 I was in London where I wrote, with two English scenarists, a remake of *The Blue Light,* as a ballet. In 1961, Africa again; in 1962-'63, still Africa and in 1964, I meet you, who question me, in Berlin, then in Munich, but never about Africa. Why?

CAHIERS: *We'll come to that in a little while. For the moment, I would very much like you to speak of those two big projects that miscarried: "Penthesilea" and "Voltaire and Frederick."*

RIEFENSTAHL: Good. The story of "Penthesilea" had a specific reason for being. During the period when, still very young, I didn't know that one day I would become a cineaste and saw myself as remaining a dancer for life, I made the acquaintance of Max Reinhardt. When he saw me he cried, "I have finally found my Penthesilea!" At that time, I had no idea at all of what this could be, but I set about informing myself, and then I knew who the Queen of the Amazons was and who Heinrich von Kleist was. From that moment on, I began to seriously read everything concerning this Queen, everything by Kleist (I read all of his work, while I was at it), as well as everything by the Ancients. I thus read a great deal, and what I read was very curious and very remarkable. The more so since, at the outset, I experienced a particular feeling: Penthesilea and I formed an indivisible entity. Each of her words, each of her expressions—I had the feeling of having already lived them myself.

It was then that I made the acquaintance of another theatre director: Tairoff (who had just directed "Girofle-Girofla"); and Tairoff, too, as soon as he saw me, cried, "Penthesilea!" . . . Decidedly . . . Well at that point, there was already talk of making a "Penthesilea" in which I would have acted, but it would have been a silent film. In my opinion, the film would have lost its *raison d'etre*, for the most beautiful thing in it was Heinrich von Kleist's language. However, the idea stayed with me and, after *The Blue Light*, I envisaged concretizing it. Shooting "Penthesilea" became my greatest desire.

Years went by before things began to take shape. But in the end, I had lived with that story for so long that I felt mature enough to give it its proper style. I was persuaded that Kleist's "Penthesilea," in full, could be filmed. There was a moment when I had the idea of filming the play in a reduced version, but no: it was necessary to keep everything. As a play, it is made for the ear. As a film, it could be concretized with a stylized architecture that would give the word its full resonance. The representation I had of "Penthesilea" called for an action of image, decor and frame that would be the equivalent of verse; a rhythmic unity.

Do you know the film by Emil Jannings, after a play by Kleist, called *The Broken Jug* (The Cracked Jug?)? It is an excellent example of what shouldn't be done. The film begins, in a realistic fashion, in a room. But when you show an ordinary room in a film, with ordinary furniture, like a bed, and on this bed there is a man who suddenly starts speaking in verse, you have a rupture that ruins everything. On the contrary, it should have been possible in "Penthesilea," with the step back in time implied by the play, to make the verse correspond to the spirit of the times, at least such as we imagine them in mythical recreation. This authorizes a super-dimensional representation in the stylization, in the spirit in which the verse itself constitutes a stylization. From this one could obtain unity, harmony: what I am looking for.

I don't really see the film in studio decors. I see nature. But nature magnified. There would be, for example, the sun, the real sun, but ten times as big. A tree, a real tree, with branches, but enlarged ten times. And in the middle of all that, the face, and the characters, but each at another level. And without ever forgetting that the language, it too, must be composed with the images in terms of the harmony.

And now, "Voltaire and Frederick." This concerns another very dear project, and this was done with the complicity of a very dear friend: Jean Cocteau. I made his acquaintance shortly after the war, in Kitzbuhel, where he had gone for a rest, and I was very happy when he said he liked my films. A friendship developed between us and even the beginning of a collaboration, since he did the French adaptation of the dialogue for *Tiefland*. After we had met several other times, in both Munich and Paris, he told me about a marvelous idea: "Leni, I would like to realize, under your direction, a desire I've had for a long time. I would very much like to play a double role, that of Voltaire and Frederick the Great, and the film would have as its title, let us say, 'Voltaire and Frederick.'"

I was filled with enthusiasm. We began to construct the thing right away, and an exchange of letters developed between us on this subject. His were signed "Voltaire and Frederick" and, sometimes, "Voltaire, Frederick and Jean" —which gave him the impression of playing three roles instead of two. Soon, we began to write the scenario. I met him on the Riviera for that and we set ourselves to writing. Our idea was to make a film that would have for background Germano-French relationships (this pretended Franco-German hatred), expressed in the form of light parody. Unfortunately, death did not leave this marvelous master the leisure to lead our project to a good end.

CAHIERS: *Now I ask you about Africa. What did you do there, what are you counting on doing there?*

RIEFENSTAHL: When the cinema became practically forbidden to me, I started taking photographs. And, when I discovered Africa, I took them only as a function of my interest in Africa. I started with Kenya and Tanganyika. I was carried away. After that I started, with a friend, to write a documentary fiction: "Black Cargo," whose theme was the contemporary slave traffic. I submitted this project to the London Anti-Slavery Society.

Then I had a little misadventure. We were travelling with some foresters towards Northern Kenya to mark some decors there when our Landrover fell into a dry river-bed. I had a compound fracture of the skull and some broken ribs. I had to stay in the hospital in Nairobi for some time.

It was there that, after I got better, I pursued the writing of the scenario. Everything went quickly, and, in the autumn of '56, we were ready to begin. We were doing test shots when another misfortune arrived: the Suez war. All of our equipment was on a boat that spent two months getting through the canal. When we finally recovered it, the rainy season had come. We had to do 2,000 km., with our cars, from the Pacific Ocean (?Atlantic?) to the Congo, but the trip cost us so much in time and money that, when we arrived, there was no longer enough money to do the film. Therefore I took a plane for Germany, in order to talk with a distributing company, with the aid of my associate. But on my arrival I learned that this one had just fallen into a ravine with his car, in Austria. He had to stay in the hospital for several months, between life and death. My plan had come to nothing.

But I still had a nostalgia for this country, I made other plans, and in 1961, I set out again. I had found new friends with whom I was to make a documentary on the Nile. I profited from this by coming to know Uganda, the Sudan and East Africa. When I returned to Germany, to organize the definitive expedition, everything looked good. Unfortunately, the day after I arrived in Berlin, the wall started to be built. My associate had business interests in Berlin. They underwent repercussions. The source of money had dried up again.

Today, in November '64, in Munich, I am making preparations for another expedition. Object: the Sudan. Shooting time: November '64 to June '65. But I have had to resign myself to 16 mm.

All this represents an exhausting, hellish, enormous work, but it is in this way that my life is beginning again.

The departure is set for the day after tomorrow.

Leni Riefenstahl (1902–   ):
Filmography:
1931—Das Blaue Licht (The Blue Light). 1934—Victory of Faith, Triumph of the Will. 1936—Olympia. 1945—Tiefland.

Roberto Rossellini

Roberto Rossellini had directed three obscure wartime films—La Nave Bianca, Un Pilote Ritorna, L'Uomo Della Croce—*before he emerged on the world scene with his neo-realistic classics,* Open City, Paisan, *and* Germany Year Zero. *Then he went into a Magnani-Cocteau period with* The Miracle, The Human Voice, *and* The Infernal Machine *before the advent of Ingrid Bergman in* Stromboli, Europa 51 (No Greater Love), Strangers, Joan at the Stake, *and* Fear. *During his Bergman period, he also directed* Flowers of St. Francis, Dov'E La Liberta, *an episode in* The Seven Deadly Sins (Envy), *and* We Are the Women (*with Bergman*). *Except for the brilliant, scandal-provoking documentary,* India, *Rossellini was off the screen for five years before making his comeback with* General Della Rovere, *a patriotic success, followed by* Era Notte a Roma, *Stendhal's* Vanina Vanini, *and* Viva Italia! *The most Catholic of all directors, Rossellini has always been obsessed by the inner miracles of human personality. In his oddly stylized treatment of the Honneger-Claudel* Joan at the Stake, *Rossellini sends Ingrid Bergman awkwardly soaring into Heaven, a fitting climax to his cinematic conversion of the actress into a saint. Rossellini has confronted death as a metaphysical experience with none of the histrionics of Visconti, the despair of Antonioni, the emotional causality of Fellini. The final death-images of Magnani in* Open City, *the partisans in* Paisan, *the prostitute in* Europa 51, *and De Sica in* General Della Rovere *possess a formal dignity unique in world cinema. However, like most mystics, Rossellini sacrifices fact for truth, and the ambiguities of the human condition often elude*

474

*him. With Chaplin and Bunuel, he stands apart from the
other artists of his time, irritating, inimitable, and indispensable.*—A.S.*

*Would you say it is true that you have kept aloof from the
neo-realist movement to which almost all other Italian directors have rallied?*

Yes, from a certain type of neo-realism; but that depends on what one means by the word. You know that
during a congress at Parma on neo-realism there was a
great deal of discussion of the term, but it still remains
ambiguous. Most of the time it is hardly more than a label. For me it is above all a moral standpoint from which
to view the world. Afterwards it becomes an aesthetic
standpoint, but the point of departure is definitely moral.

It is generally thought that with Stromboli *your work
underwent a change in orientation.*

That might be true; but then it is difficult to be a com-
petent judge of one's own work. As for me—not that I
think it any great merit—I feel I am very consistent in this
film. I believe I am still the same human being and that I
still see things in the same way. But one can't help becoming interested in other subjects and problems and trying
new directions; one can't forever shoot films in bombed
cities. We all too often make the mistake of letting ourselves be hypnotized by a certain milieu, by the atmosphere of a certain moment. But life has changed, the war
is over, the cities have been reconstructed. What we
needed was a cinema of the Reconstruction; perhaps I
wasn't quite capable of producing it. . . .

That is, of course, the theme that you develop in Germany Year Zero *as well as in* Europa 51; *isn't there in
these two films a sort of pessimism totally absent from*
Open City *but already perceptible in* Paisan?

I am not a pessimist; to perceive evil where it exists is, in
my opinion, a form of optimism. People have reproached
me with being presumptuous in *Europa 51;* they were
shocked even by the title; for my part, I simply wanted to
say as honestly as I could what I felt about our life today.

* The interview by Maurice Scherer and François Truffaut with
Roberto Rossellini originally appeared in Cahiers du Cinema, No.
37, July 1954, and was reprinted in Film Culture, No. 2, Vol.
1, March-April 1955.

I have also been criticized for not offering any solution—but if I were capable of finding a solution, I wouldn't have made films, I'd have done something else. . . .

Personally we think that your conception of morality gives your work its whole meaning.

You may be of that opinion—but now allow me, in turn, to interview *you*. For the past several years critics have shown not exactly hostility but a generally unfavorable reaction to my latest films. Is it because I deal with subjects usually neglected by the cinema, or is my style not considered sufficiently cinematographic? Of course it isn't the ordinary film language; I do try to avoid the usual "effects" and to explore the medium in my own fashion.

Since we admire your films and feel we understand them, the attitude of those who don't share our admiration is almost as incomprehensible to us as it is to you. The novelty of your style undoubtedly led a number of our colleagues astray at first; but the fact is that some of them have since changed their minds; for instance many of those who didn't like Europa 51 *in Venice reacted quite differently when the film came out in Paris. . . . What can of course be misleading about your style is the absence of what are known as "cinematic effects"—you don't give special emphasis to important moments, you always remain not only objective but impassive; one gets the impression that you deliberately place everything on the same level of intensity.*

I always try to remain impassive; it seems to me that what is so astonishing, so extraordinary, so moving in human reality is precisely the fact that noble acts and momentous events happen in the same way and produce the same impression as the ordinary facts of everyday life; I therefore attempt to convey both in the same manner—a method with its own very definite source of dramatic interest. . . .

Since you feel, and we agree, that your work cannot be divided into two separate periods, one is led to admit that Open City *and* Paisan *must have been appreciated for the wrong reasons.*

Yes, and it may also be that I did not quite succeed in expressing myself adequately.

If you were successful in those two films, it doesn't seem likely that you would have failed in the others. We are more inclined to think there was a misunderstanding.

Before Stromboli *the ethic underlying your work was less discernible.*

Perhaps I do not always make myself sufficiently understood. If I were to throw in ten more details, everything in my films would suddenly become extremely clear. But those ten details are just what I don't want to add. Nothing could be easier than to make a close-up; I don't take any, lest I be tempted to use them.

. . . You can't imagine how many people, women especially, have said to me: "Mr. Rossellini, we expect a great film from you. But please don't show us such frightful things: I beg of you, make it a great film, but beautiful, too." A *"beautiful* great film" is not an easy matter. I doubt whether I am or ever will be capable of producing one. Everyone is afraid of tackling problems. The political struggle has become so heated that people can no longer think freely; they react only according to their own political convictions. The world is ready for a great transformation. I don't know what it will be, but I have great hopes, even though very little is being accomplished in the direction I would like to see. But unquestionably the world is ripe for something. Take for example *Don Camillo;* I'm not speaking of the quality of the film—which does not explain its tremendous success. What does explain it is the illusion it gives that everyone can come to an understanding. I am convinced that it is quite possible to find the point of moral fusion, but not that way—it's too easy. I found that film particularly shocking. In Italy we went through a political period of "l'uomo qualunque" (the man of the street)—a period in which the general feeling was that one should not attach too much importance to moral issues. I am not at all of that opinion; man must be a participant in the struggle—with a vast compassion for everyone, for himself, for others; with a great love, it is true—but still he must always stand firm in the struggle; I don't mean literally armed struggle, I mean the battle of thoughts—and above all one must be an example. But this kind of dedication entails great difficulties, requires a constant effort of the will and the conscience. That's why a film like *Don Camillo* enjoyed such an easy success—because it would be a relief to be able to forget all about the struggle, and *Don Camillo* gave the illusion that one could forget and everything would be all right.

You have acquired the reputation of shooting without a script, of improvising constantly . . .

That is partly a myth. The "continuity" of my films is always mentally present in me; besides, I have loads of notes; still, I have never understood very well the necessity for having a script, unless it is to reassure the producers. What could be more absurd than the left-hand column: "Two shot"—"traveling lateral"—"panoramic" . . . It is almost as if a novelist were to make a script for his book: page 212, an imperfect subjunctive, then an indirect object complement . . . etc.! As for the right-hand column, the dialogue, I don't improvise it systematically but write it in the early stages of the film; I deliberately keep it back until the last moment so that the actor—or actress —will not get used to it. This control that I exercise over my actors is helped also by rehearsing little and shooting quickly, without too many shots. One must be able to rely on the "spontaneity" of the actors. . . . In short, I would say that I don't work differently from my colleagues; I simply dispense with the hypocrisy of the script.

We are impatiently awaiting your Joan at the Stake *that you were going to shoot in Cinemascope.*

Yes, but I didn't shoot it that way. It is simply a color film, in Geva-color. I am very pleased with the result. It is a strange film; I know they are going to say that my introversion has reached its maximum point, that I have withdrawn from life. This isn't filmed theater at all, it is cinema, and I will even go so far as to say that it is neorealism in the sense in which I have always aimed at it.

Roberto Rossellini
(1906–   ):
Filmography:
1936—Dafné (short subject). 1937–1938—Prélude à l'après-midi d'un faune (short subject). 1939—Fantasia Sottomarina, Il Tacchino Prepotente, La Vispa Teresa (short subjects). 1940–1941—Il Ruscello Blanca (short subject). 1941—La Nave Bianca. 1942—Un Pilota Ritorna. 1943—Desiderio. 1944–1945—Open City. 1946—Paisan. 1947–1948—L'Amore. 1948—La Macchina Ammazzacattivi. 1949—The Flowers of St. Francis. 1949–50—Stromboli. 1951–1952—Envy (*Fifth Sketch in The Seven Deadly Sins*). 1952 —Europa 51 (The Greatest Love), Dov'E La Liberta. 1953—Ingrid Bergman sketch in We Are the Women, Viaggio in Italia (Strangers). 1954—Joan at the Stake, Fear. 1957—India. 1959—General Della Rovere. 1960—Era Notte a Roma, Viva Italia! 1961—Vanina Vanini. 1962—Anima Nera. 1963—First episode in RoGoPaG. 1965—Age of Iron (TV documentary). 1966—La Prise de Pouvoir par Louis XIV.

Josef von Sternberg

Although Josef von Sternberg's directorial career spans almost thirty years, he was a meaningful force in the cinema primarily between 1927 and 1935, an interval we might ironically designate as his Paramount Period. Until very recently, even his work of this period had not been seriously evaluated since the mid-Thirties, when movies were supposed to crackle crisply to the proletarian point. Sternberg was then considered slow, decadent, and self-indulgent, while gloriously ambiguous Marlene Dietrich was judged too rich for the people's blood—it was a time for bread, not cake. Paradoxically, Sternberg and Dietrich today look deeper and more dazzling than ever, while most of the cinema of the bread lines looks excessively mannered.

Even today, however, the art of Josef von Sternberg is too often subordinated to the mystique of Marlene Dietrich, with whom the director was associated in seven of his more familiar movies. Unfortunately, the Svengali-Trilby publicity that enshrouded The Blue Angel, Morocco, Dishonored, Shanghai Express, Blonde Venus, The Scarlet Empress, *and* The Devil is a Woman *obscured the more meaningful merits not only of these particular works but of Sternberg's career as a whole. In fact, the director's filtered feminine mystique neither originated nor disappeared with Marlene Dietrich, but ecstatically embraced such other photogenic features as those of Georgia Hale, Evelyn Brent, Betty Compson, Olga Baclanova, Esther Ralston, Fay Wray, Sylvia Sidney, Frances Dee, Laraine Day, Gene Tierney, and Janet Leigh. It is also part of the record that he made films before* The Blue Angel *and after*

479

The Devil Is a Woman. *At all times, Sternberg's cinema of illusion and delusion has transcended the personality of even his most glittering star the better to reflect his own vision.*

In a sense, Sternberg entered the cinema through the camera rather than the cutting room, and thus became a lyricist of light and shadow rather than a master of montage. He concentrated on the spatial integrity of his images rather than on their metaphorical juxtaposition. Sternberg's cinema, for better or worse, represented a distinctively Germanic camera viewpoint—from Murnau and Lang—in contrast to Eisenstein's fashionably Marxist montage.

The fact remains that Sternberg's work—being more visual—was more visible than that of most of his colleagues. Even with a mechanically meaningless assignment like Macao, *his visual signature smiles through the veils and nets like the Cheshire Cat à la Chautard. That he chose to come to terms with an often uncongenial creative environment simply marks him as an artist who preferred lighting up a small shadow to cursing the darkness.*

Even today, however, critics and audiences may be reluctant to endorse Sternberg's story sense. Apart from "classical" assignments like An American Tragedy *and* Crime and Punishment, *his plots seem far-fetched, his backgrounds bizarre, and his character motivations obscure, at least by conventional standards of storytelling. As in a dream, he has wandered through studio sets representing Imperial Russia* (The Last Command, The Scarlet Empress), *China* (Shanghai Express, The Shanghai Gesture), *North Africa* (Morocco), *Spain* (The Devil Is a Woman), *Austria* (The Case of Lena Smith, Dishonored), *France* (The Exquisite Sinner), *and Germany* (The Blue Angel). *Even his American locales focus primarily on the dregs or fringes of society, from the festive criminality of* Underworld, The Drag Net *and* Thunderbolt *to the bawdy, brawling backwaters and back streets of* The Salvation Hunters, Docks of New York, *and* Blonde Venus. *Everyday life, as such, seldom appears in Sternberg's cinema. His characters generally make their first entrance at a moment in their lives when there is no tomorrow. Knowingly or unknowingly, they have reached the end of the bottom, but they will struggle a short time longer, about ninety minutes of screen time, to discover the truth about themselves and those they love. Although there is much violence and* death in Sternberg's world, there is relatively little action. The various murders, duels, executions, suicides, and assaults serve merely as poetic punctuation for lives drifting to their destinations in reflective repose. Death in this context is less a conclusion than a termination. The paradox of violence without action is supplemented by the paradox of virtue without morality. There are no codes or systems in these dream worlds; the characters retain their civilized graces despite the most desperate struggles for psychic survival, and it is their poise under pressure, their style under stress, that grants them a measure of heroic stature and stoic calm.

Sternberg's films are poetic without being symbolic. We need not search for slumbering allegories of Man and God and Life, but rather for a continuous stream of emotional autobiography. Sternberg's exoticism is then less a pretense than a pretext for objectifying personal fantasies. His equivalent literary genre is not the novel, nor the short story, nor the theatrical spectacle, but the closet drama unplayable but for the meaningful grace of gesture and movement. There persists an erroneous impression that the art of a Morocco or a Shanghai Express consists of the magnifying of trivialities. Yet there is nothing trivial about the size of Sternberg's emotions, and nothing disproportionate in the means employed to express them, critics from John Grierson to Susan Sontag notwithstanding. Also there is conscious humor in the director's awareness of his own absurdity though some spectators still imagine they are laughing at Sternberg when they are actually laughing with him. The colorful costumes, the dazzling decors, the marble-pillared palaces merely underscore by ironic contrast the painfully acquired wisdom of the all too human prisoners of grandiose illusions. The limitations of this aesthetic are self-evident. An insufficient grasp of one's time and place is hardly a positive virtue even for the most lyrical poet. It is only when we look around at the allegedly significant cinema of Sternberg's contemporaries that we recognize the relative stature of a director who chose to write with a camera in the first person long before Alexandre Astruc's "camera-stylo" made such impious subjectivity fashionable, and such personal poetry comprehensible.*

* The Editor's introduction appeared in expanded form in The Films of Josef von Sternberg by Andrew Sarris, published by the

"THE MANAGER: Not at all. Your soul, or whatever you like to call it, takes shape here. The actors give body and form to it, voice and gesture. And my actors—let me tell you—have given expression to much better material than this little drama of yours, which may or may not hold up on the stage. But if it does, its merit, believe me, will be due to my actors.

THE FATHER: I don't dare contradict you, sir; but it is torture for us who are as we are, with these bodies of ours, to see those faces. . .

THE MANAGER: (Cutting him short and out of patience) Good heavens! The make-up will remedy all that, the make-up. . ."

—PIRANDELLO

The rice fields of Java remain in my eyes as if I had been there yesterday. Standing in the center of these lovely green stretches furrowed with quiet water are the most interesting scarecrows that can be found on earth. High over the rice on bamboo stilts is a palmleaf-covered hut, and long strings with hundreds of tiny bells reach from it to the far corners of these plantations. When the birds come for the rice, a graceful Javanese woman lazily stretches out a shining copper-hued arm and frightens the birds away with an eerie tinkle.

The actor is the opposite of a scarecrow—it is his function to attract. The easiest way to attract is to be beautiful. Arnold Schoenberg's wife once said to me with a good measure of unnecessary passion: "How can a person think and not engrave the face with ugly wrinkles?" Though this is far-fetched, it may not be entirely without foundation. It is not particularly necessary to think deeply, but it is, perhaps, superfluous for a handsome person to think deeply. Fortunately, the ability of an actor to think is not subjected to the same strain as his appearance.

The sing-song girl, wheeled in a festively lighted jinricksha through the streets of China, has a simple task. The girls who live on flower boats have a simpler task. They are not required to sing or to move. Not always is entertainment expressed in this primitive form. The rice-powdered geisha in Japan is many steps higher and often

Museum of Modern Art and distributed by Doubleday, in September 1966.

Josef von Sternberg's essay appeared in Film Culture, Nos. 5–6, Vol. I, Winter 1955.

has achieved enough grace and intelligence to make her charm and wit the prime essentials. The theatre tries to make use of all these values. Generally speaking, the original attraction of the theatre was carnal rather than intellectual, and is still so today.

But no matter how beautiful men or women may be, they rarely are content to live by looks alone, and the theatre has witnessed interesting combinations of beauty and intelligence. Beauty alone has little lasting effect and so, because of the necessity to interpret elements other than empty beauty, the stage accumulated many who were forced to combine a portion of brain with a portion of beauty.

Though the balance to date is strongly in favor of good looks only, we can observe side by side with it old age and ugliness. This would not be tolerated on the stage without compensating qualities. And we often find those who have grown old with countenances so noble that we know their possessors have worked hard to remove every trace of cheap sentiment. Even when an actor has an apparently repulsive face, his features, on closer inspection, have a baseness of classic quality; and in the ugliest faces are found twinkling eyes determined to present their masks relentlessly to portray the basest instincts for critical inspection.

Trained memories that know the classics, ability to simulate age or youth at a moment's notice, joy and grief projected by precise control of feeling, personal suffering forgotten to portray impersonal happiness; a vast army of actors and actresses lurk in every cultural center to carry out the innermost thoughts of dramatists, to whom few, if any, human impulses have remained secret. What sort of human being is this actor and how does he differ from those who form his audience?

The most essential qualification in an actor must be not to conceal himself but to show himself freely. All those things which move the engine of our life and which we do our best to conceal are those the actor must do his best to show. What we are most ashamed to acknowledge he does his utmost to accent. No corner is dark enough for us to hide our love, no stage is bright enough for him to display it. The idea of killing inspires us with horror—it fills the actor with celestial delight to hold a dagger or pistol in his hand. Death to us is not pleasant, but no actor I have ever known fails to relish the idea of showing the agonies of abandoning life, gasp by gasp. His life begins when the eyes of others are levelled at him, it ends when he exits from the stage. He is helpless in the face of flattery and dreams of applause when he shuts his eyes at night. He prefers being hissed to being ignored, and his private life can be an unpleasant break in his design for living.

These traits have been registered for many centuries, and often with little affection. Lucian writes in the year 122: "Take away their mask and tinseled dress, and what is left over is ridiculous!" Hazlitt in 1817: "It is only when they are themselves that they are nothing. Made up of mimic laughter and tears, passing from the extremes of joy or woe at the prompter's call, they wear the livery of other men's fortunes; their very thoughts are not their own."

A doctor I knew had many contacts with actors and told me that when he was much younger he had been constantly puzzled by finding symptoms of claustrophobia every time he was called in to treat an actor.

Claustrophobia is the fear of being confined in a closed room. He mentioned this to Sigmund Freud. Freud took the doctor by the shoulders and shook him like a puppy when he was asked why every actor had this phobia, and roared that everyone with claustrophobia becomes an actor.

It is related that when Sir Henry Irving heard that another actor was going to play Hamlet he exclaimed: "Good God! How does he know he won't do himself a grievous physical injury!" I should like to add that the audience, too, can be badly hurt.

Acting is not the memorizing of lines while wearing a disguise, but the clear reconstruction of the thoughts that cause the actions and the lines. This is not easy. In the finest sense of the word, the actor is not only an interpreter, and not only a carrier of ideas that originate in others, but himself can be (though not without difficulty) a good creative artist. He is the mechanic who can take the word of the playwright and the instructions of the director and fuse the two with all the complicated elements of which he himself is composed to give fluent voice to inspiring ideas, with an effect so strong that one is impressed with the meaning of even the simplest word. It is his function at his best to tear emotion and mind apart and put them together again in orderly condition.

The actor also can take the loftiest sentiment and make

it ridiculous, and he can take what apparently is an absurd idea and with it illuminate the most obscure problem. He can give us clear sight instead of darkness as readily as a flash of lightning can show what the deepest night contains. He can portray sin for us in its ugliest form and can purge any evil desire by depicting the brutality of the criminal and his tormented history. He offers us breathless excitement and thrill, no less strong because it is vicarious. He can take our thoughts into his body, and return them safe and sound when the curtain falls.

He makes us laugh at human stupidity, and though we prefer not to recognize ourselves, we always notice the resemblance to a neighbor. He can make us howl at the most powerful king, and make us respect a fool.

He can make the ugliest qualities attractive by investing them with charm and grace, and he can take a fine sentiment and deliver it to be absurd.

Those who sometimes stand in the snow and rain to see a tired actor, divested of his trappings and paint, come hurrying out of the stage door may or may not know that this exhausted animal has just pulled out of himself energy enough to swim the English Channel. But there are some enthusiasts who have sensed that it can be as heroic to struggle with brain and nerves as it is to conquer the elements and have been so responsive that they have carried the actor for miles on their shoulders to his home. They still do that to bull-fighters when the bull-fighter succeeds in making vivid the qualities of skill and courage. But a maddened bull is easy to see. Not so easy to perceive is the problem of the actor.

Life itself may often teach us little except discouragement, pettiness, and care, and we are grateful to those who recall our ideals and inspire courage and give us new and unsuspected strength. The actor can make us walk out of a theatre with determination to conquer our fears, and he can empty our bag of troubles as if we were newly born. The actor can make us aware of the beauty of something we have seen every day and until now thought ugly—he can make us feel as if we have never before really seen a human being, but he can also make us feel as if we never want to see another.

Some of us are partial to the idea that all the world's a stage with exits and entrances, but for the moment, I confine myself to the man or woman who is professionally known as an actor or actress, and who is paid for it, sometimes with bags of gold, though more often with copper pennies. The pay that an actor receives is not a measure of his worth and many a strutter, making as much noise as a sack full of tin cans, has become rich. The acquisition of wealth is a study in itself. Were quality valued according to income the armament profiteer would be the greatest actor. One of the startling tragedies in our profession was caused by paying an actor ten thousand dollars a week and not permitting him to act at all.

I have known many actors and actresses. Some of them were good and some of them were bad, but among the good ones I often found many despicable traits and, among the worst, fine qualities. I don't believe that actors are essentially different from others, nor that they all get on a stage, nor that they all remain actors. I do believe that they seek exposure more than others, and that a lack of self-esteem drives them to solicit praise and applause. The key to this behavior is the same as the key to the behavior of others—it is to be found in the first few helpless years of life.

Since I cannot discuss the great actors who were before my time, my observations must be based on those whom I have myself witnessed. I did see Sarah Bernhardt both on the stage and in films, but only when she was old and crippled, and I have seen all those reputed to be great since. Not always was I impressed. I have been moved and inspired by many lesser known actors and actresses on hundreds of different stages in many corners of the world. But rarely, if ever, have I been inspired or moved by a performer in the films, though I may have been impressed by the film itself.

There is a very important technical reason for this. On the stage an actor is sent out before an audience on his own, though he may be instructed to the hilt. But, once in front of the footlights, he must establish his own contact with the audience and build a continuity of action and thought. The destiny of his performance is in his own hands.

He can gauge the response of the audience clearly—or at least not disregard its testimony easily. He would be a fool to ignore the fact that an intended joke fails to gain response or that an exaggerated gesture is greeted with tittering. (I do not rule out the possibility that fools fail to achieve success.) He is the boss of his own body and of his own mind, knows without any doubt the direction from which he is being watched and himself relays directly everything he thinks and feels to the audience.

All this is not the case in motion pictures. Though the photographed actor is popularized and reproduced so that he can be adored in Bombay, as well as in Milwaukee, and, unlike the actor in the flesh, can appear in both places at the same time, this is accomplished by a mechanism which does not confine itself to multiplication alone. This mechanism not only distributes the actor like popular dolls turned out wholesale, but it actually makes those dolls look as if they could move and speak by themselves. A child, a shark or a horse is made to act the same way as a great actor—easier, as a matter of fact, since they do not resist so much. But whether children, animals, or actors, they are invested with an intelligence that apparently stems from them. In film cartoons, when a tail-wagging duck goes into action, the audience knows at once that behind it there is someone that causes it to move and squawk. When the ventriloquist takes a puppet out of a box, it also is accepted as a unit of intelligence, but the audience is not for a moment deceived about its being a dummy, though it may not care whether it is or not. But when a film actor, who undergoes much more manipulation than a duck or dummy, begins to function, he is judged, praised and condemned, even by our best critics, on the basis of being a self-determining and self-contained human being. This is not so. Actors are usually tricked into a performance not too dissimilar from the process employed by Walt Disney or Edgar Bergen.

In films we have a large assortment of actors with a variety of looks and talent, but they are as powerless to function alone as is the mechanical dummy before he is put on his master's lap and has the strings pulled that move head and jaw. I doubt if many are intensely interested in the mechanism that moves an actual dummy, and it is possible that no one is interested in the strings which move the stars of our day, but I am going to discuss the strings anyway, though they are tangled up badly, pulled by many, and laboriously concealed, after the movements have been made.

Though not wishing to imply that the result may be favorable, it is possible for the actor on the stage to select his material and to appear directly to the audience without any distortion of purpose. But this is impossible in films. Here a complicated machine extracts an essence from the

487

actor, over which the actor has no control. He can be superior to another in proportion to his personal superiority, but his ultimate importance is regulated by manipulators who demand and receive a pliability which, given graciously, results in his advancement, and given reluctantly, causes him to be discarded.

In Paris, the artists lovingly employ a phrase of Cezanne's "Le bon Dieu est dans le détail." May that be my justification for going into detail, even where detail may be unpopular. The more I ponder on the problems of the artist, the less they resemble the problems of the actor.

Though the actor in the theatre and in films is interchangeable, and can even be active in both mediums at the same time, there are some generally observable distinctions. On the film stage, in contrast to the theatre, the actor rarely knows where the audience is going to be nor usually cares. Often three cameras are aimed at him from three different directions. He can note (to his surprise) a camera leveled at him from ten feet above and a camera looking at him from the ground, both from opposite directions and both recording his movements simultaneously. If he communicates with the camera attendant, he can persuade him to define what parts of his person will be included. He, himself, can never judge whether he is close or if his whole body is seen, since the determining factor is not his distance from the camera, but the focal length of the lens used.

His face is so enlarged that its features may no longer be viewed without discomfort. An inadvertent light can make his nose look like a twisted radish, or it can completely obliterate the expression of his eyes, which usually is a mercy. Though the actor normally is made to look better than he is, the bad use of a lens or the camera placed at a bad angle can produce an effect over which he has no control.

His voice can be garbled beyond recognition by the sound apparatus (unfortunately, it usually is only reproduced), and he can be made voiceless by the dangling microphone swinging in a direction in which he cannot aim his words.

No accumulation of emotion or continuity of thought is easy, if at all possible, to the film actor, as the technique of making a film is such that it sometimes requires the player to enter his house from the street three months after he made the street scene, though afterwards the action on the screen takes place in sequence. The exigency of film production may require the street scene to be taken on the sixth day of October and the scene of the house which we see him enter a second later on the fifth of January the following year. (That shrewd arrangement is called a schedule.) The actor has the most extraordinary difficulty in remembering what sort of necktie he wore three months ago, without adding to his concern exactly what he thought or felt. Notes and drawings on the pattern and color of his necktie help a little.

If he is a genius and gifted with great memory, even then he is at the mercy of the instructions given him by whoever happens to be the most convincing person around. The most convincing person is usually the property-man, the script-girl, his servant, or the boy who measures the distance of his nose from the camera.

I have been asked often why it is necessary to be disconnected in the making of a film. Why cannot a film be taken in continuity so that the distressed actor will know precisely what he is doing? Aside from the fact that there is rarely room enough to put up all the sets at once, or to construct, let us say, a replica of a street to connect with the house which the actor must enter, a film takes from four weeks to an occasional six months to complete. It usually takes an hour and a half to show the finished work. Somewhere in this loss of time you will find the reason for not making a film in continuity. It takes time to build sets, to place the camera and the lights, and to instruct the actors, though this last function is considered wasteful by all but a few directors.

No longer a new medium, the film has absorbed countless men who have attempted to find better ways to good results, and uninterrupted continuity of action has been found too difficult. The actor in motion pictures, as on the stage, is told what to do, but there is no dress rehearsal before an audience, nor a collective tableau to give him any indication that he has been told the right thing. Only the finished product reveals that—and then clearly.

But the finished product is not finished with the actor, but with a pair of scissors. These are flourished afterwards by someone who has little idea (usually none) of what was originally intended, and he can remove the most precious word from the mouth of the actor or eliminate his most effective expression. This posthumous operator, known as a cutter, literally cuts the actor's words and face.

He can make a stutterer speak rapidly and a person of slow thought think quickly. He can also reverse that process and does not hesitate to do this often. He can change the tempo and the rhythm of the actor's walk and his purpose. He can retain pieces of the performance which the actor fails to consider essential because at that moment he was no longer acting, but thinking of lunch; and with an easy snip of the shears, he can destroy the one expression the actor valued most—or the phrase he thought would make him immortal.

He can retain pieces which make hands and legs look like slabs of blubber (physical distortions are less ridiculous than mental ones), and he can cause the most thoughtless women in the world to think by retaining parts of her anatomy that she planned to conceal.

Not only does the cutter cut, but everyone who can possibly contact the film, even including the exhibitor who is to show it, has plans and often the power to alter the film. Actually were each one permitted to exercise his genius for improving a film, nothing would be left but the title, and that is usually debated, too, until the night before the film is shown.

Far from being responsible for his own performance, the actor cannot even be quite certain that the final result will not disclose the use of a double or even a voice which is not his. In any form of physical danger, usually featured in the motion picture, the actor is replaced by someone who is supposed to look like him, and though the actor often is willing to take the physical risks himself (rather than the mental ones), the producer is not so willing since a bodily injury means delay. As for the voice, he may for some reason be unable to sing, or what is more common, be unable to talk.

I have myself replaced the voices of many actors with their own voices from other scenes and in many cases have replaced their voices with the voices of other actors, thereby using the voice of one man and the face of another. Though this is not usual, it can always be done and is to be recommended. (The ideal film will be a synthetic one.)

In *An American Tragedy*, I replaced the voice of the man who played the important part of the judge in the famous trial. This man was not a bad actor, but only too late did I discover that his diction betrayed an accent which was inconsistent with the intended portrayal. I was asked afterwards how I had failed to notice this accent. I confessed my fault but pleaded that the actor had impressed me by not speaking when I met him. Rather than replace the actor himself and hurt his feelings, I replaced his voice, without anyone being the wiser for it except the actor, who must have experienced no mean surprise to see his mouth open and speak with a voice not his. This process is called "dubbing" and is extensively used.

I have corrected faulty diction and exaggerated sibilants by using pen and ink on the sound track that runs with the film; and it has been announced that someone had succeeded in writing on the sound track markings so skillfully resembling the photostatic image of words that, when projected, the human language was heard. Imagine writing the sound of a human language with pen and ink—or changing the human language not only with pen and ink, but with the slightest twist of a dial or alteration of speed raising or lowering the pitch of a voice.

Since few are dissatisfied with the voices of our popular actors, little such manipulation is normally indulged in, but ample sections of speech are always eliminated without the actor's participation, and every actor has been asked to make what is known as "wild track," sometimes by telephone. This "wild track" is made to be placed in some section of the actor's performance when his back is turned or when he accidentally waves a hand so that it looks as if he were talking. This "wild" part is usually some tender sentiment that has been omitted by the author or director and which is now recorded separately and then injected into the image of the actor. But normally the voice and body of the same actor are used, though long after he has finished he may be recalled twenty times by twenty different men to patch up something which afterwards passes for a memorable characterization.

Personally, I have frequently been forced to cheat sentiment into the "finished" performance by concealing flaws and revealing meanings with sound and music (all this is done afterwards without knowledge or authority of the actor), and I have had no end of trouble disguising what is technically known as a dry mouth, which means that the clicking of the actor's tongue against the roof of his mouth is recorded so that it sounds like the clatter of hail. Such an actor has to be continually lubricated by having large quantities of water funneled into his mouth, which process does not improve a performance.

Intelligent performances have been coaxed out of idiots who have not been able to walk across a room without stumbling, and I have seen intelligent men and women made to appear like half-wits without their being aware of it until they sat in the theatre and beheld the transformation.

Though one can hold the film actor responsible for his person, one cannot hold him responsible for his performance. The more the actor knows about the films, the more he will realize his helplessness and seek to determine the selection of director, cameraman and story, and that process of ultimate demolition known as editing or cutting. But worse than that, until quite recently, not even the most prominent director, except in rare cases (where it could not be prevented), was permitted to cut the film since the usually anonymous producer had only this opportunity to actively participate as a creative craftsman.

Not many actors have ever achieved the position where they can control the factors which influence their career, and when they have, they rarely, if ever, have been able to avoid failure. The history of motion pictures is littered with the wrecks of players who achieved control of their own productions, though there have been two or three unimportant exceptions.

The average film actor, capable or not, prefers to be called upon to turn on his emotions like water from a tap at nine in the morning—emotions that normally take time to develop—and at the request of even the most incompetent director, the trained star or supporting player will, without too much questioning, laugh hysterically or weep, with or without the aid of tickling or glycerine—and be content in the belief that he is considered to be performing the work of an artist.

It is naturally easier for the actor of little ability to adapt himself than for one with great intelligence, as the system of producing films is more often than not a severe shock to anyone whose mind has made some progress since childhood. But an actor is not easily shocked, and so he goes about the task of learning, as swiftly as he knows, just where he fits into the crossword puzzle of films; how he can function best and how he can sneak past the controls. When he finally is so experienced that he manages to do what he thinks is best without authoritative restraint and guidance, the result is not good.

Not the system alone, but the intricate mechanism and

unavoidable complications are against the actor. Usually organized by men who have no sympathy with problems that require thinking, the confusion of the normal studio is ghastly. Everything is ordered except the work of those who actually make a film.

When the film actor enters a set in the morning, the chances are that he has never before seen it (he may even not have heard of the director), but five minutes later he is required to behave in it as though it were a home of twenty years' standing and to be familiar with every object. That is not very difficult. He is required to act as though he were alone, but from every possible lurking place electricians and other workers inspect each movement. They are indifferent to his problems and yawn at the slightest provocation, and he must purchase their tolerance with forced good fellowship. He soon is used to that, too.

He may be required to throw his arms around another actor and call him his best friend—without having seen this individual two seconds before playing such a scene. He is induced, and sometimes prefers, to play ardent love scenes to a space near the lens which, in the absence of the leading lady, who is reclining in her dressing room or still emoting in another film, represents her until she can appear. This doesn't bother him at all, for if the woman is present who for the moment represents the love of his life, she is asked to look beyond him or at his ears, as otherwise the camera, due to the fact that film lovers are not separated by normal distance, makes them both appear to be cross-eyed.

The actor is often not given a manuscript until half an hour before having to act a part (I am told there exist actors who read an entire script and not only their dialogue excerpts) and must take instructions like a soldier to turn and walk to the left or to the right, and be content with the assurance that he is doing nothing wrong and will learn more by and by. If he rehearses too long he is put down as difficult and his reputation suffers. But he never feels that he needs much rehearsal, though he does feel that the other actors need it badly.

With the exception of a very few, whose abnormality should be discussed in detail, I have never known an actor to spend so much time on the inside of his head as on its outside. Apparently, the make-up is really worth taking trouble with, and this phase of his interpretive ability is never neglected. I am considered a martinet because of my insistence that an actor listen to my instructions without dividing his attention with a close study of his curling irons, whiskbrooms, powder-puffs and "fan" magazines. But normally, the director will not insist on being listened to very closely (he may then appear to be delaying the schedule), and his performer lends an ear while the other is belabored by a group whose sole purpose it is to make his appearance ready for the ordeal of acting. Generally speaking, an electrifying statement like: "Come on, Charles, put this over and we'll knock off for lunch" suffices. Melting make-up is then patched with hasty hands, he is brushed off, hustled and thrust into lights which generate enough heat for a Turkish bath, and given those aids, he coolly portrays a man of the world while the perspiration runs down his back and puddles at his feet.

If the words he then has to speak in a superior manner prove too much for his memory, he reads them from a blackboard, which is placed out of sight of the camera. These words are usually chalked up by someone whose spelling is on the archaic side. Some of the greatest speeches in film history have been put together from thirty different attempts to read them. Sometimes these speeches have been pieced together from efforts to get the actor to speak them that ran over a period of a month. In showing such a speech afterwards to the thrilled mob, it can be noticed that instead of seeing the actor deliver this speech, say the Gettysburg speech, one hears the words while other actors are shown listening with open mouths. Their mouths are not opened because of admiration for the orator's memory.

No, in the film world the actor loves to be known as a man who walks on the stage, views the situation with an eagle eye, establishes quick contact with all and sundry, and then if his name is, let us say, Spencer, to be known as "One Take Spencer." He will value such a nickname more than a gangster who establishes his menace by being lovingly called "Machine Gun Kelly." I once had an actor who said to me while we were rehearsing: "They call me One Take Warner." It took all day to get him to say "Good morning." But to take a scene more than once, though the acting may be execrable, is to waste film, unless the actor fumbles his lines. Believing that every time he opens his mouth the audience will be staggered with delight, the actor is offended if it is intimated that placing words in proper rotation and breathing with relief after every comma is not sufficient to embody them with meaning.

But let me continue to describe this intellectual atmosphere. Peter Arno succeeded in epitomizing the whole absurdity of the usual film stage in a cartoon which shows an actor energetically climbing into the bed where his leading lady languidly reposes and being introduced to her by the director as he prepares to lie down at her side. Of course, Arno exaggerates, as the chances are that the actor will have to introduce himself. With some exceptions, actors do not mind that. What they do mind is being ignored. There are but few actors who like to hide. Recently I passed one who was recognized in a theatre lobby by a tourist who approached him and said: "Aren't you in the movies? Your face is familiar." The actor turned pale, mumbled: "My God!" and vanished.

But as a rule, the actor does not vanish quickly enough. Particularly on the screen, where a second often seems to be endless. The one who insists on staying before the camera the longest is the star-actor, and one would think that he ought to remember that he did not become a star that way. But being a star gives him prerogatives. When he portrays, let us say, an explorer, he will do no more than don the smeared uniform selected by the wardrobe, and then enter the stage not as if after an exhausting and dangerous journey, but as if he had just left his dressing room. The director who points out the difference in distance will not long remain his friend, I presume. (Directors are usually chosen by their ability to get along with actors, and with other less essential functionaries.) As for a minor player, who, for example, is to portray a monarch, nobody bothers much with him. He is practically booted onto the set by an assistant who, in addition to this doubtful method of inducing the proper kingly mood, has just shouted, "Hey, Emperor, what the hell is the matter with you? Didn't I tell you to be here on time?" The same actor will immediately assume the part of a noble ruler distinguished for his wisdom, and issue commands to a benign minister who, yesterday, played an apoplectic sheriff in a film in which the king was a horse-thief.

It is also easy to understand that striking story about the man with a real beard, who was called in hurriedly from the street because the director suddenly had the idea that he wanted a man with a beard to walk across a scene. The beard demanded to read the manuscript. The crew on the stage, the actors who were waiting for this man, the director and his staff, could not credit their ears. Why should a man who merely had to walk across a stage demand a manuscript? The extra, who needed ten dollars very badly, nevertheless insisted, and said that unless he read the manuscript he would not know how to walk or what its purpose was in relation to the story and therefore could no more walk than he was able to fly. It is a tolerably apt commentary on motion pictures that this inquisitive actor was instantly displaced by another beard which did not care how it walked or what for. I later heard that the first man shaved.

But it is not easy to understand why the motion picture actor insists on being rated as a creative artist. He may be a hero or an exceptionally charming individual with fantastic energy. He may be worth everything he gets, which in the long run is usually taken from him. He may be one who chooses this rash way of earning a livelihood rather than another, but creative art has other servants and other standards and is based on no such nonsense.

I was the first to deal with the film machine in *The Last Command,* in which the late Emil Jannings played the part of an extra. If anyone remembers this film of long ago, he might recall that Jannings, who had been Commanding General of the Russian Army, is propelled by fate to Hollywood and there chosen from the ranks of the extras to depict his own history. The picture ended with Jannings driven mad and dying in the belief that he was once more in real command. But this ending was poetic, like all my endings. The film actor is not driven crazy—he is driven to become the idol of millions.

And the length of time in which he retains his popularity does not depend upon him, but upon his stories, current fads—and his directors. The supporting players usually last the longest in their screen life because they do not carry the burden of the failures. They are selected according to types catalogued as fat, thin, monks, doctors, baldheads, beards, soldiers, detectives, diplomats, leg girls, emperors, etc., and heaven help the man who has once played a monk and thinks that on a better day he may be a doctor.

The star is typed as much as the supporting player and strongly identified with the part he plays not only by public and critic, but by himself (though one hears once in a while that some actor or actress aspires to play something that sounds better than the piffle that made him a star), so that he usually assumes the good or bad qualities for which he has been noted and is only with difficulty weaned away from them when another part requires other qualifications. The difference in Jannings' household when he entered it as a general and when he came home as a film extra was appalling. He would on one day flick the maids with his whip when asking for a cigarette and on the next plead with them in a broken voice for permission to enter.

The nature of his work in film does not allow the actor much energy for the contemplation of abstract virtue and he therefore seeks his praise where he finds it in abundance, and he will avoid any extraneous issues by talking only about himself or about his part and will not listen to others unless he knows his turn will come.

But there is a reason for this lack of balance in the flustered life of the film actor. It is induced by the abnormal demands made on him. He is asked to play a climax first and the scenes leading to it afterwards. He may play an ardent love scene on the first day of the production, and show how he casually met the girl, originally, after he played the father of her child. These acrobatics are strenuous and exhausting and drain nerves which are needed to restore normality.

Remarkable is the stretching of emotions which must be interrupted in flow by hours of preparation for each scene, and sometimes by the finish of the day's work which, likely as not, breaks off in the midst of complications that scream for completion, say: when an actor is told that someone followed his wife and saw her enter a hotel with a stranger and register under an assumed name. The suspense will not be broken until nine the next morning.

Failing to be guided by the director, the sole guide to which he will trust is whether he feels a scene or not. And no worse guide can be imagined. Acting is not quite so simple. Nor do many directors care to guide the actor, since they thereby assume a responsibility they may not wish to carry—nor do I presume that all directors are capable of guiding the actor.

But then the vital interests of the normal film actor are above acting. Though he will battle to have as many words or close-ups as the other, he will not inspect the content of the words or the meaning of the enlargement,

He will insist that his dressing room is as good as the other fellow's and that his lunch when he motors to location is at least as palatable as the director's, and that when he returns from location only those ride with him who think him irresistible.

Acting is not make-up nor is it memorizing words. Nor is it feeling a scene. An actor must not only feel but be able to guide his feelings, and his delivery must contain criticism and comment on what he is expressing. He must know when to restrain and when to let go and his intellect must always be in advance of his impulse. He must know why the words that he speaks were written and whether they were given to reveal or to conceal his thoughts. He must be able to listen to the other actor and to consider what he hears, and not merely think of his cue and then act in his turn uncolored by what the other has conveyed. His person may be less visible than the ideas he is expressing, and he must know when his image interferes with or represents these ideas. Most of all he must be in control of the effect he wishes to cause. His humility as a human being must be genuine and not coupled with false modesty because he feels himself to be important. There is no such thing as an important actor or an unimportant one; there is only the actor who gives full expression to the purpose to which he owes his presence. Wherever such a purpose is unclear or shallow, no actor can do anything but be likewise.

We observe how enthusiastic the performance is of someone who dances, skates, sings, rides a horse, or runs to catch a train. But that is only because in those cases the actor knows precisely what he is doing. When portraying a great emotion, the film actor rarely ever can do more than guess where it ultimately will be used—or which of the many attempts to squeeze it from him will finally be shown.

There is another man who may know where all these pieces fit and who is capable of determining what is required of the actor who stands on his stage and who, on occasion with the patience of Job, compels everyone to something which can resemble a work of art. But that is not the actor.

I therefore suggest that the motion picture actor cannot function as an artist, and will deal with him not as I might deal with the actor who *appears* to dominate the stage of the theatre, but only as one of the complex materials of

498

our work. Since he has been magnified in importance, you may detect a tendency on my part to incline in the other direction. My purpose is neither to reduce nor to increase his stature, but simply to study him. In order to do so properly, further analysis is necessary of the personalities who are literally multiplied into three or four hundred images, each of whom can attract a great audience and can return to the original fame and fortune such as is not gained by a statesman, a poet, a musician, a painter, a scientist, teacher and physician, or anyone else whose approach to his work cannot be reconciled with a failure to master his profession.

Josef von Sternberg (1894–   ):
Filmography:
1925—The Salvation Hunters. 1926—The Sea Gull, The Exquisite Sinner. 1927—Underworld. 1928—The Last Command, The Drag Net, Docks of New York. 1929—The Case of Lena Smith, Thunderbolt. 1930—The Blue Angel, Morocco. 1931—Dishonored, An American Tragedy. 1932—Shanghai Express, Blonde Venus. 1934—The Scarlet Empress. 1935—The Devil Is a Woman, Crime and Punishment. 1936—The King Steps Out. 1939—Sergeant Madden. 1941—The Shanghai Gesture. 1944—The Town. 1952—Macao. 1954—Anatahan. 1957—Jet Pilot.

Erich von Stroheim

> *There's rosemary, that's for remembrance: pray you, love, remember. . .*   Shakespeare: *Hamlet*

Being some personal reminiscences of von Stroheim, recalled from memory . . .

To the Countess Maeterlinck, *"I never took myself very seriously as an actor; as a director, yes—as an actor, no."*

Driving up Fifth Avenue on a rainy night—the long ribbon of green traffic lights suddenly changed to red, like a necklace of emeralds become one of rubies, reflected in the glistening asphalt. *"That would make a nice shot in a film."*

After sitting through all three acts of the play *"Arsenic and Old Lace"* in stone-faced silence while all about him were laughing their heads off, *"Oh, you know me—I don't find anything funny anymore."*

To the query why he spoke his lines in French films so slowly and meticulously, *"To stay on the screen longer."*

Republic Pictures was always referred to as *"Repulsive Pictures."*

"Did you ever read Charles Fort's 'The Book of the Damned'? You should—it's a remarkable book, all about natural phenomena the scientists can't explain. There are lots of things we have no explanation for. I believe in extra-sensory perception and all that, I absolutely do."

He'd bought a car but never learned to drive it himself. *"I can't think behind the wheel of the damned thing."*

Trying to get him to deliver a promised article by press-time for Klaus Mann's magazine *"Decision"* while touring one-night stands in *"Arsenic and Old Lace"* in the

500

Midwest, "Unless the Holy Ghost comes down and writes the article for me, which, as you informed me, must be in Klaus Mann's hands in a week, I won't be able to contribute for the next number. That issue will greatly suffer through it, but it can't be helped."

Of Von Sternberg: "A very cultured and intelligent director."

Of Lubitsch: "Lubitsch shows you first the king on his throne, then as he is in his bedroom. I show you the king first in his bedroom so you'll know just what he is when you see him on his throne."

Of Jean Renoir: "The only man who can outdrink me."

At the "21" club in New York, Chaplin catches his eye —they smile, nod, hesitate . . . who will defer to whom? As if there had never been any question about it, he gets up, excuses himself to us, and rushes over to Chaplin's table.

Whose work did he especially like in Hollywood? (The year is 1940.) "Milestone, Ford, Victor Fleming, Capra, Lubitsch."

In Europe? "Renoir, Pagnol, René Clair, Eisenstein."

What American pictures? "The Informer, Stage Coach, Of Mice and Men, Grapes of Wrath, Gone with the Wind, Mr. Deeds Goes to Town, Ninotchka, Our Town, The Biscuit Eater, Dead End."

European films? "La Bandera, Les Bas-Fonds, La Chienne, La Grande Illusion, Souls les Toits de Paris, La Kermesse Heroique."

What projects would he like to do? " 'The Diary of a Chambermaid' by Octave Mirbeau, 'Les Civilisés' by Claude Farrere, 'God's Little Acre' by Erskine Caldwell, certain stories by Maupassant, 'Paprika', by myself."

What happened to Walking Down Broadway? "Sol Wurtzel, one of the chief moguls at Fox, did not understand the story or the picture. After it was finished he had it rewritten, remade, and rebaptized. It came out as Hello Sister!—a 'B' picture. Sol Wurtzel wanted to prove to Winnie Sheehan that his (Sheehan's) judgment had been wrong in engaging me to direct during Wurtzel's absence. I happened to be in the middle of a feud between them."

He detested the German military roles of both world wars that economic necessity forced him to play. (There was one exception, that of Von Rauffenstein in La Grande Illusion.) He found it ironic that between the two world wars he should have made an auspicious career as a direc-

tor only to wind up playing the same antipathetic German officers he started out with, as if Blind Husbands, The Devil's Passkey, Foolish Wives, Greed, The Merry Widow *and* The Wedding March *had never happened.*

When he threw a party, it was a real party—not a few miserable canapés, second-rate rye, and potato chips surrounded by a group of simpering, gushing hypocrites. I recall one in New York replete with caviar, champagne, and sweetmeats galore to delight Heliogabalus, and a guest list as succulent. (Only Tom Curtiss, of the Paris Herald-Tribune, his long-time friend, mentor, and everything else good, including "father-confessor," outdid him once in this respect by throwing a party at the old Astor designed to bring Stroheim and Thomas Mann together as a prelude to discussions which he hoped would result in Stroheim's filming "The Magic Mountain." This was a wing-ding out of a Stroheim film, indeed.)

"The Wedding March," said Erwin Piscator, "is like a novel by Balzac."

A picture post-card from Niagara Falls, during a visit there, inscribed, "So much water and no whiskey!"

A chain letter, "I am sending you this chain letter because I believe in Paul Kohner, my agent, and the guys listed ahead of him, Joe Pasternak, Robert Z. Leonard, etc. (as you can see, the sucker-list is pretty melodious), . . . and because I believe in you . . ." (Someone must have broken the chain as he predicted it would be broken —but hope sprang eternal in those wonderful days . . .)

He wrote "Poto-Poto," his African story, with Dietrich in mind to play the role of "Roulette" Masha, a flashy blonde who "works" the boats plying the Red Sea, taking on any gambler, staking herself against the cold cash of her partner. She loses a particularly high stake once to a degenerate African trader, who takes her back with him as his mistress to a steaming little green-hell up river on the East African coast. An expanded French translation of this story was recently published in Paris.

He directed a practical joke once on a young doctor friend who went calling on his girl, only to be met by another girl in his fiancée's apartment who disclaimed all knowledge of the medico's inamorata, insisting it was her *apartment. The strange girl, playing it straight-faced, had her sinister aspects, certainly, under the circumstances, but what gave the situation its most bizarre touch was the fact that, save for a pair of slippers (and smoking a cigarette in a long cigarette-holder), she conducted the entire conversation completely in the nude.*

"R. H. Cochrane, vice-president in charge of publicity at Universal, after I finished Foolish Wives, *thought its production cost of $735,000 was so close to a million that he decided to call it, for publicity purposes, the first million-dollar picture. Universal had put up an electric sign on Broadway, changed weekly as the production cost 'mounted.' They spelled my name in lights as '$troheim.' A lot of good that did me!"*

He treasured a gold cigarette case that the cast of The Merry Widow *gave him when the picture was finished, inscribed with all their signatures as an expression of their love for him.*

Returning to France at the end of the war, a farewell party was held on the deck of a nondescript French freighter on which he was to voyage across, the big liners being not yet returned to passenger service. Turkey leg in one hand, bumper of scotch in the other, he grimly regarded a snarled coil of rope on the deck, a flagrant violation of one of the cardinal rules of the sea. "Just look at that," he said. "That would never happen on a German boat. Well, if you don't hear from me anymore, you'll know why." But he loved France and had only contempt for German junkerism.

How can one reminisce of Stroheim and not also recall the role played by Denise Vernac after his first trip to France, when he was called over to appear in Marthe Richard? *She came as a journalist to interview him and remained as secretary, major-domo, and ministering angel, cushioning him against the "slings and arrows" of the world. Rarely, I think, has a woman exhibited such selfless devotion.*

There never was a more valiant trio of "musketeers" than Denise Vernac, Tom Curtiss, and Stroheim, whom Paris knew so well during the past decade.

He recalled his start in Hollywood when he, "Bull" Montana, and Lon Chaney used to walk each day to Universal City, seeking extra work. "Because of our combined overpowering handsomeness, we were known as 'The Three Graces.'"

Asked why he so often wore an armband of mourning in films in which he acted, he replied with a heavy sigh, "I don't know . . . weltschmerz, maybe."

He could think of the most startling things. "Did you

503

ever make love in a steaming barn on a hot summer after-noon?"

By 1921, when the movies were still a wilderness, he had already directed three of the most sophisticated films ever made—Blind Husbands, The Devil's Passkey, *and* Foolish Wives.

"What were the lengths of your films as cut by you for their final versions and the actual lengths in which these films were released to the public by the producing companies?"
Answer

Blind Husbands .... *9,000 ft. released in 8,000 ft.*
The Devil's Passkey . *12,000 ft. released in 12,000 ft.*
Foolish Wives ..... *21,000 ft. released in 14,000 ft.*
The version at the Museum of Modern Art is 7,000 ft.
Greed .... *24,000 ft. released in 10,000 ft.*
The Merry Widow .. *12,000 ft. released in 11,000 ft.*
* The Wedding March *14,000 ft. released in 14,000 ft.*

He never won an Academy Award in Hollywood, either as actor or director, but France made him a Chevalier of the Legion of Honor.

His last screen role was as Beethoven in Sacha Guitry's Napoleon—*fittingly, too, for what Romain Rolland once said of the master of Bonn was as applicable to Stroheim: "Beethoven would not have been what he was were it not for his excesses."*

Plagued by illness; doing one-night stands of "Arsenic and Old Lace" ("I, who never could be sure of remembering two consecutive lines of dialogue!"); following up "leads" everywhere for a possible film role here, a possible directorial post there, most of which led up blind alleys; writing scripts, articles; beset by personal anxieties that would have tried the patience of Job—he nevertheless maintained touches of optimism glinting through the somber pessimism to which he had been brought by the chicanery that kept tripping him up. Despite that . . . he could close a letter jubilantly, as he did to me once, "Vivat . . . crescat . . . floreat!" Live, create, flourish!

* Stroheim was being generous—actually, according to the original script, there was more shot. The bordello scene alone was at least 1,000–2,000 feet longer than the released version. Also, this represents only the first part.

504

He wanted to show that the whole world was kin, that there was good and evil everywhere, and not always where we would expect to find them, and sometimes in the most surprising places. Human nature was compounded of contradictory attributes, which Dostoevski realized so trenchantly, and no Stroheim character ever ceased for an instant to be a credible human being, whether cast in the role of hero or villain. A complete human being himself, with the wide latitude that this permits, he observed human frailty as he would observe it in himself, with irony or compassion, depending on the circumstances, but never losing his sense of humor, which was prodigious and, more often than not, withering. Round and round went the eternal game of lust that fascinated him as a scientist is fascinated by the developments in research he is undertaking . . . lust for the things men lust for, the lust for money, for love, for youth, before which borderlines of nationality and caste crumble. Like Asmodeus, he soared over the rooftops of the world and peered into the windows, and what he saw there is partially discernible in the pitifully few fragments that were permitted to remain of his work by those whom he angered or made afraid. But he loved life, and it was this that the buffoons who tried to "put him in his place" did not understand, for how could they know that a man can have wings and rejoice only in the flight of his creative spirit?*—Herman G. Weinberg*

The following text is a transcription of Erich von Stroheim's introductory remarks to a showing of "The Merry Widow" at the Palais des Beaux-Arts, Brussels, November 28, 1955. Jacques Ledoux of the Cinémathèque de Belgique, who has provided us with this text, writes: "You will see that it was an unprepared speech, thus full of hesitations; furthermore it was typed by an employee who was satisfied in typing only what she heard."

. . . I would like to introduce to you my friend, my collaborator, Denise Vernac . . . (applause) . . . It is always a very bad sign when a director has to speak before one of his own films . . . (laughter) . . . be-

* *Herman G. Weinberg's tribute to von Stroheim appeared in* Film Culture, *No. 3, Vol. 4, April 1958.*

The transcription of Erich von Stroheim's speech appeared in Film Culture, *No. 3, Vol. 4, April 1958.*

cause he will be making excuses . . . and that is exactly what I want to do. I have many reasons for it and for asking your patience. In the first place, because I speak very poor French. Secondly, because this film, *The Merry Widow,* was made thirty years ago. It is a very long time. In those days we did not have the techniques and equipment we have today, for instance, lighting, color, sound. . . . And then, this film that you are going to see, this copy is a . . . (Denise Vernac: *"Contretype"* . . .) a *contretype* from a completely different version. This is a 16 mm. copy and it will be projected on a regular-size screen and for that reason the images will not have the sharpness of focus. . . . Also, we don't have music. It was necessary, this very afternoon, to arrange something during the last two hours. In the old days, the M.G.M. company had experienced composers who prepared scores for the theaters which had orchestras. The smaller theaters, naturally, had only pianos —that's all. Tonight we have a very intelligent, extremely . . . (Denise Vernac: "able" . . .) able musician who will do his best. . . .

Naturally, I like drama . . . tragedy. . . . But the producers do not like it. . . . They like only what brings money, and in my youth I hated money, although today . . . (laughter and applause). Therefore I never wanted to direct stories for infantiles like that . . . (laughter) . . . but because, before I embarked on *The Merry Widow,* I had made a great tragedy . . . when I say "great," I mean in length . . . (laughter) . . . and a great story. . . . It was not my story this time—it was one of the greatest stories written by an American, Frank Norris, a student of Zola. And this film was, as the company said, a complete, a complete . . . (Denise Vernac: "fiasco" . . .) fiasco . . . (laughter) . . . because it was not this company that gave me money to make the film but another one, which had supervised me during the shooting but which did not have a money interest in the film! It is very simple—the company did not give the film enough publicity and made it also into a financial fiasco, probably. However, for me, it was a great success artistically. I had always wanted to make a great film, a good film and a long one, too, with an intermission—at a psychologically suitable moment—to give the audience time for dinner as the great Eugene O'Neill did in . . . (Denise Vernac: "Strange Interlude" . . .) "Strange Interlude." He did it several years after me. I wanted to do it in *Greed*. . . . And I made the film. But it was too long for the producer, because he did not think about screening it in two sittings, as I did. So, the company hired a man who had never read Norris' book, did not know anything about my editing ideas, and was ordered to edit it . . . so he edited it . . . (laughter) . . . he edited it. . . . When, ten years later, I saw the film myself, for the first time, it was like seeing a corpse in a graveyard. I found it in its narrow casket among plenty of dust and a terrible stink . . . (laughter) . . . I found a thin part of the backbone and a little bone of the shoulder. And, naturally, I became sick, it made me very sick, because I had worked on this film for two years of my life, without any salary. Try to play this on your piano . . . (laughter). . . . Two years with a sick woman, with a sick child, very sick, with polio—and me, working without a salary on this film, for two years! At the end of the two years, I thought: If this film comes out the way I made it, I will be the greatest film director living. . . . But, when it was edited like this. . . . And, after all this fiasco, imagine, a producer coming to me and asking me to direct for him a film called *The Merry Widow!* He bought the rights to it for a great sum of money, dollars, not Belgian francs . . . and he had nothing for his money but the title, since the success of *The Merry Widow* was in its music. The story itself was ridiculous, or almost ridiculous. Naturally, I did not want to make it. And, besides, I had never had stars, because I don't like stars—both men and women stars. Particularly, women . . . (laughter) . . . because they have ideas. . . . When I direct, it is me who has the ideas. It is me who directs. So, to please me, the Company forced me to accept two stars, not one. Two! . . . (laughter) . . . Mae Murray, who always played under the direction of her husband, a very great man, very great, six-feet-three, and a very gentle man. I could make a comparison between a Saint Bernard dog . . . (laughter) . . . She, herself, if I may say so . . . was very active, very agile, too active . . . (laughter) . . . So this *grand* man and this little woman . . . you know very well who won the battle. . . . (laughter) . . . It was always Mae Murray, it was always she who won and the big Saint Bernard did exactly what his wife told him to do. But it was very different with me, since I was not married to this woman

. . . (laughter) . . . No. She was very gentle, but she had ideas . . . (laughter) . . . and, as I said before, I have ideas myself. So these two ideas . . . (laughter) . . . clashed. One time we had a terrible battle, during the embassy ball scene, and it was terrible because I had 350 extras in it who loved me very much . . . it was always the workers who liked me, not the producers—the workers . . . do you see the difference? (laughter and applause) . . . So this woman thought . . . it was after the First World War . . . and she called me "dirty Hun" . . . Naturally, I did not like it, since I was born in Austria, in Vienna, and since she was born in Vienna, too . . . (laughter). . . As a matter of fact, she was born in Czechoslovakia, but then I did not see much difference . . . (laughter) . . . and since my workers, my extras understood that this meant the end, they took off their uniforms and threw them on the floor . . .

I want to tell you a very, very strange story. You will permit me to sit down (he sits down on the podium). Thank you. Because this is a very strange story . . . (laughter) . . . I am very superstitious, also religious, and in many cases that goes together, as you know. I had troubles with Mae Murray, as I said already, and also troubles with electricity, lamps, with the helpers, with everybody. And it was strange, because it had never happened that way before. So, after the duel with Mae Murray, I was discharged by the company, but really . . . (laughter) . . . But I almost forgot to tell you my story. . . . Since I am very superstitious and a mystic, I used to visit a certain *voyeuse* (Denise Vernac: *"voyante"* . . .) *voyante* . . . (laughter) . . . So, before I started working on *The Merry Widow,* at the time when the company approached me, I naturally went first to my friend Madame Ora . . . (laughter) . . . She was an old woman, only an EAR, so I asked her what would be the outcome, should I make the film or not? She waited a little while, just enough to give the necessary weight, and said that I should "absolutely do it" because it will be a great feather in my hat . . . (laughter) . . . In California nobody wears a hat, and I did not have a hat—but she assured me of great success, a large feather, a beautiful plume in my hat, *bon!* So I started the film, I was discharged, and I came immediately, the first thing I did, to my adviser Madame Ora. I told her that I was discharged and that the president of the company had shown me the doors himself and that, in my turn, I'd given him a few words which he will never forget, and that I am in the street now. What should I do? And you have assured me that this will be a large feather in my hat! The Madame said to me: "Monsieur von Stroheim, I can't change my idea. You will continue tomorrow on *The Merry Widow*, you will direct it tomorrow, and it will be a great success and it will be a great feather in your hat." I said, "Madame, you have not understood me correctly. I am in the street . . ." (laughter) . . ."No. Monsieur, it is you who does not understand, it is you who does not understand. You will be continuing tomorrow morning." And this was at six o'clock in the afternoon. And she says to me, further, that now, this very moment, there are four or five men in my Los Angeles home waiting to see me . . . regarding tomorrow's work. I said, "But this is ridiculous, isn't it?" And she says, "They are in uniforms . . ." (laughter) . . . And it was the time of prohibition in California, and I, like a good citizen, had plenty of whiskey in my house . . . (laughter) . . . and a few whiskeys in my car, just like that . . . (laughter) . . . That meant this . . . (laughter) . . . the years not in a private prison but on the island of Alcatraz . . . So I hurried home and, believe it or not, there were four men waiting and they were in uniforms. But they were not policemen but from the staff of the company, sent by the president himself to speak with me, to ask me to continue work on the film the next morning! That was too much . . . too strange. During the night the president sent his men twice more, just to be sure that I would definitely be at work the next morning, at 8:30—counting thirty minutes for the peace talks . . . *Oui!* Madame Ora was right. I continued directing, it was one of the great successes of its time, and it was chosen by the critics of America as the best film of 1926. That, perhaps, is not such a great credit in itself, since, probably, the other films were very bad . . . (laughter) . . . At any rate, this film has made for its company four and a half million . . . though not for me. I had twenty-five per cent of it. How much do you think I received? . . .

I thank you once more and ask you to have patience because the film is thirty years old, this print is only a 16 mm. version projected on too large a screen, and I don't have the sound or the color or the cinerama . . . I have nothing. And so I have made all the possible excuses that I could think of. All the good things in this film were made by me. The things that are no good in it were made by others . . .

Erich von Stroheim (1885–1957):
Filmography:
1918—Blind Husbands. 1919—The Devil's Passkey. 1922—Foolish Wives, Merry-Go-Round. 1925—Greed, The Merry Widow. 1928—The Wedding March, Queen Kelly. 1932—Walking Down Broadway.

Preston Sturges

Acknowledged as the foremost satirist of his time, Preston Sturges enjoyed his greatest vogue between 1940 and 1944 when his pungent wit and frenetic slapstick exploded on such topics as Tammany Hall politics, advertising, American fertility rites, hero and mother worship. Within the context of a Sturges film, a gangster could declare with ringing, heavily accented conviction: "America is a land of great opportunity." An underpaid clerk could rise to fame and fortune by coining the slogan: "If you can't sleep, it isn't the coffee, it's the bunk!" A sign in a flophouse could remind its denizens: "Have you written to mother?" Sturges repeatedly suggested that the lowliest boob could rise to the top with the right degree of luck, bluff, and fraud. The absurdity of the American success story was matched by the ferocity of the battle of the sexes. In The Lady Eve, *when Henry Fonda plaintively confesses: "Snakes are my life," Barbara Stanwyck snaps back: "What a life!" The climax of* Palm Beach Story *finds Rudy Vallee serenading Claudette Colbert's upstairs window while the object of his affections is being seduced by the subject of hers, Joel McCrea.*

Sturgean comedy was influenced both by the silent antics of Charles Chaplin, Buster Keaton, and Harold Lloyd in the Twenties, and by the crackling verbal rhythms of Howard Hawks, Frank Capra, Leo McCarey and Gregory La Cava in the Thirties. Sturges contributed to this distinguished tradition mainly through the unusual density of his scripts. His films were noted for the hilarious side effects of character and bit actors. It was not unusual for a gravel-voiced bus driver to use the word, "paraphrase,"

511

nor for a hoodlum to invoke the ruinous symmetry of "Samson and Delilah, Sodom and Gomorrah." A stereotyped performer like Eric Blore was virtually rediscovered savoring the line: "I positively swill in his ale." Similarly, Edgar Kennedy was resurrected from two-reelers to play an inspired bartender reacting to a customer asking for his first drink ever: "Sir, you rouse the artist in me." The Sturges stock company was particularly noted for the contrasting personalities of William Demarest, the eternal roughneck, and Franklin Pangborn, the eternal snob.

Sturges was criticized at the time by James Agee, Manny Farber, and other reputable critics for an ambivalence in his work projected from a childhood conflict between a culturally demanding mother and an admired businessman foster father. This unusually Freudian analysis of the director's work sought to explain the incongruity of continental sophistication being challenged by American pragmatism. Sturges himself was seen as an uneasy mixture of savant and wise guy. On the one hand, his extreme literacy, rare among Hollywood screenwriters, enabled him to drop words like "ribaldry" and "vestal" into their proper contexts without a pretentious thud. On the other, he seemed unwilling to develop the implications of his serious ideas. His flair for props and gadgets suited the popularly recalled image of the young inventor of kissproof lipstick.

His reputation today is based mainly on the eight films he directed for Paramount. The Great McGinty, a vigorous satire of big city politics marked by lusty performances from Akim Tamiroff as the Boss and Brian Donlevy as the hobo elevated to governor, was the pilot film of the writer-director movement in Hollywood. Most directors had previously risen from the ranks of studio technicians and stage directors. After Sturges led the way, John Huston, Billy Wilder, Dudley Nichols, Clifford Odets, Nunnally Johnson, Robert Rossen, Samuel Fuller, Frank Tashlin, and Blake Edwards followed from the writer's cubicle to the director's chair. Christmas in July lingered over a depression mood as Dick Powell and Ellen Drew played an engaged couple trying to make ends meet on a combined salary of forty dollars a week. The vagaries of luck and the cruelty of practical jokes developed the plot in what was to be later recognized as the distinctive and disturbing Sturges manner. The Lady Eve, a sophisticated comedy with Henry Fonda and Barbara Stanwyck, was hailed by The New York Times *as the best film of 1941. Sturges circumvented the censors with a rowdy blackout technique that began where the more discreet "Lubitsch touch" had left off. An adroit manipulation of mistaken identity aided Sturges in preserving the technical morality of the marriage contract. The duet in* The Lady Eve *was later enlarged into the quadrille of* Palm Beach Story *in which Joel McCrea, Claudette Colbert, Mary Astor, and Rudy Vallee were perpetually confused and obsessed by the permutations of what Sturges leeringly defined as "Subject A."*

Sullivan's Travels, *a Swiftian glimpse of Hollywood and its occasional flirtations with social consciousness, is generally considered the most profound expression of the director's personality. Dedicating the film to the world's clowns and mountebanks, Sturges forthrightly defended the muse of comedy against the presumably more serious demands of society. Like Shakespeare's* Winter's Tale, *the film pivots in one dance-like moment from comedy to tragedy when an old derelict is trapped in a metal jungle of switch rails and is unable to evade an oncoming train.* The Miracle of Morgan's Creek *and* Hail the Conquering Hero *represented the director's original vision of small-town America within which Eddie Bracken emerged as a Sturges folk hero. In* Miracle, *Bracken has "greatness thrust upon him" when his frolicsome V-girl sweetheart, Betty Hutton, is thoughtful enough to transcend her disgrace with sextuplets. In* Hero, *Bracken survives the ordeal of a 4-F self-exposed as a false war hero, and again he is redeemed by the generous emotions of his girl friend, Ella Raines. Many critics were impressed by the intense performance of ex-prizefighter Freddie Steele, in the film an orphanage-bred marine hero with a severe mother complex.*

After 1944, when he left Paramount to form a short-lived partnership with Howard Hughes, Sturges' career suffered a precipitous decline. His three subsequent Hollywood films were remote from the tastes of their time, and during his long exile in the Fifties, his one realized European project, the bilingual Les Carnets de Major Thompson *(The French They Are a Funny Race), was unsuccessful. His present reputation is that of a period director who ultimately lost contact with his audience. Even at the time of his greatest success, he was overshadowed by the emotions aroused by the war and the stylistic revolution introduced with* Citizen Kane. *He received an Academy Award for the script of* The Great McGinty *in 1940, and was nominated twice in 1944 for* The Miracle of Morgan's Creek *and* Hail the Conquering Hero, *though again as a writer rather than as a director.*

His directorial style depended more on the pacing of action and dialogue than on visual texture and composition. Sturges employed long, uncut, "single-take" scenes to establish the premises of his elaborate scripts, but when he shifted to slapstick, he often cut to reactions before the action had terminated. His instinct for timing comedy montage made his films the funniest of their era in terms of audience laughter. He was capable of cinematic license with a talking horse, or a portrait that changed expressions. When he wanted to speed up the plot, he dispensed with dialogue and let the crisp movement and montage of silent farce fill the screen with hurtling bodies. In Mad Wednesday, *he went so far as to begin with the last reel of Harlold Lloyd's 1925 classic,* The Freshman, *after which he attempted to recreate Lloyd's vertiginous comedy effects with even wilder Sturges variations. As a screenwriter, he had pioneered in the development of the intricate flashback with* The Power and the Glory *in 1933, and his directed scenarios remain models of structural complexity.**

My deepest critical instincts urge me to minimize the fact that I interviewed Preston Sturges in the summer of 1957. Why? Because, I suppose, I believe less than ever in the truth of direct personal confrontations between the artist and the critic. All directors, even the great ones, are human beings, but they are also something more or something less, or perhaps even something else. The link between artistry and psychology is still a tenuous one for me, and traits of character, common to millions of otherwise miscellaneous individuals, consequently seem as relevant as the signs of the zodiac. (Not that I have failed to explore the astrological potentialities of my subject, but the director's thoughtlessness in being born under the sign of the Virgin rather than the adjacent sign of the Lion discouraged this line of inquiry.) I must admit that Preston Sturges looked every inch a director. His eyes still retained

* The Editor's interview with Preston Sturges originally appeared in Film Culture, No. 26, Fall 1962.

their thoughtful glitter, and the grayness of his fifty-nine years was more an imperial gray than a sparrow gray. However, I already knew he was a director, and so how could I truthfully read the tea-leaves of character analysis? Unfortunately, what is adjudged fraudulent for a gypsy fortune teller is deemed valid for the professional investigator of the artist's mystery. It is hardly a secret that an experienced interviewer can usually mold a personality to specifications by asking the right questions, and most film directors are malleable enough to justify all sorts of preconceptions about their work. Of course, there is a grain of truth even in the lies inevitably elicited by inquisitors who know the answers before they ask the questions.

The point is that I do not wish to imply that my having met Preston Sturges confers any special authority upon my theory about his career. Nor do I believe that people who knew him intimately are any better qualified to evaluate his art than those who merely inspected his works. The conversational one-upmanship of personal intimacy seldom yields any original insights, particularly when the speaker assumes that an ounce of personal contact, however frivolous, is worth a ton of critical analysis, however dedicated. Strangely, although I have always believed in some version of the *auteur* theory, I find the cinema a particularly treacherous field for those who would establish a correlation between the personality of the artist as evidenced in his art and the personality of the same artist as displayed in a cocktail lounge or hotel suite. I am not arguing that such a correlation cannot be established, but only that I find my feeble powers of perception unequal to the task.

Anyway, to return to the summer of 1957, Preston Sturges was visiting New York to publicize what turned out to be his last film: *The French They Are a Funny Race (Les Carnets de Major Thompson)*. On a hot Sunday afternoon in July or August, I have forgotten which, I arrived at the Algonquin where Sturges always registered when he was in New York. (He died at the Algonquin in 1959, but for a creature of habit, this is fact, not irony.) A note at the desk suggested that the location of the interview be shifted to the more opulent surroundings of the St. Regis where the director was comforting an ailing pasha of the Paramount front office. (I gathered subsequently that the hospitable pasha was one of the director's few remaining friends from the palmier days in Holly-

515

wood.) The atmosphere was relaxed, the Scotch refreshing, and the director-critic relationship properly respectful on my part. We talked for about six hours, most of the time off the record, and much of the time off the subject. The setting may have been too sybaritic at the St. Regis whi.ħ is as much a producer's hotel as the Algonquin is a director's hotel. In the twilight of the afternoon, Lester Cowan burst in on us to watch an extra-inning baseball game on television. (Note: Sturges was not interested in baseball. Does that make his work less American?)

As I look back over my copiously misleading notes on the interview, I recall that I was vaguely guilty about the situation. Fortunately, I had not yet seen *The French They Are a Funny Race,* but even without this adverse information, I had the feeling that Sturges was a burnt-out talent. By the time I finally caught his last film, I saw no point in publishing the interview. It was too late for Sturges to make a comeback, but it was still too early, I felt, to treat him as a shrine. I could have spared myself these pompous rationalizations. Preston Sturges had played the hectic American game of success to the last card, but he had drawn a bilingual deuce. *The French They Are a Funny Race* is the kind of bad film which withers an enthusiast's soul. What hope is there when a comedy director loses his rhythm and timing to the extent that he is less funny than his material? At this point in one's ruminations, the time-honored theory of decline comes galloping to the rescue. Sturges had simply lost whatever it was that once made him a good director, and that was that. Or was it?

I have always been puzzled by the apparent fact that comic directors "decline" more rapidly and more frequently than do serious directors. If the terms "comic" and "serious" lack both semantic precision and the logical relationship of opposites, it cannot be helped. These admittedly vague designations are used to limit my conception of comedy to that of comedy/ha ha rather than comedy/not tragedy. It can be argued that the ability to make an audience laugh has less to do with comedy than with humor, less with wit than with slapstick, less with character than with caricature, less with a personal vision of the world than with the technical, almost totalitarian, manipulation of an audience. It can also be argued that the decibel rating of collective laughter is an absurdly impermanent criterion of lasting value.

Yet, like it or not, respect it or not, Preston Sturges once had a gift for making audiences laugh, and then one day, this gift apparently deserted him. His period of maximum craftmanship coincided with his period of maximum productivity. The co-ordinates are easy enough to chart. Eight films for Paramount (1940–1944) represent the crest, and then down into the three-film trough of the Hughes-Zanuck trauma (1945–1949) from which Sturges never recovered in a decade of exile (1950–1959). The classical simplicity of this chronology is unusual even for the allegedly heartless dynamics of Hollywood production. What Sturges understood in 1957, certainly better than many of his admirers did, was that he needed Hollywood more than Hollywood needed him. His best comedies had always been parasitic rather than creative, recherché rather than revolutionary, the art more of a gadfly than of a butterfly. Whereas Welles has been redeemed in exile by his amateurism, Sturges was destroyed in exile by his professionalism. Perhaps, it is better for an artist to abandon his audience before his audience abandons him, particularly in the realm of comedy/ha-ha. After all, Capra reigned only between 1934 and 1939, almost concurrently with McCarey. Previously, Lubitsch and Clair had been in vogue from about the mid-Twenties to the early Thirties. As for the late James Agee's "Golden Age of Comedy," who knows how long it would have lasted even without the advent of sound? By 1925, for example, Mack Sennett was viewed as an antiquated primitive. Even Chaplin was considered in decline from 1935 as far as risibility was concerned.

In most instances, the vogue for a personal comic style seems to fade with time and age. The older a director becomes, the less likely he is to be funny. As his audience turns to new approaches, the traditional director has a difficult choice. He can either change his style and thus sacrifice his personality, or he can maintain his style and thus lose his audience. Very often, the less personality a director has, the longer he will survive. Delbert Mann, for example, is presently a "hot" director because his lack of style serves as a tabula rasa for any fashionable writer who comes along. Somehow Paddy Chayevsky, Terence Rattigan and Stanley Shapiro have kept Delbert Mann's feeble talent afloat for nearly a decade, during which time gifted directors have been sinking out of sight. On the other hand, Frank Capra and Leo McCarey have endeared themselves to the admirers of directorial continuity by becoming grotesquely anachronistic. Chaplin and Lubitsch ultimately attained something more than comedy/ha ha, Clair and Wilder something less.

Yet, is not the comedy/ha ha of yesterday ultimately the comedy/not tragedy of tomorrow? Do we ever really laugh at the past, or do we just acknowledge it with a nostalgic smile? Of course, time takes its toll of audiences as well as directors, and in this subjective jumble of time perspectives, we usually end reacting to comedy/ha ha as an elusively individual experience which can only be discussed socially as comedy/not tragedy. In short, thinking about comedy is a very solemn enterprise.

Although clowns supposedly yearn to play Hamlet, they usually end up playing Lear. This is as true in the circus, the music hall, and the night club as it is in the cinema. The enjoyment of an old entertainer is often transformed into a stirring ritual of recognition. The entertainer appears and repeats a routine he has performed before and will perform again through all eternity. The time is long past for shocks and surprises. The entertainer and his audience engage in a conspiracy to hold back the clock for a few minutes or a few hours. George Jean Nathan once observed that drama critics, as a tribe, were moved more by the death of a bawdy clown than by the demise of a noble tragedian. Consequently, however high or low I might ever choose to rank Preston Sturges, the affection I have always felt for his best films would probably remain constant. The response of laughter imprisoned in a particular time and place gives Sturges a permanent retrospective value for those who want to remember the time and place, but a full appreciation of Sturges demands a full appreciation of Hollywood as well. Even though he seemed at times to be moving against the current, his films were never completely out of the stream.

What distinguishes Sturges from his contemporaries is the density and congestion of his comedies. The Breughel of American comedy directors, Sturges created a world of peripheral professionals—politicians, gangsters, executives, bartenders, cab drivers, secretaries, bookies, card sharps, movie producers, doctors, dentists, bodyguards, butlers, inventors, millionaires and derelicts. These were not the usual flotsam and jetsam of Hollywood cinema, but self-expressive cameos of aggressive individualism. With the determinism of the Sturges plots, these infinitely detailed

518

miniatures served as contingent elements, and it is these elements, and the single-take, multiple viewpoint sequences formally demanded by these elements, which establish the comedies of Preston Sturges once and for all as comedy/not tragedy.

For the record, Sturges told me that the "most perfect" film he had ever seen was Josef von Sternberg's *The Last Command*. He also admired Pierre Fresnay in *Monsieur Vincent*, but, like most directors, Sturges did not go to movies very often. Of his own films, he felt that *Hail the Conquering Hero* had "less wrong with it" than any of his other films. The producers wanted to remove Ella Raines after the first rushes of *Hero*, but Sturges refused to consider a substitute. He was still scornful of Paramount for humiliating Vera Zorina in *For Whom the Bell Tolls* by replacing her with Ingrid Bergman after the hapless dancer had cut her hair for the part of Maria.

That night Preston Sturges appeared on the Mike Wallace Show, a television inquisition of that epoch. Sturges repudiated Rudy Vallee's "sympathetic" tribute to him. Earlier that afternoon, I had gathered that Sturges was not happy with the heartwarming anecdotes Eddie Bracken's press agents were spreading in the columns about Eddie's charity to the director who had made him a star. It was the kind of acid scenario that Sturges might have written in the days of *Sullivan's Travels*, but this time there was no happy ending. Paris and New York were not Hollywood.

Preston Sturges (1898–1959):
Filmography:
1940—The Great McGinty, Christmas in July. 1941—The Lady Eve. 1942—Sullivan's Travels, The Palm Beach Story. 1944—The Miracle at Morgan's Creek, Hail the Conquering Hero, The Great Moment. 1947—Mad Wednesday. 1948—Unfaithfully Yours. 1949—The Beautiful Blonde from Bashful Bend. 1957—The French They Are a Funny Race.

Francois Truffaut

François Truffaut's quest for reality leads him to an emphasis on character. Where Truffaut breaks with conventional dramatic cinema is in his acceptance of Renoir's credo in The Rules of the Game: *"Tout le monde a ses raisons." If everyone indeed has his reasons, then the popular cinema of heroes, villains, stooges, and sexless best friends must be dismantled. When there are two or more characters on the screen, Truffaut tries to understand all the different points of view. For Truffaut, every human being, regardless of external appearance, has some poetry in his soul. There are no "chosen" characters. Truffaut frankly admits that he failed to do justice to the parents in* The 400 Blows *and that he consciously despised the Swedish impresario in* Shoot the Piano Player. *These and other mistakes are the price Truffaut feels he pays for the indispensable values of spontaneity and improvisation. In the difficult, dangerous choice between form and vitality, Truffaut has chosen vitality. His acute awareness of the possibilities of the medium has thus far averted a major disaster as he has successfully demonstrated that rules are meant to be broken. As an artist, Truffaut is torn between a love for his audience and a fear of emotional facility. As the best-liked director of the nouvelle vague, Truffaut is always tempted to be touching. His emotional commitment to and deep involvement with his players and characters generate emotional power with an occasional loss of intellectual perspective.*—A.S.*

* The conversation of R. M. Franchi and Marshall Lewis with François Truffaut appeared originally in NY Film Bulletin, *No. 3, Issue 44, Vol. III, 1962, and was reprinted in the* Melbourne Film Journal, *April 1962.*

While in Canada to attend the second Montreal Film Festival François Truffaut was interviewed by R. M. Franchi and Marshall Lewis on behalf of "New York Film Bulletin" to whom we are grateful for permission to publish this tape-recorded transcription. M. Truffaut was first asked about his critical work in "Cahiers du Cinéma" and especially about the politique des auteurs.

At that time there existed what was called the Tradition of French Quality. That is to say at that time at all the big shows and festivals they'd introduce a picture which was invariably described as a picture representing the Tradition of French Quality; and these films were generally the result of team-work—big crews—they were often directed by one of those directors who represent the so-called Tradition of French Quality. And they employed someone famous for the décors, a big name for the music, and year after year won the greatest commercial and critical success, to the detriment of the films by *auteurs,* films made by more literate people who preferred to work on a picture *not* based on a celebrated novel and who worked in a more personal, more individual way. There were at the time four or five French directors who were working in a more personal manner, Jacques Tati, Robert Bresson, Max Ophuls, Jacques Becker and Jean Renoir, and the *politique des auteurs* was a call for the kind of cinema that could be made by such directors. It was a call for a broadening of cinematic concepts. But primarily the idea was that the man who has the ideas must be the same as the man who makes the picture. This being so, I am also convinced that a film resembles the man who made it—even if he didn't choose the subject, didn't choose the actors, didn't exclusively direct them and let assistants do the editing—even such a film would, how shall I put it, profoundly reflect in depth, for instance through the rhythm, the pacing, the man who made it, because even the sum total of all those steps is inherent in the contradictions which will necessarily be in the film, because fundamentally in the cinema there are two commandments: "Action!" and "Cut!" and between these two commandments the film is made. That is to say, during one and a half minutes a day of shooting. You're a director one and a half minutes daily, and when I look at a film I like to try to guess how the man has filled that minute and a half, and you can sense it very well. Now that I make films and the question of the quality of a film hardly interests me any more, this is what I look for. When I look at a picture now what I try to spot is whether the man who made it was violent, calm, happy, angry, and I look at it scene by scene and in this way I try to get back to the source, to the beginning, to the character, the personality of the director. I can almost sense, for instance, whether in such and such a scene the director was happy with his actors or was angry with what they were doing. I now look at films almost in the way one would examine a temperature chart at the foot of a hospital bed.

Then this is no longer a critical attitude?

Not at all, any more.

I have just remembered an aspect of the *politique des auteurs* which I had forgotten. It was a critical concept, essentially polemical; for some critics there are good films and bad films and I had the idea there are not good and bad films; there are simply good and bad directors. It might happen that a bad director could make a film which gives the illusion of being good because he had the excellent fortune of having a good scenario and fine actors. Nevertheless, this "good" film would have no value in the eyes of a critic because it was just a coincidence of circumstances. Conversely, you might have a situation whereby a fine director makes a "bad" picture because of the same circumstances in reverse, but this film would have more interest for the critic than the "good" film by the poor director. Still, in the same way, because the concept of success or failure has no importance. What is interesting is the career of a good director in that it reflects his thought from his beginning to his more mature phase. Each one of the films marks one phase in his thoughts, and it is of no importance that any particular picture is successful or not, or a good film or not. I have summed it up in an example for which Jean Delannoy has never forgiven me: I said that the best film of Delannoy would never equal the worst film of Jean Renoir. And this is what is really meant by the *politique des auteurs.*

You mentioned Tati, Bresson, Max Ophuls, Becker and Renoir . . .

I would like to add Jean Cocteau.

. . . and Cocteau. These are directors with a long history of work, who have many films we can see and who are respected by even those who do not know of or ascribe to

the politique. *But what about the younger directors, or even those like Hawks, Hitchcock and Aldrich (I am speaking as an American) who even in our country are not regarded as anything but popular "entertainers" and yet seem to find with you favour for the personality shown in their work. In other words, these directors have behind them a sort of prestige but they are not regarded here either as serious or as artists. In fact, their personalities seem to be more submerged by the subject . . .*

No. I do not think this is so.

. . . or by the treatment of the subject . . .

No. I think Hitchcock is the best example of what I am talking about. Hawks as well.

The great problem it would seem for Americans in examining the politique *is to accept seriously directors like Hawks and Hitchcock primarily because they have never been presented in a serious light.*

That is because the strength of these directors is that they are not intellectuals. They are judged by intellectuals and intellectuals recognize people like themselves, those who make phrases, etc.

When you come to the young director who is making his first film, what would you think were the elements that would most show some form of personality, or betray it?

In a first film? If it appeals to me.

If you like the film you will continue to follow the man's work?

You see, the *politique des auteurs*—I don't want to renege upon it today—but the thing about it was that it was timely. I came up at a time when it was necessary to the situation as it was in France. I practise it, I believe in it today still, but on a much more limited number of directors. The absence of great *auteurs* ten years ago brought us to the point of even inventing a few, and I must admit there were many of those. At this point there are, I would say, some ten directors whose work I always go to see and whose films I look at systematically and whom I still consider tremendous. But really, for the others, unlike the critics of *Figaro* and the *New York Times,* I think there are good Bergmans and bad Bergmans, good Aldrich and bad, very uneven Aldrich, and, finally, there are very few who dominate the situation.

Do you still think the politique *is a valid critical implement?*

For critics? Yes, because when a director is a good director, has potential and is capable of going ahead, and when you love them as we used to love them at *Cahiers du Cinéma* and you have the patience to go back and examine their films time and time again, you finally succeed in seeing their pictures more acutely, more sharply, and you understand why they made this particular film and why this film marks a step in the evolution of the man.

Will you give as an example of the idea of the personality of the director being expressed in his work, good and bad, using Jean Renoir (who we believe is your favorite director), elucidating the politique *through his work?*

Jean Renoir was regularly abandoned by the French critics every two or three years. He was an excellent director at the time and was recognized as such, but because of this "law" of successful pictures and unsuccessful pictures a critic could not accept the idea of saying good things about each and every film of Jean Renoir. Consequently, it had become almost a mathematical formula: when Renoir had had two hits it was almost automatic that his next film would be denounced and busted. It was such an exact law of criticism that I came to call it the Law of Alternance: it worked the other way—after two successive flops the critic, thinking he might be useful, would describe the third as great even if it were as bad as the previous two, because the critic has a complex that he likes to feel he's useful and effective.* The career of Renoir is typical of this, because he has always tried everything and has always been far ahead. In 1936 he made a film called *Toni* which was ten years ahead of the Italian neo-realist school. The next year he made *La Bête Humaine* which on the contrary was brilliant and finished, polished as a Hollywood product in the best sense. After having explored everything and having been the first in each area in 1938 he made *La Règle du jeu*. He was deserted by everyone. *La Règle du jeu* was the first psychological film in which the notion of a good and a bad personage had been entirely eliminated. Then he left for America, and the French only saw his American-made films at the Liberation in 1945. The theme then became: "Renoir, the most French of film-makers, was lost in Hollywood and his films are now worthless." Whereas in my opinion this

* Cf. Manvell, Lambert and Beddington, "Your Critic—Right or Wrong?", *The Cinema 1952* (London, 1952).

change of atmosphere was an extraordinary help to his progress. He made a film called *Diary of a Chambermaid* which in my opinion was an immense advance, even over *La Règle du jeu,* because he used *La Règle du jeu* but the psychology of the characters no longer interested him. It was the same film, but completely poetic instead of psychological. That is to say the characters were extremely stylized—one who danced through gardens, ate roses—and this effort was entirely misunderstood. One might say that the critics are almost invariably disconcerted by a new work, and so often they don't know what to say. They search for their arguments, their points, in the most unimportant factors. With a director who is an émigré they might say if he has worked on a literary work of his new country, "he tries to take our national author who is so subtle but with his Germanic heaviness everything was a failure in advance." That's what they said of Max Ophuls in France. If Jean Renoir makes in Hollywood a film in which the action takes place in France it is obvious the streets will not be French or Parisian, and the extras will be Hollywood extras. But the critics don't have the idea of looking for a truth which has more depth; since the critic has the information that the film was made in the United States he simply says that you don't feel France at all in this picture. So that for many films it is very easy to see the reactions of the critics in advance.

This brings up the idea that an auteur's *work gets better and that his last film is his best. Is this consistent with the* politique?

Not exactly. It progresses. What is true is that the latest work should be the most absorbing. For example, first films are impetuous, a bit experimental, and often have virtuoso tricks, since it's a sort of amorous game with the camera. As the relationship stabilizes the camera gets more measured, what is in front of the camera becomes more important and, in general, a young director doesn't easily meet with success because there is invariably a large amount of provocation in his work. Then his films are seen by a middle-aged public, so that most directors are actually successful at 35-40 because then their age corresponds more with the median age of the audience and their preoccupations also correspond. Then again, following that stage, in which the director has communicated to a large degree with his public, normally he should detach himself again. That is to say he goes ahead again, because he becomes more abstract, and from that moment he is lost, lost, that is, to the industry. But it is from that point onwards that his films become the most fascinating to study. A man like Hitchcock, who has received commercial success and uses it as an additional discipline, succeeds in remaining ahead of the box-office. But others, who are *only* artists, finish their careers completely misunderstood by the public, and very often by the critics as well. That's the case with Bunuel now, Max Ophuls at the end of his life, for Chaplin right now.

Welles, too?

Yes, and Welles.

There has been some confusion as to who is part of the nouvelle vague. *The trade press and the critics now label any film arriving from France made by someone under thirty as a* nouvelle vague *film and the expression has lost all meaning as a critical tool. Would it be fair to say there is a limited number of directors who constitute the* nouvelle vague, *the people who worked on* Cahiers, *who were associated with it as working critics?*

No. They themselves wouldn't want that.

Is it true what Chabrol said: "There is no new wave; there is only the sea"?

Yes. It is an expression invented by the press, because in journalism things work only by group. Each year there was a very good film made by a young person in France but they did not discuss it because there was simply one film. At the Cannes Festival the year they had *Hiroshima, Mon Amour, Les Cousins, Orfeu Negro* and *Les Quatre Cents Coups* the *nouvelle vague* was born. That enabled them to write articles about four films, four directors; it ensured the success of the films. All those who made their first film after this initial coup automatically became part of the new wave, whatever the quality of their films.

But there is in the films of yourself, Godard, Chabrol, Rivette and a few others a certain significant way of looking with the camera, at life, which is new?

No. I see only the differences, not common grounds. I think that amongst the group formerly with *Cahiers du Cinéma* there were none who were mediocre and none who betrayed cinema. Each made, freely and in a very personal way, those films that marked our differences rather than our resemblances.

Yet in all of these films, particularly in Les Cousins, Breathless *and* Tirez sur le Pianiste *the protagonists are the victims of bizarre circumstances; for example if the knife in* Le Pianiste *hadn't fallen so close to the two struggling men there wouldn't have been the killing. If the gun hadn't been left on the table in* Les Cousins, *and so on.*

I believe you might attribute that to a scepticism towards heroic characters. Amongst us there is a great admiration for American films, but the small American films. They were, nevertheless, made with restrictions, with the necessity that the guilty be punished and always with a division between sympathetic and unsympathetic characters. It was obviously as a reaction to that that we arrived at certain points of resemblance such as the one you have mentioned.

Amongst your contemporaries whose work interests you most?

Godard, I believe.

And who among the younger French directors just making their first films?

Well . . . Claude de Givray has finished *Tir au Flanc* and has begun work on his second film.

François Truffaut (1932–   ):
Filmography:
Short Subjects: 1954—Une visite (16mm). 1957—Les Mistons. 1958—Une histoire d'eau (with Jean-Luc Godard). 1962—Antoine et Colette (Love at Twenty).
Feature Films: 1959—The Four Hundred Blows. 1960—Shoot the Piano Player. 1961—Jules and Jim. 1964—The Soft Skin. 1966—Fahrenheit 451. 1968—The Bride Wore Black. 1969—Stolen Kisses, The Siren of Mississippi.

Orson Welles

That Welles, the aging enfant terrible *of the American Cinema, is still the youngest indisputably great American director is an ominous symptom of decadence in the industry as a whole. It can even be argued that Welles' films are now less American than European in outlook, and that in ten years or less, there may be no American cinema of great artistic significance. Even today, the best American films represent the creative spasms of the last gasp instead of the first breath. No matter. With* The Trial, *Welles' career has taken a curious turn. This Man from Mars who projected radio dynamics to that RKO-Radio classic,* Citizen Kane, *has gradually gone sour on the sound-track. The ear of the expatriate has lost contact with the nuances of American speech. It may be no accident that Welles has gradually turned away from the psychological density of the biography* (Citizen Kane) *and the filmed novel* (The Magnificent Ambersons) *to the psychological abstractions of fantasy* (Lady from Shanghai), *allegory* (Touch of Evil), *fable* (Mr. Arkadin) *and hallucination* (The Trial). *The conventional American diagnosis of his career is decline, pure and simple, but decline is never pure and never simple. Welles began his career on such a high plateau that the most precipitous decline would not affect his place in the Pantheon.* Citizen Kane *is still the work which influenced the cinema more profoundly than any American film since* Birth of a Nation. *If the Thirties belonged to Lubitsch's subtle grace and unobtrusive cutting, the Forties belong to the Wellesian resurrection of Murnau's portentous camera angles. The decade of plots gave way to a decade of themes, and the American cinema had lost its in-*

nocence and charm forever. From the beginning, Welles imposed a European temperament on the American cinema. Even today, Arthur Penn acknowledges the influence of Welles. Certainly the cinema is no poorer for having been injected with a Wellesian intelligence.*—A.S.

QUESTION—*In* The Trial, *it seems that you were making a severe criticism of the abuse of power; unless it concerns something more profound. Perkin appeared as a sort of Prometheus . . .*

WELLES—He is also a little bureaucrat. I consider him guilty.

Q.—*Why do you say he is guilty?*

WELLES—Who knows? He belongs to something that represents evil and that, at the same time, is part of him. He is not guilty as accused, but he is guilty all the same. He belongs to a guilty society, he collaborates with it. In any case, I am not a Kafka analyst.

Q.—*A version of the scenario exists with a different ending. The executioners stab K to death.*

WELLES—That ending didn't please me. I believe that in that case it is a question of a "ballet" written by a pre-Hitler Jewish intellectual. After the death of six million Jews, Kafka would not have written that. It seemed to me to be pre-Auschwitz. I don't want to say that my ending was good, but it was the only solution. I had to move into high gear, even if it was only for several instants.

Q.—*One of the constants of your work is the struggle for liberty and the defense of the individual.*

WELLES—A struggle for dignity. I absolutely disagree with those works of art, those novels, those films that, these days, speak about despair. I do not think that an artist may take total despair as a subject: we are too close to it in daily life. This genre of subject can be utilized only when life is less dangerous and more clearly affirmative.

Q.—*In the transposition of* The Trial *to the cinema, there is a fundamental change; in Kafka's book, K's character is more passive than in the film.*

* *The interview with Orson Welles by Juan Cobos Miguel Rubio, and Jose Antonio Pruneda appeared in* Cahiers du Cinema, *No. 165, April 1965, and was reprinted in* Cahiers du Cinema in English, *No. 5, 1966, with an English translation by Rose Kaplin.*

WELLES—I made him more active, properly speaking. I do not believe that passive characters are appropriate to drama. I have nothing against Antonioni, for example, but, in order to interest me, the characters must do something, from a dramatic point of view, you understand.

Q.—*Was* The Trial *an old project?*

WELLES—I once said that a good film could be drawn from the novel, but I myself didn't think of doing it. A man came to see me and told me he believed he could find money so that I could make a film in France. He gave me a list of films and asked that I choose. And from that list of fifteen films I chose the one that, I believe, was the best: *The Trial.* Since I couldn't do a film written by myself, I chose Kafka.

Q.—*What films do you really want to do?*

WELLES—Mine. I have drawers full of scenarios written by me.

Q.—*In* The Trial, *was the long travelling shot of Katina Paxinou dragging the truck while Anthony Perkins talks to her an homage to Brecht?*

WELLES—I did not see it that way. There was a long scene with her that lasted ten minutes and that, moreover, I cut on the eve of the Paris premiere. I did not see the film as a whole except for one time. We were still in the process of doing the mixing, and here the premiere fell on us. At the last moment I abridged the ten minute scene. It should have been the best scene in the film and it wasn't. Something went wrong, I guess. I don't know why, but it didn't succeed. The subject of that scene was free will. It was stained with *comedie noire;* that was a fad with me. As you know, it is always directed against the machine and favorable to liberty.

Q.—*When Joseph K sees the shadow show at the end, with the story of the guard, the door, etc., does this concern your own reflections on the cinema?*

WELLES—It concerns a technical problem posed by the story to be told. If it were told at that precise moment, the public would go to sleep; that is why I tell it at the beginning and only recall it at the end. The effect then is equivalent to telling the story at that moment and I was able in this way to tell it in a few seconds. But, in any case, I am not the judge.

Q.—*A critic who admires your work very much said that, in* The Trial, *you were repeating yourself . . .*

WELLES—Exactly, I repeated myself. I believe we do it

all the time. We always take up certain elements again. How can it be avoided? An actor's voice always has the same timbre and, consequently, he repeats himself. It is the same for a singer, a painter . . . There are always certain things that come back, for they are part of one's personality, of one's style. If these things didn't come into play, a personality would be so complex that it would become impossible to identify it.

It is not my intention to repeat myself but in my work there should certainly be references to what I have done in the past. Say what you will, but *The Trial* is the best film I have ever made. One repeats oneself only when one is fatigued. Well, I wasn't fatigued. I have never been so happy as when I made this film.

Q.—*How did you shoot Anthony Perkins' long running scene?*

WELLES—we built a very long platform and the camera was placed on a rolling chair.

Q.—*But it's enormously fast!*

WELLES—Yes, but I had a Yugoslavian runner to push my camera.

Q.—*What is astonishing in your work is this continual effort to bring solutions to the problems posed by directing . . .*

WELLES—The cinema is still very young and it would be completely ridiculous to not succeed in finding new things for it. If only I could make more films! Do you know what happened with *The Trial?* Two weeks before our departure from Paris for Yugoslavia, we were told that there would be no possibility of having a single set built there because the producer had already made another film in Yugoslavia and hadn't paid his debts. That's why it was necessary to utilize that abandoned station. I had planned a completely different film.

Everything was invented at the last minute because physically my film had an entirely different conception. It was based on an absence of sets. And this gigantism I have been reproached for is, in part, due to the fact that the only set I possessed was that old abandoned station. An empty railroad station is immense! The production, as I had sketched it, comprised sets that gradually disappeared. The number of realistic elements were to become fewer and fewer and the public would become aware of it, to the point where the scene would be reduced to free space as if everything had dissolved.

Q.—*The movement of the actors and the camera in relation to each other in your films is very beautiful.*

WELLES—That is a visual obsession. I believe, thinking about my films, that they are based not so much on pursuit as on a search. If we are looking for something, the labyrinth is the most favorable location for the search. I do not know why, but my films are all for the most part a physical search.

Q.—*You reflect about your work a great deal . . .*

WELLES—Never *a posteriori*. I think about each of my films when I am preparing for them. I do an enormous sketch when starting. What is marvelous about the cinema, what makes it superior to the theatre, is that it has many elements that may conquer us but may also enrich us, offer us a life impossible anywhere else. The cinema should always be the discovery of something. I believe that the cinema should be essentially poetic; that is why, during the shooting and not during the preparation, I try to plunge myself into a poetic development, which differs from narrative development and dramatic development. But, in reality, I am a man of ideas; yes, above all else—I am even more a man of ideas than a moralist, I suppose.

Q.—*Do you believe it is possible to have a form of tragedy without melodrama?*

WELLES—Yes, but that is very difficult. For any *auteur* who comes out of the Anglo-Saxon tradition, it is very difficult. Shakespeare never arrived at it. It is possible, but up to the present no one has succeeded. In my cultural tradition, tragedy cannot escape from melodrama. We may always draw from tragic elements and perhaps even the grandeur of tragedy but melodrama is always inherent to the Anglo-Saxon cultural universe. There's no doubt about it.

Q.—*Is it correct that your films never correspond to what you were thinking of doing before starting them? Because of producers, etc.*

WELLES—No, in reality, in what concerns me, creation, I must say that I am constantly changing. At the beginning, I have a basic notion of what the final aspect of the film will be, more or less. But each day, at every moment, one deviates or modifies because of the expression in an actress's eyes or the position of the sun. I am not in the habit of preparing a film and then setting myself to make it. I prepare a film but I have no intention of making *this* film. The preparation serves to liberate me, so that I may work in my fashion; thinking of bits of film and of the result they will give; and there are parts that deceive me because I haven't conceived them in a complete enough way. I do not know what word to use, because I am afraid of pompous words when I talk about making a film. The degree of concentration I utilize in a world that I create, whether this be for thirty seconds or for two hours, is very high; that is why, when I am shooting, I have a lot of trouble sleeping. This is not because I am pre-occupied but because, for me, this world has so much reality that closing my eyes is not sufficient to make it disappear. It represents a terrible intensity of feeling. If I shoot in a royal location I sense and I see this site in so violent a way that, now, when I see these places again, they are similar to tombs, completely dead. There are spots in the world that are, to my eyes, cadavers; that is because I have already shot there—for me, they are completely finished. Jean Renoir said something that seems to be related to that: "We should remind people that a field of wheat painted by Van Gogh can arouse a stronger emotion than a field of wheat in nature." It is important to recall that art surpasses reality. Film becomes another reality. Apropos, I admire Renoir's work very much even though mine doesn't please him at all. We are good friends and, truthfully, one of the things I regret is that he doesn't like his films for the same reason I do. His films appear marvelous to me because what I admire most in an *auteur* is authentic sensitivity. I attach no importance to whether or not a film is a technical SUCCESS: moreover, films that lack this genre of sensitivity may not be judged on the same level with technical or aesthetic knowingness. But the cinema, the true cinema, is a poetic expression and Renoir is one of the rare poets. Like Ford, it is in his style. Ford is a poet. A comedian. Not for women, of course, but for men.

Q.—*Apart from Ford and Renoir, who are the cineastes you admire?*

WELLES—Always the same ones; I believe that on this point I am not very original. The one who pleases me most of all is Griffith. I think he is the best director in the history of the cinema. The best, much better than Eisenstein. And, for all that, I admire Eisenstein very much.

Q.—*What about that letter Eisenstein sent you when you had not yet started in the cinema?*

WELLES—It was apropos *Ivan the Terrible.*

Q.—*It appears that you said his film was something by Michael Curtiz . . .*

WELLES—No. What happened is that I wrote a criticism of *Ivan the Terrible* for a newspaper and, one day, I received a letter from Eisenstein, a letter that came from Russia and ran to forty pages. Well, I answered him and in this fashion an exchange began that made us friends by correspondence. But I said nothing that could be seen as drawing a parallel between him and Curtiz. That would not be just. *Ivan the Terrible* is the worst film of a great *cineaste*.

It's that I judged Eisenstein on his own level and not in a way that would be appropriate to a minor *cineaste*. His drama was, before all else, political. It had nothing to do with his having to tell a story that he didn't want to tell. It was because, in my opinion, he was not suited to make period films. I think the Russians have a tendency to be more academic when they treat another period. They become rhetoricians, and academicians, in the worst sense of the word.

Q.—*In your films, one has the sensation that real space is never respected: it seems not to interest you . . .*

WELLES—The fact that I make no use of it doesn't in the least signify that it doesn't please me. In other terms, there are many elements of the cinematographic language that I do not utilize, but that is not because I have something against them. It seems to me that the field of action in which I have my experiences is one that is least known, and my duty is to explore it. But that does not mean to say that it is, for me, the best and only—or that I deviate from a normal conception of space, in relation to the camera. I believe that the artist should explore his means of expression.

In reality, the cinema, with the exception of a few little tricks that don't go very far, has not advanced for more than thirty years. The only changes are with respect to the subject of films. I see that there are directors, full of future, sensitive, who explore new themes, but I see no one who attacks form, the manner of saying things. That seems to interest no one. They resemble each other very much in terms of style.

Q.—*You must work very quickly. In twenty-five years of cinema, you have made ten films, you have acted in thirty, you have made a series of very long programs for television, you have acted and directed in the theatre, you*

*have done narrations for other films and, in addition, you
have written thirty scenarios. Each of them must have
taken you more than six months.*

WELLES—Several of them even longer. There are those
that took me two years but that is because I set them aside
from time to time in order to do something else and
picked them up again afterwards. But it is also true that I
write very rapidly.

Q.—*You write them completely, with dialogue?*

WELLES—I always begin with the dialogue. And I do
not understand how one dares to write action before dialogue. It's a very strange conception. I know that in theory
the word is secondary in cinema but the secret of my work
is that everything is based on the word. I do not make silent films. I must begin with what the characters say. I
must know what they say before seeing them do what they
do.

Q.—*However, in your films the visual part is essential.*

WELLES—Yes, but I couldn't arrive at it without the so-
lidity of the word taken as a basis for constructing the images. What happens is that when the visual components
are shot the words are obscured. The most classical example is *Lady From Shanghai.* The scene in the aquarium
was so gripping visually that no one heard what was being
said. And what was said was, for all that, the marrow of
the film. The subject was so tedious that I said to myself,
"This calls for something beautiful to look at." Assuredly,
the scene was very beautiful. The first ten minutes of the
film did not please me at all. When I think of them I have
the impression it wasn't me that made them. They resemble any Hollywood film.

I believe you know the story of *Lady From Shanghai.* I
was working on that spectacular theatre idea "Around the
World in 80 Days," which was originally to be produced
by Mike Todd. But, overnight, he went bankrupt and I
found myself in Boston on the day of the premiere, unable
to take my costumes from the station because 50,000 dollars was due. Without that money we couldn't open. At
that time I was already separated from Rita; we were no
longer even speaking. I did not intend to do a film with
her. From Boston I got in touch with Harry Cohn, then
director of Columbia, who was in Hollywood, and I said
to him, "I have an extraordinary story for you if you send
me 50,000 dollars, by telegram in one hour, on account,
and I will sign a contract to make it." Cohn asked, "What

story?" I was telephoning from the theatre box office; beside it was a pocket books display and I gave him the title of one of them: *Lady From Shanghai*. I said to him, "Buy the novel and I'll make the film." An hour later we received the money. Later I read the book and it was horrible so I set myself, top speed, to write a story. I arrived in Hollywood to make the film with a very small budget and in six weeks of shooting. But I wanted more money for my theatre. Cohn asked me why I didn't use Rita. She said she would be very pleased. I gave her to understand that the character was not a sympathetic one, that she was a woman who killed and this might hurt her image as a star in the public eye. Rita was set on making this film, and instead of costing 350,000 dollars, it became a two million dollar film. Rita was very cooperative. The one who was horrified on seeing the film was Cohn.

Q.—*How do you work with actors?*

WELLES—I give them a great deal of freedom and, at the same time, the feeling of precision. It's a strange combination. In other words, physically, and in the way they develop, I demand the precision of ballet. But their way of acting comes directly from their own ideas as much as from mine. When the camera begins to roll, I do not improvise visually. In this realm, everything is prepared. But I work very freely with the actors. I try to make their life pleasant.

Q.—*Your cinema is essentially dynamic . . .*

WELLES—I believe that the cinema should be dynamic although I suppose any artist will defend his own style. For me, the cinema is a slice of life in movement that is projected on a screen; it is not a frame. I do not believe in the cinema unless there is movement on the screen. This is why I am not in agreement with certain directors, whom, however, I admire, who content themselves with a static cinema. For me, these are dead images. I hear the noise of the projector behind me, and when I see these long, long walks along streets, I am always waiting to hear the director's voice saying, "Cut!"

The only director who does not move either his camera or his actors very much, and in whom I believe, is John Ford. He succeeds in making me believe in his films even though there is little movement in them. But with the others I always have the impression that they are desperately trying to make Art. However, they should be making

536

drama and drama should be full of life. The cinema, for me, is essentially a dramatic medium, not a literary one.

Q.—*That is why your mise-en-scène is lively: it is the meeting of two movements, that of the actors and that of the camera. Out of this flows an anguish that reflects modern life very well . . .*

WELLES—I believe that that corresponds to my vision of the world; it reflects that sort of vertigo, uncertainty, lack of stability, that *melange* of movement and tension that is our universe. And the cinema should express that. Since cinema has the pretension of being an art, it should be, above all, film, and not the sequel to another, more literary, medium of expression.

Q.—*Herman G. Weinberg said, while speaking of* Mr. Arkadin, *"In Orson Welles' films, the spectator may not sit back in his seat and relax, on the contrary he must meet the film at least half-way in order to decipher what is happening, practically every second; if not, everything is lost."*

WELLES—All my films are like that. There are certain *cineastes*, excellent ones, who present everything so explicitly, so clearly, that in site of the great visual power contained in their films one follows them effortlessly—I refer only to the narrative thread. I am fully aware that, in my films, I demand a very specific interest on the part of the public. Without that attention, it is lost.

Q.—Lady From Shanghai *is a story that, filmed by another director, would more likely have been based on sexual questions . . .*

WELLES—You mean that another director would have made it more obvious. I do not like to show sex on the screen crudely. Not because of morality or puritanism; my objection is of a purely aesthetic order. In my opinion, there are two things that can absolutely not be carried to the screen: the realistic presentation of the sexual act and praying to God. I never believe an actor or actress who pretends to be completely involved in the sexual act if it is too literal, just as I can never believe an actor who wants to make me believe he is praying. These are two things that, for me, immediately evoke the presence of a projector and a white screen, the existence of a series of technicians and a director who is saying, "Good. Cut." And I imagine them in the process of preparing for the next shot. As for those who adopt a mystical stance and look fervently at the spotlights . . .

For all that, my illusion almost never ends when I see a film. While filming, I think of someone like myself: I utilize all of my knowledge in order to force this person to want to see the film with the greatest interest, I want him to believe what is there on the screen; this means that one should create a real world there. I place my dramatic vision of a character in the world . . . if not, the film is something dead. What there is on the screen is nothing but shadows. Something even more dead than words.

Q.—*Do you like comedy?*

WELLES—I have written at least five scenarios for comedy and in the theatre I have done more comedies than dramas. Comedy fills me with enthusiasm but I have never succeeded in getting a film producer to let me make one. One of the best things I did for television was a program in the genre of comedy. For example, I like Hawks' comedies very much. I even wrote about twenty-five minutes of one of them. It was called, *I Was a Male War Bride*. The scenarist fell ill and I wrote almost a third of the film.

Q.—*Have you written scenarios of comedies with the intentions of making them?*

WELLES—I believe the best of my comedies is "Operation Cinderella." It tells of the occupation of a small Italian town (which was previously occupied by the Saracens, the Moors, the Normans and, during the last war, by the English and, finally, the Americans) by a Hollywood film company . . . and this new occupation unfolds exactly like a military operation. The lives of all the inhabitants of the town are changed during the shooting of the film. It's a gross farce. I want very much to do a comedy for the cinema.

In a certain sense, *Quixote* is a comedy, and I put a lot of comedy in all of my films but it is a genre of comedy that—and I regret to tell you this because it is a weakness —is understood only by Americans, to the exclusion of spectators in other countries, whatever they may be. There are scenes that, seen in other countries, awake not the slightest smile and that, seen by Americans, immediately appear in a comic vein. *The Trial* is full of humor, but the Americans are the only ones to understand its amusing side. This is where my nationality comes through: my farces are not universal enough. Many are the arguments I've had with actors due to the fact that scenes are posed in absolute forms of comedy and only at the last five minutes do I change them into drama. This is my method of working: showing the amusing side of things and not showing the sad side until the last possible second.

Q.—*What happened when you sold the subject of* Monsieur Verdoux *to Chaplin?*

WELLES—I never argued with Chaplin because of *Monsieur Verdoux*. What annoys me is that now he pretends that he did not buy this subject from me. As an actor, Chaplin is very good, sensational. But in the comic cinema I prefer Buster Keaton to him. There is a man of the cinema who is not only an excellent actor but an excellent director, which Chaplin is not. And Keaton always has fabulous ideas. In *Limelight*, there was a scene between the two of them that was ten minutes long. Chaplin was excellent and Keaton sensational. It was the most successful thing he had done in the course of his career. Chaplin cut almost the entire scene, because he understood who, of the two, had completely dominated it.

Q.—*There is a kinship between your work and the works of certain authors of the modern theatre, like Becket, Ionesco and others . . . what is called the theatre of the absurd.*

WELLES—Perhaps, but I would eliminate Ionesco because I do not admire him. When I directed *Rhinoceros* in London, with Laurence Olivier in the principal role, as we repeated the work from day to day it pleased me less. I believe that there is nothing inside it. Nothing at all. This kind of theatre comes out of all types of expression, all types of art of a certain epoch, is thus forged by the same world as my films. The things this theatre is composed of are the same composed in my films, without this theatre's being in my cinema or without my cinema's being in this theatre. It is a trait of our times. There is where the coincidence comes from.

Q.—*There are two types of artists: for example, Velasquez and Goya; one disappears from the picture, the other is present in it; on the other hand you have Van Gogh and Cezanne . . .*

WELLES—I see what you mean. It's very clear.

Q.—*It seems to me that you are on the Goya side.*

WELLES—Doubtless. But I very much prefer Velasquez. There's no comparison between one and the other, as far as being artists is concerned. As I prefer Cezanne to Van Gogh.

Q.—*And between Tolstoy and Dostoievsky?*

WELLES—I prefer Tolstoy.

Q.—*But as an artist* . . .

WELLES—Yes, as an artist. But I deny that, for I do not correspond to my tastes. I know what I'm doing and when I recognize it in other works my interest is diminished. The things that resemble me the least are the things that interest me the most. For me Velasquez is the Shakespeare of painters and, for all that, he has nothing in common with my way of working.

Q.—*What do you think of what is called modern cinema?*

WELLES—I like certain young French cineastes, much more than the Italians.

Q.—*Did you like* L'Annee derniere a Marienbad?

WELLES—No. I know that this film pleased you; not me. I held on up to the fourth reel and after that I left at a run. It reminded me too much of *Vogue* magazine.

Q.—*How do you see the development of the cinema?*

WELLES—I don't see it. I rarely go to the movies. There are two kinds of writers, the writer who reads everything of interest that is published, exchanges letters with other writers, and others who absolutely do not read their contemporaries. I am among the latter. I go to the movies very rarely and this is not because I don't like it, it is because it procures me no enjoyment at all. I do not think I am very intelligent about films. There are works that I know to be good but which I cannot stand.

Q.—*It was said that you were going to make "Crime and Punishment"; what became of this project?*

WELLES—Someone wanted me to do it. I thought about it, but I like the book too much. In the end, I decided that I could do nothing and the idea of being content to illustrate it did not please me at all. I don't mean to say by that that the subject was beneath me, what I mean is that I could bring nothing to it. I could only give it actors and images and, when I can only do that, the cinema does not interest me. I believe you must say something new about a book, otherwise it is better not to touch it.

Aside from that, I consider it to be a very difficult work, because, in my opinion, it is not completely comprehensible outside of its own time and country. The psychology of this man and this constable are so Russian, so nineteenth century Russian, that one could never find them elsewhere; I believe that the public would not be able to follow it all the way.

Q.—*There is, in Dostoievsky, an analysis of justice, of the world, that is very close to yours.*

WELLES—Perhaps too close. My contribution would most likely be limited. The only thing I could do is to direct. I like to make films in which I can express myself as *auteur* sooner than as interpreter. I do not share Kafka's point of view in *The Trial*. I believe that he is a good writer, but Kafka is not the extraordinary genius that people today see him as. That is why I was not concerned about excessive fidelity and could make a film by Welles. If I could make four films a year, I would surely do "Crime and Punishment." But as it costs me a great deal to convince producers I try to choose what I film very carefully.

Q.—*With you, one seems to find, at the same time, the Brechtian tendency and the Stanislavski tendency.*

WELLES—All I can say is that I did my apprenticeship in Stanislavski's orbit; I worked with his actors and found them very easy to direct. I do not allude to "Method" actors; that's something else altogether. But Stanislavski was marvelous. As for Brecht, he was a great friend to me. We worked together on "Galileo Galilei." In reality he wrote it for me. Not for me to act in, but in order for me to direct it.

Q.—*How was Brecht?*

WELLES—Terribly nice. He had an extraordinary brain. One could see very well that he had been educated by the Jesuits. He had the type of disciplined brain characterized by Jesuit education. Instinctively, he was more of an anarchist than a Marxist, but he believed himself a perfect Marxist. When I said to him one day, while we were talking about "Galileo," that he had written a perfectly anti-communist work, he became nearly aggressive. I answered him, "But this Church you describe has to be Stalin and not the Pope, at this time. You have made something resolutely anti-Soviet!"

Q.—*What relationship do you see between your work as a film director and as a theatre director?*

WELLES—My relationships with these two *milieux* are very different. I believe that they are not in intimate rapport, one with the other. Perhaps in me, as a man, that relationship exists, but technical solutions are so different for each of them that, in my spirit, I establish absolutely no relationship between these two mediums.

In the theatre, I do not belong to what has succeeded in

becoming the Brechtian idea of theatre; that particularly withdrawn form has never been appropriate to my character. But I have always made a terrible effort to recall to the public, at each instant, that it is in a theatre. I have never tried to bring it into the scene, I have rather tried to bring the scene to it. And that is the opposite of the cinema.

Q.—*Perhaps there is a relationship in the way the actors are handled.*

WELLES—In the theatre there are 1,500 cameras rolling at the same time—in the cinema there is only one. That changes the whole aesthetic for the director.

Q.—*Did Huston's* Moby Dick, *on which you worked, please you?*

WELLES—The novel pleases me very much, but it doesn't please me as a novel so much as a drama. There are two very different things in the novel: that sort of pseudo-biblical element that is not very good, and also that curious nineteenth century American element, of the apocalyptical genre, that can be rendered very well in the cinema.

Q.—*In the scene you acted in the film—did you make any suggestions as to the way of handling it?*

WELLES—All we did was discuss the way in which it would be shot. You know that my discourse is very long. It goes on throughout a full reel, and we never repeated it. I arrived on the set already made-up and dressed. I got up on the platform and we shot it in one take. We did it using only one camera angle. And that is one of Huston's merits, because another director would have said, "Let's do it from another angle and see what we get." He said, "Good," and my role in the film ended right there!

Q.—*You are in the process of preparing for a film on bullfighting.*

WELLES—Yes, but a film about the amateurs of bullfighting, the following . . . I think that the true event in the *corrida* is the arena itself—but one cannot do a film about it. From the cinematographic point of view the most exciting thing about it is the atmosphere. The *corrida* is something that already possesses a well defined personality. The cinema can do nothing to render it dramatic. All one may do is photograph it. Actually, my biggest pre-occupation is knowing that Rosi is already in the process of shooting while I have put in four years, off and on, writing my scenario. Because of him, finding the necessary money will be more difficult: they'll say to me, "We already have a film about bullfighting, made by a serious cineaste; who wants one more?" However, I hope I will succeed in making this film, but I still don't know how I'm going to find the money. Rosi shot something last year at Pamplona, in 16 mm. He showed it to Rizzoli, and said, "Look at this beautiful thing," and Rizzoli gave him carte blanche. Now it's only a matter of knowing whether it will be a good film or a bad film. It is better for me that the film be good. If it fails, I will have even more trouble raising the funds.

Q.—*There is talk from time to time of your first sojourn in Spain, before the Civil War.*

WELLES—When I arrived in Spain, for the first time, I was seventeen years old and had already worked in Ireland as an actor. I only stayed in the south, in Andalusia. In Seville, I lived in the Triana section. I was writing detective stories: I spent only two days a week on this and it brought in three hundred dollars. With this money I was a *grand seigneur* in Seville. There were so many people thrilled by the *corrida* and I caught the virus myself. I paid the novice fee at several *corridas* and thus was able to *debut*—on the posters I was called "The American." My greatest thrill was being able to practise the *metier* of *torero* three or four times without having to pay. I came to the realization that I was not good as a *torero* and decided to apply myself to writing. At that time I hardly thought of the theatre and still less of the cinema.

Q.—*You said one day that you have had a great deal of difficulty finding the money to make your films, that you have spent more time struggling to get this money than working as an artist. How is this battle at this time?*

WELLES—More bitter than ever. Worse than ever. Very difficult. I have already said that I do not work enough. I am frustrated, do you understand? And I believe that my work shows that I do not do enough filming. My cinema is perhaps too explosive, because I wait too long before I speak. It's terrible. I have bought little cameras in order to make a film if I can find the money. I will shoot it in 16 mm. The cinema is a *metier* . . . nothing can compare to the cinema. The cinema belongs to our times. It is "the thing" to do. During the shooting of *The Trial*, I spent marvelous days. It was an amusement, happiness. You cannot imagine what I felt.

When I make a film or at the time of my theatrical premieres, the critics habitually say, "This work is not as good as the one of three years ago." And if I look for the criticism of that one, three years back, I find an unfavorable review that says that that isn't as good as what I did three years earlier. And so it goes. I admit that experiences can be false but I believe that it is also false to want to be fashionable. If one is fashionable for the greatest part of one's career, one will produce second-class work. Perhaps by chance one will arrive at being a success but this means that one is a follower and not an innovator. An artist should lead, blaze trails.

What is serious is that in countries where English is spoken, the role played by criticism concerning serious works of cinema is very important. Given the fact that one cannot make films in competition with Doris Day, what is said by reviews such as *Sight and Sound* is the only reference.

Things are going particularly badly in my own country. *Touch of Evil* never had a first-run, never had the usual presentation to the press and was not the object of any critical writing in either the weeklies, the reviews or the daily papers. It was considered to be too bad. When the representative from Universal wanted to exhibit it at the Brussels Fair in 1958, he was told that it wasn't a good enough film for a festival. He answered that, in any case, it must be put on the program. It went unnoticed and was sent back. The film took the *grand prix*, but it was no less sent back.

Q.—*Do you consider yourself a moralist?*

WELLES—Yes, but against morality. Most of the time that may appear paradoxical, but the things I love in painting, in music, in literature, represent only my penchant for what is my opposite. And moralists bore me very much. However, I'm afraid I am one of them!

Q.—*In what concerns you, it is not so much a question of a moralist's attitude but rather an ethic that you adopt in the face of the world.*

WELLES—My two Shakespearean films are made from an ethical point of view. I believe I have never made a film without having a solid ethical point of view about its story. Morally speaking, there is no ambiguity in what I do.

Q.—*But an ambiguous point of view is necessary. These days, the world is made that way.*

WELLES—But that is the way the world appears to us. It is not a true ambiguity: it's like a larger screen. A kind of a moral cinemascope. I believe it is necessary to give all the characters their best arguments, in order that they may defend themselves, including those I disagree with. To them as well, I give the best defensive arguments I can imagine. I offer them the same possibility for expression as I would a sympathetic character.

That's what gives this impression of ambiguity: my being chivalrous to people whose behavior I do not approve of. The characters are ambiguous but the significance of the work is not. I do not want to resemble the majority of Americans, who are demagogs and rhetoricians. This is one of America's great weaknesses, and rhetoric is one of the greatest weaknesses of American artists; above all, those of my generation. Miller, for example, is terribly rhetorical.

Q.—*What is the problem in America?*

WELLES—If I speak to you of the things that are wrong it won't be the obvious ones; those are similar to what is wrong in France, in Italy or in Spain; we know them all. In American art the problem, or better, one of the problems, is the betrayal of the Left by the Left, self-betrayal. In one sense, by stupidity, by orthodoxy and because of slogans; in another, by simple betrayal. We are very few in our generation who have not betrayed our position, who have not given other people's names . . .

That is terrible. It can never be undone. I don't know how one starts over after a similar betrayal that, however, differs enormously from this, for example: a Frenchman who collaborated with the gestapo in order to save his wife's life—that is another genre of collaboration. What is so bad about the American Left is that it betrayed in order to save its swimming pools. There was no American Right in my generation. Intellectually it didn't exist. There were only Leftists and they mutually betrayed each other. The Left was not destroyed by McCarthy: it demolished itself, ceding to a new generation of Nihilists. That's what happened.

You can't call it "Fascism." I believe that the term "Fascism" should only be utilized in order to define a quite precise political attitude. It would be necessary to find a new word in order to define what is happening in America. Fascism must be born out of chaos. And America is not, as I know it, in chaos. The social structure is not in a state of dissolution. No, it doesn't correspond at all to the true definition of Fascism. I believe it is two simple, obvious things: the technological society is not accustomed to living with its own tools. That's what counts. We speak of them, we use them but we don't know how to live with them. The other thing is the prestige of the people responsible for the technological society. In this society the men who direct and the savants who represent technique do not leave room for the artist who favors the human being. In reality, they utilize him only for decoration.

Hemingway says, in *The Green Hills of Africa,* that America is a country of adventure and, if the adventure disappears there, any American who possesses this primitive spirit must go elsewhere to seek adventure: Africa, Europe, etc. . . . It is an intensely romantic point of view. There is some truth in it, but if it is so intensely romantic it is because there is still an enormous quantity of adventure in America. In the cinema, you cannot imagine all that one may do in it. All I need is a job in cinema, is for someone to give me a camera. There is nothing dishonorable about working in America. The country is full of possibilities for expressing what is happening all over the world. What really exists is an enormous compromise. The ideal American type is perfectly expressed by the Protestant, individualist, anti-conformist, and this is the type that is in the process of disappearing. In reality, a very few of him remain.

Q.—*What was your relationship with Hemingway?*

WELLES—My relationship with Hemingway has always been very droll. The first time we met was when I had been called to read the narration for a film that he and Joris Ivens had made about the war in Spain; it was called *Spanish Earth.* Arriving, I came upon Hemingway, who was in the process of drinking a bottle of whiskey; I had been handed a set of lines that were too long, dull, had nothing to do with his style, which is always so concise and so economical. There were lines as pompous and complicated as this: "Here are the faces of men who are close to death," and this was to be read at a moment when one saw faces on the screen that were so much more eloquent. I said to him, "Mr. Hemingway, it would be better if one saw the faces all alone, without commentary."

This didn't please him at all, and since I had, a short time before, just directed the Mercury Theatre, which was a sort of avant-garde theatre, he thought I was some kind of faggot and said, "You—effeminate boys of the theatre, what do you know about real war?"

546

Taking the bull by the horns, I began to make effeminate gestures and I said to him, "Mister Hemingway, how strong you are and how big you are!" That enraged him and he picked up a chair; I picked up another, and right there, in front of the images of the Spanish Civil War as they marched across the screen, we had a terrible scuffle. It was something marvelous: two guys like us in front of these images representing people in the act of struggling and dying . . . we ended by giving each other accolades and drinking a bottle of whiskey. We have spent our lives having long periods of friendship and others during which we barely spoke. I have never been able to avoid gently making fun of him, and this no one ever did—everyone treated him with the greatest respect.

Q.—*As an artist and as a member of a certain generation, do you feel isolated?*

WELLES—I have always felt isolated. I believe that any good artist feels isolated. And I must think that I am a good artist, for otherwise I would not be able to work and I beg your pardon for taking the liberty of believing this; if someone wants to direct a film, he must think that he is good. A good artist should be isolated. If he isn't isolated, something is wrong.

Q.—*These days, it would be impossible to present the Mercury Theatre.*

WELLES—Completely impossible for financial reasons. The Mercury Theatre was possible only because I was earning three thousand dollars a week on the radio and spending two thousand to sustain the theatre. At that time, it was still cheap to sustain a theatre. Plus I had formidable actors. And what was most exciting about this Mercury Theatre was that it was a theatre on Broadway, no "off." Today, one might have a theatre off-Broadway, but that's another thing.

What characterized the Mercury Theatre was that it was next door to another where they were doing a musical comedy, near a commercial theatre, it was in the theatre center. Part of the neighboring bill of fare was the Group Theatre which was the official theatre of the Left: we were in contact without having an official relationship; we were of the same generation, although not on the same path. The whole thing gave the New York of that time an extraordinary vitality. The quality of actors and that of spectators is no longer what it was in those marvelous years. The best theatre should be in the center of everything.

Q.—*Does that explain your permanent battle to remain in the milieu of the cinema and not outside of the industry?*

Welles—I may be rejected, but as for me, I always want to be right in the center. If I am isolated, it is because I am obliged to be, for such is not my intention. I am always aiming for the center. I fail, but that is what I try to attain.

Q.—*Are you thinking of returning to Hollywood?*

Welles—Not at the moment. But who knows what may change at the next instant? . . . I am dying to work there because of the technicians, who are marvelous. They truly represent a director's dream.

Q.—*A certain anti-Fascist attitude can be found in your films . . .*

Welles—There is more than one French intellectual who believes that I am a Fascist . . . it's idiotic, but that's what they write. What happens with these French intellectuals is that they take my physical aspect as an actor for my idea as an *auteur*. As an actor I always play a certain type of role: Kings, great men, etc. This is not because I think them to be the only persons in the world who are worth the trouble. My physical aspect does not permit me to play other roles. No one would believe a defenseless, humble person played by me. But they take this to be a projection of my own personality. I hope that the great majority at least considers it obvious that I am anti-Fascist . . .

True Fascism is always confused with Futurism's early fascistic mystique. By this I make allusion to the first generation of Italian Fascism, which was a way of speaking that disappeared as soon as the true Fascism imposed itself, because it was an idiotic romanticism, like that of d'Annunzio and others. That is what disappeared. And that is what the French critics are talking about.

True Fascism is gangsterism of the low-born middle class, lamentably organized by . . . good, we all know what Fascism is. It is very clear. It is amusing to see how the Russians have been mistaken about the subject of *Touch of Evil*. They have attacked it pitilessly, as if it were a question of the veritable decadence of Western civilization. They were not content to attack what I showed: they attacked me too.

I believe that the Russians didn't understand the words, or some other thing. What is disastrous, in Russia, is that they are fully in the middle ages, the middle ages in its most rigid aspect. No one thinks for himself. It is very sad. This orthodoxy has something terrible about it. They live only by slogans they have inherited. No one any longer knows what these slogans signify.

Q.—*What will your* Falstaff *be like?*

WELLES—I don't know . . . I hope it will be good. All I can say is that from the visual point of view it will be very modest and, I hope, at the same time satisfying and correct. But as I see it, it is essentially a human story and I hope that a good number of stupid cinema people will feel deceived. That is because, as I just said, I consider that this film should be very modest from the visual point of view. Which doesn't mean it will be visually non-existent but rather that it will not be loud on this level. It concerns a story about 3 or 4 people and these should, therefore, dominate completely. I believe I shall use more close-ups. This will really be a film completely in the service of the actors.

Q.—*You are often accused of being egocentric. When you appear as an actor in your films, it is said that the camera is, above all, in the service of your personal exhibition. . . For example, in* Touch of Evil *the shooting angle moves from a general shot to a close-up in order to catch your first appearance on getting out of the car.*

WELLES—Yes, but that is the story, the subject. I wouldn't act a role if it was not felt as dominating the whole story. I do not think it is just to say that I utilize the camera to my profit and not to the profit of the other actors. It's not true. Although they will say it even more about *Falstaff:* but it is precisely because in the film I am playing Falstaff, not Hotspur.

At this time I think and rethink, above all, of the world in which the story unfolds, of the appearance of the film. The number of sets I will be able to build will be so restrained that the film will have to be resolutely anti-Baroque. It will have to have numerous rather formal general shots, like what one may see at eye level, wall frescoes. It is a big problem creating a world in period costumes. In this genre, it is difficult to get a feeling of real life; few films arrive at it. I believe this is due to the fact that one has not concretized, in all its details, before starting to work, the universe presupposed by such a film.

Falstaff should be very plain on the visual level because above all it is a very real human story, very comprehensible and very adaptable to modern tragedy. And nothing should come between the story and the dialogue. The visual part of this story should exist as a background, as something secondary. Everything of importance in the film should be found on the faces; on these faces that whole universe I was speaking of should be found. I imagine that it will be "the" film of my life in terms of close-ups. Theoretically, I am against close-ups of all types, although I consider few theories as given and am for remaining very free. I am resolutely against close-ups, but I am convinced that this story requires them.

Q.—*Why this objection to close-ups?*

WELLES—I find it marvelous that the public may choose, with its eyes, what it wants to see of a shot. I don't like to force it, and the use of the close-up amounts to forcing it: you can see nothing else. In *Kane,* for example, you must have seen that there were very few close-ups, hardly any. There are perhaps six in the whole film. But a story like *Falstaff* demands them, because the moment we step back and separate ourselves from the faces, we see the people in period costumes and many actors in the foreground. The closer we are to the face the more universal it becomes; *Falstaff* is a somber comedy, the story of the betrayal of friendship.

What pleases me in *Falstaff* is that the project has interested me as an actor although I am rarely interested in something for the cinema in terms of being an actor. I am happy when I do not perform. And *Falstaff* is one of the rare things that I wish to achieve as an actor. There are only two stories I wish to do as an actor that I have written. In *The Trial* I absolutely did not want to perform and, if I did it, it is because of not having found an actor who could take the part. All those we asked refused.

Q.—*At the beginning you said you would play the part of the priest . . .*

WELLES—I shot it, but, as we hadn't found an actor for the role of the lawyer, I cut the sequences in which I appeared as a priest and started shooting again. *Falstaff* is an actor's film. Not only my role but all the others are favorable for showing a good actor's worth. My *Othello* is more successful in the theatre than on film. We shall see what happens with *Falstaff*, which is the best role that Shakespeare ever wrote. It is a character as great as Don

Quixote. If Shakespeare had done nothing but that magnificent creation, it would suffice to make him immortal. I wrote the scenario under the inspiration of three works in which he appears, one other in which he is spoken of, and complete it with things found in still another. Thus, I worked with five of Shakespeare's works. But, naturally, I wrote a story about Falstaff, about his friendship with the prince and his repugnance when the prince becomes King. I have great hopes for this film.

Q.—*There is a line spoken by John Foster to his banker, which we would like very much to hear you explain: "I could have been a great man, if I hadn't been so rich."*

WELLES—Good, the whole story is in that. Anything at all may destroy greatness: a woman, illness, riches. My hatred of richness in itself is not an obsession. I do not believe that richness is the only enemy of greatness. If he had been poor, Kane would not have been a great man but one thing is sure and that is that he would have been a successful man. He thinks that success brings greatness. As for that, it is the character that says it, not I. Kane arrives at having a certain class but never greatness.

It isn't because everything seems easy to him. That is an excuse he gives himself. But the film doesn't say that. Obviously, since he is the head of one of the biggest fortunes in the world, things become easier, but his greatest error was that of the American plutocrats of those years, who believed that money automatically conferred a certain stature to a man. Kane is a man who truly belongs to his time. This type of man hardly exists anymore. These were the plutocrats who believed they could be President of the United States, if they wanted to. They also believed they could buy anything. It wasn't even necessary to be intelligent to see that it isn't always like that.

Q.—*Are they more realistic?*

WELLES—It's not a question of realism. This type of plutocrat no longer exists. Things have changed a great deal, above all economic structures. Very few rich men today succeed in retaining absolute control of their own money: their money is controlled by others. It is, like many other things, a question of organization. They are prisoners of their money. And I don't say this from a sentimental point of view; there is no longer anything but boards of directors and the participation of diverse opinions . . . they are no longer free to commit the sort of follies that used to be possible. The moment has passed for this type of egocentric plutocrat, in the same way that this type of newspaper owner has disappeared.

What is very specific about Kane's personality is that he never earned money; he passed his life doing nothing but spending it. He did not belong to that category of rich men who made fortunes: he only spent it. Kane didn't even have the responsibility of the true capitalist.

Q.—*Did* Citizen Kane *bring in a lot of money?*

WELLES—No, it's not a question of that. The film went well. But my problems with Hollywood started before I got there. The real problem was that contract, which gave me, free and clear, carte blanche and which had been signed before I went out there. I had too much power. At that time I was faced with a machination from which I have never recovered, because I have never had an enormous box office success. If you have such success, from that instant on you are given everything!

I had luck as no one had; afterwards, I had the worst bad luck in the history of the cinema, but that is in the order of things: I had to pay for having had the best luck in the history of the cinema. Never has a man been given so much power in the Hollywood system. An absolute power. And artistic control.

Q.—*There are* cineastes, *in Europe, who possess this power.*

WELLES—But they don't possess the American technical arsenal, which is a grandiose thing. The man who pushes the camera, those who change the lights, the one who handles the crane—they have children at the University. You are side by side with men who don't feel themselves to be workers but who think of themselves as very capable and very well paid artisans. That makes an enormous difference; enormous.

I could never have done all that I did in *Touch of Evil* elsewhere. And it is not only a question of technique; it essentially concerns the human competence of the men with whom I worked. All this stems from the economic security they enjoy, from the fact that they are well paid, from the fact that they do not think of themselves as belonging to another class.

Throughout the entire European cinema industry, to a greater or lesser degree, one feels that there is a great barrier posed by educational differences. In all European countries one is called "Doctor," "Professor," etc., if one has gone to a university; the great advantage in America is that there, at times, you find directors who are less learned than the man who pushes the camera. There is no "professor." Classes do not exist in the American cinema world. The pleasure one experiences working with an American crew is something that has no equivalent on earth. But you pay a price for that. There are the producers, and that group is as bad as the technicians are good.

Q.—*How did you shoot that very long sequence in Marcia's living room during the interrogation of Sanchez?*

WELLES—In Europe, there are three cameramen as good as the American cameramen. The one who made *The Trial* with me is sensational. But what there isn't is someone capable of handling the crane. In america, this man has an enormous car; he is educated and he considers himself as important to the film as the cameraman himself. In that scene in Marcia's house there were about sixty chalk marks on the ground: that tells you how knowledgeable and intelligent the man who guides the camera must be in order to do well. At that moment, I am at his mercy, at the mercy of his precision. If he can't do it with assurance, the scene is impossible.

Q.—*Was it really Charlton Heston who proposed you as director of* Touch of Evil?

WELLES—What happened is even more amusing. The scenario was proposed to Charlton Heston who was told that it was by Orson Welles; at the other end of the line, Heston understood that I was to direct the film, in which case he was ready to shoot anything at all, no matter what, with me. Those at Universal did not clear up his misunderstanding; they hung up and automatically telephoned me and asked me to direct it. The truth is that Heston said, textually, this: "I will work in any film at all directed by Orson Welles." When they proposed that I direct the film I set only one condition: to write my own scenario! And I directed and wrote the film without getting a penny for it, since I was being paid as an actor.

Q.—*In relation to the original novel, you made many changes . . .*

WELLES—My God! I never read the novel; I only read Universal's scenario. Perhaps the novel made sense, but the scenario was ridiculous. It all took place in San Diego, not on the Mexican border, which completely changes the situation. I made Vargas a Mexican for political reasons: I wanted to show how Tiajuana and the border towns are corrupted by all sorts of mish-mash—publicity more or less about American relations: that's the only reason.

Q.—*What do you think of the American Cinema, as seen from Europe?*

WELLES—I am surprised by the tendency of the serious critics to find elements of value only among the American directors of action films, while they find none in the American directors of historical films. Lubitsch, for example, is a giant. But he doesn't correspond to the taste of cinema aesthetes. Why? I know nothing about it. Besides, it doesn't interest me. But Lubitsch's talent and originality are stupefying.

Q.—*And Von Sternberg?*

WELLES—Admirable! He is the greatest exotic director of all time and one of the great lights.

Q.—*Let's talk about other directors. What do you think of Arthur Penn? Have you seen* The Left-Handed Gun?

WELLES—I saw it first on television and then as cinema. It was better on television, more brutal, and beyond that I believe that at that time Penn had more experience directing for television and so handled it better, but for cinema this experience went against him. I believe him to be a good theatre director, an admirable director of actresses —a very rare thing: very few *cineastes* possess that quality.

I have seen nothing by the most recent generation, except for a sampling of the avante-garde. Among those whom I would call "younger generation" Kubrick appears to me to be a giant.

Q.—*But, for example,* The Killing *was more or less a copy of* The Asphalt Jungle?

WELLES—Yes, but *The Killing* was better. The problem of imitation leaves me indifferent, above all if the imitator succeeds in surpassing the model. For me, Kubrick is a better director than Huston. I haven't seen *Lolita* but I believe that Kubrick can do everything. He is a great director who has not yet made his great film. What I see in him is a talent not possessed by the great directors of the generation immediately preceding his, I mean Ray, Aldrich, etc. Perhaps this is because his temperament comes closer to mine.

Q.—*And those of the older generation? Wyler, for example? and Hitchcock?*

WELLES—Hitchcock is an extraordinary director; William Wyler a brilliant producer.

Q.—*How do you make this distinction between two men who are both called directors?*

WELLES—A producer doesn't make anything. He chooses the story, works on it with the scenarist, has a say in the distribution and, in the old sense of the term American producer, even decides on the camera angles, what sequences will be used. What is more, he defines the final form of the film. In reality, he is a sort of director's boss.

Wyler is this man. Only he's his own boss. His work, however, is better as boss than as director, given the fact that in that role he spends his clearest moments waiting, with the camera, for something to happen. He says nothing. He waits, as the producer waits in his office. He looks at twenty impeccable shots, seeking the one that has something, and usually he knows how to choose the best one. As a director he is good but as a producer he is extraordinary.

Q.—*According to you, the role of director consists in making something happen?*

WELLES—I do not like to set up very strict rules, but in the Hollywood system, the director has one job. In other systems he has another job. I am against absolute rules because even in the case of America we find marvelous films achieved under the absolute tyranny of the production system. There are even films much respected by film societies that weren't made by directors but by producers and scenarists. . . . Under the American system, no one is capable of saying whether a film was or was not directed by a director.

Q.—*In an interview, John Houseman said that you got all of the credit for* Citizen Kane *and that this was unfair because it should have gone to Herman J. Mankiewicz, who wrote the scenario.*

WELLES—He wrote several important scenes. (Houseman is an old enemy of mine.) I was very lucky to work with Mankiewicz: everything concerning Rosebud belongs to him. As for me, sincerely, he doesn't please me very much; he functions, it is true, but I have never had complete confidence in him. He serves as a hyphen between all the elements. I had, in return, the good fortune to have Gregg Toland, who is the best director of photography that ever existed, and I also had the luck to hit upon actors who had never worked in films before; not a single one of them had ever found himself in front of a camera until then. They all came from my theatre. I could never have made *Citizen Kane* with actors who were old hands at cinema, because they would have said right off, "Just what do you think we're doing?" My being a newcomer would have put them on guard and, with the same blow, would have made a mess of the film. It was possible because I had my own family, so to speak.

Q.—*How did you arrive at* Citizen Kane's *cinematic innovations?*

WELLES—I owe it to my ignorance. If this word seems inadequate to you, replace it with innocence. I said to myself: this is what the camera should be really capable of doing, in a normal fashion. When we were on the point of shooting the first sequence, I said, "Let's do that!" Gregg Toland answered that it was impossible. I came back with, "We can always try; we'll soon see. Why not?" We had to have special lenses made because at that time there weren't any like those that exist today.

Q.—*During the shooting, did you have the sensation of making such an important film?*

WELLES—I never doubted it for a single instant.

Q.—*What is happening with your* Don Quixote? *It was announced so long ago.*

WELLES—It's really finished; it only needs about three weeks' work, in order to shoot several little things. What makes me nervous is launching it: I know that this film will please no one. This will be an execrated film. I need a big success before putting it in circulation. If *The Trial* had been a complete critical success, then I would have had the courage to bring out my *Don Quixote*. Things being what they are I don't know what to do: everyone will be enraged by this film.

Q.—*How do you see the central character?*

WELLES—Exactly as Cervantes did, I believe. My film takes place in modern times but the characters of Don Quixote and Sancho are exactly as they were, at least, I repeat, to my way of thinking. This wasn't the case with Kafka; I utilize these two characters freely but I do it in the same spirit as Cervantes. They are not my characters, they are the Spanish writer's.

Q.—*Why did you choose to film* Don Quixote?

WELLES—I started by making a half hour television out of it; I had just enough money to do it. But I fell so completely in love with my subject that I gradually made it longer and continued to shoot depending on how much money I had. You might say that it grew as I made it. What happened to me is more or less what happened to Cervantes, who started to write a novella and ended up writing *Don Quixote*. It's a subject you can't let go of once you've started.

Q.—*Will the film have the same skepticism as the novel?*

WELLES—Certainly! I believe that what happened to the book will happen to my film. You know that Cervantes started out to write a satire on books of chivalry and he ended up creating the most beautiful apology for them that can be found in literature. However, touching on the defense of that idea of chivalry, the film will be more sincere than the novel, even though today it is more anachronistic than when Cervantes was writing.

I myself appear in the character of Orson Welles, but Sancho and Don Quixote say only the lines given them by Cervantes; I have put no words in their mouths.

I do not think the film is less skeptical because I believe that, if we push the analysis to the end, Cervantes' skepticism was in part an attitude. His skepticism was an intellectual attitude: I believe that, under the skepticism, there was a man who loved the knights as much as Don Quixote himself. Above all, he was Spanish.

It is truly a difficult film. I should also say that it is too long; what I am going to shoot will not serve to complete the footage—I could make three films out of the material that already exists. The film, in its first form, was too commercial; it was conceived for television and I had to change certain things in order to make it more substantial. The drollest thing about it is that it was shot with a crew of six people. My wife was script-girl, the chauffeur moved the lights around, I did the lighting and was second cameraman. It is only with the camera that one can have his eye on everything in such a way.

Orson Welles (1915–   ):
Filmography:
1941—Citizen Kane. 1942—The Magnificent Ambersons, Journey into Fear (signed by Norman Foster). 1946—The Stranger. 1948—Lady from Shanghai. 1950—Macbeth. 1955—Othello. 1958—Touch of Evil. 1962-Mr. Arkadin. 1963—The Trial. 1966—Chimes at Midnight. 1968—The Immortal Story.

Richard Schickel

THE DISNEY VERSION   W148 $1.25

A biography of the Hollywood genius, a critical consideration of his films, and most importantly, a clear and careful, witty and penetrating assessment of the influence of the Disney industry on American popular art and taste

Lillian Ross

PICTURE   W134 $1.25

A classic film book and an important precursor of "the new journalism"—the novel-like account of the making of John Huston's film The Red Badge of Courage from beginning to end

PORTRAIT OF HEMINGWAY   SS18   60¢

The controversial, vitally alive profile

Lewis Funke and John E. Booth

ACTORS TALK ABOUT ACTING   W113 $1.25

Candid interviews with 14 of the premier actors of our time, including Sidney Poitier, Anne Bancroft, Sir John Gielgud, Helen Hayes